The Metropolis in Transition

The Metropolis in Transition

Edited by Ervin Y. Galantay

An ICUS Book

Paragon House Publishers

New York

Published in the United States
by Paragon House Publishers
2 Hammarskjold Plaza
New York, New York 10017

An International Conference on the
Unity of the Sciences Book

Library of Congress Cataloging-in-Publication Data

The Metropolis in Transition.

   Papers presented at the 13th International Conference
on the Unity of the Sciences, held in Washington, D.C.,
Sept. 1984.
   "An ICUS book."
   Bibliography:
   Includes index.
   1. Metropolitan areas—Congresses. 2. Regional
planning—Congresses. I. Galantay, Ervin Y.
II. International Conference on the Unity of the
Sciences (13th : 1984 : Washington, D.C.)
HT330.M46   1986   307.7'64   86-12167

ISBN 0-89226-044-0

Contents

Part I: Global and National Context

Part II: Factors Shaping the Metropolis

I dedicate this book to the memory of my beloved brother
Tibor Galantay, born in 1940,
killed in action Budapest, October 25, 1956.

Qui Ante Diem Moriit Sed Miles, Sed Pro Patria.

Acknowledgments

First of all the editor wishes to express his gratitude to the International Cultural Foundation for the financial support which enabled him to organize a Committee on the Future Metropolis within the framework of the Thirteenth International Conference on the Unity of the Sciences. The editor, as organizing Chairman, was responsible for the invitation of participants to a preparatory meeting in Paris, followed in September, 1984 by ICUS XIII in Washington D.C. where the essays of this collection were discussed. Percy Johnson-Marshall acted as Honorary Chairman of our Committee with Hans Blumenfeld and John Dyckman acting as Distinguished commentators.

Special thanks are due to the ICUS XIII Conference Chairman Professor Kenneth Mellanby; to ICUS Executive Director James Baughman and to ICUS Deputy Director Glenn Carrol Strait; to Stephen Henkin, Director of ICUS Books and to Professor Frederick E. Sontag of Paragon House Publishers, for their unflagging support in helping to get this volume produced in a very short time.

I wish to thank also Ms. Elizabeth Johnson who acted as co-editor and my wife Karla for typing the numerous revisions of the manuscript.

Preface

Percy Johnson-Marshall

The metropolis is immensely difficult to comprehend and impossible to define in precise terms. In the past it was said that the city was the most complex work of the human species, comparable in nature to the anthill or the beehive. The city was also held to be humanity's highest achievement and the key place where human society, through multifarious intercommunication, could evolve and develop to a higher level of civilization. It was only natural for people to think that as the metropolis replaced the city as the largest urban entity, so it inherited the role of the city in terms of civilization.

Patrick Geddes, the pioneer of so many innovative ideas in physical planning, was one of the first to realize that a new and menacing scale of urbanization was taking place in industrial society. For this he coined the word *conurbation*, which he thought ". . . may serve as the necessary word, as an expression of this new form of population-grouping which is already, as it were subconsciously, developing new forms of social grouping and of definite government and administration . . .", and he likened the growth of London, the first conurbation, to ". . . the spreadings of a great coral reef."[1] It is important to remember that the word *conurbation* had a pejorative meaning, whereas *metropolis* has the opposite.

More recently, Jean Gottman[2] identified an even larger urban grouping, and for this he re-used another ancient Greek word, *megalopolis*. No doubt, if megalopolis increases in size, it will be necessary to invent yet another word in the space scale.[3] For a number of reasons this may not be necessary. A new method of evaluation has evolved, different in kind from the centuries-old tradition by which urban man has dominated thinking and hence the making of decisions about societies and cities.

At last new concepts are appearing and are already conditioning ideas about human settlements. These concepts achieved their threshold of acceptance at the United Nations Conference on the Environment held in Stockholm in 1972. This conference brought about widespread realization that the days of the terrestrial "frontier" were over. No longer was it possible to accept the tendency of the human species to expand indefinitely over the planet, often moving over the face of the earth like a swarm of locusts and destroying, in many cases, the vital resources on which they depended.

The new approach, for which the term ecology has come to be used, related the human species to planetary resources as a whole. An alarming situation was disclosed, which now after 12 years, has almost been forgotten by most of the politicians of the world.

From the point of view of human survival, the land capable of sustaining the basis of life was limited, and was often the very land that was being used, or misused, for other purposes, notably uncontrolled urbanization. The mineral resources of the planet were also being exploited in an irresponsible way, so that some geologists predicted that a number of basic minerals would become unavailable within a comparatively short period. At the same time world population was increasing, notably in developing countries, where survival problems were already acute for the existing population.

The world strategical appraisal, therefore, indicated that a dangerous situation was developing with increasing rapidity, one which would be impossible to resolve even in the near future unless drastic action was taken. Even more critically, the large-scale movement of people from villages to towns and from towns to metropolitan areas was causing acute problems.

A fundamental dilemma was presented. Traditionally, the problem of total human happiness was seen as a readjustment in the distribution of resources, so that all, instead of a few, could take advantage of nature's bounty. Assuming unlimited resources, the only problem was to ensure fair shares for all.

In some respects, this has been partially achieved in a few countries, where no one starves, everyone has the minimum necessary clothing, and the majority have a minimum standard of shelter. Thus, basic needs for all have been satisfied and comforts are becoming available for large numbers, while luxuries are confidently expected in the near future. This prediction implies an ever-increasing use of land and resources; and, if the experience of the world's richest country is anything to go by, it will be accompanied by conspicuous waste.

In the conventional dream of tomorrow's world the metropolis assumed almost a magical role, like the ancient image cities of Babylon or Rome in which all the physical necessities, comforts, and luxuries of life would be available if only one could get there. How else can one explain the magnetic effect which has caused the mass migrations to metropolitan areas in recent years? Although the harsh realities of the new mass slums of the metropolitan areas in developing countries have destroyed the dream for millions, the thought of returning to their villages would be an even greater nightmare. All the while, the impossibility of providing even the basic necessities of urban life brings disaster nearer. The problems are less evident in the metropolitan areas of developed countries. In Los Angeles, for instance, it is not so much the conspicuous waste of land and resources that is critical, but the very concept of the way of life presented to the world, a way of life to be striven for as an ideal. One only needs simple arithmetic to expose the fallacy, for if one applied the ideal standard of living of Los Angeles in material terms to China and India, an impossible dilemma would be revealed. If, for instance, every Chinese family were to have two cars, the depletion of metal resources alone would cause an international crisis.

The problem, therefore, is obvious in principle, but insoluble without a basically different approach. The solution is also obvious but difficult to accept, particularly by metropolitan society as it exists today.

It begins with a consideration of the spatial problem as a whole. Human survival is the keynote and the bedrock for assumptions for the future. It depends on the best use of terrestrial resources of all kinds. In consequence, the long-held assumptions of the "frontier" are called into question.

If the human species is to survive, fundamentally new assumptions must be made. There is only so much space available, so much land capable of growing food in a non-destructive way, so many mineral resources, and a limited amount of land for urbanization. The need for the best use of resources is brought sharply into focus by current attitudes on the world's forests.

The large scale depletion being practiced at the present time is not only reducing the amount of timber that will be available in the future, but it is causing widespread erosion and complex climatic changes which may be irreversible.

The terrestrial inventory, therefore, enables human society to take a new look at the world, and at the metropolitan phenomenon within a broader context. As metropolitan growth has been based partly on the general assumption of unlimited terrestrial resources, so a new approach to the metropolitan problem is necessary, based on a new concept of human aspirations in physical terms. In the past, two opposing theories have been advanced. One is that the metropolis is an indicator of economic viability and vitality, and hence must have no restrictions placed on its growth. The other is that the metropolis must be controlled negatively and forced into a restrictive limit-of-growth concept which will cause it to be contained spatially.

Not many years ago, Lewis Mumford argued for a new approach, with an emphasis on the "invisible city." Of the metropolis he wrote, ". . . those who work within the metropolitan myth treating its cancerous tumours as normal manifestations of growth will continue to apply poultices, salves, advertising incantations, public relations magic, and quack mechanical remedies until the patient dies before their own failing eyes."[4] He argued for networks of human settlements rather than one gargantuan urban "necropolis."

Today, with the advantages of the terrestrial ecological approach, we see that the concepts flowing from Geddes, Kropotkin, Howard, Benton Mackaye and Mumford have largely retained their validity. The added advantage we have now is to be able to stand outside and above the metropolis, both mentally and physically, with the aid of Landsat and other devices, and to be able to balance urban and non-urban, to give plants as great an importance as people, and thus to see the metropolis as it exists today as an exorbitant consumer of human and natural resources, as a kind of brainless giant uncontrolled and uncontrollable, an enemy of good ecological principles and, finally, undesirable, at least in its present form.

This book is based on the discussions of a committee organized by Professor Ervin Galantay within the framework of the 13th ICUS Conference. The objective of the committee was to make a brief global review of the metropolis by means of submissions from contributors experienced in metropolitan problems in five continents and then to conjecture about future development. One problem which became clear was the great variety of metropolitan cities. Those in the most developed countries are going through a cycle of change pointing toward regression, yet some of the largest metropoli continue to expand into their hinterlands acquiring megalopolitan dimensions. It was noted that few metropolitan cities had endeavored to adopt regional plans with positive policies of restriction by means of decongestion to new towns, by the application of density controls in the inner city, and by the creation of conservation areas in order to prevent sprawl over agricultural land. The examples of cities as diverse as Greater London, Moscow, and Havana, Cuba have been cited to prove that positive policies can be quite successful if an adequate institutional-legal framework exists to permit program continuity. There was general agreement that a multi-centered regional network of human settlements of various sizes must be stimulated in order to prevent the continued degradation of the metropolitan environment and to prevent the metropolis from exerting an unhealthy dominance on the rest of the urban systems.

At least in the developed countries sufficient industrial and other resources exist to match an increase in metropolitan populations by improved infrastructure, health and other services. On the other hand, in most of the less developed countries—although wide variations exist—the resources are still insufficiently developed to provide even the basic requirements of subsistence for the majority of citizens. The problems of providing for the natural increase of the population is greatly compounded by mass immigration of impoverished rural dwellers. Under these conditions some metropolitan cities are in a state of crisis which is likely to intensify in the future. No amount of good physical planning of the individual metropoli can resolve the problem: broader settlement policies are essential to avert disasters. There can be no universally applicable panacea: programs of action must be adapted to national and local circumstances and take into account different goals. In terms of appropriate action programs, a distinction has to be made between regions where the broad metropolitan structures already exist and need only be modified: those where much growth still lies ahead and those where metropoli are only beginning to emerge and patterns have yet to be established, notably in the case of sub-Sahara Africa.

A balanced appraisal still needs to be made of the advantages and disadvantages of the metropolis in developing countries. There is a danger that decision-makers in developing countries view the metropolis as the paragon of modernization and favor them in terms of resource allocation to the detriment of the national system. The impossibility of most metropolitan cities in the developing countries ever reaching the supposedly "desirable" environments of, say, Los Angeles or New York indicates that more frugal and equitable modes of spatial organization should be pursued. Fortunately this reality integrates well with ecological thinking, and the opportunity is presented of the developing countries setting an example creating harmonious and less wasteful metropolitan environments.

It cannot be the role of a conference to develop action programs but some guidelines have been proposed. First of all, problems of the built environment should be considered against a global ecological perspective and a policy of the best use of the land in ecological terms. The new metropolitan city should form part of an urban network in which the administrative, cultural, industrial and commercial functions are equitably distributed. It should be supportive of regional development and be integrated with its hinterland so the city and country dwellers can become more equal and complementary.

Perhaps the greatest difficulty is that of perception. Many people think that, as the metropolis in its present form exists, it is therefore inevitable.

We need to start with the basic needs of the human being, with the satisfaction of the necessities of life, some of the comforts, and perhaps one or two of the luxuries. From the human person it is necessary to proceed to the family, from the family to the community, and from the community to society as a whole.

Armed with the knowledge that most of the benefits of civilization can be obtained throughout any given area by the use of appropriate technology, a network of settlements can be established which would make the metropolis in its present form not only undesirable but in fact superfluous. It would be metamorphosed into a higher order of living, with the "invisible city" becoming a reality and a harmonious distribution of settlements throughout a region the new viable and vital pattern for life in the future.

References

1. P. Geddes, *Cities in Evolution*, (London, 1915), Chapter 2.
2. J. Gottman, *Megalopolis*, (Cambridge, MA., 1961), Introduction.
3. Doxides' "Ecumenopolis" was a different conception.
4. Lewis Mumford, *The City in History*, (New York, 1961).

Introduction

Ervin Y. Galantay

The metropolis as a new type of human settlement first attracted scientific interest in the United States of the 1960s. At that time, Europe and Japan were just recovering from the destruction caused by World War II and the task of reconstruction still absorbed all creative energy. In the U.S., post-war planning first focused on housing then on urban renewal while academic research increasingly turned to explore the metropolitan phenomenon.

We might recall briefly such pioneering publications as "The Exploding Metropolis" (1958) by the editors of Fortune Magazine and "The Anatomy of a Metropolis" (1959) by Raymond Vernon and Edgar M. Hoover, followed by "Communitas" (1960), a highly original projection of metropolitan paradigms by Percival and Paul Goodman.

But far greater was the impact of the proceedings of a symposium at Tamiment Institute published in the 1961 winter issue of "Daedalus" and later also put into book form with the title of "The Future Metropolis." This volume, edited by Lloyd Rodwin and Kevin Lynch, was perhaps the first attempt to grope with the metropolitan phenomenon on a global scale. Yet even this enquiry was largely based on an analysis of the North American urban scene, and conjectures about metropolitization in other continents were extrapolated from data which may not have general validity. It is amusing to note that of the eleven authors of the articles in "The Future Metropolis," six were born in New York and two in Chicago—all were American. Further, nine of them were professors at Harvard or MIT. Only Karl Deutsch hailed from Yale and John Dyckman from Chicago. None came from the West Coast, from Europe or Asia. Although several articles made use of European data, only one, Rodwin's, mentioned the special problems of the metropolis in the developing countries.

During the following decade of 1960-1970 a number of important international meetings and publications followed, setting the foundations of our present knowledge on the metropolis:

- 1961: Publication by the 20th Century Fund of Jean Gottmann's "Megalopolis," an analysis of the U.S. Atlantic Seabord conurbation

- 1964: Meeting of the "United Nation's group of experts on Metropolitan Planning" in Stockholm (Proceedings published in 1967 by ECOSOC)

- 1965: Special issue of the *Scientific American* devoted to world-wide urbanization, with articles by Rodwin, Dyckman, Blumenfeld, et al.

- 1966: Publication of Percy Johnson-Marshall's *Rebuilding Cities*, a survey of the European experience with post-war reconstruction, heralding the change of focus to the metropolitan scale

- 1967: Publication of Hans Blumenfeld's collected essays in the volume on "The Modern Metropolis"

- 1968: Publication of Constantinos Doxiades's "Ekistics," an attempt to integrate the results of research in sectoral aspects of the evolution of human settlements into a single systemic whole

It is fair to say that by 1970 a corpus of significant publications emerged which has solidly established the metropolis as a subject worthy of scientific enquiry. During the same decade, technological progress has largely changed our consciousness of global interdependence and the world-wide interaction of population and resources on "spaceship earth." In 1960, for the first time, images of the earth were taken by the TIROS weather satellites. Color pictures of the earth were also brought back by the Gemini and Apollo astronauts. In 1972 NASA launched LANDSAT-1, the first satellite specially designed for the monitoring of changes on the earth's surface on a regular basis. Ten years later LANDSAT-4 was launched, providing regular coverage of all metropolitan areas every 18 days from the uniform height of 570 miles or 917km. This on-going monitoring provides minute information on land-use changes, the growth of urban areas, the shrinking of the vegetation, of water and air pollution, etc. This new view of our global habitat has undoubtedly contributed to the rising interest in metropolitan cities which has even reached the mass media since the rapid growth of Third World metropoli permits them to conjure up spine-tingling scenarios of urban cataclysm. But international conferences and symposia on the future of the metropolis also follow one another and the specialized publications on the subject take up ever more shelf space in every library.

Nevertheless, when I reread the "Future of the Metropolis" a quarter of a century after its inception, I felt an irresistible urge to review the findings of this seminal publication. Thus, having been invited to organize a committee within the framework of the 13th ICUS in Washington D.C., I seized the opportunity to bring together a representative group of specialists from different continents to compare notes on the likely future of metropolitan cities worldwide.

I was lucky to have been able to assure the collaboration of John Dyckman, one of the key figures at the original Tamiment Conference in

1960, to confer an aura of historic continuity on our deliberations. The success of our organizing effort was assured when Hans Blumenfeld also agreed to act as a general commentator and Percy Johnson-Marshall accepted the role of honorary chairman. From the beginning, it was my intention to compose a group including both theoreticians and academic observers of the metropolitan phenomenon and practicians deployed on the metropolitan battlefield: architects, planners, engineers and managers. In sending out invitations to some 30 participants we also tried to achieve a more balanced geographic representation than at Tamiment and, indeed, we received papers from 22 countries on five continents. As to the structure of the conference, I intended to discuss not only size-related problems common to all metropolitan regions but also the diversity of problems which may be culture-dependent, influenced by political ideology or which may simply reflect geographical constraints and the influence of such varied factors as the climate. Of the originally planned nine discussion groups, three were to focus on general issues: the metropolis as a geographical phenomenon: factors that shape the metropolis: and the size-related problems of the ecological, sociological, and psychological impact of urban giantism. The six other groups—organized on a regional basis—were asked to define the specific problems common to their geographic area, and to determine what, if anything, makes the large agglomerations in their region different from metropoli of similar size elsewhere—the key question being whether the evolution of all metropoli necessarily follows the same phases of development or whether parallel-line but distinctly different development paths are possible. Since "a world not including Utopia may not be worth visiting," we added a tenth group to discuss "paradigms for the future" to open the door for ideas based on the potentials of modern technology.

Our core group first met in April, 1984 in Paris, followed by four days of intensive work of the entire committee at ICUS 13th in Washington D.C. It was generally agreed that our group produced considerable synergy which should not be permitted to dissipate, and it was proposed that the papers should serve as the raw material for a more substantial publication than the customery "proceedings." Our proposal met with the enthusiastic support of the ICUS Books and Paragon Press staff. I agreed to serve as general editor.

All collections of essays issuing from conference material suffer from redundancy. Also, inevitably, there are some gaps in the content, less evident in a round table discussion than at the perusal of the table of contents of an ambitious publication. Although we do not pretend at encyclopedical completeness, some gaps had to be filled to assure the stability of our intellectual edifice. To achieve this we included some additional material and some articles I felt obliged to contribute myself.

As for our illustrations, I always felt that this sort of publication needs some visual material. Most planning books include some abstract information like graphs and maps and add a few photographs of street scenes or buildings as a form of visual relief. This tends to divert attention to the microscale which is not the focus of this book. Aerial photographs are more appropriate in scale and give a better idea of the urban macroform, but such is the scale of the modern metropolitan areas that it would require a complex mosaic of aerial views to give a comprehensive picture. Since I was looking for illustrations permitting a direct scale comparison of the built-up areas of metropoli around the world I was pleased to be able to acquire the false color, computer-enhanced satellite images prepared by the EARTHSAT corporation. Our images range in scale from 1 : 200,000 to 1 : 600,000, and the areas covered range from 43 × 26km = 2408 km. sq. to 129 × 168 km = 21672 km. sq. The first frame is large enough to include the built-up areas of most metropoli but it does not suffice to cover a large metropolitan region such as the San Francisco Bay Area or the Washington-Baltimore conurbation. Following a suggestion by Earthsat director Max E. Miller, we agreed to reproduce the images in a series of scales, superposing visual cues to facilitate size comparisons. Needless to say that images of a scale where 1cm corresponds to 2 to 6 km in reality are too crude to permit the identification of elements of the urban pattern; on the other hand they provide a good idea of the built-up area in its geographical setting and of its directions growth. Seeing the city at this macro-scale is a humbling experience to an architect since it demonstrates only too clearly how tiny the area is where formal design matters: in our illustrations the great walls of the imperial "Purple City" of Beijing are discernible as well as the Mall in Washington D.C. but it is difficult to make out the pyramids on the Cairo image or to locate the Kremlin on the Moscow scene.

To complement the satellite images we have also included some conventional aerial photos but we renounced using eye-level photographs: it would need hundreds of them to give a balanced picture of the metropoli, and reproducing a few at random would be misleading.

Satellite images with a fine resolution which permit us to make out an element as wide as a street will soon be available from the SPOT Image laboratories in Toulouse, France. Another promising technique is the use of radar images which can be taken independently of atmospheric conditions and even at night. However, as we went to print neither the SPOT nor the radar images were commercially available. Still, we are proud to be able to include the Earthsat images which provide useful information when viewed comparatively.

I hope that a quarter of a century from now, in the year 2010, someone will read this book just as I have reread Rodwin's "Future Metropolis" 25 years after its publication in 1960. Perhaps our future reader will be stimulated to organize yet another symposium to verify our conjectures and to compare our visions with reality. If I would live to 80 years of age I might attend such a meeting. I only wish that I could be as alert then as Hans Blumenfeld (born 1892) was at our Washington D.C. meetings proving that he still possesses one of the youngest minds in planning our profession.

Part I

Global and National Context

1.

The Metropolis in Its National and Regional Context

Dennis J. Dwyer

In recent decades remarkable changes have taken place in global, national and regional patterns of urbanization and in the structure of large cities, changes which call for reassessment both of the concept of urbanization as a process and of the sequential evolution of the urban form resulting from the urbanization process.

Traditional views of the evolution and the importance of cities are perhaps too well known to require elaboration.[1] Cities have been seen as playing vital roles in several aspects highly important both to regional and to national development, and inherent in most concepts has been the reduction in distance or the elimination of the friction of space which is implied in urban concentration. Indeed, the progressive concentration of population has been seen as being fundamental to the importance of cities. In the economic sense, it is under such conditions of urban space that the external economies associated with business enterprises can most easily be made available to neighbors. For this reason, and because of other less particularly economic characteristics outlined below, the city has been acknowledged as the principal center of change and growth in industry and commerce. The Industrial Revolution experienced in today's economically advanced countries was essentially urban based, although, of course, concomitant change in the countryside was vital to its accomplishment.

The urbanization of previously non-urban areas has also been seen as, and undoubtedly is, the mainspring of regional development. The economic history of today's more economically advanced nations shows their economic growth to have been led in spatial terms by rapidly developing regions associated with thriving urban centers, which at some stages of growth have stood in marked contrast to lagging regions in those nations: lagging regions essentially associated with poorly developed urban systems. At certain periods, counter-balancing forces, sometimes impelled by direct government policy, have acted in favor of equalization and the more even spread of growth. Such official policies have usually involved the creation of new urban centers in the more backward regions or the strengthening of existing ones, and this kind of approach has become an important feature of regional planning in both the economically advanced and the less economically advanced countries. Further, within the developing countries, the desired industrial take-off on a national scale is being sought almost wholly through city-oriented policies.

A second aspect of the advantages of population concentration traditionally held to accrue under urban circumstances lies in the role of cities as centers of change and catalysts intellectually, socially and politically. As Meier has pointed out,[2] flows of information and ideas can achieve their highest acceleration only under conditions of maximum accessibility, that is, within urban centers. Cities have therefore been designed, consciously or unconsciously, not only to provide better physical access to goods and services through concentration but also as communication centers and storehouses of information. The number of face-to-face contacts possible in a given time at urban population densities is of a markedly higher order than that possible at rural population densities. Because of their function as collecting places for the most advanced information, and also because of the concentration within their boundaries of people of diverse origins, cities have also traditionally functioned as vital social melting pots in the development of states. The concentrated nature of heterogeneous populations has, in this sense, further enhanced the catalytic role of cities.

As the above paragraphs indicate, concentration was the key note of the urbanization process in what might be called a period of industrial urbanization, that is, the period of rapid urban growth which was a feature of the Industrial Revolution as experienced in today's economically advanced countries.[3] For Hope Tisdale, writing in 1942, urbanization principally implied "a movement from a state of less concentration to a state of more concentration."[4] Europe, of course, figured prominently in terms of such population movements. In 1890 there were perhaps 20 agglomerations throughout the world of more than 500,000 population, and, of these, nine were in Europe (with another two in European Russia) compared with three in the U.S. By the beginning of the twentieth century, two-thirds of the world's urban population was located in Europe, North America and Australia. The distribution of the world's metropoli was highly correlated with that of industrialization, and the urban areas themselves were highly characterized by various aspects of concentration. Within the nineteenth century city, it was the central city that was the greatest point of concentration both for inhabitants and for work places. As Cherry has stated, "the largest cities grew territorially by the absorption of outlying smaller settlements with the economic heart being decisively at the center."[5] Sometimes such urban areas coalesced and formed what Geddes came to call conurbations (remarking in doing so that this was an ugly word for a very ugly phenomenon). As is well known, continuing population concentration not only implied the spatial growth of cities, sometimes into conurbations, but also excessive crowding and the growth of social problems which gave rise to a large nineteenth century protest literature. The great cities usually had the worst records but, for Britain at least, the decade of the 1890s seems to have constituted a watershed since during this period death rates fell and the life expectancy of urban dwellers started to rise.[6]

Counterurbanization

Even by the beginning of the twentieth century, however, processes were well under way which during the 1970s culminated in the undermining of the concept of urbanization as essentially implying a process of continuous population concentration. A long-term re-sorting process seems to have been occurring, implying essentially the rejection of congested urban areas and of further population concentration in favor of greater dispersal, initially through suburban development. As early as the last decades of the nineteenth century, the large industrial towns and cities were witnessing significant outward movement of population as a result of changes in urban transport, particularly tramway electrification and the subsequent development of suburban railways. The growth of what became known in the United States as "streetcar suburbs", as Cherry has pointed out, essentially reversed an urban locational pattern which had persisted since the Middle Ages and within which slums were located at the city gates and elite areas at the city center.[7] In the streetcar era of industrial urbanization, the central districts of the metropolis remained congested and concentrated but they were increasingly surrounded by less congested, more dispersed suburbs of higher social status. These trends were accelerated by the impact upon personal mobility made by the motorcar, which permitted the development of even less concentrated urban environments, most notably in the United States. The greatest volume of suburbanization followed the Second World War, and by 1970 the majority of the urban population of North America resided in the suburbs. Even so, however, there continued to be growth in the populations of the central cities of North America until the most recent period: that which can be most properly characterized as the period of counterurbanization.

According to Berry, the originator of the term, counterurbanization "is a process of population deconcentration: it implies a movement from the state of more concentration to a state of less concentration."[8] Berry sees the 1970s as a turning point in the urban experience of the economically more advanced countries, as characterized most clearly by the American urban experience, that of the world's most economically advanced country. Since 1970, Berry observed U.S. metropolitan areas have grown more slowly than has the population of the nation as a whole and substantially less rapidly than the populations of non-metropolitan America. This is a development that stands in contrast to all preceding decades as far back as the early nineteenth century. Further, on a net basis metropolitan areas in the United States have started losing migrants to non-metropolitan areas. The overall decline in metropolitan growth has largely been accounted for by the largest metropolitan areas, particularly those located in the old industrial heartlands of the United States, that is, in the Northeast. The large cities in this area have tended to have lost most heavily, but meanwhile, not only has rapid growth taken place in some smaller metropolitan areas but this growth has been particularly concentrated into what has become known as the Sunbelt, that is, the southern and western U.S. A further feature of the counterurbanization trend is that although the central areas of the nation's metropoli grew until 1970 (but only at modest rates compared with growth in outer urban rings), since then inner area population has started to decline. Because this decline has involved a considerable exodus of the white population, the inner areas have become much more homogeneous in terms of being characterized particularly by the black population.

These recent changes have led Berry to observe that, given the fact that only five percent of the United States' population—less than 10 million people—was left on farms in 1970, urban growth in the United States now largely consists of the transference on a regional and on a more local basis of already urbanized populations, and that consequently the concentrative migration process resulting from industrial urbanization has ended. Migration in the world's most economically advanced country now takes place between metropolitan areas on an inter-regional scale and also intra-regionally through an accelerating dispersion of people and jobs outwards beyond metropolitan boundaries. Population mobility continues to increase —at least one-fifth of all Americans move at least once a year—but largely within and between urban regions. Counties adjacent to the largest metropolitan areas now receive the most net migration and counties adjacent to the smallest the least. Urban Americans increasingly prefer the suburbs, the smaller towns, the more pleasant and the less dense environments. Declining central cities lost more people during the decade of the 1970s than did declining rural counties. At the national scale, there has been a transition to the post-industrial phase, one characterized by the creation of a service economy, the pre-eminence of the professional and technical class, and the emergence of new technology, particularly in information processing, leading to a significant growth of a quaternary sector in the economy.[9] Unlike the constituents of the older industrial economy, new post-industrial enterprises tend to be markedly footloose, and insofar as they use high grade, high-priced labor, the residential choices of such labor are often critical in the location of post-industrial economic activity. The most striking characteristic of this new locational matrix is the rapid rise of the Sunbelt cities.

Decentralization without End?

A more recent paper by Hall has updated and extended Berry's analysis.[10] For the United States, Hall observes, there now appear to be negative returns to urban scale inasmuch as the larger urban areas are either increasing much more slowly than smaller ones or else are actually declining. Hall confirms most of the processes observed by Berry but through the analysis of the most recent data he asserts that it is not true that non-metropolitan areas are gaining in population at the expense of metro-politan areas. Between 1970 and 1978, the cutoff point for his data, he observes that 41 new areas were added to United States metropolitan statistics on the basis that they satisfied the criteria for metropolitan area definition. When these new areas are included in the analysis, it is found that from 1970 to 1978 United States metropolitan areas grew in population while non-metropolitan areas actually declined. But nearly half of the net metropolitan increase in population came from the 41 newly designated areas, and these were mostly in the southern and western Sunbelt, further evidence of the powerful inter-regional shift in metropolitan population that is in process in the United States.

On the other hand, the 1980 Census Report of the United States, as reported by Hall, confirms the progressive net loss of population experi-enced by the central parts of the metropoli. The 32 largest standard metropolitan statistical areas show the same trend for the entire intercensal decade 1970-1980 inasmuch as they have recorded striking reductions in their rate of population gain after 1970. Some of the large metropolitan areas of the Northeast have lost population considerably, including New York, which lost nearly one million people during the 1970s, Buffalo, Pittsburgh, and Cleveland. Most other metropolitan areas in the Northeast and Midwest were stagnant in population. Overall, there has been a striking reduction in growth rates in the very largest metropoli, while the 32 largest as a group also experienced an almost five percent loss of population from their central cities. In general terms, central cities almost everywhere in the United States have tended to be declining or at best stagnating; however, in the South and West the vigorous growth of the suburbs more than compensated. Overall, the larger metropolitan areas are now either declin-ing or growing much more slowly than the smaller ones. Inasmuch as, except in the case of California, the largest metropoli tend to be located in the Northeast or Midwest, the inter-regional comparison is now between the still developing Sunbelt cities and the stagnant, or even declining, cities of the Frostbelt.

As to the causes of these trends, Hall agrees with Berry that in very large measure they stem from the fact that, to a greater extent than any other nation, the United States is now post-industrial; as he points out, more than 65 percent of all workers are now in the tertiary-quaternary sectors. By the same token, the manufacturing base, though immensely productive, needs fewer and fewer workers to maintain a given volume of output. But even so, changes in the geography of manufacturing account in part for the trends already noted. The older manufacturing cities of the Northeast and Midwest have for some time not only been faced with very severe industrial competition both from other parts of the United States and from overseas but also have tended to benefit relatively less from the emergence of important new industries, for example the electronics industry, which are much more footloose in character. These new footloose industries have tended to be associated with highly skilled work forces enjoying high incomes, and the concentration of such incomes, particularly in certain new cities of the Sunbelt, has in turn reinforced regional shifts in metropolitan distribution through the attraction of service industries.

According to Cherry, the European countries today exhibit a continuum of metropolitan development from centralization to decentralization.[11] However, the Netherlands, Switzerland, Belgium, and Great Britain are now exhibiting many of the same features of decentralization as have been observed in the United States. In Britain, for example, the 1981 Census gave ample evidence of significant change especially in respect of the central cities. Between 1971 and 1981 inner London decreased in population by almost 18 percent, and similarly sharp losses of population were recorded for the inner areas of Glasgow, Manchester, and Liverpool. In general, Britain's city regions are gaining at the expense of the non-urban areas but, as in the United States, there is a most significant extension of commuting hinterlands taking place and also considerable decentralization of jobs to match the dispersal of people. As Cherry has noted, "metropolitan changes continue to confirm that the pattern of urban growth is away from the largest cities and in favor of intermediate sized and smaller cities"; as far as the British metropoli are concerned, "the period of vigorous reconstruction and growth has now ended. Cities have run out of money, land and political support. As their cores have lost both people and jobs they have inevitably become preoccupied with the problems of decline."[12]

A General Model

As part of the analysis previously referred to, Hall has proposed a general model of sequential urban evolution which, he claims, fits the circumstances of most cities in most countries reasonably well.[13] This may be summarized (in parts verbatim) as follows:

1. During the early stages of industrialization and the rationalization of agriculture, population begins to migrate to cities. In many cases, local towns cannot absorb the migration flows completely and longer distance migration develops towards larger urban places, for example, the national capital or provincial capitals. One city, or a very few cities, grows more rapidly than the rest and thereby comes to dominate the urban hierarchy. A primate pattern of urban size thus develops. In this early stage of urbanization work opportunities are highly concentrated in the central cities, as they were during the early part of the Industrial Revolution in today's economically advanced countries. Population therefore tends to concentrate in the central cities.

2. In time, the rural outflow from the peripheral regions begins to exhaust itself, and the cities in these regions begin to develop as local manufacturing and service centers and also to inter-

cept more of the local rural migrants. The domination of the system by the primate city or cities therefore begins to weaken. In addition, within individual metropolitan areas central city growth is very vigorous and although, because of the weakness of suburban development at this stage, the surrounding urbanized ring on balance loses population, the system—in terms of the metropolitan area as a whole—grows because the central city growth is greater than the loss in the outer areas. This circumstance Hall terms absolute centralization.

3. In the third stage vigorous suburban out-movement begins, a process which is experienced first in the larger metropolitan areas which have experienced very rapid growth in stages 1 and 2. The outer urbanized ring is now increasing in population but the population of the central city is increasing at a still greater rate. Hall therefore calls this stage relative centralization.

4. The fourth stage reverses this process inasmuch as the rate of suburban growth exceeds that of the central city. This is relative decentralization.

5. Later, the central city starts to decline in population, and there is a marked fall in densities. The outer urban ring is continuing to develop rapidly and hence a phase of absolute decentralization has set in. During this stage, Hall observes, the growth of the largest metropolitan areas begin to slow down relative to places lower down the urban hierarchy, and primate urban distributions begin to become substantially modified.

6. The process is completed by the large metropolitan areas going into actual decline. Their suburban rings are gaining people but the gain is insufficient to counterbalance the loss of population from the central cities. This stage is termed decentralization during loss. Hall believes that it is never a general condition and that, even in the most economically advanced and post-industrial countries like the United States and the United Kingdom, it will represent the state of only a few very large metropolitan areas. There will be inter-regional forces at work elsewhere which will promote metropolitan growth in other locations.

Hall suggests that different nations are currently at different positions on this urban continuum. His data indicates, for example, that much of Europe has recently passed from stage 3 to stage 4 with some areas moving into stage 5. Eastern and southern Europe, in contrast, he believes to be still in stages 1 and 2. Japan he sees as moving into stage 5 but stage 6 so far has been restricted to a very few large metropolitan areas in the United Kingdom and the United States, at least up to about 1975.

Urbanization and Metropolitan Growth in the Developing Countries

Although Hall's model is conceptually elegant, a major problem in testing its usefulness—in terms of its predictive ability—lies in the paucity of comparative data on the world's great cities. Hall, Berry and other workers in recent years have assembled a great deal of formerly very scattered data, especially in relation to urban and metropolitan trends in the U.S. and Europe,[14] and it is clearly upon this data base that the model has been formulated. However, not only has the data situation been made immensely more complicated since the Second World War by metropolitan growth in the developing countries, but also—during the same period—the overall global urbanization trend has shifted decisively towards those countries.

In general, it is true to say that the information published by the United Nations on population living in agglomerations of 20,000 persons or more is based on census returns or reliable estimates from almost all of the industrialized countries, but that data of a similar quality is completely lacking for more than half the population of the developing countries.[15] At present, 40 percent of the world's population lives in urban places with agglomerated populations of 5,000 or more persons. But, the transition to a fully urbanized world (one as urbanized in terms of population distribution as the United States or Britain today) is proceeding so rapidly that given the continuation of present trends it could be completed within less than a century. In these circumstances, one of the most significant global happenings of recent decades has been the expansion of the revolutionary shift in the location of world population from countryside to cities, which started approximately 200 years ago, from the presently industrialized countries into the developing countries.

Today, there are two distinct facets within the general urbanization trend. The industrialized countries are showing declining rates but, because they include only one-quarter of the world's population, these declining rates have not been sufficient to retard the global urbanization trend. The huge populations of the developing countries, in contrast, appear still to be in the earlier stages of an urbanization more massive than any before. As a result, the balance of urban populations between the industrialized countries and the developing countries is currently in the process of most significant change. Urban populations in the developing countries are growing twice as fast as those in the industrialized countries. They are also growing in numbers greatly exceeding those of the industrialized countries even during the period of the latter's most rapid growth. By the end of the present century the balance of global urban population will have very definitely tipped towards the developing countries. Indeed, during the early 1970s the point of equilibrium in urban population distribution between the industrialized and the developing countries was crossed. Whereas, at the beginning of the present century, two-thirds of the world's urban population was located in Europe, North America and Australia, by the end of the century two-thirds of the world's urban population will be located in the developing countries.

This massive shift within the global urbanization trend presents immense challenges. As yet, there is not sufficient data to permit soundly based generalizations of the kind that would be necessary to extend to the developing countries the type of work on metropolitan change carried out by such workers as Berry and Hall within the industrially advanced countries. Nevertheless, it does appear that in many cases the large cities are sharing fully in the extremely rapid urban growth that is characterizing contemporary developing countries. One recent contribution has claimed that in the developing countries the bigger the urban area, the faster it grows: "Thus, towns are growing more rapidly than villages, cities faster than towns; cities with a population more than a million are growing faster than cities with less than a million, and multi-million cities with over 2.5 million are growing fastest of all."[16] But this appears to be stretching the available evidence. Rather, the available United Nations figures (for the period 1950-1970) show that in the developing countries population has grown with similar speed in all urban size groups except that of more than five million persons, in respect of which it has been much slower in growth.[17] However, the observations for the five million-plus urban size group are very much weighted by the figures for Shanghai and Calcutta. Population estimates for Shanghai are very uncertain, while the cities of India, in general, are relatively slow growing. In the circumstances, it is perhaps reasonable to reach the conclusion that while the largest cities in the developing countries may not be growing as fast as those of the other size groups, nevertheless there is much less variation in urban growth by size group at present in the developing countries than in the industrially advanced countries, and certainly nothing like the pattern which has evolved in the most highly developed industrialized countries with cities having upwards of a million people showing significantly slower population growth than that in smaller cities.

Global Urbanization: A Unitary Phenomenon?

These very basic macro-trends lead naturally into a consideration of the unity of the global process of metropolitan formation. In terms of his proposed model, Hall envisages what he calls "a continuum of industrialization and urbanization",[18] that is, not only a very close coincidence between industrialization and urbanization but also, presumably, that if appropriate data existed, it would prove possible to allocate every country to some point along the scale of his six stages. Conceptually, he embraces the idea of a single evolutionary urbanization process with the developing countries being in the earlier stages of a cycle which has already become familiar through the previous metropolitan experience of today's economically advanced countries.

The earlier stages of the urbanization cycle in today's economically advanced countries were undoubtedly ones of industrial urbanization. This appears to be very far from the case in the developing countries, however. In cases where cities evolved during the colonial period, they were almost always not industrial cities. In the period of subsequent independence much more emphasis has, of course, been placed upon industrialization in national planning in the developing countries, and undoubtedly a good deal of industrial development has, in general, been stimulated. The significant point in the present context is that virtually all of this industrial development has been carried out by means of technological transfer from the industrialized countries. Within the industrialized countries in recent decades there has been a massive replacement of industrial labor by capital in the form of ever more sophisticated machines, with the result that the industrial employment opportunities created by a given quantum of industrial development have progressively become less and less. As a result, contemporary industrial growth within the developing countries has, in general, been much less labor absorptive than was the case in the previous experience of today's industrially advanced countries.[19]

A further point of distinctiveness arises from the demographic circumstances of contemporary urban growth in the developing countries. It has become clear that a good deal of urban growth is, in fact, not related so much to the attractiveness of cities, and in particular to job opportunities (at least insofar as job opportunities have been understood within the context of the experience of the industrially advanced countries), as to the lack of opportunities—the abysmal lack of development—in the countryside. Urban populations are not being absorbed very fully into industrial job opportunities. As the United Nations has reported, "Although the Third World's industrial production increased by an average of seven percent per annum during the 1960-1972 period, it contributed very little to employment growth, especially in Africa."[20] In the case of Latin America, between 1960 and 1970 the urban population grew by 4.2 percent a year but manufacturing employment by only 2.8 percent.[21] The general conclusion must be that in the vast majority of developing countries the rate of labor absorption by industry has fallen far below the rate of growth of urban populations.

Other considerations in a similar vein relate to the evolution of the form of the large cities in the developing countries. If the theme of the recent metropolitan experience of the most economically advanced countries has been decentralization and a general lowering of urban population densities, it is as yet by no means clear that this experience is being, or will be, repeated in the developing countries. Smaller urban places in the developing countries have suffered from a marked lack of research interest to date,[22] but as far as the larger centers are concerned (cities of at least 100,000 people) certain relevant trends are apparent. The first is that rapid urban population growth has resulted in recent decades in the very significant areal expansion of such cities. Much of this expansion has not yet been properly recorded, particularly since it largely concerns unregulated residential building, for example, by urban squatters.[23] In the case of Lima,

Peru, for example, a mushrooming of squatter settlements began during the 1950s, and today squatters constitute about 40 percent of the total urban population. In all, the construction of squatter settlements probably accounts for more than four-fifths of the physical development of metropolitan Lima since 1960. Although such settlements are interdigitated with the more regular urban fabric, even very close to the heart of the city, the largest of them are of course on the periphery, some as far distant as 25 kilometers from the center. This pattern of rapid and extensive spatial extension will probably remain the city's predominant means for accommodating further population growth for the forseeable future since it has been estimated that by 1990 there may well be as many as 4.5 million people in Lima squatter settlements out of a total urban population of six million.

In addition to these trends in the residential geography of the urban poor, who of course make up by far the majority of the populations of the metropoli of the developing countries, in many cases centrifugal tendencies have been experienced in terms of the spatial movement of elites. In general, it appears that upper income groups are rapidly leaving inner urban locations for destinations on urban peripheries where they live at relatively low densities, well insulated from the poor of the city, surrounded by high walls, and sometimes even guarded at the gates. Unlike the situation in the industrially advanced countries, however, these trends do not appear in most cases to imply the emptying of inner cities. Rather the reverse tends to be the case. As inner cities have been vacated by the rich so they have become progressively more and more densely occupied by the poor through the subdivision of living space to sizes which correspond with the economic capacity of the poor to afford them. Many empirical case studies in recent years have demonstrated the smaller and smaller subdivision of existing residential units in inner areas and the further deterioration of already low environmental standards.[24]

Although these and other case studies represent valid individual instances of the consequences of the continuing growth of large cities in the developing countries, unfortunately there is a dearth of overall statistical coverage, particularly in respect of urban population densities. The kind of pioneering work carried out by Brush in the late 1960s on Indian urban population densities has unfortunately never been more widely followed up. Brush's work demonstrated repeated cases of progressive intra-urban concentration of population over the period of the present century and, in particular, found that in the great port metropoli—Bombay, Calcutta, and Madras—that concentration in the central wards was increasing while, at the same time, population was also building up on the periphery. His analysis of the statistics for Bombay, which has unusually long and continuous records, showed that during the 40 years from 1881 to 1921 the increase in the metropolitan population from 773,000 to 1.17 million was absorbed by population growth in both its central and its outlying parts. By 1961 population densities throughout the metropolis had risen to new high levels even though large areas for urban development had been opened up on nearby Salsette Island since the late 1940s. The 1961 census recorded a gross density of 3,300 persons per hectare (1,329 per acre) in one of the central divisions of the city, at that time the apex of India's urban population concentration. "It is clear," states Brush of the period up to the mid-1960s, "that a large share of population growth in Indian cities has been absorbed into existing urban areas, resulting in the progressive congestion of previously occupied tracts."[25]

More recent United Nations statistics, though by no means complete, indicate the persistence of similar trends in many developing countries. *The Global Review of Human Settlements,* prepared for the United Nations HABITAT Conference, indicated that, for cities in the developing countries for which there was comparable time series information, the cities were becoming more densely populated in all cases except two (Lima and Guayaquil in Latin America), and that, even in cases where municipal boundaries had expanded over time, overall densities had increased.[26] One notable example was Mexico City which in 1950 had an area of 242 sq. kilometers (km^2) at a gross density of 118 persons per hectare and in 1970 an area of 433 km^2 at a gross density of 227. Madras had a gross density of 134 in 1961 and, over the same metropolitan area, 193 in 1971, while the developed area of Caracas was 42 km^2 in 1945 with a gross density of 120 and 100 km^2 in 1966 with a gross density of 175.[27] Clearly, in these circumstances concentration rather than decentralization remains the theme for much of the metropolitan development of the Third World.

Conclusion

It remains to be seen whether the existing differences in metropolitan development between the economically advanced and the developing countries represent but a stage feature that will ultimately prove to have been only temporarily distinctive within the context of an urbanization phenomenon characterized by overall unity. In this respect a good deal will depend upon the future pace, characteristics and scale of industrial and post-industrial development within the less economically advanced countries.

At present, the prospect of change sufficient to radically alter the employment characteristics of the contemporary Third World metropolis does not seem bright, and the fact that a significant, and probably increasing, proportion of employment will continue to need to be found in the informal sector of metropolitan economies will probably only make for the very lengthy persistence of population concentration. Within Third World metropoli many more people are currently being supported than the economic base warrants (at least in terms of the economic experience of the industrially advanced countries) through what is essentially a shared poverty system: a type of urban employment—largely within the informal sector —that is an urban interpretation of an ethic that originally arose in response to agricultural circumstances to allow a great number of people, through a system of shared poverty, to each claim a small part of the agricultural output from a given piece of land. In these circumstances job sharing and splitting can ensure an almost indefinite increase in a metropolitan population, one largely unrelated to the progress of "formal" secondary or tertiary development. Given the absence of specific physical limitations—such as upon water supply—developing countries will thus in the near future see the emergence of metropoli of enormous size—a Mexico City of 31 million by the year 2000, a Shanghai of 22 million, and a Bombay of 17 million, for example. But these will be metropoli unrelated to industrialization for the most part, and still less to the kinds of tertiary and quaternary development that have more recently characterized the metropoli of the industrially advanced countries. They will be metropoli characterized by extensive poverty and by occupations marginal to the relatively small core of "formal" ones. They will also be characterized by continued concentration, if only because of the inability of the vast majority of their populations to pay for much intra-urban transport.

There are also other reasons why distinctiveness will probably persist. In part these reasons are social ones which involve consideration—in the migrational circumstances which strongly underpin much urban growth in the developing countries—of possibilities of alternatives to the automatic one-way adaptation of migrants to an absorptive urban culture that was characteristic of the phase of industrial urbanization in today's economically advanced countries.[28] Overall, the tentative conclusion must be at present that urbanization and metropolitan formation are not single, universally similar processes but rather processes that assume different forms and meanings depending upon historic, economic, social, and cultural conditions.

References

1. Dennis J. Dwyer (ed.), *The City As a Centre of Change in Asia,* (Hong Kong, 1972), pp. viii-ix.
2. Richard L. Meier, "The Organization of Technological Innovation in Urban Environments," in Oscar Handlin and John Burchard (eds.), *The Historian and the City,* (Cambridge, MA., 1963), pp. 74-75.
3. Brian J.L. Berry (ed.), *Urbanization and Counterurbanization,* (Beverly Hills, 1976), pp. 17-30.
4. H. Tisdale, "The Process of Urbanization," *Social Forces,* 20 (1942): pp. 311-316. (Quoted by Berry, op. cit.).
5. Gordon E. Cherry, "Britain and the Metropolis," *Town Planning Review,* 55 (1984): pp. 5-33, reference p. 7.
6. *Op. cit.,* p.8.
7. *Ibid.,* p.8.
8. *Ibid.,* p.17.
9. Brian J.L. Berry, *Comparative Urbanization,* (London, 1981), pp. 48-56.
10. Peter Hall, "Decentralization Without End? A Re-Evaluation," in John Patten (ed.), *The Expanding City,* (Oxford, 1983), pp. 125-155.
11. *Ibid.,* p.26.
12. *Ibid.,* p.30.
13. *Ibid.,* p.143.

14. For example, P. Hall and D. Hay, *Growth Centres in the European Urban System*, (London, 1980).

15. G.T. Trewartha, *A Geography of Population: World Patterns*, (New York, 1969), p. 147.

16. Jack F. Williams, Stanley D. Brunn and Joe T. Darden, "World Urban Development," in Stanley D. Brunn and Jack F. Williams (eds.), *Cities of the World: World Regional Urban Development*, (New York, 1983), p. 14.

17. Center for Housing, Building and Planning, Department of Economic and Social Affairs, United Nations, *Global Review of Human Settlements*, (Oxford, 1976), Vol. 1, pp. 8-9.

18. *Ibid.*, p. 143.

19. Dennis J. Dwyer, "Economic Development: Development for Whom?," *Geography*, 62 (1977): pp. 325-334.

20. Center for Housing, Building and Planning, *op. cit.*, p. 62.

21. John P. Dickenson, "Industrialization in the Third World," in Alan B. Mountjoy (ed.), *The Third World*, (London, 1978), p. 98.

22. See Dennis A. Rondinelli, *Secondary Cities in Developing Countries*, (Beverly Hills, 1983).

23. Dennis J. Dwyer, *People and Housing in Third World Cities*, (London, 1975).

24. Dennis J. Dwyer, "The Effect of Crowding in Cities on the Quality of Life, With Special Reference to Developing Countries," *Proceedings of the Ninth International Conference on the Unity of the Sciences*, (New York, 1981), pp. 589-612.

25. J.E. Brush, "Spatial Patterns of Population in Indian Cities," *Geographical Review*, 58 (1968): pp. 362-391, reference p. 380.

26. Center for Housing, Building and Planning, *op. cit.*, p. 74.

27. *Ibid.*, *Statistical Annex*, Vol. 2, Table 13.

28. Dennis J. Dwyer, "Urban Geography and the Urban Future," *Geography*, 64 (1979): pp. 86-95.

2.

The Emerging Metropolis in Tropical Africa

Anthony O'Connor

In an earlier paper in this collection Dennis Dwyer has emphasized the need for differentiation between developed and less developed countries in studies of "the metropolis."[1] I strongly agree with him on the need to disaggregate and differentiate, but I should prefer to take the disaggregation further than he does, and I ask why the discussion should be based on a crude and arbitrary dichotomy between developed and less developed countries. To see the world in such binary terms may assist intellectual arguments, but it generally distorts reality.[2] This applies to a wide range of phenomena conventionally discussed in terms of developed and less developed countries, but especially to urbanization when the proportion of the total national population living in cities occupies a spectrum from under ten percent to over ninety percent. Many Latin American and Middle Eastern countries occupy a position on this spectrum far closer to most of Europe than to most of Africa or southern Asia.

As for the level of urbanization so also for the character of the cities, the conventional global division may not be the most appropriate. Is there any evidence that the Latin American metropolis has more in common with that in India than with that in southern Europe? The less developed countries or so-called "Third World" will soon have two-thirds of the global urban population. Is it not then time to stop considering the "Third World city" as a distinct phenomenon, especially since some observers go so far as to suggest that it constitutes a "special case" of metropolitan growth deviating from a norm provided by Europe and North America?

I might take as my "text" the final sentence of Dwyer's paper: "urbanization and metropolitan formation . . . assume different forms and meanings depending upon historic, economic, social, and cultural conditions." I am so much in agreement with this that I feel a simple binary framework for discussion should be adopted only where it is demonstrably the most appropriate one. Far more often we should think in terms of a spectrum

—an appallingly wide one with respect to all aspects of prosperity and poverty—or in terms of a series of culture realms, of which tropical Africa is one.

The City in Tropical Africa

In 1960, around the time of independence for most African countries, "the tropical African metropolis" would have been almost a contradiction in terms, for no city had a population much exceeding half a million (Table 1). There were pre-colonial as well as colonial cities in the region, but nothing remotely comparable to the long-established metropolis of Cairo to the north of the Sahara. In most countries far fewer than ten percent of the population lived in an urban environment (Table 2). The situation is now rapidly changing, however, and with respect to the future metropolis in particular tropical Africa is highly significant. Here more than anywhere else we have "metropoli in the making," being shaped by decision-makers at every level from the highest ranking bureaucrats to the squatter settlers in a disused quarry, and including decision-makers thousands of miles away as well as on the spot. In 1980, tropical Africa still had no cities with more than four million inhabitants: yet a United Nations forecast, endorsed by the World Bank (but inevitably highly speculative), is that by the year 2025 there will be 36 cities of that size on the African continent, a quarter of the world total, and this must include at least 25 in tropical Africa (Table 3).

Table 2-1

Population growth in Tropical African Cities

| | Estimated population in thousands | | | Forecast |
	1960	1970	1980	2000
Lagos	600	1600	3000	(9000)
Kinshasa	500	1400	2700	(8000)
Addis Ababa	500	850	1300	(4000)
Ibadan	500	750	1100	(3000)
Khartoum	400	650	1100	(4000)
Accra	400	750	1100	(4000)
Dakar	400	600	950	(3000)
Nairobi	300	520	900	(4000)
Harare	300	400	800	(3000)
Luanda	250	450	750	(3000)
Abidjan	220	600	1200	(4000)
Dar es Salaam	180	380	800	(4000)

All figures are for the whole urban agglomeration.
Sources: Diverse.

Table 2-2

Levels of Urbanization in Selected African Countries

	Urban % of total population	
	1960	1980
Cameroon	8	23
Ghana	12	28
Ivory Coast	8	28
Kenya	6	14
Malawi	3	8
Mali	4	12
Nigeria	12	24
Sierra Leone	6	17
Sudan	6	14
Tanzania	4	10
Zaire	12	28
Zambia	17	36

The urban population is that in towns over 20,000.
Sources: Diverse (and sometimes conflicting).

Table 2-3

Cities with Over Four Million Inhabitants

	Number of Cities		
	1980	2000	2025
World	38	79	144
Less Developed	23	59	123
South Asia	11	23	41
East Asia	7	14	26
Latin America	6	12	22
Africa	1	12	36

Source: World Bank, *The Urban Edge*, 8 (6), 1984, p. 4.

Urbanization in all parts of tropical Africa has been occurring throughout the post-colonial period at a remarkably rapid rate. Many cities have been doubling in size every 10 years, through a combination of massive net in-migration and high rates of natural increase, together with some engulfing of formerly rural settlements. In Nigeria no reliable census data exist, but the population of Lagos has probably reached four million while there are more than one million in Ibadan and possibly that number in Kano. Elsewhere there is only one true metropolis per country, Kinshasa in Zaire

19

having over three million inhabitants and at least eight other national capitals now exceeding one million. Compared with Latin America and South-East Asia, urban development is thus relatively dispersed in tropical Africa, largely due to extreme political fragmentation. There is at present a constellation of medium-sized capital cities with around half a million inhabitants; but each of these is fast becoming a metropolis. The overall level of urbanization is in the process of surpassing that in South Asia, and also that in China. In certain individual countries, such as Burundi and Rwanda, it remains as low as five percent; but for tropical Africa as a whole it has reached 20 to 30 percent, and in Zambia it now exceeds 40 percent—though divided between Lusaka and several Copperbelt centers rather than concentrated in a single metropolis.

There is some evidence that the growth rate of the largest cities is now slowing somewhat in relative terms, but the absolute annual increment to their populations is as large as ever. United Nations projections for the year 2000 include perhaps somewhat inflated figures of 8.4 million for Kinshasa, 5.6 million for Addis Ababa, 5.1 million for Khartoum, and 4.6 million for Dar es Salaam.[3] Even cities such as Bamako in Mali and Mogadishu in Somalia are by then expected to have over a million inhabitants.

The situation at the national level is exemplified by Kenya whose cities and towns accommodated only two million people up to 1980. Between 1980 and 2000 an extra five million urban dwellers are expected. These might be highly concentrated in Nairobi, causing it to grow from one million towards or even beyond four million, or efforts could be made to spread as many as possible among smaller centers. The numbers involved are broadly similar in Tanzania, Sudan, Ghana, and Ivory Coast, despite the diversity in their economic circumstances.

Common Characteristics

Are further generalizations possible for these tropical African metropoli beyond their recent emergence as such and their continuing rapid growth?[4] With regard to functions most are very similar, serving as the administrative and commercial capitals of newly-independent nation states. Most of them also have the largest concentration of manufacturing in the country, but industrialization has certainly not provided the basis for urbanization in tropical Africa in the way that it has in parts of Latin America and East Asia, as well as in more "developed" regions at an earlier date.[5] It does not follow from this that metropolitan growth in tropical Africa is either "a special case" or "parasitic," for, throughout most of history, cities have existed largely to provide services rather than to manufacture goods, and many such services are of far greater benefit to mankind than many manufactured goods. However, even the service functions of African cities are now expanding more slowly than the population, and this provides real cause for alarm. Tropical Africa is perhaps exceptional in experiencing rapid urban growth at a time of general stagnation in the economy, with no sign, unfortunately, that this is a mere temporary phase.

One result of this situation is a rapidly increasing level of unemployment and underemployment (though these concepts are not easily applied in this region, especially since the economy of every city incorporates an "informal sector" of growing relative importance involving much self-employment). Even more critical is the low income of the great majority of the population, including many who work for long hours.[6] In part, this is a basic characteristic of tropical Africa in general rather than specifically of its cities, and, although average incomes are falling in real terms, they are still not as low as in most rural areas. However, the poverty is such as to influence profoundly the whole character of the African metropolis. Of course, average incomes mask huge disparities, and while this is a characteristic shared with cities in, say, Latin America or the Middle East, here the high-and middle-income groups are so small that the notion of "the urban poor" as a special category within the urban population is quite inapplicable.

Some indication of the low level of material well-being is provided by surveys of housing conditions. In Dar es Salaam for instance, only 27 percent of dwellings in 1976 were made of "permanent materials;" only 12 percent had piped water within the building, and 40 percent had no access to piped water at all, while only 20 percent were linked to an electricity supply. Perhaps even more significantly the situation had deteriorated over the previous decade, and this has undoubtedly continued. Kinshasa is another city in which the vast majority of the inhabitants live in flimsy dwellings and must make long journeys to fetch water. In Lagos the buildings are generally more substantial, but overcrowding is even more extreme with an average of more than four people per room.

These situations reflect not only the low incomes of individual households but also the very limited funds of most metropolitan authorities. In every case these funds are used far less equitably than they might be, and it would be hard to defend the share allocated to facilities for the elite in a city such as Kinshasa. However, even after a thorough redistribution the provision of adequate housing and public services for the majority of even the present city dwellers within the foreseeable future would be quite impossible. Meanwhile, as numbers rise rapidly, basic needs for shelter, water, school places, and health care (as well as the food and fuel which all households must provide for themselves) continue to increase day by day. Of course, many of these needs are inadequately met in most rural areas also: the horrors which are most particular to urban environments and which are intensifying with metropolitan growth arise from the lack of refuse disposal and sewerage systems in nearly all the areas where most people live.[7]

The general income differential between urban and rural areas largely explains the massive net in-migration to most African cities, though numerous other factors are also involved, including both perceived attractions and social conditioning especially among school-leavers.[8] The role of migration in urban growth has been such that the great majority of adults in most African cities are rural-born, and most of these retain strong ties with their areas of origin. Visits are made in both directions, and even those who have committed themselves to a lifetime of work in the city generally intend to return "home" eventually. This inevitably affects the extent of their involvement in the social and political affairs of the city, and helps to explain the lack of some features characteristic of the metropolis elsewhere.

However, one general feature of the metropolis found in extreme form throughout tropical Africa, and intensified by continuing in-migration, is ethnic or cultural heterogeneity. Not only does every African city reflect the meeting of African and alien cultures, with migrants from other continents still playing highly significant—positive and negative—roles in the urban economy and society, but it also constitutes a meeting ground for people of diverse African cultures. The term "meeting ground" is used in preference to "melting pot," for there is much evidence that ethnic consciousness is heightened rather than diminished by movement into the cosmopolitan city.[9] The number of people who consider themselves Nairobians rather than Kikuyu or Luo is still very small.

Associated with ethnic identity are kinship ties and the continuing significance of the extended family. These features are both cause and consequence of ongoing ties with the rural homeland, while they also influence many aspects of life within the metropolis—including the search for both housing and work.[10] The continued rapid growth of the cities, despite a desperate shortage of housing and income-earning opportunities adequate to sustain life, is made possible only by the practice whereby those who have a dwelling and a job are expected to provide shelter and food for many months for kinsfolk who come to join them. The relatives are increasingly only tolerated rather than welcomed, but there is little sign of the system breaking down, and as long as it lasts it helps to spread the wealth and the privilege so highly concentrated in the proto-metropolis of each country in the colonial and early post-colonial periods.

The high rate of net in-migration also affects the demographic structure of each city, though the heavy preponderance of males over females associated with eastern and south-central Africa in the past has now been much reduced. A high concentration of young adults, and increasingly rural school-leavers, among the migrants, together with out-migration of the elderly, produces an age structure which differs sharply from that for the nation as a whole, and this contributes to the intensity of economic activity within the city. It also means a potential for very high natural increase of population, with birth rates generally above the national average, and with death rates far below due to a combination of few elderly people and health care facilities superior to those in most rural areas. In almost every African city the relative importance of natural increase in total population growth is increasing, and the under-fives account for 15 to 20 percent of the inhabitants. It is, of course, their ideas and attitudes that will most profoundly influence the African metropolis of the future, and these must include attitudes towards the rural areas.

Meanwhile, the continuing rural orientation of many of the adult city dwellers has many implications.[11] Two examples will illustrate the range of these. Since many regard their stay as only temporary, and since some are putting savings into a house in their rural home area, the demand for housing in the African metropolis is predominantly for rented accommodation. Self-built squatter housing improved and consolidated over time by owner-occupiers, so widespread in Latin American cities, is much less in evidence in most tropical African cities where the most common pattern is for private landlords to erect relatively large structures with each room let to a different tenant household. A second implication is a softening of the urban-rural dichotomy which is so stark in some other parts of the world. In some respects tropical Africa provides extreme cases of "urban bias" in government policies, but although political power is often highly concentrated in the metropolis it is rarely exercised by people whose whole experience is thus confined. The elite are rarely members of long-established city families as they normally are in Latin America and much of Asia. In economic terms too there are counter-mechanisms, including remittance flows to the rural areas on a very substantial scale.

There is much dispute over the extent to which the metropolis in tropical Africa is a center of exploitation and a channel for harmful neo-colonial relationships, and how far it provides a spearhead for beneficial external influence and a generator of positive economic, social and political change. There is widespread agreement, however, that its relationships with its rural hinterland are intense; in this respect even many relatively small cities of a quarter-million to half-million inhabitants are playing a truly "metropolitan" role within the nation-states of which they are the political, cultural, and commercial capitals.

Contrasts and Convergence

All these generalizations should really be qualified in various ways, for there are substantial contrasts among cities even within tropical Africa.[12] Although both indigenous and alien cultures have contributed to the present character of each city, the balance between these may differ sharply. Lagos is an urban center of indigenous origin, and this has profoundly influenced its character however great the colonial contribution to its twentieth-century growth.[13] By contrast, Nairobi was a wholly colonial creation. In 1890 its site was a no-man's-land between Masai and Kikuyu territory, with a greater density of lions than of people. European influence was totally dominant, Asian influence subsidiary, and African influence a poor third, despite greater population numbers, until Kenya gained its independence in 1963.

Again polarity can be overdone, and many African cities occupy intermediate positions between Lagos and Nairobi. In Accra the indigenous component was rather smaller than in Lagos, while Dar es Salaam was not as totally alien as Nairobi. Kinshasa could be regarded as intermediate even between Accra and Dar es Salaam in this respect.[14] Conversely, the continuum could be extended in both directions, for Ibadan is a truly indigenous city in which European influence has never been more than marginal,[15] while a name change from Salisbury to Harare has not altered the fact that Zimbabwe has inherited a capital city designed by Europeans totally in terms of their own interests.[16]

The contrasts are sometimes presented in terms of a western/eastern Africa polarity, but this too is an oversimplification. Addis Ababa, the Ethiopian capital in eastern Africa, is to a large degree an indigenous city, though with a variety of external influences while Dakar, the Senegalese capital in the extreme west, still shows extremely strong French influences.

Yet another complexity is provided by the fact that some of the largest cities of tropical Africa have dual origins and retain a markedly dual physical structure even today. In Kano a colonial city was set up adjacent to an ancient walled city, and there is a remarkable balance of power between the two. In Sudan the capital city is often known as "the three towns," for it comprises indigenous Omdurman to the west of the Nile as well as ex-colonial Khartoum and Khartoum North across the river. In both these cases there is sharp differentiation even within one metropolis.

Examples of differentiation among these cities are provided by migration and demography, by economic structure and employment, and by housing, with links of course among all of these. During the colonial period men far outnumbered women among the migrants to such cities as Nairobi and Harare (then Salisbury), and most stayed only a short period in the city, whereas long-term family migration was common in Accra and Lagos. Even today the sex ratio is much higher in the former than the latter, as is the rate of return migration. Addis Ababa, meanwhile, is quite distinctive in having a majority of females in its population.

Nairobi and Harare may again be taken as examples of cities in which nearly all economic activity was, until recent years, conducted on a large scale, and in which a newly emergent "informal sector" has only recently been officially recognized. In Accra and Lagos, by contrast, small-scale indigenous enterprise has always been an important part of the urban economy. There is, for example, no Nairobi or Harare equivalent to the vigorous activity of the market women of the West African cities—which historically preceded the establishment of the large-scale sector.

With regard to housing also there is a very clear distinction in Nairobi and Harare between planned residential areas, with much housing built by government and with further sharp contrasts reflecting former racial segregation and areas of illegal squatter housing.[17] In Lagos and Accra there is much less government-built housing and also little squatter settlement strictly defined. In both cities most housing is privately owned on a legal basis, with far more of a continuum with regard to the quality of the buildings and the extent of planning for entire neighborhoods.

The differentiation extends to the morphology of each city as a whole. In Nairobi there is a very clear division between residential areas and functional areas, with the latter subdivided into very distinct administrative, commercial, and industrial zones, all reflecting colonial planning ideas which an authoritarian government was able to implement to the full. The physical planners now have to decide whether such a clear-cut structure should be retained as the city grows into a major metropolis. In Lagos a much greater mixture of land uses is found both in the central core and within the sprawling suburbs. This is due in part to a restricted site, but its origins as a part-indigenous and part-colonial city have also contributed. The physical form of Ibadan is different again, the whole central area reflecting Yoruba cultural norms while various colonial elements form appendages to this. However, here too, as in Nairobi and Lagos, decisions must be made with regard to how far future metropolitan growth can appropriately build on the existing physical structure.

With respect to all these aspects of the African metropolis the dominant trends since independence have produced convergence. In Kenya, in Zambia, and now in Zimbabwe the trend is towards the long-term family migration previously more characteristic of Ghana and Nigeria. Small-scale enterprise is expanding in Nairobi, together with intermediate-scale enterprise such as fleets of mini-buses, while the share of large-scale enterprise in the total economic activity of Ibadan is rising. In many ways Westernization is proceeding in cities of indigenous origin while those of European origin are beginning to be Africanized.

The convergence increasingly permits some generalization about the metropolis in tropical Africa, but of course this does not apply to current trends when these may be diametrically opposed. Furthermore, even if the balance between, say, large-scale and small-scale activity is similar in two cities, the relationships between the two are unlikely to be the same if small preceded large in one city but followed it in another.

National Urban Systems

The scope for generalization even within tropical Africa is also limited with regard to the issue of urban primacy, or centralization and decentralization at the national scale. My investigations over a 20-year period have indicated no clear and consistent trend. Naturally, an increasing proportion of the urban population in each country lives in cities above each size threshold as urbanization proceeds, and as more cities cross the threshold: but this does not mean that the largest cities are growing the fastest, or that primacy in population terms is intensifying.

However, evidence from censuses, adjusted for boundary change, does suggest that in the majority of African countries the high degree of primacy inherited from the colonial period has been at least maintained. The primate city has generally grown somewhat faster than most other urban centers, and in absolute terms new urban growth has been highly concentrated—following the previous pattern. In Nigeria, where the urban population was formerly very widely distributed and where there was really no primate city at the time of independence, Lagos has rapidly come to assume that position, while the pre-eminence of Kinshasa within Zaire has somewhat increased; but in neither of these cases are accurate population data available.

There is far stronger evidence of increasing primacy with regard to other indicators such as the annual wage bill, power consumption, and municipal expenditures. Wealth is certainly becoming more concentrated spatially, as well as socially, in most countries, though it might be argued that the same is true of urban poverty—or at least destitution—with a wider range of income and well-being in most of the metropoli than in most other urban centers. In most countries there is also evidence (e.g., telephone linkage data) of extreme, and increasing, primacy in terms of interaction within the national urban system. This is especially true where functions have been transferred to national capitals not only from London and Paris but also from colonial sub-regional foci such as Dakar and Nairobi.

There are conflicting views on how much primacy matters, and the issue cannot be resolved here. It is doubtful whether serious diseconomies have yet arisen in tropical Africa from sheer size, except perhaps in the cases of Lagos and Kinshasa, but if present trends continue unchecked they will soon arise in several metropoli. And even now countries such as Ghana, Ivory Coast, Sudan, Kenya, and Tanzania may have reached the point at which more dispersed urban growth would be advantageous in terms of efficiency, quite apart from equity considerations. Once equity is considered the case for greater dispersal becomes very much stronger, especially in ethnically divided countries where the location of the primate city in the traditional territory of one group tends to give great advantage to members of that group.

While continuing powerful external influence is one factor reinforcing African urban primacy,[18] the future development of the national urban systems will be influenced also by many aspects of government policy, most of which are impossible to predict even for one country let alone a sub-continent. Until the 1970s very little explicit attention was given to the matter in most countries, but the Vancouver Habitat Conference of 1976, and preparations for it, helped to bring it to the notice of governments, while the United Nations Center for Human Settlements, located in Nairobi, is particularly well placed to keep it before those of African countries. Even today, however, the influence of governments is mainly indirect, arising from ad hoc decisions on the allocation of resources. Many development plans have made a brief reference to the desirability of some dispersal of urban development, and in countries such as Kenya a series of growth poles away from the capital have been designated, but nowhere has this yet had a serious impact on metropolitan growth.

In Nigeria changes within the federal structure have had significant consequences. The shift from three Regions to first twelve and now nineteen States has brought increased centralization in some respects and some decentralization in others. The establishment of the twelve-State structure, along with the 1967-70 civil war, certainly contributed to the rapid emergence of Lagos as Nigeria's dominant metropolis; yet elevation to the position of State capital has brought cities such as Ilorin, Jos and Maiduguri closer to metropolitan status and has prompted the preparation of ambitious plans even for smaller centers such as Owerri.[19]

The most important government actions designed explicitly to modify national urban systems have been the designation and construction of new capital cities in several African countries. Nigeria is again of particular interest, along with Tanzania, since these are the countries in which the national administration is being shifted out of the main existing metropolis. In Tanzania it was decided in 1973 to move the capital from Dar es Salaam to the more centrally located provincial town of Dodoma, to escape the powerful foreign influence in the port city, to "bring government nearer to the people," and to boost the economy of what is almost the poorest part of the country.[20] It was hoped that the growth of Dar es Salaam would thus be restrained, and that Dodoma would become a modest metropolis of about 350,000 people by the year 2000. In fact, the desperate state of the Tanzanian economy has slowed the project greatly, and even by 1984 only a small proportion of the administration had moved.

In Nigeria the decision was made two years later, and there a brand new site was selected, near to the small town of Abuja. Again this represents a shift from the chief port to the center of the country, but an added factor was the location of Lagos within the territory of one of the three main ethnic groups of the country and the preference for an ethnically-neutral site. Furthermore, the extreme congestion of Lagos and the constraints on its growth provided by a site among lagoons and swamps helped to justify the move.[21] The plans for Abuja were much more grandiose than those for Dodoma, and far more rapid growth was anticipated, with the population expected to reach one million by 1995, reflecting the far greater size of Nigeria in population terms and the funds provided by oil exports. Harsher economic conditions in the 1980s have brought some restraint, but even so Abuja is growing rapidly, and several of the federal government offices have already moved there. It is not yet clear how far Abuja will become a multi-functional metropolis rather than a largely administrative city comparable to Brasilia or Canberra, but this is at least possible. Unlike Brasilia, it lies close to the center of gravity of the country's population and between the politically dominant north and the economically dominant south. For many Nigerian entrepreneurs it may soon prove to be a more attractive location than Lagos.

The new capitals of Botswana, Mauritania, and Rwanda, all formerly administered from outside the national territory, are all relatively small, as is Lilongwe which is now emerging as Malawi's capital in place of tiny Zomba as well as taking over some functions from Blantyre;[22] Dodoma now seems likely to grow only slowly over the next two decades; but at Abuja a new metropolis is being created extremely rapidly, and this provides a very exciting challenge to all the decision-makers involved. It could be a city which combines the best features of a variety of indigenous Nigerian urban traditions with the best of what the world outside has to offer: alternatively, it could be an architectural and social disaster, as costly in human as in financial terms. It is not for outsiders to predict or even to advise unless invited to do so, but it will be fascinating to watch the outcome of this massive experiment, and we can at least hope that positive aspects will outweigh the negative. Meanwhile, of course, Lagos must cope with growth which will be only slightly curtailed by the Abuja development, and this constitutes an equally great challenge of a different kind.

Conclusions

Attempting to steer a course between overgeneralization and excessive equivocation, the concluding section of this paper will start with a number of brief propositions regarding the emerging metropolis in tropical Africa. The first few are indisputable facts, but the remainder are subjective judgments which may well be challenged.

1. Tropical Africa's largest cities are growing very rapidly, with natural increase at or above the national average combining with continuing net in-migration from smaller towns and rural areas. Little de-concentration of any type has yet occurred, despite various efforts at administrative decentralization.

2. The economic base to support this metropolitan population growth is very limited, but so is the economic base for rapidly growing populations in most rural areas. Rapid urban growth is occurring in countries with very low per-capita incomes, and in the early 1980s with stagnant economies in many cases.

3. This metropolitan growth is creating intense problems of urban management, as housing provision, water supplies, sewerage systems and so on, as well as employment opportunites, fail to keep pace with population numbers.

4. Even so, material well-being is still generally greater in the cities than in the rural areas, and continuing migration is a rational response to this. The cities offer strong attractions to young people from the rural areas, though there are often advantages for older people in a return movement.

5. At present there is no sharp divide between the "urban" and the "rural" population. Just as traditional Yoruba life often involved frequent movement between town and countryside, so many Kenya families are now deeply involved in both. This applies to the metropolis as well as to smaller towns, and applies to all social classes.

6. For many African urban dwellers the advantages of maintaining strong links with their rural areas of origin outweigh the disadvantages, and justify both high expenditures on transport and temporary separation from other family members. For some families, however, continued involvement in both

28

urban and rural areas is not just a matter of preference but is, in fact, a strategy for survival.

7. Strong kinship ties and the institution of the extended family greatly assist this ongoing urban-rural linkage; and these constitute one of many elements in African culture which should be preserved in the face of the pressures of Westernization especially when this is not accompanied by Western standards of living. Indeed, the greatest hardship is now experienced by people whose extended family ties have been broken.

8. The maintenance of strong urban-rural links becomes progressively more difficult as cities expand, especially when travel budgets are severely constrained. Far more urban residents can keep contact with rural areas within easy reach from five scattered cities of one million people each than from one city of five million. In a giant metropolis a smaller proportion of the urban workforce can travel in daily from rural homes, and a larger proportion of the urban dwellers are likely to have come from areas too remote for even occasional contact.

9. At the same time, several smaller cities can provide services for the majority rural population more effectively than one giant metropolis. Of course, urban centers of any size may exploit surrounding rural populations more than they assist them, but with appropriate social and political structures it should be possible to ensure that positive influence predominates, providing rural dwellers with access to markets for their produce, goods which they require, and services such as the specialized education and health care facilities which cannot be spread through the rural areas.

10. A relatively dispersed urban system rather than intense concentration in a single metropolis may assist the development of a well-integrated national economy; and it also normally aids the political process of nation building by ensuring that urban growth is not excessively concentrated within the territory of one ethnic group. Meanwhile, the maintenance of strong urban-rural ties also contributes to this integration process.

The above propositions point towards policies involving some degree of positive response to metropolitan growth in tropical Africa, with a need for housing policies, employment policies, action on sanitation, transport and so on, in addition to a desperate need for less corrupt metropolitan administration; but they also point towards some resistance to and deflection of this growth. In most tropical African countries there are economic, social, and political arguments in favor of an urban system which includes several moderate-sized cities rather than just one giant metropolis (and which also includes many well-dispersed smaller towns). To some extent these are world-wide and well-worn arguments,[23] but they are even stronger in Africa than elsewhere. The arguments derive both from the conditions within the largest cities and from the broader national perspective. Efforts should be made to ensure that the inevitable urban growth of future decades is less concentrated in both time and space than that of the recent past. It may then be less traumatic than the current experience of Lagos and Kinshasa and more beneficial in national terms. These efforts would require, in most countries, a substantial shift in resource allocation away from the metropolis, despite its own desperate needs and the many political pressures opposing such a shift. Friedmann's stress on the spatial distribution of power is highly significant here.[24] In tropical Africa, power in terms of the state and its apparatus is highly concentrated; but in terms of the nation and its ethnic groups this is far less true, and much support for decentralization policies can normally be expected.

The whole distinction between "urban" (even "metropolitan") and "rural" should also become no sharper than necessary, and should certainly not be imposed on African countries from the outside. Deliberate efforts can be made to ensure that some aspects of urbanization as a social process extend not only to non-metropolitan centers but also into the countryside, and that many people, and especially many families, can continue to span the divide seeking the "best of both worlds." In this scenario there would be no sharp boundary to each individual urban center, as well as no rigid restriction of "urban" phenomena to the totality of such centers, as well as much movement in and out of them.

All of this must depend on improved communications, for the need for contact is the primary reason for agglomeration: but in this respect at least tropical Africa can surely avoid passing through the same stages as other parts of the world. The latest technology which is permitting the dispersal of urban activity in Europe and North America[25] is not always more costly than that which it displaces; and tropical African countries must include among their new acquisitions of the 1980s and 1990s affordable forms of communications technology which will assist them in avoiding excessive metropolitan growth. The dispersed urbanization scenario depends on continuing mobility on the part of millions of people, but no more than has already been demonstrated in Africa. It does, however, demand more mobility and flexibility than has been shown hitherto on the part of those in both state and private sectors who determine the spatial pattern of economic activity and employment opportunities.

It is widely recognized that there should be no question of Latin America, Asia and Africa automatically following a European and North American path with regard to urbanization, but neither should there be any question of a single alternative path. Latin America in particular is already far more urbanized than tropical Africa, but it would be no more appropriate for this model to be followed, even if it were feasible in economic terms. There is probably no single model that would suit even the whole of tropical Africa, the forms of urbanization most appropriate for the coming decades differing from country to country.

However, we can generalize to the extent that insofar as the giant metropolis is, in any case, a technological anachronism in the late-twentieth century world, tropical Africa should avoid it as far as possible, and decision-makers should urgently seek ways of doing this while there is yet time. The desperate material poverty of the region makes this difficult, for costs are involved in avoiding agglomeration; but in other ways Africa's material poverty, together with its cultural richness, makes it both possible and all the more essential. Few of the decision-makers in Accra or Nairobi are yet totally committed to these metropoli in the making, and few can view the prospect of concentrations of many millions of people with equanimity even with the most optimistic assumptions of economic improvement. Tropical Africa's urban population is certain to double in size between now and the year 2000, and almost certain to quadruple by 2025 unless total economic and social collapse intervenes, as Ervin Laszlo has predicted.[26] Geographical inertia is such that, without some form of planning, almost all this growth would take place in the existing major urban centers, each of which would become a large metropolis. However, there is no reason to suppose that the optimum location for the extra urban population, that is, for the next 100 million, is within or on the fringes of the existing cities, especially since most grew initially at locations suited to colonial needs. Much thought must therefore be given to the location as well as the character of this forthcoming urban growth. The aim for most African countries must be a metropolis that is modest in size, closely integrated both with a system of dispersed smaller urban centers and with the people who remain in the countryside, and culturally distinctive.

Notes

1. Dennis J. Dwyer, "The Metropolis in its National and Regional Context," this volume.
2. H. Brookfield, Interdependent Development, (London, 1975), p. 53.
3. United Nations, Patterns of Urban and Rural Population Growth, (New York, 1980), pp. 125-8. Unfortunately, this source also includes some nonsense figures, such as 3.4 million for Ado-Ekiti in Nigeria yet a mere 1.8 million for Abidjan.
4. This discussion concentrates on the metropoli as urban settlements, and does not attempt to cover such issues as class structures and urban politics. The best studies of these topics for Africa are R. Sandbrook, The Politics of Basic Needs: Urban Aspects of Assaulting Poverty in Africa, (London, 1982); and M. Peil and P.O. Sada, African Urban Society, (Chichester, 1984).
5. Even mining has led to substantial localized urban growth in tropical Africa only on the Copperbelt of Zambia and Zaire.
6. As stressed in ILO, Employment, Incomes and Equality: A Strategy for Increasing Productive Employment in Kenya, (Geneva, 1972).
7. J.O.C. Onyemelukwe, "Urban Slums in Nigeria," Journal of Environmental Management, 13 (1981): pp. 111-25.

8. See W.A. Hance, *Population, Migration and Urbanization in Africa*, (New York, 1970); and J.I. Clarke and L.A. Kosinski (eds.), *Redistribution of Population in Africa*, (London, 1982). The most useful case studies are probably still J.C. Caldwell, *African Rural-Urban Migration: The Movement to Ghana's Towns*, (London, 1969); and H. Heisler, *Urbanization and the Government of Migration*, (London, 1974) on Zambia.

9. W.J. and J.L. Hanna, *Urban Dynamics in Black Africa*, (New York, 1981).

10. This theme is explored very fully for West Africa in M. Peil, *Cities and Suburbs: Urban Life in West Africa*, (New York, 1981).

11. M.H. Ross and T.S. Weisner, "The rural-urban migrant network in Kenya", *American Ethnologist*, 4 (1977): pp. 359-75.

12. The contrasts are examined at length in A.M. O'Connor, *The African City*, (London, 1983).

13. A.L. Mabogunje, *Urbanization in Nigeria*, (London, 1968), chapter 10.

14. M. Pain, *Kinshasa: ecologie et organisation urbaines*, (Toulouse, 1979).

15. P.C. Lloyd et al., ed., *The City of Ibadan*, (Cambridge, 1967).

16. G. Kay and M.A.H. Smout, eds., (Salisbury, London, 1977).

17. A. Hake, *African Metropolis: Nairobi's Self-help City*, (London, 1977).

18. As reflected in several papers in R.A. Obudho and S. El-Shakhs, (eds.), *Development of Urban Systems in Africa*, (New York, 1979).

19. Ervin Y. Galantay, "The planning of Owerri, a new capital for Imo State, Nigeria," *Town Planning Review*, 49 (1978): pp. 371-86; G.I. Nwaka, "Owerri: development of a Nigerian State capital," *Third World Planning Review*, 2 (1980): pp. 233-42; and Galantay response, pp. 243-4.

20. A.M. Hayuma, "Dodoma, the planning and building of the new capital city of Tanzania", *Habitat International*, 5 (1981): pp. 653-80.

21. Nigeria, Report of the committee on the Location of the Federal Capital of Nigeria, (Lagos, 1975).

22. D. Potts, "The development of Malawi's new capital at Lilongwe: a comparison with other new African capitals", *Comparative Urban Research*, 10 (1984).

23. The arguments on this issue are effectively discussed for less developed countries in general in A. Gilbert and J. Gugler, *Cities, Poverty and Development*, (Oxford, 1981), chapter 8. The case for promoting secondary city growth is presented much more fully than is possible here in D.A. Rondinelli, *Secondary Cities in Developing Countries*, (Beverly Hills, 1983).

24. J. Friedmann, "The spatial organization of power in the development of urban systems", in J. Friedmann and W. Alonso (eds.), *Regional Policy*, (Cambridge, MA., 1975).

25. As noted in other contributions to this volume.

26. In a comment on an earlier version of this paper.

3.
Toward Megalopolis

Panayotis Psomopoulos

Definitions and Basic Assumption

We are asked—on the basis of whatever evidence is available—to attempt the more accurate understanding of the process of the future evolution of man's system of life and human settlements which are its expression in space.

To clarify and understand the complex thinking procedure that is to be followed, it is necessary to state clearly some fundamental definitions, assumptions or hypotheses—based on systematic observations—which implicitly or explicitly constitute the basis of our effort.

Man lives in human settlements, which are the territorial arrangements made by him for his own benefit. Furthermore, with the exception of very marginal clusters, "hunter" groups or village dwellers, all settlements are more or less part of a broad human settlements system. People tend to cluster around central facilities of various scales. One of the most characteristic scales in any city, the neighborhood scale, is defined by the overlapping "kinetic" fields of the movements of the inhabitants to satisfy their daily needs.

Throughout human history man has been guided by the same five principles in every attempt he has made to live normally and survive:

1. The maximization of potential contacts: man tries to have the best possible contact with people and other elements such as water, food, houses, facilities, knowledge. This amounts to an operational definition of personal human freedom.

2. The minimization of effort in terms of energy, time and cost: in his attempt to maximize his potential contacts, man tries to bring everything close to him. To achieve this in the best possible way, he always selects the course requiring the minimum effort.

3. Optimization of man's protective space at every moment and in every locality, whether in temporary or permanent situations, whether he is alone or part of a group.

4. Optimization of man's relationship with the other elements of his system of life, that is, with nature, society, shells (buildings and houses of all sorts) and networks (from roads to telecommunications).

5. Optimization of the synthesis of the previous four principles. This depends on time and space, actual conditions, and man's ability to create the synthesis. Human settlements have been more successful, made their inhabitants happier, and last longer when the fifth principle of balance between the other four has been applied.

In the present era old settlements like villages and cities (as they were structured in the past) are beginning to disappear and new ones like daily urban systems and megalopoli have begun to appear. This clearly shows that human settlements follow some evolutionary trends which, however, are not yet properly understood. The many different ways in which man has started his settlements could perhaps be called initial coincidental efforts. These he used as experiments; he learned which one served him best and then he continued with many mutations until he eventually found the right direction. What is certain is that, when a more satisfactory solution appeared, it was the only one that survived. We can see the truth of this statement in all types of units and at all scales of settlements.

The form, structure and texture of human settlements of all scales can be attributed to several forces deriving either from man or directly from nature.

When we move from the room—the smallest human settlement unit—to the house, the neighborhood, the city, and the metropolis, we discover that several forces are active, but their relationships change from case to case. The unit of the metropolis, for example, is too large to be influenced directly by man (in terms of his physical dimensions and senses), but it is influenced by the natural forces of gravity and geographic formation, by modes of transportation, and by the organization and growth of the system.

Following this train of thought for all categories of human settlements, we can conclude that, within every type of settlement unit, the changing forces of synthesis follow a certain pattern which, in terms of percentages, shows a decline of the forces derived from man's physical dimensions and personal energy and a growth of those derived directly from nature itself as a developing and operating system.

Future human settlements will be created by man guided by the same principles that he has applied so far, which should not and cannot be changed.

Present Conditions, Trends and Anticipations for the Year 2000

The population of the earth, which has been increasing at a constantly accelerating rate until recently, is likely to continue growing well into the twenty-first century until a level of relative stabilization is reached. According to a variety of estimates the total population of the earth by the year 2000 will be between 6.3 and 7.0 billion.

Of particular importance are the phenomena of rapid urbanization, the very high birth rates, particularly in poor countries, which result in a disproportionately large youth population, and the increasing portion of aged population (over 65) in most of the rich and industrialized countries of Europe and America.

In early forecasts—even back in the sixties—for future population distribution, major migration movements appeared highly probable. They occur and last until the population distribution reaches a level of stability on a global scale. Forecasts were based on already existing trends, on easily identifiable future conflicts, on the highly probable development of awareness among people of the comparative advantages that better climatic conditions can offer, and on a variety of studies dealing with economic, political, and other constraints that could lead to population movement. The discrepancy between the distribution of population and the distribution of resources probably to be exploited in the years to come has played an important role. In support of all the above, I quote from a recent publication of the Population Crisis Committee ("World Population Growth and Global Security"):[1]

"Although not yet a major source of international tensions, the steady increase in international migration (especially the unauthorized flow of political or economic refugees across common national borders) and the transnational effects of population growth on shared natural resources will inevitably contribute to localized conflict in regions of the globe as divergent as Central America, the Indian Subcontinent and West Africa."

"As rapid labor force growth compounds the problems of unemployment and underemployment in the developing world, incentives increase for people to seek better job opportunities by migrating, temporarily or permanently, legally or illegally. Political instability and local conflict add their share to the migrant flow. At the same time, better access to transportation and information about other countries has effectively lowered some traditional barriers to international migration."

"International migration has benefited the economies of both sending and receiving countries in many ways, but it is becoming clear that there are limits to the numbers of foreign workers or refugees receiving countries are able to absorb without precipitating serious social problems. The magnitude of current migrant flows and their impact on host countries are particularly apparent in the Western Hemisphere, South and West Africa, South Asia and the Middle East."

"While emigrant movements are not new, the scale of present flows is unprecedented and the capacity to absorb them is evidently lessening among already overburdened developing countries such as Kenya and Thailand as well as among these industrial countries whose growth rates have slowed. The doors have been closing for foreign workers in Western Europe and in a number of oil-producing countries. Furthermore, increasing ethnic consciousness and nationalism, whether a reaction to economic recession or simply a function of the present size of foreign worker populations, has produced strong anti-immigrant actions such as the mass expulsion of foreign workers from Nigeria and the violent Assam riots in India, and may be on the rise."

The continuation—and even acceleration—of such population movements are highly probable. To this should be added the impact of internal migration (i.e., toward the Sun Belt in the U.S.), major resettlement efforts, and other factors.

Accurate global figures on the total number of settlements on the surface of the earth by category (size, etc.) are not available. According to ACE (Athens Center of Ekistics) estimates in 1970 there were about 14,300,000 settlements distributed by category as follows:

10,500,000	Very small settlements
3,800,000	Villages
4,800	Poli
560	Metropoli
19	Megalopoli

Since 1950 the urban part of the total population has risen and will continue to rise very rapidly through the year 2000. This rapid increase, of which over half is due to rural/urban migration, causes extreme demands on all "infrastructure facilities" and on services in poor countries, demands that cannot be met in general. Poverty in the urban areas is growing, and a greater proportion of the poor in developing countries are now living in urban areas. Unemployment in urban areas is increasing in poor countries since the growing labor force outnumbers the available jobs and the capacity to create them.

According to United Nations estimates, the population projections for urban areas in the year 2000 for developing countries are:

All developing countries	14% of total
Market economy dev. countries	42.4%
Latin America/Caribbean	74.8%
Asia	36%
Africa	36.9%

Between 1950-1970, the urban population in market economy developing countries rose at the annual rate of:

Africa	5.0%
North and South America	4.5%
Asia	4.0%

In 1970, cities of 100,000 or more, again in market economy developing countries, numbered 644, located as follows:

Africa	123
North and South America	174
Asia	347

A total of 1,862 is projected for the year 2000, located as follows:

Africa	508
North and South America	473
Asia	873

Of the proportion of the populations in cities of more than 100,000, in the year 2000:

- 75% will be in cities over 500,000.
- 62% will be in cities over one million.
- 30% will be in cities over five million.

Latin America will have an especially high increase rate.

In the Third World cities, urban growth has caused astronomical rises in urban land prices; the sixties saw a rise of 10-20% more than the consumer price index. For the poor who spend over 50% of their income on housing, this causes extreme hardship—either squatting, substandard housing, or forced habitation farther from the central core. According to Habitat 1976, 35-60% of households in certain Third World countries cannot afford even the cheapest dwelling.[2]

Huge slums and shantytowns from the "bustees" of Calcutta and the "bidonvilles" of Dakar to the "callampas" or "mushroom towns" of Chile and the "pueblos jovenes" around Lima have a doubling time of 5-10 years and contain an ever-growing proportion of the urban population, whether in the Near East, Africa, Asia or Latin America. Currently, over one-third of the urban population in developing countries lives in slums and squatter settlements, most without clean water, sewerage systems, or electricity.

According to the United Nations, 40-60% of the urban labor force works in the "informal sector," those low-income, small-scale economic activities which receive neither recognition nor benefits from official circles.

One of the major concerns of governments, especially in poor developing countries, is the large cities which "normally" grow unproportionately to the overall population growth, the overall urban growth, and especially faster than the pace of economic development due to the difficulties in providing housing, infrastructure, education, health care and, most important of all, in creating jobs.

In 1950 there were 76 cities of over one million population of which 24 were in Europe, 14 in North America, 13 in East Asia and the rest in the other five major regions of the world.

By 1975 the number of metropolitan areas of over one million had increased to 184, of which Europe had 38, East Asia 37 and North America 32. The number of cities of this category in the USSR increased from two (Leningrad and Moscow) to 12.

In the year 2000, according to United Nations Population Studies, there will be 437 cities of over one million population, an increase of less than 2.5 times over 1975 figures, with the highest concentration in South Asia (98 cities), followed by East Asia (83 cities), and Africa (63 cities). The highest rate of growth registered for the period 1975-2000 belongs to Africa, increasing from 11 to 63 cities, slightly less than 6 times.

The order of the 35 largest cities of the world in 1950, 1975 and 2000 is shown in Tables 1, 2 and 3 respectively.

According to the United Nations, the percentage of the urban population living in cities of over one million over the entire urban population of the world was 24.6 percent in 1950 (seven percent of the total population of the world), and by the year 2000 it is expected to increase to 43.4 percent.

Human settlements are today increasing in area more than twice as fast as the rate of their population increase. The usual range of the ratio of growth rates is between one and four. It is only since about 1920 that this ratio has become spectacularly speeded up due to the advent of the car. This overly rapid rate of expansion in area shows signs of continuing unabated.

Expanding settlements eat up large tracts of cultivated areas as well as open nature. The most rapidly expanding settlements tend to be in lower-lying areas. In the universal process of urbanization, mountain settlements have tended to decrease in importance compared with those on the plains. This makes the encroachment of settlement expansion over valuable soil still more dramatic. The proportion of cultivated areas directly around the urban fringe is very high, as is the proportion of specially valuable and easily perishable food crops.

The average annual population growth rate for large settlements is about 4.5% and the average annual growth rate for their area is just over 10%. For all settlements the average annual growth rate for their area is about 5%. In

1960 all human settlements on the globe occupied 0.4 million sq. km.: in 1976 this doubled, becoming 0.8% million sq. km. By the year 2000, it is projected to reach 2.3 million sq. km.

According to a rough preliminary estimate, every year human settlements eat up about 140,000 sq. km. of arable land, 50,000 sq. km. of pastures, and 180,000 sq. km. of forests. Another way of expressing the dramatic expansion of cities is to recognize that, between 1970 and the year 2000, the volume of new buildings over the entire planet will amount to 2.5 times that existing in 1970.

Table 3-1

Slums in Selected Principal Cities and Urban Doubling Times

City	Slums and squatter settlements as percent of city's population*	Urban population doubling time**
LATIN AMERICA		
Bogota (Colombia)	60 percent	22 years
Mexico City (Mexico)	46 percent	18 years
Caracas (Venezuela)	42 percent	18 years
MIDDLE EAST and AFRICA		
Addis Ababa (Ethiopia)	79 percent	11 years
Casablanca (Morocco)	70 percent	14 years
Kinshasa (Zaire)	60 percent	14 years
Cairo (Egypt)	60 percent	21 years
Ankara (Turkey)	60 percent	17 years
ASIA		
Calcutta (India)	67 percent	19 years
Manila (Philippines)	35 percent	18 years
Seoul (South Korea)	29 percent	19 years
Jakarta (Indonesia)	26 percent	19 years

*latest documented figures available, currently used by the United Nations and other expert sources, ranging from 1966 to 1981
**length of time, at current growth rate, for the country's urban population to double in size
Sources: United Nations; U.S. Agency for International Development; Municipality of Addis Ababa, 1981.

Historically, most large cities were located on or near large fertile areas. To serve the growing and pressing needs of these cities, cultivation in these areas has been progressively improved so that the proportion of highly fertile land is much higher around cities than elsewhere on the earth.

Long before any actual buildings appear, the prospect of further expansion of the city increases land prices far out of the built-up area so much

Table 3-2

Athens Technological Organization—Athens Center of Ekistics

megalopoli added to those of the previous data

1960	1965	1970	1975
N Japanese	S Berlin-Leipzig	S Warsaw-Lodz	S Nurnberg-Munich
N Eastern (U.S.)	S Los Angeles-San Diego	S Yahata-Kumamoto	S Stuttgart-Munich
S English	S Cairo-Alexandria	S Rio-São Paulo	S Lodz-Katowice-Krakow
S Great Lakes Megalopolis		S Hong Kong-Canton	S Rome-Naples
S Paris-Randstadt		S Djakarta-Bandung	S Detroit-Toronto
S Randstadt-Stuttgart			S Chicago-St. Louis
S Ruhr-Hamburg			S Buenos Aires-Montevideo
S Ruhr-Berlin			S Shenyang-Changchun
S Shanghai-Nanking			S Changchun-Harbin
S Peking-Tientain			S Witwatersrand-Pretoria
S Shenyang-Dairen			S Milan-Turin
	"promoted" to "normal"	"promoted" to "normal"	"promoted" to "normal"
	N English	N Great Lakes Megalopolis	N Shanghai-Nanking
	N Randstadt-Stuttgart	N Ruhr-Berlin	N Rio-São Paulo
			N Paris-Randstadt
			N Ruhr-Hamburg
totals: 2N + 9S = 11 true megalopoli	4N + 10S = 14 true megalopoli	6N + 13S = 19 true megalopoli	10N + 20S = 30 true megalopoli

S = small megalopolis (10-35 million)
N = normal megalopolis (35-250 million)

Table 3-3

Type of human settlement	Population range	Estimated population	%	Estimated no. of settlements	%
very small settlement	1-100	276 million	7.7	10,440,000	73.4
village	100-5,000	1,569 million	43.6	3,747,610	26.3
polis	5,000-200,000	807 million	22.4	40,692	0.3
metropolis	200,000-10 million	455 million	12.6	580	—
megalopolis	10-500 million	490 million	13.6	19(518)*	—
total		3,597 million	100.0	14,229,380	100.0

*This 518 is an average estimate of the number of settlements included in the 19 megalopoli. This number has been subtracted where applicable from the preceding types of human settlements. (1970)

that fertile agricultural land is sold in an avalanche for non-rural (urban) purposes. This means that the zone where rural land is predominant continually recedes at a very fast rate, usually to much less fertile lands.

As a result of their expansion of buildings, industry, transportation, etc., expanding cities pollute the soil in and around them to an increasing degree through their sewerage systems, garbage disposal, industrial wastes, and the spread of other soil pollutants, quite apart from the destruction of the entire soil layer over large areas.

It is true that expanding cities sometimes encourage an improvement in the standards of cultivation in their immediate vicinity. However, this is outweighed by their far larger destruction of agricultural land.

The above statement can be considered as typical of average conditions over the entire earth. During the last four decades, parallel to the evolution of large, more or less concentrated metropoli surrounded by suburbs, and representing the largest human settlement units at that time with the continuing increase of population, the improvement of communication and transportation systems, and greater scarcity of unused habitable space, settlements in many areas became more and more interconnected until the phenomenon of urbanization on a regional scale appeared. In areas where centers relatively close to each other exceeded a critical size of some one million inhabitants, a belt connecting these centers was progressively urbanized through gravity effect; this belt was not continuously built-up but contained a predominance of urban functions. This process resulted in the formation of a "megalopolis"—a multi-nuclear band formation with a population of several tens of millions and an area 10 to 1000 times larger than the area of large metropoli.

On the basis of the "City of the Future" (COF) research project of the Athens Center of Ekistics, 12 megalopoli have been identified around the world and six more are in the stage of formation.

Projections of megalopolitan structure and growth up to the beginning of the next century, using a mathematical model developed by the COF project, show:

- a great increase in their number; over 160 megalopoli are expected to exist around the year 2000, of which 53 will be interconnected into still larger megalopolitan networks or "urbanized regions";

- a great increase in both their average and maximum populations and areas, and a great increase in their complexity.

These high-order formations are characterized by a loose and discontinuous internal structure in spite of their relatively high "regional" densities. They are not built-up areas, but areas of intensely urbanized character. Within these high-order formations large open areas are preserved for a variety of purposes such as recreation, conservation, production, etc., again according to a hierarchical system.

Economic projections indicate that the investment between 1960 and 2000 will probably be at least twice the cumulative investment of the period prior to 1960, from the beginning of history.

Rapid and large-scale increase will be one of the main factors intensifying the crisis of our urban life during the next generation, until the year 2000—a period which is likely to be the most difficult one for humanity. A large number of serious problems are expected to accumulate ranging from scarcity of basic vital resources to widespread deterioration of flora and fauna and of the quality of human life, particularly in poor regions of the world.

Such difficulties may impair the quality and efficient operation of major human settlement units, but are not expected to stop the formation and growth of megalopoli unless a total failure or catastrophe for humanity occurs. On the contrary, megalopoli attract population with a still greater force than isolated metropoli. COF estimates show that the advantages to be gained—multiple choices, such as proximity to two large centers, availability of highest order function, a standard of living considerably higher than areas outside them, etc.—will more than compensate for the disadvantages, especially around the year 2000 when between 45% and 50% of the earth's population will be living in megalopoli.

In the twenty-first century technological progress will gradually increase the availability of resources and high quality substitutes for them, and generally improve conditions of material comfort and wealth. Environmental control will become more efficient and restore the imbalance and deficiencies previously created. Higher incomes will make investments in large-scale technical projects possible, thus vastly improving man's control over his environment, the acquisition of resources, and the building of adequate settlements. And in spite of many other difficulties, the overall balance will gradually become more and more steady, as shown by the form of the S-shaped urbanization curve which flattens asymptotically toward a quasi-stable state during this period.

The areas where most of the future expansion of cities is likely to take place follow these well-defined "axes of urbanization." Most of these traverse the main inland plains or develop along coastal plains. This means that the future expansion of cities is anticipated to take an increasingly heavy toll of valuable cropland, in continuation of the historical trend.

With the continuing increase of population, the improvement of communication and transportation systems, and greater scarcity of unused habitable space, settlements are expected to become more and more interconnected until:

a. Towards the end of the first half of the twenty-first century, megalopoli will gradually be replaced by the next higher order settlement, the "urbanized region."

b. Around the middle of the twenty-first century, or later, the "urbanized region" will, in its turn, give way to a higher order settlement, the "urbanized continent" as the prevailing settlement pattern.

c. Probably less than another generation later, all major settlement units will become fully interconnected in a new pattern representing a sort of ultimate equilibrium between human settlements and their wider environment. This highest unit in the hierarchy of settlements has been called "Ecumenopolis," meaning a unified settlement system spanning the entire habitable area of the globe, not continuously but in a totally interconnected network.

According to the hierarchical concept, higher order axes will link higher order centers which also will form at the crossings of higher order axes. The approximate probable location of these primary centers was determined using a mathematical model, and taking into account "practical" considerations about the importance of oceans and coasts, hinterland, population densities, habitability and other factors, the locations were arrived at purely on the basis of achieving an ultimate global balance, and bear no relation to the present political structure or its projected trends.

If Ecumenopolis is considered as an inevitable general pattern of future urbanization—but with a large number of alternative interpretations—and if Ecumenopolis models are used as general "targets" for urban development, planners could try to connect present conditions and trends with projected future levels for certain basic variables. In fact, ACE has already used such an approach for projections of urban development on a regional scale in several areas (e.g., the Great Lakes megalopoli of the U.S. and Canada, the south coast of France, Greece, the Japanese megalopolis, and many others). It was found that this technique was quite helpful, meaningful, and capable of being considerably improved in the future.

This concept of Ecumenopolis emerges as a smooth evolutionary result of the expanding systems of settlement patterns of the preceding periods. It is also consistent with the findings of the previous approach as to population levels, greatly increased urbanization, and an internal hierarchical pattern of centers.

Ecumenopolis, and all previous high-order formations are characterized by a loose and discontinuous internal structure in spite of their relatively high "regional" densities.

Within these high-order formations large open areas are preserved for a variety of purposes such as recreation, conservation, production, etc., again according to a hierarchical system.

The spaces between the formations are not empty; they only have lower densities which allow for a large number of smaller settlements at all scales and other lower-order installations. According to various models worked out, "Non-Ecumenopolis" areas may contain from 7-20% of the earth's population, and will comprise land uses other than settlement, such as recreation, conservation of natural areas, production, etc.

It is also projected that some 3-10% of the earth's population will probably live on water in floating settlements. These may be closely related to the part of Ecumenopolis developing along appropriate coastal areas which will acquire a special importance at that time. (See K. Kikutake's article in this volume.)

Settlement both within and outside Ecumenopolis will occupy the proportion of habitable and semi-habitable areas that is consistent with the other major land uses necessary for the production, recreation, breathing, etc. of the entire global population.

Of the total 70 to 75 million sq. km. covered by mainly habitable and semi-habitable land areas, settlements may occupy up to 10 or 15 million sq. km., production 25 to 30 million, and recreation plus conservation another 30 to 35 million, in addition to a further 75 to 85 million sq. km. of "open" nature under conservation on land, and the usable parts of the oceans' surface or underwater areas such as continental shelves, etc.

A major organizing principle of the largely linear structure of Ecumenopolis is development along "axes of urbanization," which should be considered as general directions of growth and expansion along main transportation lines or as connecting links between higher-order centers.

The Process of Evolution in the Next 15 Years

Our studies confirm that the period between now and the year 2000 is likely to be most difficult; a large number of problems are likely to accumulate, many of which already exist: scarcity of food, water, and other natural resources for a growing population; slow rate of growth of the economy of most of the poor countries, leading to stagnation and dissatisfaction with the increasing gap that separates them from rich countries; environmental deterioration through air, water and land pollution and widespread danger to flora and fauna; intensification of dissatisfaction due to higher expectations and lower attainments; increasing tension and stress; violence; the possible collapse of prevailing social or political systems; and insufficient technological and organizational progress to cope with these problems efficiently.

Almost all, if not all, of these problems and their multiple repercussions are already manifest within human settlements, are harming them, and are influencing the rate and degree of growth or deterioration of their structure, function, and distribution in space. Fundamentally, these problems are causing tremendous imbalance among the basic elements of human settlements—the individual human being, society in its various expressions, constructions (shells), networks and nature—in all sizes and types of settlements and from all points of view: economic, social, political, administrative, and cultural.

Furthermore, many of these problems are also "caused" by human settlements: their distribution in relation to each other, their location on the surface of the earth, their structure, their function, and growth or decline.

To give a more specific example of this cause-effect relation in human settlements, one could only refer to just a few aspects and some of the very concrete and timely issues that have attracted the attention of or are closely connected with some of the major themes of this publication.

When we speak of the evolution of human settlements, we tend to consider the most advanced cases and rightly view them as the highest stage in human achievement. However, we all know that there do exist on this earth settlements that were characteristic of the societal organization many centuries ago, along with the new, specialized settlements, and an abundance of settlements of various levels of evolution in between.

In the context of this typology, metropolitan areas are the most successful "entities" in the spectrum of urban settlements.

These large metropoli are the most dynamic, the most complex, the most expensive, the richest in opportunities, but at the same time the most problematic (in the areas of growth and change, structure and function). For governments, universities, individuals, scholars and practitioners, the major effort so far has been concentrated on the metropolitan scale settlements.

Different and, in many cases, contradicting ideological approaches, interpretations and policies yield results that are at times positive, at times negative, and not necessarily relevant. Not rarely do they confuse the real issues. Over the years, many good policies and strategies have been abandoned, and other "bad" ones replaced them—policies that harm the physical structure of these settlements for "centuries" to come.

Lack of knowledge, partial consideration of problems, lack of ability for prediction, and lack of familiarity with "new phenomena" never experienced before are a few of the reasons why the period between now and the year 2000 is likely to be the most difficult one for human settlements.

In the past man has always been the dominating factor both in the initial creation of his environment and also in maintaining a desirable balance

45

between the various elements. However, man now seems to have lost control over the tools created by him to form his environment at a human scale; even worse, man now seems to be oblivious as to what his real needs are and "where to go from here."

Human settlements all over the world are experiencing a period of crisis; but they cannot be changed overnight. Their structure is likely to remain largely unchanged for periods of 50 to 100 years.

Not all major settlements of the world are equipped with networks appropriate to their scale. For example, in 1979 there were 61 metro systems in operation around the world, 22 others under construction, and nine in the planning stage. A comparison, however, of the list of those with metro systems with the settlements with populations of over one million will reveal that a large number of them do not have a metro system and have no chance of acquiring one in the period up to the year 2000. Furthermore, out of a world total of 33,000 airports (as reported by the International Civil Aviation Organization), only a few (from 200-500) are "large, commercial airports with sizeable airline service" and are not able to serve adequately the growing megalopolitan systems.

As all activity in human settlements takes place in space, and any decision or action implies "location" and "connection", spatial consideration within and without the settlement is of great importance.

How much do we know about the location and the connection, let us say, of "services" in metropolitan areas? How much about the appropriate "hosting" environment? Our knowledge is limited concerning the spatial extent of what "we should be looking for."

Related to this very serious problem—which must increasingly preoccupy all authorities and specialists concerned about the coming "Transactional City" and the very rapidly growing "quaternary" sector of the economy—is the international debate in the arena of development on the concentration of "services" in the center versus the decentralization or relocation of "services" from the center to the periphery "which would alleviate the standing conflict and spread public expenditure more equally to other regions of the country."[4]

Need for Immediate Action

No matter how optimistic, pessimistic or objective our studies may be, and no matter how high a probability their statements or measurements have, there is no certainty that man will find and put into effect the right solutions to some of the very critical problems in time to save the situation. And "in time" means here and now. Because whatever happens now decisively conditions the future.

There are things we might change overnight, but we never do. Instead of trying to find a new solution to the problems, most of us tend to stick to fighting urbanization—an impossible task. Urbanization seems to provide a lifestyle and a pattern of allocation of human effort and time which is desirable to most humans. On the other hand, taming urbanization by bringing existing rural and urban agglomerations together into urbanized systems is both desirable and feasible.

Many millions of human settlements—small and large, dynamic and static, closely or loosely connected, or enclosed in major systems—are now spread over the surface of our globe.

In the process of urbanization many of them may disappear, many may be embraced within major systems, many will definitely grow at various levels. Action in each case needs special consideration of the various dimensions of problems within the limits of the settlement itself, but also within the broader system or systems with which it is connected.

Although there are no globally valid principles to guide identical action for cities and villages with similar characteristics, long world-wide experience and special studies show that, in terms of probable priority, one could suggest specific action.

For each type of settlement, there is much to say on the identification of problems, the definition of goals and objectives, both short-term and long-term (ultimate and immediate), and the establishment and implementation of policies which are consistent with the immediate goals and, at the same time, lead towards the ultimate ones.

The major urbanization pressure areas are those that, it is believed, will experience the gravest and most pressing problems during the next 20 to 30 years, both for the settlements (and systems of settlements) in them and for their total environment, in view of:

a. High densities of population (increasing with time), especially in selected core areas.

b. High total population (increasing with time).

c. Megalopolitan development, i.e., development of large independent megalopoli and, what is more important, of large interconnected systems of megalopoli (urbanized regions, or small "eperopoli") that will tend to become the dominating feature within these areas. These characteristics are expected to grow spectacularly in size and complexity with time.

These major pressure areas are divided into four categories:

A. Megalopolitan systems are already developed and are evolving toward one unified complex system expected to form in them in the future. Total population and core densities are high.

B. Total population is smaller than in A; megalopolitan development is simpler (overall linear formation), but already present.

C. Megalopolitan development is still in its early phases, evolving toward several distinct megalopolitan systems which, however, have to be considered as one major unit within a unified study area because of the functional interrelations between these megalopolitan systems.

D. Same as B, but megalopolitan development still in its early phases.

Several types of problems can be distinguished within these pressure areas:

a. Problems of structure, function and development of the megalopolitan systems implying the need for measures leading to the proper organization and governance of these systems.

b. Problems of changing land uses, "eating up" of open land through expanding urbanization, and environmental deterioration due to growing megalopolitan systems, leading to proposals of environmental control and protection measures distinguished according to zones of increasing human intervention in the natural environment.

c. Problems of overall regional structure and development studied in the light of the growing megalopolitan systems within these areas, leading to corresponding proposals for regional control and development.

For each area, partial studies and modes of action could be devised, dealing either with specific problems (or groups of problems), or with specific sub-areas; in any case, the overall perspective of the total area and of the entire system of problems should not be lost from sight: this means that each partial study should always be considered as part of the total one for each major study area.

The main question is: should we allow the transition to the future to go on by itself following the present trends, or should we try to understand what is happening, conceive clearly what we want our future to be, and then guide the forces in that direction, reducing friction as much as possible?

Notes

1. Population Crisis Committee "World Population Growth and Global Security" in *Population* No. 13, (Sept. 1983).

2. Harold Lubell, in *Urban Studies* No. 21, (1984).

3. Note of the Editor: According to Jean Gottmann "The concept of the megalopolis applies to very large poly-nuclear urbanized systems endowed with enough continuity and internal interconnections for each of them to be considered a system in itself."
On the basis of this definition Gottmann sets the minimum size for the phenomenon at 25 million and found in 1975 only six cases in existence:
- the American northeastern megalopolis
- the Great Lakes megalopolis of the Canadian-U.S. border
- the Tokaido megalopolis in Japan

- the megalopolis in England
- the European northwestern megalopolis (Amsterdam-Ruhr-Northern France)
- the Chinese megalopolis centered on Shanghai
According to Gottmann, three more are in formation:
- the Rio-Sao Paolo complex in Brasil
- the northern Italian megalopolis centered on Milan
- the Californian from San Diego to San Francisco
Jean Gottmann: "Megalopolitan Systems around the World." Keynote address of the Great Lakes Megalopolis Symposium, Toronto, Canada, March 1975; also in *Ekistics* 243, (Feb. 1976).

4. Jean Gottmann, "The Coming of the Transactional City," University of Maryland Press Institute for Urban Studies, 1983.

5. C.A. Doxiades and J.G. Papioannou: "Ecumenopolis: the Inevitable City of the Future," Athens Center of Ekistics, 1975.

Part II

Factors Shaping the Metropolis

4.
Determinants of Metropolitan Structure

John W. Dyckman

Introduction

The determinants of metropolitan structure are so varied and complex as to cast in doubt the possibilities of effective treatment in a brief essay. At the least these include economic factors, demographic growth, migration forces, historic and geographic advantages, levels of national development and dominant activities, and government policies. In the face of this complexity I have chosen two emphases. The first of these is to focus on the most pervasive forces at the global scale. The second is to select, for the most part, those forces which seem to me to be the most powerful in shaping metropolitan structure. It is in the latter interest that this paper gives its main attention to economic factors. The other major metropolitan-shaping forces are introduced mainly as they modify or temper the economic pressures.

These choices are only partly a matter of editorial selection and manageability. The conviction that economic forces are powerful in shaping metropolitan structure leads one to consider the global economy and the international scope of those forces. The belief that the world economy is increasingly integrated should not blind us to the importance of the political powers of nation states or to their capacity to influence, in a variety of ways, their own settlement solutions. An emphasis on economic influence permits the author to greatly extend the range of structural effects that can be treated. The alternative of dealing with national policies across nations threatens to mire the analysis in excessive particularism.

Nevertheless, one might fairly contend that from an economic perspective the world should be divided into different groups. While there is, in some sense, a world urban system, the problem remains of partitioning the analysis of world urbanization. The commonest distinction, and one that has merit for the study of urban structure, is between the "superpowers" and the "Third World," largely a political distinction, albeit with economic implications, or between the "developed" and "underdeveloped" nations, a somewhat fuzzy, largely economic distinction. It is the latter, not the character of urbanization, which underlies this distinction. For example, the international lending and assistance agencies, such as the World Bank and the United Nations, tend to make the separation on the basis of *GNP per capita,* per capita income, and *demographic rates of growth.* The first is an economic measure, which is unfortunately not a perfectly good measure of development (e.g., are the petroleum exporting countries, which tend to high product per capita equally "developed"?). The second, while important for urban analysis, is also a gross measure. Whatever the uses of product or income per capita measures as criteria for classification, these cannot do justice to notions of *development,* a process more complex than economic level or growth.

For our purposes, some broad classification is necessary, despite the fact that the measures are very summary and mask many internal differences. Since most of the countries in both the "underdeveloped" and "Third World" categories are in Asia, Africa and Latin America, it seems wise to treat them on their geographical ground. While this does not correspond to the other measures perfectly, as, for example, in the case of South Africa which is both developed and metropolitan and largely underdeveloped and rural with a deceptive GNP per capita, it allows a clearer view of the internal processes in each continent.

It is useful as well that the editor has chosen to distinguish the "socialist" urbanization from the capitalist cases, since these not only belong to different economic systems but have different interpretations of the signifi- cance of the economics of metropolitan centers, different ideological per- spectives on urbanism, and different policies toward it. As a result, the socialist economic impulses and their urban expression are significantly different from those in the predominantly capitalist countries. These orientations are particularly manifest in political attitudes toward the growth and size of the largest metropoli, which are our main concern. (There are relatively few truly large metropolitan centers, outside of China, in the socialist countries.)

This is not to suggest that the socialist nations are insulated from all the economic forces affecting metropolitan structure in the capitalist world. They, too, are experiencing some shifts from manufacturing to service employment (though not on the scale of the chief capitalist centers). They also see the shifts from older types of manufacturing to higher technology production, have their share of automation and communications develop- ments, and their "footloose" industries. But in general, they are starting from a different base, have more government control of location and employment, greater power over migration, and are largely—but not entirely —sealed off from some of the capital flows of the other "worlds."

In so general a paper, there will necessarily be many generalizations which fail to do justice to the complexities hidden by the broad categories —developed and underdeveloped, center and periphery, and "metropoli- tan." The purpose here is to focus on the main economic forces shaping cities, some of which are common to socialist and capitalist urban systems, but others are not. Much of this analysis is appropriate to the capitalist system, and my remarks on the socialist urbanization are largely confined to a few obvious similarities and differences.

From the point of view of capital, central to capitalism, there is a "center"–"periphery" distinction in which the center, or centers, command major decisions. This center-periphery distinction is not simply international, for there are peripheral areas within center nations and even within metropolitan areas. These latter distinctions, however important to the economics of urbanization in the states concerned, should not hide the much greater disparities between nations. Figures compiled by the World Bank, for example, ranking nations by GNP per capita, show that the quarter of the world population in nations with a product of more than $2,000 per person account for 80 percent of the world product. And the 65 percent of the people on earth at the other end of the distribution accounted for just under 8½ percent of the total product (put by the Bank in 1977 at almost three trillion dollars).[1] While there is reason to consider the 65 percent of the world population in the poorest nations (in terms of product per person) as the "underdeveloped" world, not all of these nations are open to capital flows from the "center" (e.g., until recently at least, China) and therefore have not been in the world system for most purposes.

Tendencies in World Urbanization

The single most dramatic feature of the urban scene for demographers and urban geographers is the shift in the center of gravity of urban agglomerations from Europe and North America to Asia, Latin America and even Africa, measured by size and rate of growth. Between 1950 and 1980 the urban population of Asia grew from 180 million to almost 600 million, in Latin America from roughly 50 million to more than 160 million, and in Africa from 30 million to 90 million. Today, Shanghai is placed at 12 million persons, Mexico City at almost 18 million, Peking and Calcutta over seven million, Bombay and Cairo over six million (in the latter case, the larger megalopolis has been estimated recently at about 12 million), with cities such as Seoul, Jakarta and Rio de Janeiro already surpassing five million. The rates of growth, even at the U.N. median estimates which now seem attainable, are awesome. Planners in Mexico estimate that the city will reach nearly 30 million in the next 20 years, and according to the recent U.N. population conference in Mexico City, Sao Paulo will surpass 20 million, and Rio, Peking, and Shanghai will be in the order of 20 million in the year 2000. The same conference projections estimated, for example, that only three U.S. cities—New York, Los Angeles and San Francisco—would have urban agglomerations between 10 and 20 million at that date. Measured by population alone, Bombay, Calcutta and Jakarta will be at least as large.[2]

While these figures are not startling to the experts and appear in one form or another elsewhere in this volume, the problems attendant on this growth are likely to occupy the attention of urbanists in the next two decades. Traffic jams, pollution of air and water, subsidence, collapse of buildings, and sewer overflow (whole quarters of Cairo were flooded for 10 days by overflowing sewers in the winter of 1982-83) are familiar features in some of these rapidly growing cities. The central city densities of most of these new arrivals to megalopolitan status are still increasing. The potential for rural-urban migration in many countries of these three continents has not yet been exhausted. At the same time, there has been uneven absorption of rural immigrants, with a resulting labor surplus and informal sector. As mechanization of agriculture is extended, rural labor surpluses lead to further urban migration. The spread of business methods and technologies from the centers of world business to these nations leads to a breakdown of rural social patterns and contributes to migration. Rural unrest and agrarian revolts contribute their share of refugees to the cities.

The largest cities of what is sometimes called the Third World have perhaps the sharpest contrasts between a "modernized" sector and an intermediate area of mass communities (the "bidonvilles," "barriadas" and other "under-integrated"[3] settlements which lack most urban services). The modernized sector, where business is carried on with centers in New York, London, Hong Kong or Paris, typically has the commercial center, banks, and tall office buildings that may house branches of multi-national firms, and is served by an airport, highways and hotels. The more luxurious residences are typically not far from such centers. The apparatus of communication necessary for business, the telephone system, is centered there. In these cities, industrial districts are a growing feature of the landscape.

The metropolitan picture in the "mature" industrial countries displays some similarities and many differences. The central city remains the center of service activities in both rich and poor countries, but in the former the consumer services are much more broadly diffused in space, and the concentration of producer services at the center is much greater. The "developed" countries are increasedly marked by metropolitan spread, by a hollowing out of central residential densities, by poly-nucleated forms with major sub-centers in the open suburban areas with a diffusion of one-time central city functions to the older suburban ring, and by increasing occupation of the former rural-urban fringe. That is, there is both some decentralization of the older central city functions and greater geographical spread of residences and industry.

In part, this pattern is the result of the richer infrastructure in roads, communications and equipment, and of the higher incomes of the population which reduce the relative burden of spatial mobility. It also reflects the increased freedom of location of industries, the ability of manufacturing to separate discrete stages of the production process, and to extend the division of labor in these processes. There has been a pronounced shift in the urban economic base of these countries from manufacturing to services, and from old types of manufacturing to those employing higher levels of technology and information.

The spread of manufacturing to the periphery—both internationally and within the most powerful nation states—with a division of the production processes that leads to a search for low-wage locations for mass production and assembly portions of the work has tended to make the major metropolitan centers either international or regional service cities. These centers concentrate the financial services, legal services, accounting and marketing, and are the centers of product conception and design, engineering, and business strategy. This spatial division of labor has resulted in greater specialization of industrial activity in the lower-order urban centers, and has resulted in a growing "duality" of the service and high-technology labor forces. Many cities are saddled with obsolete and abandoned industrial plants, high unemployment, and increasing fiscal burdens.

The Economic Environment of Urban Change

The preceding very dense description of metropolitan trends deserves expansion and explanation. The influence of history, particularly colonialism, on the urban pattern of Latin American, Asian and African countries has been well argued by Celso Furtado, Andre Gunder Frank, Samir Amin and many others.[4] The policies of nation states, the role of capital cities, and the accidents of resource distribution have been well studied by urban geographers. The influence of transport costs and distance to markets have preoccupied regional economists. Urban planners have focused on infrastructure systems, environment and urban policy. This paper chooses to look at the present pattern as it is influenced by very broad economic tendencies whieh it sees as global in scope and which influence the distribution of production in space.

Economic accumulation at the centers of capital (most prominent of which is New York) is both the result of an increased mobility of capital and a spur to further mobility in its placement. Both institutional and geopolitical factors have developed to exploit the technological possibilities of this mobility. Monetary arrangements, such as the agreement to settle oil accounts in dollars, the spread of international banking,[5] the growth of stock exchanges in New York and Hong Kong, and the creation of large "trading blocs" have featured the institutional and geopolitical responses. Computerization of banking, satellite communications, and other technical developments have virtually eliminated spatial arbitrage, and make very speedy international and national transfers possible. These factors have responded to and contributed to the impressive mobility of capital in the world. What are some of the urban impacts of this mobility?

First, the mobility of capital has greatly facilitated the spatial division of labor. Michael Dunford summarizes the argument of Lipietz (in *Le Capital et Son Espace*) on this impact on the separation of production in space as follows: "This gives rise to different states of production within a single branch circuit (e.g., conception, manufacture, assembly) which can be located in different, unequally developed regions with different values of labor-power. This process results in the establishment of a new interregional division of labor with different areas specializing in activities corresponding to different stages in the process of producing commodities."[6]

A classic example of this division in space is that of the Silicon Valley electronics industry of California which centers conception and design in the San Francisco area, along with certain core manufacturing, and which uses Hong Kong or other Asian centers for other manufacturing and assembly. The examples of such spatial separation of production processes are numerous. They may take different forms, as in the case of the automobile production of Renault where design and planning are done in Paris, where many of the parts are manufactured in Spain, and where assembly and finishing is completed in a highly automated line in the North of France. Of course, such producer services as advertising, marketing, accounting and the rest take place in the capital center.

The urban impacts are felt in the loss of manufacturing and assembly jobs in the metropolitan center (Apple Computer once centered the entire production process in the San Francisco area, as did Renault in Paris) and in the strengthening of the high-skilled and professional concentrations in those centers. These impacts are also evident in the increasing "footloose" character of industries and the spread of manufacturing to new areas (in Britain and the U.S. to the southeast and southwest respectively). A study by R.B. Cohen has shown how much of the high-technology manufacturing growth of Houston, for example, has been financed by and depends heavily on the producer services of Chicago, thus increasing the specialization of each.[7] These forces of spatial reorganization are producing, in the territory of a large state such as the United States, a spatial solution which corresponds to the separation of production processes noted in individual industries. The tendency, as Stanback and Noyelle have demonstrated in several studies of U.S. cities,[8] is for all cities to have a growing economic base in services, but for those services to hierarchically nest, with only a few cities providing national and international services to producers, and for the service component to increase with hierarchical position.

At the international level, the export of technical services from the centers of the developing countries is channeled through central cities in those countries. In the global sense, the national centers of the underdeveloped countries act as regional centers in the larger system. Where in the United States the proportion of the working population in "services" is 65%, the average in Latin America is no more than 45%, and that of Asia and Africa, 25% and 18% respectively.[9] While these figures must be considered with caution—given the large agricultural subsistence populations in under-developed countries, the difficulties in measuring certain services in these populations, and the ambiguities surrounding the concept of "services"—it is possible that the real differences are understated. The structure of the tertiary sector in developing countries is complex, because of the great variations in the forms of their economic growth, and particularly of the role of the traditional sector, with its shopkeepers, officials, clergymen, military, domestics, artisans and the like. To talk of "producer services" in such countries is meaningless without specification of the forms of production, and "consumer" services depend heavily on traditional organization of the cities and countryside. In some developing countries, moreover, the construction sector accounts for up to 40% of employment, roughly twice the proportion in developed countries. And when one considers the sizable role of the state apparatus in some developing countries, with its military, police and functionaries, all of which are counted as "services", the relatively small size of production services and the heavy dependence of these countries on the import of such services is striking. Former colonial countries are notoriously dependent on the former colonial powers for technicians and experts of all types, particularly in the development of modern industrial facilities. The international "assistance" agencies provide a floating population of experts of all types which does not enter the structure of the cities in developing countries in a permanent way. Taken together with employees of multinational firms, this group helps to form the large advanced service population of the main centers of the developed countries. Finally, as the IMF (International Monetary Fund) recently noted in a report, the pressures of foreign debt in developing countries have impelled these countries to focus on their own export industries at the expense of local services and infrastructure. This tends to "freeze" the spatial and employment patterns in these countries and to inhibit the growth of advanced service centers. Indeed, an argument often leveled by planners in the developing countries is that the pattern of services in the dominant city or cities is unproductive, and that these cities are in a sense "parasitic" of national energies and an impediment to development. But this argument deserves separate treatment.

Urban Structure, Employment and Labor Markets

To this point, we have emphasized the impact of the mobility of capital on industrial location and urban specialization. Also important for cities in the "developed" countries has been the substantial mobility of persons. Two processes appear to be at work in these nations. In one, capital flows abroad in search of lower wage workers for "detachable" portions of production. In the other, lower wage workers flow into the metropolitan areas of the "center" countries to perform a variety of manufacturing and service tasks. These workers account for substantial portions of the work force in countries such as Switzerland, Germany, and France as well as in the United States. Speaking of the latter, Sassen-Koob has written:

"The large influx of immigrants from low-wage countries over the last 15 years, which reached massive levels in the second half of the 1970s, cannot be understood separately from this restructuring. It is a mistake to view this new immigration phase as a result mostly of push factors and as being absorbed primarily in backward sectors of the economy. It is the expansion of the supply of low-wage jobs generated by major growth sectors that is one of the key factors in the continuation at even higher levels of the current immigrants."[10]

The processes of automation, division of production tasks, and the replacement of middle-income skilled workers by machines have, at the same time, increased the demand for both highly qualified and very low-wage workers. The latter effect has, for a variety of cultural and institutional reasons, created opportunities for immigrants. If industrial restructuring continues along these lines, that demand may continue. Such restructuring is not available to all industries, but the pressure for it is greatest in industries where technology is well known internationally and where the competitive pressure on labor costs is greatest. The continuing role of immigrants also depends on the degree of their insertion or integration into the economy, as Moulaert and Deryckere have shown in a comparison between the time-paths of employment of migrant workers in West Germany and Belgium.[11] But in many countries we may expect it to remain an important element of the workforce.

The important presence of an immigrant work force has a number of impacts on urban structure. On the one hand, the presence of a large immigrant population may make an area attractive for industrial location by certain industries. Sassen-Koob finds this immigrant population an important factor in the industrial expansion of the San Diego area near the Mexican border of the U.S.[12] Secondly, cities with such high immigrant populations show a greater-than-average polarization of their income structures. Looking at New York and Los Angeles, both of which have very high numbers of such immigrants, she observes:

"The combination of these various trends expresses itself in an increased income polarization in these two cities. Comparing household income for 1969 and 1979, there is an increase in the high-and low-income strata and a shrinking in the middle stratum. Considering the 1969 and 1979 median income and including the bracket immediately below and immediately above the middle-income stratum, we find that almost 49% of the Los Angeles and 51% of the New York City households were in the middle stratum in 1969, compared with 38% and 39% respectively in 1979. The higher income stratum increased from 21.5% to 29.5% in Los Angeles and from 19% to 23.5% in New York City. In considering the city rather than the metropolitan region there may actually be an overestimate of middle-income households."[13] Thirdly, there has been substantial social segregation of immigrant groups, creating higher indices of segregation in such metropolitan areas. A 1981 report of the Ad Hoc Group on Urban Problems of the Economic Commission for Europe found that the operation of housing systems and labor markets tended to distribute population in a polarized fashion and to create segregation of social and racial groups. The report found:

"This is accentuated in some European countries by the inflow of foreign "guest workers." This concentration and the perceived disparity between the well-being of inner city areas inhabited by low-status and minority groups and suburban areas inhabited by higher-status, more dominant culture groups, spark social tensions and raise questions of social equity. Indeed, one study of urban decline in the U.K., Netherlands, Belgium, France and Germany concludes that it is the increasing concentration of all kinds of minority groups in terms of age, income and culture added to the dilapidating physical urban fabric and declining economic strength of the central cities that together are the building blocks for what is called the urban decline problem."[14]

The bi-polar income distribution in major metropolitan centers of the United States such as New York, Chicago, Los Angeles and San Francisco has been a major spur to the "gentrification" of central city areas. This development has sometimes been exaggerated to mean a "back to the city" movement. Nationally and numerically, it is relatively unimportant, since the population active in this movement is predominantly childless, and displaces a larger number of persons than it introduces. But with the impact of economic restructuring which reduces the number of blue- and white- collar workers in the "middle" income categories, taken together with the movement of lower-middle and middle-income families to cheaper suburban or exurban locations, it is likely to be a continuing feature of the occupancy pattern of the major metropolitan areas which provide the bulk of producer services.

These advanced producer services appear to benefit significantly from clustering—from "agglomeration effects."[15] The highly specialized firms providing these services are consumers of each other's outputs and engage in much joint production.[16] The numbers of highly-trained persons engaged in these activities form a significant part of total employment in these major centers. According to Sassen-Koob, such producer services accounted for 31% of employment in New York City and 25% in Los Angeles in 1981.[17] Not all of these employees seek central city residential locations, but enough of the accountants, lawyers, brokers, designers, and computer specialists do so to contribute to the expansion of central city demand for higher income housing, a factor which swells the demand for gentrification and piecemeal redevelopment. And whether or not such employees choose central city residences, there is evidence that they prefer to have access to the attractions of the major centers.[18]

At the same time these centers are developing the technological capacity to decentralize substantial portions of their traditional office employment. With the expansion of ownership of home computers which can be linked by telephone lines to central offices, the computer has the potential to become the traditional sewing machine equivalent in the "putting out" or "home work" system. Such a development would provide firms with the capacity to "suburbanize" substantial portions of their office work while retaining central control and management at the center. Of course, the possibility also exists for decentralizing such work much farther. Major credit card companies in the U.S. have already decentralized central billing and accounting to relatively remote locations, in smaller cities with lower living costs. The possibilities do not stop with this level of decentralization. Sassen-Koob comments that "Barbados and Jamaica are two key locations for overseas office work because of their high literacy rates and English speaking population. And they earn about $1.50 an hour for work which in the United States ranges from $4.00 to $12.00 an hour."[19]

61

A likely scenario for those metropolitan areas that are most highly integrated into the world economic system, then, contains some of the following elements. These centers will continue to locate management, control, finance and headquarters functions in the downtowns of those cities. The downtowns are likely as well to house scientific and design functions. The employees of the firms who are engaged in these central functions are likely to swell the demand for gentrification. Their income and lifestyles contribute to the demand for high-level consumption activities, cultural facilities, and personal services. But the lower-income populations engaged in the provision of the relatively low-paid services are probable candidates to inherit the aging inner-ring suburbs whose more affluent inhabitants move to more remote suburbs. The inner-ring suburbs are, in turn, candidates for economic decay. In the less "central" or "international" cities the effects will be weaker, and the demand for gentrification and high-style consumption less. These are likely to retain the bulk of the low-paid and unemployed in the inner city. (If, as Stanback and Noyelle contend, there are only four major producer service centers in the United States—New York, Chicago, Los Angeles and San Francisco—the bulk of American cities will be in this category.)

There are also many cities whose base has been heavily in older manufacturing industries whose technology is well-diffused in the world. In Europe as well as in North America these cities are experiencing crises of employment and fiscal capacities as demand declines, as competition from less-developed countries grows, and as old plants are shut down and industries move to new locations. The north of England and France, upper New York State and the Great Lakes in the U.S., the Ruhr valley, and many older industrial regions face these problems. The city of Liverpool, which has an overall unemployment rate of 21% and as much as 80% in some quarters of the city, is bankrupt. In such cities the prospects are indeed bleak for, with declining activity and employment, local revenues and ability to maintain services also suffer. As services decline, so does the ability—however small' it is at best—to attract new activities. These urban areas confront the prospect of substantial depopulation. Between 1960 and 1980 many of the older cities lost population at a high rate—not only in the central city, but also in the metropolitan area. Merseyside in England, for example, experienced a loss of 12.7% in the city and almost 7% in the metropolitan area. In other cases, the metropolitan area continues to grow, but the central cities are losing population at a high rate. In some cases, this rate amounts to a virtual "hollowing out" of the centers. Between 1961 and 1971 in the U.K., for example, losses in the inner areas amounted to 37% in Glasgow, 32% in Liverpool, 27% in Birmingham, and 27% in Manchester.[20] These numbers mean something quite different for cities that are predominantly manufacturing, and at best, regional service centers than they do for cities such as London, New York, and Chicago which also lost substantially in inner city population (from roughly 11% in London and New York to 7% in Chicago between 1960 and 1980) but which are major producer service centers.

The cities of Europe and North America which were once the industrial heartlands of those continents too frequently find themselves holding the wrong end of the "product cycle" in the international economy, that of the mass production which is diminishing in importance in their own national economies and which faces brutal international competition from the less-developed countries that have been rapidly industrializing. The general strategies for such local economies are to "modernize" by adopting new technologies of production, by changing the product mix, and by searching for new, usually "high technology" industries. All of these steps, which involve increasing capital investment in automation and new plants, specializing in the high-value items of the production, and searching for technological growth industries, respectively, have some promise. But none is likely to replace the employment lost in the recent past in the older industries. For even if these policies could be successfully pursued, they would involve the substitution of capital for labor, and some retreat from previous levels of production, and would employ a substantially different labor force. Success in attracting a semi-conductor activity, for example, is almost certainly to be followed by the "off-shoring" of the mass assembly portions of that output to low-wage regions of the world.

The prospect for many older industrial areas of the world, then, is for some continued decline in employment and population. Very few of these areas have locations favorable with respect to markets and financing. All suffer from the historical disadvantage that newer, growing industries in their own countries have in recent years located elsewhere. Short of large-scale policies in their countries to direct investment and industrial location and massive reformation of the labor force, the cities in these regions must await still another cycle of international industrial restructuring and hope they may be advantaged by it.

The impacts of economic restructuring have been very different for the developing and under-developed countries. The "middle level countries" —with metropoli that include Seoul, Taipei, Hong Kong and Singapore in Asia and Sao Paulo, Rio, and Mexico City in Latin America—have experienced the most rapid economic development. This development is manifest in a number of ways. First, they have begun to change the composition of industrial activity and exports from low-cost consumer goods towards intermediate products having higher capital composition and more sophisticated technology.[21] A good example is the Hyundai Group of Korea, which as Mucchielli observes, "is the second firm in the world in the mechanics sector and which comprises a vast conglomerate working as well in construction, automobile and ship-building."[22] Secondly, these centers have begun to "farm out" work in some of the older, less sophisticated industries such as textiles. As an example, Hong Kong has dispersed some of its textile operations to Malaysia, Sri Lanka, Macao and the Ile of Mauritius.[23] The latter are able to use older machinery which requires large inputs of labor at competitive costs. The metropolitan centers of these "middle" countries thus play, in an analogous if less dominant manner, the role of the major centers of the developed countries. There are, nevertheless, major differences in the internal structure of the main metropolitan areas of these "middle" or developing countries and that of the principal centers of the "developed" nations. Despite the high pace of growth of exports, local collective and individual consumption lags well behind that in the older industrial cities of Europe and North America, not to mention the great service centers. The growth of services is still another aspect of "export" activity, with hotels and services for tourists and international business but with relatively underdeveloped infrastructure for local populations. Enclaves such as Hong Kong and Singapore have achieved high levels of public housing and "standard" accommodations at astonishing densities. Yet many cities in the same class of national development, such as Sao Paulo and Mexico City, are ringed with layers of squatter or minimal housing settlements, poorly served even by basic utilities. So pervasive are these extensions of the city that open land around these centers is virtually preempted.[24] The great population concentrations in these centers are a relatively recent phenomenon, even in Latin America where functional primacy dates from colonial times. Chase-Dunn has demonstrated that the overwhelming population primacy of Latin American cities did not emerge until well into this century.[25] Of course, developments in agriculture and the force of demographic effects in many developing countries are relatively recent.

Services in many cities of the developing world depend heavily on the "informal sector." (The term "informal" is somewhat fanciful, given the high level of organization of these activities and their degree of integration into the larger economy.) All kinds of activities, from food vendors to shoe shiners to waste collectors, are lumped in this "informal" category, largely because the workers are outside the normal wage and tax systems. Increasingly, many types of small manufacturing and repair, fashioning of parts, and tax-free merchandising fall into this class. (In Bogota, for example, there is a very large and well-developed district for the selling of "duty free" items outside the normal "legal" channels.) Such activities are not limited to the developing countries—the importance of the "black" economy in Italy, for example, is considerable, and such extra-legal work flourishes in developed countries as well.[26] But the relative importance in the developing world is generally very great, and is in fact essential to the functioning of the cities.

In contrast to the metropolitan areas of the developed world, where the virtually ubiquitous infrastructure permits the middle and upper classes to find congenial ex-urban residential locations, the elite residential areas of developing countries are typically in closer-ring suburbs or quarters of the city. (The "ex-urban" locations are relatively self-contained ranchos or estates at a considerable distance.) The commercial middle class, in Asia particularly, remains in central city residences. In Arab countries it is common for the commercial class to have residences, often very large, in the same structures that house commerce on the street level.

The rapid pace of urban construction in developing countries—often of a speculative nature—poses many future problems. In addition to the difficulty of a time-concentration of obsolescence to be faced in the future, there is frequently inadequate maintenance and shoddy construction. The governor of Cairo declared last year that "40% of the buildings in Cairo are threatened with collapse."[27] While this is a rather alarmist view, there is no doubt that much urban building is hasty and below standard. Under the pressure of demand and with the financial stakes in construction, building controls are likely to be absent or ineffectual. This problem is not confined to Cairo, though it may well be extreme there; it is common to many under-developed countries.

The growth of metropolitan centers in the under-developed countries has, to date, generally outstripped even these important gains in industrialization. In his paper for this conference, Dwyer notes that:

"Within the industrialized countries in recent decades there has been a massive replacement of industrial labor by capital in the form of ever more sophisticated machines, with the result that the industrial employment opportunities created by a given quantum of industrial development have progressively become less and less. As a result, contemporary industrial growth within the developing countries has, in general, been much less labor absorptive than was the case in the previous experience of today's industrially advanced countries."[28]

He goes on to cite a United Nations report that found that "although the Third World's industrial production increased by an average of seven percent per annum during the 1960-1972 period, it contributed very little to employment growth, especially in Africa."[29] In some regions, industrial growth in employment is barely half the rate of urban population growth. Despite the development of the "informal" manufacturing and service activities, these differential rates insure the presence of substantial unemployment and under-employment in these urban centers. Indeed, it is the presence of this "labor surplus" which keeps wages low and endows these areas with much of their labor cost advantage. But it also contributes to the scale of urban problems in these nations, particularly in managing growth, providing necessary services, and achieving standard housing conditions.

The socialist countries of Eastern Europe have not experienced the same population pressures, nor have they the phenomenon of metropolitan giantism and primacy to the degree found in Asia, Latin America and Africa, or for that matter, in France and Britain. In part this may be due to policy, which has emphasized regional equalization, "filling up" the developable space, and attempts at restriction of urban population size. (Though these latter have not been wholly successful in attaining desired numbers, as witness Moscow, they have probably maintained city size below what it might otherwise have been.) As Mihailovic has pointed out in a study of Eastern Europe, the success of these socialist countries in regional equalization and occupancy of the national space has depended upon the degree of industrial development of the countries concerned. Thus, he found much more equalized and pervasive development in East Germany and Czechoslovakia than in Yugoslavia, Bulgaria or Albania, with Poland and Hungary in an intermediate position.[30]

Paradoxically, some of the success of these efforts may result in a situation where the major metropolitan centers of Eastern Europe are actually too small to play a role in the exercise of metropolitan functions and in the competition of metropolitan areas in Europe and the world. As an example, Szelenyi and others have made the argument that development policies in Hungary have actually kept Budapest too limited in size, and have prevented it from the full exercise of the metropolitan functions.[31] In any event, the size of the principal metropolitan area even in countries with the greatest regional inequalities and lowest levels of development within this group are not very large as metropolitan areas go. (In Yugoslavia, for example, the largest city, Belgrade, is just over one million, and Zagreb is just slightly smaller.)

In a comparative study of London and Hamburg with East Berlin, Warsaw and Moscow, Friedrichs and associates found that all had:

- a similar urban structure in land use distribution and specialization;

- similarity in planning policies for shared development patterns;

- a relatively low success rate in implementing urban policies.[32]

Given the difficulty of characterizing "structures," spatial organization and social organization across national and cultural lines, such findings must be treated carefully. But all such cities showed distinct social differentiation, leading to the spatial differentiation. That social differentiation exists in socialist as well as capitalist countries cannot be doubted, but the nature of distinctions and the impact on spatial differentiation is not as well understood.[33]

Whatever the similarities of structure *within* metropolitan areas in socialist and capitalist countries, there are clearly differences in the workings of national urbanization policies. An excellent study by Banerjee and Schenk comparing "Lower Order Cities and National Urbanization Policies: China and India" concludes that, despite some similarity in policies and objectives, "much of the available evidence suggests that the lower-order cities have played a much more significant role in the urbanization and economic development of China than in India, although the latter's performance may not have been as dismal as it appears on the surface, or as in some other developing countries."[34] The main reason for the difference, they find, is between the capitalist and socialist ideologies and institutions. They say flatly that "the most profound difference between China and India is related obviously to their two different political institutions."[35] The Chinese appear to believe that industrialization and modernization are not inexorably linked to greater or more concentrated urbanization, while Indian planners have accepted greater polarization and spatial inequality as the price for industrialization. The Chinese are also more committed to a "bottom-up" and total resource mobilization model.

What will be the evolution of urban structure in socialist countries is a matter for history to say. That the Marxian and Maoist national urban policies have much overlap with the strategies advocated by such capitalist institutions as the World Bank, however, cannot be denied.[36] The push for development of middle-sized and market cities in developing countries and for more "even" development has become part of the conventional wisdom of international development agencies.

Economic Forces and Human Values in the Metropolis

In the preceding sections the emphasis has been placed heavily on economic forces determining metropolitan structure. This is the result of the choice of a vantage point from which to approach the explanation of that structure, not a plea for economic determinism in urban policy. It is not a case for structuring cities according to the efficiency of capital. Economists are concerned with such efficiency, but citizens of metropolitan areas have other values and objectives as well. The most "livable" cities are not necessarily the most efficient locations for capital investment, though they may well attract the skilled persons indispensable for the deployment of that capital. Whether or not they perform this function, however, they are desirable ends in themselves.

Nor do I wish to suggest that urban problems are a simple function of economic development and growth. The most strikingly "successful" of the Sunbelt and West Coast cities of the United States in attracting growth and "post industrial" economic activity are also cities marked by the most dramatic income inequalities and segregation, as are the "international metropolitan centers." At the same time, one should not conclude that urban problems are the exclusive province of the centers of world capitalism. Bensman has argued that the "general problematics of urbanization, industrialism, population density, and the struggles for control over scarce resources by organized elites, classes, regional groups, and rural and urban dwellers exist in all societies whether capitalist or socialist, developed or under-developed, colonial or neo-colonial."[37] He adds: "Of course, the problems that become the basis of theoretical problematics are experienced differently in different societies, depending on their history, their culture and their stage of economic, political and social development, as well as on the character of their structures."

History and culture not only affect the form of development, they contain their own embodied value systems as well. Values at the level of social needs and wants are particular historical products. Urbanization itself has, as many writers have observed—often ruefully—an impact on needs and wants, particularly in under-developed countries experiencing mass migrations from primitive rural conditions to at least partially "modernized" cities.[38] The term "civilization," which derives from "civis" or membership in an urban community, has come to stand for a certain constellation of values. There is a level of values which is broadly cultural, racial or national, but the concrete expressions of the broader values are local and come from local, social interaction.

These social forms and the relation of individuals to the production processes of their economic life must be placed in a specific historical context. The level of generalization of this paper has not permitted the development in appropriate depth of this type of analysis. In this sense it must be considered a prolegomenon to the theory of metropolitan structure and not an adequate explanation. But at least implicitly, it calls attention to the profound *delocalizing* forces in the world economy. If these forces are not to prevail, it will be because local values attached to local places will be mobilized by citizens whose defense of this localism finds effective form, and who gain control of some of these forces. The abstraction of production that characterizes this paper is not simply a device of the argument; it is, in my view, an actual tendency. That production seeks to overcome space in all its manifestations, including the national spaces. In its realization, it would make people as mobile as capital. In so doing, it threatens to depreciate the local shared experience that is so essential to the formation of local values and the history of people.

It is not an accident that in Italy, where localism is relatively strong, and where the "state" remains for many an undeveloped abstraction, the so-called "black" economy of small, flexible, informally arranged enterprises is strongest. (It is estimated that firms employing 10 or fewer persons account for almost 20% of the Italian output.) The organization of local communities and local responses is a mediating force between "civil society" and the state. Localism has justifiably been associated with narrowness and provincialism, but it may also appear increasingly as a defense of a specific place where social values are nurtured. Decentralization and the development of strong local governments is not simply a matter for administrative reform for, without some transfer of power, including economic power, such reforms are likely to be empty. If democracy is among the values to be preserved, local direct participation must also be preserved. In the end, this can be made meaningful only if there is movement towards economic as well as political democracy.

Bibliography

Berry, B. and Kasarda, J. 1977. *Contemporary Urban Ecology.* New York: Macmillan.

Bluestone, B. and Harrison, B. 1982(?). *The Deindustrialization of America.* New York: Basic Books.

Bradbury, K.L., Downs, A. and Small, K.A. 1982. *Urban Decline and the Future of American Cities.* Washington, D.C.: Brookings Institution.

Friedrichs, J., ed. 1978. *Stadtenwicklungen in Kapitalistischen und Socialitstischen Landern.* Reinbek: Rowohlt.

Grassman, S. and Lundberg, E., eds. 1981. *The World Economic Order, Past and Prospects.* London: Macmillan.

Hawken, P. 1983. *The Next Economy.* New York: Holt, Rinehart, and Winston.

Lacaste, Y. 1984. *Geographie du Sous-Developpement.* 5th edition. Paris: Presses Universitaires de France.

Massey, D. and Meegan, J. 1983. *The Anatomy of Job Loss.* London: Methuen.

Meltzer, J. 1984. *Metropolis to Metroplex: The Social and Spatial Planning of Cities.* Baltimore: Johns Hopkins Press.

Moulaert, F. and Wilson-Salinas, P., eds. 1982. *Regional Analysis and the New International Division of Labor.* Boston: Kluwer-Nijhoff.

Osborne, A. 1979. *Running Wild: The Next Industrial Revolution.* New York: McGraw-Hill.

Pred, A. 1977. *City Systems in Advanced Economies.* New York: John Wiley.

Sauvy, A. and Klatzmann, R. 1984. *Le Travail Noir et l'Economie de Demain.* Paris: Calmann-Levy.

Smith, M.P., ed. 1984. *Cities in Transformation, Urban Affairs Annual Reviews.* Beverly Hills: Sage Publications.

Stanback, Jr., T.M. and Noyelle, T.J. 1982. *Cities in Transition: Changing Job Structures in Atlanta, Denver, Buffalo, Phoenix, Columbus, Nashville, Charlotte.* New Jersey: Allanheld Osmun.

Stanback, Jr., T.M. et al. 1981. *Services: The New Economy.* New Jersey: Allenheld Osmun.

Timberlake, M., ed. 1979. *The Changing Structure of the City.* Beverly Hills: Sage Publications.

Notes

1. Y. Lacoste, *Geographie de Sous-Developpement,* 5th ed. (Paris, 1984), pp. 62-64.

2. *Ibid.,* pp. 149-50.

3. The term "under-integrated", says Lacoste, is attributable to the Moroccan urbanist Mohamed Naciri.

4. See, for example, C. Furtado, *Analyse du Modele Bresilien,* Anthropos, Paris, 1974 and other writings; A. Gunder Frank, *Le Developpement du Sous-Developpement,* Maspero, Paris, 1970, and similar literature.

5. See S. Sassen-Koob in M.P. Smith, ed., *Cities in Transformation, Urban Affairs Annual Reviews,* Sage Publications, (Beverly Hills, 1984), p. 145. She writes: "From 1971 to 1981 foreign branch assets of U.S. banks had a sixfold increase, from \$55.1 billion to \$320 billion. A study by the Center on Transnational Corporations (1981) of the United Nations found that six countries accounted for 76% of the assets of all transnational banks in 1978. The United States was the leading owner."

6. M. Dunford, "Capital Accumulation and Regional Development in France," *Geoforum* vol. 10 (1979): p. 105, note 9.

7. R.B. Cohen, "The New International Division of Labor, Multinational Corporations and the Urban Hierarchy", in M. Dear and A. Scott, *Urbanization and Urban Planning in Capitalist Society,* (London, 1981).

8. T.M. Stanback, Jr. and T.J. Noyelle, *Cities in Transition: Changing Job Structures in Atlanta, Denver, Buffalo, Phoenix, Columbus, Nashville and Charlotte,* (New Jersey, 1982).

9. Lacoste, *op.cit.,* p. 161.

10. Sassen-Koob, *op. cit.,* p. 158.

11. F. Moulaert, and P. Deryckere, "The Employment of Migrant Workers in West Germany and Belgium: A Comparative Evaluation of the Life-Cycle of Economic Migration (1960-1980)," *International Migration,* September, 1984.

12. Sassen-Koob, *op.cit.*

13. *Ibid.,* p. 159.

14. Ad Hoc Group on Urban Problems, Managing Urban Decline, O.E.C.D., (Paris, November 9, 1981), p. 25.

15. Stanback and Noyelle, *op.cit.*

16. *Ibid.*

17. Sassen-Koob, *op.cit.*, p. 141.

18. Castells cites the evidence to this effect in a study of the electronics industry in the San Francisco area; A.L. Saxanian, "Silicon Chips and Spatial Structure: The Industrial Basis of Urbanization in Santa Clara County", MCP thesis, Department of City and Regional Planning, University of California, (Berkeley, 1980), in Smith, *Cities in Transformation*, note, p. 257.

19. O.E.C.D., *op.cit.*, Annex, p. 64.

20. H. Chenery and D.B. Keesing, "The Changing Composition of Developing Country Exports," in S. Grassman and E. Lundberg, eds., *The World Economic Order, Past and Prospects*, (London, 1981).

21. J.L. Mucchielli, "Evolution des Avantages Comparatifs et Specialisation Optimale: La Lecon des Annees Passees," Cahiers Lillois d'Economie et de Sociologie, 1st semester, 1984, p.46 (my translation).

22. *Ibid.*, p. 50.

23. This point is made by Dieter Kunckel, in "The Latin American Metropolis" prepared for this conference.

24. C. Chase-Dunn, "Urbanization in the World System: New Directions for Research" in Smith, *Cities in Transformation*, p. 117.

25. A. Sauvy, with R. Klatzmann, *Le Travail Noir et l'Economie de Demain*, (Paris, 1984).

26. "Le Caire menace de s'effondrer", *Liberation*, 18 and 19 (August, 1984).

27. D.J. Dwyer, "The Metropolis as a Geographical Phenomenon" p.17.

28. *Ibid.*

29. K. Milhailovic, *Regional Development: Experience in Eastern Europe*, (Paris, 1972).

30. Richardson, for example, (in H.W. Richardson, *The Economics of Urban Size*, London, 1977) argues that in less-developed countries, the primate cities offer a higher rate of return on investment than alternate locations. This argument about the economies of scale in large cities is much debated by economists. It is worthwhile to remember that it is a "competitive" claim not always accepted in Eastern Europe.

31. J. Friedrichs, ed., *Stadtenwicklungen in Kapitalistischen und Sozialististchen Landern*, (Reinbek, 1978).

32. For an interesting study of this differentiation, see M. Voslensky, *La Nomenklatura: Les Privilèges en U.R.S.S.*, (Paris, 1980).

33. T. Banerjee and S. Schenck, "Lower Order Cities and National Urbanization Policies: China and India", *Environment and Planning A*, (1984), Vol. 16, p. 507.

34. *Ibid.*

35. This position is increasingly advanced in the literature by non-Marxian urbanists such as Dennis Rondinelli and Walter Stohr.

36. J. Bensmann, "Marxism as a Foundation for Urban Sociology," *Comparative Urban Research*, (1978), vol. 6, quoted along with the following citation, in R.C. Hill, "Urban Political Economy: Emergence, Consolidation, Development", in Smith, *op.cit.*, p. 129.

37. *Ibid.* p. 130.

38. This view is often expressed as the "explosion of expectations" with their demand for consumer goods and services which foreign critics feel must be dampened in the interest of capital accumulation in developing countries.

5.

Factors Shaping the Metropolis: Land Use, Accessibility and Transportation

William K. Mackay

Introduction

The preparation of transportation policies for major cities is an evolving process. Early procedures concentrated on solving obvious congestion problems. This was followed by extrapolation of measured demand and led to the highway-based solutions which are expensive and disruptive. In cities whose urban form and land-use distribution is static the emphasis then moved to mode transfers, in particular to restraint of cars and promotion of public transport. In cities in the developing world where urban development and growth are substantial the opportunity exists to adapt the land-use distribution and the urban form.

The preparation of alternative transport policies for testing requires the specification of goals disaggregated into assessable criteria. These will include some representation of the search for efficiency, quality and social equity.

All alternative transport policies should conform to national and regional policies. All will have to define the role of motor vehicles, and the prospects for cheap public transport. The possibilities of new transport technology will have to be incorporated, as well as the effects on travel demand of new communication processes such as computerized visual display units for stay-at-home shopping. Most urban travel occurs on the existing street networks, and this requires a policy of rationing and management.

Current preferences from the transport sector seek to disperse city center land-use activities, to create zones of dispersed, mixed development instead of large single land-use zones, and to foster high-density corridors rather than concentric town forms.

The former techniques of projecting demand and user cost benefit evaluation are being replaced by examination of needs for travel and the use of accessibility studies for the evaluation of development implications and levels of transport service.

In times past transportation planning in major cities was concerned with solving the problems of congestion, especially that arising from the increased ownership and use of motor vehicles. Traffic congestion, conflicting street activities, accidents and deterioration of the environment are all problems whose overt immediacy commands pressure for problem-solving action. Such activities, executed haphazardly, are an expedient response to much deeper problems posing fundamental questions which require a more coherent policy.

Early transport studies attempted to plan further ahead by surveying trends in travel demand—extrapolating these to the future and then designing expansions and extensions to the existing travel modes and networks to accommodate the forecasts. This process led to large-scale construction of highways and parking areas in major cities in the sixties and the seventies.

The cost and the urban disruption of highway works in major cities have led to an examination of the possibility of changing the demand for travel in two ways: firstly, by devising methods of transferring demand from one travel mode to another, principally from private cars to public transport; secondly, by using opportunities, as they occur, to re-arrange the land-use activities of the city into urban forms which are more conducive to transport systems which will provide an equitable and efficient service.

In the major cities of developed countries, where changes in urban land-use are unlikely to exceed 1% or 2% each year, the emphasis has to be on mode transference. Alterations to the urban form can only be long-term and marginal. The most probable locations for such changes will be in the central districts, where redevelopment tends to be continuous and on the periphery where marginal expansion usually takes place.

In the major cities of developing countries land-use changes are much more rapid. Urban activities and areas often double within 10 years. This situation offers the possibility for significantly altering physical urban patterns within a few years by integrating the transport policy with other policies for promoting desired land-use distribution.

A comprehensive transport policy for a major city is concerned with movement demand and how to cater to it. It is concerned with the probable number, nature, origin and destination of trips for moving people and goods between the various urban activities. It is concerned with the existing and possible modes of movement and with techniques for changing the way in which the available modes are used. It is concerned with processes to change the distribution of land-use activities, with costs and benefits, and with the effects on different groups of people and on the urban environment. In the face of such an array of issues, it is not surprising that many transportation engineers and politicians prefer to concentrate on the day-to-day problem solving approach!

Goals and Criteria

The search for optimal policies for urban transport, in relation to land-use and urban form, implies alternatives and choice. The process of selection therefore requires some goals against which competing policies may be assessed. These goals will probably have different levels of importance assigned to them by the assessors.

A danger here is the setting up of transport goals which are not compatible with other sectors. For example, a planning policy might be that, for reasons not connected with transport, all development was, and would continue to be, dispersed and low-density. An incompatible transportation goal would be a preference for a high-occupancy, mass-haul public transport system.

Within the transport sector itself mutually contradictory goals can exist. For example, an expressed preference for a policy which optimized the vehicle usage of available road space could be contradictory to a desired goal to eliminate non-essential traffic from roads in areas of environmental sensitivity.

The importance of the goals and, indeed, the goals themselves will vary between different cities, but it is almost certain that they will include a search for efficiency, for quality and for equity.

For use in judging alternatives such generalized goals need to be disaggregated into sets of criteria which can be used to test the performance of alternatives. Thus, the goal of efficiency may be disaggregated into assessable criteria which are used as a measure of efficiency. These might be:

- minimum average trip time or cost

- highest ratio of user benefits to expenditure

The goal of quality might be disaggregated into assessable criteria such as:

- least environmental impact on activities adjacent to transport networks

- highest levels of service in terms of accessibility, safety, and user comfort

The goal of equity might be disaggregated into:

- best response to the needs of various groups of users

- best distribution of financing obligations

The setting of clearly defined goals and their disaggregation into assessable criteria in some ranking of categories of importance is invaluable, and perhaps essential, not only for selecting from a number of candidate options, but also in setting up the candidates themselves.

Analysis and Evaluation

The techniques of analysis of alternative transport policies are varied and complex. In the past, the emphasis has been on *forecasting demand* by survey and extrapolation or by calibration of mathematical simulation models. Efforts to influence the predicted demand have concentrated on simple restraints, such as control of parking for cars, and inducements to transfer modes, such as from cars to public transport or for goods from road to rail. These attempts to influence the demand have not, in general, been very successful.

More recent techniques do not depend on an extrapolation of current behavior and demand as a basis for policy-making. Instead an attempt is made to establish the *travel needs* of groups of people and of categories of commodity. The base knowledge of current supply and demand is then examined to identify the strengths and weaknesses of the system to satisfy the identified needs. The transport policies and proposals are designed to improve the areas of weakness while maintaining the areas of strength.

The establishment of travel needs introduces to transport planning the techniques of social science and market research. It entails specialized attitudinal interviews of carefully stratified samples. In order to secure results with an adequate level of confidence the expertise of experienced social scientists should be used in conjunction with the full survey experience of market research organizations.

The ability of a transport system to satisfy the travel needs of its users can be examined by the use of *accessibility indices*. In the same way that need for transport is not synonymous with current travel behavior, so accessibility is concerned with the potential to reach and take part in activities rather than with current behavior. Accessibility studies measure the opportunities to reach particular activities.

The relation between accessibility, travel behavior, and participation in activities is illustrated in Figure 1.

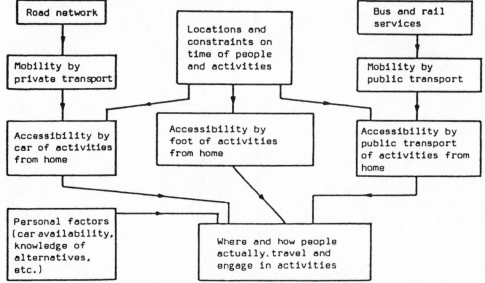

Fig. 5-1: The relation between mobility, accessibility and travel.

Development of Land Use and Transport Options

General

In cities where changes and development in land-use are anticipated to be of sufficient scale and rate to offer significant opportunities to adjust and create urban forms conducive to the transportation goals, a number of principles are worth bearing in mind in preparing the options for testing.

In applying these principles, it is important to recognize that the preparation of policies and plans for testing is essentially a trial-and-error process. Alternative policies and plans are postulated, and the performance of each is tested against the predetermined goals and criteria. It is clearly important, therefore, that the alternatives are of the highest possible calibre and represent as wide a range as possible of credible options.

A two-stage approach is recommended. In stage one, as wide a range of transport strategies, and the related land-use distribution strategies, as is credible should be examined and a preferred strategy selected. In stage two, variations within the theme of the preferred strategy are then subjected to more refined analysis and evaluation.

A fundamental principle for the transport policy of a major city is that all credible options should conform with national and regional policies to ensure compatibility of transport modes and transport interchanges, cohesion of energy policy, and adherence to budget constraints.

One of the major transportation issues to be faced in most of the world's major cities is the determination of policy with respect to motor vehicles in general and private cars in particular.

Private cars

The developed parts of most cities of the world suffer from traffic congestion in which the growth in the number of private cars is a major source of pressure. A policy of responding to this pressure by building the appropriate highway capacity is costly in terms of national resources and damaging to the urban environment, and generates patterns of urban development which are often neither economically efficient nor socially desirable.

If the appropriate highway capacity is not provided, then re-routing and/or restraint is inevitable. It may happen by laissez faire congestion or it may be managed as part of a comprehensive transportation policy.

The search for an appropriate transportation policy for a major city must therefore address itself to the following questions in relation to private cars:

1. What is the present demand and supply balance between private vehicle use and public transport use?

2. What is likely to happen if there is no planned intervention?

3. What kind of intervention is possible and in accord with the transport planning goals for the city?

Taxation and road user charges

The rationale for a price mechanism derives from the fact that private car usage produces external costs considerably in excess of the user benefits. For example, congestion costs are imposed on other forms of transport including commercial vehicles, public transport and pedestrians. There are environmental costs in terms of pollution, noise, visual intrusion, community severance and so on. There is inefficient use of high-value urban land in the provision of parking areas.

The incremental costs of providing additional road and parking space, particularly in city centers, are high apart from such opportunities as exist in traffic management and minor works.

The logic is that vehicles should be charged realistically for the urban space which they occupy in travel and parking. In setting a charging policy it is possible to:

- prepare estimates of congestion costs for peak and off-peak periods for different classes of vehicles.

- estimate the marginal costs of increasing the provision of highways and parking areas.

- differentiate between charges aimed at restricting general ownership and usage (taxes on car purchase, general use licenses, fuel taxes) and charges specific to particular areas (special licenses, tolls, parking fees, in-vehicle meters).

Increased general taxation and charges aimed at reducing overall ownership and usage of private cars on a national scale is not politically attractive and may not be economically or socially justifiable. However, increased charges on the use of low-occupancy private cars at peak periods in selected parts of urban areas have obvious attractions. The Area Road Licensing Scheme in Singapore provides a noteworthy example.

The example of Singapore

The Singapore scheme obliges motorists to buy and display supplementary license stickers before entering the central area of the city. An important task was therefore to define the area which was to be restricted, the hours during which the scheme was to operate, and the classes of vehicle to be affected.

The restricted zone envelops the congested area of the city center, it provides diversion routes for motorists who do not have destinations in the zone, it minimizes the number of entry points that have to be monitored, and it offers a number of peripheral car parks for transfer to public transport. The zone covers about 500 hectares and has 22 entry points.

The requirement to display a license does not apply to buses or commercial vehicles. Cars carrying at least four people are also exempt, as are motorcycles. Taxis are not exempt.

The aim was to reduce peak-hour congestion by encouraging work-journey travelers to change mode and to share car space. The restriction was therefore confined to the morning rush hour—initially from 7:30 a.m. to 9:30 a.m.—but later it was extended to 10:15 a.m.

The most dramatic result is the change in morning inbound traffic (see Figure 2). The proportion of car trips by vehicle-owning households fell from 58 percent to 46 percent, and the bus share of trips rose from 33 percent to 46 percent. The greatest switch was to car pooling, which rose from 14 percent to 41 percent of all car trips.

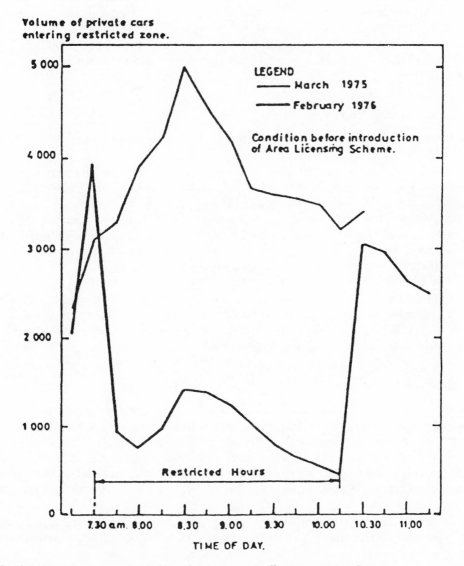

Fig. 5-2: Singapore: morning inbound private car traffic into restricted zone.

There was some apprehension as to the possible effect of the Singapore scheme on business activities in the central area. The general conclusion is that the scheme has not had an adverse effect. City center street congestion and the high cost and scarcity of parking was previously generating a trend towards decentralization. This is still continuing, but not at an increased rate. There is a marked improvement in the movement of goods.

The bus companies enjoy higher revenues and improved operating conditions, and they meet their schedules. Also pedestrians move more easily.

A public opinion survey revealed that the citizens of Singapore believed that the Area Licensing Scheme had relieved congestion and improved conditions in the city center. Pedestrians, bus riders, and cyclists believed that they were better off as a result of the scheme. Central area residents reported that it was easier and safer to cross roads and that noise and fumes had been reduced. Motorists reported that they were worse off but all, including the motorists, believed that the effect on Singapore as a city was favorable.

Physical restrictions

Restriction by charging can produce social inequity, in that it does not affect all car users equally—it lifts the threshold of the cost of car usage. *Physical design measures* are usually required to complement pricing policies. Physical measures may consist of "Comprehensive Traffic Management" whose components are summarized in Table 1.

In practice few of the measures listed in Table 1 stand alone; most are nearly always applied in association with others (e.g., bus lanes imply clearways, pedestrian areas imply restraint on vehicle movement, and labyrinths imply one-way streets and prohibited turns).

It is obvious that a particular tactic does not rely for its effect on an individual measure but on how different measures are used and integrated into a single system. Although most of the measures in common use today are well tried and familiar to traffic engineers, new and more effective measures are continually being developed.

Public transport

While good *public transport* does not match the convenience of the private vehicle, a poor standard of public transport increases pressure for the use of private vehicles and makes it politically very difficult to restrict private car usage. In many cities the cycle consists of poor public transport services generating usage of private cars which causes further deterioration of public transport. Clearly intervention is required in order to reverse the spiral.

In developing countries the majority of urban families cannot afford private cars nor is there any near prospect of their doing so. These urban

Table 5-1

Components of Comprehensive Traffic Management

Objective	Individual Measures	Common Measures
Manage	Turning restrictions	
	One-way streets	
	Clearways	Urban traffic control
	Tidal flow	
Capacity	Box junctions	Traffic route signing
Manage	Bus lanes	Traffic laning
	Bus priority at signals	
	Pedestrianization	Street parking control
	Pedal cycle priorities	
Priority	Car park allocation	Junction design
Manage	Partial closure of streets	Traffic signals
	Labyrinths	
Demand	Car park control	

citizens are therefore captive patrons to public transport or to walking and bicycles.

It follows that in the cities of both developed and developing countries the emphasis of the urban transport policy should be directed towards promoting public transport at levels of service and costs which will be acceptable to all social and wage categories of citizens, including car owners.

Buses generally provide the cheapest and most efficient form of mass transport. Buses are up to 10 times more efficient in terms of road space per passenger than private cars, and they are more flexible and less costly than rail. The initial approach to a policy for urban public transport accessibility should clearly examine what can be done to improve bus services.

At present, bus services usually lack both adequate capacity for peak-hour demand and the quality of service to attract, or hold, marginal passengers. Improvements to administration, repair, and number of buses can improve both capacity and frequency of service. Provision of priority bus lanes can bring similar improvements and also greatly reduce the journey time relative to private cars. Some recent experiences suggest indeed that in congested conditions bus lanes can enable bus speeds to be increased above those of private cars thus offsetting longer walking and waiting time at trip ends. For the marginal passenger, the improvement of bus service quality, particularly speed, often appears to be more important than cost differentials.

It may be helpful to introduce more than one class of public transport. Fast minibuses, air-conditioned buses, or first-class compartments on subways, though charged more heavily, may have a greater impact on marginal private vehicle use than a uniform system. Similarly, multi-passenger taxis and jitneys have sufficient advantages in terms of greater flexibility in origin and destination to warrant serious consideration as part of the total transport system.

In many cities the greatest problem for mass transport is the peaking pattern of demand. Restraint on peak-time usage of cars could have the effect of increasing the peak-time demand on the public transport system and also decreasing the off-peak demand through more off-peak use of the left-at-home private car.

The experience of buses and rail transport jammed to capacity at peak hours is common in most major cities. This situation is exacerbated by many city administrations operating restrictive practices on taxicabs. The numbers are restricted by licensing. Fares are kept artificially high by banning group riding. Some cities have zoning systems which restrict the freedom of taxis to collect and deliver passengers, and so on.

Multiple passenger taxis, or para-transit in the jargon of transporting, being free enterprise vehicles looking for a market, can fill these gaps and do so in many cities of the developing world. They emerge in large numbers at rush hours when demand is greatest. They offer a flexible form of public transport on dispersed road networks not suitable for bus services. They offer a real alternative to private cars and they provide a useful work opportunity. Undoubtedly some licensing and registration of vehicles and drivers is needed as well as some control on over-provision on the lucrative routes at the expense of the less attractive.

The potential role of para-transit in urban transport policy relates to the following main factors:

1. Income distribution

2. Size of city

3. The degree of "freedom" of the system

The graph shows transportation-mode preference (walk, cycle, bus, para-transit, private car) as functions of income in percentage of users in various income groups.

Figure 3 is an illustration of the Ladder Principle showing relative changes in the patronage of transport modes for a set of income distributions. It also attempts to introduce the effect of "free market" (upper part of Figure 3). A free-for-all situation could push the boundary between bus and para-transit to the left (line a), squeezing the market for buses, and restrictive legislation on para-transit could extend the market for buses (line b). Similarly, advantageous conditions for importing private cars could reduce the market for para-transit (line c).

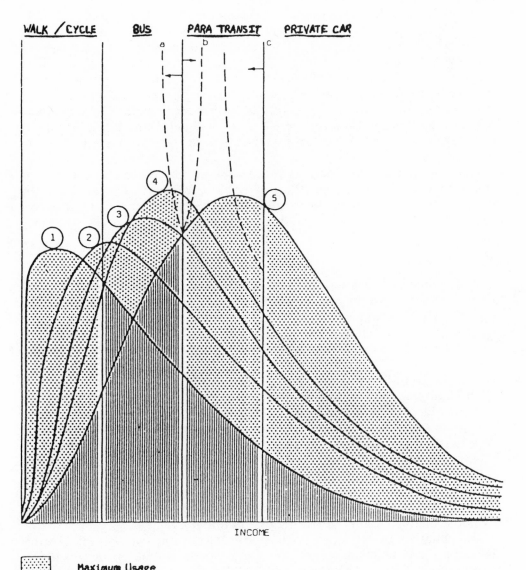

Fig. 5-3: Income distribution and mode usage; showing transportation-mode preference (walk, cycle, bus, para transit, private car) as functions of income in percentage of users in various income groups.

The provision of public transport as a social service for the poor and the disadvantages raises the problem of subsidization or of a lowest common denominator of transport services. There are many ways to finance public transport other than fares in proportion to distance traveled. Concession fares, flat fares, and community fares (transferability between transport systems) are all refinements to the fares system.

A possible new line of thought suggests a "transport club" subscription. This proposes a split revenue policy whereby the variable costs of running the service are met by fares, but the fixed costs of keeping the service available for use are to be paid not just by actual users but by all who have an interest in having the service available. Public transport would then approach the pricing structure of many other public services, such as telephones, power supply, and even highways. More wide-reaching proposals for financing public transport include a general urban tax on all city dwellers, an employee tax deducted at source by the employer, or an employer tax.

The relevance of these financial measures in relation to city planning is that where the financial position of public transport is weak then the opportunities to influence the spiral towards independent private transport may turn out, in practice, to be theoretical and not real.

New technology

The development of options must start with the existing transport modes, their networks, and the role and usage of each. From that base the adopted policies will determine what changes, if any, should be pursued in the existing modes and networks and what new transport technology should be introduced. The essential principle here is that the evolution of the policy must embrace a comprehensive knowledge of developments and possibilities in the technology of transport modes and networks.

The land-use implications of the evolution of transport technology are considerable. For example, how would the urban form of a central business district change if corridors of people-mover conveyors were inserted? What will happen to shopping centers, offices, and educational premises if micro-processors and computerized visual display units allow people to fulfill their shopping, work and educational requirements without leaving home? Clearly no transport policy or indeed urban planning policy for major cities for the year 2000 can ignore these questions when we have now the demonstrated feasibility of shuttle flights into space.

And what of the prospect that in the electronic twenty-first century personal travel will not be necessary and goods will all go by pipelines? Commonly referred to as "telemobility," the idea is that instead of people moving from point A to point B in order to work, shop, play or meet, the same thing can be achieved by means of video communications and computerized data processing. For the movement of goods a network of high-technology pipelines could transmit pallets of goods suspended in electro-magnetic fields or even in fluids.

Although these developments are already taking place it would be false to assume that, as a consequence, overall travel and movement demand will decrease. The same logic could have been applied to the development of the telephone. All the indications are that, although the nature of travel will change in respect of its purposes and its distribution, the overall demand for travel is increasing and will continue to increase. Modern technology expands the dimensions of living so that people will seek to do more and different things with their time, including more and more travel.

As far ahead as can be seen therefore, there will be demand for a transport mode that has the following characteristics: it will be ground based, independent, highly maneuverable, and its minimum size will contain two adults and some baggage. The body material will probably be a plastic derivative; it may expand and contract or have interchangeable bodies for weekend family use and for individual use; the power unit may be electric or solar; it may have only three wheels for maneuverability or perhaps no wheels at all; it will have many electronic devices for environmental control, for safety, and for route guidance. Despite all these developments, both in motion and at rest, this transport unit will still demand much the same kind of highway and parking space as the motor vehicles we have today.

The current dependence on oil as a base for the propulsion of motor vehicles and the dramatic apparent increases in oil costs may produce some reduction in the rate of growth of vehicle ownership and usage, but these seem likely to be short-term. In the longer term alternative sources of oil and alternative fuels will be available and all indicators suggest that even with a three times real increase in pump prices for gasoline in the next 20 years, vehicle ownership and usage will still increase.

This emphasis on the continuing demand for independent private transport does not imply that there is no place in the planning of major cities for innovation systems because there certainly is—in particular situations. The horizontal travelator is a continuous, segregated pavement moving at speeds of about 10 to 15 miles per hour with boarding points incorporating speed transfer integrators. The horizontal elevator is an automated train of small cars which can couple and uncouple themselves. The mini-electric car is a familiar sight on golf courses but is rarely used as a street vehicle because it is incompatible with high speed cars and trucks and would require a separate network.

"Green field" new towns, amusement parks, and exhibition centers are obvious locations where these innovative systems have application—the Paris Exhibition of 1905 had a moving pavement people mover system! The time is now overdue for some courageous use of those systems in the busy city centers of existing cities where severe restraint on private vehicles must be coupled with some attractive and radical mass transit alternatives.

One of the most promising innovations is probably the segregated travelator which would form a transport spine between conventional bus and/or rail terminals and car parks. The land-use planning and plot ratios within walking distance of the flanks of the spine would be set high and the lower densities and greenways would be parallel to and behind the high-density corridor.

Another promising innovation is the car-free central area zone which is too dispersed for a travelator spine but within which mini-electric cars are available for use by holders of the appropriate club credit card which also activates the vehicles. They are then used like self-drive taxis.

The major thrust in twenty-first century urban transport technology will be:

- Development of the technologies already in existence

- Better control and use of existing transport networks

- Control of the nuisance effects of transport

- Restraint on private vehicles in particular areas

- Innovations in areas where there is intensive activity and a powerful need for restraint on existing transport modes

Evolution of street hierarchy

Suburban rail networks, metros, tramways, perhaps the rail bus, and other forms of segregated or partially segregated mass and rapid transit are all possibilities to be considered in a review of possible modes and networks. However, the basic transport network of any major city is the street system.

Commonly more than 90% of urban trips take place on city streets and highways. Policies for the use and development of the street system are therefore paramount in transport planning. The principle to be pursued here is identification of primary street function and the subjugation of non-compatible activities. Thus, some streets may be designated for priority use by pedestrians, others for service access, others for public transport, others for general vehicle use and so on. This segregation of function may be total or partial.

The evolution of streets for particular functions has many possibilities with interesting consequences for urban transport and city form. The possibilities stem from questions such as "why should all city streets be designated to be used by the largest and heaviest vehicles on the road?" The concept of separate walk-ways and cycle-ways is now established, so why not have separate routes for heavy trucks, separate routes for buses, separate routes for small commercial vehicles and cars and perhaps even separate routes for mini-electric cars? Minicars and heavy goods vehicles are really almost as incompatible as bicycles and motorcars.

Consider an urban freeway system for light vehicles only (cars and vans)—the possibilities are interesting. Access would be controlled by gantries approximately six and a half feet wide and six and a half feet high. Headroom at intersections would clearly only need to be about six feet; structural depth for such light–weight vehicles would be reduced by at least 50%; lane widths need be no more than nine or ten feet wide, and a dual three-lane freeway would have an overall width of one-fifth of a full scale conventional freeway.

The reduction in scale would clearly reduce the land-take and construction cost. Another major advantage would be the reduction of disruption to the urban fabric since mini-freeways could be inserted into many existing corridors between buildings. The major benefit perhaps is that the conventional street network would be relieved of the pressure of motorcars and small vans whose growth in numbers is the basic cause of most traffic congestion. Buses, lorries, service vehicles and emergency vehicles would enjoy freedom of movement on these relieved streets.

Ideally the urban street hierarchy should probably be evolving towards:

- Courtyards, service areas, and access streets where terminating vehicles, pedestrians, trolleys, etc. all mix together

- Segregated walkways and pedestrian precincts

- Segregated routes, if appropriate, for bicycles, electric mini-cars or any other intermediate technology

- Distributor roads for mixed vehicles where the emphasis is on surface junctions

- Roads or lanes reserved for buses and perhaps taxis and para-transit

- Mini primary routes for cars and vans only

- Primary routes for mixed vehicles with the emphasis on through-way capacity with perhaps segregated facilities for buses and heavy commercial vehicles

Transport and Town Form

Land-use planning and transport are, of course, closely interactive. Physical urban patterns greatly influence the merits of different transport systems, and, conversely, transport modes and networks greatly influence the form of urban development. The potential for influencing urban form, deliberately, through the transport policy has not been widely used especially in the major cities of the developing world, yet it is in these cities that the scale and rate of change offers the best opportunities. Some aspects of the interaction between land-use planning and transport policy are elaborated in the following paragraphs.

Large areas of single land-use zoning clearly create a compulsion to travel. When housing is concentrated in extensive suburban zones, and shops, commerce and offices are equally concentrated in central business districts, then, clearly, the land-use distribution has created the transportation nightmare of work journey tidal flows. The creation of dispersed, mixed, land-use developments would clearly reduce this compulsion to travel.

Traditionally, towns have developed around a commercial, business, and industrial center, and expansion has followed a peripheral, concentric form. This concentration of employment and commercial interests at a central node generates tidal peaks of transport demand and, with increasing affluence and the higher levels of personal mobility achieved by the use of private transport, this leads to traffic congestion in city centers and on the radial approaches to them. The conditions which optimize public transport do require concentration of generators to maximize the number of people and activities within easy reach of the transport route and thus induce a high level of usage.

On the other hand, the characteristics of private transport suggest a dispersal of generators in order to achieve maximum accessibility. Different arrangements of residential, industrial and commercial land activities will generate different movement patterns, and it is possible to quantify the transportation implications of such variations.

In a study with which the author was associated, different hypothetical land-use and transportation structures were considered and, of these, some reflected the traditional cartwheel or ring-and-radial form of development, while others represented variations of linear forms. In order to make comparisons of the alternative transport networks, the land-use structures were evaluated on a series of common test beds in respect of total population, jobs, vehicles owned, and so on. Some of the transport networks examined are illustrated in Figure 4. The conclusions from the study are summarized in Table 2.

Table 5-2

	Capital Cost (excluding land)	User Cost	Average Trip Duration
Cartwheel	100%	100%	100%
Single Strand	72	61	65
Two Strand	85	80	84
Three Strand	66	71	75
Four Strand	93	80	86

The cartwheel or traditional ring-and-radial pattern is taken as the base, and the differences between this 100% base and the figures for the other town forms indicate by what percentage they are cheaper in capital cost and user cost, and also by what percentage each has a lower average journey time. The main conclusions were that the arrangements which offered the quickest travel times and the least cost to the travelers were also the cheapest in terms of capital cost. It is also clear that the corridor or lineal grid arrangements were better than the cartwheel or ring-and-radial arrangements.

This elementary work has been developed and applied to a number of new town, urban renewal and town expansion projects. In general, the conclu-

Fig. 5-4: Basic Town Forms.

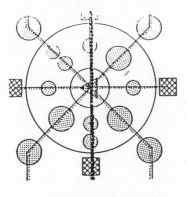

CART WHEEL

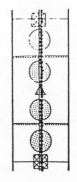

SINGLE STRAND

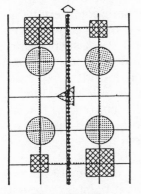

TWO STRAND

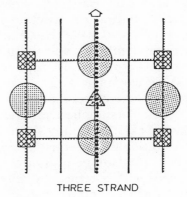

THREE STRAND

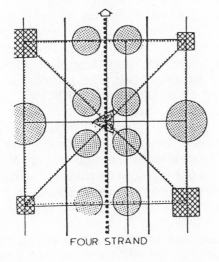

FOUR STRAND

LEGEND

————	High speed road
••••••	Express public transport
··········	Local public transport
△	Centre
▤	Proposed industrial area
░░	Proposed residential area

sions have been strengthened in the rigorous process of application to particular cities.

The concept of corridor development, or finger plans, is gaining momentum worldwide, particularly when more and more emphasis is being put on the development of public transport. Many cities are now developing rapid transit corridors to promote urban expansion, and the associated internal urban renewal is integrated to these transit corridors.

Opportunity for Change

The rate of change of urban land-use in industrialized countries is unlikely to exceed one or two percent each year. Alterations to the urban form can therefore only be long-term and marginal. The major change has to be in the way in which the existing urban area and its systems are used.

The most probable locations of significant opportunities for physical change are in the central business districts where commercial pressures generate a continuous redevelopment process, on the periphery of the central business district where urban decay and obsolescence and neglect tends to predominate, and in the outskirts and suburbs where the new planned neighborhood developments are usually found.

These development and renewal processes do allow a slow planning evolution to take place, especially if coupled with control on the use of the static areas. This implies comprehensive and integrated management and planning of existing and new urban development.

The traditional concentric or cartwheel form of cities, surrounded by a green belt, needs to be re-thought. High-density corridor developments or linear grids with a series of dispersed centers can be shown to satisfy the criteria for efficient urban systems more flexibly, more efficiently and at less cost. This is the area in which Panayotis Psomopoulos has, in a preceeding article in this volume, I believe correctly, counseled us to stop fighting urbanization and, instead, to seek to tame it. He also has identified "multi-nuclear band formation" along well-defined "axes of urbanization" as the evolving form of most of the world's megalopoli. The increase in the number of megalopolis structures from 12 to 160 between 1970 and 2000 will be dominantly in the developing parts of the world.

Paradoxically, in the developing world their greatest problem—rate of growth—is also the source of their greatest opportunity. Urban areas often double within 10 years. The scale of land development and change is very rapid. This raises the possibility that, if only it could be planned, managed and controlled, then innovative urban forms and systems could be developed which would promote the general criteria of efficiency, quality and equity.

Unfortunately the omens are not good. The lack of resources of all kinds makes it very difficult. There is a lack of knowledge, there is a lack of institutional authority, there is a lack of effective control, there is a lack of money. Those responsible for planning and for urban services can barely keep up with what is happening much less get ahead of it and control it.

The key must surely lie in the development of some international consensus on land utilization. Land is currently the main source of wealth and is consequently the battleground between the rich and the poor. The introduction of change is thus complicated politically and technically difficult, being inhibited by vested interests, by cultural attitudes, by extensive bureaucracies, by abuse, and by corruption. Despite these problems it is vital that we respond to the challenge presented to us by Psomopoulos in his article in which he states that: "we must discover what the inevitable future is which has been decided by nature and man; what can be controlled by us; what the most desirable city for man is, and, finally, how we can write the specification for it, lay its foundations and build it."

It would be naive, however, to assume that if "we"—the technocrats—did come up with the recipe which would tame urbanization and offer hope to the urban poor, then the world at large would be motivated to use it.

A useful study on Future Development Dimensions identified three possible attitudinal scenarios. The first is the prevailing one of "Stubborn Persistence" characterized by a resistance to change in consumptive lifestyle, ignoring symptoms of dysfunction and warnings of disaster. There would be a continuation of nationalism, of political ambition, of economic greed and of international distrust. Global problems are seen as somebody else's concern. The second scenario is labelled "Big Brotherhood" and assumes a large base of popular support for a strong central leadership which can, even dictatorially, take bold and forceful action on global problems. The insidious aspect of this scenario is the danger that the controlling mechanism would persist and grow into a George Orwell type of monster. The possibility of a gradual change in direction is the basis for the third scenario called "Forward to Basics." This would be characterized by a general awareness that we live in one world and not three, that uncontrolled population growth anywhere affects everyone, and that global conservation and resource management is good for everyone. There would be a widespread feeling that global and national institutions will never agree on solutions and therefore never take collective action to avert disaster. As a result, a grass roots movement could gather momentum throughout the industrialized world. Eventually the dispersed elements of such a movement would influence regional and national politics as a first stage to promoting international action. There are clear signs of such a process happening now. The disturbing question is whether it can gather sufficient momentum before it is too late.

John Galsworthy wrote: "If you don't think about the future, you cannot have one" and Robert Theobald said: "the challenge is whether we shall recognize that there are no solutions to our present problems within our present pattern of thinking." Thus, we need new patterns of thinking about the future to find solutions to our problems.

References

1. N. Arge et al., "Gothenburg — A Case Study," *Managing Transport*, (Paris, 1979).
2. T. Bendixson et al., "Singapore — A Case Study," *Managing Transport*, (Paris, 1979).
3. H. Baum and W. Kentner, "Tariff Policies for Urban Transport," ECMT Round Table 46, European Conference of Minister of Transport, (Paris, 1980).
4. D. Greenwood and R. Ham, "The Organization and Management of Urban Traffic," Bulletin of Permanent Association of Road Congresses, Vol. 233-II, (1979): pp. 9-43.
5. E.P. Holland and P. Watson, "Measuring the Impacts of Singapore's Area License Scheme," Paper presented to World Conference on Transport Research, (Rotterdam, 1977).
6. J.C. Holmes, "An Ordinal Method of Evaluation," *Urban Studies* vol. 9 no. 2, (1972).
7. G.B. Jamieson et al., "Transportation and Land-Use Structures," *Urban Studies* Vol. 4 No.3, (1967).
8. S.R. Jones, "Accessibility Measures," TRRL Laboratory Report No. 967, (1981).
9. S. Mayers and R. Schwartz, "Technology," *Architectural Forum*, vol. 132 no. 5, (1970).
10. I. Megas, "Para-Transit in the Developing Countries," Para-Transit Workshop Document No. 16, (Paris, 1977).
11. OECD Working Group, "Transport Choices for Urban Passengers," (Paris, 1980).
12. F.R. Shaw, "Mini-Motorways," Paper presented to Seminar on Transport Technology at Loughborough University, (1970).
13. World Bank, "Urban Transport—Sector Policy Paper," (Washington D.C., 1975).
14. McNamara—on Population, Finance and Development World Bank, June 1977 vol. 14 No. 2.
15. World Bank Development Report, (1979).
16. World Bank, "Urban Transport—Sector Policy Paper," *op.cit.*
17. Future Development Dimensions, Daon Corporation.

6.
Who Creates the Built Environment?

Anthony H. Penfold

*M*etropolitan structure is concerned with the location, arrangement, and interrelationships between social and physical elements of the city, their spatial distributions, and the interactions between these distributions set in the context of changing urban environments, real and perceived, that residents of the metropolis create and inhabit. This understanding of structure (Bourne et al., 1971) reinforces our interpretation of the city as a system comprising a set of linked elements that, in turn, constitute multitudinous subsystems made up of subsets of elements that interact with each other in a complex way over the spatial domain of the metropolis.

This notion of metropolitan structure, positioned as a backdrop to Dr. Dyckman's paper, "The Determinants of Metropolitan Structure," suggests that the choice of the paper's title could imply the presence of three underlying assumptions, stated below, that may be relevant to the discussion at hand.

1. That a heightened knowledge of the complex and dynamic interrelationships and behavior of the myriad vector components that determine metropolitan structure can serve to enhance our potential to intervene, directly or indirectly, at the metropolitan level to modify and shape more decidedly the structure of the metropolis as it grows into the future.

2. That the increasing understanding we gain from our knowledge of the way the determinants of metropolitan structure operate can also enable us, in some corresponding measure, to develop our insight and appreciation of the nature and role of the interlocking sets of individual and collective values that mold and color the multiplicity of incremental decisions and actions over time. These are manifest in the spatial arrangements of activities and related built elements that comprise

the accretion we recognize, in the aggregate, as the metropolis.

3. That the continuous striving between metropolitan activity elements that takes place to secure operationally an acceptable spatial structure to achieve activity ends is potentially responsive to metropolitan system-wide intervention. This would be true especially if such intervention is oriented towards optimizing the performance of the component subsystems to which the activity elements pertain.

These three assumptions lead to a fourth, expressed as an hypothesis in tandem:

That the structure of the metropolis is susceptible to manipulation and guidance, and that this susceptibility constitutes a real potential to create urban environments having the capability of molding more appropriately built responses to perceived activity needs and desires in accordance with the value systems held by metropolitan communities.

The goal or aspiration that this hypothesis represents is, of course, somewhat utopian in character, and its achievement requires, perhaps, heroic optimism about our ability to shape the structure of the metropolis in the future. Nevertheless, it behooves us to explore ways to reinforce progressively progressively the potential to manage the development of metropolitan structure, and realize this potential. But to identify the ways of doing so is not a simple task even at the individual metropolitan scale; viewed on the world scale that this conference committee is concerned with makes the task a very difficult one indeed. We are well aware that metropoli exhibit their own particular sets of developmental opportunities and restrictions, rooted largely in socio-cultural, economic and physical factors that, in different combinations, impress through varied mechanisms their unique character stamps on extant structures—and will continue to do so—in terms of systems configuration, constituent components, and overall clarity and quality. As a result, it can be argued, there are as many solutions to the structural shaping of metropolitan growth as there are metropoli.

The realists among us, however, may assert that we must scale down our sights in line with resources likely to be available, and that these will probably be far too few, especially in developing countries, to promote and manage the future structuring and restructuring of the metropolis in any radical way to bring about living environments better than those presently existing. Merely to seek ways to conserve present environmental levels into the future will, they hold, constitute a challenging goal.

Be that as it may, our discussion of the determinants of metropolitan structures, and of the means we have of manipulating or conditioning them, might fruitfully start by examining objectively some of the conventional wisdom that surrounds and influences our thinking on the matter so that we can sweep away cobwebs to reveal a common base of understanding with regard to the potential we have at hand to mold the metropolis and its physical environment in the future. While we are probably in agreement with Dr. Psomopoulos' prediction that the metropolis will continue to grow in size and proliferate in number, accommodating over time proportionally more of the world's growing population, our notions about the future conditions of the metropolis may well be prejudiced by some unsubstantiated assertions that tend to be accepted on sight by both the planning profession and academia. It is appropriate, therefore, to initiate this review process by examining some relevant assertions and discuss their validity.

Problems of the metropolis are not always metropolitan problems so T.A. Broadbent reminds us: many so-called "urban problems" are social problems pre-existing (at the national scale) that are revealed and laid bare by economic processes that concentrate these wider-ranging problems within the metropolis in a highly perceptible way (Broadbent, 1977). Examples include problems of income distribution and of shelter and services for the urban poor, also problems of management in cultures that fail to value management's worth—of little relevance at the village scale but critical to the well-being of fast-growing metropolitan areas. The metropolis itself did not create these problems; thus, their cure calls for measures that stretch far beyond metropolitan limits.

Metropolitan size is the crucial metropolitan problem: a questionable assertion if we can intervene to shift more effectively the form and structure of future metropolis away from radial growth patterns, and instead, towards lineal and multi-nuclear configurations, for instance, that allow for the interpenetration of urban/non-urban space with reduced activity concentrations, and the emergence of specialist centers that articulate metropolis by providing functional identification and comprehension. If there exists for the metropolis a single crucial problem in this context, it resides in the rate of population growth that can outstrip the resource ability of the metropolis to cope with its consequences, especially in developing countries, rather than in the need to impede metropolitan growth, even at moderate rates, to meet some preconceived size model in physical or population terms.

With scale, the metropolis becomes unmanageable. We are perhaps correctly inclined to believe that most organisms created by man become exponentially more burdensome and costly to manage efficiently as they increase in size and complexity; human settlements appear not to be an exception to this rule, especially those administered in conformity with democratically based mandates.

This tendency, in the case of settlements, is compounded by the failure of urban government to transform its administrative structure in pace with stages of settlement growth; the consequent management lag this creates compounds local governments' inability to deal with settlement problems at the scale they deserve. There are numerous reasons for this governmental capability lag in the process of settlement transformation from village to town to city, at times to conurbation, and finally to metropolis; but, at rock bottom, the reason touches on considerations of economic efficiency and the importance urban governments decide to attach to this value.

However, since response to a value is conditioned by the value system in which it is set, optimization of urban efficiency is compromised by a variety of other linked considerations acting within and outside of the human settlement but vital to its health. Furthermore, promotion of urban efficiency as a value is not made easier by the fact that it has been late in taking its place in the urban decision-making process, being of little consequence historically in early settlement growth.

Because most human settlements initially found purpose in an array of functional objectives—some compatible, some conflicting—their physical form solutions evolving over time evidence compromise responses to competing and shifting value criteria operating within a framework of transient resource parameters. Be that as it may, the early stages of a settlement's internal organizational development paid little heed to efficiency as a value simply because small settlements typically have insufficient activity generators to allow for inefficient deployment. Their order and cohesiveness responded in practice more to socio-cultural criteria borne out of the collective and often homogeneous expressions of their community members.

With further growth, however, settlements commenced to lose their cultural identity, and, in the physical absence of community-scaled structuring frameworks, exhibited disorderly traits which distorted the coherence of their initial formal environments and eroded their functional viability. In any event, the inertia inherent in the increasing scale and permanence of urban development exacerbated the difficulty of subsequently reorganizing and redeploying the components of these previous patterns of development to bring them in line with reassessed community values in which the concept of efficiency enjoyed its initial role as an ingredient of community well-being. Though the implementation of ameliatory processes of physical adjustment and adaptation do provide some functional improvements to settlements as they transform themselves into metropoli, the benefits bestowed fail to prevent steep rises in congestion and other social costs that, as a consequence, call for high levels of metropolitan productivity to support the heavy fiscal and financial burdens that result.

Given the difficulty of radically restructuring the metropolis in physical terms to reduce operating costs and to meet the exigencies of high productivity, metropolitan communities have perforce turned to the potential benefits that "good management" offers. But this potential is not easily tapped and realized. For a start, local governments have to reassess their objectives and make major adjustments to their administrative apparatus to meet more numerous and onerous management obligations; and those that drag their feet eventually pay the price of lost confidence on the part of their constituents due to declines in community prosperity. If metropolitan areas in economically advanced countries find it difficult to organize themselves to further these management endeavors, it is understandable that similar efforts tax to breaking point the very limited administrative capabilities at the disposal of the fast expanding metropolitan areas in less developed countries.

We have, of course, no hard and fast criterion of universal application against which to measure metropolitan administrative success or failure, since these concepts in the public sector are highly relative and intimately related to performance levels conditioned by cultural norms; and even success or failure in the fiscal sense is hard to define since the extent to which the metropolis is considered to be an autonomous, self-financing entity is variously interpreted between nations. Notwithstanding, we can hypothesize that, in any cultural context, a fundamental but albeit implicit design determinant of metropolitan government structure is the consideration of its viability or "effectiveness" under severe conditions of stress.

If, for a moment, we conceive of a generalized model of the determinants of metropolitan administrative options, we might include in it possible roles played by the state, at one extreme, local jurisdictions at the other, and the metropolis as an entity in between. The relative strengths of these roles would most likely be controlled at the national level, perhaps according to ideologies at play. Support could be unequivocally given to the concept of metropolitan government or else negated, trading off its potential advantages of functional efficiency in favor, for instance, of the expression of township values at the local level, as is prevalent in the U.S.; or, in exceptional cases, it could be withdrawn from established metropolitan government for political or other reasons, as evidenced by the decision to disband the Greater London Council, allegedly to remove from the power hierarchy its authority and influence over an important segment of a nation's population that is held to warrant a closer identity to its local jurisdictions. Weaker controls, more indirectly applied, would also exist in the model at the local level, by providing districts, for instance, with the option to pool advantages in the interests of the metropolitan good, or to withhold these, as in Caracas, where largely for this reason only a few services operate at the metropolitan scale by agreement while national government takes care of major infrastructure. The model would also identify the metropolis with internally generated forces prepared, if necessary, to counteract or capture pressures operating at levels above and below it, and to redirect this energy towards the goal of creating a metropolitan tier of government as evidenced in a variety of guises, and with varied success, in different parts of the world, such as Toronto, Paris, Buenos Aires, Miami, and Tokyo.

That man is the most adaptable of animals can perhaps be applied also to the metropolis in the sense that it will always find ways to adapt itself to existing hierarchical frameworks of government while responding to strictures imposed by the state on the one hand, and to the values of the people it accommodates on the other, in some places mostly discarding the concept of metropolitan government, in others applying it in its most comprehensive form. Generally, the metropolis will continue to seek compromise solutions by carefully balancing the consequences of efficiency criteria against the need for local value expressions and the power in its hand against the powers that allow it to flourish. Thus, we are unlikely ever to witness metropolitan growth to "unmanageable" proportions if only because of the capability we observe it possesses to adapt symbiotically to the realities of its context without having recourse to set models inherently inflexible and vulnerable to collapse.

City residents create the environments, real and perceived, that they inhabit. This allegation (taken from Bourne) may have validity at the small town level, but in the metropolis residents have virtually no role in the creation of their high rental environment. Capital formation, concentrated in relatively few private financial institutions, "floats" across national and metropolitan borders seeking to optimize investment returns, while national government agencies invest directly in the metropolis, or approve investment aid, according to their own criteria. Those that "call the shots" are increasingly divorced from the locale, responding to market factors and national "norms" insensitively attuned to the particular needs of a given metropolitan area.

Individual values find satisfactory responses more readily in the metropolis environment. There is truth to this assertion in that the metropolis offers its residents a wide selection of goods and services to satisfy individual lifestyles and a wide range of "off-the-peg" built commodities—houses, apartments, offices—built by third parties that, in the mass, constitute, in effect, a "metro-condominium" development complex. The metro-condominium, however, offers the occupants of its "units" few, if any, opportunities for external expressions of individual identity through design, color, landscaping and other means of adaptation and characterization, and in this sense is much more restrictive as a vehicle for individual creativity than are the component elements of squatter settlements in the metropoli of developing countries where "marginal" populations enjoy freedoms, albeit severely circumscribed by resource limitations, to shape their household environments and express the results openly to the street. But it can be argued that the metropolitan inhabitants of more advanced nations are too physically mobile to find a root need for seeking means of expressing physically and overtly their collective individuality within the community environment.

The metropolis is too unwieldy to shape. This depends on our determination to do so, the skills available, the methods we use, and the strategic level at which we are content to operate. We can define a "cone of opportunity" for setting limits on future growth options, and recognize within it metropolitan "inevitabilities"—and attempt to capitalize on these—policy plans incorporating operational strategies at the structure level that employ infrastructure design and investment programs, especially for transport facilities, as development spearheads; we can then stand some chance of molding the structure of metropolis to some purpose.

This "carrot" approach requires funds, and its concomitant "stick" calls for legal enforcement resources, both difficult to come by in developing countries. Nevertheless, if we can inculcate in decision-makers' minds a systems approach to metropolitan problem-solving in place of a reliance on independent, politically-oriented projects, we will take a positive step towards establishing metropolitan growth frameworks more conducive to providing structured opportunities for institutionalized and individual development initiatives—flexibly responsive to community needs, yet integrated into the multiplying metropolitan matrix.

This brief discussion of some of the conventional wisdom surrounding the future metropolis encourages us to believe that the outlook for its continued development is not as black as some would like to make out; and though the rate of its population increase is a factor mostly beyond control, it does seem as though the metropolis will continue to find the means to manipulate and manage its growth, at least at the structural level, in ways that will provide the frameworks for obtaining tolerable levels of environmental quality and functional convenience for its inhabitants. While this view is probably quite valid for the metropolis in the developed world, it may turn out to be true also for metropolitan areas in the developing countries, if one is content to apply criteria concomitant with those operating within national contexts.

There is no doubt, however, that an improved future for the metropolis in the so-called Third World, especially in those countries in the early stages of development, will be highly susceptible to adjustments made to national policy factors that presently tend to favor the popular perception of the metropolis as a superior medium to satisfy human aspirations in economic and socio-cultural terms as against life in smaller urban centers and the rural interior. Thus, in the absence of these policy adjustments, economic and social inequalities will become, at increasing rates, more highly profiled in the metropolitan areas of these countries, making it all the more difficult to satisfy the physical and cultural needs of the growing concentrations of underprivileged populations in terms set by the formal urban frameworks that typically, though not always appropriately, attempt to maintain their dominion metropolitan development.

There seems to be some validity too in the notion that, while the conventional structure of the metropolis is, of necessity, gearing itself to improve its functional efficiency, this endeavor is being achieved at a cost of community identity, resulting in an increasing loss of a live sense of touch on the part of its inhabitants with the reality that creates and controls its built environment. However, the experience in some areas of the metropolitan world is that this effect can be ameliorated. Residential area populations are observed to be breaking themselves down into small political units to reinforce their identity, defend their interests and, if possible, participate more actively in decisions that effect at least their own communities if not the metropolis as a whole, while local government is becoming more concerned with strengthening the civic identity of commercial and other activity centers.

Clearly, the metropolis is in flux, and needs to be in order to maintain its capacity to respond fully to the changing and divergent requirements of its inhabitants actively involved in the varied local, national and international roles that the metropolis is asked to play. It is this ability of the metropolis to adapt to contextual circumstances, albeit severely constrained by physical and other factors, that enables us to visualize its horizons with sufficient optimism to plan for its growth and management needs in the future with some measure of confidence.

References

Larry S. Bourne et al., *Internal Structure of the City: Readings on Space and Environment*, (New York, 1971).

T.A. Broadbent, *Planning and Profit in the Urban Economy*, (London, 1977).

Part III

Metropolitan Gigantism and its Impact

7.

How Big Should Cities Grow? The Concept of Optimal Size and its Relevance to Spatial Planning in Developing Countries

Ervin Y. Galantay

Let us assume for illustrative purposes that some form of extra-terrestrial intelligence succeeds in establishing an orbiting laboratory to gather information about the earth.

The observers would soon distinguish land masses and oceans, mountain ranges, forest zones and deserts. Next they would become intrigued by the phenomenon of numerous mold-like blots emitting heat, carbon monoxide, sulphur dioxide, hydrocarbons, nitrogen oxides and dust.

Observation over a period of years would reveal that the areas covered by oceans, land and mountain ranges remain constant while the forest areas are slowly receding as deserts advance—and more dramatically, the strange blots are spreading rapidly and tending to coalesce to a contiguous tissue in some areas. The observers would have discovered our fast-growing metro-politan regions and conurbations, each covering thousands of square miles.

This spectacular spread of urban agglomerations is of course the result of the exponential growth of the human population triggered off by the industrial revolution and the corollary phenomenon of urbanization which led to the rise of cities of unprecedented size.

Compared to the history of life on our planet, the time span of organized civilization is but a short episode—a mere 150 generations separate us from urban society's humble beginnings. Yet speculating about the future of mankind, we hardly dare to project forward the same time span and, in fact, most scenarios cautiously stop at the magic year 2000.

If projections venture further, they often touch on the absurd, as in the case of the United Nations' ECOSOC 1970 statement that if the global population continues to grow at the present rate, then by the year 2570—or 24 generations hence—there will be only one square meter for each human to live on.

The studies of the Club of Rome and of the Bariloche group were useful and courageous in pointing out why this can never happen. Yet I believe that the pressure of global population on global resources need not be our immediate concern: I believe the first barrier to unlimited growth will come from the pressure of humans on other human beings—resulting from the very uneven distribution of the world's population and its concentration in vast metropolitan areas, particularly in the so-called developing countries.

Between 1975 and 2000 world population will increase by some two billion people: of this, 1.5 billion is the share of the Third World, and the cities of the developing countries will add about one billion more people to their present populations.

A large proportion of this increase will be accounted for by the growth of large metropolitan areas.

According to United Nations figures, already 33% of the urban population of the Third World is concentrated in cities with more than one million inhabitants—and the "million-plus" cities will number over 300 by the end of the century.

As recently as 1950 there was but one city in the Third World—Buenos Aires—with a population in excess of five million, yet according to United Nations projections—"medium tempo, medium variant"—there will be 40 Third World metropoli by the year 2000 with populations ranging from five to 30 million.

The biggest Third World cities are growing at yearly rates of 4-7% doubling their size every 10–15 years. In numerical terms, cities like Mexico City or Sao Paulo are adding half a million persons to their population each year, lesser giants like Jakarta or Seoul well over a quarter million.

Projecting forward two or three generations—say to the year 2050—still well within the lifespan of our grandchildren, we would have to envisage cities of the 50 million population range, even if we assume greatly reduced migration and fertility rates.

Reducing migration to these cities would not in itself stop their growth, of which one-half to two-thirds can be attributed to natural increase (i.e., natural growth share of Nairobi is 50%, of Bogota 67%). Without further migration but with a natural growth rate of 2%, cities double their population within 35 years.

No less disturbing than the absolute size of Third World cities is their dominance with respect to the rest of the national urban system and to total population. In a small country not unlike a city-state like Denmark, Hungary or Uruguay, it may make economic sense to have a capital 10 times the population of the next sizeable town: in large countries like Argentina, Peru or the Philippines, such disproportion is likely to result in parasitical dominance.

However, in the less developed countries, giant cities can also arise in the absence of marked primacy: i.e., the four largest Indian cities only account for 3.5 percent of the national population.

In some primate cities, the polarization of resources is truly impressive:

i.e., in Peru—a country five times larger than the UK—the capital Lima concentrates 71% of all manufacturing employment. Lagos with only 2% of the national population contains one-third of all manufacturing employment and consumes one-half of all electricity produced in Nigeria.

Apart from dominance another ominous aspect of the Third World's giant cities is their vast extension which results in spatial segregation and the emergence of large homogeneous areas. In many cities, half of the population is crowded into central city slums or peripheral squatter settlements containing hundreds of thousands of "marginal" people in a degrading and increasingly dense environment.

To illustrate the rapidity with which spontaneous marginal settlements arise, one may cite the example of Netzahualcoyotl, a squatter agglomeration occupying the dried-out bed of Lake Texcoco just outside the boundaries of the Federal District of Mexico.

In the 1960 national census, no place of that name appears. In the 1970 census, Netzahualcoyotl magically appears as the fourth largest Mexican settlement with 571,000 inhabitants. Yet, at this point, the agglomeration hardly amounted to a city since it did not possess any infrastructure, water supply, hard-topped roads, schools or municipal administration of any kind. Since then, the government provided numerous improvements, but in the meantime the vast slum has passed the mark of a million residents. Other slums of Third World cities, like Tondo in Manila, North-Rio or the Thonburi zone of Bangkok are of similar dimensions.[1]

Since national economies cannot possibly cope with the infrastructure needs of city populations doubling every 10 or 15 years, further degradation of living conditions by a process of "cumulative causation" has to be faced. By the end of the century, urban slums of the Third World may contain one-sixth of the global population. Will such a world be still governable, will it be worth living in?

However, common sense whispers that "trees cannot grow to the sky" and it is axiomatic in engineering that every structure has its maximum span as well as its optimum range for economic performance. Nor is the "optimum size" concept unknown in other fields of science. It is therefore logical to infer that there should also be an optimum city size which one might define as "the upper limit of the population for maximum living conditions with minimum cost" (Chapin, 1957).[2]

Indeed, throughout history there has been some awareness that there must be a right size for human settlements which according to Aristotle would enable the inhabitants to live "temperately and liberally in the enjoyment of leisure" or in the words of Sir Thomas More permit "sufficiency without frivolity," or to cite contemporary Soviet theory "adequate amenities with the lowest public expenditure."

But what are "adequate" amenities and "maximum" living conditions? Obviously, both are culture-specific variables and there is a strong normative element in any definition of these criteria. Optimality only makes sense in the context of goal achievement: one might distinguish, for example, between efficiency-maximizing, creativity-maximizing or welfare-maximizing paradigms. Often multiple goals are posited which may not be entirely compatible.

Apart from the cultural determinants, the optimum range for a city will also depend on the complexity of the society and the wealth and education of the population. This explains why the theoretically established "optimum size" for cities has constantly been adjusted upward even within the context of Western civilization.

As recently as 1829, Fourier argued that a mere 1620 persons are adequate to provide sufficient occupational diversification within a community—far less than the number recommended in the fifth century B.C. by the sage Kung-Fu-Tse who proposed 625 families or about 3000 persons, or the figure of 5040 citizens put forward by Plato which, adding family members and slaves, amounted to an "optimum" size city of 30,000 inhabitants. The same number was later endorsed by Leonardo da Vinci and rediscovered in 1898 by Ebenezer Howard who argued that 30,000 inhabitants is the right size "to make possible the full measure of social life . . . and for this reason, the city needs not be any bigger"—further growth should occur by colonization.

In post-World War II Britain, the arguments of Howard and his disciples found general acceptance. The "target" sizes of the British new towns were first fixed at 50,000–60,000 people and later revised upward to 100,000 –120,000, acknowledging the fact that only bigger towns can support a full range of modern urban services.

In the U.S. of the 1960s, James Rouse, the developer of the New Town of Columbia (Md), also concluded that "a city of 100,000 was about the minimum that would provide sufficient markets . . . variety, choice and opportunities—the full fabric of life." More recent New Towns in the UK such as Milton Keynes or the French Villes Nouvelles set their minimum target size even higher in the 250,000 population range. Thus it appears that, while the "minimum threshold" concept maintains some operational relevance, the Garden City concept of fixing an upper limit beyond which the town should not grow has been quietly abandoned.[3]

It has been pointed out correctly that optimum size cannot be evaluated independently of location and of the city's function. Further, the variables affecting cost and efficiency are often interrelated, thus costs related to population size are also affected by density, i.e., in the case of network cost for transport. Yet it seems obvious that each city function must have an optimum range beyond which diseconomies occur, and I tend to agree with Lillibridge who argues that, although an optimum size cannot be generalized, "the best size of a given city is perhaps discernible." [4]

Recently some economists—not content with ridiculing the "traditional utopianism of optimum size" (Richardson)[5]—turned into advocates of the big metropolis arguing that "the bigger the better." This school of thought claims that the larger the population, the greater the possibilities for the division of labor, external economies and economies of scale.

There can be no doubt that larger cities have a more diversified employment structure and are, as a result, less prone to economic instability. Their larger market supports services that cannot be provided in lesser centers. Studies show that higher wages are paid in the largest cities and higher incomes are indeed the chief attraction for migrants from smaller towns or the countryside. There is some evidence—at least in the U.S.—that the incidence of poverty is inversely associated with urban scale.

Further it is claimed that innovation potential is related to city size and there is a positive correlation between city size and the concentration of "eminence groups" per thousand population (Seeley, 1968).[6] This is contradicted by more recent analyses by Paul Bairoch[7] (1977) who demonstrates that the influence of city size on innovation and creativity peaks out at 500,000-700,000 population and finds this range also optimal with respect to access to education.

In the context of the developing countries, a recent study of Koito Mera[8] (1973) reveals an apparent correlation between increasing primacy and aggregate growth performance. This encouraged Richardson in 1977 to argue that the primate cities of the less-developed countries "offer a higher return on investment than alternate locations" and other authors to claim that the Third World cities as large as five or six million are essential for innovation diffusion and the formation of an efficient urban hierarchy (Herrera, 1971).[9]

However, even these apologists of the big size must admit that agglomeration economies decay with distance and thus higher order function cannot be supplied efficiently from a primate city to a nation as large as the Philippines or Peru.

The fallacy of the arguments in favor of very large towns seems to be that they are based on comparisons between small- or medium-size towns and the metropolis rather than cities in the one to two million category and agglomerations of 5-10 million inhabitants. Manifestly, there exist economies of urban concentration but beyond a certain size the costs of centralization are likely to increase more rapidly than the benefits.

While certain services operate with advantage to economies of scale, other, user-oriented public services (such as refuse collection, fire and police protection, libraries) do not profit from scale economies. Size also imposes important constraints on management and accessibility.

The costs of traffic congestion rise rapidly with size for very large centers (above two million, Neutze 1965)[10] and the transportation cost borne by the private sector increases above a city size of 50,000 (Stone, 1973).

Physical constraints often compound size-related diseconomies and inefficiencies, and topographical or water-supply problems can make the social costs of very large cities unreasonably high.

In the case of Mexico City where water has to be piped from the 350 km. distant Papaloapan Valley and pumped up to the 2300 m altitude of the capital, it is rumored that the production cost of 1 liter of water is equal to the cost of 1 liter of gasoline.[11]

In Venezuela, the "Caracas 1990" study[12] proved that the container capacity of the valleys in which the capital is located—including all land up to a 40° slope—cannot accommodate more than five million inhabitants, and any further increase of the population beyond that threshold will result in excessive land development and infrastructure cost.

The already-mentioned study by Bairoch also examines the variation of threshold sizes between cities in developed and less-developed countries. It appears that the hypothetical size that would equate marginal costs and benefits would be greater in developing countries, but it is significant that Bairoch finds that the optimal threshold is in the range of 600,000 to 900,000 population, well below the size of the giant metropolis.

It would be hard to disprove that very large cities also generate "negative social benefits" or "negative externalities" such as pollution, long journeys to work and public sector inefficiency. Higher incomes earned in large cities are often associated with higher living costs and higher levels of taxation. Higher wages paid do not translate into higher welfare and may indeed represent compensation for the stress created by noise, congestion, pollution and crime.

Comparative statistics are often misleading since only the quantity of the service rather than its quality, scope, reliability or continuity are compared. Yet the number of hospital beds per 1,000 population is meaningless without knowing about the quality of the hospital service. There is some evidence that the quality of services declines in very large cities and the optimal threshold is in the one to two million city size.

Statistics showing a positive correlation between city size and the per capita product of the inhabitants can be farcically misleading. Air pollution is a classic example of external diseconomy associated with city size: the volume of pollutants varies directly in function of population size and density. If air pollution levels require the installation of costly filters, then the expenditure in acquiring, installing and maintaining this equipment is considered as "output" and appears on the positive side of the ledger as goods and services produced—just as the cost for increased police protection corresponding to the size-related increase of urban crime appears to give a higher per capita "product" for the large city dweller.

In yet another way, statistics of urban incomes and welfare are grossly misleading: because of the segregation of the giant city in large homogeneous sectors, incomes and services will vary widely from one district to another, giving hardly a clue about the extent of deprivation in the vast slum areas. Yet we know that in the Manila slums, infant mortality, tuberculosis, gastroenteritis, undernourishment etc. are eight times more prevalent than in the "formal" districts of the same town. In Mexican slums, buying water from a cistern-truck will cost the slum dweller 10 times more than piped water supplied by the municipality in the better neighborhoods —this alone will wipe out the advantage of the higher wages earned in the capital.

If, nevertheless, the metropolitan areas remain attractive for migrants, this is partly due to their ignorance and the fact that they are attracted by varied employment opportunities rather than by gain. Once arrived in the big city, there seems to be no return back to the village or the small town without loss of face.

Comparisons of rural and urban incomes are further misleading since they do not take into account the non-monetary income more abundant in rural areas or the simple fact that poverty in the city is more degrading than in the village or small town.

Our chief objection to very large cities in the developing countries is based on the fact that they inevitably give rise to very large slum areas. It has been argued that this phenomenon and, in general, environmental degradation is "not so much a result of size per se but of a too rapid pace of achieving that size," i.e., of absorption capacity (Richardson).

This seems to me somewhat beside the point since the emergence of large slums and degrading living conditions are directly size-related phenomena. A small slum or squatter settlement may be a relatively cheerful place to live with some hope for gradual improvement. By contrast, a slum settlement with hundreds of thousands of inhabitants becomes a "closed universe" perpetuating a "culture of poverty" with many inhabitants never going beyond its limits. As an example, I may mention that in direct questioning of the inhabitants of a Northern Rio slum, I found to my astonishment that many have never been to Copacabana or indeed seen the waterfront at all.

Studies made in such urban slums prove that schizophrenia, neuroses and other personality disorders are much more common than in smaller towns or rural areas (Strotzka, 1964).[13] There exists also a strong association between overcrowding and increased aggressivity (Marler & Hamilton, 1966).

Density does not seem to be the major factor, rather the rate and quality of social interaction: studies show that in a large metropolis, within 10 minutes of walking or driving, a person will encounter 20 times more persons (220,000) than in a small town or suburb (11,000). Inasmuch as this increased "average rate of collision" produces increased stress, it will manifest itself in loss of productivity and creativity, heightened aggressivity and other indices of breakdown of accepted behavior.

It has been suggested (Dohrenwend, 1972)[14] that an incubation period of at least three generations is needed for the socio-pathological effects of crowding to become fully manifest. Since it is notoriously difficult to carry out experiments with large human groups under controlled conditions —and it may be impossible to do so over several generations—it is perhaps not inadmissible to extrapolate from animal experiments.

Current opinion holds that insect populations will expand to the limit of the carrying capacity of the environment—according to a "logistic" curve like the Drosophilia flies embottled in Pearl's "dipteran microcosm."[15]

By contrast, in higher species certain "territorial rights" are enforced which prevent the population from heading toward Malthusian demise. Territorial skirmishing forces some individuals into marginal situations. Animals that fail in competition become exposed to shortage of shelter and may not reproduce or survive, while others, finding areas suitable for habitat, extend the range of the species.

The burden of saving the optimum habitat from resource depletion thus falls on the minority of displaced individuals forced to adapt to marginal situations or to die (Bartholomew & Birdsell, 1953).[16] In this context one cannot fail to draw a parallel to the "marginal populations" of the Third World slums forced to adapt to their "suboptimal habitat."

Animal experiments also prove that in a population confined to a "closed environment" competition becomes so severe that it will lead to the breakdown of normal behavior. If the population "overshoots" the maximum carrying capacity of the environment, adjustment will occur by a series of catastrophes.

Since very large urban slums constitute practically "closed" environments, John B. Calhoun's[17] experiments are particularly relevant.

By increasing rodent densities in a "closed utopian universe," Calhoun proved that increasing stress will lead to frantic aggressivity or withdrawal; sexual deviance and cannibalism among males; high rates of miscarriage among females; high infant mortality; and eventually regression and demise of the entire population.

As Calhoun describes it, the young are prematurely rejected by their harassed mothers and start independent life without having developed sufficient bonds and survival skills. Again one cannot fail to be reminded of the thousands of street urchins in Bogota or the legions of subteen whores in South-East Asian cities. Reading how young adults—capable of involvement in species-specific activities but unable to fulfill their potential—turn to frantic aggression or withdrawal, the image that comes to the mind is that of the teenage gangs and zombies in urban slums from Bedford-Stuyvesant to Soweto.

I am familiar with the objections to easy generalization from rats to human behavior—of what Ludwig von Bertalanffy[18] called the "ratomorphic fallacy."

Counterindications have also been listed by Prof. Mellanby. At a 1973 symposium on "Man and his Place" he notably recalled certain "restricted" neighborhoods of London where high densities did not keep the cockneys from cheerfully reproducing. The example of Hong Kong is also often cited where extreme overcrowding has not produced a corresponding increase in the incidence of socio-pathology (Mitchell, 1971).[19]

Certainly, men are more adaptable than rats—their higher intelligence, technological and organizational skills enable them to increase the resources of their environment, and they have also invented "conceptual space" where they can take refuge in times of extreme stress and physical discomfort.

However, the examples of London and Hong Kong are misleading exceptions to the rule. Located in the proximity of the central areas of prosperous and well-administered cities, the residents profit from good access to services and amenities: this unusually resource-rich environment compensates for the stress created by overcrowding.

High density "per se" is not an evil—witness the Upper East Side of Manhattan which is among the most coveted urban habitats yet it possesses the highest residential density in the world. (Dwyer 1980)[20]

In the slums of the Third World, social breakdown will come from a combination of size-related factors in an overcrowded "closed environment" and the increasing friction of such resources as employment and services.

To avoid or at least to postpone the likelihood of such breakdowns, let us consider some policy implications.

One useful insight derived from Calhoun's experiments is that stress and the incidence of socio-pathology can be minimized by a meaningful structuring of the physical environment: as Calhoun puts it, "the stochastics of social interaction demand that in order to maximize gratification from social interaction, intensity and duration must be reduced in proportion to the degree that the group size exceeds the optimum."[21]

To urban planners this would indicate a strategy of breaking up the large homogeneous slums into smaller units to reduce the "rate of random collision" but maximize meaningful contact. On the macro-scale of the megalopolis, this strategy would call for intraregional decentralization and the creation of a poly-nucleated urban structure with new subcenters. This should also make economic sense since the smaller urban units within the megalopolis will profit from many of the benefits of agglomeration without suffering from the diseconomies and negative social cost of large size.

Such a strategy has been recently put forward in the Master Plan for Bogota (Llewelyn-Davies et al., 1974).[22] This strategy proposes the formation of more or less self-contained cities within the metropolis and a judicious redistribution of employment opportunities and other urban activities. The plan permits an increase of the population of Bogota to about 10 million by the year 2000 yet most people would live within walking distance from their work. The insertion of "employment cores" in existing squatter areas and the fostering of the so-called "informal sector" would permit the provision of a comprehensive range of activities in all areas.

A similar policy has been proposed for Mexico City by Prof. Carlos Hank Gonzales. This plan provides for the restructuring of the urban fabric by the superimposition of a grid of 34 avenues with a minimum separation of slightly more than half a mile. The grid roads would enclose urban cells with a maximum density of about 500 people per hectare and populations varying from 10,000 to 50,000 inhabitants. The size of these cells is not just determined by optimalization of the traffic flow, but based on the conviction that 10,000-15,000 people represent the "right size" for participation and for social cohesion and identity.[23] (op. cit.)

The poly-nuclear cellular approach also has its validity in the creation of New Towns. In our own plan for Owerri, capital of Imo State in Nigeria, the city structure consists of "environmental areas" grouping 6,000-10,000 inhabitants, considered optimal for social interaction in the specific context of Nigeria (Galantay, 1978).[24]

We have thus come full circle and the "optimum size" concept as proposed in the eighteenth century pops up in the new guise of the "right size" for the "urban cell," "sector" or "environmental area."

However, adjustments of the spatial structure of the metropolis can only be carried out if the growth rate is reduced drastically. Although there is some evidence that, at a certain level of economic development, "polarization reversal" arises as a spontaneous phenomenon, in most cases a deliberate decentralization policy will be needed to restrict the growth of the metropolis and to guide development to the smaller cities.

That such a policy can be successful even in a mixed economy can be seen in the example of London where the population of the present Greater London has been reduced from a peak of 8.6 million in 1950 to about seven million at present. Continued out-migration will further reduce the size of London to six million by 1991—a remarkable shrinking of the population by 30% within a period of 50 years. As a result of this policy, the total population of the London metropolitan area is likely to stabilize at a 12 or 13 million level, making possible the upgrading of the quality of the physical environment in all neighborhoods.[25]

These policy choices and strategies of deliberate intervention bring us to a major dilemma confronting the planning profession.

Social sciences such as economics and planning have always operated on the basis of a theory with underpinnings from concepts borrowed from the physical sciences, still largely based on deterministic description, a mechanistic view of closed systems and reversible processes not unlike nineteenth century thermodynamics in which "time" never played much of a role.

The traditional view of the urban system is further tied to a belief in progress made possible by rational intervention and to the optimistic view that human ingenuity will always find a way to confront the forces of chaos and degradation.

But what if the metropolis is an unstable and dynamic "open system" in a highly entropic state and subject to irreversible processes?[26] In such systems, the entropy of interacting units can only increase. In such a context the notion of "optimum size" is meaningless.

Recent research by Ilya Prigogin (1977)[27] has proved that highly entropic systems lead to increasing order as a result of self-organization. Prigogin also says that, although we cannot predict the future, we can project "bundles" of scenarios: "irreversibility" is thus explained as the common characteristic of all possible scenarios which permit the description of the system in terms of stochastic processes.

It is hoped that analogies of the social system with non-equilibrium systems in biology, chemistry and thermodynamics will provide useful insights of operational relevance.

Urban society may be subject to entropic degradation although—unlike energy—human society is heterogeneous and its component units possess a high degree of specificity.[28] Urban entropy could perhaps be defined as the degradation of the diversity and innovative energy of the urban social system to an ultimate state of inert conformity and, in terms of spatial distribution of the population, the disappearance of the difference between the city and the country.

Assuming that the disequilibrium and instability of the present urban system is due to spatial concentration and excessively rapid population growth, will entropy work toward a state of higher order by a reduction of the concentration of interacting humans, i.e., by a series of catastrophes?[29]

Or would entropy rather imply that the unstable urban system characterized by extreme concentration and primacy will tend to correct itself by a
spontaneous process of "counter-primacy" and decentralization?

Bibliography

Alonso, W. 1970. *The Question of City Size and National Policy.* IURD. UCLA
Berk. WP 125.

_____ . 1970. *The Economics of Urban Size.* PPRSA 26, 67-83.

Berry, B.J.L. 1964. *Cities as Systems within Systems of Cities.* PPRSA 13;
147-63.

Blokhine, P.N. 1961. Provision of Welfare and Cultural Facilities and Public
Utilities in the USSR, Paper No. 31, submitted to the United Nations meeting of
planning experts.

Calhoun, John B: "Environment and Population" Prager Scientific Publishers,
N.Y. 1983

Duncan, Dudley, Otis 1957. Optimum Size of Cities in Hatt, P. and Reiss, A., eds.
Reader in Urban Sociology. 2d revised ed. Glencoe IL., Free Press.

Galantay, E.Y. "The Impact of Increasing Density on the Spatial Structure of
Human Settlements" in Calhoun, J.B: "Environment and Population" pp. 177
New York, 1983

Geisse, G. & Coraggio, J.L. 1972. Metropolitan Areas and National Development in
Geisse, G. and Hardoy, J.E., eds. in *Latin American Urban Research.* vol. 2,
Beverly Hills: Sage.

Hamburg, D.A. 1971. Crowding, Stranger Contact and Aggressive Behavior in
Levi, L. ed. *Society, Stress and Disease.* London: Oxford Univ. Press.

Hoch, I. 1972. Income and City Size. *Urban Studies* 9:299-328.

Krapf, E.E. 1964. Social Change in the Genesis of Mental Disorder in David, H.P.,
ed. *Population and Mental Health.* H. Huber, Berne.

Leven, L. 1968. *Determinants of the Size and Spatial Form of Urban Areas.*
Papers of the Regional Science Association, vol. 22, 7-28.

Milgrim, S. 1970. The Experience of Living in Cities. *Science* 167:1461-8.

Rothenberg, J. 1970. The Economics of Congestion and Pollution. *Am. Economic
Review Papers* 60:114-21.

Shapiro, Harvey 1963. Economies of Scale and Local Government Finances. *Land
Economics.* 175-86.

Singer, S.F., ed. 1971. *Is There an Optimum Level of Population?.* New York:
McGraw Hill.

Thring, J.B. 1977. Scenarios for Urban and Regional Planning. *Financial Context.* London, Department of the Environment.

Winsborough, H.H. 1970. The Social Consequences of High Population Density.
in Ford, T.R. and Dejong, G.F., eds. *Social Demography.* New York: Prentice
Hall.

Notes

1. E.Y. Galantay, "Les problemes de l'urbanisation rapide au Tiers Monde: le cas
   de Mexico," in *Schweizer Baublatt,* no. 35, (May, 1979), pp.1-8.
2. Steward F. Chapin, Jr., "How Big Should a City Be?" in *Urban Land Use
   Planning,* (New York, 1957).
3. E.Y. Galantay, *Nuevas Ciudades,* Gustavo Gili, (Barcelona, 1977).
4. Robert M. Lillibridge, "Urban Size: an Assessment" in *Land Economics*
   XXVIII, no. 4, (November, 1952), pp. 341-352.

111

5. Harry W. Richardson, *The Economics of Urban Size*, (U.K., 1973).

6. J.R. Seeley, Remaking the Urban Scene, *Daedalus 97, (1968), pp. 1124-1139.*

7. Paul Bairoch, *Taille des villes, conditions de vie et developpement economique*, Editions de l'ecole des hautes etudes en sciences sociales, (Paris, 1977).

8. Koito Mera, *On the Concentration of Urbanization and Economic Efficiency*, (1974).

9. F. Herrera, "Nationalism and Urbanization in Latin America," *Ekistics*, 32, (1971), pp. 369-73.

10. G.N. Neutze, *Economic Policy and the Size of Cities*, (Canberra, 1956).

11. E.Y. Galantay, *op.cit.*, ref.1.

12. Caracas 1990, Concejo Municipal del Distrito Federal *Plan de Desarrollo Urbano*, (1968).

13. H. Strotzka, "Town Planning and Mental Health," in Ph. P. David, *Population and Mental Health*, (1964).

14. B.P. & B.S. Dohrenwend, "Psychiatric Disorder in Urban Setting," in G. Caplan, ed., *American Handbook of Psychiatry*, vol. III, (New York, 1972).

15. Carlo M. Cipolla, *The Economic History of World Population*, 6th ed., (New York, 1975).

16. G. Bartholomew and J. Birdsell, "Ecology and the Protohominids," *Am. Anthropologist* 55, (1953), p.485.

17. John B. Calhoun, "Death Squared: the Explosive Growth and Demise of A Mouse Population," *Proc. Roy. Soc. Med.*, vol. 66, (Jan., 1963), pp.80-89.
    ———— , *From Mice to Men*, US Dept. H.E.W., National Inst. of Health, (Bethesda, 1973).
    ———— , "Scientific Quest for a Path to the Future," in *Populi*, vol. 3, no. 1, (1976).

18. Ludwig Von Bertalanffy, *Robots, Men and Minds*, (New York, 1967).

19. R.E. Mitchell, "Some Social Implications of High Density Housing," *Am. Sociological Review* 36, (1971), pp.18-19.

20. Dennis J. Dwyer, "The Effect of Overcrowding on the Quality of Life" in *Proceedings of the 9th ICUS*, Miami Beach, (I.C.F. Press, New York, 1980), pp.589-612.

21. John B. Calhoun, "Population Density and Social Pathology," in *Sci. Am.* no. 206, (1962), pp. 139-46.

22. Llewelyn-Davies, Weeks, Forestier, Walker & Bor: *Bogota Urban Development Study*, Phase 2, BIRD/UNDP, 1974.

23. E.Y. Galantay, *op.cit.*, ref.1.

24. E.Y. Galantay, "The Planning of Owerri, New Capital of Imo State in Nigeria," in *TPR*, (July, 1978).

25. Klaus Muller-Ibold, see article in this volume, Chapter 10.

26. Ervin Laszlo, see article in this volume, Chapter 8.

27. N.I. Prigogin, *Self-Organization in Non-Equilibrium Systems*, (New York, 1977) and N. Roegen-Georgescu, *The Entropy Law and the Economic Process*, (Cambridge, MA, 1971).

28. Ervin Galantay & Christian Eberegges "Self-Organization in Spontaneous Human Settlements" in Proceeding of the Committee on Non-Equilibrium Systems, 10th ICUS, Seoul, Korea 1981.

29. Ervin Laszlo, *Transformation Dynamics in Metropolitan Systems*, see the following article for his conjectures. Laszlo seems to assume that the evolution of urban systems has reached a "bifurcation" point and systems breakdown will inevitably precede further "saltatory" evolution. I disagree with this conclusion. For my somewhat more optimistic interpretation of the future see "Conclusions" at the end of this volume.

8.
Transformation Dynamics in Metropolitan Systems

Ervin Laszlo

$\mathcal{T}$his chapter attempts to apply the latest insights of non-equilibrium thermodynamics and the theory of paleological macroevolution to the historical process of societal change.

A critical discussion of urbanization trends will demonstrate that skepticism in regard to a continued growth of giant metropoli—particularly in the developing world—has solid roots in the latest insights into the basic nature of change and transformation in complex systems.

Scenarios of Metropolitan Growth for the Coming Decades

Belief in a single, continuous and generally positive growth curve with regard to large metropoli has been shattered in recent years. In a preceding article Dennis Dwyer rightly insists that "urbanization and metropolitan formation are not single, universally similar processes but rather assume different forms and meanings depending upon historic, economic, social and cultural conditions." Anthony O'Connor, in turn, points out that differentiation in the process of urbanization is so divergent in different regions that we should avoid thinking in binary terms of a "developed" and a "developing" country model or standards but envisage a broad spectrum of processes encompassing a series of evolutionary lines. Peter Hall's general model, quoted by Dwyer, is esthetically pleasing but empirically false. It is reminiscent of the familiar "railroad" theories of development which assume a single-line development process of sequential phases. Developing and developed countries are located at different points along a single "track," with the developed countries closer to some vaguely defined terminus called the "developed condition" and with the developing countries lagging behind on the line depending on their particular level of underdevelopment. Dwyer and Hall correctly emphasize that the process of urbanization in the developing world is so different from that in the developed countries that no single, multiple-stage model can apply to all. However, their suggested solutions are unrealistic. Faced with the continued concentration of population in Third World cities, Dwyer suggests that job sharing and job splitting could ensure an "almost indefinite increase in metropolitan population." This is highly questionable, given the fact that the majority of Third World metropolitan populations is already living on the edge of survival. The meager job opportunities which exist in the "informal" sectors of these cities are not jobs at all in the Western sense of the word but ways of squeezing out a living on the subsistance level. Any more splitting of such "jobs" and the "self-employed" of this sector will cross the line from semi-starvation to below. It does not follow, therefore, that the developing countries will "in the near future see the emergence of metropoli of enormous size" such as Mexico City with 31 million and Shanghai with 22 million inhabitants. Such population projections seem academic in the face of the stark reality of Third World urban life. In some cases there are very definite upper limits to further population growth and concentration—for example, the water supply for Mexico City, an oversized settlement located on a high plateau lacking natural sources to supply water to a projected population of 31 million people. No wonder that Elias Gomez-Azcarate seriously envisages a "theratoplan" or planning measures to deal with impending catastrophies! (See Part 7, Chapter 23.) At the edge of survival the result will not be population decompression by dispersal but epidemics, social breakdown, political unrest and a generalized system breakdown. The fact that the world has not yet experienced this kind of breakdown does not prove that it cannot occur: never before have so many millions been concentrated quite so densely on a limited surface. We are facing a qualitatively new phenomenon. It is rather weak to conclude, as Dwyer does, that the giant metropoli "will be characterized by extensive poverty and by occupations marginal to the relatively small core of "formal" ones . . . (and) also . . . by continued concentration, if only because of the inability of the vast majority of the population to pay for much intra-urban transport." The reality will be destitution to such a point that informality or formality of employment or ability to pay for urban transport will hardly matter at all.

What will happen after the year 2000 which statisticians like to quote in connection with urban population figures? If metropolitan concentration in the Third World continues, would then cities like Mexico City grow to encompass 35, 40, 50 million inhabitants?

If the human and physical constraints are underplayed and only the socio-economic processes are modeled as though in a vacuum, growth might seem to continue exponentially. But it is unlikely that a metropolis would reach absolute saturation density like a lily pond in which the water-lily population doubles at given intervals, so that one day the pond is only half full of lilies but the next critical day it is entirely choked. Human systems break down much before they fill up all available space. They are reaching the point of critical instability already.

Thus Dwyer's and Hall's conjectures have only limited validity: Third

World cities do not behave like First World (or Second World) cities—but their process of population concentration cannot indefinitely continue in the future since a breakdown will intervene very likely within the next decades. This is why I also disagree with O'Connor with respect to urbanization policies for tropical Africa. After pointing out that the rise of the large metropolis creates immense problems of management, housing, infrastructure etc., he recommends a small-towns development strategy to counterbalance the concentration in a single large metropolis. Yet it seems utopian to suggest that "efforts . . . be made to ensure that the inevitable urban growth of future decades is less concentrated" since O'Connor himself points out that this policy would require a substantial shift in resource allocation away from the metropolis against the powerful political pressures supporting vested interests opposed to such a policy. Nor is it realistic to propose that the nations of tropical Africa attempt to leapfrog the historic process of urban concentration, making instant use of the latest communication technologies to create the kind of low-density "invisible cities" which have so far only appeared in limited subregions in the most developed countries (California, Japan, the Dutch Randstad, etc.). This scenario of using telecommunications in place of spatial concentration of population for maximum interaction depends not only on a high degree of mobility of millions of people and great flexibility on the part of the private and public sector decision-makers, it depends also on an entire culture shift, the absorption and adaptation of a post-industrial civilization—a slow process even in Europe or in America. Thus, one can wholeheartedly agree with O'Connor that "the aim for most Third World countries must be a metropolis modest in size, closely integrated both with a system of dispersed smaller urban centers and with the people who remain in the countryside." It seems unrealistic to want to exhort decision-makers to urgently seek this goal "while there is yet time." It is precisely time that is lacking from the equation, even if political will—another dubious variable—was granted.

What then, is the likely outcome? The crystal ball of urban future is admittedly cloudy. But it contains two points of reference: continued population growth in the Third World and outer limits to urban growth. When we add the inability of governments to carry out rational policies we get a linear progression toward breakdown. As Sumet Jumsai points out in his article (Part 9, Chapter 30), decentralization must begin with the nation's power base. Yet, such decentralization is not occuring anywhere at the required speed to starve off the collision of population concentration with resource constraints. Perhaps the first collision will bring the opportunity for radical change. As the ancient Chinese well realized—and as contemporary non-equilibrium thermodynamics and the theory of paleontological evolution has rediscovered—*crisis and opportunity are one and the same*, and system transformation emerges in the wake of system breakdown.

In his preface, Percy Johnson-Marshall gives us the required perspective in describing the metropolis "as it exists today . . . an exorbitant consumer of human and natural resources . . . a kind of brainless giant uncontrolled and uncontrollable, an enemy of good ecological principles, and finally *unnecessary*, at least in its present form." Perhaps we shall have to wait until this "brainless giant"—uncontrollable and unnecessary—begins to crack under its own weight and the processes of system overload. Then, and probably only then, will the metropolis of the future be born like Phoenix on the Ashes of its predecessor.

Saltatory Evolution in Nature and in Society

The prospects of urban system breakdown in the Third World are consistent with a major breakthrough in our understanding of systems change and transformation in general. The origin of the new insights is simultaneously the theory of irreversible processes in the non-equilibrium thermodynamics developed *inter alia* by Ilya Prigogin and the theory of biological macro-evolution propounded by Gould and Eldredge. Both theories show change and evolution to be discontinuous and non-linear processes, contrary to the previously dominant perception of an essentially smooth, linear and continuous evolution.

The concept of critical instability in complex systems appears in both of the above-mentioned theories. In the thermodynamic theory critical instability refers to a state in a system far from equilibrium which is triggered by a level of perturbation beyond the error-correcting range of the feedback loops. It damages the essential auto- and cross-catalytic cycles responsible for the persistence of the system and thus endangers its very existence: unless the system settles into a new steady state it faces decay and disorganization.

In the biological theory of macro-evolution critical instability refers to a state of dominant species in its milieu: that state in which the species is less able to maintain balanced relations with predators and preys than some other species within the clade. If such imbalance continues, the more fit species can invade the territory of the destabilized population and become dominant. The critically destabilized species may eventually face extinction. Critical instability is correlated with the notion of bifurcation points in both theories (the term itself stems from thermodynamics). Bifurcation points are the sudden bursts of evolutionary transformation attendant upon basic instabilities. This takes the form of "speciation" in the biological theory. The tempo and mode of evolution are isomorphic in both theories: saltatory evolution is an invariance lying at the heart of the new understanding of evolutionary processes in the physical as well as in the biological realms.

These invariances are not superficial analogies and coincidences. They are basic features rooted in the core of each of the theories. To appreciate this fact we should restate the main outlines, first of the theory of non-equilibrium systems in thermodynamics, and then of the theory of macro-evolution in contemporary paleobiology.

According to non-equilibrium thermodynamics, systems in the real world may exist in one of three states. Of these states the third—the one in which systems are far from thermodynamic equilibrium—is the typical state produced and maintained in the course of cosmic as well as biospheric evolution. In this state the systems are neither at equilibrium nor tend toward it, the fluxes are no longer linear functions of the forces, and structure is maintained by non-linear processes manifested by multiple feedbacks in cross- and auto-catalytic cycles. Systems in this state can have more than one steady-state: they are bi- or multi-stable. Their stability is dynamic rather than static: it is maintained through a constant balancing of environmental perturbations by internal adjustment controlled by complex feedbacks. When such meta-stable systems are exposed to perturbations which surpass the critical threshold, the self-maintaining cycles are disrupted and the system is destabilized. At that point of bifurcation it either finds another steady-state, which can absorb and correct for perturbations, or it disorganizes to its stable components.

In their meta-stable states, non-equilibrium systems are resilient to perturbations within the range of error-tolerance and are dominated by the parametric values of the critical forces and concentrations. Consequently, the behavior of the systems is relatively determinate and predictable. At the points of bifurcation determinism vanishes: an external observer is unable to determine in advance which of the fluctuations will be amplified in the system and become dominant. Small modifications may spread rapidly across the entire system: the choice among them is not determined by boundary conditions.

In the theory of biologic macro-evolution change does not occur by means of linear adaptations of existing species to their environment, as in the Darwinian theory (such adaptations exist but are relegated to a secondary role in perfecting the fit of the emerging species with their niche): genuine change, i.e., evolution, is species-selection. It involves the destabilization of a dominant population by critical changes in the species-environment relation, and multiple explorations or experimentations by hitherto peripheral isolates as the latter invade the territory of the previously dominant population. Such a process of "allopatric speciation" is not predeterminate and inherently directional but occurs stochastically. If some of the "invasions" produce an improved fit of species and environment, reproduction rates are increased and the invading population may become dominant. This process is called "saltatory evolution" through speciation rather than ortho-selection in gradually changing lineages. While gradual adaptations keep fine-tuning organisms to their environment, critical instabilities make for the appearance of new species. The time-span of existing species (i.e., the interval between speciations in a given lineage) varies with changes in environmental conditions and the range of environmental adaptability of the given species: species that are adapted to a wider range of conditions speciate less often than those that are locked into relatively narrow environmental niches.

The process of speciation changes the composition and distribution of populations within their ecosystems. The relations that bind populations of species within ecosystems undergo changes, and these changes can be better absorbed in a resilient rather than in a rigidly stable ecosystem. Resilient systems can cycle through different sets of relations, constituting a varying sequence of ecological steady states. Stable systems, on the other hand, may be efficient in buffering out a limited range of perturbations by using the feedback loops typical of their basic steady states, but are unable to switch over to alternate states when the perturbations surpass a critical threshold. It is of great importance for given species, especially if there are major speciations in the milieu, to find themselves in resilient rather than inflexible stable ecosystems. Interactive relations can be restructured in resilient systems without endangering the survival of the populations to depend on them.

This theoretical core can be applied to a wide variety of complex systems not excluding those formed by human beings. Human societies, including the urban subsystems, constitute complex systems far from thermodynamic equilibrium, maintained by multiple catalytic cycles complex feedback loops among themselves. In the stable, or more precisely meta-stable state, a society operates within the error-correcting thresholds of these feedbacks, assuring the reproduction of all subsystems and substances critical for its persistence. In such a state the human population of a society is reproduced in a manner that enables all individuals living in it to sustain themselves by satisfying their basic needs and requirements. However, human reproduction is not merely a biological but also a sociocultural process, conditioned by all the ramifications of the economic, social, political, and cultural dimensions of society. These processes are constituted according to certain codes or norms which are the common property of all of society's members, although no single member possesses them in their entirety. Such codes and norms include a language, a value system, an organizational and institutional code, a more informal behavioral code, and an entire system of technologies (taken in the broad sense to include skills and knowledge required for the production of artifacts as well as the production and processing of natural resources). The set of codes and norms makes up the "cultural information pool" of a society.

In a meta-stable state, society's information pool is adequate to permit the reproduction of its members, by coding and controlling the major catalytic cycles involved in the production, distribution and consumption of the resources needed for survival. Society remains in balance with its resource base and also with other societies in its milieu. Such balance may apply to a relatively narrow or to a wider set of conditions: in the "specialist" societies stability is restricted to a narrow band of conditions (whether in the natural or in the societal environment), while in "generalist" societies the range of stability extends over a wide spectrum of environmental states and conditions.

If the state of societal stability is defined as the adequacy of society's information pool with regard to the reproduction of its human population with adequate access to resources, the state of societal *instability* can be defined as that state of the information pool which signifies a critical imbalance either in the man-nature interface of society, or in the man-man interface. The former refers to all inputs and outputs which connect the given society with its natural environment through the exploitation of natural resources, renewable as well as nonrenewable. The latter interface concerns societal relations, domestic as well as foreign, pertinent to the persistence of the given society. The state of instability signifies that the information pool of the society is "out of sync" with its natural and/or societal milieu.

The critical destabilization of a sociocultural system means the imperative need to transform the system's information pool, and therewith its organizational and institutional structure, its mode of production and communication, and its relations to the natural and the societal environment. It means reaching a point of bifurcation in which either a new steady-state is found, or the system faces dissolution and decay. In the processes of history, types of cultural information pools are selected through a form of natural (more exactly, natural-cum-societal) selection acting on the "phenotype," namely the human population together with its production systems and inter-societal relations. Thus, evolution in the societal domain is the transformation of societies in consequence of the "speciation" of their cultural information pool. It is an essentially saltatory process which calls for the destabilization of one type of social system (and hence the critical malfunctioning of its information pool) and its replacement by another. This process, we may assume, is random with respect to the overall directionality of history in any given instance. Any small fluctuation in the information pool can be "selected": in periods when the dominant pool is destabilized it can become amplified. Hence, fresh socio-ideological currents can achieve dominance, whereas in previous, more stable epochs they are kept on the periphery by the stabilizing feedbacks of the dominant system.

The issue of the nature and maintenance of societal stability may be of particular importance at the present juncture in history. It is possible that numerous societies may find that they are losing the vital match between information pool and environment that is the determining condition of their stability. They would have to prepare for the re-coding of the cultural information pool, i.e., for a major evolutionary transformation, as the means to assure their persistence and development. Other societies may find that their current steady-state is steady enough to allow them to persist without a total transformation. But giant metropoli, especially in Third World societies that are near the point of destabilization, come into the category of imminently and critically unstable systems. They are not self-sufficient "generalist" types of social systems but highly specialized agglomerations directly dependent for their persistence on a stable societal setting. As societies suffer crises and approach conditions of critical instability, urban systems are prone to breakdown. Their resource base becomes inadequate, and the metropoli themselves become unable to provide their inhabitants with the wherewithal of human existence.

When the dynamics of change in contemporary societies brings about unstable conditions in various national and regional economies, in particular in the developing world, such highly specialized subsystems as major cities can only survive if they manage to control their vital environment and assure an uninterrupted flow of the basic economic, financial, material and technical resources. Third World metropoli may face major crises precisely because they can neither control the mushrooming problems of the national and regional economies in the context of which they operate, nor can they decentralize and diminish in size and concentration rapidly enough to adapt to the existing resource flows. The evolutionary dynamic may be manifested in the human sphere first in the area of big cities: it is here that the saltatory nature of change and transformation will appear with greatest force. The kind of decentralized urban-rural system that is currently envisaged by urban planners may have to await the transformation of Third World societies themselves. The lesson of the new insights of evolutionary processes are clear: change is discontinuous, rapid and nonlinear, and it concerns the total system and not its individual members or subsystems alone. As societies change, so do metropoli. The current growth-trend in giant Third World metropolitan centers is a manifestation of the progressive destabilization of scores of Third World societies, and can be radically modified only when these societies themselves become modified. Under such conditions urban planning is not a separate field of endeavor: it is an element in the overall planning for change in human sociocultural systems. We can apply Hegel's dictum, *"Das Wahre ist das Ganze"* . . . the reality of urban futures is the future of human societies themselves.

References

I. Self-organization in non-equilibrium systems.

Konequilibrium Thermodynamics and Related Works.

Manfred Eigen and P. Schuster, *The Hypercycle: A Principle of Natural Self-Organization,* (New York, 1979).

Irving Epstein et al., "Oscillating Chemical Reactions," in *Scientific American,* (March, 1983).

Ervin Y. Galantay and Christan Ebenegger, "Self-organization in Spontaneous Human Settlements," in *Proceedings of the 10th ICUS,* Seoul, Korea, ICF Press (New York, 1980).

P. Glansdorff and I. Prigogine, *Thermodynamic Theory of Structure, Stability and Fluctuations,* (New York, 1971).

Hermann Haken, *Synergetics,* (New York, 1978).

Hermann Haken, ed., *Dynamics of Synergetic Systems,* (New York, 1980).

Aaron Katchalsky and P.F. Curran, *Nonequilibrium Thermodynamics in Biophysics,* (Cambridge, MA, 1965).

Erich Jantsch, *Design for Evolution,* (New York, 1975).

————— ,*The Self-Organizing Universe,* (Oxford, 1980).

G. Nicolis and I. Prigogine, *Self-Organization in Non-Equilibrium Systems,* (New York, 1977).

Ilya Prigogine, *Etude Thermodynamique des Phenomenes Irreversibles,* (Liege, 1947).

Ilya Prigogine and I. Stengers, *Order Out of Chaos (La Nouvelle Alliance)*, (New York, 1984).

Rene Thom, *Stabilite Structurelle et Morphogenese*, (Paris, 1972).

II. *Macroevolutionary Theory of Punctuated Equilibrium.*

D.V. Ager, *The Nature of the Stratigraphic Record*, (New York, 1973).

H.L. Carson, "The Genetics of Speciation at the Diploid Level," in *American Naturalist*, (1975).

Niles Eldredge and S.J. Gould, "Punctuated Equilibria: an Alternative to Phylogenetic Gradualism," in Schopf, ed., *Models in Paleobiology*, (San Francisco, 1972).

————— , Punctuated Equilibria: the Tempo and Mode of Evolution Reconsidered, in *Paleobiology*, (San Francisco, 1977).

Niles Eldredge, "Stabililty, Diversity and Speciation in Paleozoic Epeiric Seas," in *Journal of Paleontology*, vol. 48.

Stephen J. Gould, *Ontogeny and Phylogeny*, (Cambridge, MA., 1977).

C.S. Holling, "Resilience and Stability of Ecosystems," in Jantsch and Waddington, eds., *Evolution and Consciousness*, (Reading, MA, 1976).

III. *General Theory and Philosophy of Systems*

Ludwig von Bertalanffy, *General System Theory*, (New York, 1968).

Walter Cray and N. Rizzo, eds., *Unity Through Diversity* (2 vols.), (New York, 1973).

Erich Jantsch and C.H. Waddington, eds., *Evolution and Consciousness*, (Reading, MA, 1976).

Ervin Laszlo, *Introduction to Systems Philosophy*, (New York, 1973).

Henry Margenau, ed., *Integrative Principles of Modern Thought*, (New York, 1972).

Paul A. Weiss, et al., *Hierarchically Organized Systems in Theory and Practice*, (New York, 1971).

9.
Urban Stress in the Metropolis: Psychobiological Consequences

Jesus Martin Ramirez

In this chapter on metropolitan gigantism I want to discuss the effects of the size and density of very large agglomerations on the human being, on his value systems and on his psychology. I would prefer to say on his "psychobiology" because there is no clear demarcation between somatic and psychic effects; biological and sociocultural factors are closely interwoven and their separation is almost impossible.[1]

I must confess that I am not prone to predictions or conjectures about the future, for the following reasons: experience often shows that predictions are not as easy and straightforward as they sometimes appear to be; and I also believe that the future of mankind is far from being determined. On the contrary, it will become what people want it to be.

I hope that the future metropolis will not develop toward a "necropolis" and that the metropolitan megastructure need not be inevitably an inhuman and restrictive urban environment. Indeed, some recent trends seem to point toward more rewarding and viable directions.[2] However, in this paper I shall examine the possible psychobiological consequences of very large human agglomerations.

Before addressing the variety of pressures exerted by the man-made urban environment, in particular focusing on their deleterious effect on the human psychobiology, two things should be clarified. First, most of the problems to be discussed are *not specifically urban* ones, although it is in the urban environment where they are the most frequent; they are the price we pay for the progress of the human civilization. Second, it would be unjust to leave a too-pessimistic impression of the urban phenomenon. If we focus only on the negative side, it is just because that is what needs a remedy. We should not lose sight of the positive aspects of urban society. Urbanization is a desirable world-wide phenomenon that provides both an irresistible lifestyle and a pattern of allocation of human effort and time.[3] G. Nobelo justly reminds us of the superiority of urban life over life in the rural environment.[4] Krivatsy, in his paper on the San Francisco Bay Region, even asserts that the modern metropolis—while not perfect—may be the best form of urban settlement now. To try to mitigate the negative consequences of urban gigantism does not imply a bias in favor of ruralization.

One of the major "stressors"[5] brought by urban development is the excessive crowding produced by the spatial concentration of a heterogeneous population. Overcrowding is the root cause of a number of severe socioeconomical and psychobiological problems.[6] Although high density per se is not an evil, a combination of factors related to overcrowding results in various "negative social benefits."[7]

The scarcity of open space in the metropolitan environment, coupled with the use of mechanized conveyances—cars, elevators, etc.—deprives the inhabitants of healthy physical exercise. Negative physiological effects on the organism have been observed in Hong Kong where children living in high-rise apartment buildings and getting little exercise have 8% less lung capacity than the children of hillside squatters who lead a very active outdoor life.[8]

The fast life, the fatigue, the isolation, the stress caused by traffic congestion in the big cities produce other acute negative effects on health besides traffic accidents. The physical pollution resulting from the accumulation of harmful industrial wastes, garbage disposal, leaking sewage systems, the emission of smoke carbon dioxide and other toxic gases, and "deafening" noises and vibrations may be the cause of even more serious disturbances since their symptoms are chronic and difficult to detect due to their subtle nature.[9] Likewise, the morbidity rate increases in crowded environments due to stress factors such as fatigue which weakens the organism, making it more susceptible to disease. Malnutrition and the lack of proper hygiene and sanitation facilities add to the misery of living in many urban environments. Respiratory-tract diseases are more serious in nature when they occur in places like crowded urban settings which lack proper ventilation. Dr. Diana L. Mendoza reminded us at the 13th ICUS Conference of the results of experiments attempting to determine how socio-environmental factors such as overcrowding affect the organism and how psychological and nervous stimuli affect the heart function and the circulatory system. For obvious reasons, experimentation with human beings is often impossible but it is entirely justifiable to extrapolate the results of animal experiments.

Experiments carried out by Richard Venier of the Harvard School of Public Health in Boston suggest that people suffering from heart disease increase the risk of early heart failure by living in a stressful urban environment.[10] It has been demonstrated experimentally[11] that crowding can alter feelings, increase anxiety and influence other affective behaviors. In crowded cities the competition for scarce resources and the latent aggressivity causes feelings of anxiety. An individual who feels "threatened" yet unable to flee physically—like his primitive hunting-gathering ancestors —will try to escape into mental space. However, this psychological defense mechanism burns out adrenaline and other toxins and the energy stored in our muscles. The result may be a long-term alteration of the heart function or immediate death by "asystole" which is a form of heart failure.

Crowding can also take the form of an excess of nonphysical contact and communication resented as a form of harassment typical of modern urban life. Most of us are familiar with the rise of bad temper when the phone rings at an improper time: it is a small example of those too-many contacts with strangers bombarding us with an excess of stimuli and information.[12] Conflict, tension and stress bring about a fatigue of our social reaction processes. Every inhabitant of a modern city is familiar with the surfeit of social contacts and knows the disturbing feeling of not being as pleased as he ought to be at the visit of a friend, even if he is genuinely fond of him. For this reason every year more telephone numbers are unlisted in the directory to avoid unwanted calls. An accelerated life-pace with an excessive number of contacts with strangers leads to a weakening of the family bonds and the disappearance of personal relationships within the social groups defined by spatial proximity such as the neighborhood. The result is that people, especially young ones, feel lonely and alienated, less "visible" and therefore less responsible. This explains, at least partly, the higher rates of suicide in larger cities, especially in the so-called "welfare" societies. Social deviance can also be induced indirectly by crowding which destroys the feelings of identity and of solidarity.[13] The fact that unemployment leads to a higher rate of deviant behavior, crime and aggressiveness does not seem exclusive of our species. It has also been observed in captive wolves and Rhesus monkeys.[14] When their chief occupation of hunting for food was taken away due to human feeding, there was an increase in quarreling. An effective way for decreasing violence, therefore, seems to be to guarantee full employment.

Given the characteristic sensory overload of urban environments, it is advisable to apply a selective principle with regard to the hour in which to use time and energy, blocking the reception of those with less priority and to filter them out to decrease the stimulation intensity.[15]

Are pathological characteristics inherent to the modern megalopolis? Psychobiological aberrations show a higher rate in congested areas. There are various somatic illnesses and respiratory diseases due to the increased possibility of contagion, humidity and irritant gases. Due to the lack of sunshine, rickets also presents a problem, and there is a greater incidence of ulcers, diabetes, arteriosclerosis, obesity due to inactivity, loss of hearing from the excess of noise, and hypertension.

Of special interest are the psychic consequences of urban over-crowding. A simple index of tension may be the speed of walking: people in big cities have been observed to walk twice as fast as those in small towns. It is widely agreed that crime, deviant behavior and human segregation are higher in urban areas, that they increase as the cities grow in size, and that slums are a source of unrest, violence and delinquency.[16] The erosion of the quality of life and of social relationships is a consequence of many interrelated stress factors, such as overstimulation or an excessively rapid generational change and the coping problems which usually follow migration.

Such factors bring on the further degradation of living conditions by a process of "cumulative causation".[17] Stress caused by living in big cities is one of the reasons for the decline of social cooperation, a hypertrophy of competitiveness, a lack of consideration for others and the rise of aggressivity. The lack of altruism is a characteristic of big cities. Darley observes that people are more ready to help others in the underground than in the airport. He found that novelty is an inhibitor to helping. People are more ready to help one another in the subway because most of them use it for daily commuting. Being familiar with the subway environment they are not as inhibited by novelty stimuli as in the airport.[18]

Another factor of urban stress, according to Tinbergen[19] is the high pace of generational change whereby, with each new generation, it becomes harder for young people "to understand" their parents. This produces great anxiety and uncertainty.[20] Socially disruptive behavior develops, as does rebellion, against restrictions through too many regulations and rules limiting an individual's own freedom of decision and of action.[21] Continuous dissatisfaction makes them look for happiness through other ways. Most often, escape through alcohol and drugs is attempted, leading to an increased rate of deviant behavior and violence in urban environments.[22]

An experiment carried out by Eliasz and his Polish colleagues shows how people of different temperament are also differently influenced by the urban environment. Boys of 15 and 16 years of age were observed in an industrial city of Silesia, and their spontaneous activities and their behavior recorded during their free time down-town where there were more sources of stimulation (noise, danger, novelty), and also in the periphery of the city with a less stimulating atmosphere. Two groups were assessed by a temperament inventory: high-reactive persons, very sensitive even to low stimuli but with less endurance to them, and low-reactive people, with a low susceptibility to stimuli but with high endurance to strong ones. Whereas high-reactive boys behaved most of the time in the same way in both places, low-reactive ones showed a more spontaneous and independent behavior, adjusted to the space and the possibilities.

There are also frequent behavioral disorders resulting from new social circumstances. Current figures from psychiatric sources indicate that in our particular form of urban culture there is a high occurrence of disorganized personalities: schizophrenia, neuroses and personality disorders are much more common in big cities than in rural areas.[23] One person in five has serious psychiatric difficulties during his lifetime, and one in ten will at some time enter a mental hospital. What is disorganized in them? Primarily, it is their social relationship which seems to be maladaptive.[24]

Such problems of human maladjustment are often caused by migratory movements.[25] Frequently there is a strong anti-immigrant sentiment among the original population which is shown in aggressive reactions towards alien newcomers of different ethnic, religious, linguistic or social groups. The problem of cultural and social integration of such minorities is even more difficult when large numbers of people have been separated from their family, friends and cultures. The fact that such situations are prone to social disintegration and to the breakdown of interpersonal relationships explains the prevalence of aggressiveness and violent situations.

How may we interpret those data? The threshold for stimuli and the range of optimum differs according to the individual temperament: low-reactive people are more resistant to social pressures; they behave in the same way in different environments regardless of high or low level of stimuli—also they are more tolerant. On the contrary, high-reactive people adjust their behavior to social regulation, trying to be in conformity with others to avoid punishment and personal tensions; they are more susceptible to changes in their motivation. Since there is a high level of stimuli in our urban society, there will always be a lot of problems with high-reactive people. Individual differences, therefore, have to be taken into account when we study how people behave under environmental pressures. Individual conditions require individual approaches.

Even though we have noted a few "stressors" which are common to any metropolis, we should avoid over-generalization assuming that people react in the same way to environmental pressure variations. We cannot ignore that there is a diversity in the supply of environmental situations as well as in the psychobiological and genetical idiosyncrasies of each person. The quality of living conditions reflects a great variety of needs and wants, depending upon historical experiences, social background, religious convictions, current ideologies, cultural conditions and economic circumstances. The feeling of crowding, for example, depends upon the cultural and sexual context—males seem to need more space than females—and even on situational differences. ("Was man in der U-Bahn Ueberfüllung nennt heisst in Nachtlokalen Atmosphere"[26] i.e., the degree of crowding resented in the subway is enjoyed in a disco or in a bar.)

Each person perceives the same environment in a different way and is influenced by it in a particular way. To demonstrate this fact all that is needed is to ask a group of people to draw from memory the map of their city or to describe a place known by all of them. Their subjective interpretation will differ from the same objective reality; each observer will emphasize what is important to him. Although the harsh realities of the mass slums in the metropolis have destroyed the urban dream for millions, the return to their villages would be an even greater nightmare. The urban lifestyle offers great advantages in comparison to the country: lower mortality rates due to more effective health services, improved access to cultural and educational facilities, higher incomes. Cities have always been the prime movers of innovation in all civilizations, intellectual, social and political catalysts.

As the articles by Dwyer, Blumenfeld and Robertson indicate, the historic trend toward enormous conurbations is increasingly checked by centrifugal forces causing out-migration. This phenomenon of "counterurbanization"[27] heralds the rise of more dispersed, non-metropolitan yet urban areas and of a more harmonious regional distribution of networks of human settlements that offer work, living and recreations in close proximity. This pattern of human settlements is similar to that described by Lewis Mumford as the "invisible city."[28]

Since I have pleaded from the beginning against any determinism of our future, I have no doubt at all that there is a real alternative to the deleterious effects of the present megapolis. If we want a better social environment, remedial measures have to be directed, first, to a change of the environment, reducing its most damaging pressures, and second, to changes of the society, making future humans better able to cope with their habitat. As Dubos reminds us,[29] man can adjust himself quickly to harsh, unusual and even potentially dangerous environments. I do not believe that we are helpless victims of urban society which is a product of every one of us rather than imposed on us from the outside.[30] Based on this insight we should search for ways to master our habitat and to make our environment more suitable by avoiding the disadvantages of an urban gigantism. But trying to prevent gigantism does not mean a return to the rural setting. Rather, we must adjust the architecture and the urban design to make the city qualitatively better—with more space, cleaner air, less congestion and decreased sensory overload—and let its inhabitants have a more pleasant and attractive lifestyle so that it becomes a place apt not only for "living" and "surviving," but also for "living together" ("convivir" in Spanish).

Scholars should commit themselves to "producing" a new type of man with expertise in many sciences—mainly in those concerned with education and knowledge of the psychobiological development of humans—who is motivated to participate in the creation of a better urban environment. For that, Tinbergen[31] suggests a biologically more balanced form of education with more scope for playful, exploratory and imitative self-teaching. I would add to such a regimen more self-control and seek to eliminate the sense of indifference towards others. Antisocial behavior could be counteracted by mutual interaction, and mechanisms of adaptation could be developed adequate to the peculiar environmental tone and experiences of each city.

Some of the articles in this collection may give the impression that man has lost control of his environment. It may even seem that "he is oblivious to what his real needs are, to what he wants to do, and, of where to go from here," to cite Psomopoulos.[32] But we should not fall prey to defeatism faced with menacing trends. On the contrary, we must help man in finding his own road.

As the Spanish proverb says: "prevenir vale mas que curar," or in English, "an ounce of prevention is worth a pound of cure."

Notes

1. J.M. Ramirez, "Fundamentos biologicos de la personalidad," G.E.R. 18 (1974): pp. 366-368.
   ———— , "Vida humana y biologia," G.E.R. 23 (1975): pp. 509-511.
2. Dwyer, Johnson-Marshall and Robertson have pointed out that rather than a trend toward a future enormous conurbation—in its pejorative meaning of "spreading of a great coral reef" (Geddi 1915)—today we can observe a centrifugal force of out-migration from many big cities; this "counter-urbanization" in terms of Bryan Berry (1981): "implies the growth of non-metropolitan areas, of more self-sustaining and harmonious distribution through the region, of independent networks of human settlements that offer

work, living and recreation in close proximity."

3. P. Psomopoulos, in this volume Chapter 1, Article 3.

4. G. Nobelo, (1984), Contribution à l'étude du développement de l'enfant à travers l'analyse comparative de trois groupes d'enfants appartenant à des communautés d'origine indigène, Thèse de doctorat, Université de Paris X, (1984).

5. For our present purpose we define "stressors" as any outside antihomeostatic stimulus eliciting stress, i.e., anything in our external world that deflects our organism from the ideal or optimal state at which it operates.

6. R.L. Snyder, (1958), "Reproduction and population pressures," in F. Stellar and J.M. Sprague, eds., *Progress in Physiological Psychology*, vol. 2, (New York, 1958).

7. E.Y. Galantay, in this volume, Chapter 7, Article 2.

8. J. Nicholson, (1984), *Men and Women: How Different Are They?*, (Oxford, 1984).

9. D.C. Glass and J.E. Singer, *Urban Stress: Experiments On Noise and Social Stressors*, (New York, 1972).
   J.M. Ramirez, Einführung in die Anthropobiologie, (Bern, 1978).
   _____ , (1984), Vida, ambiente y biologia, 2 volumes, (Madrid, 1984).

10. Richard Vernier of the Harvard School of Public Health in Boston has exposed healthy dogs to stress situations such as overcrowding before and after inducing heart damage. He found that the healthy dogs exposed to stress respond by *arrhythmia*, slowing down of their normal heart rate. As a result severe uncoordination of the fibers of the heart, *"fibrilation,"* occurs. And finally, the heart ceases to function as a pump, becomes *"asystolic"* causing the death of the animal.

    When dogs are electrically induced to arrhythmia, the amount of current needed is greater than when they are exposed to stress factors such as overcrowding.

    To simulate human disease in dogs, Dr. Vernier has blocked the dog's coronary artery. After complete recovery he has moved the dog to a stress environment and arrhythmia was produced. This suggests that people suffering from heart disease enhance the risk of dying when living in a stressful metropolitan environment (communication by Dr. Diana L. Mendoza at ICUS 13th).

11. Ramirez, *op.cit.*, (1978 and 1984).

12. K. Lorenz, "On Aggression," (London, 1966).
    Z.J. Lipowski, "Surfeit of attractive information inputs: a hallmark of our environment," *Behavioral Sciences* 17 (1971): pp. 467-471.
    Ramirez, *op.cit.*, (1978).

13. P.G. Zimbardo, "The human choice: individuation, reason and order vs. deindividuation, impulse and chaos," in W.J. Arnold and D. Levine, eds., Nebraska Symposium on Motivation, (Lincoln, NB, 1969): pp. 237-309.

14. A. Murie, "The wolves of Mt. McKinley", Washington D.C. Government Printing Office, (1944).
    G. Southwick, et al., "Rhesus monkeys in North India," in I. DeVore, *Primate Behavior*, (New York, 1965): pp. 111-159.

15. S. Milgran, "The experience of living in cities," *Sciences* 167 (1970): pp. 1461-8.

16. P. Wyss, in this volume, Chapter 28, Article 1.

17. E.Y. Galantay, in this volume, Chapter 7, Article 2.

18. C.U. Daly, ed., *Urban Violence*, (Chicago, 1969).

19. N. Tinbergen, "Ethology in a changing world," in P.P.G. Bateson and R.A.

Hinde, eds., *Growing Points in Ethology*, (Cambridge, Mass., 1976).

20. Ramirez, *op.cit.*, (1978 and 1984).
21. K. Mueller-Ibold, in this volume, Chapter 10, Article 1.
22. J. Goldstein, *Aggression and Crimes of Violence*, (New York, 1978).
23. B.P. Dohrenwend, "Psychiatric disorder in urban setting," in S. Caplan, ed., *American Handbook of Psychiatry*, vol. 3, (New York, 1972).
    H. Strotzka, "Town planning and mental health," in Ph.P. David, *Population and Mental Health*.
24. J.P. Scott, *Aggression*, (Chicago, 1958).
25. P. Psomopoulos, in this volume, Chapter 3, Article 3.
26. J.M. Ramirez, *Einführung in die Anthropobiologie*, (Bern, 1978).
27. B.J.L. Berry, *Comparative Urbanization*, (London, 1981).
28. Lewis Mumford, *The Invisible City*, (1970). See also P. Johnson-Marshall's "Preface" in this volume.
29. R. Dubos, *Man Adapting*, (New Haven, Conn., 1965).
30. L. Valzelli, *Psychobiology of Aggression and Violence*, (New York, 1981).
31. Tinbergen, *op.cit.*
32. Psomopoulos, *op.cit.*

Additional References

Y. Booth, *Urban Crowding and Its Consequences* (New York, Praeger, 1976).
J.J. Christian, "The adreno-pituitary system and population cycles in mammals," *J. Mammalogy* 31: 247-259, 1950.
T.A. Ferrar, (ed) *The Urban Costs of Climate Modification* (New York, Wiley, 1976).
E.T. Hall, *The Hidden Dimension* (New York, Doubleday, 1966).
P. Helwig, *Charakteriologie* (Stuttgart, Erns Klett, 1965).
R.A. Hinde, *Ethology: Its Nature and Relations with Other Sciences* (New York, Oxford University Press, 1982).
H.E. Landsberg, *The Urban Climate* (New York, Academic Press, 1981).
A. McCord, *Urban Social Conflict* (Saint Louis, Mosby, 1977).
J. Peschier, *Wind and Temperature Profiles in an Urban Area* (Austin, University of Texas, 1973).
U.S. Congress "Urban unemployment: Hearing before the Sub-committee on Economic Development of the Committee on Public Works and Transportation", *97th Congress* (Government Printing Office, Washington D.C., 1982).

Part IV

Western Europe

10.

The Western European Metropolis: An Overview

Klaus Muller-Ibold

Development of the Western European Metropolis

Population and urbanization

For over three centuries, Europeans emigrated to other continents in several major waves. This emigration process has contributed considerably to a balanced western European population which has avoided overpopulation and has not produced giant metropoli. A second major factor has been the decline in birthrate since the 1960s in all these countries. The total population of Western Europe presently is 350 million. Britain, Italy, and West Germany come quite close to one another in population (roughly between 52 and 61 million) and area (between 244,000 and 301,000 sq. km.). France, similar in population (53 million), has twice the area of the other countries (547,000 sq. km.).

Urbanization in Western Europe is highly urbanized. In Britain and West Germany, approximately 80 percent of the population lives in cities. Whereas demographic developments have affected the growth rate of urbanized areas and overall population is stable or even decreasing, migration from rural to urban areas still continues.

Territory and urbanization

Western Europe is densely populated. Countries such as the Netherlands (334 inhabitants per sq. km.), Belgium (320), West Germany (249), and Britain (229) feature high-density populations. Italy (185) is above average in density, while Denmark (117) and France (100) range in the average. Sweden, Norway and Finland with less than 20 inhabitants per sq. km. feature very low densities.

Each Western European country has developed a specific urban structure —the product of centuries of history. In France, since the monarchy, Paris has emerged as the dominant urban and economic hub due to the centralization of decision-making, the national economy, and the transportation and communication networks. Recent policies to reduce this domi-

Fig. 10-1: Land use in Ile-de-France Region.

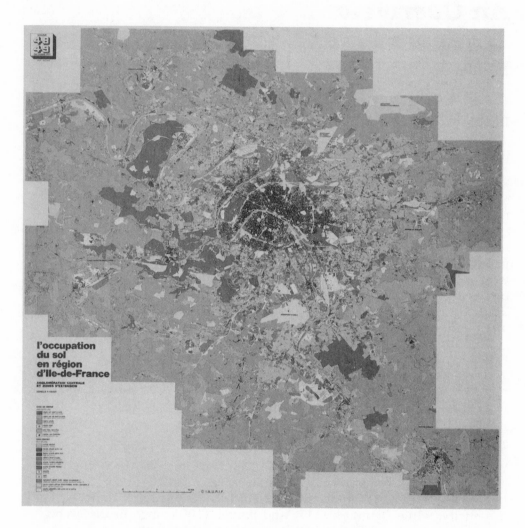

nance have produced few results thus far. (See Figure 1.) Unlike Paris, London has not impeded the development of other very large cities which have emerged largely due to the vigor of Britain's nineteenth century industrialization. Nonetheless, London's position is dominant in Britain, compared with the more dispersed urban pattern in West Germany. (See Figure 2.)

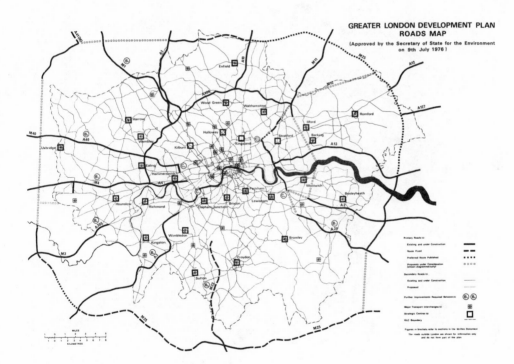

Fig. 10-2: Greater London Development Plan road map, 1976. (Courtesy: Her Majesty's Stationary Service)

Many of Italy's cities are former capitals of principalities and their role to and share in Italy's economy remain highly differentiated.

West Germany has preserved a very strong balance and diversity of urban structure. With 11 cities with more than 500,000 inhabitants and two with more than one million, West Germany is a country notable for its balanced urban distribution. (See Figure 3.) On a smaller scale, Switzerland and the Netherlands have a similarly decentralized urban system.

The emergence of the "Randstad-Holland" in the Netherlands, the growth

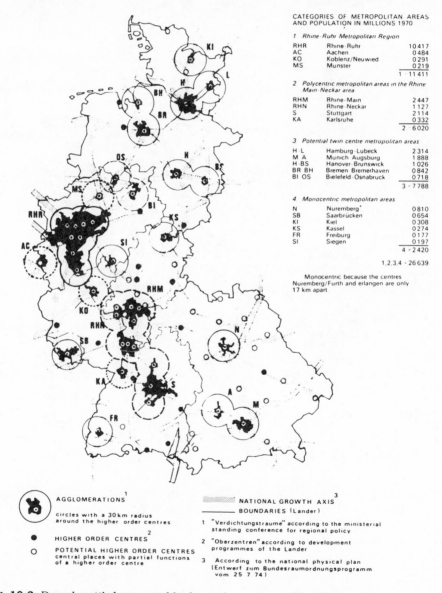

CATEGORIES OF METROPOLITAN AREAS
AND POPULATION IN MILLIONS 1970

1 Rhine-Ruhr Metropolitan Region

RHR	Rhine-Ruhr	10 417
AC	Aachen	0 484
KO	Koblenz/Neuwied	0 291
MS	Munster	0 219
		1 · 11 411

2 Polycentric metropolitan areas in the Rhine Main-Neckar area

RHM	Rhine-Main	2 447
RHN	Rhine-Neckar	1 127
S	Stuttgart	2 114
KA	Karlsruhe	0 332
		2 · 6020

3 Potential twin centre metropolitan areas

H-L	Hamburg-Lubeck	2 314
M-A	Munich-Augsburg	1 888
H-BS	Hanover-Brunswick	1 026
BR-BH	Bremen-Bremerhaven	0 842
BI-OS	Bielefeld-Osnabruck	0 718
		3 · 7 788

4 Monocentric metropolitan areas

N	Nuremberg*	0 810
SB	Saarbrücken	0 654
KI	Kiel	0 308
KS	Kassel	0 274
FR	Freiburg	0 177
SI	Siegen	0 197
		4 · 2 420

1,2,3,4 · 26 639

* Monocentric because the centres
Nuremberg/Furth and erlangen are only
17 km apart

AGGLOMERATIONS[1]
circles with a 30 km radius
around the higher order centres

● HIGHER ORDER CENTRES[2]

○ POTENTIAL HIGHER ORDER CENTRES
central places with partial functions
of a higher order centre

▨ NATIONAL GROWTH AXIS[3]
―――― BOUNDARIES (Lander)

1 "Verdichtungstraume" according to the ministerial
standing conference for regional policy

2 "Oberzentren" according to development
programmes of the Lander

3 According to the national physical plan
(Entwerf zum Bundesraumordnungsprogramm
vom 25 7 74)

Fig. 10-3: Densely settled areas and higher order centers in West Germany
(Courtesy: The Town Planning Review".)

of Antwerp, and the recent investments in northern Belgium are expressive of balanced industrialization and urban structures in the Benelux countries.

In Austria, Denmark, Finland, Norway, Portugal and Sweden, in the capital cities hold 30 percent of their populations. The remaining population is widely dispersed.

European towns of 100,000 to 500,000 inhabitants are quite evenly distributed. In Britain, France and West Germany, roughly the same population lives in a similar number of towns. France and West Germany feature 45 towns with nine million inhabitants, while Britain has 50 towns with approximately 8.5 million inhabitants.

Metropolitan urbanization

In regions with population of more than one million, a different scenario emerges:

Country	Population (millions)	Regions	Percent of total population
Britain	26.5	6	47
West Germany	16.0	7	26
France	13.2	2	25
Italy	13.2	4	23

Britain and France differ from Germany and Italy in the overriding size of their national capitals, London and Paris.

Many European metropoli have experienced stagnation or even decline in population, largely due to the loss of central functions. This trend is best exemplified by Vienna, once capital of the Holy Roman Empire then of the Austro-Hungarian Monarchy and a leading metropolis of central Europe. After World War I, with the Austro-Hungarian Monarchy dissolved, Vienna lost its function, leaving it a somewhat oversized, capital of Austria.

Similarly, the loss of colonial empires reduced or removed the central functions of cities such as London, Paris, Madrid and Lisbon. Berlin lost its function as capital of a united nation, and Hamburg its port function for the vast hinterland. Yet with the exception of Vienna, most of these cities continued to expand well into the second half of the current century.

The different patterns of urbanization and population concentration in Britain, France, West Germany and Italy are best explained by the differences in centralized and non-centralized government. Britain and France were traditionally ruled by strict central government systems. Germany and Italy, on the other hand, are rather young nations and have been formed by the union of a large number of formerly autonomous smaller states with capitals of their own.

West Germany has preserved the strong federal system. The legislative functions and financial resources of states and municipalities are protected by the federal constitution which greatly reduces the influence of the central government. To eliminate sharp fiscal disparities, revenue-sharing provides that the "poorer" states receive a portion of tax revenues from "richer" states, and "poor" municipalities from "richer" ones. Only in Switzerland is there a comparable distribution of power and resources. Such distribution of power and resources has created and continues to nurture strong local initiatives and activities as well as competent local administrations.

West Germany's industrial, management, and other decision-making centers are scattered throughout her territory. A multi-nodal financial and political structure corresponds with the decentralized concentration of industry in the 11 federal states.

West Germany's population is likewise well-distributed throughout the country. Following World War II, West Germany hosted 12 million East German refugees in the midst of war-time devastation and scarcity. These refugees poured into West Germany's villages and small- to medium-sized towns. In addition, millions of urban dwellers moved from the large cities destroyed by war into the countryside, and industries were relocated as well. Thus, towns of 10,000 to 50,000 have grown far faster than the cities of 100,000 or more since the 1940s. In the 1950s and 1960s, industry followed the population in search of labor.

During the 1950s, federal legislation mandated a remarkable program of property redistribution. Citizens paid into a public fund 10 percent of the value of their property to support all persons of German origin who had become refugees or lost property in World War II. Millions of citizens have used this fund to provide start-up capital for new activities within the small towns and villages where they have settled.

West Germany's population distribution is relatively well-stabilized, and no overriding national metropolis has emerged. Thus, there has been no need for an urgent national policy comparable to the New Towns program in Britain, as described in Dudley Leaker's article in the following chapter.

The situation in Britain, France and Italy was different. Migration in these countries was concentrated excessively in London, Paris and northern Italy. These migrations created a serious imbalance of population distribution and economic strength.

The conurbations of the Midlands, South-East England, the Benelux countries, the Western Ruhr Valley, the Rhine Valley, Switzerland and northern Italy together constitute a potential megalopolis. Offshoots of this megalopolis include the Paris region, the Eastern Ruhr Valley, and—to a lesser extent—the regions of Hamburg, Munich, Lyon-St. Etienne and Marseille-Fos.

The disparities of population distribution in Western Europe are primarily due to:

- The location of coal and mineral deposits, though less important in recent years

- The location of favorable transportation networks which is increasingly important

- The location of central government offices

Since 1945, Britain has launched a national policy, combining legislative and administrative efforts, in order to:

- Counteract the centralization of industries by the nationwide control of factory and office building
- Steer growth into desired areas, "new" and "expanding" towns
- Prevent the physical expansion of large cities, especially London, by the creation of large-scale green belts
- Improve environmental conditions by renewing the inner districts of existing large cities

Since 1945, almost 30 "new" and "expanding" towns have emerged in Britain. In addition, migration out of London to existing, smaller towns and villages has increased. In spite of successes, Britain's policies have not managed to renew the decaying urban cores. The policies have not included incentives to rehabilitate existing housing and business facilities or to attract new businesses, services and industries. The urban cores continue to lose population to the new and expanding towns.

In response, Britain has undertaken additional steps:

- To strengthen the decentralized power and financial resources of local administrations
- To create development corporations to increase urban renewal efforts in decayed areas, such as the London and Liverpool docklands
- To increase the means for modernizing existing housing stock and to encourage rehabilitation efforts
- To give higher priority to encouraging the growth of existing towns over the building of New Towns

In hindsight, it appears that the increase of local resources in Britain has been too half-hearted, and the creation of development corporations limited to spectacular rather than commonplace sites, leaving the problems of the decayed or derelict areas largely unsolved.

France, since the 1960s, has also encouraged the building of New Towns. Further, the French "departements" were transformed recently from a regional state administration into regional autonomous administrations, albeit with restricted rights and resources.

New Towns and metropolitan urbanization

Until the mid-1970s, the rapidly expanding needs for new housing predominantly shaped metropolitan development in Western Europe. These housing requirements were largely due to:

- Changes in demographic structure

- The large-scale destruction and decay of the housing stock during World War II

- Foreign immigration, including guest workers

- In the case of Germany, the in-migration of refugees from East Germany and other Eastern European countries

In Switzerland and West Germany, the distribution and development of new housing remained a cantonal and local function in the context of private initiatives within existing villages and towns.

One-sided migration in Britain and France, and even in smaller countries like Sweden, has created the need for new satellite towns. In France and Sweden, contrary to Britain, such satellite towns are not intended to be self-sufficient in terms of employment and services.

By contrast the first British New Towns were planned for a population of 30,000 to 50,000 were set at a sufficient distance from London or other major cities to assure economic independence. Today, the 14 New Towns created after World War II are well integrated within their respective regions. However, the New Towns did not stop London's growth.

Britain's second generation of 11 Expanding Towns shows a change in conception and scale. The Expanding Towns are planned to accommodate up to 400,000 inhabitants eventually, to be developed from existing towns, and to attract large-scale producing industries and some managerial functions as well.

The New Towns in France and Sweden, on the other hand, were intended to play a structuring role within highly developed regions such as Paris or Stockholm. Even the four New Towns in the French "provinces" are not intended to redistribute population, but to restructure and strengthen those provinces which already enjoyed a strong industrial base.

Non-European immigration

Many metropoli, especially in Britain, France, and West Germany and to a lesser extent in the Netherlands and Sweden, have experienced significant non-European immigration in recent decades (including Maghrebians, formerly inhabitants of western North Africa, in France; Pakistanis and West Indians in Britain; Yugoslavs and Turks in West Germany and Sweden;

Surinamese and Ambonese in Holland; and more recently Tunisians, Maltese and Lebanese in Italy). Due to economic motives, this population moved into urban rather than rural areas. Differences in religion, cultural background, and subsequent lifestyle and social behavior created stressed relations between the host population and the newcomers.

In West Germany, no less than 25 percent of the population of Frankfurt-am-Main are non-European aliens. Likewise, the Turks in West Berlin (approximately 150,000) constitute the largest community of Turks outside of Turkey.

Western Europe's leaders have tried for some time to develop policies which would foster the integration of these minorities. In the beginning, policy-makers believed that the best policy called for dispersal of the minority population throughout the country. Since the mid-1970s, however, policies tend to encourage decentralized concentrations of immigrants, recognizing that immigrants have stabilized metropolitan populations and employment in many cases.

Housing, Transportation, and the Economy

In Western Europe, the welfare of the human being is central to planning. Therefore, a high proportion of housing is now subsidized. Housing subsidies have become a major problem in budgetary policies. Subsequently, subsidies have been and will continue to be reduced considerably. The situation is worth remembering with reference to the housing needs and financial means available in developing countries.

Rents in West Germany have increased significantly, requiring increased personal subsidies. Even with personal subsidies, many more families are being forced to move to less expensive housing. Compounding the problem is the fact that West Germany lacks substantial amounts of older housing stock with very low rents. West German cities lost 20 to 30 percent of their housing stock due to wartime destruction. These losses occurred primarily in the core of the cities, where buildings were old and therefore rents lower.

The loss of inexpensive, older housing also has a slowly emerging positive side, as the housing stock to be maintained in the inner cities is relatively new. This means that, in West Germany, the cost of maintenance of an average unit is lower than in most other industrialized countries.

In Britain, fixed rents, strict housing regulations, high interest rates and taxation have "overburdened" the broad mass of old housing. The state of maintenance in vast areas of Britain's cities is therefore poor. In both Britain and West Germany, and in most other European countries, the standards for new housing—and for the modernization of old houses—are too high. A number of countries, therefore, are carefully reviewing and revising existing standards.

In the post-war period, Western European countries have constructed unparalleled quantities of high quality housing. The following table illustrates this boom in housing construction from 1964 to 1973 (peak years of production):

Country	Millions of units	Number per year
Britain	3.8	383,000
France	4.4	440,000
Italy	3.1	310,000
West Germany	5.8	580,000

These figures imply that Western Europe will face a corresponding peak of general maintenance and rehabilitation costs for housing in the 1990s which will have a considerable impact on housing policies.

Although never in European history has the population been better housed, housing conditions are not fully satisfactory. In industrialized countries, approximately 3.6 persons lived in one dwelling unit before World War II, while today the average unit is occupied by only 2.1 persons. This means that, whereas before the war 280,000 dwelling units accommodated one million inhabitants, today 470,000 (!) units are needed to house the same one million persons. This also means that, due to the increased area required for housing, the inner cores of the cities lost considerably more population due to structural changes than any other cause. This also has resulted in a significant increase in daily transportation distances (and time) for the population.

Transportation

Telecommunications experts foresee that workplaces will be decentralized to such an extent in the future that a large proportion of the employed population will work out of the home. This trend, might reduce some of the city's traffic congestion and financial needs.

New technologies for mass transportation are no panacea. To date, no such device has effectively replaced (or even significantly reduced) reliance upon the individual automobile and the existing public transportation system. For example, in West Germany, since 1960 at least 12 cities with populations of 400,000 or more have invested tremendous sums in rapid transit systems which will not be abandoned before they are fully amortized.

One factor, which strongly affects the structural development of public transport, is the reduced number of inhabitants per dwelling unit. Before World War II, 360,000 citizens occupied 100,000 dwelling units. Today those 100,000 units accommodate only 210,000 inhabitants. The daily transportation needs of the working population can be considered the backbone of public transportation systems. The decreasing density within a district also means a drop in the working population—in this example, a drop from 170,000 to 100,000—which results in a severe loss of user potential for public transportation.

For a short period in Western Europe, planners tried to compensate for the declining inhabitants/dwelling unit trend by advocating higher building densities. However, several factors led planners to impose certain limits on housing density which currently allow a maximum floor-area-ratio (FAR) of 0.8 to 1.0 in Northern Europe and 1.0 to 2.0 in the Mediterranean countries. Obviously, these density levels will not compensate for the reduced number of inhabitants per dwelling unit.

Industries and services

During recent decades, mechanization and automation of industries demanded one-level production procedures and subsequently more physical plant space. Therefore, industries search for locations in the outlying regions of the cities. Old production sites in the inner core were abandoned and seldom rehabilitated for other uses due to the expense. This created a new kind of "urban erosion" in industrial and mixed-use areas of the older cities. With no new users in sight, such derelict areas have persistently expanded to consume larger and larger portions of the cities. Urban erosion of this kind has plagued British metropoli more than any other, as Britain's industrial infrastructure is the oldest and most outdated in Europe.

Smaller, tertiary industries automatically tend to concentrate in city centers. As office space requirements have grown, businesses have moved into these tertiary industrial areas, creating tremendous pressure on the city center and reducing or eliminating mixed-use and housing areas within the city center.

Types of Metropoli

As John Dyckman points out in his article, the dominant economic structure of the metropolis strongly influences its macroform and physical environment.

The multi-centered metropolis

The multi-centered metropolis is characterized by several large and almost equally strong cities, complemented by a number of smaller towns which have grown to form a large conurbation. Originally, many of these incipient metropoli developed at the sites of coal or mineral deposits. Outstanding examples of this pattern are the British Midlands or West German Ruhr

Valley. Within such regions, three problems predominate:

1. Heavy industries are still intermixed with housing.

2. The "industrial erosion zones" of such regions provoke the decay of adjacent residential or mixed-use quarters.

3. Organizing, operating and maintaining a public transportation system in such very large, but decentralized, conurbations has become extremely difficult due to the scattered physical structure of such regions, the effect of the "erosion zones," and the general drop in population density.

While the Ruhr Valley and the Midlands are dominated by the secondary sector, a new kind of multi-centered conurbation has emerged in the case of the "Randstad Holland," where manufacturing no longer plays the dominant role

The multi-centered metropoli of Europe therefore have two main physical configurations:

1. The multi-centered grid structure such as the Ruhr Valley of West Germany

2. The multi-centered linear structure such as the Randstad Holland

The mono-centered metropolis

This type of metropolis is dominated by the tertiary and quarternary sectors which developed in the same neighborhoods in city centers and thus created a mono-nuclear configuration. Most national capitals are of this kind. Usually these metropoli also have a considerable amount of modern industrial development. These regions suffer from the following problems:

- A too-high concentration of working places in the city centers, which generate traffic congestion, severe environmental and life-style disturbances, and high development pressure on land use

- The continuing expansion of the tertiary and quarternary sectors, which have grown faster than the secondary sector in recent decades

- Pressure on housing in areas adjacent to the city center

The situation is changing again, as automation has begun to intrude upon the tertiary sector. This could mean that, in the future, the number of workplaces in such regions is likely to decrease.

The mono-centered metropoli of Western Europe have two primary physical configurations:

- The ring-structure such as Paris and London

- The radial-axis or finger-structure such as in Hamburg

Tertiary expansion in such metropoli threatens to destroy the social and cultural function and the historical tissue of the city centers, including valuable housing areas.

Administration and the Metropolis

Strategic development action

Previous sections of this paper demonstrate that administration must continually adapt its role, approach to solutions, management methods, and techniques of administering the metropolis. The efficiency of planning and its transformation into reality stand and fall with the ability of public administration to act and react.

During recent decades, the classical exercise of sovereign administrative jurisdiction has changed to one of strategic development operation and action within public administration. When the first European conurbations began to grow rapidly, planning philosophy was based on the principle that private enterprise alone could bring about a sufficient system of physical order. Public authorities would attend mainly to overt threats to rational land use and the needs of the population. In the context of growth, increasing complexity of social development forced public authorities to widen their scope of activities. In physical planning, the first step in this direction was the introduction of land-use plans, covering the entire area of a town or city. However, until World War II, such planning merely defined guidelines for future land-use, when such areas would be ready for development. It did not plan in a strategic manner the timing for development.

Broadening the scope of administrative action appeared after the war, first in Britain and Sweden and later in the other countries. Increasing attention has been paid to:

- The structure and function of urbanization

- Its social and economic needs and potentials

- The related areas of land-use and investment goals

Following this analysis, concepts and programs were increasingly developed in a more comprehensive way. Since then, medium-term financial and investment planning frequently have been applied to spatial planning. In post-war development, planning administration gradually became part of a multi-dimensional system of decision-making, which strongly differs from traditional administration. New methods have evolved, a task which was made more difficult by the simultaneous increase in the demand for public participation. Presently in large West German cities, the biggest land agency is the city administration itself, active on a broad scale to ensure the transformation of plans and programs into reality by means of a promotional land policy and day-to-day land purchasing and selling.

Subsidies and other incentives

Plans are only of value if they are transformed into reality. Local authorities must take action to ensure the coordination of public infrastructure measures.

The various districts of a metropolis differ strongly in their quality due to age, location, and structure. Infrastructure deficits of districts, especially in the inner core, vary considerably—some having a deficit in educational infrastructure, others in social, technical, or service infrastructure. During the past decade, municipalities have begun to try to balance the varying qualities by district-specific improvement programs, in slums *and* in areas on the verge of becoming slums. Western European countries have increasingly implemented state financial provisions and subsidies explicitly connected with urban renewal and modernization of housing to support such municipal policies. Within such a guideline of municipal policy, a framework for public and private investment areas has been developed, especially in high priority areas such as the inner core. Such improvement areas usually are not expected to remain priority areas in the long term. As soon as public intervention has created a reasonable standard of facilities, buildings and environment in one area, another area will be designated as a priority location for public and private efforts.

Due to the lack of maintenance during World Wars I and II, the immediate post-war periods and the world economic crises, the total environment of buildings, housing, blocks and districts must be improved by measures of basic renovation and rehabilitation.

Public—especially municipal—financial resources began to shrink in the late 1970s. In response, Hamburg, for example, designated special improvement areas and created a series of small investments designed as a "program of small steps in district development."

Increasingly, major public infrastructures were planned not only to serve their own function but also to assist special improvement areas in their district development. In Hamburg, for instance, a new public rapid transit line serves six such improvement areas with its stations. Similarly, Hamburg sited a new technical university in a special improvement area (rather than in an undeveloped area), on former industrial lands, to create a nucleus for new economic impulses, and created a new center of five professional schools in another of these areas for the same reasons.

Identity of areas of planning and administration

Several municipalities must coordinate their policies to assure harmonious regional development. For example, in 1965 the installment of the Greater London Council replaced the London County Council (LCC), founded in 1889. Prior to this, only 30 of the roughly 90 boroughs which were part of the Greater London region fell within the administration of the LCC.

In West Germany, the Ruhr Valley Council, the country's first regional body, was founded in 1920 as a corporation of the Ruhr Valley municipalities. Other regional agencies were created after World War II, including Frankfurt, Hannover, and Mannheim-Ludwigshafen. Such regional administrative bodies achieved remarkable results in coordinating regional tasks such as public transportation, water supply, sewerage, green belts, and irrigation. Clearly, individual municipalities could not have achieved such high-quality results alone.

In very recent years in Britain and West Germany, there is a tendency by national and state governments to weaken or dissolve regional planning bodies. Perhaps it is too soon to comment on the results of such a trend. Nevertheless, observation and comparison suggest that decentralization plays a major role in preventing the rise of giant metropoli. Metropolitan bodies (with the necessary statutory and administrative powers) should be created or strengthened, as instruments of decentralization.

General Conclusions

This paper will offer general conclusions about aspects of the European metropolis which might have some relevance for future development of metropoli outside Europe. However, major differences between Europe and developing countries must be taken into consideration.

In Western Europe, large metropoli developed over a period of many decades. In developing countries, metropoli of previously unimagined size have emerged within a very few years. Metropoli in developing countries grow not only through migration but also through a higher-than-average birth rate within their own populations. Europe has never experienced comparable growth, as its population was periodically decimated by war or disease, by large-scale emigration to other continents, and by the current lower-than-average birth rate.

Not growth, but maintenance and modernization of the existing infrastructure and the spread of new communication techniques, will be the principal issues of development in Western Europe. By contrast, in Third World countries, in addition to rapid growth, mass poverty will determine all policies, and programs. The lack of a general and reliable social security system contributes to the continuing high birth rates and related poverty— as poverty requires family "insurance" in the form of many children!

Western Europeans who have become dependent upon technical services cannot live without reliable water, electricity and sewerage supplies. However, such services will only be provided to buildings erected in compliance with formal zoning and building code requirements which permit control of urban expansion. In developing countries, the peasant, having moved to the metropolis, is still willing to walk a mile to a public well for water-supply, to use an oil lamp, and to disappear behind the bushes for certain personal needs. His television set is battery-operated. Little can be done to prevent people from building their primitive shelters at the edge of the metropolis in developing countries. Lacking the means to enforce formal development, it seems rather academic to try to fix optimum or maximum sizes for metropoli. With this proviso, the following set of guidelines can apply to metropolitan cities both in Western Europe and in market-economy countries of the Third World.

Measures of the metropolitan and local levels

General

Statutory and administrative metropolitan bodies should be created. Such a body should not represent central government, but rather the respective municipalities.

The quality of living conditions is basically defined by the social, cultural and economic needs and wants of the individual citizen which reflect a great range of variety. Further, the individual citizen's needs and wants will change throughout his lifespan. Therefore, a choice of living qualities of a wide range should be offered in a diversity of environmental settings.

Human settlements must strive to create and maintain a human scale. Experiences of recent decades indicate that high-rise buildings dehumanize their inhabitants. The slogan "low-rise, high-density" promotes the goal of human scale development.

Existing structures and buildings should be maintained and utilized, as they provide a reference to history.

A comprehensive concept combining public transportation corridors with a central places system, including guidelines for land-use and building densities, should be introduced on the metropolitan level as a framework for sectorial and local plans and programs.

Industries

A central places system helps a metropolis to develop a framework for the distribution of basic services. Such a system should be hierarchal and should determine the location of non-local services.

Big and disturbing industries will need to find their own specific locations, but small-scale industries with a service character should be permitted to locate in central places.

Housing

The provision of adequate shelter is a primary goal. It is not the technical quality or the standard of equipment that is most important, but rather:

- adequate room for at least limited privacy and family development, including the aged.

- an environment, providing places for social contact, especially for children and the elderly.

- location with reasonably good access to social and cultural services, especially health and education.

- location with good access to public or semi-public transportation.

Citizens should be offered a choice in housing in terms of difference in age, standard, location, size and rent, so as to enable them to find a home in accordance with their preferences and financial means.

- New neighborhoods should not be uniform. The citizen should be able to identify himself with his environment due to its individuality.

- Housing districts should be developed in such a way as to avoid a negative image.

- Qualitative improvement of the environment should be accorded priority.

- New housing, modernization and maintenance of older housing are complementary and not as alternatives.

- Maintenance of housing should regain its normal character as a permanent, private-sector activity.

- Modernization of housing should receive limited subsidies as stimulus and to temporarily retard the subsequent increase in rents.

- Minimum standards in housing are necessary, yet there is no need to set them extraordinarily high.

- Burdens of rents on one side and of subsidies on the other should create a balance in the community. It is the prime duty of political leaders to communicate the importance of adequate shelter to all members of the community.

Transportation

Opposition to private automobiles, and more particularly to the roads, is growing in Europe. In the context of the comprehensive metropolitan concept, transportation policies should be based on the following principles:

- Mobility is characteristic of and indispensable for modern society.

- Wants of commuters for unlimited use of their private cars cannot be met, especially for environmental reasons.

- The quantitative needs of services should be the major criterion for the sizing of the road system and of short-term parking facilities.

- The through-traffic in residential areas must be reduced parallel to the creation of environmental zones.

- Relieving residential areas from through-traffic results in further concentration of traffic on main roads. Along such main roads lives a non-negotiable proportion of citizens. These citizens are often among the socially and economically underprivileged in the society.

- This effect calls for relief of main roads by the means of by-passing expressways. The imposition of tolls on these expressways reduces their efficiency.

- The size and density of city centers and subcenters that generate traffic must be limited. To avoid pressure of tertiary activities on residential areas, zones for such uses must be offered in central places.

- Absolute priority must be assigned to the development of the public transportation system. A rapid transit network, complemented by a suburban train system and a connecting bus-lines network, is essential. Such a system must include interchanges at train stations and a park-and-ride system, all coordinated by a metropolitan transportation authority.

Environment

During the past decade, Western Europe has focused increasing attention on the care for the environment. This is best illustrated by the creation of departments, authorities, and ministries of environment on all levels of government in many countries.

In many countries of Western Europe, environmental conservation enjoys a substantial tradition. The green-belts in Britain or the green-zones of the Ruhr Valley are the result of planning action taken at a time when the public was not yet very environmentally conscious.

Many European metropoli are located on bodies of water providing access to cheap transportation. Such water facilities have long lost their original function. Even large cities located in the inner zones of the continent such as Paris, Cologne, and London have large-scale port facilities. Some of these cities have made strong and systematic use of their waterfront resources in combination with free and greenspace zones. A good example is the nineteenth century artificial Alster Lake Project in Hamburg (see Figure 4), which inspired the city of Boston to create the Charles River Project.

Closing remarks

Post-war urban development policies in Western Europe have been frequently criticized, with claims that policy priorities have been assigned disjointedly. Three main phases can be identified:

- Urban reconstruction in the 1940s and 1950s

- Urban expansion in the 1950s and 1960s

- Urban regeneration which has occurred mainly since the mid-1970s

In general, this has been a plausible sequence. Post-war conditions required the identification of priorities accompanied by the temporary neglect of less urgent needs. A "balanced" policy would not have been possible during this time period.

With the widespread completion of major reconstruction and expansion in the 1970s, a more normalized development pattern emerged. The present "third phase" of policies is therefore more balanced than the previous two. Thus, the present emphasis on the regeneration of existing city centers is to be understood as complementary to urban expansion rather than a new alternative.

Urban policies in Western Europe are now part of a balanced, multi-dimensional process involving continuous maintenance, reproduction and new production of urban substance with the primary goal of safeguarding the already existing, high-quality, built environment.

With close to two million inhabitants, Hamburg can serve as an example of the ecologically friendly city of just the "right size."

The view is taken toward the Southwest. In the foreground is the Alster Lake created by damming a river. An arc of green trees marks the line of the fortifications which encircled a town of less than three sq. km. until the mid-nineteenth century.

Beyond the green arc are the suburb of St. Pauli, the Northern Elbe River, and, on its south bank, the port and shipyards. In the distance is the horizon of the Atlantic.

Fig. 10-4: Oblique aerial view of Hamburg. (Stuttgarter Luftbild Elsaber GambH) With close to 2 million inhabitants, Hamburg can serve as an example of the ecologically friendly city of just the "right size." The view is taken toward the south-west. In the foreground the Alster Lake, created by damming a river. An arc of trees marks the line of the fortifications which encircled a town of less than 3 square kilometers until the mid-19th century. Beyond the arc is the suburb of St. Pauli, the Northern Elbe river, and on its south bank the port and shipyards. In the distance is the horizon of the Atlantic Ocean.

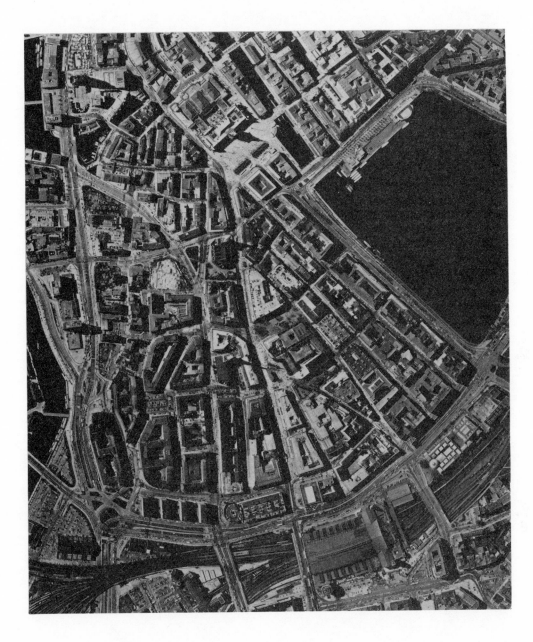

Fig. 10-5: The Hamburg CBD. About 1 square kilometer area densely built up with office buildings. Scale: 1 centimeter = 60 meters. (Institut fur Angewandte Godasie permit NR 847/82)

11.

Decentralization: The Lessons of the British New Towns Policy

Dudley Leaker

In 1950 there were only six cities with a population of a million or more, and their combined population was 44 million. By the year 2000 this number will rise to 60 cities with an estimated population of nearly 650 million. 45 cities with more than five million inhabitants will be in the less developed countries" . . . (Draper Fund Report)

Against the enormity of such predictions, one cannot but feel helpless and totally inadequate. In this short paper, I will relate my comment and opinions to my own 40 years of experience in the planning, designing and implementation of various British New Towns. (Perhaps, more importantly I have lived with my family in these new communities over that period as well.) I am very aware that the problems faced in Britain are quite different from those of the less developed countries, and therefore the experience gained in the British New Towns Program must be seen in context. The following are some relevant questions to ask:

- What is the role of New Towns with respect to the metropolis?

- Can New Towns serve to restrain the growth of the metropolis?

- Can New Towns serve to revitalize decaying "grey areas" within the metropolis?

- Were such goals explicit or implicit in the British New Towns policy?

- What experiences can be passed on to developing countries?

- How successful was the British New Towns policy in restraining the growth of the metropolis (London, Glasgow, etc.)?

- How successful was the British New Towns policy in revitalizing decaying areas or derelict land within the metropolis (Merseyside, Runcorn, Glasgow)?

- What is the potential for the use of the Development Corporation mechanism in other than the New Towns context (i.e., London Docklands)?

More than 70% of Britain's people live in towns and cities of more than 100,000 population. Of greater significance is the fact that nearly 20 million people, or 36% of the population, live in the eight conurbations—clusters of separate cities, towns and villages, which have coalesced into continuous urban areas or metropoli. Each of these metropoli support a constellation of lesser towns and villages, and provide opportunities for work and a principal focus for department stores, specialist shops, theatres, concerts and other cultural facilities. Together, the eight conurbations and the catchment areas form recognizable city regions and metropoli in which 60% of Britain's people live and work. The largest by far is the London Metropolitan Region in which 12.3 million people live. Within the core areas of the conurbation and other large cities, especially those in the northern half of Britain, are concentrated most of the nation's sub-standard houses and tenements, a legacy from the nineteenth century. These must be demolished and replaced by modern homes, with more space for recreation, schools and areas for leisure activities which have become essentials for modern living. These interventions will reduce housing density and, at the same time, also the population capacity of the renewed areas resulting in the need for town extensions or the reconversion of derelict sites for housing purposes on a considerable scale.

On the national scale, an imbalance in terms of economic strength and prosperity and in the quality of the urban environment exists between the southern half of England and the older industrial regions of the rest of England, Scotland and Wales. For this reason the opportunities for change by active intervention are the greatest in the decaying, derelict, and economically lagging pockets of these areas. On the other hand, the London region—which contains the nation's largest concentration of modern industries, commercial, governmental and other public organizations—also provides opportunities for the upgrading of the quality of the environment, due to the very dynamism of the area which is attracting investment capital from both national and international sources.

Planning Policies Since 1945

In an attempt to deal with these problems and trends, Britain has, since 1945, pursued certain major policy objectives and set up programs to pursue these policies:

Fig. 11-1: The Greater London Metropolitan area. Landsat image. (ICUS XVIII)

1. A national policy to control new factory and office building. The location of factory development, until recently, has been controlled by the government in an effort to inject as much new industrial growth as possible into the old industrial regions or so-called development areas. Generous financial aid is offered as an inducement.

2. A major policy to conserve land and to secure the proper planning of development and of urban redevelopment. Regional plans and studies are prepared for areas such as the Clyde Valley, Greater London and the South East, giving a context to more detailed planning. The 1947 Town & Country Planning Act and successive acts made the local authorities responsible for preparing and reviewing critical plans to guide, to promote and to regulate all development and redevelopment in their

157

areas. As a result, development has been better located, better related to central services, and far less wasteful of land than in the inter-war years. Ribbon development along roads has been stopped. Unplanned and sporadic building has been prevented, and advertisement boards banned outside the towns and cities. The preservation of countryside around the conurbations of large cities has been achieved with the creation of "Green Belts" to limit urban spread and to prevent physical expansion of the conurbations, a most successful program.

3. The program to build New Towns and to plan small country towns to which industry, commerce and people could be attracted from the overgrown and overcrowded cities. New Towns were, to a large extent, intended to decongest existing metropolitan areas by creating semi-independent communities with their own employment, shopping, social and cultural facilities to cater to the surplus population. These New Towns, and later cities of up to 200,000 people, created counter-magnets to the growth in the conurbations. It is generally thought that they have been successful, some think too successful in this particular objective. However, with the current economic situation and the falling birth rate, the need for further New Towns in Britain has disappeared. Further, a change in political attitudes currently insists that major development work should be predominantly privately financed.

4. A complementary objective to clear large slum areas and to renew the inner city areas themselves.

New Towns

The new and expanding towns are therefore an essential feature of a four-part policy for Britain's great cities, city regions and metropoli. Some of these policies have been more successful than others.

The New Towns of Britain have been developed in a very different economic, political and climatic context from conditions in Third World countries. Britain is a small, overcrowded island where comprehensive planning legislation and New Towns are a preferred alternative to suburban sprawl. In developing countries, however, there is a greater need for development to accommodate rapid population growth. This development occurs in an atmosphere of limited planning legislation, less effective development control systems, and a limited number of locally-produced technicians, professionals and administrators. It is thought that developing countries could learn useful lessons from the relative weakness of non-executive regional planning in Britain, and thereby develop much more effective regional planning policies to support New Town development.

According to Prof. Walter Bor ("Reflections about Planning New Towns," 1979), the 40-year-old British New Town development corporations have proven to be successful executive bodies in planning and building New Towns. Increasingly developing countries are adopting this model, albeit with appropriate modifications to suit local circumstances for the planning and implementation of their own New Town programs.

The expeditive assembly of land is a critical factor common to all major development work. The public acquisition of land required for the development of New Towns, at existing land values, is essential for a realistic program. Where land must be acquired from many private owners, such land acquisition should precede, or at least coincide with, the publication of plans for New Towns in order to avoid land speculation. A thorough development brief for New Towns must state explicit goals and objectives and establish clear criteria for the selection of alternative strategies, design concepts and the organization of infrastructure and services. In developing countries, most practitioners find that briefs must include specific references to the informal sector of the economy and squatter housing. Some realistic and pragmatic lessons learned from the British New Town experience might interest those facing even greater problems of rapid large-scale urban and metropolitan expansion. The following are just a few examples.

- The need for a national and regional context and affecting national policies, outlining the preferred locations of industry and employment, and the provision of transportation and communications. To be successful major planning projects and major development on this scale must secure stable, multi-partisan political support. Also, the legal framework for the development should attract multi-partisan support so that private, as well as public or government interests, support the program.

- Any plan, especially a New Town plan, should be a basic plan only: it must provide a broad, flexible framework. A program is the main device and means of concentrating the energies of all the involved agencies. The plans themselves should be prepared by multi-disciplinary professional teams which include indigenous experts with local knowledge, and professionals who will see the scheme through to its implementation. Wherever possible, there should be continuing public consultation. The inhabitants actually create the town and its community: their support is essential. The plan must concentrate responsibility for the construction of as many community facilities as possible with one agency.

- One of the objectives of the British New Towns policy was to "draw off" population from the over-populated areas. This objective has been achieved, far too successfully in the view of some. Some have argued that the program has impoverished the inner areas of cities such as London and Liverpool and has reduced their employment and commercial facilities. Some have criticized the New Towns for attracting the best of the inner city's people, including the young and skilled adults. These criticisms are not substantiated. Further, there has undoubtedly been a natural migration to the suburbs from inner city areas, quite independent of New Towns. The renewal of cities and their centers, which is a part of the four-part national policy, has not yet taken place.

Although there are no more New Town proposals and the political emphasis has recently been shifted to privately financed development, development corporations have been set up in the dockland areas of London and Liverpool. Professor Gosling (Paper, I.F.H.P. Conference, 1984) cites the creation of the London Docklands Development Agency in 1980 which subsequently became the London Docklands Development Corporation in 1981. In 40 years the New Towns had provided homes for more than one million people and, just as importantly, had provided much-needed industrial growth and employment opportunities. In both London and Liverpool, the city docks were made obsolete by revolutionary changes in container cargos. The economic revitalization of Liverpool and the eastern sector of London was seen as politically and socially important.

Professor Gosling found an important difference between the New Town development corporations and the proposed London Docklands Development Corporation. The New Town development corporations were not only the planning authority for the designated area, but also the design and implementation authority for the subsequent construction. Conversely, the London Docklands Development Corporation was not granted powers of implementation which, for political and economic reasons, were reserved for the private sector. This factor has contributed to the less than satisfactory overall planning policy in this inner city.

Nonetheless, these new development corporations are instigating development, attracting industry, and generally acting as catalysts. Their marketing and commercial aggressiveness in particular is achieving results.

The Relevance of the British New Town Policy for the Third World

The British New Town Program has gained much experience which, in my view, could be applied to other areas of accelerated urban development. Of course, British or European New Towns must not be taken as patterns to be arbitrarily copied, and local conditions will always impose their own over-riding influences.

British New Towns performed their primary functions and, to a large extent, met their goals. Paramount among these goals were those to provide new growth points and to help limit and control the expansion to existing metropoli. But, as one part of a four-party policy, the New Towns were never thought to be answers in themselves to rapid urbanization and its problems. But they were important elements in the British National Plan.

Those of us living in the industrialized countries can so easily be complacent and ignorant of the realities of expanding metropolitan and urban development elsewhere. The industrialized countries comprise only 25% of the world's population, and urbanization for us is mainly a middle class phenomenon. Middle-income people are mobile, own cars and show an increasing preference for living in smaller towns, including New Towns and less dense areas in the suburbs. In the less developed countries, slum and squatter settlements increase at twice the speed of the urban population and at four times the speed of overall population increases (Habitat, Nairobi, 1984). The poor, who are the majority of those affected in the developing areas of the world, face a bleak future. As pressures on the urban areas increase, the drive for self preservation and human nature being what they are, the attitudes of the "haves" could harden towards the "have nots" and vice versa, creating serious social unrest and untold misery. As urbanization accelerates in many countries, solutions such as subsidized mass housing become hopelessly inadequate and insufficiently funded in the face of declining financial resources. If disaster is to be averted, plans of action must be formulated which are realistic, pragmatic and immediate. Any relevant experience which can be applied or can help in any way should be made available wherever it is needed.

References

1. Frederick J. Osborn and Arnold Whittick, *New Towns: The Answer to Megalopolis*, (London: Leonard Hill, 1977).
2. Walter Bor, *The Making of Cities*, (London: Leonard Hill, 1972).
3. Ervin Y. Galantay, "New Towns from Antiquity to Present," 1975 Braziller, New York.
4. Dudley Leaker, "Chairman's Introduction," E. Galantay & H. Hague (eds.) "New Towns in National Development." Report of the Working Party on New Towns (The Hague: IFHP, 1980).
5. A. Constandse, E. Galantay & T. Ohba (eds.) "New Towns World-Wide" (The Hague: IFHP, 1985.
6. David Gosling, "The Application of New Town Planning Systems to the London Docklands," in "New Towns World-Wide" (The Hague: IFHP, 1985).
7. Dudley Leaker, "The Experience of the British Towns," Proceedings of the International Seminar on New Towns, Japanese Ministry of Construction, Tokyo, Japan, 1986.

12.

A View from the Randstad

Adriaan Constandse

Introduction

At the end of the nineteenth century, Europe was the most urbanized part of the world. Now, the largest metropolitan areas are found outside Europe, and the fastest growth is observed in a number of developing countries. Apparently, the urbanization processes in developing countries are different from those which created the European urban pattern. They are so different in fact that some believe that the study of European urban development has little relevance to planning the future metropolis. This is not my point of view. I believe that to understand the history of urban development is of utmost importance to the quality of urban planning throughout the world.

Europe's Experience

Europe should be studied as a whole because its history of urban settlement and development is so varied. Urbanization in socialist countries may require separate study; however, the cities of Eastern Europe are older than socialism and very European in character. Cities were formed in the course of time for many reasons. Those varied reasons created many different types of cities and an irregular pattern of dispersal and concentration. In time, processes of growth and decline emerge to reflect changing political powers and the development and depletion of resources.

In ancient times, cities emerged and sometimes disappeared, leaving only ruins such as Troy, Carthage and Ephesos. Later, destroyed and declining cities were generally rebuilt in the same location, perhaps using the existing infrastructure. In modern times, the physical structures and built areas represent a huge investment, and thus, existing urban areas tend to remain in use even when the original functions lose significance and the physical structures are reconstructed.

Built *by* people, cities have an influence *on* people. On the one hand, cities absorb and diffuse change and foster the growth of a world culture with many common traits. On the other hand, the older European cities conserve the local, regional or national culture. Often, this latter process is neglected in urban studies.

While Europe is largely composed of nation-states, notwithstanding the federation of smaller states and the creation of political and economic communities, it is an area of diverse cultures. The large number of moderately-sized cities is attributable to the absence of large, centralized states until recent times in most parts of Europe. In fact, only two European cities can be considered as giant metropoli, namely, London and Paris. It is difficult to judge whether the large, centralized states emerged so late (as in the cases of Italy and Germany) due to the older patterns of small urban centers, or whether these patterns remained intact due to the absence of centralized states.

Of course, changes in political boundaries have influenced the development processes. For example, if the Austro-Hungarian Monarchy still existed, then perhaps Vienna, Bratislawa and Budapest would have united to form a single metropolis by now. On the other hand, Spain's capital is an isolated big city, and a constellation of other strong urban centers is found dispersed throughout the country. In a number of cases, the strong regional identity of these centers leads to tension.

One should look for common traits in studying the European town, although there are many differences. The Netherlands, one of the most densely populated countries in the world, is often selected to illustrate the relation between the degree of urbanization and population density. Western Germany is far larger and less densely populated. Yet the state of Nordrhein-Westfalen—though smaller than the Netherlands—has a larger population. Sweden has a very low density, but it is certainly not a rural country.

The densely populated Benelux countries have no big cities, while Denmark, Austria and Hungary have an oversized capital with respect to their national urban system. As an extreme example in Greece, almost half of the total population lives in the Athens region.

Special maps have been drawn which eliminate national boundaries to reveal Europe as a series of dense zones, such as the It-Brit axis, stretching from the south of Britain to the north of Italy. It has been suggested that this zone reflects a socio-economic-spatial system, yet it spans seven different countries, at least five languages, different development levels, and various types of government and trade.

Even on a smaller scale, one must interpret maps cautiously. The Dutch Randstad or Greenheart Metropolis, with its six million inhabitants, is among the largest population concentrations in the world. However, the structure of this metropolis differs significantly from that of a city like Paris. Within dense networks of communication, the metropolis can be considered as a system and as a kind of unity. But many relatively small towns, all less than one million in population and most smaller than 200,000, can be observed within the metropolitan system. In addition, there are significant amounts of open land reserved for recreation and also for agriculture. Thus, although many Europeans live in vast urbanized systems, most live in physical structures or systems which they experience as relatively small places.

Nevertheless, the stagnation and decline experienced by the metropolis in the industrialized countries is also manifest in smaller urban areas. This process is often described as an urban exodus and a dangerous phenomenon. Yet, for the most part, it is a healthy decrease in the city's density or the average number of people per dwelling. In the nineteenth century, the countryside was not "depopulated" but rather, relieved of overpopulation by the growth of the cities. Similarly, today the overpopulated urban areas are relieved by out-migration.

The problem is not so much that the central cities are losing inhabitants, but that the migration is selective, leaving the poor, the young, the old and the socially deviant in town. This is obviously a problem for urban management, and if not contained, a threat to the city's existence. However, out-migration can also stimulate the search for better solutions to the inequity among population groups. New ideas about space-time budgets and about the integration and segregation of age and status groups are likely to emerge.

The Urban-Suburban System

For Europeans, the center, the "downtown," is where the action is. This urbanity can exist only on the basis of a large number of people supporting such a center; activities of the highest order require millions of people. The problem is that most people in the metropolis do not and cannot live in the center, while the vast residential areas around the center are not regarded as very attractive. Many, probably most, people would like to live in semi-urban/rural environments. Yet this does not mean that these people are willing to lose contact with the center city.

Perhaps if planners would abandon the ideal of balanced urban/suburban communities as a goal, both urban and suburban needs could be better met. Young people tend to prefer living downtown; young couples prefer to raise their children in green and quiet suburbs, new towns or rural villages; the old choose to live in either setting. This implies that mobility is a positive force—mobility of residence over time as well as daily mobility among residence, workplace, services and recreation.

For many planners, it is difficult to accept the concept of mobility as a positive one. Mobility, after all, creates traffic, consumes energy, pollutes the environment, and contributes to the deterioration of the landscape. These disadvantages should not be dismissed, for they pose serious problems. Nevertheless, the efforts to reduce mobility and promote higher densities in the inner city will not alone significantly improve the quality of life in urban environments. This is not to suggest that urban sprawl is acceptable. People *should* live in concentrations of the size that permits public transportation systems to operate effectively and discourages the use of the private automobile in commuting to work. Likewise, it is important to channel the traffic in corridors in order to preserve the open countryside between the urban areas.

In Europe, several examples of urbanized regions can be found where many people live in moderately-sized cities and small settlements. In addition to the Netherlands which has been mentioned already, the Swiss Mittelland is another example. The Mittelland, stretching north of the Alps from Geneva to St. Gallen, has four to five million inhabitants and no single major city. Many people live near or virtually *in* the countryside, and urban facilities are close by. This provides many opportunities for people to maintain and create differentiated environments for living. As a growing number of people do not work or work part-time, and as tele-communication technologies improve, this mixing of town and country offers a successful alternative to the model of compact metropolitan development.

Unfortunately, as population shifts to smaller settlements, derelict areas in older cities are not redeveloped or renovated. The erosion of the older cities is a major, but probably temporary, problem. With concerted efforts, such as the New Towns program in Britain, cities can probably be revitalized.

The City as A Gathering Place

It is crucial that the city center is lively and attractive and that it is visited by many people often. That many people *use* the city center is even more important than that many people *live* in and around it.

The city as a gathering place for people living dispersed is older than the city as a dwelling place. In Antiquity, Delphi and Olympia had no permanent residents other than priests, yet they functioned as centers for a large population. Although it is not possible to explore fully this point in a short paper, it is evident that in the city center, the streets, restaurants, and theaters are filled primarily with visitors, many of them residing in hotels, rather than actual residents.

The Municipal-Regional-National System

Ideas about the future of the metropolis will remain wishful thinking until clear concepts are developed about government and about the public support government needs. In many cases, the municipalities are unable to manage the metropolis. This often prompts the national government to interfere in local affairs, which many believe is undesirable. Further, many argue that the national government should be decentralized and the old municipalities restructured and made more powerful on a regional level. But for the citizen, the small municipality *and* the national or federal state are the real things: the *region* means much less to the individual. If each region adopts different policies which lead to different taxes or different restrictions, this would disturb the citizen, who is accustomed to national policies which treat every individual alike. Clearly, centralization has certain advantages.

The plea for deregulation and decentralization in order to allow the individual greater freedom sounds attractive. However, it is doubtful that greater citizen involvement in decision-making is possible or desirable in matters of physical planning and urban development. There are many conflicting interests between the metropolitan level and the local or neighborhood level: it is difficult for people to solve non-local problems in an informal way. The average citizen lacks the technical competence to make rational choices between alternatives of regional or metropolitan development.

Appendix: "The Randstad Holland in 2010"

The Ministry of Housing, Physical Planning and the Environment of the Netherlands developed alternate scenarios for the future development of the Randstad. These were published in 1984 with the title "The Future of the Randstad Holland." The following information, supportive of Dr. Const-andse's arguments, is taken from this document.

1. A trend scenario:

This scenario depicts the settlement pattern (see Figure 2) that will result if the urbanization policies of today cannot be made efficient and the quirks of Dutch nature predominate over responsibility towards the future.

We see a pattern of settlements which slowly but surely grows inwards into the Randstad and occupies a growing part of the open space of this conurbation. In the basic analysis the probability was expressed that about 400,000 new houses should be built in the Randstad area in the next 20 years. In this scenario, assuming an average of 2.7 persons per household in 2010, not more than 200,000 houses will be built, the majority constructed in the fringe area on the inside of the ring of cities. This means that many of the existing open zones will change into urban fringe areas. In encroaching upon the open space people will have to pay a higher cost of transport in order to live in the countryside.

2. The compact cities. A scenario of a concentrated pattern:

This scenario attempts to conserve and to re-strengthen the traditional functions and the unique character of the Randstad as a world-city with a polycentric spatial structure as much as possible, while, at the same time, to restore the traditional, regional functions of large cities like Amsterdam, Rotterdam and Utrecht.

In the early 1980s some tendencies indicating a renewed orientation of people and activities towards large cities were already discernible. Migration away from the city continued but at a much lower rate than in the period before. The new attention societal elites gave to urban life made the "back-to-the-city" movement even more important. It resulted in a process of "gentrification." Especially younger people and ethnic minorities prefer to stay in the large cities instead of moving to suburban areas. After the motto "the city is full up" had been generally accepted for a long time, a new mentality started to develop around the idea that "the city is worth living in."

3. A scenario of a deconcentrated pattern:

Location trends since the beginning of the economic crisis show a further deconcentration of economic activities from the large towns toward medium size towns. The principle of this scenario is that this natural trend will be strengthened by national policy and a number of selected medium-size towns will be developed in a balanced way. The extension of these medium-size towns will benefit from the existence of major infrastructure. The scenario provides for a great diversity in the locational possibilities, both for households and for enterprises. The main centers are the four large cities (Amsterdam, Rotterdam, The Hague, Utrecht) as well as the centers of technological development—Eindhoven, Wageningen, Twente and perhaps Groningen. In the future, a not inconsiderable part of economic activities will spread to medium-sized towns situated within a distance of roughly 100 miles from the centers mentioned above.

The final image will show decongested large towns: a number of medium-sized towns will have expanded. The whole process will (need to be) supported by national policy.

These three scenarios show what might happen to the Randstad with its forecasted 6.5 to 6.7 million inhabitants in or around 2010. The trend scenario, or projective scenario, projects a situation in which the policies and measures concerning physical planning will remain unadapted to new ideas and conditions and no effort will be made to change the (uncontrolled) development processes into strategic processes which may result in a more desirable situation. In the two contrasting scenarios such an effort is indeed made. As a result, the traditional function of the "Green Heart" as an open space can be maintained.

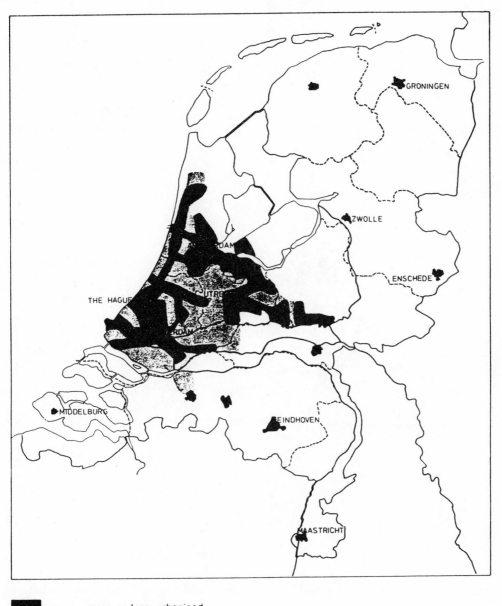

areas more or less urbanised

areas with suburban characters

existing cities anno 1980

rural areas

Fig. 12-1: The Randstad in 2010—a trend scenario.

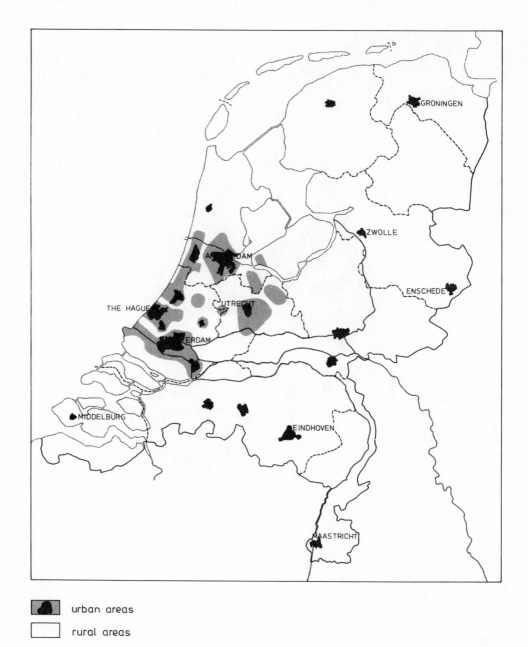

urban areas

rural areas

Fig. 12-2: The Randstad metropolis—a scenario for growth in concentrated settlements.

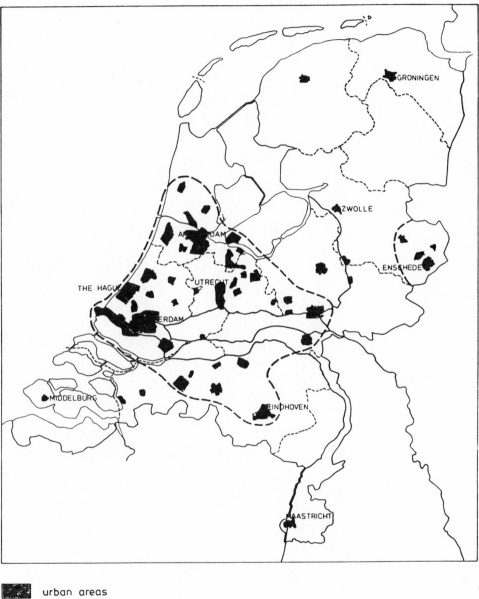

■ urban areas

□ rural areas

— — boundary for deconcentration policy

Fig. 12-3: The dispersed settlements—a scenario for a deconcentrated pattern.

13.

Switzerland: A Discontinuous and Polycephalous Metropolis

Michel Bassand

Argument

In Switzerland, specialists in the fields of planning, geography, economy and sociology are seriously debating whether the entire country forms a single great metropolis. Switzerland is known for its exceptionally high standard of living and its world-wide economic influence. Consequently, a metropolitan type of urban structure should exist. This reasoning, however, is far from unanimous, and there are at least three different points of view.

One viewpoint defines Switzerland as a giant, international metropolis of 6.2 million inhabitants, multiform and multifarious, which includes the entire Swiss territory. "It has swallowed up former cities as well as towns/villages, lakes, fields and forests (. . .). Political boundaries still exist between the various communities, but in relation to urbanism and culture they have broken down."

A second viewpoint holds that the above statement is exaggerated. There is a dichotomy in Switzerland between central and urban regions, and peripheral regions. The world-famous Swiss metropolis only includes the central and urban regions that are spread out in the shape of a cross, more or less contiguous, from Geneva to Rorschach and from Basel to Lugano. These urban regions are so well linked to each other by networks of transport and telecommunications that they constitute a whole. In short, this cross forms a giant metropolis of world-wide importance, and includes nearly four million inhabitants. Some observers deny the validity of the cross-shaped macroform and prefer the more limited concept of a triangle incorporating the territories between and within the regions of Zurich, Basel and Bern, the Golden Triangle. This metropolis is slightly smaller than the preceding one but still hosts about 2.5 million inhabitants.

The third viewpoint claims that Switzerland lacks a true metropolis. It is instead composed of a network of noncontiguous urban regions (or agglomerations) with populations varying between 20,000 and 800,000. Differentiated by political, linguistic and religious characteristics, these urban

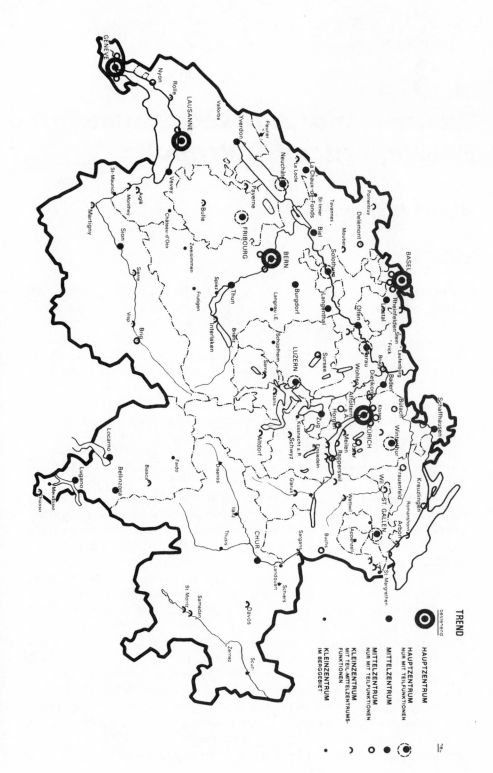

Fig. 13-1: The national settlement network of Switzerland, 1973. (ETH-Zurich Institut ORL)

regions by no means form a single territorial whole. Therefore, it can be argued that Switzerland lacks a metropolis.

In order to settle the matter, the metropolitan phenomenon must be defined. I believe that three criteria are determinant:

1. A metropolis is an extensive and *contiguous* territorial ensemble of at least two million inhabitants who interact socially, economically, politically and culturally.

2. The metropolis exerts influence (or dominance) on a national and international level.

3. Issues of civil order and change are central within the metropolis due to often vague geographical and political boundaries. These issues are the focus and subject of complex interactions and negotiations among the various inhabitants. Political groups, communities, districts and regions, and decentralized administrative agencies concerned with public education, health, science, culture, transportation and telecommunications defend and promote the interests of specific social actors.

In light of these criteria, is Switzerland or has Switzerland an important metropolis?

Spatial Organization in Switzerland

Research on the trends, behavior and indicators of spatial mobility provides a first answer. This study divides Switzerland into 12 regional types (see Table 1). The first five types define the Swiss urban phenomenon: large and average-size cities with their suburban zones. The seven other types are agrarian, touristic and industrial, composed of towns of at least 10,000 inhabitants. The urban regions account for more than 60% of the Swiss population despite stable demographic growth in the 1960s and 1970s. The peripheral regions continue to lose population. A factorial analysis of the regional demographic, social, economic and cultural indicators suggests that the five urban regions form a unit. This unit is characterized by a strong spatial mobility, modernity and urbanity. The urban regions constitute clearly the center of Switzerland. The seven other region types are characterized comparatively by rural traits and constitute peripheral Switzerland.

Another recent study focuses on the role of the tertiary sector in Swiss cities. By linking the size of the city with the importance and nature of the tertiary sector, this research reveals a network of 26 cities, divided into four hierarchical levels. The first level is Zurich, which leads in terms of its size and tertiary structure (369,000 inhabitants). Level 2 includes Geneva, Lausanne, Bern, Lucerne, Basel, and St-Gall (between 70,000 and 200,000

Table 13-1

CENTER-PERIPHERY TYPOLOGY

Type of Region	% Swiss Population	Size at Center (1000)	Relative Migration 1965/70	1975/80
1—Large Centers	22.7	195	−0.9	−0.8
2—Suburban Residential Areas	8.2	9	6.5	3.3
3—Suburban Job Areas	3.3	13	9.7	4.3
4—Average Tertiary Centers	11.2	33	1.7	0.6
5—Average Industrial Centers	15.4	35	0.7	−0.3
6—Small Industrial Centers	15.5	14	−0.5	−0.6
7—Industrial Peripheries	5.7	7	−3.7	−2.5
8—Small Tertiary Centers	5.6	7	−2.2	−1.9
9—Touristic Centers	1.2	6	−4.2	−2.5
10—Agro-Tertiary Peripheries	1.4	2	−7.1	−3.6
11—Agricultural Peripheries	1.9	4	−7.4	−3.3
12—Agro-Industrial Peripheries	7.9	4	−1.8	0.3

inhabitants), and exhibits a strong tertiary sector. These seven cities possess a strong national and international outlook. The third level includes 13 smaller cities of 10,000 to 50,000 inhabitants. Level 4 consists of six small cities similar to the third level in size. The tertiary sector in the fourth level is relatively weak, and member cities support a regional rather than national outlook. The cities of Levels 3 and 4 are dependent upon the seven cities of Levels 1 and 2. (The Map superimposes the results of these two studies and provides a concrete illustration of the Swiss urban framework.)

Taking into account our definition of the metropolis and these studies, it is clear that a metropolis of a particular kind exists in Switzerland. This metropolis incorporates the urban regions of Zurich, Winterthur, Zug,

Lucerne, Baden and Aarau. This contiguous area contains more than one million inhabitants and exerts an unquestionably national and international influence. However, these analyses do not support the idea that Zurich, Basel and Bern (the Golden Triangle) constitute a single giant metropolis.

Nevertheless, those who, like Professor Galantay, claim that a large Swiss metropolis exists challenge the contiguity criterion in defining a metropolis. They give priority to functional proximity over physical proximity. They can easily demonstrate that all the urban regions on our map are inserted within a highly dense and intensely used network of railways, highways and airways. Each point of this network can be reached in one or two hours. Moreover, telecommunications are up to date and common throughout the territory (95% of Swiss households have a telephone). Therefore, for those specialists, territorial discontinuity loses its meaning since it is offset by functional proximity.

A Metropolitan Social System?

A metropolis is not only a form of spatial organization but a social system as well. If it can be shown that a social system extends over a very large area of the urban regional network, then it can be argued that a single large Swiss metropolis exists. How does this metropolitan social system function?

According to recent studies, the social relations that structure the Swiss urban regions are characterized by two antagonistic forces. On the one hand, there is technocracy and, on the other, the social movements of inhabitants, users and consumers. The social relations of the capitalistic, industrial society have not yet disappeared, but they are no longer dominant.

Increasingly technocracy is the central actor in the urban region. It manages modernization and investment through large private and public organizations of manufacture, distribution, transport, consumption, planning, health, information, education, and research. With great autonomy, technocracy defines the objectives and means of these organizations essentially in terms of efficiency. Performance, functionalism, international competitiveness, techno-economic rationality and output are its fundamental criteria of action. In this way, technocracy conveys messages, norms, rules and codes that create a systematic program of daily life and that tend to reduce the significance and autonomy of the individual citizen.

Nevertheless, technocracy claims to defend the common welfare and general interest. Through its plans and programs, it identifies with collective investment, with "reason," with the "nature and order of things." Technocracy also tends to monopolize the management of knowledge and information. However, technocracy, for the time being, exists only as a professional network composed of engineers, economists, sociologists, planners, architects, urbanists, jurists, and public relations and advertising specialists.

The category of consumers, users and inhabitants consists of many

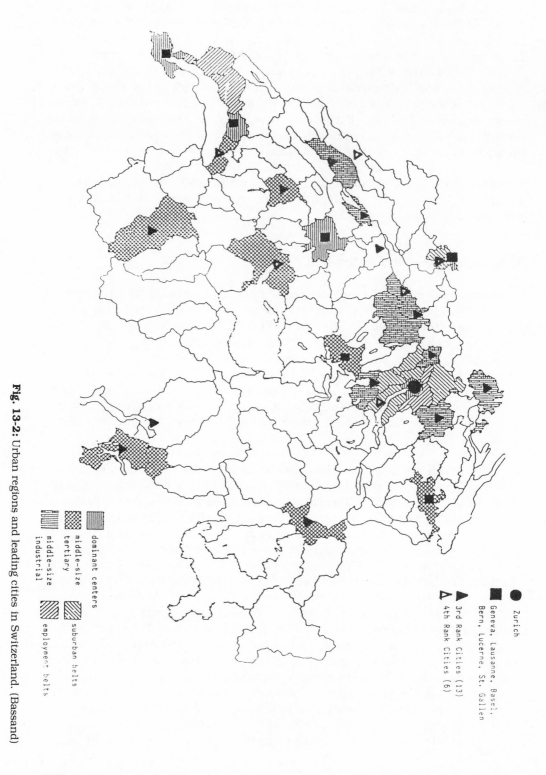

Fig. 13-2: Urban regions and leading cities in Switzerland. (Bassand)

dominant centers

middle-size
tertiary

middle-size
industrial

suburban belts

employment belts

● Zurich

■ Geneva, Lausanne, Basel,
Bern, Lucerne, St. Gallen

▶ 3rd Rank Cities (13)

△ 4th Rank Cities (6)

Fig. 13-3: Satellite image of Switzerland. The densely settled "Mitteland" is in the arc between the snow-covered Jura Mountains and the Alps.

individuals who are subordinate in relation to manufacture, usage and consumption. This category is opposed to technocracy. It no longer knows of the economic, moral and political misery of the nineteenth century working class. The demands of manufacturing have broadened its education; its health and housing conditions have greatly improved; its income is higher than ever. Its misfortunes and hardships are different: dependence, resignation, and moral, cultural and political alienation. Numerous movements manifest this opposition to technocracy though disorganized, scattered, short-lived, without coherence. Moreover, these social movements do not seem to mobilize all those whose interests they claim to defend.

The actions of these social movements are characterized essentially by three traits:

- a search for identity

- the elaboration of social-group projects based on autonomy, participation, spontaneity, the desire to be oneself and the quality of life

- the designation of an adversary, typically technocracy or the "establishment"

In the beginning, latent movements are manifested by mainstream opinion or a masked discontent. Later, they become active in struggles (that may become violent) to protest in the mass media, to create specific media, to debate, to occupy premises, to organize street demonstrations (more or less pacific), and to reject law and order.

There are five movements presently active on the Swiss urban scene.

Student and youth movements

Within the emerging programmed society, youth's future is vague. Youth considers its education and training authoritarian and inadequate; the life style proposed to them is not convincing. The youth of every generation experiences a search for identity, but today, this is a demand for autonomy in every area: political, cultural, emotional and social. Youth denounces constraint and repression in all forms; it claims material space for autonomy. Such confrontation identifies technocracy as the adversary. Because it calls all of society into question, it runs into harsh refusals, often a source of discouragement, withdrawal and despair. These movements often led to violence in Zurich and Lausanne in the 1970s and early 1980s.

Women's movements

Feminism dates back a century. Although its achievements are considerable, they are accompanied by new problems; the economic, social and political dependence of women is slow to change. Women's struggles are multiple: their central theme is collective, as well as individual, autonomy.

Women are fighting for abortion rights and the creation of autonomous health, education and cultural centers, and against masculine prejudices and family structures that reinforce dependent roles.

They are protesting against mistreatment, unpunished and tolerated by men, for example, rape, physical violence, and the overt eroticism of everyday life. In these struggles, they discover their most obstinate adversary—those men who, from their ivory towers, develop the norms, rules and laws for women without the collaboration of women: the technocrats.

The ecologist movements and urban struggles

These movements are the most well-known and turbulent of the urban phenomenon. Their battles focus on nuclear power plants, highways, public works in general, concrete construction, improper renovation and pollution. They defend the natural environment and cultural heritage. In so doing, they encounter technocracy which promotes efficiency, performance, rationality, modernity at any price. Consequently, they challenge current trends of functioning and change. They fight to create, defend and promote a *humane environment* as well as a more democratic system of administration. They advocate, among other things, a management of everyday life within the neighborhood and its surrounding areas by procedures developed by local democratic government.

The anti-state and anti-bureaucracy movements

The movements protest especially against state bureaucracies and all forms of private corporatism, regarding them as ineffective, costly and counterproductive. Hospitals breed disease, schools stultify minds, nation-states provoke dissent and war, transport companies slow down exchanges, prisons harden their "boarders," the churches father atheism, and families engender divorce. Further, these large organizations are repressive, endanger basic freedom, and belittle human dignity. These anti-bureaucracy movements are sometimes dramatically violent and destructive, but more often are nonviolent and pacifist movements.

Alternative movements

Alternative movements promote alternative lifestyles on a local level, as much from the viewpoints of family, nutrition and education as culture or profession. They are sociable and self-managing *hic et nunc*.

All are related; they often have a common culture, style of dress and physical appearance (hairstyles, postures, gestures), language, music and specific feelings and emotions. The theme of autonomy is quasi-generalized throughout these movements, as is the rejection of economic growth.

In most Swiss urban regions, technocracy and the new social movements can be observed as the principal social actors, typically urban actors. It is also clear that their actions are strongly disjointed by the cantonal and linguistic boundaries and barriers which divide Switzerland. For example, the youth and ecology movements exist in all urban regions, but in each region they take a specific form that derives from the cantonal, political context and linguistic differences. These movements have been unable to successfully organize on a trans-cantonal or trans-linguistic, inter-urban basis. In short, these movements seldom occur on a metropolitan or inter-urban scale in Switzerland, but rather are confined to the cantons and the specific linguistic areas of each urban region, none of which overlaps any linguistic boundary.

Political fragmentation as a barrier to metropolitanization

The Swiss Federal system—comprising twenty-six strongly autonomous states—presents a barrier to the rise of a socio-politically integrated metropolitan system. For a long time all urban and regional planning was the quasi-exclusive responsibility of the cantons. Federal policies that influence the cities such as the national highway program, public housing or regional development had to be translated into cantonal policies for approval and implementation. The only exceptions are policies and programs concerning the railroads the postal service or telecommunications.

Switzerland became industrialized and attained a high degree of socioeconomic development without experiencing a corresponding degree of urbanization and centralization. The fragmentation of life and of the political institutions in twenty-six cantons within four linguistic regions continues to hinder the emergence of a fully integrated Swiss metropolis.

Conclusions

The network of urban regions that polarizes Zurich constitutes a metropolis as defined by our three criteria. But, a giant Swiss metropolis? The answer is incomplete. Rather, Switzerland appears to feature a discontinuous and polycephalous metropolis. The network of urban regions, excepting Zurich, does not make a contiguous habitat. Each urban region reflects a specific, autonomous social system. Despite the lack of physical relation, the functional proximity of the urban regions is intense. Therefore, Switzerland does have a kind of metropolitan system without a metropolis: a discontinuous and polycephalic metropolis. Is this an exceptional situation? Or could it serve as a model for a desirable metropolitan pattern to be emulated elsewhere? There is considerable evidence to show that this type of metropolis offers more advantages and less inconveniences to its inhabitants than the model of the mono-nuclear centralized metropolis of comparable population size.

Bibliography

Bassand M. and Fragniere J. P. 1978. *Le pouvoir dans la ville.* éd. Delta, Vevey.
Bassand M. 1982. *Villes, régions et sociétés.* Lausanne: Presses Polytechniques Romandes.

Bassand M. et al. 1982. *Les Suisses entre la sédentarité et la mobilité.* Lausanne: Presses Polytechniques Romandes.

Bernfeld D. 1980. *Groupement de citadins-participation-cadre de vie.* Venise: Ciedart.

Burnier T. et al. 1983. *La mise en oeuvre de la politique des routes nationales.* Lausanne: CEAT.

Camenzind A. 1982. "La ville une image anachronique?" in *La ville expression de dialogue et de conflit.* Lausanne: IREC.

Duvanel L. and Levy R. 1984. "Politique en rase-mottes. Mouvements de contestation suisse." *Réalités sociales.* Lausanne.

Joye D. 1984. *Structure politique et structure sociale.* Université de Genève (thèse non encore publiée).

Perret-Gentil J. G. et al. 1984. *Centres régionaux de développement: rôle des petites et moyennes villes dans la distribution du tertiaire supérieur en Suisse.* Urbaplan. Lausanne.

Rossi A. 1983. *La décentralisation urbaine en Suisse.* Lausanne: Presses Polytechniques Romandes.

Rohr J. 1972. *La Suisse contemporaine.* Paris: A. Colin.

Schuler M. 1980. *Les agglomérations en Suisse en 1980.* Lausanne: IREC.

Part V

Eastern Europe

14.

Moscow: Model Socialist Metropolis

Ervin Y. Galantay

Introduction

It could be argued that there should be only one chapter in this book on the European metropolis. No doubt, a visitor from Africa or from South-East Asia is overwhelmed by the unity of our shared heritage: classicistic buildings from Dublin to Moscow echo the memory of the Roman civilization; towers of Christian churches dominate the skyline from Lisbon to Leningrad; the vast gothic Parliament of Budapest reflects in the Danube the spirit of the British Parliament on the Thames. And no doubt an attempt to classify the German cities by "East" and "West" would amount to a crude overvaluing of the idiosyncrasies of recent history and a denial of the mainstream of European culture.

Nevertheless, current development is characterized by undeniable differences between the liberal ideals and market economy cherished in the West and the central planning practice of the socialist states. The impact of this practice varies widely: in 800-year-old Moscow the soviet state had nearly 70 years of opportunity to turn its capital into a model socialist metropolis. By contrast in Budapest, the 40 years of socialist rule do not weigh heavily if we take into account that Aquincum—the direct ancestor of Buda—had been the flourishing capital of the Roman province of Lower Pannonia in 125 A.D.!

To understand the recent development of the metropoli of Eastern Europe, it is indispensible to study the metamorphosis of Moscow under central planning. For this reason I solicited a contribution for this volume from Vladimir Belousov, Director of the Central Scientific Institute of Town Planning in Moscow. He could not comply with my request, no doubt due to the temporary freeze in U.S.–USSR "detente." However, based on material mailed to me by Mr. Belousov previously, papers read by Soviet authors at a recent Paris symposium, and my personal acquaintance with Moscow, I shall attempt to give an objective survey of the achievements and weaknesses of Soviet planning as an introduction to the following case studies of Warsaw, Budapest and Belgrad.

The USSR extends over a land area which is bigger than the territory of the U.S. and Canada, combined. 35% of the Soviet population lives in rural areas as compared to 52% in 1959. For over 50 years the Soviet state has pursued a consistent policy aiming at the rational distribution of the population over the national territory, a policy which included the creation of hundreds of new settlements. As a result, urbanization is proceeding at a controlled speed with towns of 50,000 to 250,000 population growing the fastest. The urban system now includes 22 cities with a population in excess of one million inhabitants (see Table 1) but only three of these —Moscow, Kiev and Leningrad—qualify as metropoli. In terms of international "connectedness" only Moscow ranks as a true world city. Beautiful and historic Leningrad—even though it has 4.8 million inhabitants—has a role as an international cultural center like Kyoto, Florence or Edinburgh but it is more like a *regional* metropolis.

Table 1

Million-plus cities in the USSR 1984

Moscow	8,301 000	Tbilissi	1,110 000
Leningrad	4,719 000	Odessa	1,085 000
Kiev	2,297 000	Yerewan	1,076 000
Tashkent	1,901 000	Cheljabinsk	1,066 000
Kharkow	1,503 000		
Gorkij	1,373 000	Omsk	1,061 000
Minsk	1,370 000	Baku	1,060 000
Nowosibirsk	1,356 000		
		Donezk	1047 000
Swerd lowsk	1,252 000	Perm	1,028 000
Kuibyschew	1,244 000	Kazan	1,023 000
		Uta	1,023 000
Dnepropet rowsk	1,114 000	Alma ata	1,001 000

Soviet Ideology and the Metropolis

The Moscow metropolitan region comprises an area of approximately 13,378 km, with a population of 12.7 million inhabitants. Thus, it is comparable in size to the Paris region of Île de France. But while 18% of the French national population is concentrated around Paris, the Moscow region only accounts for 4.5% of the population of the USSR.

Moscow is not only the capital of the USSR and of the Russian Federated Republic but since the end of World War II also the seat of the leading organs of the Warsaw Pact and of the COMECON, and may lay claim to be the model metropolis of the "socialist" countries. In fact both V. Promyslov, the longtime mayor of Moscow, and M. Grishin, the Party Secretary of the capital, aspired to demonstrate through the example of Moscow the "superiority of Marxist-Leninist principles."[1]

The use of a city for the exemplification of a political ideology is not pursued as a policy in the capitalist countries. New York or Sao Paulo may look as embodiments of unfettered capitalism but certainly no efforts are made to strengthen this image—in fact such intervention would be contrary to the liberal philosophy of a market economy. By contrast, in the "socialist" countries, to cite Prof. Goldzamt: "city planning is not only a tool to provide for the needs of the present but must also serve as an instrument of societal transformation."[2]

Oleg Tulinov reminds us that, in accordance with the constitution of the USSR, the entire country is viewed as "an integral economic complex comprising all the elements of social production, distribution and exchange on its territory." City planning is a mere subsystem of this economy run on the basis of state plans and centralized direction." [3]

The goals of Soviet spatial planning can be summarized in three points:

- reduction of the differences between city and the country

- elimination of regional inequities

- optimization of the relation between production, leisure and dwelling areas

Some of the principles involved are:

- the elimination of speculation by the restriction of private ownership of real estate

- the integration of all projects within a general plan (i.e., no *ad hoc* decisions)

- the sound organization of land use and the planned provision of public facilities

- the limitation of the growth and size of large agglomerations based on the development potential and constraints of the sites and rational estimates of future populations

- the utilization of standard designs for residential projects and the use of industrialized methods in the production of buildings

All these goals and principles are derived from the ideology of Marxism-Leninism. With respect to the metropolis we are particularly interested in the goal of limiting the growth of large agglomerations. This attitude can be traced to Karl Marx's hostility to big cities because of their pollution and the degradation of living conditions due to crowding, as observed in the nineteenth century industrial slums by Friedrich Engels. Echoing Marx, V.G. Davidovich claims that "a large city is neither economic nor pleasant to live in . . ."[4]

As recently as 1974 V.K. Stepanov wrote that "long range development plans . . . should be based on a strict limitation of growth of cities with a population over 500,000 people. It is forbidden to build new industrial enterprises there."[5] Since then, however, it has been noted that large cities are not necessarily "parasitical." On the contrary, the productivity of industry in the largest cities is 38% higher than in cities of 100,000 to 500,000 inhabitants. Returns on capital investment in the million-plus cities is double of that in the medium-size, or small, towns.[6] Further, it appears that Soviet people much prefer to live in the big cities. As an example, newspaper ads frequently offer to exchange a three-room apartment in a provincial town for a small studio in Moscow.[7]

Small wonder that the growth of some big cities turned out to be much faster than planned, even though the Soviet Union possesses fairly efficient means of influx control. Nevertheless, these controls are not uniformly enforced as became evident in the case of Kiev which had a target population of half a million fixed for 1990 by a master plan developed in the sixties; yet in 1975 the population was found to be in excess of two million![8] Similarly, as we are going to demonstrate, the growth of Moscow consistently outstripped the forecasts, and in many other cities the population targets fixed 25 years ahead have been overtaken by reality only five to seven years later.

As a result of these experiences the "optimum size" dogma developed in the sixties by Davidovich has been somewhat discredited: there is no *single* optimal size, although there may be an optimal size for every given city, and this size may even vary depending on changing economic circumstances.[9] This insight explains the fact that, after many attempts to fix an upper size for the population of Moscow, the latest Master Plan shows great flexibility while still aiming to slow down and then to stabilize the growth of the metropolitan agglomeration.

In the USSR, matters of population distribution over the national system of settlements are decided by the highest central planning body, GOSPLAN, established in 1921. In spatial planning Soviet practice distinguishes between the socio-economic plan, "planirovanya," and the corresponding physical development plan, "planirovka." For a city like Moscow, plans are worked out in two different offices: GIPROGOR, the State Planning Institute, and GOSTROIPROIEKT which is the urban design office.

The development of Soviet planning theory and practice can be conveniently divided into four phases:

> 1917-1931: the experimental phase
>
> 1932-1944: the transitional phase
>
> 1945-1953: the reconstruction phase (socio-realism)
>
> 1953-present: the pragmatic post-Stalin phase

During the initial phase there was much theoretical discussion about the nature of the socialist city. Around 1925 S.G. Strumilin developed the concept of the "microrayon" or comprehensively planned neighborhood for communal living with appropriate services.[10] This pioneering work—which is contemporary with similar concepts developed in the U.S. by Clarence Stein and Clarence Perry—is the source of the familiar building blocks of

Soviet spatial planning: modern "microrayoni" are composed of 4-8 (more seldom of 7-15) multi-story apartment blocks or "kvartaly," grouping 3600 to 7500 people on roughly 9 to 15 hectares. Their equipment includes nurseries, kindergartens, elementary schools, a community center and some shops. Such neighborhoods are formed into districts or "raiony" which contain up to 100,000 people.

Planning Moscow

Among other achievements of the initial phase that keep inspiring the actual planning of Moscow were Shestakov's proposal[11] for the integrated development of the entire Moscow "Oblast" and the creation of a double ring of satellite cities around the center (1925), and Ladovskiy's scheme for a linear growth axis from the center of Moscow toward the northwest along the Leningrad Highway.[12] Elements of both proposals found their way into the first general plan for Moscow in 1935 and into the presently valid 1971 General Plan. The initial phase of planning experimentation ended in 1931 with Kaganovich's famous speech in which he rejected "utopianism."[13] The same year drastic measures were decided to restrain population influx to Moscow by introducing the internal passport and residency permit system. Work started on the first General Plan. It was completed in 1935. As described by Prof. S.E. Chernysev in his report to the First All-Union Congress of Soviet Architects: "For the first time in history we are setting a definite limit to the spread of the city . . . In the new socialist city the difference is removed between the rich center and the poor outskirts . . . by the planned distribution of public and cultural buildings over the entire area for accessibility and convenience . . ."[14] The plan also introduced neighborhood organization on the principles of the "microrayon" equipped with sociocultural amenities. The 1935 plan proposed the extension of the city's area to 600 square kilometers and simultaneously fixed the upper limit for the city's population at five million. To prevent sprawl, a 10 to 15 kilometer wide "forest-protective belt" was designated (well ahead of Abercrombie's 1943 "green-belt" proposal for Greater London!). Although the General Plan became State Law and integrated into the overall national economic plan, the city government, "Mossovjet," found loopholes in permitting new industries to move to Moscow on the basis of temporary permits and lacking vigilance in the control of residency permits. As a result the city reached 4,182,916 inhabitants already in 1939 and only the war managed to slow down the migration to the capital which led to severe overcrowding.

During the post-war reconstruction phase, violations of the General Plan became "so frequent as almost to amount to the rule" and in 1949 a Ministry of City Building was set up to ensure implementation in conformity with the guidelines of the plan.[15]

A Census taken 10 years later, in 1959, proved that the size-limit of five million inhabitants has been passed. Next year, in 1960, when a 100

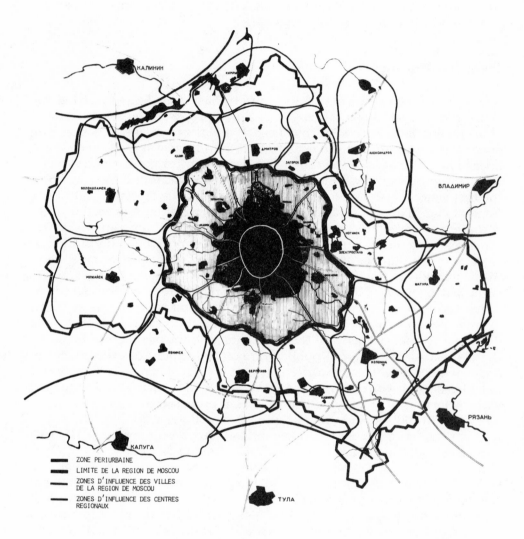

Fig. 14-1: The Moscow Metropolitan Region. The city of Moscow is within the oval ring—road. The surrounding region includes numerous satellite towns. The outer ring consists of twelve territorial units, each with its service center. In the outermost ring are the more autonomous towns of Tula, Kaluha, Kalinin, Valdimir and Ryazan. ("Construction and Architecture of Moscow," Moscow, 1971, No. 7-8)

kilometer long peripheral motorway had been completed, the city area was extended to the new ringroad, and it was found that within the new area of 877 square kilometers the population amounted to 6,045,000 people. Confronted with this fact, the planners now proposed to fix the ultimate size of the city at 6.8 million and asked for immediate measures to prevent the implantation of new industries in Moscow. The Council of Ministers approved this proposal in 1971 but in the meantime the population rose to over seven million.

The Actual General Plan for Moscow

The present General Plan elaborated in 1971 proposes to gradually reduce the population within the ring motorway but permits moderate growth in the forest belt and in the outer suburban area. It fixes the outer limits of the metropolitan region which now encompasses 13,500 square kilometers. In 1971 it was found that the yearly population increase of the capital amounted to some 90,000 people, mostly due to immigration. It also became manifest that the composition of the working population has changed considerably: only 26% of the actives were employed in industry with another 10% in construction, with still 6% engaged in agriculture in the periphery of the vast region, leaving 48% in "services" of whom a full 20% were in educational, research and development institutions. This employment profile increasingly conforms to that of the Paris agglomeration where 24% of the actives work in industry, 6.5% in construction and 68% in "services."

Yet Moscow is still an industrial city of importance, accounting for 14% of the national production of cars and trucks, automated and robotized machine tools, and 7% of the national production of textiles. The present directives permit the re-equipment of exisiting industries in Moscow only under the condition that the number of employees remains stable or be reduced: this is forcing industries to modernize by introducing automated processes.

Soviet theory distinguishes between "city forming" (basic) and "city-servicing" (non-basic) employment. The first also includes export services provided by government and by educational or research institutions consid-ered "directly productive" in terms of investment. Since the expansion of industrial employment is forbidden, the expansion of the sector providing export services has expanded accordingly. The present structure of the Moscow region is focused on the historic center of the Kremlin, site of the first settlement some 800 years ago (first mentioned in 1147). Around the Kremlin is the historic core area of approximately 103 square kilometers with 1.26 million residents—in size comparable to the city of Paris (110 square kilometers) although the latter has a higher residential density. Between the core of Moscow and the ring motorway is a suburban zone of 774 square kilometers with some seven million residents. The 1971 General Plan proposes to reorganize this zone in a polycentric fashion by creating seven distinct sectors each with a population of about one million and with a sizeable, fully-equipped subcenter.[16] The sectors have as their spine the radial suburban railroad lines and roads built in the late nineteenth century. They are supposed to be separated by green wedges leading to the peripheral forest belt beyond the ringroad. Further development will take place in linear fashion along the preferential development axes within the forest belt and in a nucleated fashion in the outer peripheral zone of the metropolitan region. Detailed plans now being prepared for the year 2010 envisage a continuous built-up area of 3,250 square kilometers for Greater Moscow with a population of 11 million with another two to four million inhabitants in the outer suburban zone of the region.

Mossovjet, the city government, will continue to administer the area within the ringroad, as well as Sintsevo and the satellite town or "gorod sputnik" of Zelenograd.[17] The rest is to be administered by the Regional Soviet in 17 different administrative districts. This outer area beyond the forest belt is not entirely undeveloped but includes some 39 towns with populations ranging from 45,000 to 200,000 with a total of 2.5 million inhabitants. Mossovjet has a stable budget and assured income from its enterprises, state duties, taxes, rents and also receives subsidies from the budget of the RSFSR, and from the budget of the central government. One-third of its budget is assigned to capital construction.[18]

Housing

According to Goldzamt, "the human being is the most important factor in the socialist economy" and therefore there should be "no contradiction between the two goals of the development of the productive forces and the pursuit of social justice."[19]

In practice however, whenever a choice needs to be made in resource allocation between directly productive investment or social-cost type investment such as housing, the latter is invariably shortchanged and indeed in the field of housing the Soviet achievement is far from satisfactory.

As early as 1935 a "sanitary norm" of close to 11 sq. meters of living space per capita was postulated by Soviet planners. A more modest goal has been set at just over 6.5 square meters for the five million inhabitants at the end of the 10-year development period. However, due to priority accorded to industrialization, then because of Stalin's craving for ostentatious public buildings and the resulting low priority given to the housing program, average living space per capita sank to about 4.8 square meters by 1956. In 1957 Khrushchev launched his mass building program promising to provide free housing for everyone. Inexperienced crews erected massive five-story brick apartment blocks in record time, but in sloppy construction: complaints poured in about cracked walls, leaky roofs, jammed doors, faulty radiators.

In the following years there was a change to industrialized speed-building methods with the quality of finishings sacrificed to quantity building and time schedules. The size of rooms was gradually increased, with average size dwellings of 46m^2 in the 1966-70 period and 55m^2 in 1976-80. At present, the per capita floor space provided is 17m^2 (by comparison, the average space per capita for all of Switzerland is over 40m sq.)

The 1977 Soviet Constitution declares the access to adequate dwelling to be a "fundamental right" for all citizens. However, satisfaction of this right needs to be delayed in this period of the "construction of socialism." The distribution of dwellings is subject to social control and some people—such as party worthies—have priority which annoys ordinary people whose name is on the waiting list for five years before their application is considered.

After 25 years of relentless production of mass housing, one-fourth of the Moscow population is still obliged to share dwellings with strangers, often assigned at random. This promiscuity is the source of much friction. J.V. Trifonov's famous novel, *The Exchange,* describes the vicissitudes of a family trying to exchange two separate rooms in distant parts of the city for a single two-room unit.[21]

Fast building still results in shoddy construction, and occupancy permits are frequently delivered to buildings lacking doors, insulation, chimney caps, gas or water connection, toilet bowls, etc. In 1980 the Council of Ministers had to pass a menacing directive to punish not only inspectors who sign an occupancy permit for an unfinished building but also those "who persuaded them to sign in violation of the law . . ."[22]

To mobilize private savings for housing construction it is now possible to buy cooperative apartments. Private construction amounts to 10% of the output and it is anticipated that it will rise to 25% by the end of the century. In the early 1960s a cooperative apartment could be bought for some 6000 rubles, then equal to three years of the earnings of a worker. Such an apartment can be passed on as a heritage to close relatives if they have lived in the apartment before the death of the owner. Otherwise the heirs are obliged to sell the apartment back to the cooperative although they would want to enter into possession.[23]

In Moscow the possibilities of building industrial mass-housing are completely exhausted in the central area within the ring-motor road.[24] New sites are developed within the forest belt along the preferential axes. To save as much of the green area as possible, high density construction is pursued. In some areas 22 to 26 floor-high buildings are used.

According to Makarevich most buildings are "erected in accordance with standard designs and constructed of the articles of the Moscow Single Catalogue of Standard Prefabricated Units and Assembled Components."[25]

Some of the new housing projects accommodate up to 300,000 people (e.g., Ikargest at 18 miles from the center toward the south). The architects seek to provide variety by using colors and varying building height, shape and finishing materials but such is the scale of the new housing projects that monotony invariably results. Relics of historic or rural architecture provide a welcome accent and are carefully preserved and integrated.

It must be mentioned that rental charges are extremely low[26] and generally only amount to 5% of the take-home income of a family for an apartment providing just under 11 sq. meters living space per head. A problem is that buildings are both poorly built and also poorly maintained. As a result the quality of the building stock is decaying rapidly and many buildings erected under Khrushchev already require replacement or very costly repairs.

Open Space and Water

Much more satisfying than the housing situation is the provision of open space and green areas. Present provision is 20 sq. meters per capita which will be increased to 30 sq. meters by the year 2000.[27]

In Moscow the 9 mile-wide forest and protective belt includes 78% undeveloped green space. In addition, the green wedges separating the seven large development areas between the forest belt and the core are all sizeable forests of 600 to 700 hectares each. A continuous linear green space is being formed along the Moskva River.

In addition, since 1973 four new "zakaznik" or conservation areas have been designated. These are: the Gorki Leninskye historic park; the Elk Island nature park in the northeast; the upper Moskva River flood bank; and the lower Moskva River. Three more zakazniks with a total surface of 460 square kilometers will be developed until the year 2010.[28]

Of the 10,000 square kilometer peripheral zone of the Moscow Metropolitan Region 91% is open agricultural or forest land. 6% of the active labor force of the region still works in agriculture and the zone is highly productive since it provides 5% of the national meat production, 8% of the milk products, margarine, etc. which makes the capital self-sufficient in many vital food products.

The water supply of the metropolitan area is also resolved due to the 128 kilometer-long Moscow-Volga Canal which permitted the level of the Moskva River to be raised by 3 meters.[29] Numerous reservoirs have been built in the forest belt around Moscow and in the Volga River basin. The consumption of drinking water amounted to 241 liters per person already in 1953 and total consumption including industrial use, actually approaches 700 liters per person.

Due to the low degree of motorization and the fact that most new housing projects receive steam provided from central heating plants burning natural gas, there is less air pollution than in comparable size large cities elsewhere. Within the city distant-heated water and steampipes are running in utility tunnels alongside the subways.

These tunnels also include water mains, sewerage lines, and electric and telephone wires, reducing air and noise pollution which otherwise results from the periodical digging up of the utility lines laid in the traditional ways.

The air pollution of Moscow can then be traced mostly to its industries. But the problems of ecology have received much attention lately and noxious emissions have already been reduced by half.[30]

Thus, in terms of environmental protection and the provision of green open space, Moscow is indeed in the vanguard among metropoli of its size. In contrast to Tokyo's green belt which the planners were unable to save from the speculators, Moscow's green belt exists and is constantly expanded. There is hardly any restriction to free access to these vast green zones and people use them very intensely for picknicking, mushroom picking and other activities.

Transportation

Soviet planning accords priority to the development of efficient public mass transportation. This goal is supported by the principle of compactness in the layout of the residential areas.

As a result of this policy, only 3% of trips in Moscow are made in private automobiles, and the motorization has been kept at 45 per 1000, with less than 400,000 units circulating in the metropolitan region.[31]

Metro and suburban trains carry over 50% of the traffic. By comparison, in Beijing—with 9,179,000 inhabitants in 1984—where private cars also account for less than 3% of all trips, 60% of all deplacements are made on bicycles—and there is no subway system.[32]

This contrasts with the "modal split" in the metropoli even of the poorer capitalist countries. In Buenos Aires the number of private cars is estimated to amount to 2.5 to 3 million units.[33] In Mexico City 2,331,000 private cars circulated in 1984, taking up 97% of the street space while accounting for only 21% of the trips within the metropolitan region![34]

In the USSR in the 1960s, there was much discussion about what role to assign to the private automobile in Soviet society, and it had been decided to promote taxi-fleets and car-rental pools and to discourage private ownership. However, soon after, there had been a shift in policy and a giant Fiat-designed car factory was set up in the new town of Togliatti to increase domestic production. Yet in Moscow, snow removal is a serious problem during four months of the year and there is a dearth of underground parking space. During the winter most cars are kept in improvised and unsightly shacks taking up the open space of the microrayons. This —combined with the high cost of the cars and the difficulty of servicing them and finding spare parts—keeps car ownership down. A modest increase is expected to bring the stock up to one million units by the year 2000, but no more than 10-15% of the trips are expected to take place by private automobile. In fact, cars are mostly used for recreational use. This results in peak traffic volumes on the weekends, particularly on Sunday evenings with cars mingling with the fleets of trucks used to transport groups of workers returning from outings for organized collective merriment.

Another problem causing many headaches in Moscow is the inefficient use of truck-fleets making half-empty runs in cross-hauling merchandise or transporting people. But rationalization of freight movement is supposed to reduce the average distance moved by one ton of freight from 20.2 km to 17.6 km in the next decades.[35]

In Moscow priority is assigned to electrically-powered mass transit: metro, suburban trains, trolley-buses and tramways. The first subway line of 11.6 km was opened in 1936 and by now the length of metro lines totals 215 kms, soon to be extended to 330 kms. This is the subway system with the greatest carrying capacity in the world, moving 3.5 billion passengers yearly; trains of 6-7 carriages are run at only 90 sec. intervals. Suburban trains of 10-12 carriages are run on 2½ minute intervals. Their lines consist of four parallel tracks to permit omnibus and express trains to run side by side. The building of a high-speed Metro—on the model of the Paris RER System—is now proposed with stations spaced 2 to 3 km to permit average speeds of 60 to 70 km/h. However, between the rail corridors bus service is still not adequate and some commuters need four hours daily to get to their work place and to return home. The goal is to assure that commuter trips do not exceed 40 minutes each way. The interstitial areas between rail lines are to be served by fast trams running on reserved right-of-way with priority assigned by signalization at intersections. Trolley buses will also have their reserved lanes.[36]

Conclusions

To make a balance sheet of Soviet planning achievements in Moscow one might ask the following questions:

- How satisfying are the results *per se,* i.e., within the framework of the given politico-economic system, the disposible resources, and the parameters set by the traditions and character of the Russian people?

- What aspects of Moscow's planning can be emulated by the metropoli of the Western industrial countries?

- Can Moscow serve as a model for the planning of the metropoli of the Third World?

The answer to the first question cannot be anything but that positive central planning can be credited for the fact that the USSR does not know the phenomenon of a decreasing metropolitan population due to a shrinking of the employment base as does Greater London. There are no "footloose industries"—managers go where they are told. Of course spatial planners are often overruled if their proposals conflict with production targets set by the economic plan. Soviet managers—always eager to "overfulfill" their production targets—do not easily agree to disrupt or reduce their production to comply with environmental directives or to move their factory to a new site. But interest in ecological problems seems to have been awakened in the highest levels of decision-making, and the Council of Ministers repeatedly ruled in favor of spatial planning objectives even against objections of the Gosstroi.

There is no question that the practice of *influx control* has shown favorable results. Not only did it slow down the growth of the capital and keep it within manageable limits but the *selection principle* and the practice of granting residency permits—based on a priority list for skills needed for the fullfillment of the plan—permitted the composition of the population according to an *optimum profile.* The growth of the city is now largely due to migration since the resident population has such a low birth rate that it barely replaces its numbers. Thus, it is no accident that the age-cohorts of the Moscow population show a pleasing symmetry: children under 16 years of age account for 20% of the population, the same percentage as the old and retired people, while the active population is 60% and nearly totally employed.

Selection has also resulted in a remarkably *homogeneous* population: apart from a sprinkling of foreigners and Soviet citizens from the Asiatic republics, the Moscow population is overwhelmingly Russian. This homogeneity fosters great pride in being a Muscovite and a high level of civic discipline. If we consider that still one-fourth of the population lives in forced promiscuity, sharing kitchens, toilets, etc. with strangers, the self-control of the Muscovites is even more remarkable. Rates of vandalism and criminality are very low in Moscow compared to such Western metropoli as New York, London or Sao Paulo. Even more impressive is the fact that the criminality rate of Moscow is not even half of the national average.[37]

The vast Soviet bureaucracy is certainly an irritant in the daily life of the Moscow citizen and its rigidity is blamed for much inefficiency. Yet the very inertia of the system also assures a remarkable program continuity which is a very essential aspect of the Soviet economy. In planning, little effort is made to involve the public in consultation, let alone participation in decision-making, or to monitor the popular approval of decisions. This insensitivity permits imperial gestures, like the cutting in half of the beloved old Arbat district by the wide Kalinin Prospekt—very much like Baron Hausmann's "percée" of the Avenue de l'Opéra in the Paris of the 1860s. There has been some grumbling about the Arbat but its memory already fades and pride in the modern Kalinin Avenue is on the ascendance.

While in many Western countries it may be "urgent to have patience" with respect to decisions effecting the ecology or the high-quality built environment, there is a greater sense of urgency in rapidly developing countries, the Soviet Union included. The "fast-tracking" of decisions has priority over participation in an economy of frugality. With respect to the shaping of the built environment much can be said in favor of decisions taken by competent technocrats rather than by populist politicians, speculators, real estate men and what in the U.S. is called the "grass-roots." As Edgar Banfield has pointed out, the little people are unabashedly "self-regarding," have notoriously short "time-horizons," are unable to think in terms of solidarity with future generations, and are only interested in the immediate satisfaction of their urges and needs.[38] Soviet planning technocracy is of course "immensely strong in relation to the customer" and P. Hall even accuses the Soviet planners of creating a permanent scarcity of housing—a sort of "seller's market"—to cow the humble citizen: "bureaucratic provision flourishes on brute shortage"[39]—a situation vexing to Western observers who are used to seeing the customer as king. The aspirations of the Soviet customer are in fact very modest; according to a survey taken in 1978 only 26% of the sample dreamed of a single family house while 48% would have preferred an apartment in the center-city area. They asked for 22m² of floor space per person, or one room per person—not unattainable goals in the future.[40]

Western critics make much about the privileged lifestyle of the elites in the presumably "classless" Soviet society. However, an analysis of the lifestyle of the "nomenclatura" class reveals that they hardly live better than the upper-middle class in Western countries. Moscow elites own larger apartments, may also have a "dasha," a private car, access to imported goods; they eat in better restaurants and may occasionally travel abroad. None of this is viewed as a "privilege" in the West but part of the lifestyle of the middle classes. The difference in the lifestyle of soviet elites and the lowest income workers is not nearly as great as the abyss separating the rich and the slum dwellers in the metropoli of the developing countries.

In fact Soviet society may err more by attempts at reducing income differentials than from building up an elite. The price of the egalitarian policy is a certain greyness and a lack of initiative and creativity. The very competitive educational system provides numerous social awards for outstanding performance but the linear programming in education lacks the random, spontaneous exchanges which, in Western society, yield a ferment for dynamic intellectual mobility. This may explain the Soviet need for borrowing and copying of advanced technology—a strictly one-way flow since there is little evidence of America's or Japan's copying of Soviet inventions. Rigidity and lack of imagination also characterizes Soviet spatial planning in its restrictions of mobility and private initiative. This is why Moscow can hardly serve as a model for Western planners.

Contrary to Marxist doctrine which views capitalism as an intermediate step on the path toward communism, it appears more likely that Soviet-type central planning may be a convenient intermediate step toward a more liberal market economy. On this path, not only the inhabitants of Warsaw, Prague and Budapest are ready for change but also the populations of Moscow, Leningrad and Kiev who have reaped the benefits of central planning and now could profit from a loosening of the system and a bit more social and spatial mobility.

Seen from the developing countries, the Soviet model offers an alternative to the example of the Western metropolis. The question is not so much which model is superior but rather which system is "affordable" and provides a better "safety net" against the threatening crisis situations. As in war, an urban emergency may require a command economy and a restriction of individual liberties. Many less-developed countries may opt temporarily for the centrally planned model to be able to put their house in order. Elias Gomez-Azcarate who visited Cuba has pointed out that Havana may be the only metropolis in Latin America where metropolitan growth has been brought under control and Cuba the only country where regional inequities are fast disappearing.[41] The stability of the centrally planned system assures program continuity which is an essential condition for the development of a country lacking investment capital.

Soviet-type metropolitan planning is not good at delivering quality goods and services or in providing choice. However, the goals of choice and of quality clearly need to be subordinated to the goal of the "satisfaction of basic needs" in the giant metropoli of the Third World.

The Soviet-type metropolis is compact and energy-saving. It makes frugality into a virtue based on a command economy. It is good at delivering collective services—transportation, infrastructure, recreation areas—even a clean public environment. By its quantitative orientation it is geared to production in conformity with "minimum adequate standards."

The USSR, with an economy only one-third of the gross domestic product of the U.S. invests about the same amount yearly in its defense and space programs. What is left of the budget obviously cannot be stretched to provide an abundance of consumer goods such as housing. Yet this should not be taken as proof of an inherent structural defect of central planning since, in the case of the USSR, the shortages result from constraints due to "superpower" competition on the global level. A reduction of the military and space budget would greatly benefit internal development, and the present greyness and monotony of the built environment of the Soviet cities could be upgraded rapidly.

Notes

1. V. Promyslov, "Osnovnye printsipy . . .," in *Urbanistica Contamporalis*, (Budapest, 1972).
2. Edmund Goldzamt, "Stadtebau sozialistischer Lander," VEB Verlag, (Berlin, 1974).
3. Oleg Toulinov, "The Solution to the Economic Problems of the Moscow Agglomeration," paper read at the "Metropolis 1984" symposium in Paris.
4. V.G. Davidovich, ". . . Tendencjach gorodskogo rasselenija v.SSSR," in Goroda mira, Izd.Mysl, (Moscow, 1965).
5. V.K. Stepanov, "USSR," in A. Whittick (ed.), *Encyclopedia of Urban Planning*, (New York, 1974).
6. V. Perevedentsev, "Urbanizatsia v triokh rakursakh," in *Drujba narodov*, (Moscow, 1976), pp. 206-225.
7. *Ibid.*
8. *Ibid.*
9. E.Y. Galantay, "How Big Should Cities Grow?," see Chapter 7 in this volume.
10. M.B. Frolic, "The Soviet City," *Town Planning Review*, 34, (1964): pp. 285-287.
11. V.V. Kirillov, "Idei rekonstruktsii Moskvy v proyektah 20-kh . . .," in V.L. Yanin, (ed.) Russkiy Gorod, Moskva. Izd. Moskovskogo Universiteta, (1976).
12. R.A. French, and F.E. Hamilton, "The Socialist City," (Chichester, 1979).

13. ———, "Architecture in the Land of Socialism," in *Arkhitetura S.S.S.R*, nos. 17-18, (Moscow, 1947).

14. S.E. Chernyshev, "General'nyi Plan Rekonstruktsii Mosky i Voprosny Planirovki Gorodov SSSR," (Moscow, 1937).

15. M.F. Parkins, *City Planning in Soviet Russia*, (Chicago, 1953).

16. Promyslov, *op. cit.*

17. Mossoviet is presiding over the "zaisovjets" into which the whole of Moscow is divided.

18. Toulinov, *op. cit.*

19. Goldzamt, *op. cit.*

20. A. Beliakov, "Bolshoe novoselie," in *Literaturnaia Gazeta*, no. 18, (Moscow, 1980). This provision of 20 sq. yards floor space is contested by Western experts. They assert that the norm is still 15.6 sq. yards and most people have no more than 3.6 to 7.2 sq. yards per capita. Only if actual floor space is less than 3.6 sq. yards can a person join the waiting list for a new apartment and it may take as long as 8-10 years to have completed the move. Communication by Prof. A. Shtromas, University of Salford, U.K.

21. J.V. Trifonov, "The Exchange," in *Der Tausch*, (Munich, 1974).

22. S. Dementiev, "Verkhnii etaj" in *Literaturnaia Gazeta*, no. 27, (Moscow, 1982).

23. Communication by Prof. A. Shtromas, University of Salford, U.K.

24. Gleb Makarevich, "The Development of Moscow, New Residential Areas," paper read at the "Metropolis 1984" symposium in Paris.

25. *Ibid.*

26. B. Batishchev, "Spetsifika kvaternoi platy," in *Gorodskoe Khoziaistvo Moskvy*, no. 8., (1983), pp. 22-26. This is contested by recent emigrants from the USSR who claim that rentals can amount to 35-40% of family income.

27. Valentin Ivanov, "Natural and Cultural Heritage in the Moscow Agglomeration," paper read at the "Metropolis 1984" symposium in Paris.

28. *Ibid.*

29. Parkins, *op. cit.*

30. Makarevich, *op. cit.* These figures are contested by recent emigrants from the USSR. See Boris Komarou's book "The Nature Extinguished."

31. Rostilav Gorbanev, "Transport Development Policy in the Moscow Agglomeration," paper read at the "Metropolis 1984" symposium in Paris. Most of the following information is taken from Gorbanev.

32. Ph. Jonathan, "Municipalite de Pekin," in *Cahiers de l'IAURIF*, no. 74, (1984).

33. Concejo de Planificacion Urbana: "La Region de Buenos Aires 1984."

34. E. Gomez-Azcarate, "The View from Mexico," see Chapter 23 in this volume.

35. Toulinov, *op. cit.*

36. Gorbanev, *op. cit.*

37. Louise Shelly, "The Geography of Soviet Criminality," in *American Sociological Review*, vol. 45, (Washington D.C., 1980).

38. Edward C. Banfield, *The Unheavenly City Revisited*, (Boston, 1968).

39. Peter Hall, "Metropolis 1940-1990," in A. Suthcliffe, (ed.), *Metropolis 1890-1940*, p. 439.

40. A.V. Baranov, *Sotsialno-demografitcheskoe krupnovo goroda*, (Moscow, 1981).

41. E. Gomez-Azcarate, *op. cit.*, (ref. 34).

15.

Warsaw: Conservation and Renewal

Krzysztof Pawlowski

As an historian of town-planning, I intend to introduce a retrospective element. As a specialist in the conservation and rehabilitation of historic districts and monuments, I wish to emphasize the role of the historic core areas in the life of the socialist metropolis. Finally, since I am most familiar with Warsaw, I shall focus on the Polish capital as a case study of the transformations of an old European city during the relatively recent period of scientific socialism.

The focus on Warsaw seems justified since the development of the capital of the Polish State is in many respects representative of the successive shifts of theory and practice which have also shaped other socialist metropoli. I believe this assertion is born out both by Vidor's article on Budapest and Peroviç's paper on Belgrade. Of course in Warsaw—due to the immense war damage—the "opportunities" for physical planning were greater than elsewhere.

However, these opportunities have often been overestimated by foreign observers uninformed about the extremely precarious economic situation of post-war Poland and the need for the maximum possible reutilization of the surviving elements of the city's technological infrastructure. Many fine urban design proposals had to be modified and subordinated to these considerations.

The example of Warsaw illustrates the effectiveness of central planning in controlling population influx to the leading city. As a result of administrative measures Warsaw's growth has been stopped so effectively that its present population does not exceed 1.5 million inhabitants, concentrating only 4.5% of the country's population—exactly the same proportion as that of metropolitan Moscow to the population of the Soviet Union.

The on-going socio-economic crisis has not spared Warsaw. At present city planners participate in discussion on the national level of how to improve the state of affairs. Their arguments carry considerable weight in decision-making on the national level.

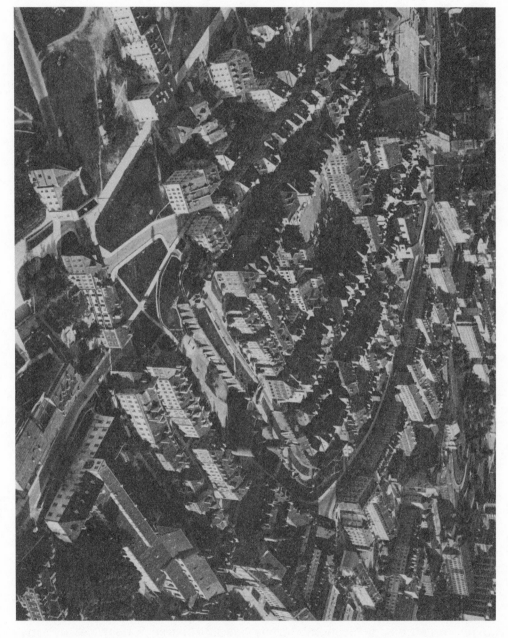

Fig. 15-1: Warsaw, The Old City, "Stare Maisto." It was totally rebuilt after World War II destruction. (Osrodek Dokumentacjy Zabytkow, Warsaw)

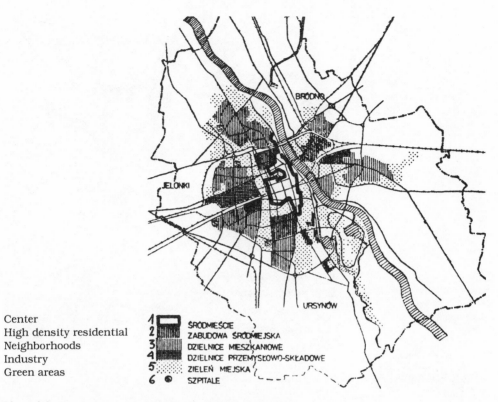

Center
High density residential
Neighborhoods
Industry
Green areas

1 ŚRÓDMIEŚCIE
2 ZABUDOWA ŚRÓDMIEJSKA
3 DZIELNICE MIESZKANIOWE
4 DZIELNICE PRZEMYSŁOWO-SKŁADOWE
5 ZIELEŃ MIEJSKA
6 SZPITALE

Fig. 15-2: First post-war reconstruction plan of Warsaw.

An analysis of the history of town planning will help us to realize that *the concept of the socialist city is older than the existence of socialist states.* My research on the origins of modern townplanning indicates that Tony Garnier's design for "Une cité industrielle," elaborated in 1901-1904, may be considered as the first blueprint for a socialist city.[1] In this conceptual model, satisfaction of the needs of the working classes is the primary objective. The model city was conceived as an integral part of the metropolitan region of Lyon and it posited a target size of 35,000 inhabitants. All land was to be communally owned and as a result there was no need for a subdivision of the blocks. Buildings could be placed free of lot boundaries and the pedestrians could move unhindered, independently of the street-layout. Open green space also played an important role in the layout of industrial areas in an attempt to humanize the working environment.

The key element of Garnier's ideal city is the *social control of land,* and it is no accident that his ideas found a favorable echo in the planning theory developed in the Soviet Union by Miliutin and his followers. This permits the observation that the concepts of the socialist city are most appropriate for the creation of New Towns, which does not imply that existing cities are not subjected to ideologically motivated attempts at redevelopment.

Another prototype of the socialist city was J. Chmielewski's and S.

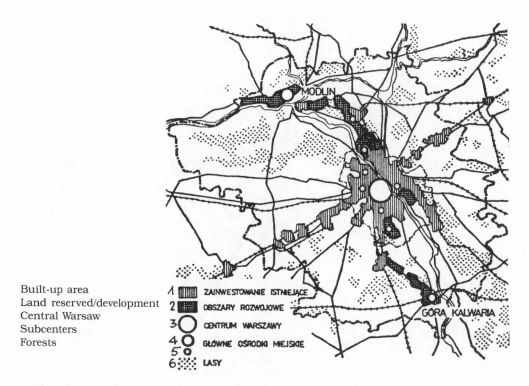

Built-up area   1   ZAINWESTOWANIE ISTNIEJĄCE
Land reserved/development   2   OBSZARY ROZWOJOWE
Central Warsaw   3   CENTRUM WARSZAWY
Subcenters   4   GŁÓWNE OŚRODKI MIEJSKIE
Forests   5
    6   LASY

Fig. 15-3: Warsaw Metropolitan Area. (After A. Kolewki)

Syrkus's design for a "Functional Warsaw" dating from 1934.[2] This concept called for the development of so-called "equipment zones" in a metropolitan region extending far beyond Warsaw's administrative borders. Development axes were proposed along the major national and regional highways and along the course of a natural waterway, the Vistula River. The major functional center was defined by the intersection of the axis of the "capital zone" with a linear "commercial zone." The authors of this vision of the future Warsaw emphasized that they were aware of the contemporary economic depression, unemployment and housing shortage, and they knew that their study would only become useful "when social and economic forces finally regained their balance." The advent of this moment was forestalled by the dramatic events of World War II. In 1939 the noble vision of a "maximal Warsaw" was supplanted by the minimalist concept of a "Warschau die Neue Deutsche Stadt."[3] Work on this design was launched in the Würzburg city planning office before Hitler's invasion of Poland. The project was officially approved by the German authorities in February, 1940. According to this so-called "Pabst-plan" the Polish capital with its 1,300,000 inhabitants was to be reduced to a provincial town of 120,000 German settlers implanted within the area of the historic city, complemented by a satellite labor-camp for 20,000 Poles on the right bank of the Vistula. The Royal Palace—symbol of Polish independence—was to be pulled down to yield its place to the NSDAP (German National Socialist Workers Party) headquarters.

Fig. 15-4: Warsaw 1990, proposed land use.

1.   O   Ośrodki usługowe
2.   Zabudowa mieszk. intensywna
3.   Zabudowa mieszk. ekstensywna
4.   Centrum miasta i funkcje centralne
5.   Przemysł
6.   Zieleń urządzona
7.   Lasy
8.   Granice administracyjne miasta

In this light the logic of the successive stages of the destruction of Warsaw becomes more apparent: first the bombing of the Royal Castle in September 1939, then the destruction of the Ghetto in 1943, and finally the systematic demolition of the surviving buildings by special Kommando units after the ill-fated uprising in 1944. As a result 84% of the city was destroyed, including 90% of its monuments. The entire population of the capital was dislodged: the city ceased to live.

Soon after the liberation of the capital in January, 1945 a decision was made to rebuild Warsaw and to restore it to the rank of the capital of Poland. Reconstruction could be launched thanks to the central control of the modest financial means and the organization of a national fund for the rebuilding of the capital. Work started on the basis of plans elaborated before the war and during the occupation adapted to the tragic realities.

Numerous proposals were discussed with respect to the fate of the entirely destroyed "Old Town" including the idea of leaving the ruins as a memorial to the heroic resistance. Finally it was decided to faithfully reconstruct the external form of the historic core area, as a symbolic act of defiance, to demonstrate the will for survival of a nation condemned to annihilation.[4]

This decision reflected the nationalistic feelings of the Polish society. The high priority accorded to the reconstruction of the Old Town had public approval. I am not going to dwell on the complex methodology used in the reconstruction of the Old Town. Suffice to say that the quality of work was so meticulous that the Old City has been subsequently placed on UNESCO's "World Heritage" list. However, I want to stress the town-planning aspects of this conservation scheme. The historically inspired reconstruction of Warsaw is responsible for the present peripheral location of the Old Town. Its functions and amenities correspond to that of a standard 50-acre housing estate, and 5,000 inhabitants and its commercial facilities are scaled to serve the needs of the local residents. However, some of the cultural institutions in the Old Town area are of city-wide importance. To permit the creation of a pedestrian precinct, transit traffic has been routed on a new east-west route passing in a tunnel under the Old Town. Close collaboration by the city planners with the conservators of historic monuments assured the success of this project. The Old Town became the nation's showcase and the scene of important political events.

For various reasons the reconstruction of the Royal Palace could only be undertaken with great delay. This building now fills what used to be a jarring gap in the panorama of Warsaw and it is playing an increasingly important role as a scene of cultural and political events. Significantly, the reconstruction of the Royal Palace was entirely financed by public subscription. Unlike some of the ostentatious public buildings erected in the first post-war reconstruction period which have since lost their public prestige, the Royal Palace is an object of civic pride: public interest in the progress of its rebuilding has been remarkable.

Apart from this example, the protection of historic monuments is now less patriotically motivated and, instead, their role in conferring unique identity to the built environment is emphasized. The presence of some old buildings breaks the monotony of the environment composed of industrially produced modern buildings. This argument is often invoked to secure the protection of relatively modest elements of the cultural heritage. Increasingly such historical elements are considered as "center-creating" assets in the planning theory of all socialist countries.

The debate with respect to the optimal use of reconstructed historic centers led to a variety of solutions in the socialist countries. The rebuilding of Budapest, for instance, was carried out by inserting numerous modern elements in the tissue of the medieval buildings of the Castle area. The recent construction of the Hilton Hotel within the ruins of a former monastery illustrates the experimental Hungarian approach. In Moscow the Kremlin complex and the Red Square—the city's symbolic center—is handled with the utmost care. Yet in the immediately adjacent Rossya Hotel the priority accorded to functional exigencies resulted in the intrusion of a scale and proportions alien to the historic environment. Yet interesting effects have also been created by the introduction of modern architecture, as in the case of the Assembly Palace built within the Kremlin walls. The contrast between a small seventeenth century orthodox church and the adjacent modern office buildings lining Kalinin Avenue is equally stimulating. These examples show that the values of cultural heritage are treated with reverence everywhere in the socialist countries, although the methods of their integration into the modern environment vary from country to country.[5] The "museal" reconstruction of the totally destroyed Old City of Warsaw must be considered *sui generis*, dictated by unique historic and political circumstances.

To return to our case study of the development of Warsaw it must be stressed that the successive plans reflect changes in theory as well as the evolution of social and political factors. The first plan for the rebuilding of the capital proposed to limit the size of the city to 680,000 inhabitants. The fact that after the war most of the land within the city boundary became municipal property greatly facilitated large-scale planning measures. Vast areas were set aside for recreation. In 1951, the 120 sq. km municipal area was almost quadrupuled to encompass 446 sq. km. In the north of the city, a new satellite town was built around a vast metallurgical complex. In similar fashion the new town of Nova Huta has been developed in the vicinity of the ancient city of Cracow. These moves were justified by ideological reasons, to give a more working-class character to the two historic capitals of the Polish nation. The high level of air pollution in both cities is the price that had to be paid for the subordination of rational planning to the ideological objectives.

The 1950s were the years of "socialist realism," bequeathing to Warsaw such bulky edifices as the Russian-donated "Palace of Culture and Science" located on Europe's largest and least satisfying urban space. "Constitution Square" is another relic of the period, characterized by heavy formalistic design. 1956 and the well-known political events brought increased criticism of "socialist-realism" and the search for modern, functional solutions. The group of skyscrapers and shopping centers on the so-called "Eastern

Wall" are the landmarks of this phase-transition.

The 1960s brought a basic change with respect to the further development of the capital. Up to that point Soviet-inspired planning theory held that the cost of a metropolis is inherently greater than that of a number of medium-sized cities with the same combined population. Accordingly, attempts were made to shrink the size of Warsaw by reducing industrial employment. At the same time, expenditure on housing and on municipal facilities was cut to one-fourth of its former magnitude. However, the attempt of shifting industrial workers to the services failed because the under-developed service sector did not have a sufficient labor-absorption capacity.

A new strategy for the accelerated development of the Capital was adopted after 1970. Priority was now accorded to the creation of new branches of industry, i.e., the making of television equipment. Numerous departures from the plan were tolerated, for example, encroachment on agricultural land. The existing communication system, lacking a subway rail network, became severely overstrained. The new situation prompted the town planners to work out variant plans for the development of the Warsaw agglomeration. From among the four basic variants, the one promoting the development of the Northern Zone around the huge international airport of Modlin was chosen for implementation.[6] The institution of the Warsaw Metropolitan Voivodship was conducive to the comprehensive treatment of the 3,800 sq. km large metropolitan region. This amounted to a resuscitation of the pre-war concept of the "Functional Warsaw." Professor Helena Syrkus—co-author of the original concept in 1934—told me how pleased she was to see the confirmation of the validity of her 40-year-old design.

In the 1970s the project of the Warsaw West Center was also launched. The design of this complex turned out to be particularly difficult as it had to be compatible with the historical skyline of Warsaw. The controversy revolved around a skyscraper which was intended to close the perspective of the city's main artery, Marszalkowska Street, but its shape visually intruded upon the image of the Royal Palace in the panorama of Warsaw. There are grounds to hope that similar errors will not be repeated in the future. The latest version of the plan for the city center includes guidelines with respect to "architectural elements crystallizing the urban landscape" and places restrictions on the use of high buildings. Also, important design issues will be tested by public architectural competitions in the future.

It is common knowledge that 1980 brought a serious socio-economic crisis in Poland. However, this crisis did not result in any major change in the ambitious plan which had been adopted previously, and only the implementation schedule has been modified.

The construction of an underground railway system has finally been launched. The success of the plan now depends on whether economic recovery will permit making the necessary capital investments.

It is worth noting that the authors of the new Master Plan made an attempt to describe the flaws of the current model of spatial planning.[7] They traced planning errors to the same causes which were also responsible for the acute socio-economic crises in Poland. These include "the excessive concentration of power in the hands of a narrow group of people beyond social control, extreme centralization in the management of the economy, and the disregard of social and professional criteria in the decision-making process." The directivity of "socialist centralism" has proved very useful during the phase of the reconstruction of the war-damaged country. It permitted the re-accumulation of wealth, the creation of new values and the materialization of new concepts. But this model lost its validity as soon as the problems of reshaping and modernizing the metropolis came to the foreground.[8]

This is what the authors of the new Master Plan for Warsaw have to say about the methodology of planning: "Town-planning methodology must be adjusted to the existing economic situation . . . it is necessary to formulate realistic development prognoses, particularly in the field of investments and the implementation of social goals . . . Unrealistic postulates contained in a plan deprive it of authority and multiply the departures from it . . . It is indispensible to resume the economic analysis of the cost of the functioning of the city, the policy of siting major projects, analysis of the costs of the development of sites, and of overcoming technological and economic thresholds."[9]

Participation in planning is also stressed: "We observe an increasing involvement of the population with the problems of spatial planning, regional planning and architecture. Society should be our ally, not just a critic. Several conditions must be fulfilled however: an organizational platform for dialogue must be provided, plans must be worked out in a form intelligible to non-professionals, and the mass media must be prepared to explain plans and programs as they are being elaborated."

The private sector is still playing a very minor role in the Polish economy. The vast deficiencies in the field of municipally sponsored housing might act as a stimulus for individual initiative. Yet the shortage of building materials, particularly sanitary equipment and fittings, and the insufficient provision of motor transport constitute a major hindrance to private sector construction. Privately financed single-family homes now amount to 15% of the dwelling units produced yearly. These modest and often poorly designed individual houses result in a disorderly appearance of certain suburban areas. In manufacturing, the private sector does not exceed 1% of the national production yet it is important because of its complementary character in commerce, handicrafts and services. As pointed out by French geographers a great number of small shops and service establishments are needed to give vitality to the city center.[10] In Poland the private sector is also relatively strong in the sphere of agriculture but this has relatively little relevance for the planning of the metropolitan region. In any case, the private sector as a group has little influence on decisions based on the premises of the relevant development plans.

In conclusion, let me attempt to answer the question of whether the socialist-type metropolis can serve as a model for the large cities of the Third World. My opinion is based on my experience with the rehabilitation of historic urban centers in Algeria, Iran, Mozambique and Senegal. In all these cases the problems had to be solved within the framework of economic and spatial planning. Complex projects require the efficient marshalling and management of appropriate means, and their implementation is often blocked by land speculation. In dealing with such problems the experience of the socialist countries may indeed be useful. Yet, in line with our self-criticism, active participation must be included in the process of planning to achieve a built environment which is not only technically adequate but also psychologically satisfying.

Notes

1. K. Pawlowski, *Tony Garnier et les débuts de l'urbanisme fonctionnel en France*, (Paris, 1967).

2. J. Chmielewski and S. Syrkus, *Warszawa Funkjonaln*, (Warsaw, 1934).

3. A. Ciborowski, *Warszawa*, (Warsaw, 1964).

4. K. Pawlowski, *L'expérience polonaise dans la reconstruction des villes historiques*, (Brest, 1982).

5. W. Ostrowski, *Les ensembles historiques et l'urbanisme*, (Paris, 1976).

6. A. Kowalewski, *Warszawa, Problemy Rozwoju*, (Warsaw, 1981).

7. A. Kowalewski, and P. Rafaljki, *Warsaw—The Past and the Prospects*, (Warsaw, 1981).

8. *Ibid.*

9. *Ibid.*

10. S. Savey, *L'espace central de Varsovie, commerce et artisanat—Analyse organisation et gestion de l'espace*, (1978).

16.

The Metropolis in Socialist Countries: The Case of Budapest

Ferenc Vidor

Introduction

Socialist principles and the ideology of town planning became intertwined in the late nineteenth and early twentieth century when the concepts of "Town and Country Planning," "Stadtebau" or "Urbanisme" emerged in Europe.

The pioneers of these progressive movements agreed with Marx that, as a consequence of the industrial revolution, the urbanization process of Western Europe was likely to have a global impact triggering off rapid growth in most cities of the world.

Millions of people streaming into the cities wanted better housing, infrastructure and public transport, and a higher standard of living in general. Town planners had to live up to those expectations.

Although socio-economic problems were more or less similar in the highly developed and medium-developed countries, the policies pursued after World War I differed in function of the political structure, level of development and historical traditions of the individual countries.

After the devastations of World War I and the ensuing civil war, the Soviet Union followed the path of socialist planned economy, in which the means of town planning and development were subject to central decisions and all targets were centrally set; in other words, the industrial, residential and communal development of cities and regions was controlled by central/ planning mechanism.

In countries with social-democratic governments, the spontaneity of the market economy was also counterbalanced by the application of Marxian principles; it is sufficient to refer to the record of the labor governments of Britain or of the Scandinavian countries and the "low-cost housing" policies adopted by many other countries. In the Central-European context, characteristic products of this trend were the large housing projects built in Vienna in the framework of the "Gemeindebauten" policy.

Between World War I and World War II most Eastern-Central European countries lagged behind Western European countries, not only in providing low-cost housing but also in the introduction of social-welfare principles.

Such developments came about only after World War II when socialist governments did their best to implement these principles.

Countries which differ widely from one another regarding their geographical position, historical development and economic level now call themselves "socialist." Besides the Soviet Union and the Eastern-Central European countries, China, Vietnam, Laos, Cambodia, Cuba and some smaller African countries also claim to be in this "category." The latter ones, beyond any doubt, could be classed with equal justification among the "developing countries." Thus it would be difficult to generalize about the "socialist metropolis." In the context of this book we shall focus on a case study of Budapest which is, with 2.2 million inhabitants, the largest metropolis of Eastern Europe outside of the Soviet Union and comes closest in size and in structure to such Western European metropolitan agglomerations as Vienna, Hamburg, Barcelona or Milan.

The Eastern-Central European region has not produced such vast agglomerations like New York, London, Paris, the Netherlands' "Randstad" or the Rhein-Ruhr. Such excessive concentrations of population should not be expected in the future either not only because of lagging historical development of this region but also due to the increasing efficiency of socialist regional planning in Eastern Europe. The roots of the economic lag of Eastern-Middle Europe go back several centuries. The shift of world trade to the oceans in the sixteenth and seventeenth centuries and the simultaneous advance of the Turks leading to the partial occupations of the Kingdom of Hungary and the total occupation of the lands now known as Romania, Yugoslavia and Bulgaria were significant factors which slowed down urban development in Eastern-Middle Europe. Although the nineteenth century Austro-Hungarian Monarchy induced a spectacular metropolitan development in Vienna and Budapest, it was a somewhat artificial flowering which came to an abrupt end after World War I.

Among modern socialist countries the metropoli of Prague and Budapest emerged within the territory of the one-time monarchy. Berlin is a special case not only because of its present dividedness but also because of its standing as the former capital of the powerful German Reich; by contrast the Rumanian capital Bucharest, the Yugoslavian capital Belgrade, and the Bulgarian capital Sofia have been imprinted by Byzantine traditions, the Eastern Church, and long-lasting Turkish rule. In Bucharest and Belgrade metropolitan development only began in the 1920s triggered by Rumania's and Yugoslavia's territorial gains (having sided with the victorious powers in World War I).

These sketchy historical references indicate how different historical backgrounds and various socio-economic and political forces had worked in this region before the advent of socialist planning which made its mark some years past the end of World War II. This development is hardly 40 years old, and it is no overstatement that the predominant character of the aforementioned cities is still determined by historical development predating the socialist state—and most importantly by the industrialization and speculation booms of the second half of the nineteenth century.

Budapest: A Historical Survey

Before examining the Budapest Metropolitan Region in the socialist era, a brief survey of the historical process of urbanization in Hungary seems indicated.

The nomadic Hungarians from Asia conquered the Danube basin from the Carpathians to the Adriatic and settled amid Slavs, Germanic tribes and remnants of Romanized ethnic groups. The Hungarian Kingdom flourished from 1001 to 1490 and reached its zenith under the great renaissance ruler Mathias Corvinus (1458–1490); however, in 1526 Hungary was defeated by the Ottoman Turks and Buda was occupied in 1541. Urban development stagnated during the Turkish conquest until 1686 when the capital was recaptured by the Christian armies. Reconstruction in the eighteenth century brought about a growing German/Austrian influence. Yet, it is fair to admit that Buda and Pest remained quite provincial. Count Istvan Szechenyi was the most significant personality of this epoch. This intelligent and anglophile aristocrat can be considered the very first "regional planner" of Hungary. His ideas led to the construction of the Hungarian railway system, river regulation, irrigation, etc. in the mid-nineteenth century. The comprehensive characteristics of his concepts are still valid today. Szechenyi was also one of the initiators of the unification of Buda and Pest, which were at that time separate municipalities.

As a result of the establishment of the Austro-Hungarian Dual Monarchy in 1867, Buda and Pest—due to their central location within the Carpathian basin—have grown into a leading metropolis. The two towns were unified in 1873.

In 1869, soon after the Compromise with Austria, Hungary had 15,509,455 inhabitants and Budapest a mere 280,349 which amounted to only 1.8 percent of the country's population. By the turn of the century, the capital's population had grown to 733,358, or 3.8 percent of the total population of Hungary. Budapest then ranked fifth among the European capitals after London, Paris, Berlin, Viena and St. Petersburg (however, Moscow and Glasgow also exceeded it in population). The population passed the one million mark in 1910.

The pace of development was the highest in the last decades of the nineteenth century. Influx from 1890 to 1900 was 226,974—almost as much as the total population in 1869. In this period the villages around the city grew at the same rate; later on they became the outer suburbs of Greater Budapest. The total population of those villages was only 20,000 in 1869; by the turn of the century it rose to 126,000.

Light and heavy industries, central administration, commerce and transport were all centered in the capital. Budapest built the first underground railway on the continent in 1869, the second in the world after London. By the turn of the century, Budapest became a true metropolis both in terms of infrastructure and in cultural influence as well.

At the end of World War I and as a result of the Versailles Treaties (1919–1920), Hungary lost more than two-thirds of her territory, shrinking from 325,000 sq. km. to a mere 93,000 sq. km. Many Hungarians fled from the occupied territories to Budapest, and Budapest's population grew again to one million. But the formerly harmonic relation between the capital and the Carpathian Basin had been disrupted.

Budapest and Her Hinterland

Between World War I and World War II Hungary remained a primarily agricultural country. During the last 35 years, however, there has been a powerful shift toward industrialization, and today approximately half of the national income of Hungary comes from industrial production. The center of industry is still the Budapest metropolitan region. One-fifth of the population of the country lives in the capital and Budapest provides approximately half of the industrial production of the country. Nearly three-fifths of the industrial workers of the country work in the Budapest Metropolitan Region. The proportion of those working in the tertiary sector is similarly high.

In the 1960s the total increase of the population of the metropolitan region of Budapest exceeded the total growth of the population of the country. During this period 48 percent of the labor force concentrated in the medium and large towns of industrially developed areas. The increase of urban population was approximately 30 percent, compared with that of 1949. One-third of this increase boosted the capital while one-fifth went to the five large provincial towns—Miskolc, Debrecen, Szeged, Pecs and Gyor—situated near the frontiers of the country along an arc at a distance of about 90–120 miles from the capital with 120,000 to 220,000 inhabitants in the early 1980s.

The development of an inner line of provincial cities (Szolnok, Kecskemet and Szekesfehervar) is most significant regarding their industrial and supply functions. During the 1980s their population increased from 70,000 to 100,000 inhabitants.

Within the new municipal boundaries extended in 1950 to include the peripheral settlements, the capital covers 525 sq. km, accommodating over two million people. The density of population within that area is relatively low: 3,600 persons/sq. km compared to Vienna with 3,800 persons/sq. km.

The morphology of Budapest is essentially radio-centric. This characteristic was given to her in 1870 when the winning design of a competition proposed a main boulevard surrounding the core of Pest in a large semi-circle, similar to the Vienna "Ring." Although Budapest boulevards are not as rich in artistic monuments as Vienna, Budapest has an edge in the very favorable adaptation to topographic features offering magnificent views from the Castle area and the hills of Buda toward the geometrical pattern of the city on the plain of the Pest side. The topological situation of Budapest can be compared to a huge amphitheatre.

Budapest still bears the stigma of cities developed in the frenzied years of "laissez faire" capitalism. The most striking sign of this inheritance is the contrast between the compact, high-density inner core and the random low-density development of the peripheral settlements composed of detached homes. The urban structure of Budapest is adjusted to the geographical features of the area: it developed along the north-south axis formed by the Danube between the plain area of Pest in the east and the rolling hills of Buda on the western side.

The present Budapest Metropolitan Region covers 1,670 sq. km and embraces 44 communities including four towns. Its area only amounts to 1.7 percent of Hungary yet almost one-quarter of the country's total population lives here (22.7 percent in 1970, and 23.1 percent in 1980). In 1970, 27.2 percent of Hungary's labor force lived in this area.

A few maps illustrate the distribution of the population in 1920 and 1970 and the development of the concentration of buildings between 1930 and 1970 within the municipal boundaries. Some more information is presented on the emergence of the Budapest agglomeration between 1900 and 1970, on the changes in the population between 1880 and 1970, and also on the 1970 density of population. Table 1 shows changes in the number of inhabitants in Budapest and her agglomeration between 1960 and 2000.

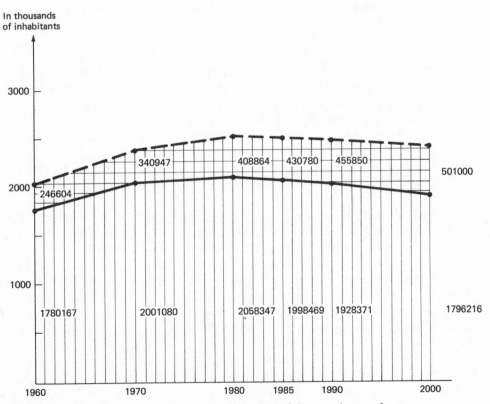

Table 16-1: Real changes and the estimated number of the population of Budapest and its agglomeration between 1960 and 2000.

Budapest and the Socialist Planning Directives

Some features of socialist town planning were implemented in Eastern-Middle European countries, also in Hungary, after World War II. While leaving a heavy mark on the latest strata of historical urban structure these features also limit future development. Since the principles applied are equally valid in all socialist countries, the Hungarian experiences can be used as an example.

The elimination of capitalist exploitation is a principal tenet of the Marxist-Leninist interpretation of socialist principles.

This policy very soon resulted in nationalizing all privately owned land with the exception of single-family homes, condominiums, and household plots. The real estate business was wound up almost completely, along with speculation in real property. Settlement planning and development were subjected to wider regional concepts which, in turn, formed part of medium-term (five years) and long-term (15 to 20 years) plans. The first "5 Year Economy Plan" pushed egalitarian tendencies aimed at eliminating the differences of levels of development not only within the individual settlements but also within the entire national territory. These social aims of ideological character were accompanied by practical measures. Under the top-priority development programs of developing the heavy industry, almost all socialist countries strove after building heavy industrial New Towns (e.g., Nova Huta in Poland and Sztalinvaros, now Dunaujvaros, in Hungary). This effort drew off vast resources from the development of housing and infrastructure in the capital and all other towns and communities as well. Later, the rigidly directivist planning of the 1950s gave way to more flexible measures, taking into account local interests. As the value of land in socialist countries is not a prime regulator and thus, in theory, there is no land speculation, the opportunities for ideal location of housing projects and industrial plants could be optimal. But in socialist cities we come across "optimal" solutions only rarely since the preliminary studies on which centralized decisions are based too often lack critical evaluation of alternative solutions.

It should be mentioned that forms of unemployment which exist in the capitalist countries and—even more markedly—in the developing countries are unknown in Eastern-Middle European socialist countries. But in a number of workplaces the absence of external unemployment has led to a reduced speed of work that may be considered a form of limited intramural unemployment. This "hidden" unemployment is yielding a low level of productivity and is one of the main reasons for the search for a new economic policy in Hungary. It is to the merit of the socialist state that it contributed to the decrease of the inherited pattern of social segregation. However, this levelling-off occurred chiefly at a lower level. In the seventies and eighties income differentiation tendencies have reappeared especially in Budapest where this phenomenon is regarded as one of the concomitant features of the New Economic Policy.

The built environment of Eastern-Middle European cities still bears the

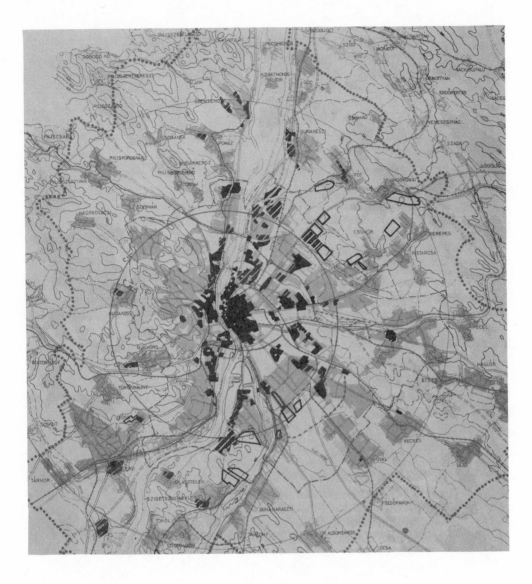

Inner circle: r = 10km
Outer circle: r = 20km

Settlement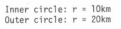

Highway

Freeway

Other roads

Railroad

River or Canal

Budapest City boundary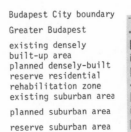

Greater Budapest

existing densely
built-up area

planned densely-built

reserve residential

rehabilitation zone

existing suburban area

planned suburban area

reserve suburban area

Fig. 16-1: The Budapest Metropolitan Area.

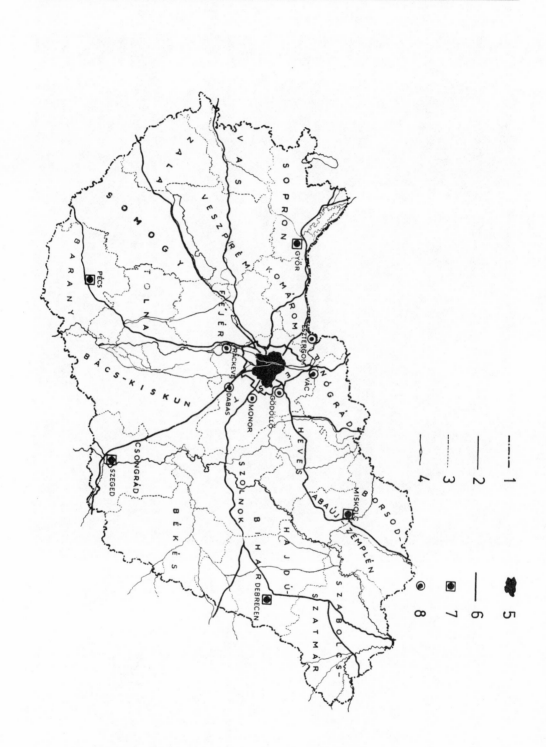

Fig. 16-2: Budapest and the National urban system of Hungary.

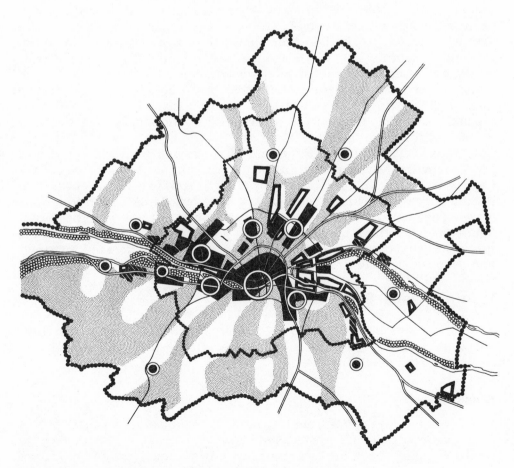

●	1	Centers
■■■	2	Built-up urban area.
▨▨	3	Reserve residential area.
▭	4	Industry
▦	5	Leisure and recreation
▭	6	Green areas
=	7	Urban Freeways
—	8	Other important Highways
••••	9	Boundary of the Budapesz agglomeration
••••	10	Boundary of Budapest Region

Fig. 16-3: Conceptual scheme of the general development plan, long-range.
(BUVATI, Pudaeest City Planning Office)

marks of periods of development that preceded the socialist state. This flavor is most evident in the inner cores of the metropoli. The most conspicuous monuments of the 30 to 40 years of socialist construction are the huge housing projects, matching in size the historical inner core. The design of these housing projects can be traced back to the quantitative view imposed by the housing shortage and the need to provide a great number of cheap and rapidly built apartments. The tens of thousands of pre-fabricated new apartments and buildings contributed to the alleviation of the post-war era housing shortage but the majority of these dwellings units are too small and the residents are now clamoring for more floor space.

It is often asserted that planners in the developed Western countries are unable to curb speculation and have difficulties in providing adequate public transportation and amenities. By contrast, the socialist states provide more long-range comprehensive planning. Instrumentation is less hampered by the need for popular consensus and is much less sensitive to market-pressures than in consumers-societies. However, all these are over-simplified statements. In many Western countries urban and regional planners represent ideas which are close to the socialist positions. By contrast recent approaches in the socialist countries—both in administration and in planning—tend to be more market-oriented. The State control is becoming looser and more private ventures are tolerated in the field of housing. All these tendencies have been pioneered by Hungary while maintaining a profile of essentially socialist ideals. Even more flexible regulations are being worked out within the framework of the New Economic Policy of the government.

In Budapest, more than 80 percent of the housing investment is now financed by the private sector. In the peri-urban, low-density areas of the Capital and in the villages, practically only the private sector is engaged in building homes, making use of short- and long-term bank loans and various forms of self-help. As the economic depression is not over yet, the output figures are lower than those of the 1970s, yet there is a hope that the private initiatives will contribute to satisfy the ever-increasing demand for larger and better-quality apartments.

Future Regional Scenarios

Within the framework of Hungary's long-term national economic plan three alternate scenarios have been developed with respect to national and regional spatial developments.[1]

Scenario I

The first alternative starts from the *trend projection* of actual development of the various regional units, considering that these would be likely to persist in spite of modified circumstances. It assumes that the growth of towns will continue to determine regional development, and that the population of a limited number of towns will continue to increase albeit more slowly. Thus, the current supply problems will continue to exist and social tensions due to *regional inequities will persist.*

Scenario II

The basic assumption of this scenario is that social and *ideological goals* will be *more emphatically asserted* in the period until the year 2000. Developing settlements—numbering hundreds—will be spread throughout the country to permit a *gradual reduction of the differences between* the development of various *regions.* Some smaller settlements and villages will be able to preserve their populations owing to their progressing urbanization as well as an improved infrastructure and provide residence for a part of the population from the stagnating or regressing settlements. This may contribute to the slowing down of the growth of urban populations and alleviate existing social tensions.

Scenario III

This scenario assumes a more differentiated and, at the same time, more dynamic urbanization. It aims at the acceleration of the development of rural areas by way of conscious, planned control of the agglomerations. It assumes that, owing to their geographic position, smaller settlements may grow together to form a more contiguous agglomeration pattern.

In order to implement this scenario, it is intended to promote a *selective village-development* policy which would ensure the *preferred development of the peripheral near-city settlements.* The introduction of such a system of preferences is vindicated by the assumption that, if present conditions prevail in near-city settlements, people will prefer to move to the cities instead of commuting 45–60 minutes each way. Further rural-urban migration would require more extensive development of the cities. The comprehensive development of near-city villages may decrease the population pressure on the older central districts. This development would also permit upgrading the presently substandard rural infrastructure. The marshalling of local resources supplemented by central control and assistance could increase the current sluggish rate of development.

The Master Plan for Budapest

Budapest stopped growing in the early 1980s and it was expected that her population would drop below two million by 1985, in line with regression trends in many Western metropoli. The fast growth of the peripheral agglomeration is also likely to slow down; an increase of 100,000 immigrants as recorded for the decade of 1970–1980 would now require 20 years. In 2000, the capital with some 1.8 million inhabitants will be surrounded by an agglomeration of about half a million people, giving Greater Budapest a total of 2.3 million inhabitants—nearly one-fourth of the total population of Hungary.

The growth of the Budapest agglomeration contrasts with the diminishing population of the country. Hungary is one of the few states in Europe where the natural increase of the population has stopped, and since 1981 the number of Hungarians started to drop by approximately 30,000 to 35,000 people yearly. The background of this phenomenon could be characterized as a "multicausal" syndrome where the low birth rate, the relatively high suicide rate, and factors rooted in the transitory nature of the social-economic transformation play an interrelated role.

Economically, the socialist countries of Eastern-Middle Europe are poorer than the leading states of Western Europe. With respect to their GNP they are lagging behind the latter, owing both to their histories and to their geographical positions. These constraints have consequences independent of the social system, not only on general welfare but also on the quality of the physical environment.

The Master Plan of Budapest, completed in 1980, considers both the economic and the physical limitations of the country.

According to the Plan, Budapest is developed chiefly within the present settlement boundaries. Within this framework a main trend of development optimizing the natural assets of the region seems to be emerging. By taking into consideration the disposible vacant areas and the economic feasibilities of transport and public utilities, a preferential axis of development running roughly parallel to the Danube appears to be the most desirable.

Over the period of time encompassed by the present plans, the residential areas of Budapest will be further increased by releasing plots suitable for building an additional 100,000 dwelling units. As a result, a belt of new settlements will be drawn around the periphery, mainly in the north and in the west. Nearly half of the capital's population will be accommodated in that belt. With the bulk of the population shifted to the north, the network of public transport will also be modified, and two new subcenters will be built north of the city on either side of the Danube. This development will extend the capital to her extreme territorial limits.

Once the quantitative housing requirements have been met after 1990 through new developments in the outskirts, the emphasis will be gradually shifted to qualitative development and to rehabilitation. By proceeding from the outskirts towards the internal districts, significant problems will be encountered. The present technological standards will have to be surpassed and significant reorganization be undertaken. It is expected that a "critical phase" will be met when the technological intrastructure of the past must be replaced.

The above-mentioned strategy will make the outskirts more compact, inasmuch as the stock of buildings will increase by 30 to 40 percent within the individual areas. Provided that construction will meet high standards, the outskirts which, at present, are somewhat transitional in character, will become more urban; the outer sections of main throughfares and the outer district centers can be tidied up, and the still obvious differences between the built environment of the internal and external boroughs can be reduced. At the same time, the entire city will be "loosened up" by spacious green areas which should reduce inequities between the two sides of the river. (Pest lacks green areas in contrast to Buda which is well endowed.)

Parallel to the restructuring of Budapest, some new areas will have to be reserved for the relocation of a number of industrial plants from the center and for providing appropriate sites for new industry. Non-polluting manufacturing will be permitted in the vicinity of residential areas or traffic junctions. Traffic lines are main generators of urban growth. It is not envisaged to modify the present network of railways and suburban railways, main throughfares, ports and airports; the goal is their qualitative development.

As apparent from the guidelines of the Master Plan, the Budapest of the future will retain many features of the present. What town planners and decision-makers will have to achieve through common efforts could be put as follows: imagination must be harmonized with the exigencies of political realities in order to preserve and enhance the matchless topographical features of the Hungarian metropolis.

Epilogue

The climate of the Eastern-Middle European countries is determined by the influence of three great seasonal air-currents. These are: the Oceanic current coming from the Atlantic, the Mediterranean breeze and the Continental current originating in the vast spaces of Eastern Europe and Asia.

Inasmuch as these meteorological facts can serve as a metaphor, we can state that the national character of Eastern-Middle European countries has always been subject to the varying mix and impact of three great cultural and economic influences: the Western (mainly German), the Mediterranean (mainly Italian) and the Eastern (Byzantine-Orthodox). In the last four decades these influences have been tempered by a common socialist layer. In examining the physical pattern of the capital cities in this region the mix of influences results in a morphology akin to a "collage." The spatial realities of Budapest, Prague, Warsaw and even of Bucharest or Belgrade can be best understood as a mosaic formed from the juxtaposition of smaller or larger heterogeneous components. The national differences manifest themselves in the relative importance of the various components and their integration.

The mosaic keeps changing since every city requires constant renewal; new tissue must replace the atrophied or decaying cells. The challenge is how to solve the continuity-discontinuity equation and how to ensure that out of the conflict of tradition and modernization a high-quality environment will emerge.

There is no easy answer: the town or metropolis does not easily reveal its essence and permit us to know its hidden processes such as the strength of its ties to the past. Questions pertaining to values cannot be answered by the new fashionable computer techniques. Many errors can be attributed to false attitudes or to basing decisions on insufficient knowledge of the nature of the mosaic and the relation among its components on the micro-level.

The mosaic character of Eastern-Middle European metropoli is linked to their bridge-like role between East and West and to some extent the North and South as well.

This interim position between the principal European cultures increasingly finds its reflection on the level of management and the instrumentation of policies. This can be attributed to the importance accorded to the interpreting role of the intelligentsia of these metropoli, which explains the fact that so many scientists and artists coming from this background have become not only interpreters of the world's culture but also initiators in the unfolding of human values.

Note

1. Department of Regional Planning of the Ministry of Town Planning and Building, "Regional Development Prognosis Related to Long-Term National Economic Planning," vol. 1, (Budapest, 1980).

17.
Toward a New Belgrade

Milos Perovic

The Evolution of Town Planning in Belgrade

Belgrade is the capital of the Socialist Federal Republic of Yugoslavia and has at present close to one and a half million inhabitants. It is a city of medieval origin but not much can be said about its genesis and early development because of a lack of information. We do not know all the phases of the gradual erosion and internal transformation of the urban structure of the ancient settlement which took place in the course of the Middle Ages and later under Islamic influence.

With the liberation from the Turks and the beginning of the free development of trade in Belgrade there began a long process of transformation. The town's access roads gradually turned into streets of commerce and the tissue of the town itself lost its oriental characteristics.

An extremely important document for the development of Belgrade was the first plan for the reconstruction of the town published in 1867 by Emilijan Josimovic. Four projects from the period before and immediately after the First World War also deserve particular attention.

What all these projects have in common is their exceptionally selective artistic approach towards town planning. Sitte and his "Der Städtebau nach seinen Kunstlerischen Grundsätzen" were the most frequently quoted author and work of that time.

The crucial period in the concept of the shaping of Belgrade came around the year 1930. The most important factor was Dobrovic's prize-winning proposal for the Terazije Terrace, a major endeavor to apply architectural concepts to the transformation of the traditional structure of the city.

Around 1950 prevailing ideology brought the systematic neglect of the valuable historic fabric of Belgrade. The predominant opinion was that the traditional core of the city should be allowed to go to ruin and then be rebuilt on the principles of the functionalistic concept of the city.

The first intrusions upon the traditional structure of the city—the construction of certain semi-open blocks and the commencement of New Belgrade could have—on account of the innovations they brought, aroused a certain amount of good will for the principles of modern architecture and town planning. However, the public soon reacted strongly in protest against

227

later mass town planning activity, especially against planning proposals during the period 1960 to 1975, some elements of which are still being implemented today.

With the construction of a ring of new settlements on the rim of the continuous built-up area of Belgrade and the construction of New Belgrade and Upper Zemun, the historic tissue of Belgrade has been reduced to a narrow strip.

New Belgrade, a new town planned and built on the deserted marshlands between the clay plateau of Bezanijska Kosa and the left bank of the Sava River, has, over the last four decades, been virtually completed—according to approved planning documents—over more than three quarters of its territory. During this period there has been the construction of over 54,000 apartments with a total net floor surface of some 320,000 square meters and a communal infrastructure over some 4,000 hectares of land.

There are a number of characteristics which make this undertaking unique. Foremost is the fact that New Belgrade is a new town located between two historical entities—Belgrade and Zemun. It also represents a rare example of a town built in the spirit of the Athens Charter a key document of the International Congress of Modern Architects (C.I.A.M.) dating from 1933.

The proximity of established urban centers gives New Belgrade great comparative advantage over other parts of the metropolitan region of Belgrade. So far, these advantages have not been exploited due to the unfortunate development strategy for the central part of New Belgrade, reflecting imported models. It is to be hoped that in the future a more natural concept of spatial organization will be implemented. New Belgrade still has many different alternatives open for its further development.

The Sava Amphitheater presents a somewhat different situation. The planned relocation of railway installations, opens up exceptional developmental opportunities for this part of the city.

This paper will examine one of the possible alternatives for the future construction of New Belgrade and the Sava Amphitheater. Attempts were made to shape this alternative on the basis of scientific theories on the nature of town growth.

The Center of New Belgrade and the Sava Amphitheater 1: Intentions

The central zone of New Belgrade took on its present appearance during the second half of the 1950s. In 1959, as a result of a national architectural and town planning competition, the final overall concept for the center of New Belgrade was completed.

This central zone was to consist of nine macro-blocks on the exterior of which are the Federal Executive Council building and a vast transportation center made up of the railway station, the bus station and the metro station. Within the nine basic blocks, in adherence to the spirit of the "Athens Charter," there was to be a strict segregation of urban functions. It was planned that six blocks should be residential in function, while the three blocks situated along the axis formed by the Federal Executive Council building and the New Belgrade railway station should contain exclusively town center functions. Thus conceived, the center of New Belgrade was to be, alongside the historical core of Belgrade and the center of old Zemun, one of the three centers of the metropolitan region of Belgrade.

Excerpts from a text by Aleksandar Djordjevic,[1] at that time director of the Town Planning Institute of the City of Belgrade, are the best illustration of the spatial organization of the central part of New Belgrade.

"The monumental axis from the Federal Executive Council building to the new railway station was given great importance . . . It is no longer the local center for the 200,000 inhabitants of New Belgrade, but a point to which . . . all guests and visitors to the Yugoslav capital will be attracted.

"Although inspiring in its breadth, this monumental axis is not for pageantry but is a living city center which meets the needs of the citizens of a large city.

"Three large squares, each with its own particular function, are included in this axis: the ceremonial square in front of the Federal Executive Council, the central town square and the station square.

"The square in front of the Federal Executive Council is a place of ceremony, parades, meetings and large gatherings. The central square represents the focus of the cultural and entertainment life of the town, a pleasant place for strolling.

"The square in front of the railway station is for the reception of travelers.

"Between the station and central squares there lies the commercial section of the center.

"On the axis between the central square and ceremonial squares are facilities of high-ranking institutions.

"The new residential blocks in the central part are not meant to be the idyllic neighborhood units of some exclusively residential zone. They retain the advantages of "living among verdure," while creating a firm "urban" composition.

"A new quality was envisaged with respect to composition relations. The architects abandoned the method of the uniform distribution of free-standing, small buildings in unlimited verdure. Repeated over a huge area, this practice leads to a new type of monotony, that of infinite lines of row upon row of isolated, similar buildings over an undefined area. Attempts have been made to avoid this monotony through the establishment of firmer relationships between the buildings and through the clearer defining and shaping of the internal, open areas intended for recreation and sport."

In contrast to New Belgrade, planners did not devote much attention to the Sava Amphitheater, with its criss-crossing railway lines and installations.

In 1946, Dobrovic published a sketch for the layout of this area, proposing to turn the Sava Amphitheater into a large city park containing ministry buildings.

In 1975, when it appeared that the railway installations would soon be removed from this area, it was proposed that a range of cultural, banking, scientific and tourist facilities be located in this area and in the area on the opposite bank of the river Sava.

Fig. 17-1: Plan of Greater Belgrade, including New Belgrade and Zemun. The Sava Amphitheater is the open land on the Belgrade bank of the Sava. (Perovic-Computer Atlas of Belgrade 1976)

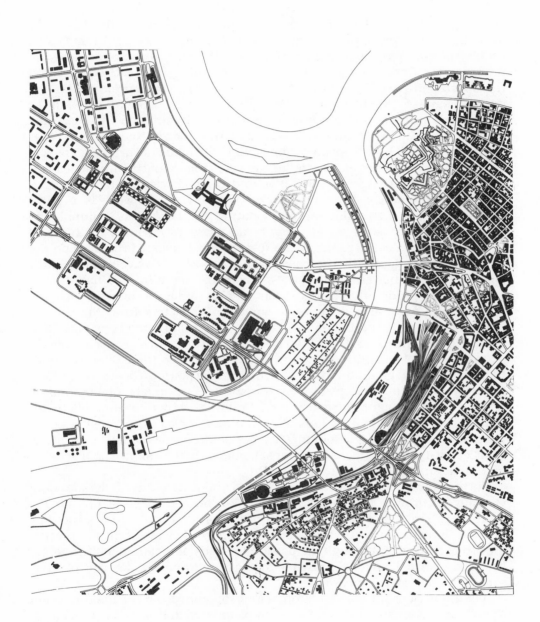

Fig. 17-2: The center of New Belgrade and the Sava Amphitheater.

It is easy to identify the models for the concept implemented in the construction of the center of New Belgrade. They are Le Corbusier's, the "Radiant City" project of 1930,[2] and the project of Lucio Costa for Brasilia of 1957.

Le Corbusier's Radiant City project represented one of the bases for formulating the principles of the "Athens Charter." Costa's Brasilia is a consistent example of the implementation of the same principles. Land-use provision is reduced to only four activities—dwellings, recreation, work and transportation—strictly separated from one another. Both projects plan the development of the town around a powerful institutional axis. In Le Corbusier's project, the administrative quarter is situated in a separate zone surrounded by verdure. It is set apart from the zone containing other central functions by a transportation center, the focus of various transport systems. In Costa's project, a similar unit is made up of the ministries and the group of the Congress, Executive and Legislative buildings. Situated about 2.5 kilometers from this Plaza of the Three Powers is a giant multi-level traffic interchange accommodating the central bus terminal. The space in between is made up of a broad grass promenade. In both Le Corbusier's and Costa's projects, the residential zones are organized on the super-block principle: in the case of Le Corbusier, twelve-story setback apartment buildings and in the case of Costa, free standing, six-floor tracts.

In New Belgrade, the composition is also axial in nature. On this monumental axis, at a distance of some 1,100 meters from the Federal Executive Council building, is the transportation center made up of railway station, bus terminal and metro station. Central activities are accommodated in three blocks of 400 × 400m in the area between the Executive building and the railway station. In the axis, on a raised platform of 400 × 1,200m, there is a 100m wide pedestrian prospect. The axial composition is strengthened by eight extremely high buildings which accommodate administrative and hotel functions instead of ministries as in Brasilia. As in the case of Le Corbusier's Radiant City, residential zones consist exclusively of collective-type apartment buildings, some of them designed in a setback pattern as in Le Corbusier's Radiant City.

All three projects, Le Corbusier's, Costa's and central New Belgrade, have virtually no growth possibilities. Expansion on the edges of the already built-up urban tissue through the addition of identical units is the only possible growth form for the town. The more delicate form of internal growth of the center through adaptation to needs of greater densification of the urban fabric is made impossible by the functionalistic doctrine of strict separation of urban functions.

Looking back at the construction of New Belgrade from the first project of Nikola Dobrovic up to those being implemented today, it is possible to perceive two phases. The first, which lasted a short period of time, was the planning of New Belgrade by Nikola Dobrovic in 1946, and Edvard Ravnikar in 1947, then up-to-date with the latest insights of planning theory. The second period, extending to the present day, differs from the first in that the

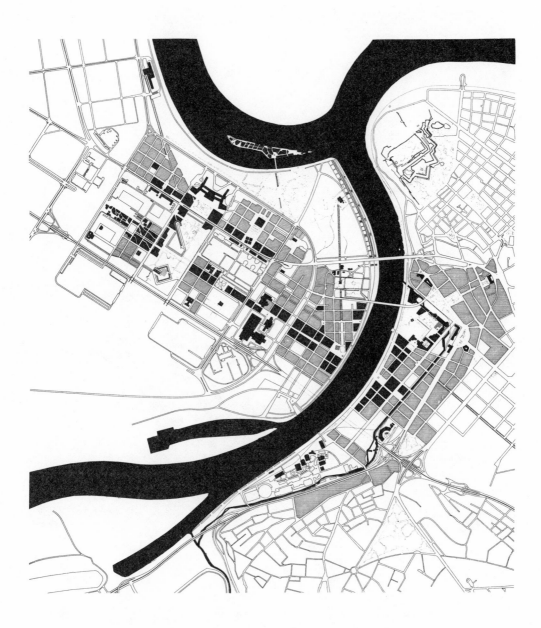

Fig. 17-3: Milos Perovic and Branislav Stojanovic. Proposal for the reconstruction of the central part of New Belgrade and the Sava Amphitheater. On this plan the Danube is to the right and the Sava River and Sava Amphitheater are at the bottom of the page. New Belgrade lies southwest of the Danube.

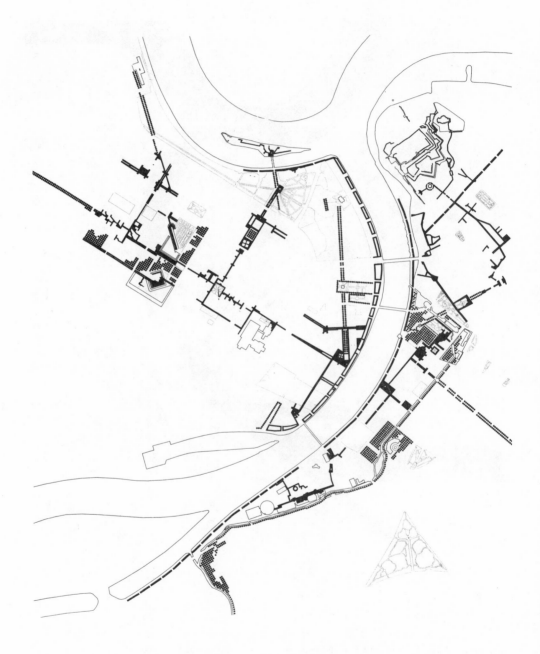

Fig. 17-4: Scenario for the development of the center of the metropolitan region of Belgrade.

great names in Yugoslav architecture and planning no longer participate in the formulation of concepts and policies. At present, research goes no further than the pursuit of partial results and the application of outmoded doctrines of modernism. These two stages closely correspond to the periods of close contact with CIAM (Congrès Internationaux d'Architecture Moderne). The point at which that contact has been lost can be defined precisely.

CIAM, an informal association of modern architects and town planners, was founded in 1928 with the aim of coordinating individual experiments and research and channeling efforts towards a common formulation of new principles. Congress themes have gradually developed from the examination of the rational organization of the apartment via the study of the housing problem as a whole to an examination of the town and the problems of towns.

CIAM activities can easily be divided into three stages. The first congresses (1929 and 1930) were dominated by housing problems under the influence of uncompromising German Marxists led by Ernst May.

By contrast, the fourth CIAM congress in 1933 was taken over by French bourgeois reformers. At that congress, Le Corbusier succeeded in having the basic assumptions from his three experimental town designs for the "Modern City for Three Million Inhabitants" (1922), the "Plan Voisin" (1925) and the Radiant City (1930) entered into the congress document entitled the "Athens Charter" which was to have profound influence on the development of towns in the world.

At the post-war congresses, representatives of the younger generation were present for the first time alongside the already legendary personalities of contemporary architecture. The congress in Hoddesdon in 1951, the subject of which was "The Heart of the City," spotlighted the rigidity and inflexibility of the Athens Charter and the intellectual inflexibility of the "old guard." The congress held in Aix-en-Provence in 1953 brought about the final break between the generations.[3] The new generation was interested in finding principles and laws in the structural organization of urban growth. They made it known that the simplified model of the functionalistic town built in line with the principles of the Athens Charter did not reflect all the complexities of modern life. They demanded the search for a framework for complex urban interactions instead of the image of the "ideal town" projected by the Athens Charter.

The architects and planners of New Belgrade have not followed the creative efforts of progressive CIAM development after the congress of Aix-en-Provence and persist in implementing the clichés of an outmoded pre-war CIAM ideology.

Scientific Theories on Urban Growth

Urban growth and development and the changes in structure which these changes bring about are extremely complex, and it is therefore very difficult to develop a comprehensive theory. Urban growth can be seen as a dual process: firstly, a change in the composition and intensity of land use, and secondly, the taking over of new land for urban functions. A number of theories exist, both descriptive and analytical, which endeavor to describe the contemporary town and its growth processes (e.g., the rent theory, the central place theory, the density gradient studies and various descriptive diagrams such as those elaborated by Burgess, Hoyt and Harris and others), but not one of them is operational.

In order for such a theory to be operative, it must be able to meet the following four criteria: first, the theory must contain a dynamic aspect if it is to demonstrate the true processes which form the structure of the town and the processes according to which its growth evolves; second, the theory must be able to stand up to empirical verification; third, the theory must have a firm internal logic and consistency; and fourth, the theory must not lose contact with reality. It must give the basic elements of structure, growth and their interactions, and show them as they evolve in reality.

Today there exist two theories which comply with these criteria. These are the corridor and wave theories.

According to the corridor theory,[4] the town, and thereby also its central functions, develop predominantly in the direction of the main communication lines and the lines of marked attractions. The intensity of communications and the intensity of the gravitation of neighboring settlements determine town development.

The wave theory,[5] put in a similarly simplified manner, explains the processes of the intensification of land use in the town. Population and activity growth give rise to increased demand for space on the outskirts of the town and also in the core areas. The growth of the activity in the town center increases the pressure on land in the limited number of accessible locations. When the land reserves in the town center are exhausted and the intensification of land use in the center reaches a high degree, central activities tend to invade neighboring residential zones. The evicted residential activities then begin to exert pressure on the residential parts of the town with lower population density along the main arterial roads, and the wave of transformation gradually moves from the town center towards the periphery.

In a metropolitan region with several growth poles or in a continuously built up metropolis with a number of secondary town centers the situation is considerably more complex.

Historic examples such as the successive transformations of the Piazza San Marco in Venice support the wave theory and help in refuting the static models of "rational" town planning.

The Center of New Belgrade and the Sava Amphitheater 2: Reality

There is today abundant literature offering criticism of a planning practice based on the principles of the Athens Charter. It is sufficient to point out the basic criticism that its concepts are founded more on aesthetic ideals than on scientific findings on the nature of urban growth. They reflect the desire to form an ideal urban environment through a series of preconceived solutions and to subordinate all design action to the ultimate vision of overall future development.

These preconceived solutions which are offered as a panacea for all problems include: the strict partition of town functions into separate zones; the forming of physically isolated and static neighborhood communities around a primary school which contain some other central activities such as a supermarket, library or outpatients' clinic; and the construction of unnecessarily high apartment buildings which sociologists frequently call "vertical ghettoes," surrounded by large unbuilt areas, around a town center raised on a special platform served by an efficient system of transportation.

The desire of planners to subordinate all design to the ultimate vision of the town in the distant future results in the reservation of disproportionally large areas for the future development of the individual activities. Such large areas then lie unused for decades, and the result is depressing.

New Belgrade, one of the more consistent examples of the implementation of the Athens Charter principles, is not immune from these faults. The errors are built into its development concept as the consequence of the adherence over many years to an outmoded ideology. Particular difficulties have been encountered in the development of the center because of the static planning procedure, the provision of excessively large open areas and over-sized building structures and, thereby, the loss of the human dimension. All this has led to New Belgrade becoming a monotonous, unattractive town—a town without vitality. Due to its comparative locational advantages, New Belgrade should be in great demand for the location of banks, embassies, hotels, department stores, design offices and cultural and entertainment facilities in the overall urban system of Belgrade. Yet, only 12.5 percent of the total volume of private cars entering New Belgrade is destination traffic, while 87.5 percent of the traffic uses New Belgrade only as a transit area. These figures show that New Belgrade is not a zone which attracts people, where people come and linger. By contrast, within the area of the circular route of the No. 2 tram in old Belgrade, over 60 percent of the total volume of private cars entering that zone do actually stay there. New Belgrade's town planning concept—juxtaposed identical neighborhood units—results in a minimum of traffic movement within the super-blocks or from one super-block to another, for no-one wishes to travel from one dull environment to another.

The analyses of residential density also give an unsatisfactory picture of the current situation. The construction of the residential parts of New Belgrade is almost completed and the population density per hectare is only 42 inhabitants. This is to be compared with 104 persons per hectare in the Stari Grad (Old Town) and 260 persons per hectare in the Vracar district. In New Belgrade there are an average of 18 apartments per hectare, while the figures for Stari Grad and Vracar are 36 and 93 respectively.

In order to make these figures more realistic let us exclude from the analyses the villages which still exist on the territory of the municipality and the larger green areas and parks. The number of inhabitants per hectare in the older Belgrade municipalities varies from 173 to 271 while in New Belgrade it is only 109. A complex index of the degree to which an area is built up can be calculated by giving a ratio of the total gross floor space for commercial purposes and the total residential gross floor area minus the large parks, recreation areas, rivers and other open spaces. For the municipality of New Belgrade this index amounts to 0.18, being especially unfavorable for its central part; while it is 0.21, for the municipality of Stari Grad. The index of the built up areas for business purposes is 0.35 for the municipality of Stari Grad and only 0.07 for the central part of New Belgrade.

These results lead to a number of conclusions. After 20 years of construction, the center of New Belgrade does not show signs of vitality despite marked locational advantages. Secondly, the organization and design concept of the broad central zone of New Belgrade does not permit the formation of a sufficient "critical mass" to act as the generator of attraction for various town activities. Thirdly, the static planning concept is the cause of a number of negative effects with respect to economic requirements. One of the reasons for these problems probably lies in the fact that the center of New Belgrade occupies an unnatural position with respect to the directions of the city's main transportation lines and the gravitational effect of the historical urban centers of Belgrade and Zemun.

One of the causes for the lack of "critical mass" lies in the fact that only 2.4 percent of the jobs in Belgrade are to be found in New Belgrade, which is the lowest percentage of jobs in any Belgrade municipality. The percentage of jobs is four times less than the percentage participation of the New Belgrade inhabitants in the overall Belgrade population. The largest number of jobs are still to be found in the Old Town (Stari Grad: 27 percent). The situation is similar concerning the number of enterprises located in the New Belgrade municipality. New Belgrade, with only 2.6 percent of the commercial enterprises located on its territory, has the lowest percentage in the whole of Belgrade, and once more the highest percentage of enterprises is in the Stari Grad municipality—36 percent.

The total built-up area of the central part of New Belgrade amounts to 771,420 square meters. This area is distributed according to function as follows: 83 percent apartments and 17 percent in services and institutions. The total number of jobs in the central part of New Belgrade is 16,768; 83.7 percent of this is office employment.

Viewing large urban territories as architectural entities, that is, insisting that everything should be planned in detail in advance, obstructs the natural processes of change and adaptation to real needs which is the source of vitality in town centers.

What will happen to such a center in the future when new needs arise? Such a center can only meet the need for which it was planned at only one moment in its existence. The totality of central activities is in direct correlation to the national product, disposable income and its regional distribution. This total is a variable, and therefore the concept based on development toward an ultimate picture is not realistic, especially as it requires the equipment of large areas of land with costly infrastructure and holding it in reserve for the highly uncertain volume and form of future development.

This reservation of infrastructurally equipped land in New Belgrade, combined with the complete lack of vitality of its center, results in major losses to the economy. The extent of these losses can be roughly calculated. Agricultural land outside the zones planned for future urban development has a stable value. This value is calculated on the basis of the 10 yearly cadastre earnings. This value increases considerably if the land is divided into plots and sold privately for residential construction purposes. On the basis of data provided by a United Nations work group of land values in different towns throughout the world, the average land value in city centers is 10 to 20 times higher than the increased value of agricultural land. It is clear that reserving of land for future construction in cases where this land cannot be put to use in the foreseeable future is dyseconomic, for the losses on such communally equipped land are proportional to the losses for its non-use and increase every year.

Due to the desire for a pre-defined "total form" by means of which an as yet unknown quality of life can be achieved, the current concept of the development of the center of New Belgrade is a utopian vision of the ideal town rather than a realistic proposal.

Meyerson[6] distinguishes two types of utopia: the literary utopia and the visual design utopia. He considers that literary utopias construct a desired future by changing the organization of society and social institutions, while visual design utopias sketch out a desired future by creating a new spatial organization. If literary or social utopias deal with elements of the physical environment at all, they do so in an extremely superficial manner. The forms and relationships follow as by-products of the proposed changes in society, the family, ownership, changes in political and other institutions. By contrast, the visual design utopias neglect the social structure and economic basis by aspiring towards a desired image of the spatial distribution of activities. However, Meyerson believes that there are some points of contact in these two utopias. The primary similarity lies in the belief that if a man is placed in an "ideal" environment—social or physical—he will behave according to the expectations of the creator of the utopia. The second point of similarity is that they are caricature-like. Caricature-like forms are the consequence of our inability to comprehend all the complexity of the urban environment. The creators of utopia usually reduce reality to a number of principles on which they then build their system to various kinds of exaggeration.

Comparing New Belgrade with three historical models—the towns of Korcula, Dubrovnik and Diocletian's palace in Split—we find that even a single apartment block in New Belgrade is bigger than all of Dubrovnik within the ramparts, while Korcula could easily fit into the space in front of the Federal Executive Council building. Diocletian's palace, still the center of animation in modern Split, is smaller than any of the open spaces between the huge buildings in the center of New Belgrade.[7]

Some of the most famous squares in the world seem minuscule in comparison with the planned square in the center of New Belgrade.

The loss of contact between the planners of New Belgrade and the CIAM also represents a loss of contact with experiments and research into urban structure and growth. Towards the end of its existence CIAM members made a major contribution by rejecting their own highly influential doctrine, the Athens Charter. They focused attention on the problems of internal urban growth and on the functional transformation of urban centers for which a theoretical framework has already been formed by urban geography and space economy. Losing contact with CIAM, the New Belgrade planners also lost the contact with science.

Scenario for the Development of the Center of the Belgrade Metropolitan Region

The metropolitan region of Belgrade emerged through the gradual growth of two urban cores, Belgrade and Zemun, and the settlements within their narrow gravitation zones.

In the first half of the nineteenth century the center of Belgrade was situated along Dubrovacka Ulica, today the Ulica 7 Jula. This street linked the local urban centers of two ethnically and politically different groups of inhabitants—the Serbian section of the town, which at that time was situated around the Serbian Orthodox Cathedral and the residence of Princess Ljubica, and the Turkish section of the town, situated in the vicinity of today's remnants of the Bajrakli Mosque. When Ulica Kneza Mihaila cut through the Dubrovacka Ulica, the center of Belgrade gradually began to expand along it and then, as a result of the sudden growth of Belgrade, it spread into many transversal streets. Today the center includes the wide area situated, roughly speaking, within the circle defined by the route of Belgrade's old and popular No. 2 tram.

At the same time, a similarly complex process was taking place in the second large urban core of today's metropolitan region of Belgrade—in Zemun. In the 1820s the center of Zemun was situated around the City Hall, today's Trg Pobede. In the middle of the nineteenth century the center gradually extended along today's Lenjinova Ulica, and at the turn of the century it was already situated at the place of today's Ulica Marsala Tita.

The commencement of the construction of New Belgrade should, theoretically speaking, have introduced new relationships into the system of the centers of Belgrade. However, New Belgrade shows a low degree of vitality and its influence on other centers within the metropolitan region of Belgrade is still negligible. If the problems of its functioning were to be overcome through channeled activity, then one scenario for the development of the system of centers in metropolitan Belgrade could take on the following form:

The operational technique known as the "scenario" represents a complete contrast to the numerical or quantitative planning techniques for perceiving the future. This technique lies in the realm of speculation, but speculation founded on reason. The aim of the scenario is not to foresee the future in all its complexity but to render those concerned "sensitive" to the various possibilities which might occur and the wide range of factors which could influence such a future.

Under normal conditions, as defined in the corridor and wave theories of urban growth, the gravitational forces of the centers of Zemun and historical Belgrade should draw the main mass of central activities in New Belgrade to today's Bulevar Lenjina and along the planned pedestrian zones of the Bulevar AVNOJ–a, but not to the monumental axis between the Federal Executive Council and the railway station as is now planned. This is a natural process: the town center always expands along the main streets, not laterally from them.

The next important factor in the development of the center of metropolitan Belgrade could be one of two alternatives, not mutually exclusive, depending on construction priority. These are a bridge downstream and the relocation of the railway lines and installations away from the Sava Amphitheater. With the construction of this bridge, the inhabitants of peripheral areas would gain an important link to the center of Belgrade via New Belgrade. At the same time the central part of New Belgrade becomes more accessible to these districts. The removal of the railway installations from the Sava Amphitheater would allow the natural descent of the city center to the river banks and its expansion along the river Sava to the area of the Sava Amphitheater. Besides central functions, this large territory would probably also have to contain a considerable volume of residential buildings and recreational facilities. With the expansion of the historical center of Belgrade onto the right bank of the Sava River, the attraction of the opposite river bank would suddenly increase.

This stage in the development of the metropolitan region of Belgrade would give rise to great structural changes in the historical cores of Belgrade and Zemun, drawing away from them administrative and large-scale commercial facilities and liberating the central parts of the city for culture, artisans and small, exclusive shops. On the basis of this, it is clear that the center of New Belgrade could in no way be limited to the narrow strip from the Federal Executive Council building to the New Belgrade railway station; but would comprise a wider band of complex activities.

Notes

1. Nikola Dobrovic, "Obnova i izgradnja Beograda: Konture Buduceg Grada," *Tehnika*, I, no. 6 (1946), pp. 176–186.
2. Le Corbusier, *The Radiant City*, (1935; New York: 1967).
3. Alison Smithson, ed., *Team 10 Primer*, (Cambridge, MA.: 1968).
4. C.F.J. Whebell, "Corridors: A Theory of Urban Systems," *Annals of the Association of American Geographers*, LIX (March, 1969), pp. 1–26.

5. Cf. Ronald R. Boyce, "The Edge of the Metropolis: The Wave Theory Analog Approach," *Internal Structure of the City: Readings on Space and Environment,* ed., Larry S. Bourne (Oxford: 1971), pp. 104–111; Richard L. Morrill, *The Spatial Organization of Society,* (Belmont, CA., 1970), pp. 173 f.

6. Martin Meyerson, "Utopian Tradition and the Planning of Cities," *Daedalus,* XC (Winter, 1961), pp. 180–193.

7. The boulevards of New Belgrade bear no resemblance whatsoever to creations of the same name in the world. The width of the Bulevar Avnoja from building to building is 120 meters, while the Bulevar Jurija Gagarina is as wide as 240 meters. In comparison, the width of the profile of the Avenue des Champs-Elysees in Paris is only 80 meters.

1. *The San Francisco Bay Area*

The scene covers an area of 129 × 168 kilometers or 21,672 square kilometers.

Note that the area covered is four times larger than that of our images of Chicago, London or Tokyo and nine times larger than that of the images of Sidney, Montreal, Athens or Beijing.

The San Francisco peninsula separates the silted waters of the Bay from the Pacific.

The bluish-grey of the built-up areas forms a continuous horseshoe pattern around the Bay. Urbanization is encroaching on the Bay by land reclamation.

Starting with the Golden Gate Bridge, we may distinguish clockwise, the Bay Bridge; Oakland and Alameda; the Oakland Airport; Fremont; San Jose—and moving up on the east shore of the Bay—Palo Alto; San Carlos; the San Mateo Bridge; San Francisco International Airport; the San Bruno Mountain; the Giants Baseball Stadium; the neat street grid of San Francisco with the 10 kilometer long Golden Gate Park, and the Presidio.

2. Chicago

The scene covers 64.4 × 84 kilometers or 5,418 square kilometers.

The built-up area stretches along Lake Michigan from Evanston, Illinois in the north to Gary, Indiana in the southeast corner of the scene. Toward the east, suburban subdivisions are spreading over the fields for 60 kilometers from the Lake shore.

The image is dominated by the orthogonal pattern of roads defining checkers of 1 mile square, derived from the 1785 Continental Land Ordinance.

Superimposed on the checkered pattern are the fine radial lines of railroads and highways converging on the center of Chicago, the "Loop," a dark spot east of the finger like Navy Pier.

Some 20 kilometers inland and parallel with the Lake shore, the Des Plaines River runs south into the Chicago Ship Channel, joined further down by the Calumet Sag Channel.

Major recognizable features are the giant O'Hare Airport; Midway Airport; Lake Calumet; Wolf Lake; the US Steel plant at Gary and the major roads and thruways.

In its geographical location, size and growth pattern Chicago is very similar to Buenos Aires (map number 5, reproduced at the same scale). Both cities grew to importance as ports and meat–packing centers.

3. Montreal

The scene covers 43 × 56 kilometers or 2,408 square kilometers.

Montreal is on the island between the St. Lawrence and the Riviere des Prairies. St. Labert is on the east bank of the St. Lawrence. Laval on the Isle Jesus between the Riviere des Prairies and the Rivieres des Milles Iles. The core area is facing St. Lambert and the islands of Ste. Helen and Notre Dame, between the red spot of the Mt. Royal and the St. Lawrence. The other red spot further north is Maisonneuve Park.

The Trans-Canada Highway forms a spine to Montreal. The urban pattern derives from the subdivision of the typical french "long lot" fields contrasting with the checkered pattern of Manila or the majestic axial pattern of Beijing (these reproduced here at the same scale as Montreal).

4. Baltimore and Washington D.C.

The scene covers 82.25 × 98 kilometers or 8,050 square kilometers.

The centers of the two cities are located barely 60 kilometers apart, and the two are linked by an increasingly urbanized corridor between Routes 1 and 29 with the Interstate Route 295 in the middle. The new town of Columbia, Md. is half way between the two major centers. This is the southern leg of what Jean Gottman called the Northeast Seabord Megalopolis or BosWash, stretching from Boston to Washington D.C.

Baltimore within the perimeter of the Route 695 ring–road includes an area of about 440 square kilometers, about half the size of the area within the Route 495 ring–road of the Washington area.

In Washington the geometric pattern of Major l'Enfant's plan is clearly distinguishable between the Potomac and Anacosta Rivers. On the Virginia side the built-up area with Arlington and Alexandria is as important as the District of Columbia.

Apart from the blue-colored strip development along Route 1, several other growth corridors are visible. Baltimore has a particularly neat finger-like growth pattern.

To the east of the image Annapolis can be seen with the white line of the Chesapeake Bridge over to Delaware.

5. Buenos Aires

The scene covers 64.5 × 84 kilometers, or 5,418 square kilometers.

Greater Buenos Aires consists of the Federal Capital and 19 surrounding communes, an area of 3880 square kilometers and a population of nearly 10 million inhabitants—42% of the urban population of Argentina or 35% of the total population of the country.

On the image one can clearly distinguish the dense core area of the city defined by the arc of the 24 kilometers long Avenida General Paz and the dark line of the Riachuelo canal. The city is spreading over the small-scale checker-field pattern. The planners are trying to create a "cinturon ecologico" or forest-belt about 30 kilometers center.

The location of Buenos Aires on the La Plata River is similar to that of Chicago on Lake Michigan. Buenos Aires stretches to the northwest to Escobar and Pilar and to the southeast 64 kilometers to the city of La Plata, just outside of our scene.

247

6. Rio De Janeiro

The scene covers 86 × 112 kilometers or 9,632 square kilometers.

The area of this image is four times larger than the ones in our images of
Sidney, Beijing, Manila, Athens or Montreal.

The deep–water Baia de Guanabara separates Rio from Niteroi on the east
side, but the two have been linked by the 8 kilometer long Bay Bridge. The
entrance of the bay is guarded by the Sugar Loaf rock on the Rio side and
the facing Parrot Beak. To the south of center Rio, the red Barra de Tijuca
creates a barrier to the famous beaches of Leme, Copacabana, Leblon and
Gavea.

The built-up area spreads both to the north with its industrial suburbs and
squatter areas, and in westerly direction toward the Baia de Sepatiba. A
planned satellite town is being created in the triangular area of the
Jacarepagua lagoon with its 20 kilometer long beach west of the Tijuca range.

The swamps on the north end of Guanabara Bay have so far prevented a
horseshoe-form continuous growth between Rio and Niteroi as in the San
Francisco Bay area. The main growth direction is toward the west along the
highway to the industrial town of Volta Redonda and toward São Paulo.

The aerial photographs reproduced in this volume show the central area
with Santos Dumont Airport halfway between the new bridge and the Sugar
Loaf. The main airport of Rio is on the large Ilho do Governador in
Guanabara Bay. The smaller curly island is the site of the University City.

7. Greater London

The scene covers 64.5 × 84 kilometers or 5,410 square kilometers.

The snake line of the River Thames crosses the image from east to west. In the middle of the image, Hyde Park with the Serpentine can be identified; to the east lies Westminister and the City of London, only one square mile in size. The dockland area with the Isle of Dogs and further toward Greenwich can be distinguished, also the construction site of the London Flood barrage. To the east the red dots of Richmond Park and Hampton Court as well as Heathrow Airport are easy to recognize. The M25 outer Ring Motorway can be traced in white or blue line segments about 20 to 30 kilometers from the center, well within the Green Belt, which of course appears red in our image. Just outside the Green Belt some of the "First Generation" New Towns can be identified: Hemel Hempstead, Hatfield and Harlow. The area administered by the London County Council is about 1,600 square kilometers. The orbital M25 Motorway includes a somewhat larger rectangular area of 48 × 54 kilometers or 2,500 square kilometers.

The vast sprawl of London is very evident in a comparison with Moscow or Buenos Aires. Another aspect is the poly–nuclear nature of the London agglomeration. There is less evidence of axial development although one may be emerging along the M1 Motorway toward Luton and another one along the M4 toward Reading.

8. *Amsterdam*

The scene covers 53.75 × 70 kilometers or 3,762.6 square kilometers.

The historic core of Amsterdam—a mere 170 hectares—is on the south side of the Nordzee Canal connecting the Ijselmeer with the Atlantic. Planned extension has been the rule, and the large development areas are clearly legible: Amsterdam west; Amstelveen to the south; the Bijmelmeer to the southeast. To the west—beyond the port—is the old town of Haarlem and from there linear development is also discernible both from Zaandam and from Ijmuiden toward Aalkmar.

To the east are the newly reclaimed lands of the Flevoland-polders. The older east Flevoland with smaller fields and the new town of Lelystad in construction contrasts with the larger scale pattern of South Flevoland on which the new town of Almere is being built facing the old fortress town of Naarden.

To the east the string of cities making up the northern arc of the "Randstad" continues with the towns of Busseum and Hilversum (just under the visual cues). South of Amsterdam and Haarlem are the planned fields of the Haarlemermeer which include the vast Schiphol Airport, larger than the historical city of Amsterdam.

250

9. Moscow

The scene covers 64.5 × 84 kilometers or 5,418 square kilometers.

The Moscow Metropolitan Region now encompasses 13,378 square kilometers. On this image the eggshaped central area within the peripheral motorway has been enhanced by a yellow overlay. Within this area of 877 square kilometers live 8.2 million of the 12.7 million inhabitants of the Moscow Region. Of this the clearly discernible core of 103 square kilometers concentrates 1.2 million; the rest of the area is divided into seven sectors each with about a million inhabitants.

The monocentric, annular structure of the city strongly resembles that of Paris. The winding Moskva River crosses our scene from east to west. The Moskva-Volga Canal running north is crossing the Khimki, Priogovskiy and Uchinskoye reservoirs.

Diagonally to the Northeast runs the Moscow-Leningrad Highway with the satellite town of Zelenograd. To the right of the road is Shemenestvo International Airport. Other development axes are to the north to Pushkino-Aagorsk, east to Elektrostal, and to the southeast to Ramenskoye cutting wedges out of the wide forest-protective belt.

251

10. Athens

The scene covers 43 × 56 kilometers or 2,408 square kilometers.

The core of Athens is situated somewhat inland from its port Piraeus on the Gulf of Saronica. The climate is arid and the image shows a marked absence of vegetation.

To the southeast is the large island of Salamis. Athens is expanding both toward the Gulf of Salamis as well as to the north, and from Piraeus along the shore toward Cape Sounion, already stretching 16 kilometers to the beaches of Glifagha.

Another urbanization axis is discernible toward the northeast and the Gulf of Petali. Most of the new development is unplanned and illegal.

Over three million people, one-third of the Greek population, lives in the Athen metropolitan area.

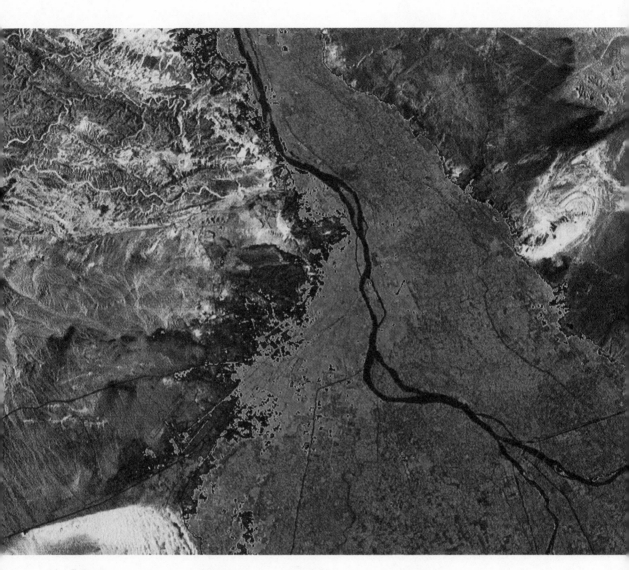

11. Cairo

The scene covers 43 × 56 kilometers, or 2,408 square kilometers.

Greater Cairo, including the Governorates of Cairo proper, Gizeh and Kalubiah concentrates some 11 million people on only 2,900 square kilometers. The image shows that most of this area is desert land, some of it intensely cultivated with a small built-up area implying very high residential densities.

The Nile crosses the image running north. The core of the modern city is on the east side facing the large island of Zamalek. The historical core is further south toward Mogattam Hill. Between the Nile and an irrigation canal marking the edge of the desert to the east is cultivated land. An 8 kilometers long urban corridor cuts across the red of the vegetation, corresponding to the Pyramid road to Gizeh. The pyramids are barely discernible on the edge of the desert.

Major growth corridors are emerging toward Helwan on the right bank of the Nile some 12 kilometers south of the city, to the north along the Alexandria Delta Road, and along the Ismailia Delta Road to the northeast passing the large new airport.

253

12. Beijing

The scene covers 43 × 56 kilometers, or 2,408 square kilometers.

Planned urban form and imperial scale are manifest in this image of Beijing. The core is the rectangle of the old imperial "Purple City," a rectangle of about 5 × 6 kilometers within the thirteenth century walls. To the south is the Outer City, 3 × 8 kilometers, to the north the area once surrounded by the Mongol earth walls.

The commune of Beijing extends over an area of 16,800 square kilometers, the inner city to be limited by a planned ring–road is no larger than about 24 × 30 km or 688 square kilometers, much of it intensely cultivated in tiny plots alternating with houses.

In 1982 the 62 square kilometers of the old city had a population of 1.8 million, the larger agglomeration of 688 square kilometers 5.5 million. The city is growing by planned extensions primarily along its east-west axis. To the west, some 20 kilometers from the center is the Shijingsan industrial area. Universities and research institutes tend to be located to the northwest in proximity of the former summer palace and Yiheidan area, its large lake visible as a black dot on our image. The long white stripe to the south is Nanfan Airport.

254

13. Tokyo

The scene covers 64.5 × 84 kilometers or 5,418 square kilometers.

Just west of Tokyo Bay in the middle of this image is the dark red rectangle of the imperial palace. More than 30 million Japanese live within a 60 kilometer radius from this center. Tokyo proper occupies the table land between the Tamgawa and Arakawa rivers and the flat land between the Arakawa and the Edogawa. To the east of the Edogawa is Chiba prefecture with the towns of Ichikawa, Chiba and Kisarazu. To the south of the Tama River are Kawasaki and Yokohama. To the east the conurbation stretches to Tachikawa and to the new international airport. Like San Francisco Bay, the shoreline of Tokyo Bay also shows the result of large scale land reclamation. Most of the port facilities as well as Heneda Airport are built on filled land. The very fine grain of the built-up area indicates the very tiny plots. Note that this image in only one-fourth of the area shown on our scene for San Francisco Bay.

Metropolitan Tokyo includes Tokyo proper and the three prefectures of Kanagawa, Chiba and Saitama, with a combined area of 8,431 square kilometers. Tokyo proper covers 2,156 square kilometers and had a population of 11.61 million in 1980.

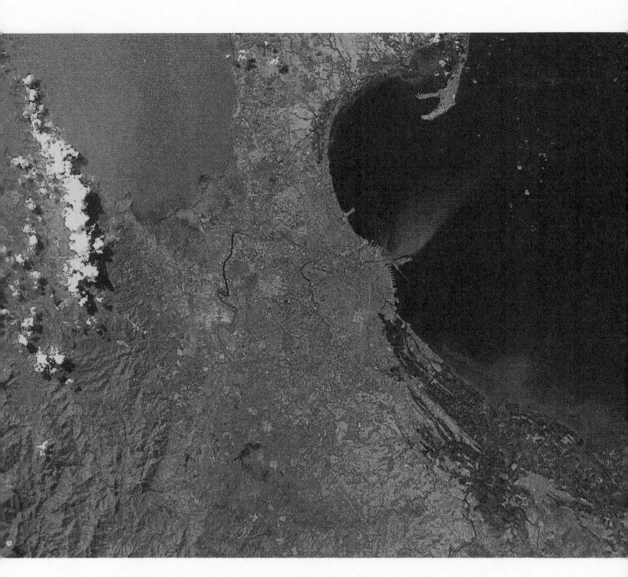

14. Manila

    The scene covers 43 × 56 kilometers or 2,408 square kilometers.

    Metro-Manila is the greenish-grey area between the dark waters of Manila Bay and the sedimented Laguna de Bay which appears light blue. The Passig River connects the Laguna to the Bay. To the north of the Passig is Tokyo Harbor and further north the notorious Tondo Foreshore squatter settlement. On the northeast edge of the scene are mud flats studded with commercial fish ponds.

    Manila has a fan-shaped agglomerate pattern with some radial avenues visible on the satellite image.

    The very high residential densities become evident by comparing this image with that of Montreal which is at the same scale.

15. Sidney

The scene covers 43 × 56 kilometers or 2,408 square kilometers.

The center of Sidney can be located by the thin white line of the harbor Bridge in Port Jackson. To the right of it the white dot is Bennelong Point with the famous Opera House. From this point the city stretches some 40 kilometers east in the direction of the Blue Mountains range. To the south on the Pacific shore is Botany Bay with the runway of Sidney Airport jutting into it. The city spread beyond Botany Bay north of rugged Port Jackson are the suburbs of Mosman and North Sidney.

The Sidney metropolitan region covers 12,407 square kilometers and has a population of 3.3 million people. 90% of this, or close to 3 million, live within a distance of 30 kilometers from the center. The pattern of Sidney shows both axial and poly–nuclear development with numerous green-colored service centers distinguishable within the reddish-grey suburban areas.

Part VI

North America

18.

Where Did All The Metropolitanites Go?

Hans Blumenfeld

The Conceptual Framework of the Problem

For several centuries a trend toward concentration of activity and population in relatively few urban centers has been observed. This trend has been generally accelerating and spreading from the "developed" to the "developing" countries. For at least a century this centripetal trend has been supplemented by a centrifugal trend from urban centers to their "umland." The resulting new form of human settlement has been recognized as a "metropolitan area" by the Census of the U.S. and under the same or another name by many other countries. The metropolitan area is essentially defined as a commuter watershed, constituting a common labor and housing market. It has long been recognized that such a concentration leads to a substantial increase of activities and population well beyond its boundaries, up to a travel distance of about two hours from its center.

These activities are of two kinds—productive, primarily manufacturing, which draw on the services of the center, and recreational services to the population of the central area. John Friedmann, while expressly recognizing only the second function, has proposed the term "urban field" for this large unit. I have called it a "metropolitan region," consisting of a "fringe" surrounding a "core," constituted by a metropolitan area. The boundary between core and fringe is blurred and becoming more so as work places move increasingly from the center toward the periphery of metropolitan areas.

In no country have these "metropolitan regions" been defined officially, nor their characteristics investigated systematically. While "growth pole" and "satellite town" theories and policies are widely accepted, few comparisons have been made between the growth rates of towns within or outside of metropolitan orbits. A small study of the 17 towns in Ontario which passed the 20,000 population mark between 1941 and 1969 showed that the growth rates of 10 towns located within metropolitan orbits averaged more than twice those of the seven located outside such orbits.[1]

Metropolitan regions are potentially very large: if two hours travel time is identified with 90 miles, one such area could cover almost 28,000 square miles, over twice the size of Belgium. Indeed, in the most urbanized parts of the world such as West Central Europe, the northeastern U.S. and most of Japan, there is hardly an area left outside such regions. If their inhabitants are defined as "metropolitanites," there is no place for them to go (or to come from) except abroad. The question formulated by the title loses its meaning. The United Kingdom has established "metro economic labor areas." Although these by definition are less extensive than "urban fields," they accounted in 1971 for all but 4.3% of the population and 4.0% of the employment of the British Isles.

In most parts of the world, however, including most of North America, extended areas are definitely "non-metropolitan," and have been defined as such by the U.S. Census. A difficulty arises because the census definition of a metropolitan area includes numerous areas which are much smaller than those denoted in common parlance as "metropoli," generally thought of as units of at least half a million or a million population. On the other hand, an investigation limited to these large units encounters the difficulty that their number in most countries is so small that the potential weight of random deviations makes statistical analysis somewhat hazardous.

Renewed discussion of the problem has been touched off by the fact that the U.S. Census showed an actual decrease in the population of some of the largest metropolitan areas in the country since 1970. Prior to that time a reversal of growth had been observed in only two cases. Vienna and Berlin (both East and West), after they had lost their roles as imperial capitals, are both located in countries with decreasing populations. Other cities which have lost their roles of national capital—Istanbul, Leningrad, Calcutta, Rio de Janeiro—continue to grow.

An added impetus was given to the discussion when U.S. census figures on internal migration showed a sizeable reversal of the long established flow from non-metropolitan to metropolitan counties. While from 1965 to 1970 the sum of all metropolitan counties gained 352,000 persons from the non-metropolitan counties, from 1970 to 1975 they lost 1,594 to them. The trend continued with a loss of 396,000 from 1975 to 1976.

This surprising phenomenon gave rise to various explanations, not necessarily mutually exclusive. A few observers saw it merely as a repetition of the return of the unemployed to their home communities, a situation which had been observed during the depression. This may be a contributing factor, but probably a minor one. Most scholars interpret it as a continuation of the historical centrifugal trend beyond the metropolitan boundaries established by the census; others see a "clean break," a return to life in the countryside and the small town.

There can be no question that metropolitan life extends increasingly beyond official boundaries. Residential "sprawl" has been amply documented. Perhaps even more significant is the fact that a rapidly growing percentage of the workplaces of the metropolitan population is located beyond these boundaries. Table 1 presents the relevant data for the five largest metropolitan areas of the northeastern United States, all of which have lost population since 1970. It is evident that this loss is inconclusive and that much larger areas must be analyzed before jumping to the conclusion—which may or may not be valid—that the diseconomies of city size now outweigh long established economies. Even less founded is the hypothesis of a "return to the land." Farm population continues to decrease; in the U.S. four out of five "rural" dwellers are now classified as "non-farm."

In opposition to those who believe that the "overspill" resulting from the historical centrifugal trend provides a complete explanation, a number of observers have emphasized the growth of counties located well beyond metropolitan overspill. These have been defined by two different measures: first, counties not adjacent to metropolitan areas, and second, counties with less than 3% of the labor force commuting to metropolitan areas. The former accounted for only 12.5%, and the latter for 13.1% of the population of the United States in 1974.

TABLE 1

Percentage distribution by workplace location
for workers resident in five S.M.A.'s in the U.S., 1960 & 1970

S.M.A.	Central City		Other S.M.A.		Outside S.M.A.	
	1960	1970	1960	1970	1960	1970
New York	79.2	71.0	18.7	24.4	2.1	4.6
Chicago	68.1	51.9	30.3	46.0	1.6	2.1
Philadelphia	55.6	45.8	41.0	48.5	3.4	5.7
Detroit	55.9	37.5	42.3	60.0	1.8	2.5
Boston	42.8	36.0	53.6	59.0	3.6	5.0
unweighted average	60.3	48.5	37.2	47.6	2.5	4.0

Alex Anas and Leon N. Moses, "Transportation and Land Use in the Mature Metropolis," in: Charles L. Levin, *The Mature Metropolis*, Lexington Books, 1978, p. 158, Table 8-1.

*S.M.A. stands for SMSA or Standard Metropolitan Statistical Area.

An interesting new twist was given to the discussion by the studies of Daniel R. Vining, Jr.[2] Vining is interested in the most spectacular form of centripetal movement, the trend toward concentration in one (more rarely two or more) primate cities. In order to encompass any conceivable overspill, he overbounds their area. This in fact shifts the investigation from a comparison between non-metropolitan and metropolitan regions, and between various size classes of the latter, to the relation between core and periphery, or the regional distribution of a nation's population. This is an even more complex problem, related to the former one in ways which may be contradictory as well as concurrent. Another peculiarity of Vining's approach is his emphasis on net internal migration as the most significant factor of population change. I have had the benefit of a wide exchange of views with Mr. Vining which, in fact, provided the stimulus for this chapter.

Problems of the Data Base

All the relevant data for study of population change are derived from official statistics. While their authors never fail to point out the margin of error of these data, their precise numerical form makes it easy to forget that they cannot be more reliable than the individual answers which they summarize. If deviations of answers from facts are entirely random, they are irrelevant because of the "law of large numbers." Estimates of biased deviations are always speculative, but may be still worth considering.

The primary data in dealing with population change are periodic census counts, based generally on oral or written replies of the head or other member of the household. Overcounting of persons with two residences is probably eliminated with modern methods of data processing; a seasonal bias dependent on the date of the count may exist, but is probably not significant. However, undercounting may be serious. It may be assumed that persons distrustful of public authority will try, often successfully, to avoid being enumerated. This certainly applies to illegal immigrants but may include other groups hostile to "the Establishment." It is probable that these are concentrated in metropolitan areas, and increasing in number. A significant and growing undercount of metropolitan populations is a distinct possibility.

Population changes are the combined results of births minus deaths and of net migration. Probably the substitution of place of occurrence for place of residence which has long bedeviled vital statistics has now been practically eliminated in developed countries. Net migration is given as the difference between the change derived from vital statistics and that found by successive census counts, and is as reliable as these. Gross migration, however, is elusive. No data, nationally or locally, are available for out-migration. National data on in-migration are notoriously deficient because of substantial illegal immigration.

For movements between different areas of a given country the main sources are answers to census questions concerning a person's place of residence at a previous (usually five years) point in time. By processing these data, movements between areas can be defined, including movements from (but not to) places abroad.

On this basis a distinction has been made between "internal migration" and "foreign immigration." Vining and most other authors treat them as clearly distinct and independent variables. This is questionable. First, some of the persons who lived abroad at the defined previous point in time are not "immigrants" but returning from temporary residence abroad. Second, illegal immigrants, and quite likely some legal ones also, will substitute a place within the country—almost certainly a major city—for their actual previous location abroad. Third, when does an "immigrant" become an "internal migrant"? According to the questionnaire classification, the moment he arrives in the country. In Canada almost all immigrants "land" in one of the three largest metropolitan areas: Montreal, Toronto, or Vancouver. Most of them stay there for shorter or longer periods of acculturation until they find jobs and permanent residence all over the country, approximating the general population distribution. A case in point is Toronto; from 1971 to 1976 there was a "net internal migration" loss of about 20,000, but immigration of 200,000. In the preceding five-year period immigration had been even higher. Certainly far more than 20,000 of these moved to other places in Canada between 1971 and 1976. Should they be counted as "internal migrants"?

Another point raising doubts about the reliability of figures on net internal migration derived as residuals from gross internal migration is the fact that the former usually represent a small fraction of the latter. In the city of Munich, Germany, a gross migration (both directions) of 217,000 resulted in a net migration of -546. It is evident that an error of less than 1% in the data for either gross direction could have reversed the sign of net migration.

Finally, the large size and irregular shape of the territorial units of measurement—counties in the U.S.—is a potential source of error, e.g., a county with less than 3% commuting may well contain municipalities from which 10% of the labor force commutes to a metropolis.

For all these regions the following findings must be regarded as highly tentative.

TABLE 2

Metropolitan and non-metropolitan population U.S., 1940 to 1977

Year	Percent of total	Metropolitan Average annual 1000	change (%)	Non-metropolitan Average annual 1000	change (%)
1940	52.8	69,535	—	62,135	—
1950	56.0	84,854	2.2	62,135	0.0
1960	62.9	112,886	2.8	66,438	0.7
1970	68.6	139,419	2.2	63,793	−0.4
1975	72.7	155,021	2.2	58,153	−1.8
1976	73.0	156,754	1.1	58,114	−0.1
1977	73.0	157,968	0.8	58,570	0.8

Note: Average annual growth is calculated as equal fraction of period.
U.S.A., S.M.S.A. Population, Statistical Abstract 1979, No. 14.

Observed Changes in the U.S.

The changes in population between 1940 and 1977 of metropolitan and non-metropolitan counties are summarized in Table 2. In their interpretation it should be kept in mind that counties may shift from non-metropolitan status, while the opposite shift has not occurred. Somewhat surprisingly, the data do not indicate any decrease in the annual growth rates of metropolitan populations up to 1975; only the last two years show a definite slowing down, but not yet a reversal of growth.

A reversal can, however, be observed in the annual growth rate of non-metropolitan areas—from 1.8% between 1970–1975 to 0.8 from 1976 –1977. It may be noted that this rate is only nominally higher than that observed between 1950–1960 (0.7%). More significant is the fact that in 1976–1977 the growth rate of non-metropolitan equalled that of metropolitan areas. Also, a definite slowing down of the growth rate already during the 1970–1975 period occurred in the largest Standard Metropolitan Statistical Areas (SMSA's), those with populations over 1.5 million, together with a nominal slowing down in the smaller SMSA's and a tripling of the growth rate of the non-metropolitan counties (Tables 3 and 4).

TABLE 3

Percentage distribution of population of SMSA's, U.S., 1970 and 1977

Size group (1000)	1970 1000 percent		1977 1000 percent		Percent change 1970 to 1977
over 3,000	39.3	26.3	38.8	24.6	−1.1
1,000-3,000	45.8	30.6	49.3	31.2	7.5
500-1,000	23.8	15.9	25.3	16.0	8.4
250-500	22.9	15.3	25.0	15.9	9.1
100-250	15.8	10.6	17.4	11.0	10.2
under 100	2.0	1.3	2.1	1.3	5.9
All groups	149.6	100.0	158.0	100.0	5.6

U.S.A., SMSA population, Statistical Abstract 1979, No. 15.

It can be hypothesized that it is precisely the largest SMSA's which have overflown their boundaries and that this overflow accounts for the increase of the non-metropolitan population. Some support of this hypothesis can be derived by a breakdown of the data by four major regions of the U.S. (Table 5). These show that only in the Northeast, where SMSA's account for almost 60% of the population, has the share of the non-metropolitan population shown an increase between 1970 and 1975, from 14.2% to 14.3%. In the other three regions their share continued to drop; in the South, with only 22% in large metropolitan areas, the drop was precipitous, from 38.8% to 33.4%.

A valuable contribution to the analysis of the problem has been made by Peter A. Morrison and his associates,[3] by breaking down the non-metropolitan counties into those "adjacent" and "non-adjacent" to SMSA's. They have also divided the 2,469 non-metropolitan counties of the U.S. into

Table 4

**Population of the U.S.
by three size groups of settlement units,
1960, 1970 and 1975**

Unit	1960	1970	1975	Percent change 1960-70	1970-75	1960-75
SMSA						
over 1.5 m	69,262	81,472	82,899	17.6	1.7	19.7
under 1.5m	58,676	68,355	73,198	16.5	7.1	19.7
non-SMSA	51,373	53,478	56,954	4.3	6.6	10.9
U.S.	179,311	203,305	213,051	100.0	100.0	100.0

U.S. Census, Estimates of the population of counties and metropolitan areas, July 1, 1974 and 1975.

Table 5

**Population of SMSA's with population over 1.5 million
and of non-SMSA counties
as percentages of four regions, U.S., 1960, 1970, 1975**

Region	SMSA's over 1.5 million 1960	1970	1975	Non-SMSA 1960	1970	1975
Northeast	58.9	59.0	58.0	14.7	14.2	14.3
North-Central	38.8	40.0	39.4	33.3	31.3	30.8
South	18.4	22.0	22.1	41.2	38.8	33.4
West	45.2	46.7	44.2	23.9	21.2	20.0

U.S. Census Estimates of the population of counties and metroplitan areas, July 1, 1974 and 1975.

321 "urban," 865 "less urbanized," and 1,283 "rural" (Table 6).

A comparison between Tables 4 and 6 indicates the fragility of the data. A lowering of the threshold of "large" from 1.5 to 1.0 million population and a one-year reduction of the period from 1970–1975 to 1970–1974 results in the disappearance of the relative decrease of the "large SMSA" population. In Table 6 growth rate is positively correlated with the population size of SMSA's. However, the large SMSA's are the only one of the nine groups in which the 1970–1974 growth rate has dropped below that of the preceding decade. Growth has accelerated far more in the adjacent than in the non-adjacent counties, and in the rural than in the urban ones. The significant net result is an equalization of growth rates among the nine groups, the range being reduced by about 70%. By contrast, within SMSA's the difference between core and fringe areas has increased by almost 65%. The importance of the overflow as a source of the apparent reversal of metropolitan growth is strongly confirmed by data presented in the study by

Table 6

Non-metropolitan counties in 26 U.S. states which
showed growth from 1970 to 1974;
Annual net migration 1960-1970 and 1970-1974
for three groups of counties

Group of counties	1960-1970	1970-1974	Change from (1960-1970)-(1970-1974)
Urbanized	−.23	.52	.75
Less urbanized	−.77	.83	1.60
Rural	−1.00	1.30	2.31

Kevin F. McCarthy, and Peter A. Morrison, The Changing Demographic and Economic
Structure of Non-Metropolitan Areas and in the United States, Rand Corp., Santa Monica,
January 1979, p. 34-37.

McCarthy and Morrison which show an opposite reversal in the counties
adjacent to SMSA's. The study divided the U.S. into 26 regions. While from
1960 to 1970 more than three-quarters of these (23) showed a migration
loss, including five with a total population loss from 1970–1975, all but
three showed migration gains.[4]

Of the three regions in which non-adjacent counties showed a net
migration gain already in the 1960s, two—"N-E Metro Belt" and Florida[5]
—have a metropolitan structure which makes overflow beyond adjacent
counties highly probable. In the N-E Metro Belt the migration gain in the
non-adjacent counties accelerated to an annual rate of 1.7%.[6]

All data so far presented indicate continued strength of the centrifugal
trend within metropolitan orbits, both within SMSA's and in the adjacent
counties, defined as the "Fringe." Of the 0.75% loss by metropolitan
counties of share of national population, 0.62% were absorbed by "fringe"
and only 0.13% by non-adjacent counties. In the 1970–1974 period, 82.6%
of the metropolitan loss appears to be due to "over-spill" and only 17.4% to
"reversal." This is a very tentative conclusion; post-1974 data may show a
different picture.

Some Canadian Data

The Canadian Census identifies, in addition to 23 metropolitan areas with
populations over 100,000, another 88 smaller "urban areas." From 1971 to
1976 the median growth of the former was 6.80%, of the latter only 0.25%.
Twelve of the 23 metropolitan areas, but only 27 of the 88 smaller urban
areas, increased by more than 6.79%; only two of the larger areas lost
population (only 0.4% in both cases), but 23 of the smaller ones showed
decreases, in nine cases exceeding 5.0%.

Within the universe of 23 metropolitan areas growth rates were not
consistently correlated with size, either positively or negatively, but were
clearly determined by specific local factors. The very small (2.2%) growth of

Table 7

**Percentage distribution of population of Japan
by three major metropolitan regions,
rest of central (Tokaido) region, and rest of Japan,
1920, 1970 and 1975**

Region	Percent of Population			Annual percent change	
	1920	1970	1975	1920-1970	1970-1975
Tokyo, Nagoya, Osaka	29.6	44.6	46.1	0.3	0.3
Rest of Tokaido	19.5	14.5	14.5	−0.1	0.0
Rest of Japan	50.9	40.9	39.4	−0.2	−0.3
Japan	100.0	100.0	100.0	0.0	0.0

Daniel R. Vining, Jr., and Thomas Kontuly, Population dispersal from major metropolitan regions: an international comparison, RSRI Discussion paper series, No. 100, September 1977, p. 7. Table 1.1.

the largest (in 1971) area, Montreal, is clearly due to adverse shifts in economic geography and an unfavorable industrial profile. The two other areas with populations over one million, Toronto and Vancouver, each grew by 7.7%, above the median rate. The highest growth rate occurred, not surprisingly, in the oil-boom area of Calgary. It was closely followed by Kitchener (14.0%) and Oshawa (12.3%), industrial towns within the metropolitan orbit of Toronto, at distances of 60 and 30 miles, respectively, from its center. The other nine areas with growth rates above or at the median are all capitals, federal or provincial, reflecting the fact that during this period government was one of Canada's leading growth industries.

Table 8

**Percentage distribution of population of Sweden,
by three major metropolitan areas,
their umlands, and rest of Sweden,
1900, 1960 and 1975**

Region	Percent of Population			Annual percent change	
	1900	1960	1975	1900-1960	1960-1975
Stockholm, Goteborg, Malmo	23.8	33.7	35.9	0.167	0.147
Their umlands	37.8	32.5	33.3	−0.090	0.053
Centers with umlands	61.6	66.2	69.2	0.770	0.200
Rest of Sweden	38.4	33.8	30.8	−0.770	−0.200
Sweden	100.0	100.0	100.0	0.0	0.0

Daniel R. Vining, Jr., and Thomas Kontuly, Population dispersal from major metropolitan regions: an international comparison, RSRI Discussion paper series, No. 100, September 1977, p. 7. Table 2.1.

A comparison of the 1951–1976 growth of Canadian towns, urban areas, and metropolitan areas by five size groups shows a consistent positive correlation between growth rate and size, from 25.2% for those between 5,000 and 10,000 to 46.6% for those over 500,000. It appears that in Canada the centripetal trend to larger agglomerations has not been reversed, though it is certainly slowing down.

The opposite, smaller-scale, centrifugal trend within metropolitan orbits is certainly continuing vigorously. From 1971 to 1976, the three inner municipalities of the Municipality of Metropolitan Toronto lost 8.6% of their population and the three outer ones gained 10.4%, while the surrounding municipalities within the Toronto SMSA increased by 36.2%. There is little doubt that a sizeable overspill over the SMSA boundaries has occurred in this and other Canadian metropolitan areas. This overspill may account for most or all of the increase in the national share of the "rural" population from 24.0% in 1971 to 24.5% in 1976.

The Role of Migration

While overspill clearly accounts for most of the relative, and in some cases absolute, population loss of metropolitan areas which has been observed so far, reversal toward non-metropolitan forms of settlement certainly is the more surprising and interesting phenomenon. As differences in birth and death rates between metropolitan and non-metropolitan areas have almost disappeared in developed countries, the shift is due to changes in net migration which, as noted previously, is a generally small residual of much larger volumes of two-way gross migration. It is worth noting that the net movement of 396,000 persons from metropolitan to non-metropolitan areas of the U.S. represents only 5.7% of the gross two-way movement between these two types of areas.

Caution in the use of census data on internal migration is also advisable because of incomplete reporting. Out of a population of 183.5 million persons over five years of age enumerated in the United States in 1975, 19.0 million lived in non-metropolitan areas at both periods. A group more than half that numerous, 10.4 million, is listed as "no report on mobility," in addition to 3.6 million who "moved from abroad."[7]

It is well known that migration is highly selective. In the period 1970 –1975 no less than 72% of those aged 25–29 and 60% of those aged 30–34 but only 20% of those over 65 changed residence.[8] A comparison of the population by age group anticipated in Metropolitan Toronto by moving forward the age cohorts of 1971 to 1976 with the age groups enumerated in 1976 indicated a strong net migration gain of the same young adult groups and a net loss of all others.

While the influx of young adults testifies to the continuing attraction of the metropolis as a labor market, the movement in the opposite direction, from metropolitan to non-metropolitan counties, is strongly concentrated among persons relying on sources of income other than labor. Of every 100 males aged 16 or over that had made this move between 1970 and 1975, no less than 35 were not in the labor force.[9] It may well be that the growth of genuinely non-metropolitan areas is due mainly, maybe exclusively, to an increase in the number of persons permanently or temporarily not working. Both the first ("retirement") and the second ("recreation") group also induce, of course, a growth in the number of persons working to service them.

This hypothesis receives some support from the aforementioned study by McCarthy and Morrison. If I understand the study correctly, it identified 753 non-metropolitan counties which showed positive net migration gains from 1970 to 1974, by "concentration" of one or more functions; in 98 cases there was more than one concentration, resulting in a universe of 671 cases in 26 selected states of the U.S. Out of these more than one-third (244) were identified as "retirement" followed by 135 for "recreation." Government accounted for 125, energy for 124, and manufacturing only for 43 cases. If my understanding of the study is correct, it did not identify concentration in counties with population loss; their number may well be higher in the case of manufacturing, and possibly also in the cases of energy and government.

The changes in the rate of change between 1970–1974 versus 1960 –1970 were least pronounced for "urban," more pronounced for "less urbanized" and strongest for "rural" counties, both for net population (0.33, 1.16, 1.85) and for net migration (0.75, 1.60, 2.31).[10] The most significant changes, are those of net migration in rural counties. By far the greatest change, 3.46 annual net migration, was found in recreation counties which also were the only category which had experienced a net migration gain in the 1960s. They are followed by "retirement" with 2.54 and lower values for the three other, work-based categories.

Interaction Between Metropolitan—Non-Metropolitan and National Core-Periphery Population Shifts

As already noted, this important area has been opened up by Vining. His studies attempt to deal with both at once by applying the general concept of "concentration." By an ingenious application of the "Hoover Index of Concentration" to areas of different sizes in the United States he shows, first, that the results vary strongly with size of area and, second, that for the first time in the history of the United States the Index showed increased deconcentration for all size units. He concludes that the secular trend toward concentration has been reversed since 1970.

He then proceeded to an investigation of the same problem in 20 other countries and summarizes his conclusions as follows: ". . . suggests a law of spatial development whereby deconcentration becomes possible only in the mature phase of a country's industrialization." It is true, as Vining states, that in the "developed" countries the trend toward concentration in major urban areas is "exhausted," while in "developing" ones it is still continuing apace.

As noted earlier, Vining's studies provide information primarily on population shifts between core and peripheral regions of nations rather than on those between metropolitan and non-metropolitan regions (however defined). However, shifts between national regions cannot be understood in terms only of the two "classical" trends: national-scale centripetal towards major agglomerations, and smaller-scale centrifugal towards the expanding periphery of these agglomerations. At least five other general trends can be identified:

1. Older-to-newer regions

2. Unpleasant-to-pleasant climate and scenery

3. Declining-to-growth industries

4. Depression-to-boom (the business cycle)

5. Catastrophe-affected to safe

The meaning of "old" and "new" is different for long-settled countries and for those of relatively recent white settlement such as the U.S., the USSR, Canada, or Australia. For these "old" areas are, by definition, the core areas. In long-settled countries the "old" regions are those first industrialized, usually comprising both the region of the capital and of location of the "old" industries, coal-steel and/or textiles.

The interactions of shifts between geographic regions of a country and shifts between metropolitan and non-metropolitan regions are multiple and complex.

In developing countries, a substantial part of the population, frequently the majority, is employed in agriculture. Only in the core region is a substantial part of the population urban. As urbanization proceeds, even if it proceeds at the same or faster pace in peripheral regions, the share of the core region is bound to increase. It is therefore erroneous to conclude from this that the metropolitan share or urban population must have increased. A separate investigation of this share is required. In the case of the Soviet Union and other Eastern European countries such an investigation shows an actual decrease of this share absorbed by the largest cities,[11] contrary to Vining's conclusions.

If and when development in one or more peripheral regions proceeds faster than it does in the rest of the country, generally—though with significant variations—the growth rate of both rural and urban (not necessarily metropolitan) population will be above the national average. Frequently one or more urban nodes in such a growing region will transcend the metropolitan threshold, and further growth of such a region may indicate strength rather than weakness of metropolitan concentration.

Vining's studies, which take into account only the inverse, less ambiguous effect of growth rate of a metropolis being reflected in the growth rate of their region, are therefore inconclusive as to the problem which has been brought to the fore by recent developments in the United States population shifts between metropolitan and non-metropolitan forms of settlement. However, their significance as pioneering efforts in the field of international comparisons warrants further discussion of at least some of his cases.

Vining's "classical" first two cases are those of Japan and Sweden. In both countries he compares the population growth rates of the three largest metropolitan areas, first defined more narrowly, roughly corresponding to the U.S. concept of "metropolitan areas" and, second, defined much more broadly, corresponding to my concept of "metropolitan regions." However, by regrouping his data (Tables 7 and 8), I arrive at different conclusions.

In Japan the share of the three "metropolitan areas" continued at the same annual rate of 0.3% from 1970 to 1975 as during the preceding 50 years. In the "metropolitan fringe," here "the rest of Tokaido," the modest annual decrease of -0.1%, observed 1920 to 1970 has stopped after 1970. I interpret this to mean that the centripetal "country-to-metropolis" movement is now being balanced by the centrifugal "overflow" from the three "metropolitan areas." The decrease in the share of the "rest of the country" has accelerated from an annual rate of -0.2% during the half-century prior to 1970 to -0.3% after that date.

In Sweden the centrifugal movement has been stronger, resulting in a slowing of the annual share increase of the three metropolitan areas from 0.167 during the period 1900–1960 to 0.147 from 1960 to 1975. Correspondingly the annual change in the share of the fringe, or "umland," has reversed from -0.090 to 0.053. In the rest of Sweden it has slowed down from -0.770 to -0.200. As the second period presented for Sweden includes also the 1960s, these data do not preclude a reversal after 1970. However, this appears highly unlikely in light of data for net total (internal plus external) migration to the three metropolitan areas, also given by Vining, which I have summarized as follows:[12]

1973	-9,940
1974	2,337
1975	6,542
1976	11,314
1977	16,392
1978	10,502

Vining is of course correct in showing that internal net migration alone has been negative for the three metropolitan areas in recent years. However, for reasons presented earlier, I consider this to be less relevant than total population change.

Of the other countries investigated by Vining, I will deal only with the two Germany's. Vining notes that the strong population shift towards the provinces ("Laender") located in the watershed of the Rhine, which was characteristic of Germany since the middle of the nineteenth century, has stopped in the post-war Federal Republic. He defines this very large area, which comprises five of the ten provinces, as the "core" and interprets the change as a "long-term secular decline in net immigration from peripheral regions." I believe that a more adequate explanation of recent changes is provided by the shift from north to south (Tables 9).

Certainly it cannot be interpreted as a shift from metropolitan to non-metropolitan areas, because five of ten areas identified by German geographers as agglomerations ("Ballungen") are located in the south and have

Table 9

**Percentage of population
in northern, middle, and southern provinces
of German Federal Republic, 1960 and 1975**

| Region | Percentage of Population | |
	1960	1975
North	51.1	49.3
Middle	17.3	17.3
South	31.8	33.5
F.R.G.	100.2	100.1

North: Nordrhein-Westfalen, Niederschsen, Schleswig-Holstein, Hamburg, Bremen.
Middle: Hessen, Rheinland-Pfalz, Saar.
South: Bayern, Baden-Wurttemberg.
Daniel R. Vining, Jr., and Thomas Kontuly, Population dispersal from major metropolitan regions: an international comparison, RSRI Discussion paper series, No. 100, September 1977, p. 7. Table 9.1.

considerably increased their national share in recent years. In the north the growth of three of its four metropolitan areas has been slower because of their industrial profile: in the Ruhr-Rhine region coal-steel and in Hamburg and Bremen overseas trade, which has largely shifted to Rotterdam and to the Baltic ports of East Germany and Poland.

In East Germany Vining recognizes the decreasing share of its industrial heartland, formed by its four southeastern provinces, but assigns it to the group of countries in which "net migration into the core regions remains high and positive." This conclusion is based on the assumption that the growth of the two eastern provinces (Frankfurt and Cottbus) contiguous to East Berlin is due to overflow from the capital. This assumption is in error. There is no overflow from East Berlin, as was confirmed orally by East German planners in 1980. The growth of these two provinces is due entirely to the growth of five new (or enlarged) towns on the Oder River, which from 1969 to 1976 increased the population of Berlin itself, which had dropped from its pre-war level of 9.5% to 6.3% in the 1960s and increased to 6.6% in 1976 as a result of a reversal of government policy. This reversal applies, however, only to the capital, apparently for reasons of prestige. The general shift from larger to smaller towns continues from 1967 to 1975. The five cities with populations over 200,000 (in 1969) increased only by 0.7%, while the 16 with populations between 50,000 and 200,000 increased by 7.9%. The conclusion of my earlier study appears still to be valid: the countries with centrally planned economies have achieved some "deconcentration," with population shifts both from core to periphery and from larger to smaller urban units.

Perhaps the most interesting result that can be derived from Vining's data on the share of national population concentrated in the core area is its almost miraculous stability (Table 10). In conjunction with the previously noted stability of the shares of national population living within and outside of "metropolitan regions" achieved in the United States in the 1970s, this points to the tentative conclusion that population distribution, in these terms, in the most developed market (including "mixed") economy countries has reached maturity. It is significant that this term is being used not only by Vining but also by another astute observer of the phenomena under study, Charles L. Leven.[13]

Table 10

**Range of change
for share of national population concentrated in core areas,
five European nations, various recent periods**

Country	Region	Length of period years	Range percent
Sweden	Stockholm, Goteborg, Malmo	4	0.1
Italy	Piedmonte, Lombardia, Ligure, Toscana, Lazio	5	0.1
Norway	Ostlandet	5	0.3
Germany	Nordrhein-Westfalen	14	0.4
France	Paris Region	14	0.3

Daniel R. Vining, Jr., and Thomas Kontuly, Population dispersal from major metropolitan regions: an international comparison, *International Regional Science Review*, Vol. 3, No. 1, 1978, pp. 56, 57, 58, 62. Same authors and title, RSRI Discussion Paper Series, No. 100, 1977, p. 45.

Three Possible Interpretations of Recent Stability

It should be noted that the observed stability is, in fact, compatible with the three previously mentioned different interpretations of net migration from metropolitan to non-metropolitan counties in the United States.

It is compatible with the hypothesis of a temporary interruption of the trend to metropolitan concentration by the economic stagnation of the 1970s, presumed to be part of a business cycle.

It is compatible with the hypothesis of "reversal." In this case it would represent the moment at which the pendulum is at rest between swings toward concentration and deconcentration, respectively.

Finally, it is obviously compatible with the hypothesis of achievement of "stability" or a "stable state."

Only the analysis of future events will enable us to determine which hypothesis is the true one.

The Significance of the Concept of "Metropolitan Region"

It must be emphasized that the stability of the share of the metropolitan regions does not apply to their cores, the metropolitan areas. It is maintained because their loss in terms of share of national population is compensated by the gain of the "fringe" of the metropolitan region.

For the United States this conclusion is strongly supported by data from Morrison's studies. Morrison has broken down the non-metropolitan counties by percentage of the labor force commuting to SMSA's into four groups: over 20%; 10%–19%; 3%–9%; and less than 3%. Their annual rates of growth between 1970–1974 averaged 2.0, 1.4, 1.3, and 0.6 percent respectively, compared to 0.8% for the SMSA's.

I tentatively identify the counties with less than 3% commuters (which accounted for only 13.1% of the U.S. population) as genuinely non-metropolitan, and those with higher percentages of commuters (accounting for 13.5%) as the fringe. My rationale—not tested, but plausible—for rating counties with a commuting share of the labor force as low as 3% as part of a metropolitan region is as follows.

By definition, the fringe is the area beyond normal commuting range which attracts both residents seeking recreational services and establishments seeking business services within the range of easy accessibility of the metropolis. Commuting requires about 240 round trips annually. Both recreational services (e.g., summer cottages) and establishments needing intermittent metropolitan services (e.g. factories) may need no more than 24 round trips annually, an average of two per month to induce them to choose a location within the metropolitan orbit rather than beyond it. It can therefore be hypothesized that their number is likely to be 10 times that of the commuters who make the same trip 10 times as frequently, or 30% for 3% commuting. Together with the population serving them, they will account for the majority of the population of such a county.

As Charles L. Leven notes: "It is not so much that metropolitan life is being forsaken for a return to a small town or rural existence, but rather that the metropolis is actually moving to the countryside."[14] It is, however, equally valid to note that these moves *do* reflect a preference for a location other than a metropolis.

The debate whether these moves should be interpreted as a continuation of the centrifugal trend toward metropolitan expansion or a reversal of the centripetal trend of metropolitan concentration is really a quarrel about semantics. They are both. We are dealing with a dialectical process which can be adequately explained only by the concept of "reversal (Umschlagen) into its opposite," so dear to Hegel and Marx. The continuing urban or metropolitan expansion into the countryside reaches the point where it becomes "ruralization" of urban population and activities. ("Rus" includes many small and some not-so-small towns.) The age-old distinction between city and country is beginning to lose its meaning.

Tentative Causal Explanations

In the social sciences incontrovertible identification of cause-effect relations is never possible. In trying to explain the recent population movements away from metropolitan areas, the small size of the universe and the small number of years during which this phenomenon has been observed make such attempts particularly speculative.

There is fairly unanimous consent that the reason for metropolitan concentration is primarily the economic one of greater productivity of labor, due to agglomeration economies which are reflected as "external economies of scale" for the individual enterprise. The preference of enterprises for metropolitan location sets in motion the well-known cycle—vicious or virtuous—of enterprises attracting workers and supplementary enterprises, and the presence of these two factors attracting more enterprises. The concentration of people and of purchasing power also greatly enlarges the choice of services and contacts of all kinds. In addition to its primary attraction as a place for "making a living" the metropolis also has attractions as a place for living.

It has been argued that the observed "reversal" is due to the "diseconomies of scale" having outgrown the "economies of scale." This is questionable. The strictly economic "diseconomies" affecting enterprises are time losses in short-distance transportation due to street congestion and higher local taxes due to higher cost of services. There is no evidence to show that either of these has increased more in metropolitan areas than in smaller agglomerations, or even has increased at all, though it may frequently be perceived as having done so.

It is more likely that the "external economies of scale" have decreased, though the changes are not all one-way. Access to the most effective forms of long-distance transportation for both persons (frequent and direct air and rail service) and goods (big and specialized ships, unit trains, pipelines) is increasingly concentrated in the largest metropolitan areas. However, improvements in transportation and, in particular, in communication have made many business services as accessible to small communities as to the metropolis. This is particularly true for those located in the "fringe" which continue to have substantial advantages over more distant ones in access to services requiring personal presence as well as to highly specialized goods.

However, it is likely that the recent acceleration of the movement away from the metropolis, and in particular from its core, to more dispersed forms of settlement, both within and beyond the fringe, is due primarily to a basic shift in attitude, encouraged by prosperity, from seeking a place "to make a living" to choosing a place for "living." This is reflected in the greatly increased emphasis on "environment" and on the "quality of life." Most of the goods and services previously found only in the metropolis are now to be found almost everywhere in developed countries; those that are not, in particular personal contact, are becoming more accessible by greater ease of travel. The relative advantages of the metropolis as a place for living have been greatly reduced.

On the other hand, its relative disadvantages are weighted far more heavily and perceived as growing inexorably. They are numerous: congestion, pollution of air and water, noise, anomie, and, particularly in the United States, insecurity of person and property and unsatisfactory schools. The rural and small-town environment is attractive not only, as it has always been, because it offers access to the world of nature, more space and privacy, but also as providing stronger community ties.

The growing importance of environmental amenity is confirmed not only by the previously mentioned dominant role of retirement and recreation in the growth of non-metropolitan counties and the correlation of their rates of growth with "rurality," but also by the fact that out of the 14 areas which showed the highest growth among the SMSA's in the U.S. since 1970, nine are located in Florida.

It is also important to keep in mind that any net gains of non-metropolitan areas are residuals of a much larger and highly selective two-way movement. Despite the rejection of the "consumer society" by a significant minority, the majority of young adults is still attracted by the economic opportunities of the metropolis. As Charles L. Leven notes, on the basis of migrations observed in the U.S. from 1970 to 1975, the chances of a person moving from a non-metropolitan county to a metropolitan county were 1.7 times greater than the reverse.[15]

What May the Future Hold?

In very general terms, probably "more of the same."

The contrast in the rate of metropolitan growth between "developing" and "developed" countries is bound to increase simply because the former have a much higher rate of growth and a huge and growing "surplus" of agricultural population. By contrast, the population of the developed nations is approaching stability or even beginning to decrease, and the total non-metropolitan population is small in relation to the majority already concentrated in metropolitan regions. There is little left "to come from," except foreign countries.

In the developing countries, metropolitan concentration is reinforced because the infrastructure and services making a place attractive both for economic activity and as a living environment are to be found only in primate cities. This increases their advantage in productivity, because the small number of educated and qualified people strongly resist living in "backward" areas.

I am also hypothesizing that these same factors generally will limit metropolitan expansion to areas much smaller than the metropolitan regions of developed countries. An exception is China which has implemented a policy of locating industry in "New Towns" at considerable distances from the center. This has, however, led to time-and energy-consuming commuting from the central cities, the volume of which, in places like Peking and Shanghai, far exceeds that of inbound commuting. It remains to be seen if, with the present emphasis on the "four modernizations," this policy will be fully maintained.

In the Soviet Union, after exhaustive discussions, the policy of limiting the growth of big cities has been somewhat relaxed. Soviet policy now favors small and medium-sized cities within "agglomerations," or, in my terms, metropolitan regions. East German planners consider their present population distribution as generally satisfactory. Moderate preference is, as before, given to development of the less industrialized northern and eastern provinces and of some provincial capitals, to which more recently Berlin has been added. In addition, there is a strong effort to contain the spatial expansion of all settlements, large and small, in the interest of preservation of agricultural land.

In the developed market economy countries, the main shifts to be expected are, first, those between regions. These will be determined in part by the predominance of new industries but primarily by the increasing importance given to climatic and scenic amenities. Second, and even more important, will be the rate, location, and form of the outward shift within the metropolitan regions.

In the "old" and relatively small countries of Europe and Japan, and also in the equally densely populated and highly urbanized northeastern part of the United States, these are the only questions. In the large "new" countries, including the U.S. as a whole, most of the areas, though only a relatively small part of the population, are certainly non-metropolitan and the question of their development is highly relevant.

Growth in these areas, and to a considerable extent also in the "fringe," is likely to be increasingly selective in terms of environmental amenities. This means that the majority of municipalities in non-metropolitan regions, and many in the fringe, are more likely to lose than gain population. Planning theory so far has always been dealing with growth; we are ill-prepared to deal with conditions of decreasing population. Such decrease will increasingly occur not only in scattered small communities but in a rapidly extending area of all core cities. Here the task is to provide a higher quality of urban environment for a smaller quantity of people.

The toughest problem, however, will be posed by increasing scatteration of "urban" activities and population. The danger is twofold: first, exclusive reliance on and greatly increased use of motor vehicles for *all* movements, of goods as well as of persons, and second, loss of agricultural production, both by direct occupancy of land and by disruption of farming by other uses.

The obvious remedy is channeling of development into relatively compact clusters. Continuing and increasing conflicts are predictable between such attempts and the apparently insatiable desire for more space, supported by a strongly rooted belief in the right of the individual to freely own and use land.

Many observers believe that the increasing price of oil will force a reversal of this trend. I consider this unlikely for two reasons. First, the wellhead price of oil is now well above the cost of producing an equivalent amount of coal in the United States; it is therefore more likely to decrease than to increase, in real terms, in the future. Second, the traditional American cars are so fantastically inefficient that fuel consumption can easily be reduced by two-thirds by a switch to smaller, lighter cars. This argument has been countered by the statement that "smaller, lighter cars . . . do not lend themselves to one-way work trips of 30 and more miles because they are uncomfortable."[16] To this writer, who has traveled all over Canada from coast to coast in a Volkswagon Beetle, this statement is not convincing. Nor is the same author's expectation that multi-nucleation will induce people to work in the nearest nucleus confirmed by experience.

Desirable Future Research

As noted earlier, the data published by the U.S. Census on metropolitan and non-metropolitan counties do not provide an adequate basis to evaluate changes in metropolitan concentration for two reasons. First, the definition of "metropolitan" is much broader than that normally and meaningfully associated with the term "metropolis," and, second, the country may contain areas with radically different characteristics.

I suggest a special study of the metropolitan areas in the United States with a population over one million and of their surrounding regions up to a distance of 90 miles from the metropolitan center. In Canada, because of the paucity of areas of this population size, half a million is a more suitable lower limit. A supplementary study of U.S. areas with populations between 500,000 and 1,000,000 would, of course, also be welcome.

All smaller metropolitan areas, whether outside of or within metropolitan regions, would have to be treated as non-metropolitan in dealing with all movements, commuting as well as migration. This should, of course, not preclude additional studies dealing with them. In many cases neighboring metropolitan regions will overlap. The boundary between two such neighbors can easily be determined by the preponderance of commuting to one or the other. Within the metropolitan regions I recommend collection of data by census tracts or, where these are not available, by municipalities, and their grouping by concentric circles around the metropolitan center as well as by location in the fringe and its SMSA, respectively. With the aid of available computers, this is not excessively laborious.

As for the population shifts and migrations affecting the distribution of the national population by major regions, only a detailed investigation of all relevant factors can provide valid answers. I completely agree with the statement made by Daniel R. Vining, Jr. in a letter to me dated October 10, 1978 in which he stated "that a satisfactory theory of the phenomenon of deconcentration will be more complex, richer, and more interesting than mono-causal explanations."

Notes

1. Hans Blumenfeld, *Metropolis—and Beyond*, (New York, 1980), p. 132.

2. D.R. Vining, Jr. and A. Strauss, "A Demonstration That The Current Deconcentration of Population in the United States is a Clean Break with the Past," *Environment and Planning A*, 1977, vol. 9, pp. 751–758; also: Daniel R. Vining, Jr., Robert L. Pallone and Chung Hsin Yang, Population Dispersal from Core Regions: A Description and Tentative Explanation of the Patterns in 20 Countries, Working Description and Tentative Explanation of the Patterns in 20 Countries, Working Paper No. 26, University of Pennsylvania, February 1980.

3. Kevin F. McCarthy and Peter A. Morrison, The Changing Demographic and Economic Structure of Non-Metropolitan Areas in the United States, Rand Corporation, Santa Monica, January 1979; Also: Peter A. Morrison, "The Current Demographic Context . . ." in L.S. Bourne and J.W. Simmons, *Systems of Cities*, (1978), pp. 473–479.

4. *Op. cit.*, p. 14.

5. *Op. cit.*, p. 17, fig. 4.

6. *Op. cit.*, p. 16.

7. U.S. Bureau of the Census, Series p. 20, No. 285, October 1975, Mobility of the Population of the United States, March 1970–March 1975, Table 1.

8. *Ibid.*, Figure 1.

9. *Ibid.*, Table 10.

10. *Op. cit.*, p. 37, Table 5.

11. Blumenfeld, *op. cit.*, pp. 181–187.

12. Daniel R. Vining, Jr., Robert L. Pallone, Chung Hsin Yang, Population Dispersal from Core Regions. Working papers in Regional Science and Transportation, University of Pennsylvania, No. 26, p. 12, Table 2.

13. Charles L. Leven, *The Mature Metropolis*, (Lexington, Mass., 1978).

14. *Op. cit.*, p. 7.

15. *Op. cit.*, pp. 29–30.

16. Alex Anas and Leon N. Moses, "Transportation and Land Use in the Mature Metropolis," in Charles L. Leven, *op. cit.*, p. 164.

19.
Urban Settlement Patterns in the North American Metropolis

Rebecca Robertson

In 1963, Melvin Webber, in an article entitled "Order in Diversity: Community without Propinquity," predicted that non-spatial cities and nucleated dispersion were the logical next steps in the chain of technological advances that had shaped the structure of urban settlement in North America.[1] Twenty years later, a decline in big-city populations, rapid growth in non-metropolitan areas and an increasing "foot-looseness" of jobs and population appear to be bearing out his prognosis. However, the picture is not totally clear. Not all metropolitan areas are losing population, and even among those that are, there are unmistakable signs of vitality, particularly in the central cities where the luxury housing market is strong and office construction is booming.

The present paper explores urban settlement patterns in North America, drawing on trends and experience of the past and present and on projected changes in communications, technology and economic activity in the future. The objective is to learn from the past, not only to predict more accurately the future of metropolitan structure but also to consider the planning policies that would most successfully accommodate the new order.

The Past: 1860 - 1970

In 1790, the U.S. had just under four million inhabitants, 95% of whom lived in isolated rural areas or in settlements of less than 2,500 people. The largest city was New York, which boasted a population of 49,401. It was not until the Civil War in the 1860s that urban growth exceeded that of rural areas in absolute numbers, and it was not until the early part of this century that the majority of Americans lived in cities. Absolute urban growth reached a first peak in the 1920s fueled by massive immigration from abroad and high fertility rates. Between the wars, cities increased at an average of 12 million persons per decade. Urban growth declined precipitously during the Depression, but began to rise again in the forties. It reached its highest levels in the fifties and sixties. During these two decades, net migration from the farms exceeded one million per year, and the birth rate soared.

However, even as the vision of the American megalopolis and of cities of more than 20 million people were being raised by Gottman (1963) and others, the trend that had been sustained since 1860 was beginning to reverse itself. In the 1960s, Pittsburgh became the first metropolitan area in the history of the country to suffer a net loss in population. In fact, as Alonzo points out,[2] the net migration from many of the older cities had started well before the 1970s (when the trend was first noticed), but was obscured by the fact that natural increase exceeded out-migration.

The causes of the rise and fall of metropolitan areas in North America are linked to a number of factors but foremost among these are communications and the nature of the economic base.

Early American cities developed as new technology pushed workers off the farms and pulled them in to nascent urban areas. The absence of labor in America in the early nineteenth century encouraged entrepreneurs to reinvest heavily in technology,[3] and, as a result, American industrialization took root quickly. Cities grew up around two types of industry, both of which benefited from agglomeration and concentration.[4] The first type, which can be described as "large-scale materials-intensive manufacturing," relied heavily on large (and bulky) quantities of input with respect to output. These industries profited from close proximity, with other like concerns, to a transportation terminus where the cost of delivery of materials was minimized and where the economies of scale intrinsic to rail or canal transport could be exploited. The second type of industry that formed the base for big-city growth involved "small-scale labor-intensive manufacturing" of such goods as furniture, apparel, printing and publishing, etc. These activities, although carried out in small units of production, were extremely interdependent and tended to cluster into "complexes of productive enterprise." They also located at central points to insure accessibility to a large labor pool, and to their market.

Early advances in transportation and communication such as the telegraph, the telephone and the inter-urban railway system contributed to further centralization of economic activity. They favored the growth of the larger cities by permitting them to dominate an increasingly large hinterland. In addition, although the telegraph handled interregional communications, it could not sustain the heavy volume of intra-urban messages. This had to be accomplished through face-to-face contact or by messengers, a fact that played a role in the clustering not only of manufacturing but of commercial and business activities.

Municipal services were also more cost-effective when serving a concentrated demand, and city governments responded to growing industrial needs by massive investments in infrastructure which further assured a prosperous economic base. By the end of the nineteenth century, New York had spent $24 million in subways, bridges, paving and water supply, and was projecting another $86 million for the further expansion of its rapid transit, tunnel and bridge system. Chicago had spent $225 million in similar infrastructure improvements.[5]

In response to the influence of these concentrating forces, an identifiable urban structure began to emerge. The labor force accommodated itself around the highly centralized economic activities, with the less economically advantaged population located in a ring around the core and the wealthier inhabitants "commuting" short distances in carriages. Cities in the early 1900s, for the reasons cited above, were necessarily compact and densely built and, up until World War I, 90 percent of the employment in cities was within one to three miles of the center. This is all the more amazing when one considers the size of the larger urban areas in 1910: New York City—nearly five million, Chicago—just over two million, and Philadelphia —one and a half million.

It was only shortly before the First World War that motorized transport affected the structure of cities. The use of the truck had an important role in reducing the cost of inter- and intra-urban transport and in permitting the deconcentration of industry within the core. In addition, the waves of inmigration from abroad (which accounted for more than 48% of national growth in the first two decades of the century) led to an expansion of the lower and lower-middle class areas around the core and a further withdrawal of the middle classes. Nevertheless, the central city remained the undisputed hub of economic, social and cultural activities.

The initial steps in the disintegration of the geographically contained and center-dominated structure of metropolitan areas occurred between 1940 and 1960, when urban growth reached an all-time high. It began with the suburbanization of the population, permitted by the widespread use of the automobile, and accelerated by a number of other factors: the national home finance program that favored new construction in the suburbs over rehabilitation in the central cities; the influx of poor and minorities to the core in large numbers; an erosion of the tax base in the central cities that resulted in a decline in municipal services; and a lifestyle preference for cleaner air, less congestion, and more space to raise growing families.

The fifties also witnessed the decentralization of manufacturing during what was one of the most significant periods of industrialization in America's history. Between 1948 and 1954, central city manufacturing employment in the 40 largest SMSA's decreased relative to suburban employment, although it increased in absolute terms. Between 1954 and 1963, the central cities actually lost manufacturing jobs, while the suburbs gained in roughly equal numbers.

The long-distance truck and the greatly expanded urban road system were key factors in providing industry with more locational flexibility. The suburbs offered a number of advantages—cheap land, proximity to airports, cheaper labor, less government regulation. In the central cities, on the other hand, land was a scarce commodity, wages and taxes had risen, and there was increasing regulation of industry. In addition, as industry became more capital intensive, efficiency increased and the ratio of output to input grew larger. Thus, the importance of material inputs decreased, and with it the economies of scale that prompted industry to cluster around transportation nodes in the first place.

Retail, and to a lesser extent, commercial activities, also moved out to the suburbs, sapping the city core of some of its economic vitality. In the 1950s and 1960s, retail employment opportunities in the suburbs increased substantially, while the central cities suffered a net loss of jobs in this sector.[6] By 1967, nearly half of all metropolitan retail jobs were located in the suburbs.

In summary, the forces that first propelled the growth of cities were inherently centripetal. Industries needed to locate near like industries and a major transportation node. Labor and ancillary commercial activities gathered around, trapped by the high cost of personal travel and poor communications. The population of the cities grew, the cores became increasingly congested, and advances in transportation technology permitted the more affluent to distance themselves from the industrial core and the ring of immigrant areas that surrounded it. The spurt of economic and demographic growth in the fifties, coupled with the widespread use of the automobile and truck and deteriorating conditions in the central city, resulted in the suburbanization of the population and the era of the commutershed. Jobs, particularly in the manufacturing and retail sectors, followed as the central cities began to relinquish their roles as the centers of economic and cultural activity for an increasingly disperse suburban area.

The Present: 1970 - 1980

The 1970s witnessed further fundamental changes in the traditional pattern of urban settlement. Notable among these were the regional shift of population to the south and west, the decline of large cities, and the rapid growth of non-metropolitan areas. Basic economic activities shifted from manufacturing to "advanced" services, and became increasingly "footloose," i.e., indifferent to geographic location, and suburban areas outstripped central cities in employment growth. The population profile experienced some significant variations from previous years: there were more elderly; the "baby-boomers" started to work, buy shelter and consume goods and services; and households became smaller.

The growth rate in the U.S. dropped from 13.3% between 1960 and 1970 to 11.4% over the last decade, due, in great part, to a significant decline in the fertility rate which plummeted from 123 live births per 1,000 women in child-bearing age in 1957 to 66 per 1,000 in 1976. By the end of the 1970s, the rate of natural increase stood at 1.8 children per woman, considerably below the estimated replacement rate of 2.1. Explanations for this decline include a decrease in the "desirable" family size, an increase in the number of women postponing child-bearing, and a rise in divorces and marital separations.

Despite the slow growth, the mobility of Americans manifested itself in significant regional shifts in population. The North-central and North-east increased 4.1% and 0.2% over the decade, while the South and West registered growth of 20.0% and 24.1%. The population shifts can be explained in part by the rise of new industries in these regions, e.g., oil in Houston, computer technology in Santa Clara, California, retirement communities in Florida and Arizona, etc. However, they are also indicators of a weakening of the "spatial barrier" that previously dominated the location of economic activity, and the ascendency of amenity and quality of life as major locational determinants.

Urban growth reflected these regional adjustments, but was also marked by an internal reconfiguration, in which central cities experienced negative or stagnant growth while the suburbs flourished. Between 1970 and 1977, 95 or 62% of the 153 largest cities in the U.S. lost population, including New York (-840,000), Chicago (-360,000), Philadelphia, Detroit, Baltimore, Indianapolis, San Francisco, Cleveland, Boston and New Orleans. Overall, cities over 100,000 in population increased 1.9% over the decade—a virtual no-growth situation. The suburban areas grew at the healthier rate of 18.25%, with major increases in the growth regions of the South and West, and in the outer fringes of the older metropolitan areas.

The 16 largest conurbations increased by only 4.3%, and seven of these lost population. Only one (Houston-Galveston) grew at a faster rate than during the previous decade.

One of the more anomalous trends of the seventies was the rate of increase in the number of households that was almost three times that of the population. Household size nationwide dropped from an average of 3.17 in 1970 to 2.74 in 1980. In central cities, the household size had traditionally been smaller, and decreased over the last decade from 2.98 to 2.57, resulting in a 14.7% increase in households. In the suburbs the household size dropped more markedly (from 3.25 to 2.6) and the number of households rose by 50.6%, an indication that couples and singles increasingly seek out suburban locations.

Perhaps the most startling demographic trend of the seventies was the rate of growth of non-metropolitan areas, which, for the first time since the 1800s, exceeded that of urban areas. SMSA's grew at 10.2%, while the population outside SMSA's grew at 15.1%. In addition, there is evidence that the migration from SMSA's to non-metropolitan areas was greater in absolute terms than in the migration in the reverse direction.

One obvious explanation for non-metropolitan growth is the spillover of the metropolitan area across official boundaries. However, 40% of the growth registered by non-metropolitan areas was in counties not adjacent to SMSA's. This trend cannot be accurately described as a "back-to-the-country" movement, despite media articles to the contrary. The farm population continued to drop in the seventies, totaling losses of 1.4 million inhabitants between 1970 and 1976 alone. It was, in fact, the small and medium-size towns that experienced the highest rates of increase. Places with less than 25,000 inhabitants grew 24.1%, while places with 25,000 to

100,000 increased 24.9%.

In the 1970s, the U.S. economy entered into what is variously known as the "information," "knowledge" or "advanced services" era. The manufacturing industry, although still a major force, continued to grow slowly. Jobs in the service sector, on the other hand, surged with substantial gains in personal services, but more importantly in services related to the handling and processing of information, e.g., in fields of corporate and production management, research and development, branding, customizing, etc. As Noyelle[7] explains:

> "By any measure, the U.S. market has grown enormously during the post–war years. Between 1950 and 1980, the population grew from 152 to 222 million (sic), the civilian labor force from 62 to 102 million and disposable income from 362 to over 1,000 billion dollars (1972 prices). . . . This has led not so much to the development of broad homogeneous markets as to the creation . . . of a large number of specialized markets. . . . The result has been a proliferation of products and services and an increased emphasis on product differentiation and styling."

National employment grew at about 25% during the decade, more than twice the rate of the population. In the 50 largest SMSA's, employment grew at the same rate as the U.S., but the geographic pattern of gains and losses continued to favor the ascendency of the suburbs. In 1967, the central cities offered 19,861,000 jobs, which increased to 21,262,000 jobs in 1977. During the same period, employment in the suburbs increased from 10,602,000 to 16,879,000.

The central cities lost over 1,000,000 jobs in manufacturing as well as jobs in the related fields of wholesale and transportation. The greatest absolute gain was in government, followed by services and FIRE (finance, insurance and real estate). In the suburbs all sectors increased but services and retail showed the greatest gains.[8]

Overall, the number of new jobs in the suburbs exceeded those of the central city in a 4 to 1 ratio. The suburbs captured 95% of new employment in the retail sector, 63% in services, 99% in construction and 47% in FIRE. By 1980, nearly half the jobs were located in the suburbs. The central cities had lost their dominant share in manufacturing and retailing, and they were losing their share in other sectors as well.

Nevertheless, the "boom" in the office market and widespread "gentrification" of older residential areas near the core led some observers to predict a return to the city in response to rising energy costs, increases in housing prices in the suburbs, and decreasing household size. A study conducted under the auspices of the Urban Land Institute[9] found that, in the 143 cities analyzed, 48% had experienced some degree of private rehabilitation activity. Clay, in a later study, found private housing reinvestment in all 30 cities considered, and identified 53 areas of substantial "gentrification." The office market was strong not only in the major cities—New York, Chicago, Los Angeles—but also in "declining" cities; Philadelphia added 5.6 million new square feet of office space between 1970 and 1975; Detroit, 8 million square feet, between 1965 and 1975; and Pittsburgh, 3.5 million square feet, between 1970 and 1975.

However, both the housing reinvestment and the new office construction have tended to occur in or very close to the city core. This revitalization trend, which exhibits every sign of continuing in the future, is unfortunately paralleled by a serious decline of the inner suburbs, as indicated by the bleak picture presented by socio-economic indicators in the central cities. In 1975, the crime rate in the cities was nearly twice that of the metropolitan areas. Per capita real income between 1969 and 1974 increased 9.9% in the SMSA's and only 8.3% in the cities. In 1980, the unemployment rate of the central cities was 5.8% as opposed to the SMSA rate of 5.2%. The proportion of households with incomes under $7,000 was 27.4% in the central cities while in the suburbs it was 14.8%. Between 1970 and 1977, central cities suffered net losses of population in all income categories, except the lowest (under $5,000) for which it registered a net increase.

The Future

The urban settlement patterns of the coming decades will continue to be shaped by three factors: communications technology, the new "service" economy and demographic trends.

The impact of communications technology on the structure of future urban areas probably cannot be overstated, in that it will create an economic system in which locational determinants are qualitative rather than spatial and in which physical proximity no longer serves as an indicator of functional relationship. The "foot-looseness" of employment does not necessarily mean continued dispersion but rather deliberate choice of location based on: (1) amenity, i.e., the quality of life available to the labor force; (2) regulations sympathetic to specific business needs; and (3) availability of the utilities required to support the necessary telecommunications infrastructure, e.g., power sources that are cheap and reliable, a local telephone system with available circuits and switching capacity.

Consider operations such as credit card and check processing, car rental, hotel or airline reservation operations, insurance claims processing, or any other similar routinized or automated office function. From a communications or transportation point of view, the only locational determinant is availability of the basic technical infrastructure. The mode of communication with head office and with customers is an area code, 800 number, a computer installation, or the mail. Thus, the location of many of these facilities has been determined by the quality of life factors: better weather, less crime and lower housing prices.

The regulatory environment for business is also a key locational consideration. A few years ago, a major bank requested the State of New York to increase the interest rate limit on credit card outstandings. Public officials, concerned over the political ramifications on an increase in the usury limit, denied the request. The bank subsequently moved its credit card operations (which employed over 2,000 people) to South Dakota which was only too happy to accommodate the bank's needs. A second similar operation is being established by the same bank in Nevada.

Another major effect of advances in communications technology is that the capacity of management to control operations over a large geographic area will greatly increase. With the rise of the giant "multilocational" corporations, the "headquarters" function in large cities will greatly expand.

Advances in communications technology will continue to dramatically diminish the barrier of geographic distance with regard to social interaction and cultural diffusion. With the divestiture of AT&T, it is expected that long distance calls, which formerly subsidized the high cost of the local infrastructure, will in the near future be priced at the same levels as local calls, thus eliminating distance as a factor in one's choice of a partner in socializing via the telephone. The television has already had a like effect in reducing cultural isolation. Paradoxically, it is increasingly used now not only as an instrument of cultural homogenization but also to heighten local awareness and identity. Community cable stations that can respond more closely to the tastes and interests of its local viewers are proliferating and may soon prove to be strong competition to the national networks.

Projected trends in economic activities indicate increased "footlooseness" for routinized processes, smaller units of production, increased market segmentation and specialization, and a continued need for face-to-face contact among high-level executives and decision-makers. The experts predict that further expansion of the service sector will be the major trend, but it is also likely that manufacturing will continue to be a significant contributor to the economy.

Manufacturing, with smaller units of production and more widespread separation of processes, will tend to continue to locate where land cost and wages are low, regulations are sympathetic, and accessibility to highways and/or airports is maximized. These factors will favor an ex-urban location in the future. There is evidence, however, that certain consumer-sensitive industries may relocate in cities or in dense urban centers as market segmentation becomes more important.

The locational propensities of various components of the new service sector are not completely clear. A number of functions, especially those that are routinized, will have tremendous locational freedom. Other information industries where daily personal contacts are unnecessary (e.g., research and development) will also be increasingly "footloose." On the other hand, "headquarters" functions will locate in what Thierry Noyelle[10] calls "diversified advanced service centers" in order to insure face-to-face contact among high level executives. The largest cities will have a particular advantage in that they will increasingly provide centers for both national and international business. "High touch" services such as advertising, legal services and financial advisers will also continue to locate in these centers near the decision-makers. It is not clear to what extent this latter group will separate functions internally, locating routinized operations in one location and high-level personnel in another.

Greater locational flexibility and increasing emphasis on market speciali- zation could also mean that headquarters employment will be relatively reduced, as regional offices will locate closer to their markets. These branch functions will also spawn a myriad of "high touch" business services outside the "diversified advanced service centers."

Population growth at the national level is projected to decelerate further in the future, increasing by only 9.6% between 1980 and 1990, and 6.9% between 1990 and 2000.

Fertility rates, which are now below the replacement rate, will probably level off, although there is disagreement on this subject. On the other hand, there may be some increase in births as the number of women in childbear- ing age rises as a result of the "baby-boom." Immigration is also likely to maintain its present level as America continues to present comparative advantages over its Latin American neighbors.

The anticipated shifts in the age pyramid are expected to have a signifi- cant effect on urban life over the next 10 to 15 years. An increase of 30% in persons aged 25 to 44 will produce a higher rate of household formation than in the previous decades. Between 1980 and 1990, it is estimated that 17 million new households will be formed, 51% of which will be single- person. Many of these will be occupied by the elderly who will increase in number by 4.1 million over the next decade.

Adolescents and young adults as a group will decline from 10.6% of the total population in 1978 to 7.9% in 1990. Bradbury et al.[11] have hypothe- sized that a result of this decrease could be a reduction in crime which has traditionally registered much higher rates among males aged 14 to 24. The reduction in the number of young adults could also have the effect of lowering the unemployment rate as fewer people enter the labor market.

So what does this all mean for future population and job location? How will urban settlement patterns respond to the expected advances in commu- nications technology, the changes in the economic base, and the new demographics?

It would appear that there will be two opposing forces acting on urban settlement patterns over the next few decades. One will be an increasing locational freedom of both jobs and people; the other will be a greater need for a certain level of concentration and density.

The "concentrating" factors include:

- Face-to-face contact for decision-making functions

- Face-to-face contact for social interaction as a lifestyle prefer- ence

- Critical mass of population required to support increasingly diversified consumer services and goods

- Smaller households

- Increased housing and land costs that favor multiple-unit dwellings

- Rising energy costs

- High cost of new infrastructure

- Agglomeration advantages for certain activities: live arts and culture, headquarters functions and related business services

Factors that allow and, in some cases, favor increased "footlooseness" include:

- Rise of information industries that are based on "knowledge" products as opposed to "material" products

- Cultural diffusion via telecommunications

- Separation of processes and small units of production in manufacturing

- Disadvantages of central city: high wages, land and housing costs, decaying infrastructure, and high crime rates

- Over-regulation in urbanized areas

- Increased ability of management to efficiently control branch operations over any distance

Expert urban observers[12,13] predict three possible scenarios for future settlement patterns: a revival of the core as the dominant urban component, continued dispersion around a declining center, and a multi-nucleated system in which central cities become just one of many higher-density nodes.

The revival of the central city is unlikely, although there may be substantial rejuvenation in the core. Land and housing prices are exorbitant, crime rates are high, the infrastructure is in decay, and there is an increasing number of poor and minorities. These are not the conditions that will pull back either the middle class population or economic activities that have the option of locating elsewhere.

Dispersion is also doubtful and, in fact, does not really characterize accurately the trends of the seventies, as much of the population movement was to small and medium-sized towns inside or outside the SMSA's. Classic dispersion occurred in the 1950s when families with automobiles bought three-bedroom houses on large lots and commuted to work in the city. It should be noted that this dispersion occurred around a central core, not as a phenomenon in its own right. It is not probable that we will see a revival of this trend. Costs and other inconveniences discourage commuting, and single and two-person households tend to seek a certain level of density for

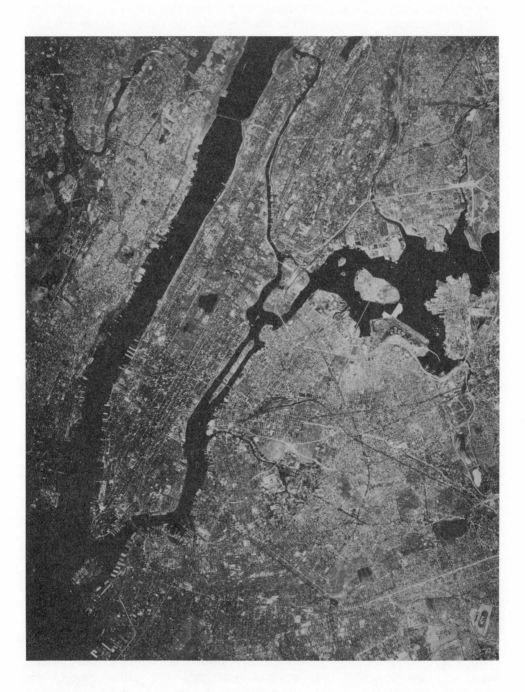

Fig. 19-1: Landsat image of New York. (Landsat Archives, Chaire d'Urbanisme EPFL, E. Galantay)

reasons relating to social preference, and choice and costs of housing.

The most likely scenario is a system of independent nodes or centers that offer work, living and recreation in close proximity. These centers will have a certain level of density to allow social and business interaction, and will be of sufficient scale to support a strong retail and service market. It will be a new urban form in the sense that—unlike a metropolitan area where the component parts have a clear relationship with the center in terms of employment, culture and entertainment—in this new configuration, economic, social and cultural interdependencies will not be spatially defined.

The existing large cities that can successfully exploit the opportunities available in the new service sector are likely to experience decline in the older suburbs and continued revitalization within their cores. The scale of agglomeration represented by these areas will continue to have comparative advantages for the highly affluent and the poor. The highly affluent, the decision-makers, require face-to-face contact to carry on business; they can afford the escalating housing prices; they support the live arts that are agglomeration oriented; and they are less affected by poor services in infrastructure. The poor will continue to locate in the old cities for completely different reasons: the greater availability of social service infrastructure, the increasing political base of minorities at a local level, and the greater opportunities for unskilled labor. Thus, the central city will survive, but at a certain cost as the economic gap between its inhabitants widens.

Some Directions for Future Policies

What does all this augur for the development of planning policies in the future? What will be the role of planners in the evolution of this new urban structure?

Planners in the United States have a curious role. The basic purpose of their activity is somewhat at odds with a society that puts a high value on individual freedom and the rights of the free marketplace. Thus, American planners tend to act as regulators rather than initiators, followers of trends rather than trendsetters. As members of a vocally pluralistic democracy, they play the role of mediator and middleman between various interests. They do not have the status or the influence of technocrats in more socialist or communally oriented countries, and thus tend to largely reflect political realities—the views of the voting majority or compromise solutions between political opponents.

This is not to say that planners have not had or will not have an impact on the evolution of U.S. cities. As we have noted, regulatory policies in the past have been responsible for stemming and spurring trends in growth and location of people and jobs. However, the nature of the future changes and the dynamics of the market for housing and jobs must be thoroughly understood so that regulations and policies may be developed to optimize the opportunities for an improved quality of life. Planners should focus their efforts to ensure that the rising centers develop in an orderly and desirable manner, and that the problems of decline and decay in the old cities do not become insurmountable.

Land-use regulations outside the older metropolitan areas should be shaped to facilitate the development of centers that include multi-family dwellings and allow a mix of work, residence and leisure activities. If the overly restrictive and complex regulations that presently govern many suburban areas will force new jobs in housing outside urbanized areas, incurring unnecessary costs in new infrastructure, and restricting the development of the critical mass that will be necessary to maximize choices and diversity in living conditions, services, goods, employment and leisure-time pursuits.

A combination of strategies should also be adopted to prevent severe decay of central cities. Architecturally and historically significant areas should be protected to encourage private reinvestment. There should be an increase in transfer payments so that the tax burden on central cities is on more of a par with other centers. Privatization of municipal services such as sanitation and garbage pickup should also be considered to relieve the tax burden.

Land-use controls should encourage expansion of growth industries such as personal services (e.g., health clubs, restaurants, entertainment), consumer-sensitive manufacturing (e.g., apparel), and components of the information industry (e.g., data processing). Tax breaks should be made available to a targeted group of major employers, and programs should be undertaken to train the unskilled worker for employment in the growth sectors.

Technology and communications will continue to shape the cities of North America. The challenge for the planners of the future will be to acquire the sophistication and knowledge necessary to deal with the new phenomena competently and humanely.

References

1. Melvin Webber, "Order in Diversity: Community without Propinquity," in L. Wingo (ed.), *Cities and Space: The Future Use of Urban Land,* (Baltimore, 1963).

2. William Alonzo, "The Current Halt in the Metropolitan Phenomenon" in Charles Leven (ed.), *The Mature Metropolis,* (St. Louis, 1968).

3. Christine Boyer, *Dreaming the Rational City - The Myth of American City Planning,* (Cambridge, MA., 1983).

4. Allen Scott, "Production System Dynamics and Metropolitan Development", *Annals of the Association of American Geographers, (June, 1982).*

5. Boyer, *op. cit.*

6. Alonzo, *op. cit.*

7. Thierry J. Noyelle, "The Rise of Advanced Services," *JAIP,* (Summer, 1983).

8. Robyn S. Phillips and Ana C. Vidal, "The Growth and Restructuring of Metropolitan Economies," *JAIP,* (Summer, 1983).

9. Thomas Black, "Private Market Renovation in Central Cities: A ULI Survey," *Urban Land,* (November, 1975).

10. Noyelle, *op. cit.*

11. Katherine Bradbury, et al., *Urban Decline and the Future of American Cities,* (Washington, 1982).

12. George Sternlieb, and Robert Burchell, *Planning Theory in the 1980's: A Search for New Directions,* (New Jersey, 1978).

13. Harvey Perloff, *Planning the Post-Industrial City,* (Chicago, 1980).

20.
Comments

Hans Blumenfeld

$\mathcal{M}$ s. Robertson's paper presents an excellent summary of the historical development of the North American metropolis, followed by a closely reasoned scenario of its probable future and thoughtful proposals for future policies based on a realistic evaluation of the limited role of planning in North America.

I have only a few minor additions to Ms. Robertson's presentation of historical development. The peak of urban growth in the 1920s was due to massive internal migration in addition to the factors mentioned. Some heavy industries developed early at the urban periphery along rail lines; their workers mostly lived nearby.

I have more questions on Ms. Robertson's treatment of the 1970–1980 period, misnamed "The Present."

Industries have become "indifferent" to location of raw materials, but are more dependent than ever to access to business services, including major airports. The decrease in average household size is not new, but has been going on for 100 years. The main reason for the precipitate drop of the fertility rate is the coincidence of the long-term increase of women working outside their home with fear of the future resulting from the (probably) cyclical downturn of the economy. "Gentrification" does not mean "return" to the cities. Most of the people who "up-grade" old houses have previously lived in the city. By replacing poorer and larger households, gentrification accelerates the population loss of the central city but improves its financial conditions.

Increase in office space does not necessarily mean an increase in office employment, because per head absorption of office space is also increasing. Some office construction is occurring in inner suburbs, generally in those of high socio-economic status.

When it comes to the future, two very different scenarios can be developed, dependent on two different anticipations of the future of the economy. It may be that late corporate capitalism has entered a period of permanent stagnation, with only short minor cycles. It may be that capitalism has retained its historic resilience and will produce another period of strong growth. Ms. Robertson bases her prediction on the second hypothesis, anticipating continuing growth of GNP per head. She enumerates a number of factors working for "concentration and density," and of opposing ones working for "footlessness." Both concentration and footlessness have very different effects if they work on a national or metropolitan scale. Concentration induces density only on the metropolitan scale.

As for the enumerated concentrating factors, I know of no evidence that preference for face-to-face social contact is increasing; it seems to be a constant. It is income rather than population which has to reach a critical mass to support consumer services and, more important, business services. As for "increased housing and land cost," their recent increase was entirely due to demand pull and is already beginning to be reversed. "Rising energy costs" are more likely to resume their secular falling trend; for oil this is already happening.

A significant shortcoming, to be attributed less to Ms. Robertson than to her sources, is the excessive reliance on the census distinction between "central cities" and "suburbs" within SMA's and between "metropolitan" and "non-metropolitan" counties on the national scale. I have explained in my paper entitled "Have the secular trends of population distribution been reversed?" why I consider my concept of "metropolitan regions," or "orbits," or "urban fields" better suited to answer this question. As for the distinction between central cities and suburbs, it has little meaning given the fact that in the U.S. the central city's share of SMA population varies from 20 to 99%.

Nor is the often quoted fact that many "non-metropolitan" and "not-adjacent" counties have grown at above-average rate between 1970 and 1980 conclusive. Such growth has also occurred in the preceding decades of unquestioned metropolitan concentration, albeit to a lesser extent.

I believe that the development of the pattern of human settlements since the emergence of towns can be understood in terms of Ebenezer Howard's two magnets, urban and rural. Howard did not fully spell out why these magnets attract: the first by providing access to other human beings, the second to extra-human nature. In both cases the object of attraction is sought both as resource and as environment.

As technical progress has reduced the number of workers required for on-site work to use nature as a resource to 3–4% of the labor force, the balance has tended to agglomerations where they could use each other, increasingly specialized skills as a resource, the more effectively the greater the number and variety of skills accessible to each other. Also, the greater the number of human beings accessible to each other, the greater the chance to meet those which each individual might enjoy as environment.

The centripetal trend to larger and larger agglomerations, which gained speed with the Industrial Revolution well over two centuries ago and is still gathering momentum in most areas of the world, has almost run its course in the most "developed" regions.

But while the rural magnet as resource has lost much of its power, as environment its attraction is as powerful as ever, if not more so. The rich and powerful have always had their country villas. The mass of the urban population could not follow them because they could not move far from their work, as long as persons could move only on foot, or at best on hoof.

This changed when technical progress provided faster means for the movement of persons, goods and messages. The change started with the steam railroad which created the "railroad suburbs" of the wealthy, and of horse-drawn busses and street cars which created the "inner suburbs" of the middle class. It gathered momentum toward the end of the nineteenth century with the bicycle, electric traction and the telephone. It was further accelerated by the motor vehicle and by wireless communication. As a result, the time required to move a given distance has been reduced ten to one for persons and goods, and from ten to zero for messages. As a consequence, human beings can maintain access to their fellows, both as resource and as environment, while gaining access to the rural environment, or at least to its most important attractions, space and vegetation.

Hence, the second, centrifugal trend from city center to periphery which started more than a hundred years ago. The centrifugal trend can be observed all over the world. In the Northeastern United States, as in West-Central Europe and in Japan, it has completely overflowed the centripetal one. In these regions practically everybody lives within the orbit of one or another metropolis. Ms. Robertson refers to these two opposing trends, but does not always clearly distinguish the different scales at which they operate.

She starts her discussion by referring to Melvin Webber's paper on "Community without Propinquity." This significant paper overstates its case. A-spatial communities have always existed; their existence in no way precludes the existence of definite patterns of human settlements.

In connection with Webber's paper, Ms. Robertson refers to "increasing footlooseness of jobs and population." Jobs certainly are becoming more footloose. However, data from several developed countries, both "West" and "East," indicate that internal population migration has actually decreased.

I emphatically agree with Ms. Robertson's statement that planning policies should "accommodate the new order"—accommodate, not change. Certainly Albert Mayer's statement "trend is not Destiny" is true, but neither is trend just a line on a graph. It is the net result of contradictory actions of many human beings undertaken to satisfy their aspirations. It can be changed only by devising means to satisfy these aspirations equally well, or better—which is difficult, or to change the aspirations—which is even more difficult.

Ms. Robertson's last point is an elaboration of her first one. As for the factors favoring footlessness, "knowledge" industries may require more rather than less face-to-face contact than those making commodities. "Disadvantages of central city" are relevant on metropolitan, not on national scale.

As to the conclusions, I agree that "a major revival of central cities" (are they really dead?) is unlikely. I also agree that "dispersion" on a national scale (different from a shift to South and West) is improbable. However, "decentralization" on the metropolitan scale will probably continue and even accelerate. It has most vigorously proceeded during the seventies when all the concentrating factors enumerated by Ms. Robertson, including the two which I expect to be reversed, were fully operative. This is proof of the strength of the rural magnet. Contrary to Ms. Robertson's assertion, the growth rate in the metropolitan fringe has been higher for rural than for urban areas.

However, the radius from the metropolitan center within which decentralization occurs is likely to be no more than 60 miles, maybe 75. Small communities beyond this distance are likely to lose population, except those that can offer environmental attractions, primarily climate and scenery.

Branch plants, if they are to be efficient and innovative, require easy access to face-to-face communication and to highly specialized business services as well as to major airports, all to be found only in the metropolis.

The development of "secondary" centers should be encouraged within as well as outside metropolitan areas, and of newer as well as of older areas.

A final remark. Population decline and decay are not the same. Where large-scale gentrification occurs, population decline means "upgrading." Both population decline and decay may be a greater threat to small towns than to big cities.

21.
The San Francisco/ Oakland/San Jose Metropolitan Region

Adam Krivatsy

Introduction

This paper examines metropolitan phenomena in a still evolving, multi-nodal urban concentration on the west coast of the North American continent: in the San Francisco/Oakland/San Jose Metropolitan Area.

In search for means of controlling metropolitan growth, the writer reviews the metropolitan community through the key factors which act as "value determinants" in shaping people's lives around the Bay.

Three Cities, One Metropolis

San Francisco has a population of 695,000 and Oakland 184,000, while San Jose's population reached 740,000 in 1984. With an aggregate population of 1,619,000, these three cities are part of a nine-county metropolitan region of over five million. San Mateo, Alameda and Santa Clara Counties are quite urbanized, while Marin, Sonoma, Napa, Solano and Contra Costa Counties still experience steady urbanization. Regional indicators of metropolitan growth are presented in Table 1. A map of the nine-county area is featured on the next page.

Presently only the San Francisco/Oakland Metropolitan Area is recognized as a Standard Metropolitan Statistical Area (SMSA). In spite of its significant role in the region, the U.S. Census Bureau regards San Jose as a separate statistical area. In view of the fact that this city functions as an integral part of the San Francisco/Oakland Metropolitan Area, this analysis treats it as part of the metropolitan environment.

Table 1

Regional indicators of growth in the nine-county San Francisco Bay Region

	1980	1985	1990	1995	2000
Population	5,179,793	5,496,000	5,745,000	5,955,000	6,142,000
Household Population	5,058,613	5,364,000	5,609,000	5,815,000	5,997,000
Households	1,971,000	2,090,000	2,239,000	2,405,000	2,552,000
Labor Force	2,702,000	2,906,000	3,089,000	3,420,000	3,664,000
Annual Average Net Migration Over 5-Year Period	—	20,800	24,000	25,400	26,000
Mean Household Income in Constant 1980 $	$31,614	$32,600	$33,400	$34,300	$35,300
Total Births Over 5-Year Period	—	403,000	369,000	350,000	354,000
Household Size	2.567	2.566	2.510	2.420	2.350

Source: ABAG Regional Economic-Demographic Information System.

Evolution of the Metropolis

More than two centuries have passed since Father Junipero Serra established the missions which became foundations for cities throughout California. During this eventful period, the San Francisco Bay Area has witnessed the Gold Rush. It was destroyed by the 1906 earthquake, and served as a staging area for the Pacific Theater during World War II. Many waves of newcomers added to the steady stream of people who made the Bay Area their home. There were many reasons which prompted people to move to the Bay Area: the Gold Rush, Kaiser's shipyards, the Silicon Valley computer industry, or simply trade with the Far East.

For many years, San Francisco, Oakland and San Jose lived separate lives. However, what functioned as three separate cities 30 years ago now lives as a three-pronged metropolis. San Francisco has long lost its importance as a major port and is now recognized as the bastion of corporate business in the West. Oakland has evolved from the subsidiary role as the "other city across the Bay" to a major western container port and distribution center. San Jose changed its role from the "prune capital of California" to one of headquarters of the computer industry in the United States.

Yet, at this point, none of the three cities could perform its present role without the support of the other two. None of them has either the size nor the resources necessary to be competitive. By now, San Francisco relies on

Oakland for goods and access, industry and affordable housing; the city also benefits from the scientific community in the San Jose area. In turn, Oakland has become dependent on the exposure, services and business represented by San Francisco and San Jose. Many believe that San Jose would still be a sleepy village surrounded by plum orchards if it would not be for Stanford University and San Francisco, which have attracted the scientific community to the Bay Area.

Each of these cities has a distinct social profile of its own: San Francisco being the recipient of immigrants from Europe and the Pacific Basin; Oakland housing a significant black community; and San Jose with its established Mexican American neighborhoods. Today, these cities—and their respective hinterlands—function as compatible components of the larger, complex and colorful metropolitan community.

In urban planning terms the conurbation of three individual cities is logical: the very centrifugal forces within their shared labor/housing markets have contributed to expansion of each growth pole until their interdependence caused them to function as complementary parts of a metropolis.

During the past two decades, the benefits of this trend have become increasingly clear. While, as observed by Ms. Robertson in her paper on the North American metropolis, most mature metropolitan communities seem to be on the decline, the very trend of decentralization that is said to undermine the vitality of the North American metropolis continually reinforces the metropolitan community which has emerged on the shores of San Francisco Bay.

Of course, in the process, the centrifugal trend is causing a constant transformation in the nine associated counties. Practically all of the buildable bayfront has become urban; most of the valleys are either built-up or are rapidly urbanizing; and the major highway routes and transit corridors are being developed.

The result of this urbanization process is that the "rural" and "less developed," "non-metropolitan" counties—so classified by Peter A. Morrison—are swiftly becoming "urban" in character and beginning to perform metropolitan functions. In the Bay Area—using Charles L. Leven's words—the metropolis is indeed "moving to the countryside" and does so without detriment to its vitality!

The centrifugal growth patterns first followed the safe route. They tended to expand along the two transit corridors which connect San Francisco and Oakland with San Jose, spanning distances of 40 to 50 miles. (San Francisco and Oakland are linked by a bridge across the Bay.) This caused the intensive urbanization of San Mateo and parts of Santa Clara and Alameda Counties. After 1975, urban growth reached out along valleys, simply seeking accessible land, or expanded along the Route 80 corridor that connects the San Francisco Bay Area with Sacramento, the State's capital.

In keeping with established trends, outlying farmland in rural counties was first usurped by housing developers seeking cheap land. Housing has soon followed by industries in pursuit of labor. Thus, the metropolitan

303

region has further expanded within the limits of up to one-hour "commute time" from the three hubs of the tri-nodal metropolis: in the east as far as Fairfield and Livermore, in the north to Santa Rosa, and in the south to Gilroy and Morgan Hill (see Figure 1).

Within a decade, miles of rural countryside have been urbanized, and formerly remote, extensive farmland has become part of the metropolis' urban life. Today urban concentrations dot Sonoma, Solano and Santa Clara Counties, and especially the rapidly urbanizing Contra Costa County.

This trend validates Hans Blumenfeld's observations presented in this publication that the exodus of middle-class families to the suburbs is now followed by the move of the workplaces from the center to the periphery of metropolitan regions. The small towns of Santa Rosa, Concord, Fairfield, Walnut Creek, Pleasanton and Morgan Hill are inundated with re-zoning applications by industries and businesses which seek suitable sites for their new plants in those small, outlying communities.

Thus, in the San Francisco Bay Area region developable parts of the former "umland" are rapidly absorbed into the expanding metropolis. This trend seems to justify Hans Blumenfeld's concern that the increasing decentralization of urban activities and population will cause: (1) increased reliance on automobile transportation (in an age of potential fuel crises!), and (2) disturbance of agricultural hinterland.

Many members of the San Francisco/Oakland/San Jose metropolitan community are also concerned about these issues. San Franciscans' attitude toward regional growth—and their potential for guiding and controlling that growth—will be best understood through a glimpse at their socio-economic characteristics.

Economy, Jobs

The Bay Area, and particularly San Francisco, has never been heavily industrialized, although the Bay has always served as an important port. The San Francisco Bay Area has undergone a considerable re-structuring over the past 50 years. By now San Francisco can be viewed as the archetypal post-industrial city. It is expected that economic trends that powered the Bay Area's transformation will continue in the future. Information and service activity will increase, while the residual manufacturing activities will decline.

It is quite likely that within the information and service sector, employment may become compartmentalized even further. The higher-level executive and professional jobs will converge in the urban centers of San Francisco, Oakland and San Jose, while office workers will move to the adjacent counties, perhaps near one of the regional rapid transit stops. By the end of 1982, the Bay Area Rapid Transit district (BART) has already devised plans to encourage such concentration in the vicinity of its Pleasant Hill Station.

The Bay Area:
Cities and Open Space

North

Sonoma County

Napa County

Santa Rosa

Sebastopol ●

● Rohnert Park

Napa ●

● Vacaville

● Petaluma

● Fairfield

Solano County

Marin County

Novato ●

Vallejo ●

San Rafael ●

● Martinez

● Antioch

Richmond ●

● Concord

Brentwood ●

● Walnut Creek

Contra Costa
County

Oakland ●

● San Ramon

San Francisco

Daly City ●

● Livermore

● Hayward

● Pleasanton

Alameda County

San Mateo ●

● Fremont

Redwood City ●

Santa Clara
County

San Mateo
County

● San Jose

● Morgan Hill

● Gilroy

☐ Urban areas, 1980
☐ Open lands, 1980
   (Includes some rural
   development)

0   10   20 Miles

Source: People for Open Space

Fig. 21-1: The Bay Area: Cities and Open Space. (People for Open Space)

Social and Demographic Trends

The San Francisco Bay Area is in the vortex of the change from an industrial society to the information-centered society. Values are being transformed to focus on quality of life and health. People want to experience things and want to fulfill their potential.

Through Silicon Valley, the Bay Area has become a center of new technology, and it is also the home of venture capital. The business community thrives on information exchange throughout the Pacific Rim. The Bay Area is also the place in America where civility and tolerance are widely practiced. According to James W. Haas, in the new "American Renaissance," San Francisco has the distinction of being the new "Florence."

Socially and demographically, the area is quite distinctive. The population is dynamic, composed of many transients. In 1984, only 30 percent of the population was native born, another 30 percent had lived in the Bay Area for less than three years.

The area has attracted many people from all over the world and from small-town America. Migration trends and projections are presented in Figure 2. Within the past decade, many Asians and Hispanics have migrated to the area. The Bay Area community has a higher ratio of foreign-born residents than any other area in California. Political conditions in Asia and Latin America will effect further immigration.

In San Francisco, the Anglo population, now down to 53 percent, does not reproduce itself; only 11 percent of the Anglo population is under the age of 20! Anglos are also reluctant to form traditional families: less than 40 percent of Anglo families consist of related individuals, and almost 40 percent of the adult males are single. This population maintains itself in the Bay Area through young, working age immigrants, especially young males, often from out-of-state.

Middle-class families prefer to live in surrounding counties. When families start to have children, they will leave San Francisco for one of the region's suburbs.

It is expected that, due to the influx of new arrivals, the population will continue to be unstable. Among the transient population, those segments least likely to leave are Asians and gay males. These are urban people who are tied to large communities within the urban core. Many of the Asian immigrants are poorly educated and economically deprived; however, they are quick to learn, and they tend to prosper in the metropolis. The gay males are generally well-educated and relatively affluent.

The main concern of this dynamic versatile population is to preserve the very qualities which first attracted them to California, and more particularly, to the Bay Area—a certain lifestyle and the physical and social setting that supports that lifestyle.

Fig. 21-2: Migration trends and projections, average annual net migration, San Francisco Bay Area. (Historical Data, California Department of Finance; Projected Data, ABAG)

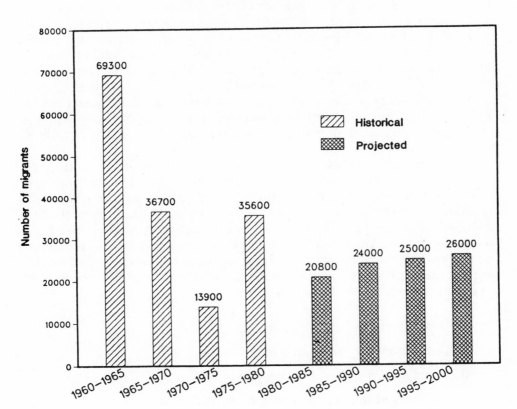

Migration Trends and Projections
Average Annual Net Migration

San Francisco Bay Area

Value Determinants

During the past two decades, Bay Area residents have manifested distinct preferences for a lifestyle. They strongly associate this lifestyle with their metropolitan environment. Planning for the future, preserving the benefits that the San Francisco/Oakland/San Jose metropolitan area represents, will be possible only if these preferences are understood.

Sense of openness

Perhaps the most important concern of Bay Area residents is to preserve what is strongly associated with the American West—a sense of openness in the form of human settlements. Interpreted in scientific terms, this represents low densities, and consequently a cavalier use of the land resources, and inefficient modes of urban services. Table 3 illustrates that the planned densities are lower than the established densities. This insistence upon maintaining sufficient "elbow room" in urban areas has manifested itself in total reluctance to accept any proposal by the regional planning agency, ABAG, which suggested increased development intensities in the vicinity of rapid transit nodes.

This concern for openness in the built-up urban environment is in sharp contrast with simultaneous efforts to preserve agricultural lands through a green belt program in the nine-county area. Authored by the grassroots organization, People for Open Space (POP), the 1983 plan promotes five strategies for meeting Bay Area housing needs without further encroaching on open land. POP claims that, if the five strategies would be fully accepted, 150 percent (!) of the metropolitan's housing needs could be satisfied for the next 20 years without losing open space **and** without loss of the character of the urban environments. These five strategies are:

1. Use vacant land more effectively,
2. Build more housing along major roads,
3. Bring homes and people downtown,
4. Add second units on existing homesites, and
5. Recycle lands no longer needed for industry.

Of course, POP's recommendations are based on a logic that is contrary to the people's desire to keep densities low and to secure ample room for private outdoor spaces on the ground. Yet, POP is determined to maintain a green belt around the urban area in perpetuity. It hopes to achieve this goal through a massive public education program and through financial assistance from the Trust for Public Lands, a non-profit organization dedicated to acquiring and preserving threatened open space.

Table 2

Planned and Existing Densities by County

	Existing Density[1,2] (units/acre)	Planned Density (units/acre)
Alameda	9.3	7.4
Contra Costa	6.3	5.2
Marin	4.6	1.7
Napa	5.1	4.2
San Francisco	31.2	72.5
San Mateo	6.6	9.9
Santa Clara	7.3	8.1
Solano	7.0	5.3
Sonoma	5.7	4.7
Total Region	**8.2 units/acre**	**5.8**

Notes: 1. **Net** density within urban planning areas
2. Density per net acre as of 1975.
Sources: Existing density data is from ABAG, "1975 Base Data." Planned density data is from POS.

Bay Area residents' changing values are reflected in their concern for the San Francisco Bay as an important amenity. While in the past it was normal practice to create new waterfront real estate by filling the Bay, today any attempt to encroach on the Bay is viewed as a social crime. In the early 1960s, the Bay Conservation and Development Commission (BCDC) was established to safeguard the Bay. Through its effective police powers, this watchdog agency not only fights against pollution of Bay waters and prevents further filling of the Bay, but also actively pursues a program of creating public access to the waterfront. Should BCDC's plans be realized, there will be a 200-mile long, continuous public walk along the Bayshore. Again, this concern for the Bay, a central asset of the metropolitan community, will strongly influence further development of the metropolis and the urban form of the metropolitan environment.

Of course, the quality of life in California, this affluent, avant-garde state of the Union, is also affected by the quality of air and water. Bay Area residents had ample opportunity to learn from their distant neighbors in Los Angeles about the adverse effects of air pollution. Their interest in wildlife and in recreational uses of the Bay also focused their attention on the quality of Bay waters. This concern for the quality of air and water was manifested in the creation of the Bay Area Environmental Management Plan.

In agreement with the state's regulatory measures affecting air quality, this plan monitors industrial and vehicular emissions and works toward enforcement of increasingly strict air and water quality standards. The plan is administered by the staff of the Association of Bay Area Governments (ABAG), an inter-governmental agency established to coordinate planning in the 95 cities and nine counties of the metropolitan region.

Fig. 21-3: San Francisco Bay Area. Scale: 1 centimeter = 5.77 kilometers; area covered is approximately 7,000 square kilometers. (Copyright: Gropic 1984 Earthsat)

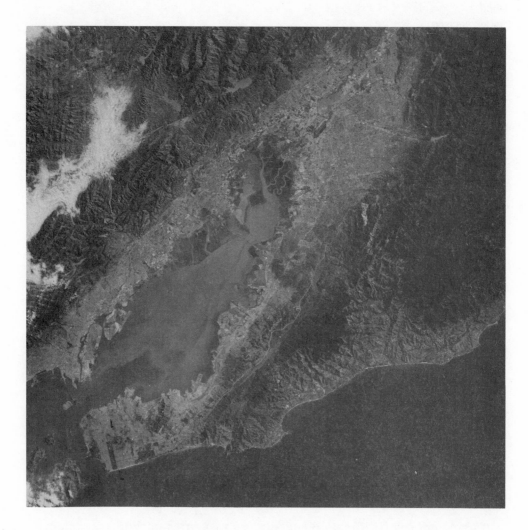

Environmental goals of the plan are realized primarily through a creative manipulation of industrial emissions and waste. Old plants can expand if they *reduce* their total emissions. New plants can "buy" emission capacity by paying for the installation of scrubbing devices in existing plants. (Automotive air pollution standards are enforced by the state.) Water pollution is being reduced through an area-wide waste-water management program coordinated by ABAG.

Mobility

As are most Californians, San Francisco Bay Area residents are wedded to their cars, even if the freedom that automobiles provide also represents financial sacrifices and occasional frustration. While several routes within the regional highway system are often congested, residents are reluctant to abandon their cars for public transit. In 1984 the average number of passengers per vehicle was only 1.47, and this figure increases only slightly with growing peak traffic congestion along major commute routes.

Yet, characteristic of the environment-oriented values of San Francisco Bay Area residents is the fact that, it would be regarded as political suicide to suggest increasing vehicular capacity across the Bay by building a twin to the San Francisco-Oakland Bridge, or to add a second deck to the Golden Gate Bridge. In this case, beauty wins over convenience! Who would dare to destroy the graceful lines of the Golden Gate Bridge with a second deck?

Regional transportation is coordinated by the Metropolitan Transportation Commission (MTC), an agency which closely collaborates with the land-use planning staff of ABAG. Unlike ABAG, the MTC has strong powers and serves as the agency responsible for coordinating local, state and federal transportation programs. Regardless of most residents' preference for private automobiles, the MTC vigorously promotes public transit programs. One outcome of this work is the Bay Area Rapid Transit system (BART), serving the metropolitan population since 1972, with 71.5 miles of tracks.

MTC's 10-year plan focuses on further extension of the transit system through a combination of BART, light-rail and bus routes. Still, it will be mostly the poor, the old, and the disabled who will avail themselves of the public transit network.

Education

Another value dear to Bay Area residents is the education of their children —and more increasingly—continued education for themselves. In this regard, local population is not unlike the rest of Americans; most everyone knows that basic education is a necessary "ticket" to a decent life, and many believe that continued education is essential for individual success in today's changing world.

Concern for education affects the location preferences. Most parents with school-age children tend to live in the racially and economically segregated suburbs. Those interested in one of the institutions of higher learning generally choose to live nearby.

Facilities and services

Perhaps less essential, yet historically proven, values to metropolitan population are represented by the facilities and services which respond to need for specialty goods, which offer cultural experiences, or which simply provide a forum for social interaction. The most, and the best, of these can still be found in the inner cities in the three growth poles of the San Francisco/Oakland/San Jose metropolitan region, with emphasis on shopping, music, theater, the visual arts, and dining in San Francisco.

As Hans Blumenfeld so aptly states, we are ill-prepared to deal with decreasing population in our urban centers in mature metropoli of North America. However, continued migration to the "sunbelt" states assures the vitality of urban centers. The San Francisco/Oakland/San Jose Metropolitan Area is living proof of this phenomenon: the urban "plant" is continually rejuvenated by the steady flow of immigrants. These newcomers are quick to adapt to the local lifestyle, and—according to their cultural preferences —are eager to patronize local arts, sports and organizations.

Thus, the urban centers of the San Francisco/Oakland/San Jose metropolitan region are still gaining vitality, attracting new programs and further investment in programs which must depend on widely based support and substantial individual contributions. Concert halls, museums, theaters, racquet clubs and par courses built during the past two decades attest to commitment to the culture, the arts, and the cult of good health in this rejuvenated, vigorous society.

Summary

In summary, we can conclude that, in the past 20 years, the Bay Area has re-oriented itself in many ways:

• Goods-producing jobs have been replaced by service-oriented activities to a greater degree than has occurred nationwide.

• While the Bay Area still attracts many foreign immigrants, a great majority of the (domestic) "immigrants" are more concerned with the quality of life than with the job opportunities that the Bay Area represents.

• This lifestyle regards private and public open space, clean air, clean water, access to nature, mobility, good education, and access to culture, arts and opportunities for self-improvement as values essential in life.

• To achieve—and to safeguard—these values, residents are prepared to support organizations that are dedicated to preserving the natural environment and to plan for a better future.

The Future

Lacking a metropolitan form of government, the Bay region's future will not be shaped by decisions made by one agency in a single location. Rather, it will be the cumulative product of many decisions made in each of the region's cities and counties. It is likely that the form of the growing metropolis will reflect a certain compartmentalization of work, living and leisure activities:

- Of the growth poles, San Francisco will increasingly attract executive jobs, Oakland will be the destination of overseas shipping, and San Jose will expand as the center for high-technology manufacturing.

- Due to a lack of willingness to accept higher density living, and due to the lack of housing sites, the population of San Francisco will remain stable in size. Yet, as a result of continued immigration, it will churn with mobility and vitality. Of the two other growth poles, Oakland and San Jose, the first one has no room for growth, and the second has elected to expand slowly through a carefully managed annexation program.

- In time, it is expected that the city of San Francisco will gradually relinquish its leading role as the cultural capital of Northern California, as residents will increasingly patronize events in Oakland/Berkeley and San Jose.

The future form of the metropolis will be determined by several factors, including:

- established development patterns
- constraints and opportunities represented by permanent open space and topography
- dominant values of the metropolitan population

The Bay Area metropolis of the future will take the form of the multi-nucleated system of *interdependent* urban nodes, unlike the system of *independent* nodes suggested by Ms. Robertson as a potential scenario for the future. Each of those nodes will have a special business profile and a certain cultural, if not ethnic, flavor. These nodes in the metropolitan structure will represent the leadership, closely tied to the surrounding economic and employment bases and institutions of higher learning.

The expanding metropolis will reflect the values of the society which is active in shaping it for convenience, for comfort, and for a healthy way of life. Most probably, the champions of open space, the advocates of the green belt system, will lose out to the insatiable urban sprawl. Only a total failure of the metropolitan transportation system could cause restraint in the rate of urban expansion, and at this time such a breakdown is inconceivable to the public. It has been suggested that, in case of a transportation crisis, there is always the Bay to be used as the most flexible route of surface transportation. Sydney Harbor and Istanbul's waterways provide ample evidence of possibilities for effectively complementing land-based transportation with a variety of water-transport systems.

Conclusion

Examination of the San Francisco/Oakland/San Jose metropolitan community lead to the following conclusions:

- A new, conservative point of view, based on quality of life concerns, is replacing the liberal positions based on economic justice.

- In the post-industrial society, values shape the metropolis which affect the quality of life within the metropolis.

- Continuing in-migration has a beneficial effect on the vitality —and perhaps the viability—of the metropolis.

- Given certain conditions, the poly-nucleated metropolis is more viable that the mono-nucleated metropolis.

- People less often expect government to do things for them, and do not even have much faith in representative government.

- Planning for the future is often initiated at the grassroots level, and such plans are implemented without government participation or through the initiative process.

- The urban plant can be kept livable—and reflective of contemporary value systems—through the partnership of private entrepreneurs and public leaders.

- While the driving force and direction for development and redevelopment is the market place, the public planning process must play a responsible guiding role.

- Effective planning will require clearly defined policies and well-chosen incentives that safeguard the cherished amenities and encourage developers to build in response to future needs.

- Finally, it is evident that it is futile and perhaps wasteful to aim for an "ideal" metropolis conceived to serve yet unknown, future values and needs. The metropolis must respond to the population's needs in the present, the best it can, every day of the year. This can be accomplished through a metropolitan super-agency that has both powers of implementation and methods of funding major public improvements.

Bibliography

American Planning Associates (APA). 1984. New Downtowns.

Association of Bay Area Governments and the Bay Area Council. October, 1979. San Francisco Bay Area Economic Profile.

——————— , 1980. San Francisco Bay Area Historical and Projected Household Size, 1970–2000.

——————— , 1980. Developed Land.

——————— , 1980. Land Available for Development, 1980–2000.

——————— , 1980. Jobs in the Bay Region, 1980–2000,

——————— , 1980. Regional Projections,

Chafee, Dr. D. 1984. Economic Trends in the San Francisco Bay Area.

Center for Real Estate and Urban Economics, University of California at Berkeley. 1984. An Update on Retail Trade and Retail Space in California.

DeLeon, Dr. R. 1984. Political Trends.

Dowall, Dr. D. 1984. Possible Employment Patterns.

Holliday, R. 1984. Housing Costs,

Inman, B. 1984. Housing Demand in San Francisco.

Livingston, D.G. 1984. Downtown Retailing on the Rebound.

Lubliner, A. and Libermann, E. 1984. Downtown Transportation and Planning for People.

McCarthy, Dr. Kevin. 1984. San Francisco's Demographic Future,

Macris, D. and Williams, G. 1984. City of San Francisco Department of Planning. San Francisco's New Downtown Plan.

Metropolitan Transportation Commission (MTC). December, 1983. San Francisco Bay Area, New Rail Starts and Extensions.

Mollenkopf, Dr. J. 1984. San Francisco's Economic Development.

Oakland Tribune. 1980–1984. Selected Articles.

City of Oakland, Department of Planning. 1980. A Downtown Plan for Oakland.

Phillips, Dr. E.B. 1984. Questions on Social Relations.

People for Open Space. December 1983. Room Enough: Housing and Open Space in the Bay Area.

Rudin, Hedgecock & Whitehurst. 1984. Three Mayors Speak Out,

San Francisco Bay Architects. 1983. Review: San Francisco's Future as a Port City.

San Francisco Chamber of Commerce. February, 1983. San Francisco Business Special Issue.

——————— , 1981. San Francisco's Strategic Plan.

San Francisco Chronicle. 1980–1984. Selected Articles.

San Francisco Forward. November, 1984. A City We Share.

San Jose Mercury News. 1980–1984. Selected Articles.

City of San Jose, Department of Urban Planning and Transportation. 1981. San Jose's Future: A Growth Control Plan.

Schwartz, Dr. G.G. 1984. ENO Foundation for Transportation, Inc. Where's Main Street USA?.

Shory, Paul 1984. Mental Maps of the Future.

Spalding, J.F. 1984. Los Angeles Downtown Redevelopment Program.

U.S. Census Bureau. Census of Population. 1960, 1970, 1980.

——————— , Census of Business. 1960–1980.

Wolff, G. 1984. The Human Cost of the Downtown Boom.

Part VII

South America

22.
The Latin American Metropolis

Dietrich Kunckel

When trying to define the specific qualities of the Latin American metropolis, it becomes quite apparent that there is probably not just one type of Latin American metropolis but rather a number of diverse and different metropoli throughout the continent, depending on factors of historic development, location, climate, cultural circumstances, and other factors relevant to city form and structure.

The Latin American context comprises countries such as Argentina where urban development has started relatively early and where over 80% of the population is considered urban, and at the other end of the scale, countries such as Bolivia or Honduras with only 29% and 23% respectively of their total population living in urban settlements.

The climatic differences between the southern tip of the continent, the tropical and subtropical regions of the majority of the countries and the highlands of Mexico or Bolivia are considerable and not only affect settlement patterns and possibilities of agricultural development but also the requirements for housing and other services. There are other differences, such as the racial composition of the population, which ranges from 95% of European origin in Argentina, Uruguay and the southern part of Brazil to 45–60% Indian in Bolivia, Peru and Ecuador, while countries like Chile, Colombia and Venezuela show the highest percentage of mix between the races with about 65% of mestizo population.

With all these obvious differences between the countries of the Latin American continent, there are also a lot of similarities and common characteristics which will allow for some generalizations and the identification of development patterns within the region.

Historical and Geographical Context

The Latin American continent which stretches over 7,000 km north to south, and over 5,000 km at its widest point east to west, comprises 24 countries with a total surface area of about eight million square miles and an estimated total population of 393 million inhabitants in 1984. This enormous mass of people is due to the unparalleled population growth of the continent, which increased by 100 million people between the years 1900 and 1950 and since then has added more than 200 million new inhabitants.

These numbers are particularly startling if one looks at the situation during the last century when Latin America was considered underpopulated: Brazil in 1823 had a total population of 4.7 million inhabitants (about the population of Sao Paulo in 1960), with a gross density of less than one person per square kilometer, while Argentina exhibited similar characteristics in 1852, with 1.2 million inhabitants and an even smaller gross density than Brazil.

Although the Spanish colonization founded cities largely for the purposes of conquest and domination of the continent, many of these cities never grew beyond a few thousand inhabitants, while others were abandoned or had to be founded anew, perhaps several times, before they took root. The only major exceptions to this rule can be found in the highlands of Central America and Peru where the Spanish cities relied heavily on the existing infrastructure and population of pre-Colombian settlements.

The Portuguese colonization of Brazil developed mainly along the seaboard to support the agriculture of coastal plantations easily accessible to ports for the export of produce, leaving the large hinterlands for centuries without any major settlement.

Richard M. Morse[1] cites five factors common to the history of urbanization of Latin America:

1. The colonization was in great part an urban adventure brought about by people with an urban mentality. The municipal nucleus was the parting point for the colonization of the land.

2. In spite of elaborate regulations, urban site selection was often arbitrary, incorrect or obedient to momentary pressures.

3. The first to arrive tended to assure priority in buying up the land around the cities (even municipal land was often handed over to private persons) and to reserve special rights for their dependents. Therefore, the initial moment of social democracy was soon followed by the consolidation of an oligarchy based on land ownership and priority of arrival.

4. In Brazil and much of the rest of Latin America, the continuity of the institutions and municipal processes was menaced by the movement of the 'mayores' from the city to their rural holdings. By radiating centrifugal energy towards the surrounding land, all but the large commercial and administrative cities tended to become appendices of the countryside.

Actually, a municipality (municipio) included the rural areas with no interstitial land between municipalities.

5. The system of cities developed weakly. Geographical barriers were often formidable, while the mercantilistic policy of the Crown did little to foster centers of complementary economic growth. The cities of the New World used to relate individually with the overseas metropolis and to stay isolated between each other.

Many examples can be cited to prove these points, and the consequences of this historical heritage can still be felt today. To mention only two examples:

- In 1950, 86.5% of the total population lived in the areas along the seaboard, comprising only 50% of the continent.[2]

- Communication between the major cities of Venezuela—Caracas, Maracaibo, Cumaná and Ciudad Bolívar—was faster and safer by sea than by land until well into the twentieth century.

One of the decisive factors which changed the situation of Latin America, especially of its southern half, was the influx of European immigrants. This influx became dominant during the 1880s. Until then, lack of industrial growth, the difficulty of acquiring land and a sense of personal insecurity on the continent combined to retard migrant flows from Europe that instead sought a more hospitable reception in North America. Once these flows shifted to favor Latin America, with a bias towards Argentina and Brazil and later Chile, the continent's first two metropoli began to materialize: Buenos Aires and Rio de Janeiro.

The Present Situation

Of the total population of Latin America, 61% was classified as urban in the year 1975, making Latin America one of the most urbanized areas in the world. The growth of cities on the continent has been formidable and has been closely related to the overall growth of the population, which has been, for extended periods of this century, the fastest growing in the world. Over half of the countries had inter–annual growth rates of total population of more than 2.9% between 1960 and 1975, while only four had growth rates below 2%.

These rates, however, have been much higher in the cities. The inter–annual growth rate of the urban populations in nine countries reached over 4.5% between 1960 and 1970, and over 4% in the period 1970–1975 in 10 countries, leading to a high concentration of the population in the urban

areas. The resulting contrast between the very highly concentrated populations of the urban areas and the sparsely inhabited rural areas (or
unexplored and unexploited zones of the continent) is quite evident to see,
and is highlighted quantitatively by statistical comparisons with European
countries and the United States. For instance, though Chile and Venezuela

Table 1

Inter–annual Growth of Urban Population (%)

	1960-70	1970-75
Mexico	5.0%	4.6%
Brazil	5.0%	4.5%
Colombia	5.4%	4.9%
Peru	4.3%	4.2%

Source: World Development Report, 1978, The World Bank, August 1978

have roughly half the overall population density of that of the United
States—13.9 and 13.6 inhabitants per square kilometer versus 2.3 inhabitants per square kilometer—the populations of the two Latin countries are
more concentrated in urban areas: 83% for Chile, 82% for Venezuela as
against 76% for the United States. On the other hand, while the Netherlands show a degree of urbanization comparable to that of Argentina (79%
vs. 80%), the overall population density of that country is 36 times that of
Argentina (33.6 persons per square kilometer vs. 9.3).

But not all of the countries are equally urbanized or show the same degree
of concentration in their populations. At the individual country level, there
were four countries in 1975 with over 80% of their population in urban
areas: Argentina, Chile, Uruguay and Venezuela, while at the other end of
the scale there were six countries with 40% or less of their population in the
same condition: Bolivia, Honduras, El Salvador, Guatemala, Paraguay and
Costa Rica. Neither of these two groups, it should be noted, included the
countries where urban growth is expected to be most dramatic: Mexico,
Brazil, Colombia and Peru.

The two giants of the continent, Brazil and Mexico, account for almost

Table 2: The 4 largest Latin-American metropoli in 1975.

Rank		Country	Population (in million)
4	Mexico City	Mexico	11.9
6	Sao Paulo	Brazil	10.7
10	Gran Buenos Aires	Argentina	9.3
12	Rio de Janeiro	Brazil	8.9

54% of the total inhabitants of Latin America. In 1976, Brazil possessed 51% of South America's population and Mexico 58% of that residing in Central America. If Colombia and Peru are considered as well, the four countries together accounted for two-thirds of the continent's population, or 212 million people.

There are also marked differences in the growth rates of urban populations. Three of the four countries in Latin America with over 80% of their population in urban areas—Argentina, Chile and Uruguay—show for the period 1970 to 1975 inter–annual rates of growth for their urban populations between 1.7 and 2.7% (less than the overall population growth rate for Latin America). At the same time, these rates are among the highest for the four crucial countries:

Not surprisingly, the fastest growing metropoli of the continent are located in these countries, and their enormous growth will make them the largest urban agglomerations in the world. According to United Nations statistics, there were four Latin American metropoli among the 35 largest cities of the world in 1975:

The same statistics list six Latin American cities for the year 2000:

Table 3: The largest Latin-American metropoli in Year 2000.

1	Mexico City	Mexico	31.0
2	Sao Paulo	Brazil	25.8
7	Rio de Janeiro	Brazil	19.0
15	Gran Buenos Aires	Argentina	12.1
26	Bogota	Colombia	9.6
31	Lima	Peru	8.6

Clearly, the problem is not only a question of rate of growth but also of overall size of the urban agglomeration and its administration and management.

Growth of the Metropolis

It has been argued with good evidence that the change of a country from rural to urbanized is a finite process with a beginning and an end, and that it is necessary to distinguish between urbanization and growth of cities.

However, while a country is undergoing the process of urbanization, its cities grow at a much faster pace than at the beginning or the end of the process.

As Kingsley Davis has pointed out, the typical growth-form for the cycle of urbanization is a curve in the shape of an attenuated "S."[3] This logistic curve has also been observed and established in ecological studies of population growth under the condition that "there are no marked changes

323

in exploitable potentialities of the environment"—in other words, assuming that no new resources are made available.

If we try to apply this concept to the growth of cities, it could be observed that, in recent history, technological innovations have opened up innumerable resources for the cities to continue to grow, although, in the numerous mountainous areas of Latin America, the availability of the basic resource —space—and its utilization have become so restrictive as to imply a very limited supply.[4]

Assuming that serious restrictions of resources would be a feasable way of limiting the growth of the metropolis, measures to reduce the availability of land, to limit access and to increase cost would possibly divert growth from the metropolis to other, less limited areas.

The problem with resource restriction, however, is that it affects not only the potential future inhabitants but also the existing population. It has been noted that the phenomenon of growth of the cities changes its character and meaning when occuring at the speed and scale of the modern metropolis. In ecological terms, each stage in the historic urbanization process (city building) represented a significant expansion over the preceding one in terms of the components of the system, increased densities and size of the territory of the "effective population unit." As cities continue to grow, their territory of the "effective population unit" becomes larger and larger. At present this "effective population unit" and its related territory have reached unprecedented proportions if we look at metropoli like Sao Paulo and Mexico. It might be asked, however, whether these urban agglomerations are still representing "effective population units" or whether they are rather undergoing structural changes that transform them into several related but, to a certain degree, independent units requiring a new definition of the metropolis or metropolitan area.

Fig. 22-1: The maturation of urban settlements. (Richard Meier)

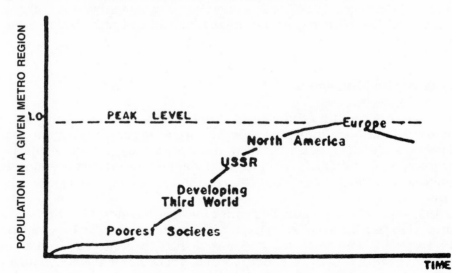

While cities continue to grow, new resources—physical, technical, social and spiritual—will have to be made available which might substantially alter the urban environment.

It is doubtful that these resources can be generated in sufficient quantities and fast enough, so only a reduction in the demand of resources could alleviate the problem of urban growth, which calls for new less wasteful ways of building cities, especially in the developing nations.[5]

In Latin America a large proportion of the population is living in metropolitan agglomerations and increasingly will be living in this type of urban settlement. As John D. Durand and Cesar E. Pelaez have pointed out,[6] the majority of the Latin American countries show a megalocephalic urbanization or concentration to a large extent in one primate city. According to their study, two–thirds of the Latin American countries had over 50% of their urban population concentrated in one city or metropolitan area (1960).

This absolute dominance of the primate city cited also by Castells[7] has established a pattern of dependence in terms of goods and services of the rest of the country from the capital which will prevail for a prolonged period, although recent trends indicate for some countries a decrease in the participation of the primate city in the overall urban population. This slow-down of growth of the primate city is accompanied by a more accelerated growth of the settlements of a lower order.

Characteristics of the Latin American Metropolis

When Hans Blumenfeld defined the 'modern metropolis' in 1965[8] he modeled it mainly on the European and North American examples in terms of size of population and the basic characteristics which set the metropolis apart from traditional cities. Of these characteristics—concentration of political and economic power, size of population and surface area, inclusion of open space, separation of workplaces from place of residence and high mobility in choice of jobs and occupations—some can be used to describe the Latin American metropolis. However, looking more closely at the major components, there are some important differences from those of Europe and the United States.

The first difference is one of overall population; at present, cities of 500,000 to one million inhabitants are not classified as metropoli in Latin America as they do not offer the specialized urban services which are characteristic of the metropolis.

The effective population to generate these services is only a portion of the total. Taking into account the limited resources of the majority, larger numbers are needed to provide the critical mass.[9]

With respect to the location and importance of the central business area in the Latin American metropolis, it is normally located around a very small historic center, concentrating government, banks and related services such as lawyers' offices, maintaining the primacy of the original center as the most important workplace concentration of the city. Specialized retail operations and offices of major corporations do not necessarily concentrate in the same area, often creating specialized centers in other parts of the city. There is generally more dispersal of commercial activities than in European cities. The lack of effective controls and regulations has contributed to a situation where commercial establishments are relatively footloose and locate according to convenience.

Manufacturing has played a less important role in the maturing of the Latin American metropolis. The typical fringe areas of the centers of European cities are almost nonexistent, or are rather of a different character.

The biggest difference, however, can be observed in the area of housing. Central city slums versus high-income suburbs is not the typical pattern, although some deteriorated housing does exist at the fringe of the old centers. It is the contrast between formal residential developments and the informal housing areas of the poor which characterizes the Latin American metropolis.

Location and extension of these areas do, of course, differ, but a typical growth pattern has been a series of ring–like developments with the high–income groups at the center and the lowest income sectors at the fringe. In Caracas, for example, there are several such rings, the original being the old center, where the most prestigious residences were located as close as possible to the central square while the poor settled in the surrounding areas of difficult topography.

While elaborate planning and design rules were set up and applied to the new developments of the formal sector, no such controls were established for the informal sector, to the effect that different standards are observed for services, densities and other indicators. Eventually the metropolis gets to a stage where the informal and formal parts of the city grow outward in different directions, leading to an ever–increasing social segregation.

The fourth major component of metropolitan land use—open land—is a scarce commodity in many of the Latin American metropoli. Continuously built-up areas without any major open space are characteristic, for example, of cities such as Sao Paulo and Mexico City. The access to open space for leisure and recreation is a privilege of the rich and middle class. In Mexico City, thousands of the poor have benefited from the subsidized fares of the Metro to cross the whole city from Ciudad Reforma east to west on weekends to get to the only major park of Chapultepec. There are, of course, noted exceptions where nature has provided for spectacular natural assets and measures of protection have been taken, as in the case of the beaches of Rio de Janeiro and Mount Avila towering over Caracas.

Problems of the Metropolis

In most of the Latin American countries the main problem for their major

Fig. 22-2: Lima, Peru. The checkerboard pattern of the original colonial "traza" of the Center, left of the Rimac River. (Servicio Aerofotografico Nacional, Courtesy: E. Galantay)

Fig. 22-3: Montevideo, Uruguay. Typical Latin-American grid pattern. Scale: 1 centimeter = 200 meters; area covered is approximately 4 square kilometers. (Servicio Geografico Militar, 1971, Archives, Chaire d'Urbanisme EPFL, E. Galantay)

Fig. 22-4: Caracas. Aerial view of Central Caracus looking north. In the middle, the Centro Simon Bolivar. Directly beyond the 25 squares of the original "traza" of the colonial foundation. (Courtesy: E. Galantay, 1971)

Fig. 22-5: Caracas areial photo, 1971, showing the juxtaposition of a planned urban extension on the flat land between squatter settlements occupying the hill ranges, an the abandoned "Helicoide" shopping center. (M.O.P. Cartografia Nacional, Permit 15930, Courtesy: Archives, Chaire d'Urbanisme EPFL, E. Galantay)

Fig. 22-6: Caracas. Juxtaposition of high-rise "superbloque" public housing and squatter settlement on the hillside, 1971. (Courtesy: E. Galantay)

metropoli is the continuing high rate of growth, leading to ever-enlarging metropolitan areas of gigantic size which require an unprecedented effort to supply goods and services for the population.

The notion of progress which traditionally has been associated with the process of urbanization has become questionable. However, without entering a socio-historical argument, a data comparison between countries with different degrees of urbanization shows a remarkable interdependence between the level of urbanization and the GNP per capita, as well as the availability of services. The six countries with the lowest degree of urbanization in Latin America (40% or less) together showed substantial differences with respect to the four most urbanized countries of the continent in terms of indicators such as access to safe water, population per physician, adult literacy rate, and percentage of enrollment in the different levels of the educational system.

Table 4 shows, for instance, that, in the six countries exhibiting low levels of urbanization, an average of 42% of the population had access to safe water compared to 78% for the highly urbanized countries. In the latter group there is a physician for every 1,163 people while in the former there are 2,925 persons per physician. Adult literacy rates are 89% vs. 63.5%, and attendance of higher education 19.5% vs. 8%. These figures clearly show that the more urbanized countries, aside from offering better economic conditions (GNP per capita of US$ 1,640 vs. US$ 597), on the average provide for better social services in terms of health care and education. It is, however, erroneous to assume that these services are available on an equitable basis to all of the population of the more urbanized nations. Large sectors of the urban population of these countries have limited access to the services of the metropolis. Nevertheless, this limited access is still a considerable improvement over the complete lack of services in many parts of the countryside and the smaller towns.

If one distinguishes the problems *of* the metropolis from those *in* the metropolis, it is obvious that those *of* the metropolis have to be dealt with on a larger national scale. It is at this level where policies have to be established and measures taken to balance the distribution of resources and turn growth into development.

Lack of continuity in planning policies and goals, however, is characteristic for many of the Latin American countries, not only at the national but also at the local scale. This, consequently, has prevented many good plans from being executed over the years.

Of the many problems in the metropoli of South America, a most pressing one is the low level of social equity expressed in many forms in the city. In social terms, the South American metropolis is hardly catering to its citizens in an equitable way. Community services are unevenly distributed. Infrastructure of water and sewer lines prevail in the formal sector but are absent in many of the informal areas. Access to lots by paved (or unpaved) streets is rarely provided in the low–income areas, and the highway system favors the parts of the population with higher incomes.

On the other hand, rules and regulations are applied in the formal sector

Table 4

Urbanization and Socio-economic Indicators 1975

Country	% Pop. urban areas	GNP per capita US $	% Pop. with access to safe water	Persons per physician	Primary school enrollment % age group		Higher & sec. school enrollment % age group		Adult literacy rate
					M	F	Sec.	High	
Chile	83	1040	70	2420	119	118	48	17	90
Uruguay	81	1390	98	910	103	103	62	14	91
Argentina	80	1550	66	450	108	109	55	28	93
Venezuela	82	2570	NA	870	96	96	43	79	82
Average highly urbanized countries		1640	78	1163					89
Bolivia	37	390	34	2120	72	65	31	10	40
Honduras	28	390	41	3360	89	88	13	4	61
El Salvador	40	490	53	4070	71	69	18	8	63
Guatemala	35	630	39	4200	62	56	13	4	47
Paraguay	37	640	13	2200	106	102	20	6	81
Costa Rica	40	1040	72	1580	109	109	52	17	89
Average less urbanized countries		597	42	2925					63.5

Source: The World Bank

but are totally neglected in the informal sector; residents of the formal areas have to pay property taxes, while those of the informal areas do not even have title to the land.

These incongruencies lead to abuse in both areas—the better-off evading taxes and the less well-off evading regulations.

In terms of space consumption, inner-city low-income areas—be they formal or informal—tend to show higher densities, less open space and fewer services than the higher income areas. In Caracas, the overall density of the informal areas is more than twice the density of the rest of the city. The overall density in the formal areas has gone up in recent years due to the large numbers of families moving into apartment buildings, but they are, on average, much lower than the densities reached in areas of single-family dwellings of the informal sector. This is also an indicator for the degree of crowding in the individual dwelling.

Access to jobs is another factor where the poor are at a disadvantage with respect to middle and higher income groups. Places of residence for the majority of the poor are located now on the fringe of the metropolis, resulting in very long journeys to work, often by several modes to reach the places of work which are mostly located in central areas.

Another important problem has been the lack of provision of urban infrastructure including streets due to the runaway occupation of new territory by rich and poor alike. Traditional planning strategies to guide development by building the urban infrastructure have widely failed when trying to move against established trends and growth patterns.[10] While the political system normally favors higher income areas eventually supplying the required systems, the low-income areas are often neglected.

Planning of the Metropolis

Efforts to guide and control growth of the metropolis in Latin America started in the twenties, became more visible by 1940, but gradually formed part of official policy only toward the middle of the century when the first negative effects of rapid urban growth became apparent. Faced with the unproportionate concentration of population in the major cities, most countries established a policy designed to slow down metropolitan growth and to organize the urban areas.[11] Urban renewal programs and the building of an urban highway system often went hand in hand with goals for decentralization of industry and decongestion of the major urban area by, for instance, the creation of New Towns.

Urban renewal projects and highway construction probably helped to attract more people to the metropolis and industry was still looking for locations near the metropolis—the place of the biggest supply of labor and the best market. A lot of study is still needed to identify and explain the specific growth-form of the metropolis. Present evidence is indicating that a prolonged growth-phase is an inevitable phenomenon of the metropolis, a transitional phase from one stage to another later stage at which urban population might become stable.[12] While growth itself is difficult to curb and control, it can be ordered and, to a certain degree, guided into desirable directions to achieve the goals of society. In a highly informal environment such as the South American continent, however, it will take strong measures of control to achieve stated planning goals.

Some of the difficulties are due to historic circumstances such as the conflict between national and municipal authorities in matters of urban planning laws which regulate titles to land and "bienhechurías" (any improvement on the land—houses, etc.).

The planning effort of the metropolis for the future should be undertaken outside as well as within, "outside" meaning that the growth of the metropolis cannot be curbed within its boundaries or sphere of influence, but rather has to be part of national policies and strategies.

If the Latin American continent wants to explore its resources, it must look inward towards the enormous extension of uninhabited land, with natural and mineral resources of great value and with a largely underutilized reservoir of agricultural land. If cities of second or third degree size are strengthened in terms of infrastructure, services and job opportunities, they will become more attractive as places of residence, especially if supported by agricultural production nearby, as has happened, for example, with the city of Mérida in the Andes of Venezuela.

As national policies will have effect only over a prolonged period of time, the metropoli will continue to grow in numbers of inhabitants and territory requiring an internal planning effort of the metropolis at least as demanding as those at the national and regional scales.

This planning effort within the metropolis will have to be directed to improve the living conditions of the marginal population and to incorporate this sector into the formal economy and city structure. The disparities between formal and informal, between rich and poor, have to be reduced by attacking the most pressing problems of these areas:[13] lack of land tenure, lack of infrastructure, lack of community services and excessive distances to places of work. Housing itself ranks relatively low on this scale, as it is the element that can be provided most easily by the residents themselves.

While planning for the underprivileged is urgently needed to improve the balance of social justice, there is a second aspect of major concern for the future of the metropolitan areas: the protection of the environment and the preservation of nonrenewable resources of all kinds. Urban populations tend to consume many times the resources of rural populations. The development of new habits (or, maybe, going back to traditional habits) of energy consumption and resource preservation, together with the use of less wasteful technologies, are needed for a more balanced development of the overall environment.

The Individual in the Metropolis

The individual's situation in the urban environment of the metropolis is characterized by the extremely limited relevance of his actions and the wide freedom of choice (if not conditioned by economic factors). This kind of environment is probably unsettling for many individuals who not only depend on feedback to evaluate the effect of their actions but also need identification with an environment that fits[14] their needs and aspirations. Urban environments, however, are not built to fit the individual but rather to cater to a hypothetical statistical average citizen, applying standards of different kinds according to cultural and economic circumstances. Depending on housing type, location and regulations, this pre-established environment allows some limited modifications. Paradoxically, in South America, at both ends of the social scale, the individual interferes more directly in the shaping of his environment: one building his house according to his needs, the other building his 'rancho'[15] according to his means. In any case, the individual will look for additional elements which allow him to establish his identity, be it by locating near family and friends, within ethnic neighborhoods, close to special services, place of work and so on.

While the single individual's possibility to influence planning decisions and to shape his environment is extremely restricted, he can join pressure groups—neighborhood associations, professional groups, chambers of commerce, etc.—to try to widen his influence. Until now, however, participative planning has been quite limited in the South American context as the urgency to provide infrastructure and services did not allow for prolonged processes of consensus-building. Thus, capital budget programs, infrastructure and road improvement plans have had more weight in planning decisions than social cohesion and organization or individual well-being. As the metropolis becomes more structured and more organized over the years, the process of consolidation will result in more conservative attitudes of the residents, defending their environment against physical and social disruption and slowing down the pace of change and replacement which has been extremely fast over the last decades.

The Venezuelan Metropolis

As an example of recent trends in urban and metropolitan development, Venezuela offers some interesting aspects, as certain shifts in trends have developed over the last ten years. Already highly urbanized in 1970, this trend has continued and seems to have reached a certain level where qualitative changes are as important as quantitative ones. While overall population growth of the country has remained quite high and constant at about 3.6% annually over the last 20 years, the growth of cities has varied considerably. The only metropolis, Caracas, has slowed down from 6.14% annually between 1950 and 1961 to 1.91% annually between 1971 and 1981, while all towns located in the metropolitan fringe have increased their rate of growth dramatically. While the growth rate of Caracas fell below the overall population increase, almost all of the cities of the interior had rates well above the natural increase. The result of these trends can be seen in Tables 5 and 6. These trends seem to indicate that:

Table 5

Venezuelan Cities with Population of 100,000 Inhabitants or More—1950-1981 (in thousands)

City	1950	1961	1971	1981
Maracaibo	272	458	677	954
Valencia	139	237	485	817
Maracay	105	198	381	638
Barquisimeto	132	234	373	566
Puerto La Cruz			122	154
Barcelona				178
Acarigua-Araure				152
Guarenas-Guatire				152
Ciudad Lozada			101	200
La Victoria				130
Los Teques				122
Valera			111	142
Lagunillas			115	116
Mérida			115	188
Cumaná			133	195
Maturín			133	199
Barinas				118
Coro				120
Punto Figo			102	133
Puerto Cabello			109	155
Cabimas		117	139	177
Ciudad Bolívar			125	200
Ciudad Guayana			153	325
San Cristóbal		117	162	213
Depto. Vargas		141	202	254
Caracas	712	1372	2184	2640
Total	1360	2874	5922	9238

Source: Census 1981

- The relative importance of the capital diminished not only with respect to the total population but also with respect to the population in cities over 100,000 inhabitants.

- Two other cities will soon reach the one million mark: Maracaibo and Valencia.

- Venezuelan cities or metropolitan areas of 100,000 people or more grew from five in 1950 to 26 in 1981, increasing their share of the total population from 27% to 63.4%.

Table 6

Indicators of Urbanization
Venezula: 1950-1981

	1950	1961	1979	1981
Caracas, as percentage of total population	14.14	18.24	20.37	18.12
Caracas, as percentage of cities of over 100,000 population	52.35	47.74	36.88	28.58
Cities with over 100,000 population as percentage of total population	27.01	38.2	55.23	63.4

Source: Census 1981

All these trends seem to indicate a more balanced urban development in recent years, due to a series of factors of which we can cite a few and others will still have to be identified:

• Restrictions to development in the capital due to limited land supply and high costs

• Decentralization policy of the government for industrial establishments, including the oil industry's administrative apparatus

• Improved and widened services in cities of second order

The figures might also indicate that Caracas is about to amplify its "effective population unit" and related territory. As the towns and cities of the fringe continue to grow, their interrelations with the capital will increase proportionately and eventually will require mass transportation links (perhaps the extension of the metro, presently under construction in Caracas), converting them into effective parts of the metropolis.

Historically, technological breakthroughs helped to set off the first geographical expansion of the city beyond the colonial precinct of the present center. Steel and reinforced concrete construction of bridges and tunnels and the new means of transportation expanded the urban area many times, resulting in a marked decrease of urban densities during the years 1920-1940, as shown in Figure 7.

Within the newly enlarged urban area, enormous population growth was responsible for bringing densities back and beyond the pre-automobile level, resulting at present in a gross residential density of 72 inhabitants per acre, or 180 persons per hectare.

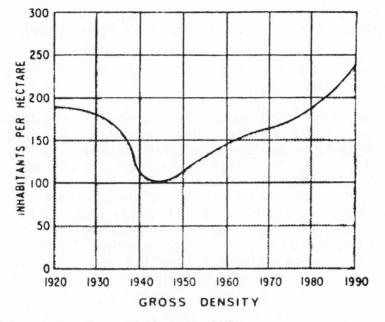

Fig. 22-7: Caracas. Gross density in urban area. (OMT)

As urbanizable land has become a sparse commodity in the urban area of the city, growth has been diverted to the surrounding towns and slowed down the growth of the central city.

Qualitatively, there has been a constant increase of the population living in informal urban areas in proportion to the total population. While in 1959 this proportion was 21% of the total and in 1966 it was 32%, it rose to 42.5% in 1979. It may be that general scarcity of land, high costs and overregulation have forced major portions of the population into the informal areas or into the outlying towns, thus producing the double effect of a decreasing role of the central city and a decreasing role of the formal sector within the central city.

Admittedly, more data will be needed over a longer period of time to confirm this trend. However, official planning goals have shifted to take account of the situation and to direct a major effort towards the marginal areas of the city, reducing the budget for highways and urban infrastructure and orienting investments towards the creation of community services and employment opportunities within the marginal areas. While the Venezuelan example might not be typical for overall trends of urban development on the continent, as the country is already highly urbanized, there are aspects to its urban environment which allow the raising of general questions with respect to the future of the South American metropolis:

• Will the cities of the continent be able to satisfy the aspirations of its future inhabitants by providing an acceptable environment and social justice?

- Will the metropolis continue to offer better services, more opportunities and wider choices than other types of settlements?

- Will it be possible to control costs, violence, pollution and congestion in the metropolis?

As world population and metropolitan areas will be faced with a period of growth well into the twenty-first century, the goals for planning the future must be revised as well as the means of their fulfillment.

Waste of resources is becoming increasingly unacceptable, more equitable distribution of wealth ever more urgent.

Planning the future will need the reconfirmation of basic values of the human society—equal rights, freedom of thought, respect for the individual, social justice and the willingness to sacrifice a portion of one's own wealth or happiness for the good of the community. This is not meant to be the call for the plan of another "ideal city" but rather a reminder that, in planning, one will always have to mediate between the ideal and the possible.

Notes

1. Richard M. Morse, "Una Investigacion Reciente sobre la Urbanizacion Latinoamericana: Un Estudio Selective con Comentario," en Gerald Breese (ed.), *La Ciudad en Los Paises en Vias de Desarrollo*, Editorial Tecnos, Madrid.

2. Manuel Castells, "La Cuestion Urbana," Siglo Veintiuno, Editores.

3. Kingsley Davis, "The Urbanization of the Human Population," in "Cities," *Scientific American*, September, 1965.

4. The city of Caracas is a good example for such a situation, as shown later on.

5. Taken from Richard Meier, "A Stable Urban Ecosystem," *Third World Planning Review*, vol. 2, no. 2, Autumn 1980.

6. John D. Durand and Cesar E. Pelaez, "Pautas de Urbanizacion en America Latina," en Gerald Breese, *op. cit.*

7. Castells, *op. cit.*

8. Hans Blumenfeld, "The Modern Metropolis" in "Cities," *op. cit.*

9. As happens with the term "urban," the term "metropolitan" not only is used as a description of size, but also as a description of specific qualities of the environment.

10. This has been shown in detail in studies on Ciudad Guayana, Venezuela. See: Maria Pilar Garcia and R.L. Blumberg, "The Unplanned Ecology of a Planned Industrial City: The Case of Ciudad Guayana, Venezuela" in *Urbanization in the Americas*, 1977.

11. A recently adopted policy of the Venezuelan Government prohibits the government-owned utility companies from providing water or electricity to newly established illegal housing (ranchos).

12. The World Bank includes projections of size of "hypothetical stable population" and year of reaching it in the tables of the World Development Report, 1978.

13. The recent food riots in the cities of Brazil indicate the potential for social unrest which exists.

14. The "good fit" as understood by Christopher Alexander ("Notes on the Synthesis of Form," Harvard University Press), might in this case be provided by environments where there are no "misfits."

15. Venezuelan term for squatter house.

23.
The View from Mexico

Elias Gomez-Azcarate

Four topics seem basic to me in any attempt to shape the future of our main cities:

- Inequity in resource allocation
- External dependance
- The limits of physical planning
- The limits of strategic planning

Resource Allocation

Let us take for granted the aspects that we all recognize as meaningful in the life of a metropolis and examine them in the light of the latest trend projections:

- 90% of the population growth in the next 20 years will take place in the developing countries; 60% of this increase will swell the ranks of urban dwellers, and half of them will be concentrated in giant metropolitan agglomerations.

  By the year 2025, 80 of the 93 cities with more than five million inhabitants will be in Third World countries.

- As Dietrich Kunckel explains in the preceeding article, the urbanization process began early in Latin America and, at the present, six out of 10 persons live in urban areas. The population of the capital cities together accounts for almost one-third of all urban dwellers and 17% of the total population of the region.

- In the next 20 years the rural population will remain stable at about 170 million and the entire increase of the population will take the form of urban growth (+ 200 million). The capital city regions will concentrate more than 20% of the total population, some 130 million people in all.

In spite of these figures the problem stems not so much from the size of the population but rather from the very uneven resource allocation, an historically determined distribution of the population in the national space which is far from optimal in terms of accessibility to fixed resources and a lack of attention to implement policies for regional development.

The real challenge in the metropoli of Latin America is not their great size or rapid rate of growth but the nature and characteristics of this growth and the environment and living conditions which result. Each city is striving to offer the same sophisticated goods and services to its elite and at the same time produces slums and traffic bottlenecks, be it in Santiago Chile, Sao Paulo or Ciudad de Mexico.

Underdeveloped or "Dependant" Metropolis?

No doubt much research has been done on this subject, much of it from what we may call an "ethnocentric perspective," i.e., taking the metropoli of Europe or the U.S. as yardsticks for "proper" performance. Obviously, from this point of view, not many Latin American cities would qualify as "developed" in any but purely quantitative terms. Yet it is perhaps not unfair to ask here whether Aztec Tenochtitlan with its 300,000 inhabitants in the fifteenth century and its sophisticated urban services was not the first "metropolis" of the American continent and a leading city, even in comparison with the capitals of the contemporary European kingdoms.

For a fair analysis we need a new framework: not the simple dichotomy of developed/undeveloped as proposed by Dennis Dwyer, but one incorporating the economic abyss between the "North and the South" as defined in the Brandt Commission Report. Only the review of the historical evolution—its origins and unfolding in Latin American development and colonial development—can give us the adequate background highlighting colonialism and post-colonial dependence, i.e., the use of a given country's resources for the benefit of foreign subjects and nations.

The above two characteristics explain the origin and present structure of our regional economies and urban systems. They also explain the rise of local power structures closely related to the North (as seen from the "South") and the quasi-colonial relations between the leading metropolis and the other cities of the national system. In Mexico there is no hierarchical spatial order of settlements, nor can we find a "logical" relation between the primate city and the next largest ranks. The country of Mexico has 33% of its urban population concentrated in the metropolitan zone of Mexico City (ZMCM).

Most population centers, including the largest ones, are located on the high plateau, far from the coasts. Brasil, with a different colonial economy, has a different pattern, with most of its population and its largest cities hugging the Atlantic coastline. Yet both cases, the Mexican and the Brasilian one, prove that metropolitan formation in Latin America does not follow the pattern of development stages familiar from European and American studies. It is also evident that, although resource-scarcity tends to level off metropolitan growth, there are other forces—still incompletely understood —that shape the Latin American metropoli.

These forces derive from a common Latin origin (with its Catholic and even Moorish traditions) and a shared Ibero-American colonial evolution. Whatever ethnic and cultural differences have existed have largely been evened out in 300 years of Spanish and Portuguese domination. It helped, of course, that the pre–Columbian urban pattern blended perfectly with the Spanish conceptions for the ideal city—and, in fact, the physical features of Aztec Tenochtitlan were largely incorporated into the plan of the Mexico City founded by Cortez.

The Limits of Physical Planning

I agree with Dietrich Kunckel's perception of the role of the formal and informal sectors in Latin American metropoli and his description of the duality of attitudes toward urban processes. However, it is important to recall the origins of the informal sector by recent rural migrants, their low educational level and their slow integration into the urban economy due to underemployment. The impact of these factors on urban marginality is as important as the lack of housing, urban services or infrastructure.

In this context we must admit that physical planning is not very effective in Latin America, except in such cases as Brasilia where a master plan had been partly implemented before the first settlers arrived. But then, physical planning is not succeeding in reshaping the cities of the rich industrial countries either, where tighter controls exist and financial means can be more easily mobilized to support programs and policies. With weaker resources in Latin America we must find alternatives to the constant renewal of expensive center-city land or the development of peripheral (and inaccessible) housing estates resulting from the extension of the built-up area of the metropolis.

Let me enumerate some of the main problems confronting Mexico City:

- *Increasing social disintegration:* Social solidarity is being substituted by social antagonism among classes and gathering momentum due to the financial crisis. This is reflected in spatial disarticulation and in problems related to constraints to physical and social mobility.

345

• *Pollution and environmental decay:* A social mass with a density of 160 inhabitants per hectare providing 50% of the gross domestic product, concentrating 25% of the active population, 28% of the federal budget, and accounting for 45% of the national energy consumption cannot avoid the ecological consequences of its 17.5 million inhabitants, 130,000 industries and three million motor vehicles packed together in the largest urban agglomeration of the world.

Mexico City generates 12,000 tons of garbage daily, and 11,000 tons of dust and other pollutants are released into the atmosphere. Due to a weak environmental policy, the capital is likely to remain one of the most polluted areas in the world for the next generations. Pollution combined with environmental decay, particularly in the marginal areas, produces a vicious circle swallowing up capital investment in urban support systems.

• *Mass transportation:* Until 1977, priority had been accorded unabashedly to the needs of the owners of private automobiles. Starting in 1977 enormous investments were made in mass transportation. Nevertheless, private cars continue to take up street space with 97% of the vehicles accounting for only 15% of all trips. Fare policies complicate the problems: the subway (a trip costing less than one U.S. cent for a 20 kilometer ride) is now carrying four million passengers daily, about one-sixth of a total of 25 million trips. However, an expansion of the subway system to meet the demand cannot be financed without a drastic fare increase which would then take about 18% of the minimal daily wage. Since more than 50% of the employed population earns only the minimal wage, raising the cost of public transportation is a socially explosive issue.

• *Water and Sewerage:* The closed valley of Mexico does not have sufficient water resources for the needs of the giant metropolis, and water must be brought in by pipelines from distances of 100 miles and more and pumped up to the 7000-foot altitude of the capital. Apart from the pumping requiring enormous quantities of energy, the waste waters must again be evacuated by pumping to avoid the inundation of the central city area due to soil subsidence. Also, the taking of water from remote regions deprives those populations of "their" water for irrigation and, thus impoverished, they tend to migrate to the capital. Garbage collection, including industrial waste-disposal, presents serious logistic, administrative and financial problems compounded by the traffic congestion which makes truck movement slow and expensive. These problems cannot be tackled without planning and regulative measures for the informal sector. Yet massive investment in improvements further enhances migration to the metropolis.

This brings us back to the basic problem of regional inequity. It could perhaps be remedied by decentralization of power structures (and not only of the politicians, as Sumet Jumsai correctly insists), followed by the strengthening and reorganization of regional development with imaginative measures. But so far, in Mexico, every peso invested to finance regional development programs only increased capital returns to the metropolitan banking system where 60% of the movements occur. After nationalization in 1982, the banking system was restructured to more properly serve the policy of regionalization with sectoral financing areas, decentralization of the financial flows and their multiplier effects.

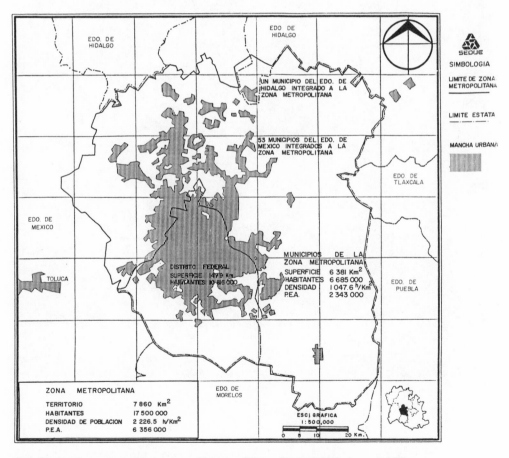

Fig. 23-1: The metropolitan zone of Mexico City or "Z.M.C.M.". Area: 7,860 square kilometers. Population: 175,000,000 (1984). This includes 53 municipalities of the State of Mexico and one municipality of the State of Hidalgo. (Sedue: Mexico, D.F.)

347

Fig. 23-2: Relief map showing the geographic location of Mexico City. (Cahiers del'IAURIF, Paris, No. 74. Dec. 1974)

Fig. 23-3: Mexico. The colonial core of Mexico City with the "Zocalo." (Archives Chaire d'Urbanisme EPFL, E. Galantay)

Fig. 23-4: A "New Town in town." The Tlaltelolco-Nonoalco housing project built on the site of a formal railroad yard. (Archives, Chaire d'Urbanisme EPFL, E. Galantay)

Fig. 23-5: "Informal" housing in the Netzahualcoyotl squatter settlement just beyond the Federal District boundary. (Courtesy: E. Galantay)

Fig. 23-6: Mexico. The modern city. Paseo de la Reforma. (Cīa Mexacana Aero-foto S.A., Obrero Mundial 338, Mexico DF)

The Limits of Strategic Planning

If the decentralization policy works we shall still be faced with a sprawling 25 million people in the metropolitan area of Mexico by the year 2000. At the same time, another 25 million people will need to be accommodated in 14 large cities, some of them undergoing a metropolitanization process. Thirty-five million more urban Mexicans will live in medium- and small-size cities and 20 million in hamlets and villages. The policy of promoting the 14 regional metropoli holds out the hope of being able to rescue the capital as the center of national cultural life and as a generator of cultural and social change.

However, it will be impossible to finance the regionalization strategy unless radical changes occur in international trade and financial relations, i.e., unless a new economic order becomes the base of more equitable sharing of global resources.

A simple trend projection conjures up the image of a giant agglomeration of 25 million people in a core area with 15 to 20 million more in a radius of 80 miles around the center. Increasing out-migration of the well-to-do, of those on higher educational and income levels, would be compensated by an inmigration of the less trained, the unskilled. The low-income population will surround the remaining enclaves of the rich, isolated by high walls, protected by armored surveillance in a climate of increasing hostility among income groups and the specter of social instability. The environmental decay in the informal sector (which will amount to three-fourths of the total built-up area) will continue, and public health will decline due to ever worse conditions of atmospheric pollution.

Since the total breakdown of urban systems is not an improbable eventuality, we propose a set of strategies called "Theratoplan" (from the Greek word "theratos"-monstrosity) defining ways to cope with the crisis when it arises.

To conclude, let me emphasize once more that the increase of the national population is not the origin of our problems: the problems arise from our internal economic structure, our dependant role in the international division of labor and, above all, from the burden of the foreign debt which is almost impossible to repay. We have arrived at a point in our history where people say that "not even our future is what it used to be."

References

Robert W. Fox, "The World's Urban Explosion," *National Geographic*, August, 1984.

Comission Brandt, "Dialogo Norte-Sur," Editorial Nueva Imagen, Mexico.

Dietrich Kunckel, Chapter 22, Art. 1 in this volume. Kunckel explains Richard Meier's model of the maturation of urban settlements, not necessarily agreeing with it.

Ervin Galantay, in Chapter 7, Art. 1 in this volume. See his description of the rise of Netzahualcoyotl.

Kingsley Davis, see his article in the "Cities" issue of the *Scientific American*, September, 1965.

Sumet Jumsai, Chapter 30, Art. 3 in this volume.

Ervin Laszlo, Chapter 8, Art. 2 in this volume.

24.
The View From Brazil

Geraldo Nogueira Batista

Introduction

This paper focuses on the case of Brasilia for two reasons. In the first place, the young Brazilian national capital is a fast-emerging metropolis. Brasilia is classified as a metropolis in light of the following facts:

- The city is the capital of the largest and most populous country in Latin America. Therefore, it is strongly linked with the international political and economic system, and is a focal point for the rest of the nation.

- Brasilia is a rapidly expanding urban area with over 1.5 million inhabitants and the highest rate of growth in the country, compared with other large–to medium-sized cities and metropolitan areas in Brazil.[1]

Secondly, Brasilia is perhaps *the* largest urbanistic experience based entirely upon the ideals of the international modern architecture movement. Not to dismiss the importance of an integrated and holistic study of the metropolis, this paper will address the interrelated cultural, political, institutional and economic aspects of the metropolitan phenomenon.

The Cultural Issue

Generally speaking, two basic social groups coexist in Brasilia, as in most other Latin American metropoli. The first group is an elite subculture which tends to adopt the values of the higher classes of the industrialized countries of the Northern hemisphere. The second group is a popular subculture characterized by rural or urban proletarian values.[2] Until now, the management of urban and metropolitan problems has been the exclusive province of the first social group, involving an intellectual, governmental and private enterprising class. As a privileged minority, this group enjoys access to high-priced goods and to relatively high-quality housing

Table 1

Brazilian Urban Agglomerations and Metropolitan Areas
1970-1980
(in thousands)

Area	1970	1980	Rates of growth 60-70	70-80
*Sao Paulo	8.206	12.708	5.53	4.47
*Rio de Janeiro	7.173	9.153	3.62	2.47
*Belo Horizonte	1.628	2.584	6.25	4.73
*Recife	1.824	2.399	3.93	2.78
*Porto Alegre	1.554	2.284	4.19	3.92
*Salvador	1.170	1.795	4.77	4.37
*Fortaleza	1.053	1.615	4.87	4.37
*Curitiba	838	1.471	5.04	5.79
*Belem	665	1.016	4.85	4.32
Brasilia	546	1.202	11.56	8.22
Goiania	512	975	8.43	6.64
Campinas	382	680	5.99	5.94
Natal	270	428	5.21	4.73
Santos	350	424	2.80	1.94
Sao Luiz	270	400	5.42	5.45
Teresina	230	388	5.69	5.39
Joao Pessoa	228	338	4.17	3.82
Aracaju	186	299	4.91	4.84
Sorocaba	177	273	3.92	4.39
Jundiai	170	261	4.93	4.40
Vitoria	136	215	4.81	4.66
Florianopolis	143	195	3.83	3.18
Taubate-Temembe	112	171	3.64	4.32
E. Mansa-V. Redonda	102	160	4.88	4.59

*Designated metropolitan areas
Source: Instituto Brasileiro de Geografia

and public services. Their economic, social and technological judgments reflect their own life experiences. Therefore, it follows that members of this elite tend to emulate imported standards. This creates a divergence between the quality-of-life concepts defined by this class and the aspirations of the majority of the population.

A second, more flagrant, dichotomy has emerged between the academic/ professional/ideological discourse and the action of the groups involved with urban problems. For example, although planners and public officials, in theory, emphasize more efficient, energy-saving public transportation systems, they generally adopt density and land-use models which perpetuate inefficient and inequitable transportation and accessibility patterns.

This ambiguity between ideology and reality is apparent in Brasilia which was planned to reflect perceived collective and communal values. Yet, due to low densities and the scattered settlement patterns used, Brasilia's current bus system carries five times fewer passengers than the bus system of any other large Brazilian city. Similarly, affluent barrios in the same city provide up to 600 liters of water per person per day, while poorer neighborhoods do not even have simple taps and pipelines installed.

The plan of Brasilia does not reflect the national culture of Brazil. It incorporates American and European socio–cultural patterns as a basis for planning, with little regard to the behavior, traditions or customs of the Brazilian people.[3] This issue is an important economic force in the city. As Professor Johnson-Marshall points out, the standards of living in Western industrialized cities are not suitable ideals for less-developed countries.

The work of planners who are insensitive to the underlying culture sometimes produces tragic, unforeseen results. After the National Housing Bank was created in 1965, the "super–block" concept used in Brasilia's residential areas was adopted as an ideal model throughout the country. However, while in Brasilia federal subsidies funded reasonable maintenance of the super–block green areas, in less privileged housing projects the open spaces between the buildings cannot be properly maintained and have become a kind of "no man's land."[4]

If urban public infrastructures and utilities are to be supplied to undeveloped areas, clearly it is inappropriate to apply the standards already used in more affluent or central sections of the Plano Piloto[5] (the formally planned, central area of Brasilia which accommodates about 500,000 inhabitants within the framework of Lucio Costa's Master Plan). It is unlikely that adequate housing, public transportation and infrastructure can be developed for the growing population of Brasilia or any other Latin American metropolis unless planners and other experts eliminate cultural bias and Western industrialized standards from their thinking.

Political and Institutional Issues

Twenty years after its foundation, Brasilia is already facing complex legal, political and institutional problems related to land-use control. Although the local government owns almost half the territory of the Federal District, the supply of new housing areas remains a main question facing planners.

Public ownership of land, by itself, has been unable to prevent the spatial segregation which is the hallmark of the current Latin American urbanization process. Actually, spatial segregation in Brasilia tends to be more rigid than in other Brazilian metropoli. Poor migrants are forced to locate in legal or semi-legal subdivisions in areas outside the Federal District or to squat in more central locations.

One of Brasilia's most important problems is the intense urbanization, speculation and subdivision of rural land, beyond public control. Planning action to control these activities is mainly obstructed by the very limited power of local governments to regulate the use of rural land. Rural peripheral sectors are usually incorporated into urban areas as the result of land subdivision for private profit. This has created an enormous quantity of idle areas and also a rather scattered and low-density pattern of settlement. Peripheral municipalities of the Brasilia metropolitan region already have an estimated 400,000 non-utilized residential plots. These plots can be legal, quasi-legal or illegal, but buildings constructed on them, as a rule, do not obey municipal regulations.

The subdivision of rural land does not exclusively benefit the poor. Subdivisions for the wealthy are usually located within the Federal District in the basin of the Saint Bartolomeo River. This river is the best and largest source of future water supply, and careless development of the basin can seriously disturb the use of the river as a supply of water for the expanding metropolitan population. Controlling development in the river basin is surely a most critical and urgent problem for public authorities.

Among other issues, the "institutionalization" of planning on a metropolitan level is a key question—how to bring together the operations of local, state, regional and national authorities, agencies, public corporations and related bodies operating within the metropolitan territory for effective and cooperative action. Recent efforts to "metropolitanize" government or to create "super-municipal" planning agencies in Brazil are inconclusive and cannot be evaluated yet. A clear political and institutional solution must be found. In Brasilia, this problem is especially acute as the future metropolitan area is expected to expand beyond the Federal District into two adjacent states.[6]

The political weakness of the local administration is another major institutional hindrance to problem-solving. As in most Latin American countries, Brazil's government is highly centralized. In addition, Brasilia's local executive government derives its power exclusively from the Federal Government, and there is no elected representative local council. Urban planning in this context cannot perform well at the local or metropolitan level. For example, Brasilia has been unable to incorporate a planning system within the administrative machinery of the Federal District. Six years ago, a first attempt was made to guide Brasilia's future expansion, but it failed from the *very* beginning. Successive efforts also failed because they were unable to secure the necessary political support.

Economic Issues

Now 20 years old, Brasilia is still a young city and its economy largely depends on the public administration sector. As a consequence, most economic activities are concentrated in the Plano Piloto area of the city. This area is the central source and location of business, employment and leisure for the new capital and its surrounding areas.

While industry accounts for only 11 percent of the total employment, the tertiary sector, which is heavily concentrated in the Plano Piloto, employs more than 75 percent of the labor force. The tertiary sector includes activities which are directly and indirectly derived from public sector activities.

Poverty and under-development in the geo-economic region of Brasilia is another problem. Although the new capital, as a growth center, was expected to diffuse modernization and economic development, its surrounding region still offers few opportunities for economic growth or better living conditions for its inhabitants. Some argue, however, that the region was previously an empty territory, and that the processes of modernization and economic development require more than 20 years to achieve significant results.[7] Nevertheless, even in Brasilia, urban expansion is not necessarily followed by matching economic growth.

The demographic tendencies and the political-economic context of Brasilia suggest several alternative or complementary growth trends for the near future.[8] First, a planned, linear, poly-nucleated urban structure model may be consolidated. Six years ago a plan to guide the further growth of Brasilia proposed this alternative. If this plan's recommendations are not implemented, urban growth will concentrate in several isolated settlements, creating a scattered and uneconomic urban structure. Second, demographic growth may be located either in peripheral, lower-density subdivisions, or in areas within existing satellite cities of the Federal District. In this second scheme, Brasilia could follow the general Latin American trend of increasing density in the lower income areas, as noted by D. Kunckel. Third, the Plano Piloto area may become an elitist enclave, mainly due to land speculation. Lower-middle class groups have already moved away from the Plano Piloto. Fourth, in time the building construction sector may become less important. The worsening economic and external debt crisis suggests that the tertiary and informal sectors are likely to expand. Fifth, the agricultural sector will expand in the geo-economic region. Publically funded agricultural research stations located in Brasilia have successfully introduced several new crops in the region. This is perhaps the only effective way to slow down in-migration to the Federal District.

Final Remarks

Until now, urban planning in Latin America has been a governmental function and a strictly top-down activity; Brasilia is no exception. Planning objectives in this context are often meaningless to common people, and even to mid-level public administrators or politicians.[9]

Many authors suggest that the present situation can be reversed only with a shift in orientation towards a new concept of "development from below." This concept includes issues such as decentralizing the economic and institutions, securing greater participation by lower income groups in decision-making, and fully utilizing available financial and manpower resources.[10] Clearly, this is a monumental task for planners and for society at large.

In this perspective, Brasilia and other Latin American cities face the question of how to overcome the gap between planning and society. In order to make planning a meaningful activity, planners must express their aims and objectives in a language easily grasped by the public. They must also help build a more collective approach to solving the urgent problems of the metropolis.

Notes

1. This figure is for the Federal District and does not include adjacent urban areas located in peripheral municipalities. If considered, these areas would add at least 500,000 more inhabitants to the total population of the area. The rate of growth for the period 1970-1980 was 8.22% (see Appendix I).

2. See Alfredo Gastal & Geraldo Nogueira Batista, O Habitat Urbano Brasileiro: Paradigmas e perspectivas, *Revista do Serviço Público*, ano 40, vol. III, no. 1, Jan/Mar, 1983, pp. 5-16.

3. See Paulo Bicca, *Brasília: Da Apologia à Crítica*, IAU, UnB, University of Brasilia.

4. See Carlos Eduardo Comas, O Espaço da Arbitrariedade, *Revista do Serviço Público*, ano 40, vol. III, no. 1, Jan/Mar 1983, pp. 21-29.

5. The formally planned, central area of Brasilia which accommodates about 500,000 inhabitants within the framework of Lucio Costa's Master Plan.

6. For example, during the program to institutionalize the metropolitan regions in 1973, the metropolitan region of Rio de Janeiro was blocked for almost three years. No legal, political *and* institutional solution could be found to assemble areas belonging to the states of Guanabara and Rio de Janeiro under the same metropolitan administration. Solution to this problem emerged only when the two older states were integrated as a single new political entity.

7. Ricardo L. Farret, The Justification of Brasilia: A Political-Economic Approach, *Third World Planning Review*, Vol.5, no. 2, May, 1983.

8. Aldo Paviani, *Brasilia Anos 80: Uma Visão Econômica*, Universidade de Brasília—Departamento de Urbanismo, March, 1981.

9. In relation to this problem, the programs of the recently organized Brasilian political parties do not even mention urban planning as a prominent issue.

10. See, for instance: John Knesi, Town and Country Development from Below: The Emerging Paradigm for the Decade, *Ekistics* 292, Jan-Feb, 1982, pp. 14-22; Michael Safier, Habitat for Development: An Action Planning Approach, in *Report of Proceedings*, Town and Country Planning Summer School (RTPI), September, 1974, pp. 72-79.

Fig. 24-1: Central Rio de Janeiro with Santos Dumont Airport. (Crùzeiro de Sul S.A., Courtesy: Archives, Chaire d'Urbanisme EPFL, E. Galantay)

Fig. 24-2: Central Sao Paulo. (Courtesy: E. Galantay 1978)

Fig. 24-3: Central Sao Paulo. (Courtesy: E. Galantay 1978)

Fig. 24-4: Brasilia. Central area with the East-West "Institutional axis" and the curved North-South residential axis. (EMBRAFOTO. Courtesy: CODEPLAN 1984)

Part VIII

Islamic Countries

25.
The Metropolis in Islamic Countries

Abdulaziz al-Saqqaf

I have chosen to divide this essay into four sections, all of which aim at providing a summary analysis of the subject at hand.

Why Urbanize?

The growth of urban settlements is not a historical accident; it is a conscious effort in the progress of human civilization. Even with the many problems resulting from the mismanagement of the urbanization process, the city has been found to be the superior form of human social organization. Some of the reasons can be traced to the four essential functions of cities within the system of human settlements:

    A. The Generative City: The city has the primary role of generating and diffusing knowledge and information to all segments of the society and in all parts of the country. The diffusive effect of the city is evident because of its focal and central role in collecting, generating, and distributing information.

    B. The Transforming City: Cities can successfully mold their citizens in a deeply felt, continuous socio-cultural process. This is also called the "liberating effect" because of the impact of the city on eroding class rigidity and tradition-based social order.

    C. The Mobilizing City: The system of organization and infrastructure in cities allows for a rapid and continuous mobility of factors of production, i.e., labor, capital, raw materials, products, etc. This explains the concentration of major industrial and service organizations and enterprises in the cities. It also explains the high degree of economic efficiency associated with urban activities. Many studies have, for example, proved the positive correlation between the level of urbanization in a country and its per capita annual income. Societies with a high level of urban populations generally have high levels of per capita income. An additional reason for this correlation is that production in the cities can benefit from externalities, economies of scale, and other factors.

D. The Decision-Making City: Cities have become the power base in all societies. The concentration of the decision-making machinery in cities has enabled societies to make decisions regarding the different issues they face.

These four city functions combine to create a powerful drive of "circular causation" which helps to explain why the urbanization process has become the norm in all countries of the world.

The Islamic Heritage

Cities have existed in the Middle East for nearly 5,000 years. While many of the ancient cities have perished, the present pattern in modern cities reflects an older form of settlement, notably going back to the Islamic period. Therefore, "land–use" and "land–tenure" in Moslem countries and regions cannot be fully understood unless they are placed within the context of Moslem "land law"[1] and the Moslem way of life.

What is the Islamic concept of a city? How different is this from the contemporary Western model? Can Islamic cities escape the Western on-slaught and can they survive in today's world?

The rise of Islam brought into sharp focus the Ummah's habitat—the city—by settling the nomadic Arabs. From the very beginning when the Prophet Muhamed started the Islamic community, he gave them a model. Old Yathrib was renamed as Al-Madinatul Munawwarah (the enlightened city). Many new cities were then created on the basis of the model; these include Baghdad, Samarra and Tunis. In addition, there were ancient cities which, having fallen into decadence, found renewed vigor and prosperity with their entry into the "Pax Islamica," such as Balkh, Bukhara, Cordova, Damascus, Halab (Aleppo), Istanbul, Samarqand, Sana'a, Seville, etc. There is no doubt, therefore, that the Islamic civilization was an urban one, and that the urban structure expressed in concrete, material terms represented the abstract and spiritual conviction which is embodied in the social, political, cultural and economic system of the Islamic religion.

The Islamic city reflects the social cohesion and compulsory cooperation among its inhabitants. Residents have an obligation, in concrete economic and social terms, towards their neighbors as a minimum in a radius encompassing 40 houses. Therefore, neighborly cooperation and full knowl-edge of the members of the neighborhood is necessary. This contrasts with the alienation of today's city dwellers who do not know (and may not want to know) who lives next door. The togetherness of Islamic city inhabitants contrasts markedly with the loneliness of modern city people. Given that one's neighbors are determined by chance, one is neither really at home nor together.

Another aspect of the social cohesion manifested in the Islamic city is the collective responsibility of all inhabitants for the well-being of their city. This draws from the principle of "al-amr bil maroof wal nahyi anil munkar" which demanded every citizen to intercept any wrong deed and to promote useful and beneficial activities. This attitude helped control the rates of crime, pollution, and other urban malaise. Today, however, the citizens have lost much of their sense of collective responsibility, thus leading to an urban life characterized by fear, anxiety and restlessness. Modern cities, especially in the West, are making a comeback to the Islamic concept of collective responsibility through such efforts as "citizens' arrests," voluntary organizations to control crime, pollution, etc.

A third aspect of social life in cities has been the emphatic demand for a minimum of privacy. The Islamic city, through its layout, and through design, provides this privacy. Every family lives in a house surrounded by a compound which is the transition zone between the family privacy and the public space. Within the house, different rooms correspond to different levels of intimacy and privacy. In today's cities, which are troubled by exploding populations, officials import mass housing models and put hundreds of families into gigantic dormitory towns such as Nasser City in Cairo, Madinat Al-Thawra in Bahdad, the massive dormitory complex near Jeddah Airport, or al-Madinah Assakaniyyah Musaik in Sana'a. The uniform and banal structures and spaces have erased the threshold of transition, thereby leading to a total confusion as to what is private and intimate space and what is public. This kind of "new" alienation that takes away one's privacy leads to strong tendencies to protect oneself. Thus, Muslim women who have never before worn the veil in their own villages take to wearing it in the city in a forlorn attempt to shield themselves. But if the tall dormitories are not the answer, neither are the spacious pavilions a suitable solution. It is true that most Islamic dwellings were low-rise houses that resemble the pavilion in their structure, but these used to house more than just one family, given the extended family system. With the breakdown of the extended family system, more space and more houses and a different architectural concept is needed.

The layout of Islamic cities was very distinct. The city was divided into quarters (hayi, singular; ahya', plural), which in turn were divided into sub-quarters, or haraat. The focal point for a hara was the mosque around which everything else revolves. Connecting one hara to another were two things: the roads and the suq which was the lifeline of the haraat. At the hayi level, in addition to the mosque, there are public buildings representing the authorities. Depending on the importance of the hara, this could be a citadel, or the residence of a sheikh or sahib al-shurta, al-muhtasib, etc. At the city level, the "dar al-imarah" is the most important government building and in it lives the amir, or al-wali. Dar al-imarah also houses the treasury, and with it, of course, the army.

Islamic cities, therefore, had their own zoning system. Within the suqs, every profession and line of business had its own alley. The residential ahya' and haraat were separated from each other by the maidans (city squares). There were certainly large areas of open space in the pattern of Islamic urbanization but the greenery that is envisaged in many of the modern Muslim cities, whether it be Teheran or Karachi, Riyadh or Algiers, have become no more than dust collectors. In the Islamic pattern, the residents of the quarter were responsible for "their" gardens and open spaces; in today's structure, ineffective municipal authorities are supposed to take care of them.

All geographers and travelers have described Islamic cities as very clean. The linkage process which helped recycle products had created a very efficient system of sanitation. Human residue and solid garbage were used as fuel in the furnaces of the hammams (public baths). The ashes were then used as fertilizers in the city gardens, whereas the hammam water went to the farms outside the city. Even within the house, precious resources like water are recycled from one use to another in a hierarchy established by history. Today, the affluent Middle Eastern cities produce more garbage than anything else—heaps of plastics, papers, metal cans, bottles, abandoned cars, furniture, and all kinds of products. Water use per capita has tripled over the last 15 years, thereby threatening the exhaustion of the underground water supply, and also threatening the foundations of old quarters and houses.

Islamic architecture reflects a strong aesthetic value. This is manifested in the facades and gateways of buildings, street decorations, the colorful designs and writings, the different arches and geometric shapes, the gigantic public buildings (mosques, palaces, citadels, etc.), the introverted residences and private buildings, the beautifully carved stones and pillars, the meandering streets and the covered alleys, etc. Today's cities, however, have lost much of their beauty. Cost-conscious inhabitants build rush houses that are neither durable nor beautiful. The tendency has been that, once a building is constructed, a few decorative additions at the surface level are supposed to give it an Islamic touch. This is happening, for example, in many cities of the Arab Gulf. Islamic cities used to draw some of their beauty and durability from the local building materials such as burned bricks, hard stone, clay with straw, lime, and so on. In today's cities dwellings are likely to be built in cement blocks with reinforced concrete beams, glass windows, metal doors, etc. These are not only less durable and less beautiful but they also interrupt the ventilation and lighting systems, thereby requiring heating in the winter and cooling in the summer. The large glass windows, which could have provided a good lighting effect, are rendered useless by heavy curtains and drapes which are put there to provide privacy by preventing pedestrians on the sidewalk from getting a glimpse of the inside of the house.

This all proves that the Moslem city still expresses religion-centered socio-cultural values. To express this phenomenon, Oleg Grabar says: "The Moslem city reflects in its organic social structure a foundation of personal relations based on a common social and religious denominator."[2] In addition, Islamic cities of the Middle East, because of the climatic circumstances, have developed additional common characteristics. Youssef Belkacem describes this phenomenon in the following extract:

"The climatic adaptation is represented by compact urban groupings of medium-height buildings weaving a dense and continuous tapestry of structures, exposing only the rooftops and part of the facades to the harsh sunlight. This principle is based on the ratio of maximum volume of interior space for a minimum of exterior surfaces. If the houses are not grouped together, they resemble a compact cubic shape with miniaturized openings, as in the K'sour of the Dades Valley in Morocco, or the urban houses of Jeddah, of Mecca, or of Yemen. The same principle applies to urban spaces, where deep alleyways, cool and narrow, predominate shaded pathways covered with trellises and awnings. The covered street is transformed into a souk, tunnels covered by cupolas which provide shelter, light and ventilation for areas of commerce and trade."[3]

The Modern Evolution

The second half of the twentieth century witnessed the explosive growth in the size of Middle Eastern cities. The phenomenal rate of urban growth, which surpassed 10% growth per annum, has left much of the Middle East with a predominantly urban population. Virtually new cities have sprang out of nowhere at seaports, at crossroads, at the foot of mountains, and just about anywhere. The dramatic expansion of old cities and the creation of new ones could have provided a unique opportunity to re-create the architectural grandeur that has once characterized the Islamic civilization. With coherent and well-integrated urban development plans, the renewal of the original and authentic urban heritage could have been made possible. Instead, an opportunity has been missed. An uncontrollable rural exodus which has forced rapid urbanization has haphazardly expanded the cities throughout the region. The result is the present set of large urban agglomerations of unmanageable size—Cairo, Istanbul, Teheran, Karachi, Ankara, Alexandria, Algiers and Casablanca. Cities of unique architectural heritage have largely lost their character and have become just another dot on the map—Baghdad, Damascus, Isfahan, Jeddah, etc.

The present pattern of urbanization pays tribute to *two major phenomena:* a) the *nuclear family;* and b) the *automobile* transportation. Relations in Moslem countries are based on personal understanding usually strengthened by blood relationship. The overall pattern of living, therefore, has been the extended family system. Families grew larger until they become a tribe. The modern urbanization process has largely done away with this. Given that the automobile has become the principal (if not the only) means of transportation within the city, car traffic imposes its order upon the organization of urban space. "Thus roads are built first, and the remaining tissue is later filled in as well as possible."[4]

A similar erosion of traditions has taken place in terms of the materials used in house construction. The local materials which have proved to resist the harsh climate as well as the passage of time have unfortunately been replaced with imported glass, cement, steel, etc., all of which are far less durable. The situation has deteriorated further with the coming of mass-housing which uses primarily pre-fabricated concrete elements. As a result, Islamic cities have lost much of their Moslem nature, except for small isolated quarters.

Prospects

The overriding pattern of metropolitan development is the source of many worries, notably, will the cities of the Middle East lose their identity and become like cities in the West? In his paper read at the 13th ICUS Conference in Washington D.C., Professor Cyrus Mechkat expressed cautious hope: "If only for the peculiar climatic conditions and the strong Islamic revival—including urban architecture—the cities of the Middle East are bound to evolve in a different way." Yet, a conscious effort will be needed to achieve this objective.

Some aspects of the Islamic pattern of city planning still survive even in Western cities. Of course the mosque which occupied the central location has been replaced by a fountain, a garden, or a monument. Yet, if the area surrounding the center or the quarter were to be converted into "pedestrian zones," then an affinity with the Islamic model would be complete. Many city planners have already started reducing the territory claimed by the automobile, and the intention is to create "pedestrian zones" as in Bahdad, Sana'a, and Damascus. It may just be the time for architects and city planners, in collaboration with the other relevant professions, to come up with a comprehensive Islamic model for the metropolis in which harmonious human life is possible.

Notes

1. *Urban Land Policies and Land-use Control Measures: Volume I: Africa,* (United Nations Publication, New York, 1973), p. 27.
2. Oleg Grabar, "Cites et Citoyens," in Bernard Lewis (ed.), *L'Islam: d'hier a aujourd'hui,* p. 110.
3. Youssef Belkacem, "Bioclimatic Patterns and Human Aspects of Urban Form in the Islamic City," in Ismail Serageldin and Samir El-Sadek, *The Arab City,* (proceedings of a symposium held in Medina, Kingdom of Saudi Arabia, Feb/May, 1981), p. 3.
4. *Ibid.,* p. 10.

26.
Cairo: A Socio-Political Profile

Saad Eddin Ibrahim

The history and sociology of Cairo are those of Egypt; the Egyptians themselves use the name for their country and their capital city, Misr, interchangeably; and the Arabs admiringly refer to Cairo as "the Mother of the World" (Misr Um al-dinia).

This equating of Cairo and Egypt describes a state of mind and spirit. In terms of influence in so many fields, Cairo is the equivalent of the likes of Paris, the Vatican, Oxford, Hollywood and Detroit combined.

As a giant national, regional and international center, Cairo has also been gripped by giant problems. As much as the city has been enriched and stimulated by the inputs from the region and the nation, it has also carried their burdens. Still the best account for the unfolding of this dialectic is Janet Abu-Lughod's seminal, "Cairo: 1001 Year of the City Victorious."[1]

A Survey of Socio-Political Factors

Present day Cairo has evolved historically through a series of grand political designs. The four physical formations which constituted pre-modern Cairo were all envisioned and initially carried out by great military-political commanders or empire-builders. *Al-Fustat* was built by Umar Ibn al-Aas in 641 (21H.); the Abbasid dynasty built *Al-Askar* northeast of it in 751 (133H.); Ahmed Ibn Tulun added a third settlement adjacent to the second called *Al-Qataai* in 870 (256H.); and the Fatimid Jawhar al-Sikkli built *Al-Kahira* northeast of the three settlements in 969 (358H.). These four formations all started as military settlements. The four settlements were finally joined by Saladdin before he set out on his campaigns against the Crusaders in 1187. Since that time, pre-modern Cairo assumed its physical unity as a single city. Much of the developments which were to take place in the following three centuries under the Mamluks occurred within the confines of this entity of about 2 square miles. So long as Cairo remained a seat of Egyptian power, it thrived and prospered. With the Ottoman conquest (1517), the city began a decline.

At the beginning of the nineteenth century, Egypt, and hence Cairo, started to struggle for autonomy from the Ottoman Empire. Napoleon headquartered himself in the city briefly (1798) and stirred up the hitherto slumbering city.

Cairo and Egypt were never to return to their earlier state of a backwater of the Ottoman Empire. For soon was to appear Mohammed Ali (1805). Shrewd and resilient, he attempted to modernize Egypt by circumventing its traditional structures. He created modern institutions parallel to the traditional ones, and allowed channels to connect both. These arrangements enabled Egypt in a matter of two decades to emerge as a giant regional power. Not only did Egypt secure *de facto* independence, but it also posed a threat to the Ottoman Empire. But in his quest for modernization, Mohammed Ali laid the seeds for the dual development of Cairo by beginning the process of extending a modern city alongside the traditional Islamic core, to the northwest.

Since Mohammed Ali's rule (1805-1849) there have been four big modernization attempts: under Kedive Ismael (1863-1879), during Egypt's Liberal Age (1922-1952), under Nasser (1952-1970), and Sadat (1970-1981). Each created a lasting impact. Between 1881 and 1922 Egypt was under British occupation, yet Egypt and Cairo did not cease developing. But it was a development initiated by an alien power and designed to serve its interests.

Ismael's vision was to make Cairo into a European city. He seized the opportunity of the opening of the Suez Canal to hurriedly build new districts in the European style, complete with parks, broad streets, an opera house and street lights. Much of these developments were to the west of the Islamic city. Ismael's extravaganza saddled Egypt with heavy debts to European governments and banks. It led ultimately to the British occupation of the country: hundreds of thousands of foreigners settled in Cairo in the new quarters created by Ismael, and constructed their own. In those decades of late nineteenth and early twentieth centuries, the filling up of Garden City and Zamalek took place; Heliopolis and Maadi were started. The old city was left alone. While its population was steadily growing, its infrastructure was completely neglected. Population density skyrocketed, and living conditions worsened. The old city, while still containing nearly half of Cairo's population in the second decade of this century, became socially and economically marginalized. The decline of the guilds and crafts, its Ulama and Merchants had started a century earlier. With the British occupation the pace of decline was accelerated. There arose a native new social formation of technocrats and bureaucrats. The genesis of this new middle class (NMC) was laid in Mohammed Ali's time, but the birth and maturation of this NMC took nearly one century. The NMC tried in 1919 to mobilize the entire population in a two-month uprising. The gateway to power was opened for the upper half of the NMC. Between 1920 and 1950, Cairo lived a quasi-liberal age. An Egyptian banking industry was established; a modern university was built; cinemas, theaters and literature flourished. The NMC was quickly turning into a bourgeoisie. The Bank Misr group created large scale industries ranging from textile to motion-pictures. In the process it was creating a new working class.

Table 1

The Demographic Evolution of Cairo and Egypt

Year	Cairo* population	Average annual growth rate (%)	Egypt population	Average annual growth rate (%)
1800	200,000		3,000,000	
1900	600,000	1.4	10,000,000	1.5
1920	875,000	1.6	13,000,000	1.3
1930	1,150,000	3.0	15,000,000	1.1
1940	1,525,000	2.1	19,000,000	1.2
1950	2,350,000	4.8	21,000,000	1.8
1960	3,747,000	4.1	26,000,000	2.4
1970**	5,700,000	4.1	33,000,000	2.5
1980**	8,778,000	3.0	42,000,000	2.5

*Notes on sources; figures for the 1900-1950 periods are based on adjusted census figures taken regularly every 10 years from 1897 to 1947 pro-rated to even decades. The 1960 is an actual census figure.
**Estimates issued by the Governer of Cairo, published in *Al-Miswar*, July 13, 1984, pp. 22-25, for greater Cairo which includes Cairo proper, the adjacant urban areas of Giza and Qaliobiya (Shubra al-Khima) governorates.

Cairo was the center of all these socio-economic developments. Members of the upper echelon of the NMC moved to the better quarters of Cairo—now as partners, not intruders on their foreign residents. A tacit alliance was to develop between the new bourgeois class and foreign interests. The 1936 Anglo-Egyptian Treaty symbolized this new partnership.

The growing, modern working class and traditional Cairians in the old city, felt left out throughout the 1940s. New parties and mass political-religious movements appealed to them—notably the Moslem Brotherhood and the Young Egypt Socialist Party (Misr al-Fatah). Their misgivings vis-a-vis the Egyptian upper class was no less than those against the British and the royal family. The Second World War added to their alienation. The burning of the modern business district of Cairo in January, 1952 was a dramatic display of their anger.

The 1952 Revolution was to take place six months later. Led by Nasser, this revolution ushered in yet another big modernization attempt. It was undertaken by the "left-outs" of the previous three decades—the lower strata of the NMC. They soon allied themselves to the new working class and the peasantry. The structural changes effected by the July Revolution were for the benefit of this new alliance. One of the earliest acts of the revolution was to tear down the Kasr al-Nil Barracks—a symbol of both Royal and British Cairo. The whole upper class was removed from political power, and its economic power dramatically reduced. Urban rent-controls were soon to follow (in 1958 and 1960), hitting owners of real estate and benefiting the tenants. This measure was to have an adverse effect on the supply of urban housing in the long run.

Massive public housing projects were carried out in the poor districts of

Fig. 26-1: Cairo. 1982 existing land use. (GOPP-OTUI-IAURIF Greater Cairo Region-Long Range Development Scheme: 1982-1983, Courtesy: Cahiers IAURIF No 74. Dec. 1984)

Cairo. New areas were subdivided for the housing of the technocrats who provided the backbone for the development drive. It is not accidental that Nasr City was designed not only for their residential housing but was also the preferred site for the State's planning organs—the Ministry and National Institute of Planning and the Central Agency for Public Mobilization and Statistics. Likewise, the Mohandiseen City (Engineers City) was designed to accommodate the housing needs of this vital group.

Cairo grew in population and area during the Nasser years (1952-1970). Big industries were started in the southern suburb of Helwan and the northern area of Shubra al-Khima. New bridges were constructed across the river. New institutions mushroomed throughout the city. The planning in those years may have left a lot to be desired, but was far superior to what existed before.

Nasser's revolutionary drive had also turned Cairo into an Arab Capital in the political sense of the word. His pan-Arabism induced thousands of Arab students, artists, journalists and activists to make Cairo a favorite destination. The city's international flavor was further enhanced by Nasser's role in the Non-Aligned Movement.

Nasser's dreams came to a tragic halt in 1967. Following his military defeat, most of the country's resources were, for several years, earmarked for the war efforts, and Cairo's infrastructure was neglected. Earlier measures of rent-control did not encourage the private sector to help ease the growing housing shortage either.

Thus, when Sadat came to power (1970), he inherited the heavy burdens of the country and its capital city. By 1974, Sadat had evolved his own vision to deal with those burdens. His economic "Open-Door" Policy was reminiscent of that of the Khedive Ismael. Sadat wanted to develop Egypt Western-style, with Western economic aid, and with Western technology and Western experts. If Paris and Rome were models for Ismael, Los Angeles and Houston were favorite models for Sadat. He let loose private developers and land speculators. When land-values skyrocketed, he proudly declared that his policies "had made Egyptian land very valuable." Luxury high-rise buildings mushroomed all over the city; first-class hotels were built; new highways and overpasses were constructed, including the impressive bridge across the Nile over Gazira Island.

This frantic urban development in Cairo was aided by the remittances from Egyptians working in oil-rich Arab countries. A new influx of foreigners (mostly Americans) further intensified the demand for luxury housing.

The backing of Sadat came from an alliance of social forces which were bound to benefit from it. This new alliance was made up of the old bourgeoisie and landlords, the nouveau rich and leaders of Nasser's public sector. It was a very potent alliance politically and economically, but small numerically. Left out were the vast lower-middle class, civil servants, and the urban working class who saw their share in power and wealth steadily eroding. Their anger found expression in January, 1977, when rioters in Cairo burned and sacked many of the material symbols of Sadat's city —night clubs, expensive cars and police stations. The army was called in to put down this uprising. Significantly, most of those killed and wounded were from the most densely populated districts of Cairo.

Sadat's policies continued as usual. In the following four years, dissent and anger were channeled through militant religious groups. Confrontations grew rampant. The most serious of these took place in one of the poorest and most crowded districts of Cairo during the summer of 1981. A few months later, President Sadat was assassinated.

The Rise of Modern Cairo

Egypt's population has grown tenfold in the last century and half. Cairo has grown thirtyfold during the same period.

The country initiated its "demographic transition" in the early decades of the nineteenth century. Death rates began their decline; birth rates have remained at their previous high levels. The inevitable result has been a steady population increase. Egypt doubled its population in the course of the nineteenth century. By 1900 it had hit the 10 million mark. Since then, the doubling time has become shorter and shorter. The second doubling, from 10 to 20 million, took 50 years between 1900 and 1950. The third doubling took merely 28 years, i.e., from 20 to 40 million between 1950 and 1978. The growth trends are continuing with only a slight and erratic decline in rates of natural increase. For the last 30 years that rate ranged between 2.8 and 2.4 percent annually.

Egypt's urban areas grew steadily in the course of the last century and a half. This growth has accelerated in this century. Due to rural-urban migration, urban population grew from 19% of Egypt's total in 1907 to 33% in 1947, and to 44% in 1976. At present it is estimated that half of Egypt's population resides in urban areas.

Rural-urban migration has been one of Egypt's many silent revolutions, although its impact in the daily life of Egyptian cities is not so silent. Noise, crowding and oriental confusion are rampant.

Cairo—like Egypt—witnesses a steady natural population increase and it has also appropriated part of the rural areas' natural increments. The city grew from an estimated 200,000 in 1800 to 600,000 in 1900, to 2.4 million in 1950, to 5.7 in 1970, to 8.8 million in 1980. This is a fifteenfold increase in this century alone, compared to a twofold increase in rural population, and a fourfold increase in urban population. As Table 2 shows, Cairo was adding to its population as much from migration as from natural increase. Currently, the city accounts for about 25% of the country's total population and about 50% of the country's urban population.

Cairo's land area expanded steadily beyond its original Islamic core. Until the early decades of the nineteenth century this built-up core was no more than 5 square kilometers. By the end of the century it tripled to 15 square kilometers. Semi-empty quarters adjacent to the Islamic core filled up, Azbakiyya and Boulaq. New quarters to the north, northeast, and west were born in the second half of the nineteenth century. The areas west of the Islamic city to the Nile had already filled up, and bridges were constructed to connect Cairo proper to Giza on the other side. By the turn of the century, Garden City (an area between Kasr al-Aini and the eastern bank of the Nile) and Zamalek (an island in the Nile across from Boulaq) became the choice spots for residence of the upper class, foreign and native. By the end of the second decade of this century the land area of Cairo proper had expanded around the Islamic core in three directions (west, north, and south) to an area of approximately 30 square kilometers. This rapid expansion (nearly six times the original medieval city) was aided by the introduction of tramways, starting in 1896.

The first half of the twentieth century witnessed the physical consolidation of quarters built up a few decades earlier as well as the development of two new suburbs—Heliopolis and Maadi, to the east and south of nine-

Table 2

Net Migration to Cairo
1907-1980

Period	No. of migrants for entire period	Average annual rate of migration to Cairo
1907-1917	158,000	2.0
1917-1927	297,000	2.8
1927-1937	359,000	2.6
1937-1947	606,000	2.8
1947-1960	953,000	2.2
1960-1970	702,000	2.1
1970-1980	1,100,000*	1.9

*Figures for 1970-1980 are our own estimates for Greater Cairo area.
Sources: Figures for 1907-1960 are from M.S. Abdul-Hakim, "Emigration to Cairo," A
    Report submitted to the Greater Cairo Planning Commission, 1968. The figures
    for 1960-1970 are from Gamal Askar, "The Population Explosion in Cairo,"
    Al-Ahram al-Iktisadi (Dec. 1, 1972) and cited in John Waterbury, *EGYPT: Burdens
    of the Past, Options for the Future,* Indiana University Press, Bloomington, 1978,
    p. 127.

teenth century Cairo. These were designed in a European fashion. They
were to be residential areas for the foreign and native bourgeoisie who could
not be accommodated in Garden City and Zamalek. Baron Empian, the
builder of Heliopolis, attempted to give one of them an Islamic-Arab
character in outward appearance. Yet the socio-economic contents and
functions of Heliopolis (like that of Maadi) belonged to an age hardly Arab or
Islamic, but rather the age of the world capitalist system.

Between 1850 and 1950, the bulk of the present metropolis had developed. Pre-nineteenth century Cairo was to shrink further in relative size
during the three decades following the Egyptian Revolution of July, 1952.

The three decades following 1950 witnessed the tripling of Cairo's
population and the more than doubling of its built-up urban mass. The area
of Cairo proper grew from less than 100, to 220 square kilometers. Pre-1950
newer districts to the north and northeast filled up rapidly. Major new
districts have been created since 1950, notably, Nasr City to the east of the
Old Islamic core, Moqattam City to the southeast, and New Maadi to the
south. The strip stretching south along the Nile from Misr al-Qadima and
Helwan has steadily been built up on previously agricultural land. Helwan
itself has quickly transformed from a leisurely suburb to a teeming industrial district.

Across the Nile from Cairo proper, the city of Giza extended westward all
the way to the Pyramids (about 15 kilometers) and northward all the way to
Imbaba, incorporating several villages. This extension of Cairo added
another 100 square kilometers to the already built-up area of 220 square
kilometers. Giza has become the major recipient of Cairo's population
spillover. New districts were planned and developed: Mohandiseen City,
Professors City and Journalists City. Designed as single-dwelling areas in

Table 3

**Greater Cairo:
Components of Growth
1960-1976**

Urban unit	1960 Population (000)	1966 Population (000)	Average Annual growth rate 1960-1966 (%)	1976 Population (000)	Average Annual growth rate 1966-1976 (%)
Cairo Proper	3,353	4,220	3.9	5,084	1.9
Giza City	419	571	5.3	1,233	8.0
Shubra al-Khayma	101	173	9.4	394	8.6
Total	3,873	4,964	4.8	6,711	3.5

Source: Computed from official Census Data.

the 1950s, these districts soon turned into high-rise building areas in the 1970s.

To the north of Cairo proper, Shubra al-Khima has also become socio-economically an integral part of Cairo. It added an additional 20 square kilometers to Cairo's built-up area.

Thus, all in all, the socio-physical entity called Greater Cairo amounts to roughly 350 square kilometers and is the home of some 10 million people.[2] In the early 1980s, Cairo proper accounted for roughly 63 percent of that urban mass and about 70 percent of its population. Central Cairo has one of the world's highest densities—32,000 persons per square kilometer.

The Present and the Future

Over the last century and a half, the old Islamic core of the city has shrunk in relative size and population. In Table 5, the data for Cairo proper is broken down into four major divisions: eastern, western, northern, and

Table 4

**Greater Cairo:
Changing Relative Weight of Components
1960-1976**

Urban unit	Percentage of Greater Cairo's population		
	1960	1966	1976
Cairo Proper	86.57	85.01	75.76
Giza City	10.82	11.50	18.37
Shubra al-Khima	2.61	3.49	5.87
Total	100.00	100.00	100.00

Source: Computed from Table 4, above.

southern. The old medieval city is entirely located in the eastern division. The city has grown all around it. Up until 1907, the eastern division still accounted for half of Cairo's total population. By 1937, its share went down to no more than 19 percent. Measured against Greater Cairo, the population of the Islamic core would account for less than 10 percent at present.

The population of the Islamic core is only a fraction of what appears in Table 5 under "Eastern." The eastern division includes the cemeteries of Cairo, referred to in foreign sources as "the City of the Dead." Separated from Islamic Cairo to the southeast by Salah Salem Road and stretching along that road for several miles, the City of the Dead has been absorbing the spillover population of the Islamic core as well as the homeless from other parts of Cairo, including recent rural migrants. In Cairo, traditional burial places are designed to enable relatives of the deceased to come for extended visits that may even involve spending overnight on special occasions. Most of these structures are spacious and could accommodate the living as well as the dead. For centuries, the City of the Dead had a small population of watchmen, undertakers, stone-cutters, etc. At times, criminals and fugitives found shelter. But, by 1937, some 10,000 people were residing in the City of the Dead who could not find cheap housing elsewhere. At present, that population is estimated to be close to 250,000.[3]

Table 5

Cairo Proper: Differential Growth of Its Major divisions 1971-1976

Year	Cairo	Eastern (%)	Western (%)	Northern (%)	Southern (%)
1882	400,000	213,000 (54)	130,000 (32)	34,000 (9)	23,000 (6)
1897	590,000	320,000 (54)	160,000 (27)	76,000 (13)	34,000 (6)
1907	680,000	348,000 (50)	184,000 (27)	112,000 (16)	36,000 (6)
1917	800,000	376,000 (47)	216,000 (27)	170,000 (21)	40,000 (5)
1937	1,312,000	457,000 (35)	350,000 (33)	450,000 (34)	55,000 (5)
1947	2,091,000	670,000 (32)	512,000 (24)	800,000 (38)	109,000 (6)
1960	3,353,000	770,000 (23)	775,000 (23)	1,600,000 (48)	208,000 (6)
1966	4,220,000	840,000 (20)	928,000(22)	2,110,000 (50)	338,000 (8)
1976	5,084,000	966,000 (19)	1,027,000 (20)	2,645,000 (52)	458,000 (9)

Sources: Computed from official census figures, following J. Abu-Lughd's classification of districts and extending it to cover 1966 and 1967. See Janet Abu-Lughd, *Cairo: 1001 Years of the City Victorious*, Princeton University Press, Princeton, 1971, pp. 172-180.

Cairo authorities finally recognized the *de facto* situation and extended some municipal services including water, electricity, schools, bus lines and even a police station. The residents of the cemeteries engage in activities found in similar popular quarters of Cairo; groceries, bakeries and other service shops, and even some traditional industries (e.g., glass-blowing) are located there.

By international standards, the City of the Dead would be considered a slum area. But, by Cairo standards, it offers better living conditions than many other areas of the city. The population density is not even as high as it is in the Islamic core across the Salah Salem Road. The latter is about 90,000 per square kilometer, the former is only about 30,000. The general density average for Cairo as a whole is 32,000 per square kilometer. However, some districts like Bab al-Sharyya boast a density of 150,000 per square kilometer.[4]

The Islamic core of Cairo is not just densely populated, but also includes a great concentration of traditional cultural monuments. However, several new functions have intruded on that district, notably warehouses and the wholesale trade. These, along with growing population density, pose the greatest physical and cultural threat to the Islamic core. It is being squeezed from within and from without. Surrounded by other newer and faster growing districts, the demand is mounting for thoroughfares cutting across the core and for its land for modern use. The underground water level is sinking and poses an added threat to the monuments.

The Islamic core of Cairo has become an enclave of traditional urban culture surrounded by a teaming metropolis. Its fate is not entirely in the hands of its residents. Yet the enclave gallantly negotiates its survival with other modern and quasi-modern cultures of the metropolis. In this dialectic, the metropolis itself also represents an enclave in an otherwise semi-traditional society from where the Islamic enclave within greater Cairo draws some of its strength and its waves of newcomers. While some of them are "select migrants" and hence "modern-orientated," the majority of newcomers are bearers of a traditional culture. This equation has kept the terms of cultural exchange somewhat balanced within Cairo. Some of the select migrants, mostly university students or university graduates, increasingly show an aversion to modern metropolitan culture, if it means "Western culture." The growing Sufi orders and militant Islamic groups are embodiments of this trend. Thus, the Islamic enclave in Cairo is not entirely powerless in negotiating its survival. It has its secret cultural agents diffused throughout the city. In the 1970s an estimated 300 new nightclubs were opened in Greater Cairo, double the number for the previous 20 years. This was more than matched by the building of some 400 new mosques, mostly by private initiative, double the number for the previous 20 years.

To say that Cairo has overwhelming problems is merely stating the obvious. Its first problem is one of size. Greater Cairo now contains about one-fourth of Egypt's population. This in itself poses side problems of administration and manageability. Unwittingly, all of Egypt's successive regimes stimulated the city growth by concentrating power, economic activities and services (Table 6). A vicious cycle is at work; the ever greater concentration of production and service functions in Cairo is at the expense of other cities and rural areas.[5] The ambitious and needy come to Cairo at rates *faster* than the city government can accommodate. It spends a disproportionate share to keep Cairo's population (old and new) from revolting.

With only one-quarter of Egypt's population, Cairo appropriates about half of Egypt's public spending on limited-income housing. Yet the present housing shortage is still estimated to amount to 250,000 units.

Cairo consumes about 45 percent of Egypt's food. Yet, occasional food shortages are frequent in Cairo's popular districts.

Table 6

Selected Indicators of Concentration in Greater Cairo in 1976

Indicator	Percentage of Egypt's total
Population	20.0
Manufacturing establishment	55.7
Industrial workers	48.5
Industrial production	51.5
Public Investment	37.5
Public Investment in water delivery	48.5
Food consumption (1983)*	42.5
Telephone lines (1983)*	60.0

*Statement by Governer of Cairo, al-Miswar, July 13, 1984, p. 23.
Sources: Computed from official census figures, following J. Abu-Lughd's classification of
districts and extending it to cover 1966 and 1967. See Janet Abu-Lughd, Cairo:
1001 Years of the City Victorious, Princeton University Press, Princeton, 1971,
pp. 172-180.

The city consumes about one-half of Egypt's purified water, yet water shortages are frequent especially in the summer months and to dwellers of higher floors. Cairo's water consumption is over a million cubic meters daily or a luxurious 300 l/head. However, close to 40% of this is lost by seepage from poorly maintained pipes. But the capacity of the sewage and drainage network is only 2 million cubic meters. The excess gushes and creates sizeable and hazardous ponds.

As the demand on city land for housing and public buildings has mounted, Cairo's green areas have steadily shrunk. About 1 square meter per capita of green two decades ago, the share now is less than 40 square cm (compared to 10 square meters per capita in Europe).

Cairo has equity problems. In the late 1970s about 40 percent of its population lived under the "poverty line."[6] The relation between education, occupation and income is no longer congruous. Many of the poor are "new poors," often with high school or university degree. Many of the rich are nouveau riche, often engaged in smuggling, illegal currency exchange, land speculation, or other parasitic and dubious activities. Some of the new rich are in skilled, self-employed, manual occupations (e.g., plumbers, mechanics, electricians, masons, etc). Nearly all the poor of Cairo live in substandard housing. The Governor of Cairo (al-Miswar, July 13, 1984) stated that 35 percent of Cairo's 2.3 million housing units are too old and delapidated to be considered fit for human shelter. He further states that about 25 percent of all new housing units are built illegally and randomly, without proper monitoring for safety and health standards.

Another side of the equity problem of Cairo is the emergence in the 1970s of parallel service institutions with vast differences in quality. Thus, along with public schools and hospitals, for example, private ones have been established. The latter cater to the top 5 percent of Cairo's population, the former cater to the other 95 percent (the poor and middle classes). Similarly, much of the public expenditure on the city's transportation system benefits the owners of private automobiles. In the 10 years from 1972 to 1982, the number of private cars tripled; the number of public and semi-public vehicles only more than slightly doubled (see Table 7). The new highways, overpasses and Cairo ring-roads cater mainly to commuters who own private cars.

Table 7

Greater Cairo:
Motor Vehicles, 1972-1982

Year	Private autos	Public and semi-public vehicles*
1972	80,559	17,736
1974	87,388	20,710
1975	94,564	31,481
1977	133,599	33,571
1982**	250,000**	45,000

*The figures include taxi's and private buses which transport tourists and employees of public and private companies.

**Estimates by the Governer of Cairo, published in *al-Misawar*, July 13, 1984, p. 23.
Source: For the years 1972-1977, Central Agency for Public Mobilization and statistics (CAPMS), October 1978, cited in John Waterbury, "Patterns of Urban Growth and Income Distribution" in G. Abdel-Khalek and R. Tignor (eds.), *The Political Economy of Income Distribution in Egypt*, Holms and Meier, New York, 1982, p. 333.

The growing inequity in Cairo is part of that of Egypt. But it is in Cairo that this inequity is most glaring. About 200,000 of Egypt's estimated 250,000 millionaires are residents of Cairo. Another aspect of inequity is the vast salary differentials among employees of the government, public sector and "Open-Door" trade sector.[7] Three persons with equal qualifications could receive a monthly salary of $138, $276, and $1,380 (U.S.$) respectively. Such wide-range differentiation has created instability in the job market with a frantic race for "Open-Door" employment, yet the job supply in this sector is no more than 10 percent of Egypt's annual total.

Cairo's overcrowdedness, deteriorating physical infrastructure and public services are compounded for the majority of its population by glaring inequities of power and wealth. In recent years, the Cairo elite has been oblivious to the fate and living conditions of the majority. In the 1950s and 1960s, the physical development of Cairo was shaped by the lower middle class and by technocrats. It may have been austere and lacking in aesthetics but was not lacking in equity. In the 1970s Cairo's development became more vulgar and replete with social inequities. The fight over Cairo's soul and body is far from being settled in the 1980s. The poor are crowded in older quarters, cemeteries, or engaged in wild-cat developments. The *nouveau riche* still continue to ignore the rest of the city so long as their immediate districts and homes are satisfactory and as long as they spend a good part of the year abroad. It is the middle class, especially its lower rungs, who feel the squeeze, and its youngsters are teaming with frustration and anger. Much of Cairo's future, and hence of Egypt, may very well lie in their hands.

Notes

1. Janet Abu-Lughod, *Cairo: 1001 years of the City Victorious*, 1971.

2. One very important fact is that the Cairo Governorate (214 square kilometers) no longer represents the true image of Cairo today. Greater Cairo or the Cairo Metropolitan Region in the broad sense, is the true size of Cairo now. The Greater Cairo area is 2,900 square kilometers, that is, 13.5 times as big as the area of Cairo Governorate.

   In the year 2000, Greater Cairo population threatens to be 20-28 million. The total population is expected to be 66 million, 39 million urban population and 27 million rural population. Therefore, Greater Cairo is expected to be 30-42% of the total Egyptian population, and to represent the greater part of its urban population, i.e., 51%-72%

   This inflationary growth in the size of Cairo leads us to conclude that Cairo is much bigger than its proportionate size should be. This is based on the percentage share of Cairene population compared to the percentage share of the capital in other countries similar to Egypt. Such countries are old, mature, big in size and area. In these countries the share of the capital population is about one-tenth of their total population, like Cairo's share at the time of the French Invasion. In this sense Cairo today seems to be *double its proportionate size*.

   From Hoda Mohammed Mustafa, "Cairo: The Big Urban Bias," PWPA Seminar 2 on the Middle Eastern City, (Paris, 1985) (notes added by the editor).

3. Some scholarly accounts puts the figure at 900,000. See, for example, M.F. al-Kurdy, "Cairo's Cemeteries, Population" in *Annual Book of Sociology*, no. 6 (Arabic), 1984 pp. 17-132. The figure is cited on p. 19.

4. In 1984, room densities in Cairo reached a very high level. Some housing units—in districts like Bab-as-Sh'arriya—have *20 persons living in two rooms*. The usual average of the old and poor districts of Cairo today is *seven persons per room*. In such residential units, it is quite usual for two family generations to live together. (Al-Mussawar, No.3138, 30 Nov., 1984, cited by Hoda Mohammed Mustafa in "Cairo: The Big Urban Bias," *op.cit.* (note added by the editor).

5. "As Issawi, the doyen of Middle East economic historians emphasizes, Egyptian regimes have been strongly urban biased for centuries, long before import substitution industrialization strategies were invented, and which led to more serious urban bias. This urban bias has always and mainly meant a bias to the capital, Cairo. In fact, all development efforts in Egypt have accentuated regional differences, increased the degree of primacy of Cairo, and increased the lack of social infrastructure in the rural governorates. This has been effected through a strongly biased regional allocation of investments.

   a) The first 1958-60 industrial program allocated 38% of its total investments to Cairo.

Table 8

Room Densities for the City of Cairo
1947-1972

Year	City population	No. of housing units	Number of rooms	Persons per room
1947	2,090,064	448,333	1,039,742	2.0
1960	3,348,779	687,858	1,439,158	2.3
1966	4,232,663	779,789	1,559,578	2.7
1972	5,200,000 (Est.)	860,039 (Est.)	1,720,078 (Est.)	3.1

Source: Mahmoud A. Fadil, Political Economy of Nasserism. Cambridge University Press. Cambridge, U.K., 1980, p. 128.
In 1984 room densities in Cairo reached a very high level. Some housing units—in districts like Bab-as-Sh'arriya—have *20 persons living in two rooms.* The usual average of the old and poor districts of Cairo today is *seven persons per room.* In such residential units, it is quite usual for two family generations to live together. Al-Mussawar, No. 3138, 30 Nov. 1984, cited by Hoda Mohammed Mustafa in "Cairo: The Big Urban Bias," *op. cit.* (note added by the editor).

b) The first five-year plan (1960-65) allocated 20% of its total investments to Cairo. Cairo's share of industrial investments was 25%, of investments in electricity 16%, of investments in transport and communications 36%, of investments in housing 36%, and of investments in services 37%. Of course, if we add Giza and Kalyubia these relative shares would rise significantly.

c) Figures of the transitional plan (1974-75) show the same trend. The 1978-1982 five-year plan also shows the same concentration trend. Cairo got 20% of the total investment; if Giza and Kalyubia are added, this percentage increases to 24%."

Hoda Mohammed Mustafa in "Cairo: The Big Urban Bias," paper read at the PWPA Seminar on "The Middle-East City," (Paris, Feb., 1985) (notes added by the editor).

6. For details see, Saad Eddin Ibrahim, "Social Mobility and Income Distribution in Egypt" in G. Abdel Khalek and R. Tignor, (eds.), *The Political Economy and Income Distribution in Egypt,* Holms and Meier, (New York, 1982), pp. 375-434.

7. "Infitah" or "Open-Door" economic policy is the peak of the big urban bias to Cairo. Most foreign companies and businesses show their interest in locating in Cairo and its suburbs. This of course is due to government services, infrastructure availability, accessability to international communications and the huge market size.
The distribution of the inland projects that started production by geographical location up to the end of 1981 shows that:

a) The governorate of Cairo has received the largest number of these projects (totaling 196) thus representing 61.4% of the total capital assets of these projects.

b) Second in order was Giza with 74 projects representing 11% of the total capital assets of these projects.

c) Third in order came Kalyobia with a share of 38 projects representing 5% of the total capital assets of these projects.

All this means that, out of the total 436 inland producing projects, 71% are located in Greater Cairo.

Hoda M. Sobhi, "The Impact of Multinational Enterprises on Regional Disequilibria", paper presented at the 7th International Congress of Statistics, Computer, Social and Demographic Research, Cairo, 1982, p.127.

CAPMAS, "Status of the Open Door Economy in ARE up to Dec. 31, 1981," (Cairo, 1982), pp.44-45. As quoted by Hoda Mohammed Mustafa in "Cairo: The Big Urban Bias," *op.cit.* (notes added by the editor).

27.
Islamic Identity and the Metropolis: Conflict and Continuity

Ervin Y. Galantay

The built environment of the modern world has been shaped by four great urban traditions—the Far Eastern (Chinese), the Indian, the Islamic, and the Western, or European.

The Eastern traditions produced urban paradigms which expressed the high value accorded to spiritual factors and the search for harmony based on *permanent* values.

By contrast, the Western mode which has been embraced by both the capitalist and the socialist countries places a premium on efficiency in spatial organization in order to optimize production and consumption, and expresses a lifestyle in which constant *change* has become a goal in itself.

During the last 50 years—in the guise of modernization—the Western mode started its encroachement on the territory of the great Eastern traditions. As a result, the cities of Africa and Asia have lost much of their historic tissue, and the impact of modernization led to a rupture of continuity between the inherited morphology and more recent urban structure.

A living culture needs constant reference to the "collective memory" which is largely embodied in the built form of cities; the erosion of this substance results in a loss of identity and leads to cultural dependence. Due to the forced pace of modernization, the conflict between traditional values and imported ideas has been the sharpest in some of the Islamic countries and, recently, the resulting resentment gave rise to fundamentalist movements not only in Iran or Lybia but even in such secularized nations as Turkey.

Some will argue that modern technology is not a monopoly of the Western civilization but the consequence of universal progress in scientific thought. Hence, modernization is an inevitable result of global interconnectedness and, since spatial organization is no longer culture-specific, the conflicts arise simply from the difficulties of transition from pre-industrial to indus-trialized societies. In this view the world has become too small to permit cultural diversity in its urban areas; the evolution or "progress" of global society is unilineal. The modernization of Islamic cities is only a matter of time lag and of "catching-up." After all, haven't the European cities also undergone a painful metamorphosis and much loss of historical substance until a new equilibrium with modernity is reached?

On the other hand, if we value cultural diversity we should not accept the theory of single-line cultural evolution as *destiny* and examine the possibili-ty of the continuation of parallel-line development, each line keeping its distinct identity. As far as the morphology of cities in Islamic countries is concerned, the question is twofold:

1. Can we assure the survival of the special character of the historic "medina"?

2. Is it possible to infuse Islamic identity in the spatial organiza-tion of New Towns and modern town extensions?

Let us first of all attempt to define the essence of the Islamic tradition. Most of the great cities of the Islamic world were built in a hot arid zone which stretches from the Maghreb to Afghanistan between the 10th and 35th parallels north of the Equator.

Within this vast area there developed a common "pattern language"[1] which still impresses by its unity more than its diversity.

The heartlands of Islam cover regions which once gave rise to the most ancient urban civilizations. Today most Islamic nations are highly urba-nized while others are urbanizing with astonishing rapidity, i.e., the population of Lybia is now 81% urban, more urban than Italy.

Very large agglomerations have emerged due to rampant primacy: Cairo with its 10 million inhabitants may reach a population of 16-20 million by the year 2000.[2] Teheran may be close to the size of Cairo at present,[3] and Istanbul now having about 6 million inhabitants will reach 10 million within 15 years.[4] But apart from these metropoli of international impor-tance, even smaller national and regional centers show astonishing growth, i.e., Ankara which in 1923 had only 23,000 inhabitants now has over 3 million and is likely to reach a population of 6 million people by the year 2000.[5]

All these fast growing cities include as a core a relatively small historic *medina* as well as some other islands of traditional urban tissue surround-ed by a vast and amorphous agglomeration in which formally planned projects in the Western mode are juxtaposed with illegal and informal development. While the historic substance of the medinas is eroding, one looks in vain for signs of Islamic identity in the New Town extensions.

In asking the questions about continuity and identity we have to define, first of all, what exactly is *specifically Islamic* in the inherited environment. Three factors have shaped the built form of Islamic cities and, of these, two are *not* culture-specific. The first is the climate: characteristic responses, such as the intraverted court-house, the use of roof-terraces, of wind-catchers, the close packing of cubic volumes to maximize shading all go back to *pre-Islamic* civilizations. The second factor is the preference for certain building techniques and materials: it has been determined by resource constraints such as the scarcity of timber or stone which made the use of brick and of vaulting a rational choice. The recent availability of steel and particularly of cement had rapidly transformed the townscapes once dominated by brick into ones of reinforced concrete. In fact, the cement consumption of Arabic countries is staggering.[6] In the Gulf States cement used per capita is far in excess of the per capita consumption in Europe, the U.S. or the USSR.

Putting aside the parameters of the climate and of traditional building techniques, we can now identify the culture-specific determinants which are the religious practices and legal traditions of Islam and a lifestyle based on separate roles of men and women in Islamic society.

Fundamental to the understanding of Islamic tradition is the concept of the community *umma* which is based on faith rather than on kinship. Thus, Islamic ideology is democratic although—descending from the authority of the Khalifs—there has always been an elite which collected and managed the "zakat" and provided leadership in need. Basic also is the concept of social solidarity, *takaful,* and the distinction between needs (hajiyat) and absolute necessities (daruriyat) which must be met by alms if necessary. There is also provision for public consultation by open meetings (shura).[7]

The legal system is value-loaded and oriented toward the ultimate objectives of Islam: *maqasid al-shari'ah.*[8] Although the legal system, *sunna,* admits at least four different systems of interpretation, there emerged an agreement about the proper use of land and of behavior in space based on customary law (*al masalih, al musalah*) derived from the *ijmah,* a principle attributed to the Prophet's saying "my community will never agree in error."[9]

Customary law establishes that all land belongs to Allah, then to the Muslim community, i.e., to the state, and while the individual has beneficial rights of title, "this amounts to *trusteeship* or *stewardship* rather than to out-right freehold" in the Western sense. It appears that Islamic law does not condone the degree of collectivization and regulation by the state as found in socialist "regimes" but it does include the right of *expropriation* for public needs after payment of just compensation. Rights of title may not be abused to deny access to land owned by others or to visually invade the privacy of other families, i.e., by opening a window into their court. While Western law distinguishes only between free–hold and lease–hold, Islamic law permits more intricate systems of interlocking ownership and servitudes.

Customary law also caters to a refined sense for multiple layers of privacy which leads to the recognition of special rights and responsibilities of neighbors living like an extended family in a cluster of buildings, sharing access from the same cul-de-sac alley; called "Hara" in Cairo and Damascus; "Hawma" in Algiers; and "Haarat" in Yemen. In cities such as Fez, Morocco, the alley had a gate which was locked at nighttime.[10]

Islamic tradition assigns separate roles to men and women and goes to great length to safeguard privacy and female modesty. In principle, public space is considered unsafe and "to be eschewed by women," and even within the home private space is layered to permit further reclusion for individual privacy. An arrangement of a string of interconnected bedrooms "en suite"—crossed by streams of servants and visitors as in Versailles —would be quite inconceivable in Islamic society. The concern with female modesty dictated such solutions as separate entrances for men and women, separate waiting rooms, hidden or indirect entranceways (called "chicane" by the French) and the ingenious "Mashrabiyya" of Cairo, the "Kafess" of Medina or "Rawshin" in Jeddah—variations of balconies screened by wooden grillwork.

The strong sense of *sharaf,* or family honor, which includes the extended family along male blood-lines resulted in the need for controlled semi-public space serving a cluster of buildings inhabited by members of the same clan having special rights and responsibilities which later have been transferred to the proximate neighbors living around the same *derb* and often sharing communal equipment such as wells and baking ovens.[11]

On a somewhat larger scale of social organization we find the neighborhood completing the hierarchy of intraverted cells from the room to the courthouse, the cluster with its semi—private alley and to the *mahalle* with its mosque, school, hammam, etc. separated from other neighborhoods by streets carrying through-traffic.

This concept of spatial organization is based on distinct "territories" with the movement system and public open space confined to the residual, interstitial areas between cells. This is in total contrast with the spirit of Western town planning which assigns priority to the movement system by first of all reserving space for the street grid and public places and then proceeding to the subdivision of the grid squares or islands for lots and different land uses.

A basic requirement of Islam is charity. In cities the collection of the alms was based on the neighborhood units which conferred to the mahalle the status of a legal entity.

The economic institutionalization of charity gave rise to the numerous pious foundations of public fountains, schools and hospitals and the creation of the *waqf* for their administration and management. Since the waqf property was inalienable, a very sizable percentage of the real estate in Islamic cities eventually passed into public hands.

In contrast to European cities where public buildings often focus on market squares or are free-standing like sculptual objects, the major communal buildings of the Islamic city (mosques, medreses, hammama, hans, etc.) are tightly woven into the urban fabric and interlink linearly along the bazaars which run gate-to-gate as continuations of the main regional roads and, at the same time, provide the essential interface and exchange among inhabitants of adjacent mahalles.

Apart from the bazaars the other through-streets separate more than link the neighborhood territories. Unlike the extraverted European buildings where the ostentatious facade serves to advertise the social standing of the owner, the Islamic house only reveals its richness in the interior. This made possible the juxtaposition of houses of the rich and the poor and permitted the co-existence of families of different income levels within the same mahalle.

The Impact of Modernization

Let us now examine the impact of "modernization on the structure of the archetypical medina:

In a thoughtful article earlier in this volume, Dr. Abdulaziz Saqqaf[12] defined the roles to be played by the modern metropolis:

- A generative role: diffusing knowledge by education and tele-communications;
- A transforming role: molding the inhabitants to become members of a programed consumer society;

- A mobilizing role: supportive of production goals and based on efficiency principles, norms and standards;

- A decision-making role: implying integration with the international system, high "connectivity" and "coupling" with multinational technocracy.

It is obvious that every one of these roles is disruptive of the medina and incompatible with its traditional functions. Thus, policies are required to prevent new "metropolitan" functions from establishing themselves within the limits of the historic medina since this would result in its destruction.

A Professor Cyrus Mechkat[13] explained at a recent conference of the Unity of Sciences that each urban spatial system establishes its own mode of regulation. Within the framework of the international division of labor and the "Centre-Periphery Model" there is a need for the rise of a modern "central" enclave fully coupled with other international decision-making centers by high "connectivity" in terms of telecommunications.

This implies a high-technology "enclave" providing the location for the headquarters of local businesses of international stature, branch offices of international organizations and multinational conglomerates. Such a modern central business district will provide for interface of local decision-makers with members of the technocracy which is replacing the old patriarchal order. Unfortunately, the linkage needs of a modern central business district are incompatible with the structure of the medina.

Apart from offices the "enclave" requires access to a modern airport and very special amenities like luxury hotels and restaurants, entertainment areas, golf courses and, above all, street space for cars and for parking.

Needless to say, the spatial requirements of the automobile—whether in movement or stationary—cannot be met within the narrow streets of the medina in which beast of burden used to be the predominant mode of transportation, unlike the wheeled vehicles favored in the pre-industrial cities of Europe.

Unfortunately the voracious spatial needs of the automobile often resulted in clearing 30 meters and even 50 meters wide access roads through the dense tissue of mahalles and bazaars, causing irreparable damage. One of the worst offenders was Reza Shah of Iran who started with cutting two intersecting orthogonally main axes through Tehran. Similar measures of "traffic improvement" followed in Ispahan, Mashad and Yazd accompanied by attempts to "free" the view and thus physically isolate mosques and shrines. A frightening example of such an approach was Darius Borbor's project to clear a wide field by razing dense urban tissue around the Imam Raza shrine of Mashad and then circling it with eight-story office buildings sitting on a three-story parking and commercial platform. Similarly disruptive projects have been carried out in Iraq, for example, the 50 meter wide cut of Al-Keefah street leading to the Al-Gaylani shrine in Baghdad.[14]

Such cuts not only result in the insensitive severing of bazaars and mahalles but have, as a consequence, the erection of high-rise buildings along their right-of way. But high-rise buildings reduce the attractiveness of the adjacent court-houses by destroying their visual privacy, casting permanent shadows on their gardens and preventing the flow of cooling winds. By generating excessive traffic, they also contribute to noise and air pollution.

If the new central business district is established outside of the original medina, the threat of wholesale demolition of historic buildings is diminished. However, the shifting away of the center of economic activity often results in a decline of the bazaar as the prestigious businesses move out, followed by the transfer of the homes of the rich and the middle class to more fashionable areas; the slum-formation by the splitting up of large houses into small rental units; neglect of maintenance; decay of the physical structure; overcrowding and the breakdown of social coherence . . .

At the same time, the slow process of incremental renewal of the urban fabric is profoundly upset by land speculation triggered off by the search of space for the new central business district and the rapid rise of land values in zones upgraded by infrastructure improvement. The impact is often exacerbated by the insensitivity of foreign planners, architects and contractors to whom large-scale projects are assigned.

Although the outward signs of "modernization" are the most evident, the indirect impact of the imported value system on traditional lifestyles is even more destructive.

The competitive, dynamic and aggressive nature of Western capitalism and the high value given to "progress" contrasts with the importance accorded to continuity and incremental change in the patriarchal order.

The demand for ever faster production of ever larger quantities of goods and services creates a voracious appetite for the mobilization of manpower and a stimulus for bringing women out of the shelter of the home and into the active labor force.

The education of women, coupled with the impact of telecommunications (films, radio, TV, travel), is a secularizing force reducing the persuasion of the Islamic rules on privacy and female modesty. This influences authority relations within the family when it comes to mate selection, career choice, or cohabitation, for example, young wives refusing to subordinate themselves to the authority of their mother-in-law (as poignantly described in "A wife for my son" by the Algerian author Ali Ghalem).

Indirectly, the very increase of the extension and densities of the modern city are also working toward the breakdown of the extended family. The size of the nuclear family is not yet decreasing—in fact, in Lybia, average family size increased from 4.6 persons to six within the last 25 years. High natural increase coupled with accelerated rates of migration to the cities result in overcrowding in the medinas and even in the informal housing areas rising illegally on the periphery. In conditions of extreme crowding the traditional separation of the home in spheres of privacy can no longer be maintained. Standards vary; while in Istanbul[15] the average house still provides a comfortable 10 square meters per inhabitant, in the Jebel Lamar[16] "gourbi" or spontaneous settlement of Tunis, average floor space is only about 5 square meters. Similarly in Cairo[17] no less than 26% of all dwelling units (some 380,000) consist of only one room, and since the average family size is five persons, privacy is non-existent.

Another "modernizing" factor is the increasing heterogeneity of urban populations resulting in a loss of social cohesion and solidarity. Doing research in Istanbul's Kucuk Ayasofia Mahalle[18] we found considerable friction among migrants from different Anatolian regions, each mutually hostile group frequenting its own kahveh-outlet and disinclined to cooperate with any "outsiders." Such recent migrants tend to use the traditional inner-city neighborhood as a staging point for urban acculturation before moving out to settle permanently in the peripheral areas and thus have no stake in the improvement of the physical or social environment. Even more disruptive is the influx of foreigners even if they are temporary workers or refugees from other Islamic countries.

The lifestyle of foreign consultants and businessmen is emulated by the rapidly secularizing Islamic middle class. The presence of large numbers of Asiatic contract laborers, i.e., the 250,000 Philippinos and Koreans in the Gulf States, is yet difficult to fathom.

Even more upsetting than the discontinuity in lifestyles is the extremely fast rate of change of the built environment. In the pre-industrial city, change used to be slow and incremental, mostly resulting from marital and inheritance arrangements. Now most urban interventions are "mega-projects." Clusters of houses used to be settled by cohesive and compatible family groups, but now the state often builds tens of thousands of dwelling units and then assigns them at random.

As proof that the rate of change of the urban spatial environment can be a powerful irritant leading to social instability, no better example could be cited than the Iranian Revolution. The pace of modernization led to land speculation, corruption and the collusion of decision-makers with local elites syphoning off excessive and indecent profits to foreign banks.

Apart from the fact that the accumulation of excessive profit is contrary to the egalitarian and charitable principles of Islam, no doubt the ultimate irritant to trigger off the riots in Tehran was the Shah's ambitious project to create a new business and administrative center. This vast project called SHAHASTAN PAHLEVI[19] was to be located in the hills on the northern periphery of the capital on land mostly owned by the Shah's own family. The building of modern infrastructure and of a subway system using public funds would have yielded enormous windfall profits for the owners of real estate in this area. At the same time, the success of the project—planned for a daytime working population of 330,000 people—would have depressed land values in the traditional center and ruined the bazaari merchants who had to face the alternative to move to the new high-rent area in Shahastan Pahlevi or face declining sales in the neglected bazaar, already poorly served by congested narrow streets.

The anger of the bazaari combined with the distaste of the mullahs for the rampant secularization of life which threatened their power base, and both fanned the fires of revolution and prepared the ground for the advent of the fundamentalist Khomeini regime.

It is too early to tell whether the new regime can successfully block Westernization in other than its purely superficial aspects. The growth of Tehran has not been checked: on the contrary, due to the influx of refugees from the war zone and in response to unfulfillable promises to provide housing for the needy, the population has been growing even faster than in the last years of the Shah's rule. Now the Shariah has been invoked, the size of urban plots limited to 1,000 square meters, and the resale of property made difficult—yet there has been little change in the typology of buildings or the layout of neighborhoods. The building of extraverted Western-style freestanding blocks of flats continues. The only positive element is that the building of imported "megaprojects" by expatriate contractors has stopped, interventions are more incremental and also much reduced in volume.[20]

What policy recommendations can we distill from this brief critical analysis of "modernization" and the current practice of planning and building in Islamic countries?

As far as the medina is concerned, it is important to realize that, in leading cities, the historic core only occupies a tiny fraction of the area of the metropolitan agglomeration—1 to 4 square kilometers. The area of Greater Cairo is 2,000 square kilometers; of this the densely built-up area covers 261 square kilometers. The Fatimid old town is only 3.7 square kilometers—one-sixtieth of the built-up area. The medina of Tunis only occupies 2.7 square kilometers, the Medina of Aleppo 2 square kilometers, the walled city of Lahore 2.25 square kilometers, etc.[21]

The optimal strategy would be the conservation of the entire medina area by declaring it a "tradition island" to be saved from further erosion by specific legislation. If this is politically or financially not feasible, a "low-investment strategy" could still aim at the conservation of entire neighborhoods embracing a wide range of activities and a maximum diversity of elements in a compact assemblage.

Within the conservation area the reduction of densities and overcrowding is indispensable. But this should certainly not be done by clearance operations or street widening, but by relocating the numerous temporary dwellers who give the medina a transitory character—and having no stake in its improvement—are one of the chief agents of its decay. This implies that the perpetuation of the present composition of inhabitants is incompatible with the conservation goal. But what then should be the new function of the medina? As explained previously, it cannot accommodate the central business district functions, but it could profit from the proximity of a new one. In this case the medina could play a complementary "tandem" role providing a congenial setting for certain type of business and artisan activities.

Polluting, noisy and traffic-generating industries as well as wholesaling and warehousing must be removed and relocated. On the other hand, since it is desirable to maintain an optimal mix of activities, cultural and educational facilities should be attracted. The medina must remain a predominantly pedestrian precinct. The penetration of the automobile, or at least of heavy traffic, must be reduced. Truck access can be limited to certain hours of the day or night. However, it is well known that car owners want to keep an eye on their cars by parking them preferably in direct proximity of the house. This results in congestion due to off-street parking. Also, such unsightly activities as washing and repairing of cars on the curb reduce the recreational use of the street space. For this reason it seems to be desirable to concentrate on the medina residents who do not require or cannot afford automobiles, i.e., students (who primarily use motorcycles), retired educators, public servants and officers, and institutions such as old-age homes, orphanages, maternity homes and hospitals.

In any case, the upgrading of infrastructure will raise the value of real estate and of rents, forcing out the lowest income residents and leading to what in the U.S. is called "gentrification."

Hotels, guest houses, hans and certain types of entertainment activities may also be compatible with this commercial-institutional mix although not the international style nightclubs catering to foreign tourists.

The medina might be developed to attract internal—i.e., Islamic —tourism, the potential of which should not be underestimated. Traveling has a venerable tradition in Islam due to the obligation of the Hadj. With the rise of an educated and prosperous middle class and greater pride taken in Islamic identity, a visit to the splendid relics in Istanbul's Topkapi Palace, the great mosque of Kairouan, or the remnants of Fatimide Kairo may prove as attractive as a trip to Europe or the United States.

While the revitalization of the medina seems to be within easy reach, our second goal of infusing some Islamic identity in modern developments seems much more difficult to achieve.

In many countries of the Maghreb, in Egypt as well as in Turkey, much of the growth occurs in illegal settlements, in "gourbis" and "gecekondus." While these squatter settlements lack adequate infrastructure, their morphology is much more in harmony with the traditional use of space than that of planned developments. If possible they should be upgraded rather than razed as in Lybia where nearly all gourbis have been replaced by nondescript, free-standing, pre-fabricated units totally at variance with Islamic lifestyle. In such "modern" housing projects the provision of street space and so-called "green areas" is far in excess of European standards. At the same time, the size of the unit has been squeezed down to a minimum, and there is no place for private courts or gardens where receptions involving the larger family and friends could take place although there is still a demand for such gatherings in Arab households. If possible larger lots should be provided since the minimum standard may provide adequate shelter but may not suffice for the survival of the Islamic lifestyle. In the Maghreb, spontaneous housing offers the best guarantee for a continuity of Islamic traditions. In Turkey and in Iran the builders of informal housing units seem to have taken as role models the secularized middle class with their preference for Western-style isolated buildings. Maybe it is not too late to change this by enforcing appropriate guidelines.

In the formal provision of mass-housing, high-rise construction should be avoided. Most of the high-rise projects of the last decades have been provided by foreign contractors who have probably never given a thought to Islamic customs.[22] Negative examples abound. Nasr City in Cairo, designed in 1956 by Soviet consultants, packed 60,000 people in 3 to 14 story blocks on 240 hectares. The Jeddah Rush Housing Project built by American contractors can claim the dubious record of concentrating 10,000 inhabitants on only 14 hectares (in densely packed 15-story towers on three-story platforms for parking and commerce) at a net density of some 1210 persons per hectare.[23]

It can be demonstrated that reasonably high densities can be achieved by low-rise development by grouping one to-three story units and reducing public circulation space to the minimum.

In line with Hassan Fathi's[24] experiments in *gourna-el gedida* and elsewhere, 20 to 25 units should be grouped into clusters and assigned to a compatible group of inhabitants selected on the basis of common regional background, kinship, or some other social bonding force. Reasonable plot sizes should permit core houses to expand incrementally to allow at least 10 square meters floor space per habitant which is sufficient to safeguard the requirements of privacy and female modesty.

Self-help construction may offer a wide field for the application of traditional materials and building methods as pioneered by Hassan Fathy.

However these materials (such as mud-brick) and methods (such as vaulting) have never been conceived for the rapid satisfaction of mass housing needs. Therefore there is undoubtedly some merit in attempting to use modern technology consisting of the assemblage of pre–fabricated units.

The monotony of a pre-fabricated environment could be reduced by using an incremental approach, building on scattered sites rather than "mega-projects."[25] A decentralization of construction sites and reduced-scale operations would permit the maximal mobilization of local enterprises. Also less use should be made of "package deals" assigned to foreign designers and contractors. It seems that, due to the vast scale of projects preferred by the decision-makers in the Arab world, no more than 25% of all building contracts have been carried out by local companies in the last 20 years.[26]

Another attempt to break monotony would be to avoid rigid orthogonality and wide rights-of-way.[27] Hassan Fathy points out that in historic medinas even the longest straight stretch of street never exceeded 300 meters. To provide more perceptual variety various configurations of pre-fabricated houses should be tried. Inspiration should be sought in Arabic music which is not the endless repetition of the same tune but provides infinitely rich variations on a single theme—as in the stories of the "Arabian Nights" which keep unfailingly returning to the basic yarn of the narrator.

Keeping in line with the traditional size of the mahalle of 2.5 hectares, clusters should be formed with 100-250 dwelling units per hectare and not exceed 1,000 persons per hectare density. Having promoted greater social homogeneity on the mahalle level, it is desirable to restore to it some local autonomy. The institution of the waqf could be revived to take on the management of communal socio-cultural equipment on the neighborhood level, promote activities, and provide maintenance of public grounds and buildings.

Mahalles could be juxtaposed on one side on linear bazaars and on the other side on service streets with strips for car parking. Continued motorization could perhaps be slowed down by a deliberate policy of making the purchase and operation of private automobiles difficult. On this issue, of course, opinions are widely divided. Colonel Khadafi, on the occasion of an official visit in Antanarivo (Madagascar), startled his hosts by stating that the Bedouin tradition of unrestricted mobility should be met by providing each Arab with a car instead of a camel!

However, in large cities existing street space is already often congested to saturation levels. In 1973 in Istanbul there were only 70,000 registered cars, and in Cairo no more than 220,000.[28] If these numbers are going to increase tenfold until the year 2000 as predicted, there will be a dire need for more street surface and parking areas. More emphasis on public rapid transit is called for.

Major efforts are needed to control speculation. These could include the measures already introduced in Iran of limiting the maximum size of plots, making property transfer difficult and all development subject to severe control for conformity with guidelines.

Among non-physical measures it might be useful to tie property taxes to the declared value of real estate and simultaneously make it known that property can be expropriated any moment at the tax value. This would generate adequate income for municipal purposes by ensuring taxation based on a fair assessment of real estate. Positive measures of enticement, tax rebates, etc. should also be employed to assure the optimum use of land in harmony with the Islamic concept of the trusteeship of real estate, of which the ultimate owner is Allah.

It seems to me that the implementation of these simple recommendations could provide the preconditions for the rise of settlements more in harmony with Islamic principles. It is important to emphasize that these principles define an appropriate use of *space* and of *behavior* in space. By contrast, the cosmetic use of traditional decorative elements, applied skin-deep to the exterior of Western-style buildings is dishonest trickery and should be avoided.

Leaders of the modern states in the countries of Islamic tradition often seem exasperated with the conditions of the inherited environment[29] which seems antiquated, unsanitary, overcrowded, decaying and plagued by traffic congestion, noise and air pollution. Yet there is nothing outdated in the Islamic *principles* or the spatial organization derived from it. The task is to reduce the conflict of tradition and modernization to be able to enjoy some of the benefits of continuity.

Speaking as a "Western" planner and addicted to rationality and quantitative methods, I nevertheless hope that the Islamic traditions will show the way for a new paradigm of urban spatial organization based on more spiritual values.

Is it too much to hope that an Islamic urbanism will emerge that will elevate the art of city planning through levels of sublimation as asked by the sufi philosophers from the mere "world of forms" to the "world of spiritual perception," "the world of imagination" and "the world beyond form"?[30]

References

The International Symposium on Islamic Architecture and Urbanism 1930, at King Faisal University, Damman S.A.

The Arab City, Proceedings of a symposium held in Medina, Kingdom of Saudi Arabia, 1981, Ismael Serageldin, editor.

International Conf. on "Urbanization and Social Change in the Arab World," Bellaggio, Italy, 1982, and special issue of "Ekistics," May/June, 1983.

Notes

1. Janet Abou-Lughod, "Contemporary Relevance of Islamic Urban Principles," *Ekistics* 280, (Jan./Feb., 1980).

2. B. Jensen, et al., "Taming the Growth of Cairo," *Third World Planning Review*, (May, 1981), pp. 201-233.

3. Cyrus Mechkat, "The Metropolis in Islamic Countries," Proceedings of the 13th ICUS, (Washington D.C., September, 1984), ICF, New York.

4. Istanbul Master Plan Bureau & Colin Buchanan and Partners "Istanbul Urban Development Project," (1977).

5. G.K. Payne, "Ankara," *Cities*, (Feb., 1984), pp. 210-214.

6. The European Cement Association in Paris estimates that while world—wide average cement consumption was 415 lbs. per capita in 1982, it amounted to 1,584 lbs. per capita in Bahrain and no less than 7,700 lbs. per capita in the

United Arab Emirates!

7. Nur-al-Islam, al-Azhar, Matba'ah al-Ma'ahid al Diniyah, vol. 3, (Cairo, 1933), Cairo English supplement, pp. 24-25.

8. Othman, B. Llewellyn, "The Objectives of Islamic Law," *Ekistics* 280 (Jan./Feb., 1980), pp. 11-13.

9. *Ibid.*

10. Min. de l'Habitat et de l'Amenagement du Territoire, Royaume du Maroc, "Schema Directeur de l'urbanisme de la ville de Fez," PNUD et UNESCO, (Paris, 1980).

11. Janet Abu-Lughod, "Urbanization and Social Change in the Arab World," *Ekistics* 300, pp. 223-231.

12. Abdulaziz Al-Saqqaf, "The Islamic Metropolis: A Commentary," Proceedings of the 13th ICUS, (Washington D.C., September, 1984), ICF, New York.

13. Mechkat, *op.cit.*

14. J. Warren, "Baghdad, Two Cases Studies of Conservation," *The Arab City*, pp. 242-250.

15. Istanbul Urban Development Project, *op.cit.*

16. District de Tunis "Rehabilitation du *Jebel Lamar*," (1974).

17. *Cahiers IAURIF*, no. 74, (December, 1984), *La Region du Grand Caire* and text. In this document "Greater Cairo" includes the three Governorates of Cairo, Gizeh and Kaliubah with a present population of 11 million, about 22% of the population of Egypt. This metropolitan area covers 1,160 square miles, however, the built-up area is less than one-tenth, about 108 square miles.

18. Swiss Federal Institute of Technology, Zurich, INDEL-Program "Kucuk Ayas-ofia Mahalle Conservation and Renewal Study, Istanbul," report of graduate field-study group under the direction of Prof. E. Galantay, ETH-Zurich, 1977. See also: P. Schubeler, "Localization of Small-Scale Enterprise," *Istanbul ETH-INDEL*, (Zurich, 1977).

19. J. Robertson, "Shahastan Pahlevi," Proceedings of the 1st Congress of the International New Towns Association, (Teheran, 1975).

20. Sadat, student report submitted to the author, (November, 1984.)

21. Compare these areas to the size of historic Venice (1.8 sq. miles) or that of the city of London (1 sq. mile); see also: Samuel Noe, "Old Lahore and Delhi," *Ekistics* 295 (July/August, 1982), p. 306.

22. Youssef Belkacem in *The Arab City* (p. 11) states that "in Algeria people continue to sacrifice sheep on *Aid* even on the fifteenth-floor balcony. In Algeria where the sacrifice of *Aid* is observed even by the urban population, some people in modern housing projects are obliged to kill sheep on fifteenth-floor balconies."

23. A. Farahat and M.N. Cebeci, "A Housing Project: Intentions and Realities," *The Arab City*, pp. 302-311.

24. Hassan Fathy, "Interviewed by Jorick Blumenfeld," *Architecture Association Quarterly*, vol. 6, no. 3/4, (1974).

25. Entirely alien in concept are the vast projects carried out by the U.S. Army Corps of Engineers such as the King Khaled Military City in Saudi Arabia which will accommodate 70,000 people, or the Suwaihan military city in Abu Dhabi planned by the Bechtel Corp. However, equally insensitive is the concept of the new industrial town of Ariashahr in Iran provided by the Soviet State Planning Institute GIPROGOR, of Moscow and built with Russian help in 1968-76. For a discussion of Ariashahr see: Ervin Y. Galantay, *New Towns*,

(New York, 1975).

26. A. Zahlan (an Arab labor consultant) quoted in the *International Herald Tribune*, (Nov. 16, 1984).

27. It is useful to recall that Rasullah's recommendation for an appropriate street width in reconstructing Medina and Mecca as "at least seven zirahs," i.e., 9.2 yards. Somewhat later Sydgna Omar planned the main roads of Basra 15.4 yards wide (20 zirahs) while side streets were kept at 6.9 yards (9 zirahs). In fact, in traditional Islamic medinas, primary streets vary from 4.4 to 13.2 yards, and the main thoroughfares rarely exceed 13.2-22 yards. By contrast, modern roads built in Kuwait and Lybia have right-of-way widths of 77 and even 110 yards. See also: Ali Afak, "Urbanism and Family Residence in Islamic Law," in *Ekistics* 280, (Jan./Feb., 1980), p. 23.

28. "Istanbul Master Plan Study," *op.cit.* and "La Region du Grand Caire," *op.cit.*

29. "The traditional Middle Eastern city is no "paradise lost." But even if it were, it would be futile to lament its loss;" Prince Hassan Ibn Talal of Jordan in his message to the PWPA Symposium on the Middle East City, (Paris, 1985).

30. N. Ardelan and L. Bakhtiar, *The Sense of Unity*, (1973).
    The "seven levels of realization" are in ascending order:
    1. alam i tabit (the world of man)
    2. alam i surat (the world of forms)
    3. alam i ma'na (the world of spiritual perception)
    4. alam i malakut (the world of imagination)
    5. alam i jabarut (the world beyond form)
    6. alam i lahut (the world beyond Nature)
    7. alam i hahut (the world of divine essence)

Part IX

South and East Asia

28.
The Asian Metropolis

Peter Andre Wyss

Other contributions in this publication specify the world-wide phenomena of rapid urbanization, the formation of the metropolis and megalopolis. This paper shall endeavor to highlight specific characteristics of the urbanization process in Asia, a process which has generally, with the exception of Japan, only started after World War II. The phenomenon is recent in nature but, because of the large and fast growing population, it is expected that urban population will outgrow the entire urban population of all other continents.

By the end of World War II, there were only a few cities (such as Tokyo, Calcutta, Bombay and Shanghai) which had a population of more than one million. Meanwhile, many cities have been added to the "Club" of multi-million cities, growing at rates of 5% to 7% per year. If the trend continues, more than 15 metropoli in Asia will contain over 10 million people by the end of the century. By the year 2020 or 2030, some of those metropolitan areas are expected to contain between 20 and 30 (or more) million people each.

In the past, many suggestions, policies and strategies have been mapped out to contain cities to smaller sizes, to decentralize their activities, and to intercept migrants in reception centers long before they reach the urban area. But there is no doubt that cities stubbornly continue to grow and the question arises—whether this trend can be checked at all.

As E. Galantay points out in an earlier chapter in this volume: "Throughout history, there has been an awareness that there must be a right size for human settlements." Suggestions for optimal city size have been put forward throughout history and it is interesting to note that the optimal city population has been constantly adjusted (upwards, of course). From 10,000 people in 1850, the suggested size has reached the one million mark recently and a special allowance for developing countries has already been made.

As mentioned above, in Asia alone, more than 20 cities have today passed the one million mark and range from 1 to 16 million inhabitants. Thus, they have surpassed the suggested optimal city size by far and somehow do

Fig. 28-1: The emergence of numerous metropoli in Asia after World War II: a new phenomena in the largest continent before a background of fast population growth and high rural-urban migration. (Compiled by the author, based on various sources)

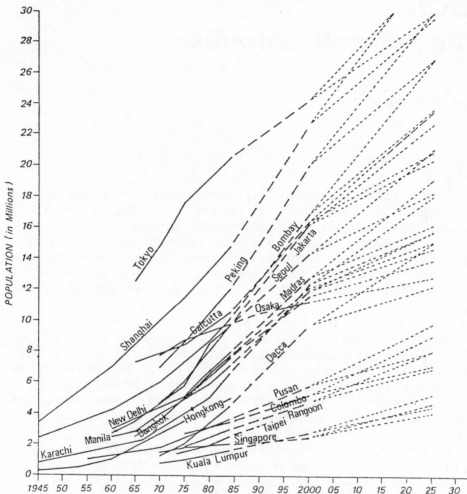

not seem to listen to those theories. It is widely agreed that large cities are more costly both to the individual as well as the public, that crime and deviant behavior and human segregation are increasing as the cities grow, and many suggestions and even policy decisions have been made/taken to restrict metropolitan growth, in vain.

There are many reasons/factors which seem to overpower theories and policy decisions. For example, if one looks at the appalling conditions of congested, flooded and filthy urban squatter settlements, one could expect those tenants to migrate back to their original rural areas. But this has not been the case. Advantages of the city, whether expected or real, keep the migrants in the city.

Thus, it is not surprising that attitudes toward large urban settlements have turned from "negative" to moderately "positive." It indicates, among other things, that human nature is adaptable to new phenomena over the course of time and, above all, that *values* are subject to change as we go along.

While in the 1960s we experienced strong contradictory views between supporters of *rural* versus *urban* development, the 1970s revealed that "rural" and "urban" cannot be viewed in isolation but rather form mutually supportive systems. This trend towards "acceptance" of what used to be "outcry" is expected to continue, and many subjects which alarmed earlier congresses are seen today with a more relaxed mind, partly because appropriate measures have been taken but partly also because value-judgments have been adapted. The "optimum size" discussion can serve as a meaningful example to this effect.

Thus, it is not surprising that fast urban growth is today widely accepted as the unavoidable scenario, and studies by Jean Gotmann, the Ekistics Center of Athens, and others point to a "positive approach" to large human settlements.

The rapid change in approaches also reflects the uncertainties of the relatively young and undeveloped urban science. Compared to other sciences, the knowledge of the complex behavior of the urban system is far behind and more efforts should be undertaken to advance the "Urban Theory" since predictions point to the urban scene as one of the predominant features of the coming decades.

We cannot speak about the Asian metropolis without mentioning two major factors for urban growth: natural increase and migration. In contrast to the low birth rates experienced in industrial cities in Europe and North America, in the Asian metropolis, natural growth is extremely high with rates of between 1.5 to 3% per year. And what is equally important, natural growth in urban areas is practically as high as it is in rural areas. Although population control is a subject by itself and cannot be discussed in this context, one should not entirely rule out that natural growth could slow down in metropolitan regions in Asia as a result of better education, higher social status and higher cost of living. But to what extent it would affect lower incomes (which constitute the majority of the population) is quite open.

Migration, on the other hand, contributes between 2½% to 5% to the urban growth, and continued disparity between rural and urban incomes is likely to keep migration high. Various measures have been tried out to reduce migration. To mention only two:

- Reduction or decentralization of industries; apart from unwanted side effects, no direct reduction on migration has been experienced. This is partly so because migration in the Asian city is, to a lesser degree, connected to industrialization than was the case in Europe and North America. This fact illustrates the difficulty of transferring experience gained in Western cities to Asia.

• Intercept migrants in reception centers away from the urban area.

Such proposals ignore the "inner chemistry" of migration, for example, the strong cohesion that exists between members of the same clan and/or ethnical groups within the urban area as well as the interdependence between metropolitan area and the provincial place of origin; the province acts as a supplier of labor force (majority of migrants are between 20 and 40 years of age), whereas the city offers higher incomes, allowing migrants to send savings back to their place of origin. Thus, the province gains indirectly through the urban migrants and reinforces the "urban-rural" interdependence. (See Fig. 28-7.)

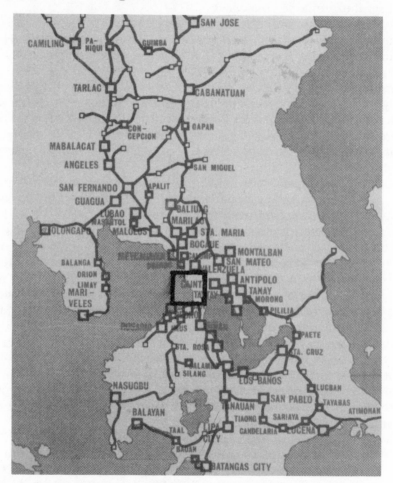

Fig. 28-2: Former villages in the vicinity of the metropolis grow rapidly to sizable towns, forming a new metropolitan conglomerate. The old concept of "boundaries" around towns can in no way do justice to this emerging new complexity full of social, economic and physical interaction. (Illustration by author)

The Loss of Borders

Cities throughout history have always been closed off from their rural surroundings by defense works. This state changed drastically during the nineteenth century when technological improvements of weaponry rendered such defense works useless: borders collapsed and cities opened towards their hinterland. Industrial development, the introduction of new transport modes, population growth and high land values were the main forces that allowed cities to grow limitlessly into the surrounding rural areas. The compact city of the past developed into the borderless, dispersed agglomeration of today. Former villages and small towns are gradually absorbed by the sprawling metropolis.

The functional zone of influence of the metropolis is changing year by year and our inherited static sense of boundaries cannot do justice to the fast–changing reality. The only boundaries left today are administrative ones which are mostly used for statistical purposes. And since boundaries for metropolitan areas are defined differently around the globe, we obtain statistical data which are not comparable with one another. Similar inconsistencies exist with the definition of the metropolitan limit where certain fringe settlements are included and others are not.

In fact, in a recent publication on Asian cities, a little accident was made in that the statistics for Colombo were only supplied for the Colombo Municipality whose 0.6 million population contributes only a small part to the 2.8 million population of the urban area.

In Manila, for example, an expansion of the metropolitan area by another 30 kilometers would increase the metropolitan population from seven to nine million and an extension by a further 60 to 80 kilometers would result in a metropolis of over 11 million people (excluding those living in villages). (See Figure 2.) The loss of physical borders has contributed to the confusion of statistical data. Therefore, speaking about sheer population numbers, without looking into the specific settlement pattern, becomes a rather arbitrary thing. Ranking of cities should be undertaken with caution.

Can We Handle the Future?—A Look-out for Strategies

Since the future starts from the "here and now," let's have a look at the present first before trying to give some thought to future policies and strategies.

The overall picture is not too encouraging. Listening to officials of major metropoli in Asia, most of them agree that:

- fast urban growth has taken them by surprise

- because of rapid urban expansion, it is difficult (or impossible) to provide even the basic amenities

- there are serious difficulties in maintaining existing services

- local governments in charge of city development have inadequate powers and therefore cannot discharge their duties

- funds for development are lacking

- many cities lack the coordination with the large number of involved agencies

- housing, transportation, congestion, pollution, poverty, slums and squatters are major areas of concern

- the absence of a relationship between physical and economic planning is a cause for ineffective planning

But there are also a few exceptions, cities that were more lucky than the majority, e.g., Singapore and Hong Kong which shall be characterized briefly.

Singapore started in the 1960s to encourage industrial investment followed by infrastructure, housing and city center development. One official remembers those days: "we started up without any masterplan, just with common sense and determination." Economic and city development went hand in hand, and Singapore since then has undergone vast social, economic and urban changes within the short period of less than 20 years. The earlier colonial city based mainly on "entrepot–trade" has become a major industrial and financial center with an extraordinary local identity and pride.

Hong Kong's planning efforts were strongest in housing and infrastructure and in the construction of several New Town schemes in the New Territories, each town planned for between 500,000 and one million inhabitants. Industrial development has been rapid and Hong Kong serves as the major financial center in the Far Eastern region. Although the border to China looks rather tightly closed, there is a strong relationship between Hong Kong and the adjoining Province of Canton; this has been further strengthened by the planned economic investment zone along the border.

The two cities of Singapore and Hong Kong are exceptions largely because of their status as City-States. Both have no hinterland and are in a better position to master their destiny. National and urban development is one and the same problem.

Other cities in the region are not as successful as Singapore and Hong Kong and, while further pressure is continuously building up, there are wide disparities on approaches and controversial views. For example:

- Believers of comprehensive master-planning are contradicted by followers of the pragmatic "Singaporean approach" where common sense and inter-governmental coordination led by a handful of strong men did the trick.

- Some advocate decentralization of industries (to relieve congestion) from the center to satellite towns while others point to longer travel distances and reduced tax income of the center city.

- Proposals to decentralize activities to smaller towns (to reduce migration and to improve medium-size cities) contrast with remarks by city officials that the shifting of Karachi to Islamabad had no impact on reducing Karachi's growth; on the contrary, it has been growing further in competition with Islamabad.

- Slums and squatters have been predicted by some to be the source of political unrest while others say that there is no evidence to this effect.

- Some advocate more direct investment in slum and squatter improvement while others would see the positive effects of investment in the formal sector to filter automatically down to the informal sector, including the slums and squatters.

- Some officials voice (in articles and congresses) the need for more "participation" by citizens but, returning back to their desks, see the difficulties of handling participation in practice.

This list can in no way be exhaustive. It indicates, among other things, only that "things" are not as easy and straightforward as they sometimes appear to be.

It also demonstrates that individual conditions require individual approaches. Although the phenomenon is global, solutions cannot be worked out globally but rather have to be tailor—made to suit local conditions.

We also realize that opposing views result from the fact that we still know too little about "how cities behave" and foremost, how people behave in cities. Are the problems that the politician or the planner identifies really the problems the people feel most strongly about?

We know, for example, that a squatter settler in New Delhi who uses wood for heating and cooking does this because it is the only affordable way. There is little concern about environmental effects of pollution and deforestation. Are our approaches able to reconcile differing values of different socio—economic groups?

Considering the strong limitations placed upon the growing metropolis by stress on housing, poverty, congestion, weak administration, lack of funds, differing value systems and uncoordinated actions, it is most likely for the majority of Asian metropoli that this state of affairs will continue into the foreseeable future. Few miracles will allow cities to follow a development path in the "Singapore style."

There is no doubt, however, that many efforts will be undertaken to improve the knowledge of the complex nature of cities to deal with housing, infrastructure, transportation and land aspects and to improve coordination among agencies. New agencies will be created to deal with urban development; procedures, bylaws and development guidelines will be created—some with more, others with less success. Some will place more emphasis on "institution building" while others will recognize the important role that great people with strong ideas and willpower can play to further development.

Taking all these limitations into consideration, there is a strong feeling that many (if not most) actions will follow pressure. Thus, the pressure exercised by the growth and transformation process will most likely be predominant. Let us therefore examine this process more closely.

The Spontaneous Process of Urban Growth and Transformation

Analyzing the immense increase of urban population in Asia over the last decades, one cannot overlook the fact that only a small percentage of development has been "planned"; the vast majority of it has happened by private initiative in small steps. The sum of all such small steps together forms a "spontaneous transformation process." The transformation process in the urban environment has various dimensions: "space," "time," "function" and one of "socio-economy."

In many Asian cities, the spontaneous process is clearly visible because of the low degree of government interference. A deeper understanding of this process is of wider interest to the future metropolis, especially in fast-developing South-East Asian countries.

Many people think that "spontaneous" is synonymous with chaos, but this is not the case. It has been found that the spontaneous transformation process follows certain rules showing strong similarities between various metropolitain areas.

The first is the interdependence between government interference and spontaneous process: the stronger the interference, the weaker is the process and vice versa. In fact, scholars interested in this subject might choose to look at sample cities where interference was minimal in order to analyze the least disturbed process. In actuality, of course, the resulting urban pattern is influenced by a complex combination of spontaneous growth and programmed action.

The evolution of the urban area shows three distinct waves of processes which follow each other.

The first is the *"settlement" process*; individual settlers take advantage of easy access and thus follow open land along major communication networks first, whereas spaces in-between are gradually filled-in later.

The road and transport network therefore assumes an important role as city-builder. Most of today's major urban radial roads have emerged from former rural links between the old city and its rural hinterland.

The settlement pattern of various cities, such as Bangkok (where waterways partly play the role of roads), Bombay, Colombo, Jakarta and Manila to name a few, have been visibly influenced by the basic rural communication grid which has gradually become part of the urban structure. Apart from roads plot boundaries have been identified as the most time-enduring element. In fact, residential plot boundaries of several hundred years ago are still clearly visible today, having undergone very few changes (subdivision or amalgamation). The layout of the initial settlement therefore pre-conditions the future settlement.

The settlement process is followed by a second process, the *transformation of "function."* Residential space on the ground floor is gradually converted for commercial and office use, repair shops, etc. pushing residential activities either to the upper floors or to the periphery. This process occurs at first mainly along major communication axes and on crossings and follows the settlement process in a distance of time and space.

The third process is one of *physical transformation.* With further economic and urban development, the new activities outgrow the former residential buildings and call for their redevelopment. This process of physical change follows the earlier two processes also in a distance of time and space. Fast economic development in a city favors fast and large redevelopment, while slow economic development does the contrary.

As indicated above, the spontaneous process of three consecutive waves of urban transformation shows a high correlation with "accessability," the better the access to transportation, the higher the chance of transformation (function, building). Therefore, transport and communication appear as strong "city-shapers" and it is indicated to make better use of this insight in city planning. Transport nodes and interchanges combined with a variety of activities tend to form the nucleus of future subcenters.

It has been noted that in the past, various planning efforts have centered strongly around land-use planning, making too little use of transport and communication as city—building elements.

While cities in Europe and North America grew rapidly in times long before the private automobile was introduced, rail-bound mass transit was the only answer to satisfy the new demand. Cities like London, Paris and New York built extensive underground mass transit networks.

The situation, however, changed dramatically with the growing availability of the automobile in the twentieth century. Contrary to European and North American cities, most Asian cities grew at a time when the automobile was becoming the prime mode of transport. Old existing tramway systems were discarded and replaced by buses and mini-buses. Roads and highways were widened at high cost, without anyone asking for its feasibility. It was simply the answer of that time.

Meanwhile, advantages of railbound mass transit have been re-discovered and many cities are today planning and/or building new systems. Although the main reason for their construction is "moving people," it is evident that they will have positive secondary effects on the restructuring of the urban tissue. Activities will concentrate around locations of "high accessibility." (Toronto has become particularly famous for high-density development around mass transit stations where developers have pursued sites around stations long before they were open to passengers.) In Asia, the best known examples are the major transport interchanges in Tokyo, such as Ikebukuro, Shibuya and Shinjuku, which are gradually developing into new, strong urban centers. In Hong Kong, the Mass Transit Authority has made

Fig. 28-3: Colombo urban area in 1978. The transformation processes (right) follow the major communication axis (well served by public transport). High accessibility accelerates the transformation process, (Author)

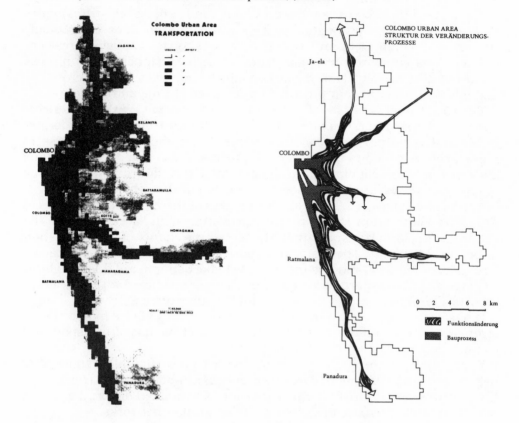

use of this phenomenon for property development around major termini, and Manila is in the process of following suit.

Transportation has most strongly influenced urban changes during this century and it is most likely to continue to play a strong role in the future. Despite this evidenced strong relationship, there is a lack of coordination between sectorial transport plans and comprehensive masterplans. More efforts are needed to deepen the knowledge of the phenomena on one hand and the practical working relationship between agencies involved on the other, in order to make better use of the available potential which public transport offers for "city-building."

Contrary to mass transit, urban "highway widening" programs react in a funny way, defeating their own objective, namely decongestion; it has been generally observed that newly widened highways simply shift the "bottle-neck" for congestion to the next area and attract new traffic, until one day, they are congested again. Cost for widening is high and benefits are questionable, apart from the fact that an overdose of highway-based urban traffic tends to scatter activities further.

Despite this fact, new highway projects can always count on support by decision—makers. A cabinet member once stated on the issue of urban highways: "but we need them (highways) since we *all* have cars," meaning: *we, who decide,* and ignoring that, in Asian cities, between 70% to 90% of all trips are made by public transport. Remembering that decision-makers and members of the strongest pressure groups all possess cars, expenditures on highways are expected to continue to be high and mass transit projects are subject to prove financial viability (something that highway projects are exempted from). Unless there is drastic change in values towards mass transit, "things" will continue the way they are today and cities will disperse in accelerated ways, eating-up more valuable agricultural land.

Segregation of Activities

In parallel with urban expansion, specific activities, once concentrated in the center, start to move out and congregate in new locations. Activities start to segregate into centers of distinct socio-economic character (sometimes even ethnic); "your address of residence and work and your shopping area will increasingly reflect your status." This process is expected to become stronger, the larger the metropolis grows.

Since each individual "uses" only a part of the entire city space, the author has carried out a small analysis in Manila to record the "activity space," i.e., areas where specific individuals spend their time for specific activities. Samples of eight persons are graphically represented in Figure 4.

The two figures (figure 4) compare the "activity space" of eight selected individuals in the course of time: left, 30 years ago, and right, today. The most striking observation refers to the completely changed utilization of the cityscape by the same people, a concentrated pattern of the past against a dispersed pattern of today.

Since this process is typical, let us observe further.

With the exception of two persons, all the others have moved their residence as well as workplace, shopping and recreation.

Places of residence and work have been moved away from the city center to the peripheral areas.

Workplace, school, shopping, recreation, etc. used to lie closer to the residence than is the case today. Average travel distance has more than doubled.

The city center of 30 years ago contained a mixture of almost all activities and all of the surveyed persons frequented the center.

The surveyed persons today visit the city center only rarely but instead visit the new dispersed sub-centers along the ring-road.

People are using the metropolitan area only spotwise and areas in

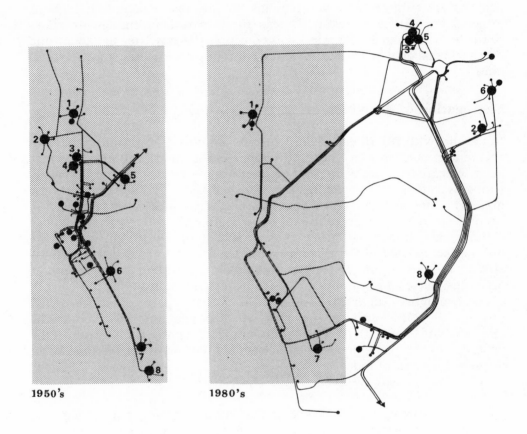

Fig. 28-4: Manila, illustrating as a typical example the dramatic process of tranformation. People have changed their place of residence, work and shopping in the course of 30 years. Spatial mobility goes in parallel with socioeconomic (upward) mobility. The concentrated pattern (1950s) has been replaced by dispersal (today) and activities are segregated. (Black dots indicate places of activity. and the dot size its duration; lines indicate movements between activities.) (Author)

416

between the activity spots are usually registered as "blank zones." Thus, the activity areas are discontinuous.

Vacated residences have either been commercialized or occupied by lower status residents (partly new migrants).

The structural change represented by this sample survey reflects the depth of urban transformation the expanding metropolis is undergoing. This sample lies in line with the general observation in Manila that two-thirds of all residents have changed their place of residence within the last 25 years. Moving the residence reflects crowding and deterioration in the center as well as "upward" social and economic mobility along the fringe.

Crowding can be observed in residential areas close to the center. It is caused by various reasons: incoming migrants are taken care of by their own kin and offered residence even if space is scarce, and high land values and high rents force many tenants to sub-rent part of the premises (students, couples, small families).

As crowding increases and other conditions of buildings and the neighborhood deteriorate, higher status residents often opt to move out while lower status residents occupy the vacant house. Deteriorating conditions of services (scarce water supply, broken sewer lines, flooding, etc.) can add to the rapid decay of once healthy residential areas. Reversing this trend, once it has reached a critically low level, seems to be extremely difficult: income levels of residents are not sufficient to pay for improvements, public funds are scarce, higher status residents are reluctant to move back and "self-help" is easier said than done.

In this light, decay of certain residential areas close to the center is to be expected as time goes by and as the metropolis increases. Government intervention, as strange as it may sound, can add further to decay. One such a dramatic experience occurred in Bombay. In 1940, a rent act was passed since authorities were alarmed by the fast-increasing rent. In essence, rents were stabilized/frozen on the 1940 values. However, because cost of living inflated as years went by, landlords were less and less in a position to pay for maintenance. Buildings deteriorated and tenants moved out. Lower status people moved in, caring little for the condition of the building. This vicious cycle led to a process of decay and, by 1970, 40% of the total housing stock in Bombay was virtually ruined.

This example shall only illustrate that the metropolis is a complex subject and that "well-meant" measures might sometimes produce more ill than good.

Informal Sector Economy

Unlike metropoli in industrial countries, metropoli in developing countries, specifically in Asia, contain a strong informal sector. Generally, between 50% to 85% of all employed persons work in the informal sector, either as

417

self-employed or in the family enterprise (in India, called "bazar economy"). Berry describes the land-use pattern in which the informal sector is located as "chaotic," a term which sounds more negative than the actual pattern is. Possibly, this stems from a desire to produce a land-use map with conventional Western-type methods, an exercise which ends in frustration since no land-use category of Western origin is able to describe the rich mixture of small scale commerce, workshops, manufacturing, trading, etc. within the basically residential areas.

Visitors to such areas usually note the active life in the public roads. Two to three-story buildings border both sides of the access roads which are full of children playing under the supervision of their mothers or relatives. Lots of men are either busy in the nearby workshops or sit at rest with colleagues, playing games or watching the children. Home and work are integral parts of this urban village, typical for the South-East Asian city which is engulfed in the large metropolis. A closer look reveals that work undertaken in the workshop is, for example, a new wooden door for one of the high-income residences, the car-service for one of the bank managers, etc. There is a strong economic interrelation between the formal economy (represented by capital-intensive business, the government and the professions) and the informal economy. But this sector also caters to the needs of middle- and low-income groups. One typical representation is the informal transport sector operating mini-buses, motor-rickshaws, jeepneys, etc. providing transport at non-subsidized rates and thus playing an important role in most Asian cities.

Squatters can be seen as the low-income arm of the informal sector. They contribute about one-third to one-fourth of the average Asian city. Fifteen years ago, slums and squatters had the highest growth rates within cities and were feared to grow endlessly. However, during the last decade, the attitude towards the once called "culture of poverty" has changed. Although the slum is different from squatter, both are seen as performing an important role in the urban economy. They:

provide housing at affordable levels (which hardly any authority can do)

serve as reception/entrance for migrants to the city

provide accommodation in close proximity to work

The informal sector areas are located close to formal sector zones, as illustrated in Figures 5 and 6.

Looking into the future, there is no doubt that efforts toward industrialization in Asian countries will continue to be strong. In fact, Korea, Taiwan, Hong Kong and Singapore are the spearheads of a new group of countries for which the term "developing countries" had to be replaced by "newly industrialized countries" (NIC's) and thus following a development trend which Japan had initiated in the Meiji area over 100 years ago.

The industriousness of the Asian people promises that more countries

Fig. 28-5: The informal sector urban tissue (light grey shade) covers the majority of the settlement area and lies side by side with the formal economy areas (black: business; hatched: industries). Note area detail shown in Fig. 6B lies in circle at northeast corner. (Author)

will be added to the list of NICs in the coming decades. Will this change the importance of the informal sector? Will this wipe out certain informal activities? If yes, which ones? Or will Asian culture and tradition maintain a strong informal sector?

These are some questions, the answers to which are expected to influence the urban activity and land-use pattern, especially those of the informal sector which today contribute a very large component. Unfortunately, no ready-made answers are available at this moment.

Looking at Hong Kong and Singapore, one notes the large percentage of population housed in multi-story housing. Many of these people are employed in new industry and services. Informal jobs have declined (there is a big shortage of household helpers, usually one of the typical representatives of the "self-employed"), and so has informal housing. There is a suspicion that decline of informal jobs and informal housing go hand in hand.

Speculating that the industrialization trend in Asia will continue along the line of Japan, Korea, Hong Kong, Singapore and Taiwan, it might be possible for informal employment to be reduced, for small workshops to disappear and for residential areas to gradually lose the mixture of activities.

On the other hand, it could also mean that providing multi-story formal housing without giving the tenants a possibility to accommodate informal activities on their premises would deprive them of the basic needs of the typical Asian settlement.

Fig. 28-6A: The informal sector in Jakarta resides side by side with modern business (along the highway). Many of those areas (hatched) are kampongs, semi-urban villages of very high density, now fully absorbed in the city. Conditions are very poor but self-improvements are also noticed. Note: Kampongs have no direct access to the highway. **B:** Typical informal sector pattern in Manila: Planned originally as low-cost housing schemes with plots of approximately 100 square meters, small scale commerce, manufacturing and trade has entered the area (hatched and dark shade). More than two-thirds of all plots contain non-residential activities. They provide important services at low cost and play an indispensable role in the urban economy. (Author)

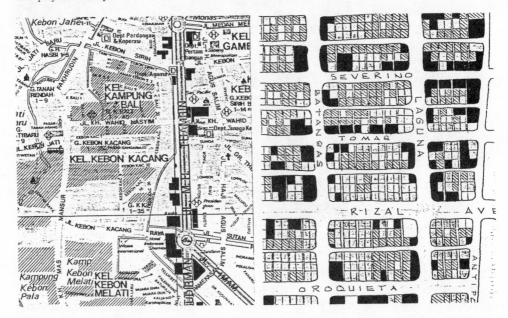

Housing development should therefore keep the option open and promote low-rise/high-density development, giving each tenement a direct access to public roadways in order to allow informal activities to take place. Metropolitan expansion areas should include large areas for such developments side by side with formal land-use and properly accessible by public transportation.

The Metropolis: A Connecting Link Between Asian Provinces and the World

Special reference is made to two contributions in this publication: Dennis J. Dwyer who writes on the metropolis in its national and regional context, and John Dyckman who demonstrates the world-wide network of world metropoli, a network which is becoming increasingly stronger along with financial and industrial role splitting.

Not everybody in a metropolis has equal international access to other world metropoli. Certain sectors of the economy play a more critical role than others but they all belong to the formal sector economy.

On the other hand, as demonstrated earlier, the informal sector in the Asian metropolis is strongly linked to the formal economy on one side and to the province on the other.

Thus the metropolis, with its intricately linked economic and social ties, has forward and backward links to the provinces through strong family cohesion, migration, rural production, etc. and to the world metropoli through export manufacturing, trade, finance, etc.

The Asian metropolis, therefore, plays a vital role as the connecting link between the Asian provincial and the world economy.

Figure 7 tries to illustrate the role of the metropolis with its very varied forward and backward linkages. Family relationships, money flows, supply of labor force, communication links and partnership agreements are just a few of them. This is why the illustration was created to resemble integrated circuits—abstract enough to allow the viewer to sense the large variety of relationships contained in this integrated model.

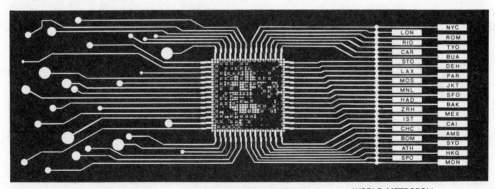

PROVINCIAL TOWNS AND VILLAGES

Strong family ties link the province with the metropolis through migration, continuous manpower sourcing and money

THE TYPICAL ASIAN METROPOLIS

A complex internal network (▦) of interactions between formal (●) and informal (O) economic activities and innumerable linkages to the world metropoli on one side and the provinces on the other.

WORLD METROPOLI

The formal economy links the Asian metropolis with the world metropoli.

Fig. 28-7: Schematic representation of the linkages between human settlements of different scale.

421

Fig. 28-8: Landsat image of Manila and Central Luzon. (Nasa-ICF purchase for ICUS XIII)

The Outlook in Summary

There are no indications at present to make us believe that the Asian metropolis will stop growing further. On the contrary, it is expected to play an important role in new manufacturing and services and contribute a substantial proportion to the nation's capital formation.

Although the metropolis is increasingly seen as a positive contributor to the nation's economy, there is still widespread belief that it absorbs unnecessary funds to the detriment of rural areas. On the other hand, the two City-States, Hong Kong and Singapore, without rural hinterland obligations seem to do better than those metropoli with such obligations. It probably confirms that urban and rural areas form a cohesive, mutually dependent system. Higher incomes in the urban area will keep a continuous migration flow to cities and more migrants will be absorbed in the urban economy because of strong family cohesion. Benefits will flow back to rural areas and squatters will play an important role as reception areas for newcomers.

Today's satellite cities around the metropolis, together with the communication axis, form the basic structure for the expansion of tomorrow's metropolis. Sufficient attention should be given to prepare the areas to take up this role.

Strong limitations on managing the metropolis will likely prevail, although few cases will emerge where strong and determined people will effectively improve its efficiency. Others will try to institutionalize city building with, most likely, little effect.

The strongly felt spontaneous process will continue to influence the growth and transformation of most Asian cities. The weaker the interference by authorities, the stronger the process will be. Scholars might be advised to learn more about the transformation process.

Transport and communication networks will continue to play a decisive role in the "long–term structuring" of the metropolis, although there are reasons to doubt that these systems will be properly utilized for city building. Public mass transit, in combination with land development, should be encouraged to enhance the mutual benefits which the urban activity pattern as well as the patronage of transport systems can derive therefrom.

There is no illusion that highway development will, in most cases, obtain priority over mass transit unless there is a strong change in attitude towards mass transit. External factors such as cost of petrol and congestion might possibly influence this issue in the desirable direction.

The larger the metropoli grow, the stronger will the mobility be, and with it the segregation of activities. If the present trend continues, each new urban generation will utilize the townscape differently than preceeding ones. Traditional personal values connected with specific parts of the city might be reduced to the family photo album, but there will be no deeper sense of belonging and heritage.

Dispersed expansion of the periphery will go hand in hand with more or less pronounced decay in the center. Maintenance of infrastructure might play an important role but reduction in tax income of the center city is likely to prevail and thus might jeopardize much needed improvements in the center. Taxation incentives might be a more effective way of handling metropolitan development rather than traditional zoning and building control.

The informal sector economy will, in most Asian cities, continue to play an important role, although the long–term effects of rapidly growing formal economies on the informal sector cannot yet be anticipated.

In this light of continued rapid urbanization, various avenues of further studies should be pursued to better understand:

the urban decay process and ways to arrest decay

423

the change of human values in the course of time and where the adaptation to lower standards will lead

the complex behavior of cities, the forces at work, and sensitive parameters

the future of the informal sector in the Asian metropolis and how cities should be prepared to cater for typical Asian needs

But above all, the Asian metropolis will continue to be a hub of human activities and an almost endless source for innovation.

Bibliography

Escap, Yokohama June, 1982. "Physical Profile of Cities in the ESCAP region." *Habitat*. Yokohama.

Berry, B.J.L. 1973. *The Human Consequences of Urbanization*. London: Macmillan Press.

Wyss, P.A. 1979. "Ueber das hartnaeckige Verhalten der Staedte" (About the Stubborn Behavior of Cities) in Walter Custer. *Festschrift*. Zurich.

Friedrichs, J. 1977. *Stadtanalyse*. Hamburg: Rohwolt.

Wyss, P.A. 1979. *Staedtebau der Kolonialzeit* (Urbanization of the Colonial Area). Zurich: ETH.

Desai, A.R. and Pillai, S.E. 1972. *A Profile of an Indian Slum*. Bombay.

Ramachandran, P. and Pillai, S.E. 1971(?). *The Bombay Rent Act and Housing Production*. Bombay.

29.

Three Asian Metropoli: Hong Kong, Singapore and Beijing

Tao Ho

Introduction

Urbanization is one of the most complex problems facing humanity. So far we are fighting a losing battle. This is due mainly to our failure to comprehend the dynamic and multi-dimensional nature of the problem. Many planners, architects, urban-sociologists, urban-geographers and urban-economists are still dealing with urban problems as if they were isolated, static phenomena. It is quite clear by now that there is no ideal, universal solution to urban problems, and that all large cities face similar crises. As Dr. Peter Wyss pointed out in the preceeding chapter: no matter what we do, it seems impossible to stop the growth of population, to prevent the influx of people to and from the city, to provide adequate services and housing, or to limit the size of the city.

These are indeed unsolvable problems if they are viewed as evils which must be controlled or overcome. But, if we recognize that these problems reflect or embody the inherent dynamic forces of cities, they can become positive factors in the shaping of the ever-changing metropolis, if used sensitively. The first approach is similar to applying the static laws of Newtonian physics to understand the dynamic behavior of sub-atomic particles; in the second approach, the new theories of relativity, quantum mechanics and high energy physics are consulted.

As Dr. Wyss points out in his paper, some of Asia's urban problems are, in fact, indigenous. Culture and traditions are important factors in the shaping of Asian communities, and to most Westerners (other than Dr. Wyss), the Asian sense of community appears to be a negative force. As Dr. Wyss understands, this Asian mentality is negative only if it is not accepted as a positive force. There are certainly differences between Asian and Western cities; these differences make the problems of Asian urbanization much more fascinating.

In my opinion, both Singapore and Hong Kong represent the Asian mentality working at its best, for better or worse, which can serve as an inspiration and guideline for other Asian cities. In 1960, Hong Kong and Singapore were under-developed, like most other Asian cities. Today, both cities have become major, highly developed and prosperous urban centers in Asia. The success stories of these twin cities result from the interaction of two vital forces: 1) a strong government policy, and 2) the hard-working nature and ingenuity of the people. In comparing Hong Kong and Singapore, the first force is somewhat different, while the second force is more or less similar.

Hong Kong

Population: 5.4 million
Land area: 1,062 square kilometers (106,200 hectares)

In Hong Kong, the government adopts a *laissez-faire* policy of non-intervention for private enterprise and also provides adequate and efficient public services, such as a transportation network, housing, maintenance and general education. Things work out and get done in Hong Kong. Although it is a British colony, there is a strong sense of identity and belonging among its 5.4 million people. In addition, the uncertainty about the future has become part of the mental condition of the residents since 1949 when the communists took over Mainland China. Both the private sector and the government practice a short-term planning policy in which quick profit and quick results dominate the decision-making process. Such an attitude, extremely versatile in all its manifestations, has created unprecedented rapid urban growth, both in physical form and economic structure. As a result, the even and continuous urban physical fabric of the homogeneous old Hong Kong has been destroyed and replaced by uneven and discontinuous, individual, isolated developments, mostly of poor design. Quantity and profit of investment are the measures of success, in which quality has virtually no place. In essence, Hong Kong has become a casino wherein the majority cares for nothing other than making money. Like all casinos, Hong Kong is an exciting place: the city is full of life. Perhaps also because of this richness of life within a well-managed, semi-controlled, self-contained environment, urban problems such as population growth and the influx of immigrants are not regarded as grave crises that cause social unrest in other South-East Asian cities.

Hong Kong has survived many crises in the past. However, the most serious will arise in 1997 when China will regain sovereignty of Hong Kong. The dream of the casino has ended. Many money-making schemes have come to a grinding halt. No one can tell what Hong Kong will be like as 1997 approaches, or thereafter. One thing, quite apparent, is that for those who have confidence in Hong Kong it has become a cheaper place to live than before. The story of Hong Kong reflects a condition created both by the government's semi-controlled policy and the versatility of the Asian mentality in which unique and dynamic patterns of urbanization take place.

Fig. 29-1: Central Hongkong. (Victoria Island, Courtesy: Tao Ho)

Singapore

Population: 2.5 million
Land Area: 618 square kilometers (61,800 hectares)

In 1984, Singapore celebrated its 25th year as an independent nation. The City State is about half the size of Hong Kong both in terms of land area and population.

Although both cities have strong economies and predominantly Chinese populations, there are fundamental differences to their success. The basic difference is, of course, that Singapore is a nation while Hong Kong is a colony. Among the Singaporeans there is a sense of community, of pride and of belonging, while selfish individualism prevails among the Hong Kong people. To the Singaporeans, the City-State is the place to build their homes, and the government's policies in public housing and in private development reinforce such attitudes. The ultimate objective of the interaction of government and the private sector in Singapore is for the common good.

The government exercises strong control over private development and promotes a very well-planned public housing program. For example, the government has the power to expropriate private land to suit its Master Plan. From time to time the government releases seized land or other publicly owned land for private development by tender. The design merit of the submitted scheme is an important criterion in awarding the contract. This policy has encouraged developers to hire quality architects. During recent years, many foreign "superstar" architects have obtained important commissions. This phenomenon has also created some undesirable effects. Occasionally these ambitious and "spectacular" proposals lack an understanding of local conditions and are both inappropriate and uneconomical. Furthermore, the invasion of foreign architects upsets the local practices and creates an unhealthy myth of foreign supremacy. Due to the insular nature of individual large-scale private developments, the flow of pedestrian movement from one large project to another is discontinuous, unlike in Hong Kong where an attempt has been made to create an inter-connected elevated pedestrianway system. (See Chapter 33 by Ian Brown in this volume.) The physical pattern of Singapore has also been noticeably disturbed by the change from a horizontal skyline to a vertical one.

On the other hand, public housing in Singapore can be rated as one of the most thoughtful in the world. It houses more than 76% of the population, most of whom own their homes. After almost 25 years, the government's public housing program has successfully achieved the quantitative objective of housing more than two-thirds of its population. Now the policy aims to upgrade the qualitative aspects of the housing stock. Within a well-planned policy, there are rules and regulations, environment support, services and enforcement support to ensure the quality of the housing estates. An incentive re-sale scheme also provides for family mobility in different stages, while retaining the traditional values of the family structure—a total integration of cultural, social and physical community planning.

The success of Singapore is based on a policy of strong control over private development within which private enterprises can make a reasonable return on investment but can never profit from speculation and greed as in Hong Kong. In the housing sector, Singapore makes private development almost impossible, except for luxury housing. The merit of this policy is that the majority is happily settled, which makes for a stable and productive society.

Both Hong Kong and Singapore are City-States of small size, relatively controllable population influx, capable governments and versatile people. These are perhaps the key factors in their success as workable, dynamic metropoli. Most cities in Asia, other than those in China, have been "modernized" with varying degrees of success. It will be interesting to watch how the major Chinese metropoli respond to the problems of China's new and determined modernization program. Certainly China can learn from the many planning and design theories, approaches and experiences of the Western metropoli and even more from the examples of Hong Kong and Singapore.

Beijing

Population: 9.3 million
Land area: 16,800 km. square (1,680,000 hectares)

Surprisingly, some of the factors shaping Beijing's development are similar to those of Hong Kong and Singapore. For example, Beijing has a strong government which can control practically every aspect of urban development including population influx. But so far, Beijing is not nearly as dynamic and lively a city as Hong Kong or Singapore although the present modernization program is already showing considerable impact.

Several major Chinese cities, including Beijing, are currently open to private enterprise development and encourage foreign investment. Economic gain is the first priority in all development projects. This can be good and bad at the same time. It is good because it helps to create more business activities in the city and thus enlivens and modernizes the lifestyle. It is bad because many indigenous qualities (especially those in the ancient core of Beijing) will be destroyed by unsympathetic and unscrupulous development schemes.

At the moment, China is very eager to transform itself from an under-developed country into a modern nation. Many decision-making officials have fixed on the idea that a modern Chinese city must feature tall, glassy, fashionable modern buildings, regardless of whether such buildings are appropriate.

Since zoning laws and building regulations in Beijing are in their embyonic stage, they can not effectively control the fast pace of new developments. So far, fortunately, new development has been confined to the outer city periphery. But the pressure to develop the inner city is mounting. Without a careful evaluation of these problems and quickly formulated, strong and imaginative zoning laws and building controls, Beijing—once the jewel of the Orient—will soon become a "Disneyland" of Western architectural styles.

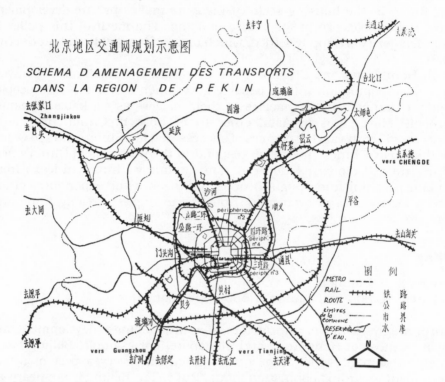

Fig. 29-2: Map of the transportation network of the Beijing region.

Today in Beijing, officials, developers and architects often debate the merit of high-rise or low-rise development. The main problem is that Beijing is a horizontal city covering a large area with very wide roads, and it lacks urbanity and human scale. What makes the streets of Beijing pleasant are not the buildings but the beautiful trees along the sidewalks. It is surprising to note that there is only one short main shopping street—Wongfujing —in all of Beijing, located in the inner city in proximity of the Palace. This is the only city street filled with lively activities and people, and it is of human scale. But how can Beijing become a dynamic, modern Asian metropolis with only one short stretch of business street?

What Beijing needs in its modernization development program is the creation of a series of mixed-use subcenters, strategically planned, through-out the city. Within each subcenter there should be a variety of elements and functions designed for the interaction of people and commercial activities on the pedestrian level. The relatively more passive functions such as offices and central housing can be accommodated above the pedestrian

Fig. 29-3: Beijing Land-Use Plan. (Municipal Planning Department, Beijing)

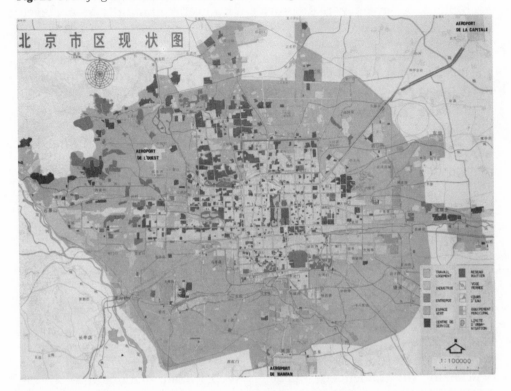

levels in the tall buildings. Some towers of landmark character can be permitted to mark the subcenters—not unlike the ancient pagodas—to set visual accents and to help orientation. The incremental development of such well-planned, self-contained subcenters will act as magnets in attracting lively action. This approach—if planned and implemented properly —could save Beijing from the redevelopment by destruction which has proved so counter-productive and unmanageable in other Asian cities.

Another important consideration in developing large-scale complexes in Beijing is the need to incorporate growth and demand into the planning and design policy to make the scheme economically viable at various stages of development. This, however, does not mean discontinuous development by completing only one or two blocks in a ten-block development scheme. The alternate approach would be to create a network of adaptable building types with a mixture of active functions (commercial and recreational) and passive functions (residential, office and institutional). The former are to be located on the lower pedestrian levels (sidewalk, subway and mezzanine levels) and the latter above. Such a system of building network should be planned to encompass the entire central area. The architectural design of the network, consisting of a flexible system of supporting services, should be capable of developing horizontally and vertically in various phases in a flexible and adaptable manner to meet the market demand. However, this system must be designed to allow a balance of active and passive spaces at each phase of development to provide for a lively community at any given phase.

When it comes to more detailed environmental and architectural design, indigenous factors such as the hot and cold contrast of the Beijing climate, the lifestyle of the residents and their movement patterns, and the traditional spatial sequences of formal and informal courtyards, should be emulated. A strong but adaptable architectural network system allows for traditional cultural values to flourish within a semi-controlled environment even in a modern context. Such an approach fosters a modernization based on Asian cultural roots. A city like Beijing, with its political system, is entirely capable of achieving such a goal while pursuing economic objectives. Otherwise, indiscriminate use of foreign building technologies will soon destroy the unique character of Beijing, turning it into just another international city, indistinguishable from similar size places elsewhere.

In the 1970s, China introduced a new economic plan called the Agricultural Responsibility System to the farmers who represent 80% of the Chinese population. Under this new plan, it gives the farmers, for the first time in recent history, an incentive scheme to make a profit for themselves. The plan is so successful that many farmers in China have become quite wealthy. They can afford to build houses equipped with such modern luxuries as washing machines, TV's and video recorders. Some farming communities even started to build hotels and to launch various commercial ventures. Rural China is rapidly changing.

Realizing the tremendous impact of such transformations, the central government responded to such rapid change with a permissive policy. In 1982, the government set up a Rural Development Unit to deal with the problems of the countryside. The previous commune system has been abandoned. Three objectives have been set for the new program:

1. To provide advice for a sensible layout of rural buildings

2. To provide information on an economic use of rural land

3. To provide technical assistance in the layout of rural communities

The ultimate aim is to prevent uncontrolled development. In fact, the program helps to stabilize the rural population and reduce migration to the metropolitan areas. As long as the farmers find their rural life satisfactory and profitable, there is no reason for them to want to migrate to the cities. If the program proves to be successful, Chinese metropoli like Beijing will be relieved from the population pressure due to in-migration while the natural increase of the resident population will already have been reduced by stern birth-control legislation. The population of the metropolis will be largely stabilized. This lesson indicates that a strong and enforceable national economic policy with incentives to raise the income of the rural population can tackle the problem of internal migration and result in the reduction of inequities between the city and the country.

Summary

In conclusion, each Asian metropolis faces a different future. Both Singapore and Hong Kong have already established an urban identity which will most likely not change dramatically. The growth of Asian metropoli, other than those of China, will depend a great deal upon the ability of local governments to effectively implement planning policies and upon the attitudes and integrity of the developers. The fate of the metropolis in China will be fascinating to observe in the coming years. Included in the main issues are those presented here:

1. A strong government policy and control in a city is essential. Such policy and control must be handled by capable hands, sensitively allowing a certain degree of flexibility to meet people's needs and the development of indigenous lifestyles.

2. The success of a city greatly depends upon the keen participation and involvement of its people. The ingenuity, versatility and hard-working nature of the people play an important role in creating liveliness in the city. Citizens must have a sense of pride and belonging. As Dr. Wyss emphasizes, the dynamic life force of the informal sector should be recognized as a positive factor in the shaping of the Asian city.

3. Asian metropoli are facing a foreign architectural invasion. Preservation of heritage and modernization must be carefully implemented and balanced. If balance is not achieved, Asian metropoli will soon lose their character.

4. The characteristics and quality of a city form rest upon *those who have the final say*—either the government or the powerful developers. Especially in Asia, it is almost impossible for architects and planners to shape the form and content of today's metropolis due to the stronger political and economic forces. The impact of economic forces grows ever stronger. Architects and planners must work hard to introduce good design and inspiring ideas in their individual projects, and then hope that these principles will influence the overall picture in the future metropolis.

5. Both designers and policy-makers must consider the multidimensional nature of urban problems in an integrated manner to achieve a richer, more dynamic result. A dynamic city features an order within which chaos is permitted—an orderly chaos.

6. For the Asian metropolis, it is not a question of high-rise versus low-rise development. It is a problem of how to design an inspiring environment which incorporates human scale

activities, a viable economy, climate, political factors and indigenous lifestyles into a unique architectural and planning synthesis.

30.
The South-East Asian Metropolis: A Viewpoint from Bangkok

Sumet Jumsai

In Chapter 28, Dr. Wyss has left his conclusions open-ended, staying clear of defining future directions and trends for the Asian metropolis. Yet if one were to read between the lines, they are there: all the existing urban problems will continue well into a foreseeable future—in-migration, failure of municipalization and the inability of national governments to even follow events, with the informal sector with its unplanned urban structure and housing becoming predominant in Asian cities of the future.

The above, however, is not entirely a negative picture. Dr. Wyss' paper points out that the phenomenon is, in fact, indigenous and an expression of the Asian sense for community and family ties which is absent in the urban West.

People who deal with macro—statistics at the United Nations and other world organizations will continue to produce staggering figures of the urban poor and the slum population in Asian cities. The purpose, besides telling the truth, is, to a large degree, to shock donor countries into giving more money to the international organizations concerned and to shock governments at the receiving end into some sort of action usually relative to the world bodies' own thinking and terms of reference.

The influence that world aid or loan agencies have on poor countries is obvious, and it is just as well to look into the agencies' thinking on matters of development strategy especially as it affects urban programs.

In the past decade or more, a new attitude towards economic development in general has taken shape, for economics has, for the first time, taken morality into account. Whereas before grant and loan projects were based on cost-benefit and return rates, the terms of reference now ask for social and environmental components. Excellent rural programs have since been carried out and slum upgrading and self-help projects have taken root in many developing countries.

This is not to say that all the projects associated with international agencies automatically include social and environmental components.

435

These are still very much wanting in many cases. When a world body makes a loan to a government, for example to expand port facilities, it might still ignore the overall impact the program has on urban decentralization, the logistics of infrastructures and the thousands of slum families facing eviction in the area. Simply stated, many such programs are still sectorial and lack comprehensiveness, causing unnecessary suffering and other negative effects.

The moral side in economic development, while producing good work, has its pitfalls. It has, on occasion, become dogmatic. For example, urban investment in mass transit (to take up Dr. Wyss' complaint) is not encouraged, while anything "soft" is insisted upon: improvement of traffic management, more one-way streets, more computerized traffic lights, more bus-lanes, etc., even if such improvements have only a minimal impact.

Perhaps all this is due to an inverted compassion for the poor, which means that if you are poor, "high-tech" is out and you are required to conform to a certain image.

This dogmatic attitude seeps down to the national governments yet, at the same time, other equally capital-intensive urban programs are implemented.

On the whole, however, planners at the national level do not know how to face the scenario of the urban poor swamping their cities. The shock effect has succeeded. But the dilemma is also due to the planners' rigid training in economics so that everything is costed in terms of hard cash which has to be accountable in the national balance sheet.

Accommodating the urban poor is therefore seen as a huge investment which no one can afford. (The odd thing in this case is that when roads are paved and pipes put in well-to-do areas of the city, they are routine expenditure and not "investment," but when miserable walkways and meager infrastructures are put in slum areas they become "investment" so that what money goes in must come out complete with interest!)

Then there are other attitudes, more blatant, toward the urban poor ranging from "we must not encourage in-migration by improving the lot of the slum dwellers" or "we must ignore the city and go to the root of in-migration by diverting all the funds to the countryside" to simply delegating any concept of slum upgrading to "creating permanent slums" in the city, a term which has a clear disdain attached to it.

To remedy such warps in the mental attitude—a pre-requisite to solving the slum problem—international agencies might start by presenting facts and figures without the shock element, that is to say, without evangelical zeal. Instead the slum problem must be presented with its positive aspects, and Dr. Wyss' paper lists a number of them.

Acceptance of and coming to terms with the urban poor, hence the informal sector of the Asian metropolis, means the beginning of a real and long-term solution. However, the solution will be different from that of the past, for the urban poor must be looked at as an indispensable economic component of the Asian city. Up-graded slums will no longer be depressed and despised, but recognized as assets in terms of their potentially beautiful indigenous character. All this can be and must be part of the future Asian metropolis standing side by side with the indispensable modern and efficient urban transportation and infrastructural networks.

Proposals for a Polycentric Structure for Bangkok[1]

In relative terms, Bangkok has two zones, one negative, the other positive.

In negative, I include areas that are already built up, congested and expensive, where utilities and traffic improvement schemes can only be realized at tremendous costs apart from continually causing disruptions, pollution, and environmental damage.

By positive, I mean areas that are relatively undeveloped or unused, and yet well within the overall urban orbit. These areas are left in between the ribbon development which follows traffic corridors, behind facades of shop-houses. Because of inaccessibility, they are relatively cheap.

It is the tendency of technocrats and bureaucrats to focus their attention on the negative zone, i.e., to tackle only problems, thus narrowing their views and confining themselves to unnecessary limitations.

To avoid endless and, in the end, useless investment in the expansion of urban infrastructures, problem areas or the negative zone should be left, if you like, as a dis-incentive zone with no more maintenance budget than it now receives. Meanwhile, the non-problem areas or alternatives in the positive zone should be looked at and properly developed so that pressure can eventually be relieved from the negative zone. When this is done, urban redevelopment and resettlement programs will become meaningful.

Looking at the existing conglomeration of the capital city one notices the finger-line pattern of urbanization, each "finger" radiating from the central area along the great radial traffic corridors of the north, east, southeast and southwest, leaving great tracks or pockets of undeveloped land in between.

The official master plan for Bangkok, "spreading over" these empty pockets and much more massively scaled, follows much the same mono-centric pattern. In this case the center is surrounded by concentric rings of decreasing densities all of which are served by the corresponding ring and radial roads. The tool for the implementation of this monocentric plan is the Town Planning Act of 1974 which has the effect of "freezing" everything for the target year of 1990, while its accompanying legislation is geared to the thesis (or antithesis?) of development through a predetermined pattern of control rather than through trends and opportunities.

A polycentric plan seems to be the answer. Instead of expanding the existing central area, other self-contained centers are to be developed. In this scheme, each center or "node" is a complete town in itself. It can also be regarded as a job center and identified in terms of predominant employment or function. In terms of facilities and utilities each is a complete system, and for drainage and flood control each is a complete polder unit. A green belt or agricultural land can circumvent and define it.

These nodes can be linked together and to the old center. To avoid traffic corridors running through them, and to avoid the strip development along the roads, they should be located in between.

What is theoretical in Figure 1 can now be applied to the actual conglomeration of Bangkok (Figure 2). Using only the positive zone and existing road network and also using the government mass housing program to act as catalysts, the following nodes can be first implemented: Node 1—Klong Toey—for export processing and as a port; Node 2—behind Petchburi Extension—for the commercial-business-service industry; Node 3—Paholyothin Superhighway—as a transportation center.

It should be noted that Node 1 will, in effect, be a town within the town. Its development priority, in spite of site constraints, is of prime importance politically since it has become a world renowned slum. Node 2 is an obvious downtown real estate property which, because of inaccessibility, remains relatively undeveloped. Node 3 is an empty government land flanked by important rail networks and a major bus terminal both of which, if coordinated, expanded and integrated into a nodal development, would become a very exciting project.

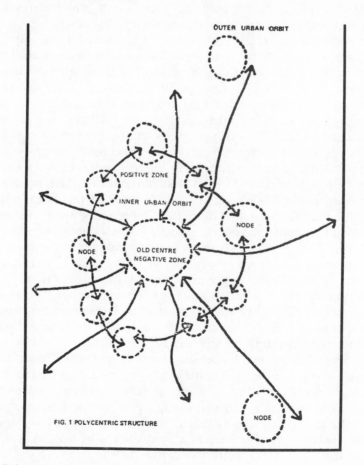

Fig. 30-1: Polycentric structure for Bangkok. (Jumsai)

Fig. 30-2: Polycentric development plan. (Jumsai)

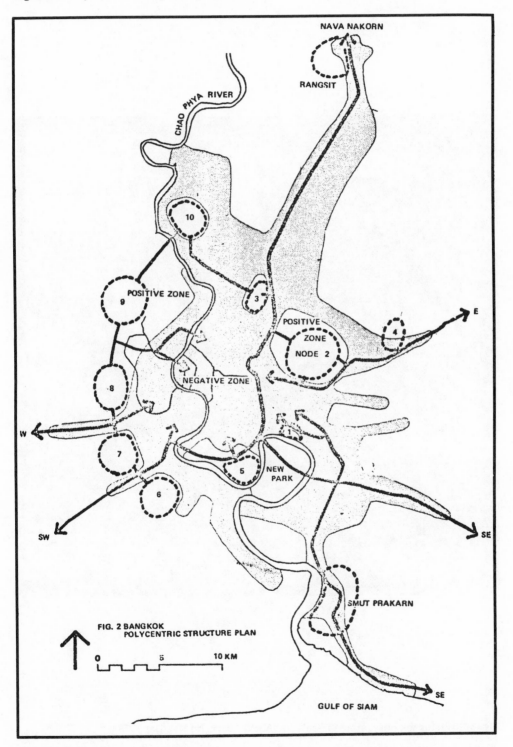

FIG. 2 BANGKOK
POLYCENTRIC STRUCTURE PLAN

0   5   10 KM

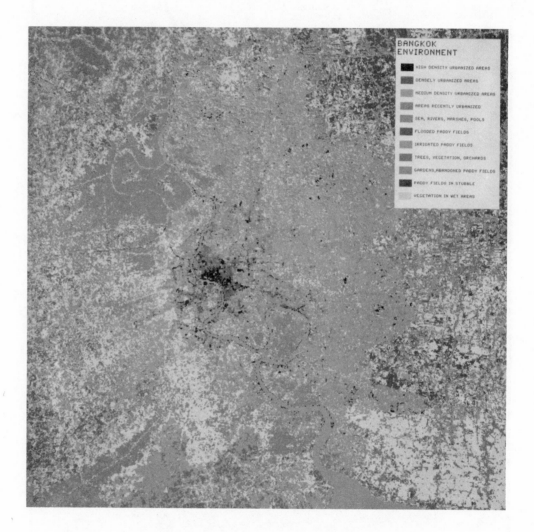

Fig. 30-3: Bangkok environment. (Cahiers IAURIF, Paris No. 74, Dec. 1984)

Fig. 30-4: Urbanization in the Bangkok Central Region, Thai University Research Associates Bangkok.

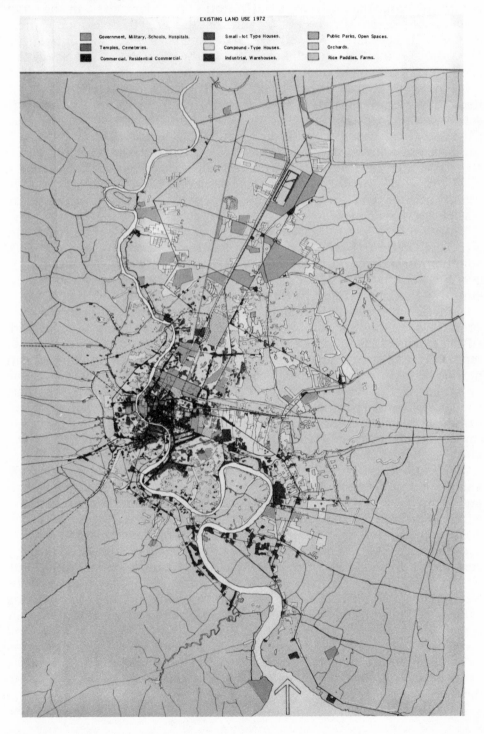

EXISTING LAND USE 1972

Government, Military, Schools, Hospitals.

Temples, Cemeteries.

Commercial, Residential Commercial.

Small - lot Type Houses.

Compound - Type Houses.

Industrial, Warehouses.

Public Parks, Open Spaces.

Orchards.

Rice Paddies, Farms.

Nodes 4, 5 and 6 can be developed two years later, followed by Nodes 7, 8, 9 and 10 after another two years. More such centers will have to be built within the immediate urban orbit while others will have to be in the outer urban orbit, preferably coinciding with natural growth poles, job centers and industrial estates. A total of 20 to 30 nodes with a population of 100,000 to 200,000 each will be needed in the next 15 years if Bangkok's projected population of nine million is to be met.

It should be noted at this point that the idea of satellites and New Towns is itself overtaken by events. In the face of a tremendous urbanization rate, satellites and New Towns will be absorbed into the overall urban region whose structure can be a uniformly distributed chaos or a definite system. If the process is anticipated and the concept is geared to the polycentric structure, then satellites and other towns within the Bangkok urban region can become integrated and interrelated as nodes. In this way, allocation of infrastructures and inter-communication networks can be much more efficient in the long run.

While building resources are rechanneled to create a more rational urban structure, decentralization of the capital must also be assumed. With administrative decentralization and with the help of other planning methods, it is conceivable that the rate of immigration can be leveled off and, in fact, substantially reduced in the next 10-15 years.

In the initial stages of the nodal development, existing traffic corridors are adequate as preliminary link-ups. Later, the system will have to be upgraded and extended. As the whole strategy is laid out, many of the expressways, rapid transits, bridges and other costly items that are being planned can now be seen to be unrelated, wasteful or secondary to other more strategic link-ups. Also, as self-contained centers emerge, the pattern of public transportation will become inter-node and node-to-old center, thus rationalizing the cost benefit of public transportation. Most importantly, private cars and traffic in general would be somewhat "frozen" as the place of living and the place of work now coincide.

Inherent in this urban development strategy is the speed of programming and flexibility. Indeed, the whole planning process is based on diagrams and approximate nodal location in contrast to the conventional master plan which is detailed, time-consuming, fixed and always overtaken by events.

For implementation and management, a new approach is also needed. In conventional urban development programs, land is expropriated at great cost and conflict, often involving lengthy legal procedures which would "kill off" any project from its inception. Here it is proposed that landowners be induced to convert properties into equities at double or triple their existing value if necessary, and to join in with the overall development of the new center. Once access roads and other infrastructures are put in, the land value will automatically increase several fold. In this way everyone is satisfied and everyone gains, the landowners, the development agency, the developers, the banks, etc., without the government having to spend money.

The development agency which should be set up for each node should be in the form of a government corporation, say the Urban Development Corporation (UDC). This is to provide a framework with which all government planning agencies, autonomy-conscious as they are, can come and work together and with the private sector. Later, UDC can become "public" and run as a normal public corporation with a minimum of government subsidy and tutelage.

The UDC area must induce quick development with incentives other than having good location, good planning and proper infrastructures. These can be in the form of tax incentives and exemption from tedious building bylaws to cater for new design concepts and building technology. UDC must be business-oriented. It must function as if it were a real estate developer itself, and it must make money. In this way the non-moneymaking elements such as public parks and low income housing can be costed in, with the result that the total sum is still profit, and the program does not have to depend on or wait for government budget allocation.

Other advantages of this strategy are that it can be implemented almost piece-meal or node by node, and that each project represents an operation which is for the first time manageable and definitive in the time frame. Of course, politically, such a nodal development immediately becomes a visible and exciting investment program.

In spite of what is said above, urban decentralization is still necessary. Bangkok (with a population approaching six million, including the surrounding conglomerations) is probably an extreme case of primate-city domination of the urban system: it is 25 times bigger than the next largest city, Chiang Mai, and almost 300 times bigger than the average municipality in the country.

Decentralization

Failure of decentralization is due, in part, to planners' concentration on physical (infrastructural and industrial) and financial aspects. In the latter case, a vast amount of funds is diverted to the countryside only to find that the banking system is such that it absorbs the money back into the capital city and more. The fact is that decentralization is really an issue outside the planner's jurisdiction. Decentralization clearly begins with the nation's power base which must be first decentralized. Money then follows power and the rest follows money.

Because of the hinterland problem that most developing countries face, Hong Kong and Singapore cannot be considered for urban comparisons. Yet this is precisely the dilemma, for both Hong Kong and Singapore are fashionable yardsticks to politicians, bankers and developers in the region so that among them there is a keen sense of competition. If Singapore can build a 70-story building, so can Kuala Lumpur. Meanwhile, Bangkok, Manila and Jakarta are nursing similar aspirations.

Future cities in this region will no doubt try to outdo or at least partially follow one another, and flashy highrises will fill their skylines. But below the skyline and behind the high rises there will be hovels, that is, if reason cannot prevail.

Note

1. This part of the paper is based on a series of articles written by the author for the Bangkok Post, notably "Polycentric Plan - The Answer to the City's Problem" (July 29, 1975) and "The Proposed Town and Country Planning Association. Towards Urban Dynamics or Standstill?" (November 17, 1974).

31.

Metropolitan Planning as an Instrument of Social Stability in South-East Asia

Ervin Y. Galantay

During the next decade the nations comprising the East Asia and Pacific region will have to adapt to a reduced capability in providing for their growing populations and in keeping up with rising expectations.

According to projections by the World Bank, the number of people living in absolute poverty will increase dramatically during the next decade, rising from 8 to 12 percent of the total population in the area's more-developed countries, and from 17 to 26 percent in the less-developed countries.

In terms of Marxist theory, such trends—or the failure to bridge the gap between housing demand and supply—are proof of the inherent "contradictions" of the market economy. As Neil Albert Salonen points out in his Ideology and Foreign Policy, such "contradictions generate harnessable resentment which can be intensified and exploited by extremist agitation to foment revolutionary upheaval."

The excessively rapid rate of urbanization is another phenomenon that creates inequities resulting in "harnessable resentment." Cultural conflicts arise, due to overly rapid change, not permitting the internalization of an achievement-oriented value structure necessary for an industrial society. This type of conflict was undoubtedly one of the main causes of the Iranian revolution.

Social stability is an essential condition for harmonious development in countries with rapidly rising populations. The threat to the internal stability of some of the key countries of the region is the real problem of the next decade.

It would be an illusion to believe that any of the region's nations can remain unaffected and pursue an isolated development. Political and social instability in Thailand, Indonesia or the Philippines would inevitably have grave repercussions on the economy and security of the industrially advanced nations such as Japan, Korea, Mainland China, Hong Kong and Singapore.

In the following, I shall examine to what extent farsighted settlement planning and an equitable housing policy can contribute to social stability and indirectly to area security. Further, I shall attempt to provide some insights and formulate policy recommendations toward the definition of shared goals for the region.

Recent information points to a remarkable drop in birth rates in all countries of the East Asian and Pacific area. For example, Indonesia's 10-year Family Program has brought down the average family size from six to just over four, while East Java and Bali have witnessed a dramatic decline of fertility to 1.2 percent. However, with so many young women entering child-bearing age, Indonesia's population increase is still 2.2 percent, while that of the Philippines is 3 percent and of Thailand 3.2 percent.

Thus, the increase of the population in numerical terms continues to present a tremendous challenge: it suffices to recall that in the next 20 years, Thailand is going to add 28 million more people to its population, the Philippines 26 million, and Indonesia 75 million—bringing the total population of these areas to 226 million by the year 2000, as compared to an estimated 133 million for Japan. (See Table 1.)

Table 1

Comparison of population growth in selected Asian Nations

Country	Total population in 1975 (in millions)	Estimated population in 2000	Increase by millions %
Thailand	42	75	33
Indonesia	135	226	91
Philippines	43	73	30
Japan	122	133	21
Rep. of Korea	37	57	20
Mainland China	935	1329	394
USSR	214	248	55

The problem is that a yearly increase of three percent in Gross National Product is necessary to absorb the dependency burden resulting from a one percent population growth. While this is well within the economic performance of the area's advanced industrial countries which have brought their population growth rate below the two percent threshold, the less-developed countries of the area have to face mounting difficulties.

For example, in 1972-1973 the Philippines enjoyed a 10 percent increase of the GNP which was sufficient to absorb a population growth of 3.1 percent. Since then, GNP growth in real terms has been reduced to six percent which is inadequate for the closing of the gap between housing demand and supply.

However, even a sustained rate of rapid economic growth does not by itself lead to a substantial improvement in housing conditions: of this Japan is a prime example.

The very uneven concentration of the population in preferred regions creates special problems. Sixty-five percent of the population of Indonesia on Java and Bali is occupying only seven percent of the nation's land area. The Suharto government very sensibly calls for "transmigration" of half a million families from congested Java to the unexploited virgin spaces of Sumatra, Kalimantan, Sulawesi and West Irian. This is a farsighted program which enjoys the support of the World Bank, the Asian Development Bank and the IDA and, once the initial management shortcomings are ironed out, it should be of great benefit to national development. Similarly, the decongestion of the overcrowded Tokaido area in Japan by "transmigration" to Hokkaido should be seriously envisaged by the Japanese government.

Excessive spatial concentration of the population also occurs through the process of urbanization. In 1970-1975, population growth for the entire region was 2.6 percent, while the growth rate of the urban areas was approximately 5.3 percent. At this rate, the urban population doubles every 15 years.

Much of this increase is concentrated in the largest cities, e.g., Metro Manila nearly doubled its population in 10 years, growing from 2.7 million in 1960 to 4.4 million in 1970 and is likely to have a population of 14.7 million by the year 2000. Bandung with an annual growth rate of 14.1 percent (1961-1970) is the fastest growing metropolis in the world. Seoul has more than tripled its population in 20 years, growing from 2.5 million in 1960 to about nine million in 1980 and is now the tenth largest city of the world.

Even more problematic than their absolute size is the dominance exerted by some of these primate cities within the national urban system and with respect to total populations. Bangkok is 30 times the size of the second largest city, Chiangmai; Manila concentrates about 10 percent of the national population and Seoul has one-fourth of the population of South Korea.

However, giant cities can also rise in the absence of marked primacy. For example, the four largest Indian cities only account for 3.5 percent of the national population, and Jakarta with over seven million inhabitants contains only five percent of the Indonesian population.

Reducing migration to these cities would not in itself stop their growth of which one-half to two-thirds can be attributed to natural increase. Without further migration, but with a natural growth rate of two percent, cities double their population within 35 years.

In the context of the developing countries, a recent study by Koito Mera (1973) reveals an apparent correlation between increasing primacy and aggregate growth performance. This encouraged Richardson in 1977 to argue that the primate cities of the less-developed countries "offer a higher return on investment than alternate locations" and other authors to claim that in the Third World, cities as large as five to six million are essential for innovation diffusion and the formation of an efficient urban hierarchy.

However, even these apologists of the big size must admit that agglomeration economies decay with distance and thus higher order functions cannot be supplied efficiently from a primate city to a nation as large as Thailand or the Philippines.

Manifestly, there exist economies of urban concentration, but beyond a certain size the costs of centralization are likely to increase more rapidly than the benefits.

Very large cities also generate "negative social benefits" or "negative externalities" such as pollution, long journeys to work and public sector inefficiency. Higher wages paid do not translate into higher welfare and more, indeed, represent compensation for the stress created by noise, congestion, pollution and crime.

Apart from dominance, another ominous aspect of the Third World's giant cities is their vast extension which results in spatial segregation and the emergence of large homogeneous areas. In many Asian cities, one-fifth to one-third of the population is crowded into central city slums or peripheral squatter settlements containing hundreds of thousands of "marginal" people in a degrading and increasingly dense environment. (See Table 2.)

Since national economies cannot possibly cope with the infrastructure needs of city populations doubling every 10 or 15 years, further degradation of living conditions by a process of "cumulative causation" has to be faced.

While Singapore and Hong Kong are able to provide piped water serving almost their entire population, 67 percent of the residents in Bangkok's Klong Toey area are reduced to buying water from vendors at exorbitant rates.

"In Jakarta, the water distribution system deteriorated to such an extent that some officials contend an increase in pressure would only increase leakage rather than supply." Approximately 40 percent of the households depend on water vendors for their supply at prices five times those of piped water. In Bandung, 66.4 percent of the population depends on open wells and streams for its water supply.

Manila's sewerage system was built in 1909 with a maximum design capacity of 440,000 people. By 1969, the system served only 12 percent of the population. Worse yet is the case of Jakarta: in 1975, the World Bank estimated that, of a total population of 5.5 million, 69 percent or 3.8 million were living in "minimum standard" inner city slums or semi-rural kampongs on the periphery. Yet Jakarta has no waterborne sewer system.

Even households having piped water flush their wastes into septic tanks, or more frequently, into open ditches along the roadside. Much of the population has no alternative to using the drainage canals for bathing, laundering and defecation. Most of the city's uncollected garbage ends up in canals . . . where it clogs drainage and causes extensive flooding during the rainy season. Flood waters seep the raw sewage and garbage out of the ditches and canals back into the kampongs. In the dry season wastes decay in exposed areas and pose a serious health problem.

Just as there is a limit to the amount of organic matter that can be

Table 2

Population growth rate and slum and squatter population in selected Asian cities

City metro area	Year	Population	Growth rate	As % of total urban population	Slum/squatter population
Bangkok/Thonbull	1970	3,051,000	6.68	67.00(1970)	600,000('70)
	1976	4,496,000			('76)
Kuala Lumpur	1961	400,000	6.93	30.97(1971)	('68)
	1971	782,000			('73)
Singapore	1970	2,300,000	1.60	100.00	345,000('72)
Jakarta	1960	2,900,000			
	1970	4,778,840	5.12	27.05(1971)	1,144,000('72)
	Est. 1985	7,700,000			
Manila	1960	2,119,000			
	1970	3,159,429	4.10	27.00	1,216,000('72)
	Est. 2000	14,500,000			
Hong Kong	1971	3,936,000	1.90	90.00	326,000
Taipei	1970	1,769,568	2.92	19.85(1975)	('66)
	1975	2,043,318			
Seoul	1960	2,500,000			
	1970	5,525,000	9.47	51.63(1975)	1,450,000('69)
	1975	8,634,000			

decomposed by natural processes within a given area, there is also a limit to the amount of carbon dioxide that can be discharged into the air. Air pollution is a classic example of external diseconomy associated with city size: the volume of pollutants varies directly in function of population size and density.

In very large cities such as Osaka, Seoul or Bangkok, temperature inversion combines with components of automotive exhaust in the presence of sunlight to create a toxic photochemical smog which blocks photosynthesis and kills plants. Seoul, with an area of 630 square kilometers and boxed in by mountains, produced (in 1971!) an air pollution emission of 611 tons per square kilometer reducing the ultraviolet radiation by 30 percent and raising the temperature (compared to the countryside) by three degrees.

Given the manifest diseconomies of urban gigantism, measures must be taken to slow down the growth of the metropolis.

Apart from promoting family planning to reduce the birth rate, much can be done to reduce incoming migration:

- The rural population can be stabilized by dispersed industrialization and generally the creation of higher incomes in rural areas. A successful example of such a policy is the Saemaul Undong (New Village Community Movement) in the Republic of Korea.

- Migration can be redirected toward new growth poles by creating New Towns or by the planned extension of existing centers.

- The attraction of the metropolis can be reduced by the moving out of important functions, i.e., decentralization. An example of such a move is Korea's 1977 decision to move the government activities out of Seoul and build a new capital in the middle of the country.

- The extension of the metropolis can be limited and its "overspill" population accommodated by building satellite towns which can also serve as reception areas to intercept incoming migrants. Along public transportation corridors, strings of satellite towns can be built by combining housing and industrial estates as in Singapore and Hong Kong.

The success of such decongestion measures is a precondition for major adjustments to the existing spatial structure of the metropolis: the breaking up of large homogeneous slums into more manageable smaller units and the insertion of subcenters and "employment cores" creating a polynucleated, cellular structure.

During the last decade, the proliferation of slums and squatter settlements have become a matter of international concern. A United Nations study reveals that, in 1960-1970, the proportion of urban dwellers in Asian cities classified as "squatters or slum dwellers" moved up from one out of five to two out of five.

For example, in Metro-Manila—with an overall population growth of six percent—the slum and squatter population is increasing by 12 percent per year.

The term "slum" implies overcrowding in dilapidated buildings, lack of urban services and privacy, and high rates of social deviation. "Squatting" is a legal concept and refers to the occupation of land or space without the consent of the owner.

The reason for illegal squatting is that the poor are practically excluded from the housing market. Land speculation has resulted in most cities in a sharp inflation of land prices, and the government social housing programs are often incapable of offering affordable housing for "marginal" people without assured stable income. In the Philippines, Malaysia, Thailand and Korea, so-called low cost housing is still built at a cost that 40 percent of the urban population is unable to afford.

Studies made in urban slums prove that schizophrenia, neuroses and other personality disorders are frequent. There is also a strong association between overcrowding and increased aggressivity and criminality. Due to a lack of proper drainage, sewage and garbage removal, most slum dwellers also suffer from diseases of the digestive tract and of the lungs. Nevertheless, municipalities often refuse to extend services to squatter settlements since this would legitimize their claim and challenge the authority of the law.

Government attitude towards squatters was at first entirely negative and resulted in massive removal and resettlement programs. However, it was soon discovered that these methods are counterproductive.

In Manila's Spang Palay, squatters were moved about 20 miles to a resettlement site on the periphery, but within a year 40 percent returned to the center city, giving rise to new slums.

In 1970, the metropolitan government of Seoul attempted the clearance of 136,000 units within three years. Few replacement units were provided and most families were transported to unserviced sites far from the center of the city. In the most notorious resettlement camp, Sung Nam City, to which 160,000 people were relocated, desperate conditions triggered off a tragic riot.

Since then, official attitudes changed in favor of upgrading and redevelopment of slum areas as it became clear that demolition only creates new problems by diminishing the housing stock. It has also been discovered that squatter settlements will be upgraded by their own residents if security of tenure is guaranteed and the *de facto* occupation of urban land is legalized.

During the last decade, large scale slum improvement programs had been attempted. Best known are those of the Klong Toey area of Bangkok affecting some 30,000 slum dwellers on a 120 hectare site, and the rehabilitation of Manila's notorious Tondo foreshore area, where some 180,000 people are crowded in single-story huts with densities exceeding 1,000 per hectare.

Land tenure has been the burning issue in Tondo leading to numerous confrontations between the authorities and the residents. A special development authority was created in 1974 and after some years of experimentation came to the conclusion that "ownership of land is basic to the Filipino's sense of security." Consequently, a Presidential decree was issued turning squatters into home owners by selling them the government-owned land at the nominal price of roughly 25¢ per square meter.

Of equal interest is Jakarta's kampong improvement program started in 1969 with the aim of mobilizing residents to improve infrastructure and existing housing in the hope of forming essentially self-sufficient residential neighborhoods. Kampong residents generally set up traditional village-type local governments, achieving a remarkable degree of social cohesion. So far, the kampong improvement program is claimed to have benefited 1.2 million people.

In addition, so-called "sites-and-services" projects have proved their usefulness in Asia: land is provided, plots laid out and equipped with access roads, drainage, water and sewage lines and electricity. Schools and health clinics are also provided. This approach yields the lowest cost solution for urban housing since the buildings are erected by the dwellers by self-help methods.

Although these pilot projects are very promising, the gap between housing needs and housing provision is still widening especially in the large urban areas:

In Thailand's Third Plan, the housing shortage in 1976 was estimated as 100,000 units, increasing to 171,000 units by 1981.

In the Philippines, the 1974 Constitution specifically recognizes that the provision of housing is a responsibility of the state, yet only two dwelling units per 1,000 inhabitants are provided yearly, while seven per 1000 are needed according to the government's own estimates.

In 1972, the Indonesian Central Planning Agency BAPPENAS estimated that to meet the total Indonesian housing shortage would require building 1.5 million houses annually, of which 3,000,000 units are needed to meet the needs of the major cities.

In Korea, the salient feature is also an absolute shortage of housing units. According to a 1972 government report, over one million units were required to meet housing needs of low-income families. During 1966-1975 the rate of construction of new units fell short of new household formations by 700,000 units. Thus, if the accumulated shortage before 1966 is added, the total deficit amounts to 1.6 million units—most of it in urban areas with populations over 500,000 people.

According to United Nations estimates, the governments of countries in the ESCAP region would need to allocate five to six percent of the GNP to alleviate the housing problem. However, most countries only spend one to two percent on housing, meeting only 15 percent of the demand.

Singapore and Hong Kong are exceptions in having developed housing programs that keep pace with the population growth. The Hong Kong board's ambitious 10-year housing program intends to provide 240,000 new dwelling units to house 1.8 million people, but this program will require 20.8 percent of all government capital expenditure.

Singapore has an even more outstanding record, having provided new dwelling units to fully house 70 percent of its population in a 20-year crash building program (1960-1980). However, this effort required the mobilization of an unprecedented 20.5 percent of the GNP for housing and community development.

The examples of Hong Kong and Singapore prove that housing can be used as an instrument to enhance productivity and provide the preconditions to sustain a rapid level of industrialization. However, the performance of these hard-working and efficient city states cannot easily be emulated by larger countries.

The contrast is striking, even if comparisons are made with the disciplined and relatively prosperous Republic of Korea. In Singapore, of the 2.5 million people provided for by the "Housing and Development Board," one million were able to purchase flats under the "Home Ownership for People" scheme. But in Korea, home ownership has continuously declined since 1960. During the decade 1970-1980, monthly household income rose threefold, but at the same time housing costs quadrupled and, according to a KRISH estimate, it would now take 32.7 years for a Korean urban family to become a homeowner.

Increasingly, the objective of homeownership or even the goal of "one household—one dwelling unit" seems unattainable within the resource constraints. This is discouraging since one can hardly overestimate the importance of homeownership to social stability. The owner of even the smallest lot or home has a stake in the community and in continuity.

The home provides a basis for healthy family life and facilitates the transmission of traditionally accepted values to the younger generations. For this reason alone, each country should aim to maximize the opportunities for home ownership to all income groups within the limits of an equitable and politically expedient housing strategy.

Conclusions

This brief survey of the housing conditions in the rapidly urbanizing countries of the East Asian Pacific area brings me to the following conclusions.

One can safely predict that unless high priority is assigned to the problem of human settlements, the lack of adequate housing will become so acute that a rational, integrated approach toward a solution will no longer be possible. Piece—meal actions to cope with the most urgent crises will not prevent the overall degradation of the quality of life of the urban underclass and will thus provide ideal conditions for agitation and subversion.

The sheer size of the urban underclass, which Leandro Viloria calls the "emerging urban majority" is such that police methods of control and containment are no longer practicable.

Hopelessness breeds aggressivity which can be easily manipulated, and the resulting confrontations with the forces of order produce an uncontrollable spiralling of riots and repression.

To avoid this, a "Ministry of Human Settlements" should be created in each country to permit an integrated approach by the coordination of all actions pertaining to the amelioration of living conditions.

Further, to help nations whose insufficient GNP growth does not permit "bootstraps" development, a Regional Housing Finance Institute should be created in which stronger partners would contribute funds and know—how to help the poorer member countries. This institute could take the form of an "Asian & Pacific Area Housing and Human Settlements Development Bank." Initially, most of its funds would have to come from Japan.

Why Japan? If Japan is searching for a new set of national goals, it seems clear to me that this great nation must play a more active role in area defense. In order to provide a credible deterrent against overt aggression, the Japanese defense forces will eventually have to acquire some offensive capacity. However, in view of Japan's "Peace Constitution" and the still lingering distrust of Japan as a major military power, this goal can only be approached gradually.

This should not be a pretext for Japan for not increasing its "defense" expenditure to a more equitable level, say, to the percentage of the budget allocated for defense by other area powers such as the Republic of Korea or the Republic of China. However, instead of over-spending on military hardware, a substantial part of the budget should be used to assure the social stability and harmonious development of other area nations, thus indirectly contributing to overall security. The instrument of this strategic cooperation could be the above-mentioned Housing and Settlement Development Bank.

I see this proposal as just one element of a new ideology based on the notion of "harmonious development." In contrast to the "conflict doctrine" of Marxism emphasizing power contest and class struggle, the ideology of harmonious development would reaffirm the time-honored Oriental tradition of a subtle balance between hierarchy and loyalty.

On the level of economic relations, a policy of "harmonious development" would aim to replace the Marxist construct of exploitative "center-periphery" linkages by the ideal of equitable exchanges based on area solidarity.

References

1. Proceedings of the Asia and Pacific Regional Conference on Human Settlements Finance and Management, UN Center for Human Settlements, (Manila, 1979).

2. IBRD, "Rapport sur le developpement dans le monde 1979, (Washington D.C., 1979).

3. N.A. Salonen et al., *Ideology and Foreign Policy*, (New York, 1980).

4. S.K. Mehta, "Some demographic and economic correlates of primate cities: a case for reevaluation," *Demography*, vol. 1, (1964), pp. 136-47.

5. Koito Mera, "On the urban agglomeration and economic efficiency" in *Economic Development and Cultural Change*, vol. 21, (1973), pp. 309-24.

6. Harry W. Richardson, "City size and national spatial strategies in developing countries," World Bank Staff Working Paper no. 252, (1977), p. 13.

7. F. Herrera, "Nationalism and urbanization in Latin America," *Ekistics*, vol. 32, no. 192, (1971), pp. 369-73.

8. Harry W. Richardson, *The Economics of Urban Size*, (1973), pp. 21-37.

9. Stephen H.K. Yeh and A.A. Laquian (eds.), *Housing Asia's Millions*, (Ottawa, 1979), pp. 39-40.

10. KRISH, "An orientation of housing policies toward the 80s," Staff working paper, (Seoul, 1979).

11. E.Y. Galantay, "New towns in national development," *Ekistics*, vol. 46, no. 277, (1979).

12. E.Y. Galantay, "How big should cities grow? The concept of optimum size and its relevance to spatial planning in developing countries," Proceedings of the 8th International Conference on the Unity of Sciences, (Los Angeles, 1979), pp. 853-68.

13. D.J. Dwyer, "The effect of overcrowding in cities on the quality of life: with special references to the developing countries," Proceedings of the 9th ICUS, Miami Beach, 1980, (New York, 1980).

14. Yung Hee Rho, "Land for low-income housing," paper presented at the VIIth EAROPH Conference, (Kuala Lumpur, 1980).

15. Tongchat Hongladaromph, *Klong Toey: A House-to-House Survey*, (Bangkok, 1973).

16. Metropolitan Manila Information Group, "The Tondo foreshore and Dagat Dagatan Development Project," (Manila, 1979).

17. R. Moochtar and A. Kartahadja (eds.), Low-Cost Housing in Indonesia, (Bandung, 1978).

18. National Housing Institute, *Housing in Thailand*, (Bangkok, 1978).

19. Yeh and Laquian, *op.cit.*

20. "Housing in the Philippines," *NEDA Journal of Development*, vol. 1, p. 553.

21. S.H. Chung, "Housing and residential land in Korea," KRISH staff working paper, (Seoul, 1979).

22. Liu Thai-Ker, "Low-cost housing in Singapore," paper presented at the VIIth EAROPH Conference, (Kuala Lumpur, 1980).

23. Rho, *op. cit.*

24. Leandro Viloria, "Land laws and their Impact," Proceedings of the VIIth EAROPH Conference, (Kuala Lumpur, 1980).

25. N. Tomita, et al., "Values and goals for Japan," in Goals in a Global Community, a report to the Club of Rome, (SUNY, New York, 1977).

Part X

Paradigms for the Future

32.
A Project for a Marine Metropolis for Japan

Kiyonori Kikutake

This paper is concerned with plans for a marine metropolis. While it offers prescriptions for the future of the metropolis, it does not present the future of the metropolis in itself.

The paper covers three major topics: first, the metropolis Tokyo is discussed from the perspective of urban planning; second, the various plans for the future of Tokyo are studied; and third, the project for a marine metropolis is examined.

Paradigms of Urban Planning

By paradigm we understand an outstandingly clear pattern or model of the future metropolis. The search for an appropriate paradigm can be based on the following propositions.

Proposition 1: Based on the conjecture that a metropolis will face specific crises, means to avoid or overcome such crises can be devised. Crises can be prevented through planning—in fact, planning is the only way to achieve a happy future.

Various crises facing cities, including overpopulation, energy problems, traffic congestion, pollution, deterioration of residential areas, and so forth, must be overcome by expert planning.

Proposition 2: Cities undergo an evolutionary process as a result of changing human needs and aspirations. Cities lack any coherent order because of the juxtaposition of the various lifestyles chosen by their inhabitants. The urban system may seem like a confusing labyrinth, yet this is precisely proof of the city's vitality; it is evidence of individualization and diversification.

The seemingly chaotic reality of cities is a transitional phenomenon of evolution. The introduction of planning into this process will only stimulate transition by providing general guidelines and incentives for change.

Through planning, chaotic conditions in cities become more ordered, only to become chaotic again with the passage of time. As this process is continuously repeated, the inhabitants adapt and modernize their cities.

Proposition 3: Cities are melting pots of culture. The laws governing culture have it that cross-cultural encounters will always produce something new. History testifies that new cultures are born in cities. This is particularly evident in a metropolis where some cultures may atrophy when new cultures become dominant, while at the same time other cultures may coexist. Such development may be characterized as a sort of cultural self-proliferation. Obviously, this process cannot be controlled by planning. However, planning can ensure that there is room for this evolution to take place.

Proposition 4: The basis of this proposition is disaster prevention. Planning is required to avoid the worst effects of disasters such as earthquakes, typhoons, fires, floods, tidal waves, ground subsidence, and so on. The effects of disasters in urban areas can be minimized if appropriate prevention strategies are efficiently implemented. This approach aims to control the urban environment by ensuring against not only natural disasters but also against man-made disasters such as accidents due to human error and social instability due to dysfunctions of the urban systems.

Experts predict the possibility of a major earthquake in Tokyo. Past city structures have been examined and suggestions were made for the creation of earthquake-proof foundations and green belts and for the re-development of urban areas to create more earthquake-resistant cities.

Proposition 5: The development of technology will bring about transitions in cities. Various "hardwares" such as new energy sources, traffic and communication systems as well as "softwares" such as new administration and laws will contribute to this.

When city dwellers are alienated by the contradictions and stagnation of the place where they live, they forget about the possibility of creating a more efficient, more rational, more economical city, and the need for searching for ways and means to provide a radically new environment.

It is necessary, therefore, to project the image of a new type of city, fully benefiting from new technologies.

These propositions may help us in addressing the question of how to deal with the metropolis on the threshold of the "metropolis age" of the twenty-first century.

Metropolitan Tokyo

The following discussion considers the current situation of metropolitan Tokyo. Edo, the predecessor of Tokyo, started to function as a metropolis in the sixteenth century. In addition to the concentration of people and goods, Edo also collected and disseminated information all over Japan since the feudal lords resided in Tokyo one year and then in their hometowns the following year.

It is interesting to note that Edo and Kyoto formed the two poles of Japan, maintaining a balance between politics and rituals, decision–making and symbolic power.

In and after the Meiji Era, Tokyo was able to modernize not only because of increasing importance over 400 years, but also due to its almost total destruction as a result of two large-scale earthquakes and war damage.

Reconstruction in and around Tokyo includes an area within a radius of 30 to 42 miles from the center with a population of 30 million people.

City reconstruction today must try to solve the following five basic problems:

1. The core area of the city is too exclusively used for business purposes. As a result, at nighttime and on weekends, the center of the city is deserted. How can this problem be solved?

2. Residential areas are increasingly far from the city center and have sprawled over vast suburban areas, with a shortage of public facilities, resulting in a lack of solidarity and social cohesion in the communities. Traffic is heavily congested. In long-distance commuting, an average of 1.5 hours is required to reach work places.

   Housing is inadequate; one-third of the housing stock still consists of small, old, wooden houses. The natural environment is degraded by air pollution, noise and vibrations. How can these problems, caused by overcrowding of the metropolis, be solved?

3. Supply of land, water and energy does not meet the demand. At the same time, problems concerning waste disposal, sewerage disposal and so forth have become acute. How can these be overcome?

4. Preventive measures should be taken to cope with large-scale earthquakes. At least one theory on the periodicity of earthquakes predicts that another earthquake may hit the metropolitan area. In order to minimize the damage, if this happens, it is necessary to plan ahead.

5. Lifestyles, and livelihoods have changed as a result of the aging society, diversified sense of values, and increased leisure hours. Such changes have affected Tokyo more than any other place in Japan, and therefore Tokyo must make special efforts to be able to adapt to these changes.

In order to address the above problems, five possible urban strategies have been proposed:

461

1. Transfer of the national government: a proposal to transfer the legislative body and its related mechanism to a new capital.

2. Transfer of productive functions: a proposal to transfer part of the functions of the capital to another city in the Kanto Plain, close to Tokyo.

3. Regionalization: a plan to divide and transfer part of the functions of the capital to areas outside the Kanto District, and to reallocate them possibly to areas all over Japan.

4. Rationalization of the capital: a redevelopment plan to drastically revise part of the capital's function, in order to eliminate uneconomic overconcentration in the metropolis.

5. Multiple shifts of working time: a proposal to alternate city functions cyclically in order to use the city space fully.

The above five strategies are being reviewed as possible ways to improve metropolitan Tokyo. So far, no agreement has been reached on the choice of the strategy to be implemented. Moreover, there are several factors restricting possible improvements, for instance, the limited space available for development within the present metropolitan area. Tokyo is presently expanding its land area by reclaiming land, using the city's refuse. Thus, space available for town extension is being created. However, closer observation reveals that the purposes for which this reclaimed land can be used are limited since it is affected by such problems as uneven soil subsidence and the emission of gases.

Metropolitan Tokyo will require 100,000 hectares of additional land for development by the year 2000. However, Tokyo will only be able to provide slightly less than one-half of the amount needed, or 46,000 hectares. There will not be enough land to meet demand.

Another example is the water supply. Annual demand for water will reach 12 billion tons. This cannot be met unless new sources of water are developed.

As far as energy is concerned, annual demand will amount to 300 billion kilowatts. However, the energy supply too has its limits. There is a shortage of energy-supplying facilities and the increased demand for energy cannot be satisfied as space to build thermal power plants is inadequate. In addition, concern has been expressed about the reliability of the supply of natural gas from abroad as Japan depends heavily on imported energy.

Tokyo is producing about 40 million tons of waste per year, and about 140 million tons of residium soil a year. How can these be disposed of?

Yet even though the resources of Tokyo are limited, the metropolis is facing increasing difficulties in the future: people do not want to leave Tokyo because there are no cities that are more attractive in terms of employment.

Fig. 32-1: Metropolitan Tokyo. (Landsat. ICF purchase for ICUS XIII)

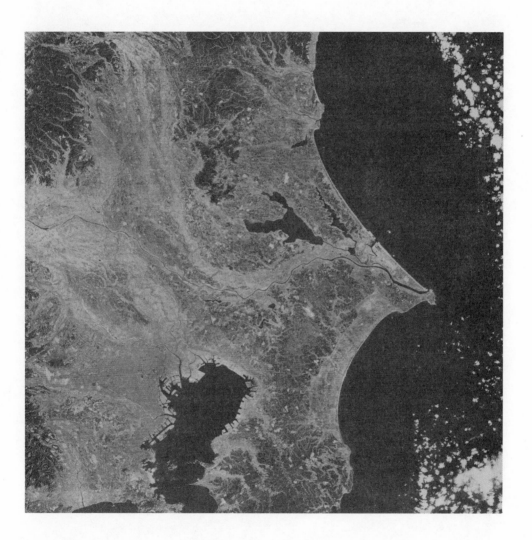

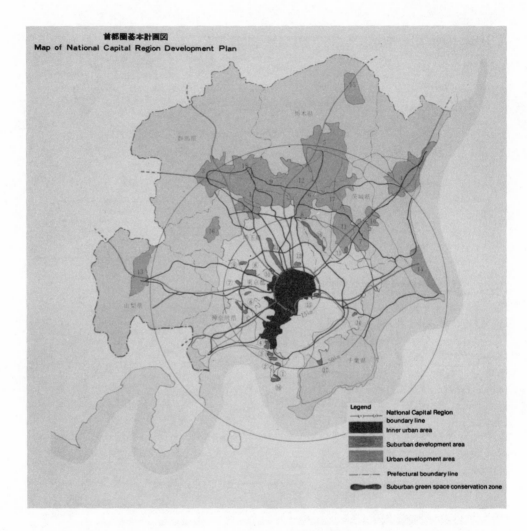

Fig. 32-2: Map of the Japanese National Capital Region Development Plan.
(City Planning of Tokyo 1983. Courtesy: Tokyo Metropolitan Government)

Fig. 32-3: Development plan for Rapid Transit, New Transport System and others.

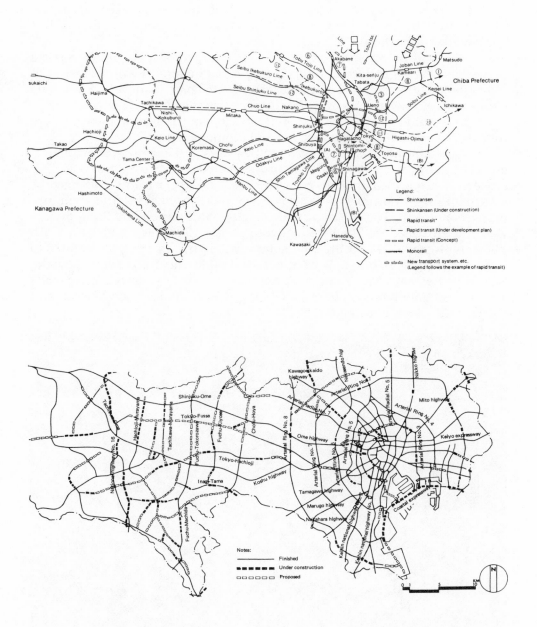

Fig. 32-4: Network of arterial roads.

Marine Metropolis

The creation of a marine metropolis will change the concept of Tokyo. The following is the outline of a plan for a marine metropolis.

It is to be located about 100 kilometers off the coast of Tokyo, on the Continental Shelf, where the depth of the sea is 100 meters. It is to be about 5 kilometers in radius.

The city will be constructed on an artificial platform on top of vertical buoyant poles, 10 meters in diameter and 150 meters in length, placed at intervals of 50 meters. Several layers of artificial land will cover this platform at a height of 20 or more meters above sea level.

The lower ends of the poles rest on the bottom of the sea. No moorings are necessary because the structure is fixed at one point.

Thus, a stable city space, unaffected by waves and currents, is created. A city is built by connecting platform units erected on every vertical pole. The city can be expanded or renewed with ease. The upper load is balanced by controlling the buoyancy of the vertical poles, thus making the structure more economical. The initial size of the city, with a radius of 5 kilometers was chosen based on the size of Kyoto in the Heian Era which was 4.6 kilometers in width and 5.2 kilometers in length, an appropriate size to walk around. It is one-half of the area inside the loop formed by the Yamanote Railway Line in Tokyo. The construction of the marine metropolis will cost 60 billion dollars (U.S.$), will require 60 million tons of steel, and will take 20 years to complete.

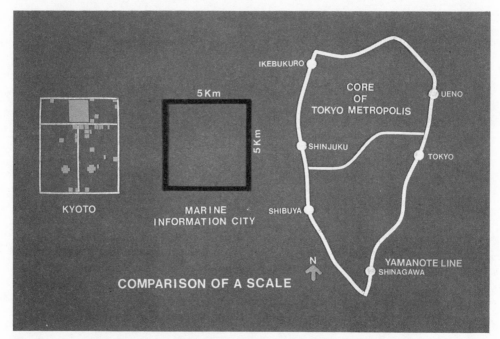

Fig. 32-5: A scale comparison of the Marine Information City with Kyoto and the core of Tokyo metropolis. (Kikutake)

Fig. 32-6: The structure of the Marine Information City. (Kikutake)

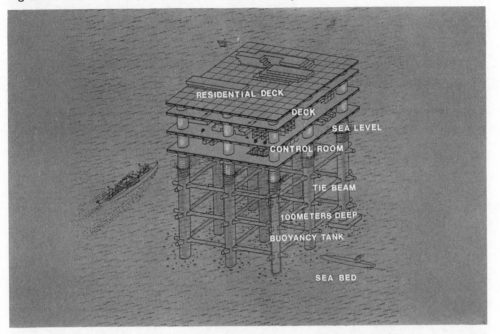

How will resources be supplied to the marine metropolis?

First of all, an infinite amount of energy can be generated from the sea itself by making use of temperature differences. Mineral resources can be obtained from the ocean. Water can be easily obtained by purifying sea water. Rainwater can also be recycled for continuous use.

The marine metropolis will be blessed with a natural environment. The surrounding ocean can be used for leisure and recreation. Looking towards the land, one will be able to enjoy the superb skyline of Tokyo with its flickering lights and distant Mt. Fuji.

More convenient traffic and communication systems can be created than those found in cities on land. Schemes for urban reconstruction pose traffic problems, as there is a shortage of land for roads and railways. However, a city on the sea will require only airplanes and ships which do not need roads or special routes. Travel between cities will become carefree. Research is being carried out to develop faster, more stable ships for mass transportation. It will be possible to travel between the city and Tokyo within one hour. Free exchange of information with other cities will be made possible by communication satellite.

The characteristic which distinguishes the marine metropolis from cities on land is the fact that the city space can be extended, revised and renewed at will. By the development of related technologies, economic and industrial capabilities, and the realization of a political and administrative structure that will enable the rational and efficient operation of a city, the marine metropolis will become an important factor in solving the problems of metropolitan Tokyo. The creation of a marine metropolis, to take over part

Fig. 32-7: The Marine Information City at night. (Kikutake)

of the capital's functions and combine advanced technologies with marine industries, is a realistic plan for the future and not just a utopian dream of futuristic urban planning. While the reconstruction of metropolitan Tokyo on land is an urgent task to be tackled, it is also necessary and feasible to seek a solution on the sea.

Various prototypes for artificial islands and other elements of a marine city provide evidence of the feasibility of the proposal.

In the future, the marine metropolis is expected to assume the functions of a centerpolis of the ocean space, 12 times larger than the present area of Japan, or 152,000 square miles, as provided by the 200-mile economic zone. The metropolis on the sea will be a good counterpart for metropolitan Tokyo on the land.

If we consider the Pacific Ocean as a whole, it is easy to predict that several centerpoli on the sea will be required to act as nuclei controlling hundreds of ocean cities in the Pan-Pacific sea area, maintaining favorable relationships with many countries.

A marine metropolis, an artificial environment, yet in harmony with nature and the sea, will make an attractive city suited to the new society of the twenty-first century, satisfying human hopes for freedom, equality and peace, a dynamic monument symbolizing a new era for urban civilization.

33.
Post-Petroleum Hong Kong: State of the Art as the Art of the State

Ian Brown

In 1997 Hong Kong will cease to be a British Colony.[1] By written agreement between the two main parties, it will revert to the sovereignty of Mainland China from which it was taken in 1842.[2]

Modern Hong Kong seems, at first sight, a counterfeit of Manhattan. Skyscrapers thrust upwards in incredible congestion along the 14 kilometers north shoreline of Hong Kong Island. On Kowloon peninsula, across the water, some of the world's most luxurious hotels look out over what has been described as the best harbor in the world. The 747's and their like, from all over the globe, land one every three minutes and take off at the same rate. (Figure 1).

Fears are now, and have been since September 1982,[3] that the days of making big money are over. The agreement between Britain and the People's Republic of China provides, astoundingly, for the continuation of Hong Kong's cutthroat capitalist way of life, not only up to 1997 but for 50 years beyond. But given the volatility of both power structure and policy in the People's Republic of China since 1949, veering between the left-wing radicalism of the Cultural Revolution and the present technological pragmatism of Deng Xiao Ping, the fears are understandable.

A city which, until September 1982, was on the point of becoming a possibly unique urban artifact, pursuing particular lines of innovation, has suddenly been brought up in its stride. It might be worthwhile to take a brief look at what had seemed about to happen in Hong Kong in terms of city formation, for there is still a slight chance that it might yet happen.

As a city, Hong Kong can be seen to have suffered or benefited from being a British Colony. In 1949 Patrick Abercrombie, fresh from completion of the Greater London Plan, prepared a similar scheme for Hong Kong. It stemmed from that preoccupation with physical environment as social justice—as distinct from efficiency in an internationally competitive arena—which has dominated United Kingdom urban planning since 1900. It included, in pursuit of this, decongestion of the older, inner-city areas and relocation of surplus population via overspill into "new quarters" that would bring

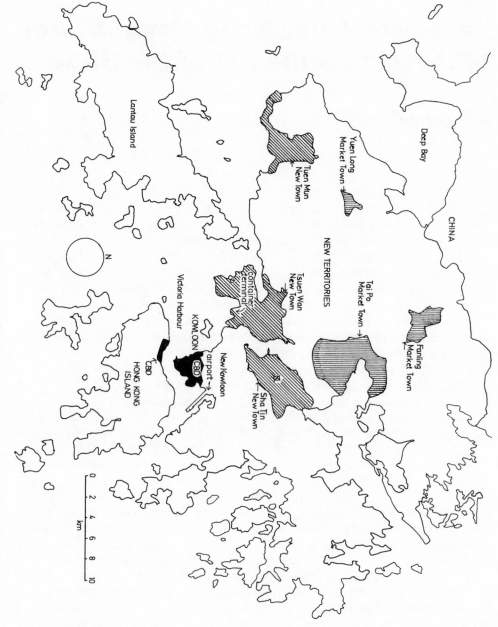

Fig. 33-1: Hong Kong: new and market towns and central business districts.

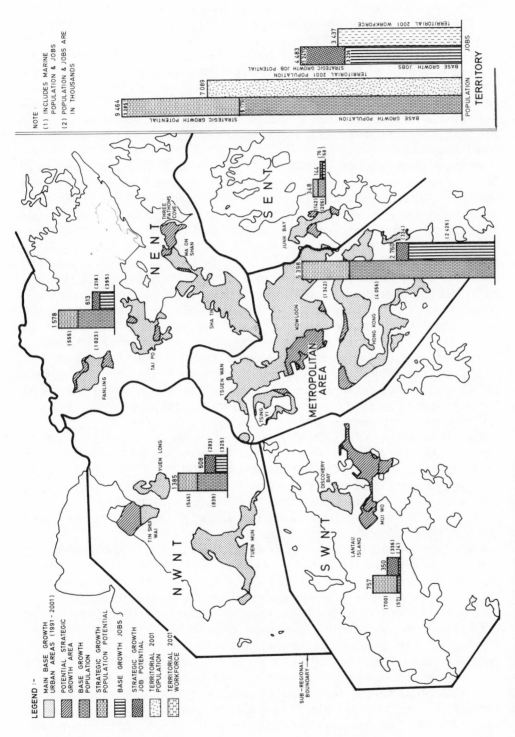

Fig. 33-2: Hong Kong: Territorial development strategy.

environmental improvement. A follow-up 1951 plan by the director of public works, referent to this, recommended the establishment of New Towns in the New Territories (Figure 2).

Since their inception in 1955,[4] the New Towns and market towns have been used to house 1,600,000 people,[5] some from the inner-city areas, some from squatter settlements. The rate of housing or rehousing has been remarkably consistent with government's declared objective of 35,000 flats per annum. In terms of sheer numbers, the Hong Kong government public housing program has been among the most ambitious and successful in the world (Figure 3).

In terms of installation of both employment and facilities to match this, however, achievement has been less. Hong Kong government has not been successful in attracting employment to the satellite areas for a variety of reasons. Among these have been resistance by firms to comply with government's often stringent rules with regard to persistence of product. For example, in its bid to raise the technological level of Hong Kong industries from, say, the making of plastic flowers, at which the territory excels, to the manufacture of electronic parts and assemblies, the government forbids, in its leases, reversion from electronic parts manufacture to plastic flowers if the going gets rough in electronic parts. Such inflexibility and regimentation made Multi-National Corporations (MNCs) weary of moving into Hong Kong as long as such rigid conditions were imposed.

In addition, industrial areas in the new and market towns find it difficult to attract firms because of lack of facilities: but more importantly, because of lack of suitable skilled residents in these towns. Skilled workers living in the older urban areas are reluctant to commute, and prefer to find employment close to their homes.

Two other reasons for this lack of success in inducing employment to locate in the new and market towns have been the strong linkages desired by locators and relocators with the mass of Hong Kong production still in the older urban and inner city areas, principally the Kowloon/New Kowloon peninsula (Figure 2) and the recent inducements from China to foreign employers to locate their firms in the Shenzhen Special Economic Zone just north of the border with Hong Kong.

Firms in the Hong Kong New Towns have maintained their linkages with firms in the older urban areas. Their ability to do this has been enhanced by the new Mass Transit Railway (MTR). As if in anticipation of the likely failure of the New Towns to provide employment congruent with resident employee numbers, Hong Kong government initiated[6] the first of several legs of construction of a potentially extensive, para-area-wide fast transit system (Figure 4). This provides personnel connection, in itself, or via modal change, between the majority of the satellite settlements and the older urban areas and between important parts of those older areas.

In addition, constant investment in road and traditional rail systems has proceeded at speed and scale. Principal among these has been the recent electrification of the Kowloon/Canton Railway (KCR) and construction of the elevated Eastern Island Corridor freeway on the northwest littoral of Hong

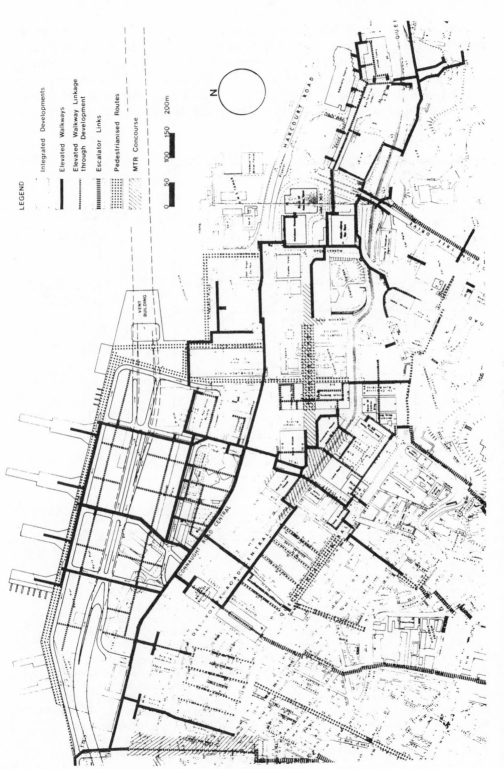

Fig. 33-3: Hong Kong Island CBD: A—Existing network of upper-level skywalks connecting main CBD buildings. B—Proposed network.

Kong Island (Figure 5). Symptomatically, a scheme is afoot for the establishment of an at-grade electrified transit system for one of the New Towns, Yuen Long. An Electronic Road Pricing System (ERPS), the first of its kind in the world, will be introduced shortly into selected parts of the older urban areas. All this is of interest as a background to other developments in integration of movement and static land use systems, the main point of this article.

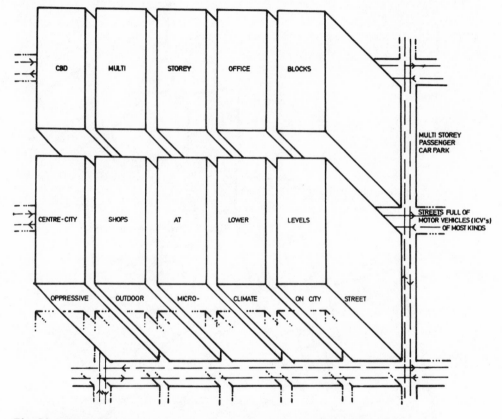

Fig. 33-4: Hong Kong Petroleum City Central Business District (CBD). Near total penetration of the external spaces of the CBD by motor vehicle restricted only by traffic management schemes (controlled parking and shopping one-way systems, bus-only lanes, etc.) But the 1930s mooted "drive in every-where" has failed. The motor vehicle is prohibited entry to the ever expanding interiors of buildings because of its noise, exhaust emission and anarchial progression. Even the "outside" is mustered against it in the form of "environmental areas." Access to the inside is horizontally by foot and vertically by elevator and escalator in the larger buildings. Even before the energy crisis, as a means of getting people from point to point in the CBD or Center City, the motor vehicle had begun to fail despite its much advertised superiority over line systems. But the size of building interiors in the center cities goes on expanding and civilizing in a revolution of building form virtually unremarked that throws more and more into prominence the "public squalor" of the city streets outside: "Manhattan Paradox." (Ian Brown)

Fig. 33-5: Route-powered movement systems for center city Hong Kong. As the medieval constraint of the notion of outdoor "street" at ground level and the "architectural" concept of the facade of a building as permanent features of the city scene both die away with the death of the motor vehicle that needs an "outside" channel, the route-powered systems begin to replicate at mid and high levels to effect ease of access across the city center at upper reaches. Concurrently, in line with this logic, the blocks perimetered by RPS lines merge across subsidiary routes into "superblocks," "digesting" upper remnants of the old streets. (Ian Brown)

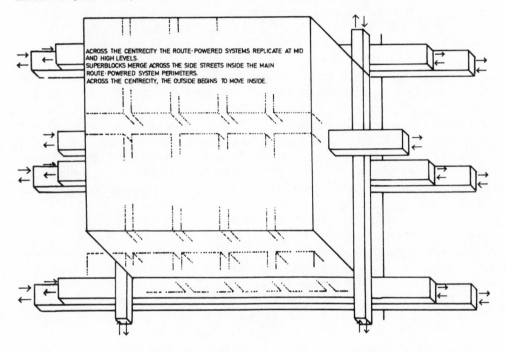

Until 1982, speculation in land and property, coupled with a real ascendancy of Hong Kong in the Far East, had produced some striking symptoms. Among these, the construction of the new headquarters of the Hong Kong and Shanghai Banking Corporation and of the new Exchange Square (Stock Exchange) Building have been the most noteworthy. The former, a 41-story high-tech tower,[7] in Central Hong Kong Island, is reputedly the most expensive building to date in the world, at HK$ 5 billion;[8] the latter, a 52-story building only a stone's throw away, reputedly stands on the most expensive site in the world, at HK$42,588 per square yard.[9]

These were pre-1982 signs of Hong Kong's transformation into a new kind of city, based upon uniquely scarce land conditions, coupled with astronomically high density and growth in GDP. These were other signs.

High density is of course not new to Hong Kong. The peak of residential occupancy reaches 61,500 per acre in Mongkok,[10] one of many such congested districts. These are poor areas in which the underclasses, who work the territory's survival and profits machine, are sequestered. Legal and illegal immigrants from across the border hole out in the multi-story warrens of the Central Business Districts (CBDs) in the in-town squatter settlements (Figure 4). It is, among other things, the *superpacked* nature of Hong Kong in general, the uncontrollable escalation of numbers in a limited area of land, which has forced it to new solutions.

In the low-income residential areas of Hong Kong, the very high density has not, in the past, generated purposive, responsive public urban formations. There has been only what the city itself has determined, which has taken two residential forms: intensification of use of internal space at all floor levels and of contiguous external space at ground level. Official response to this has recently expressed itself as an intention in government proposals for new large-scale areas of reclamation along the littoral of the Kowloon and Island older urban zones, among others, embodied in the new Territorial Development Strategy (TDS). This calls not only for immensely escalated transference of mountains into these marine areas, but for the subsequent amelioration of what will be a fearsomely violated landscape. Government ability to finance such vast plans, was based—in its capacity as sole "freehold" (Crown-hold) landlord of the territory—on the opportunity to auction land for highly profitable returns.

Since September 1982 the likelihood of government being financially in a position to see through the TDS must have seriously diminished.

Thus, if the resistance of economic activity to location in the New Towns is linked to an increasing inclination to further concentrate in the older areas, government may finally be driven to plan for even higher densities than those already current in its public housing. The present level in public housing of 2,500-3,000 persons per hectare seems at risk of being exceeded in the future in the older urban areas by planned public development.

Thus, the development of Hong Kong is moving in response to endogenous and exogenous pressures related to economic rather than received Western environmental criteria. Government, having just promulgated the TDS, is not likely to very soon indicate abandonment of its land reclamation proposals. Much will depend on the extent to which land sales and prices suffice to provide the revenue.

Some form of shoe-string solution to the issues, especially in the Kowloon peninsula, will be a result more of what the city insists on, than anything government attempts via Western-style urban planning.

The movement of these new masses of people, in conventional channelling, is handled principally by the MTR and the bus companies. But supplementary to these are *new forms of* city *networks*, pushing also to bring a new species of city to birth.

Hong Kong has a sub-tropical climate. The canyons of the city are full of particulates, of gases, garbage and fluid pollution. The hum and exhaust of air conditioners is everywhere. Sixty percent of the city's energy is devoted to keeping the inside of the city pure and cool at the further expense of the outside. Squatter settlements mingle with multi-story blocks but do not enjoy sanitary conveniences. Following conventional Western zoning theory, government policy has been to isolate non-conforming uses, but this has been successful only in the New Towns and selected parts of the CBD's. Added to all of this is a steep-sloping terrain affecting most critically main parts of the built-up area of the island. The entire territory wears the aspect, and bears the burdens, of a never-to-be-completed construction site. With the acute shortage of land, the mountains are torn down and thrown into the sea for reclamation of immense stretches of the littoral (Figure 4). The city streets, thick with people and traffic at all hours of the day, are subject to one of the most comprehensively stressful external urban environments imaginable. Traffic peaks in main parts of the city have flattened remorselessly, like the truncated mountains, into plateaus.

Up to a short while ago, the retreat to an artificial climate was possible only for the affluent or sub-affluent. This belief was enshrined in a policy of the housing authority not to provide the facilities for support of air conditioners in public housing.

The artificial environment has found its most striking expression in the two main central business districts: on the Island and in Kowloon on the facing, mainland peninsula.

Here the Croesus flow had, by 1982, begun to generate the makings of a new city machine, a new movement-specific internal and para-internal environment, one raised qualitatively and spatially above the level of the street and the pavement.

This new set of systems began to establish itself about 10 years ago with the initiation of a scheme of cooperation between government and private enterprise based on concepts of overhead movement in Hong Kong Central, with extensions to Western District and beyond. The intensifying trafficcation of this area, the creation of urban freeways through Central itself, and plans for development of an immense complex of multi-story offices and commercial centers highlighted conflict between high-number pedestrian and high-number traffic flows, often at right angles to one another. But they highlighted also the opportunities for commercial advantage to be accrued from channelling of these huge pedestrian flows.

The pedestrian overhead movement elements have been—although incrementally conceived—integrated into one system, extending not only between but through the first floors of new and existing office blocks and hotels as well as connecting to main conventional transport terminals (Figure 4). Stretches of these overhead ways, although roofed against the sub-tropical sun and rain, tend to remain open at the sides, the further the skywalks are from the high price CBD core real estate. Closer to the core, they experience enclosure with or without air conditioning, either as bridges or penetrating the buildings via upper level arcades, foyers, hotel lobbies and the like.

A result is that one can disembark from taxis, buses, maxicabs, harbor ferries, and immediately, via escalator, moving to the upper level and gain access to a 4 kilometer system of varying degrees of open or artificial environment, seldom having to descend to the conventional pavement. Another result is, however, that the raised level of this access tends to develop a class analogue. It is perceptible, first that the coolies, refuse movers and other recognizable members of the Hong Kong underclass infrequently venture to this upper level. These people are visible at work on the lower pavement, continuing to endure the dirt, noise, stench and general visual detritus of the street. As an extension of this analogue, the more sophisticated the form of the upper walkway, the more sophisticated and cosmopolitan becomes the character of the users.

A major exception to this is a space at the present approximate center of the system: the multi-floor atrium of the new "Landmark" complex. Here in lunch hours, in the early evening, on weekdays and public holidays, the general run of the petit bourgeoisie and working class throng in thousands, if not to buy the quality goods in the late-open shops, then to see and be seen. This atrium was specifically designed in consultation with government to have all the character of a public meeting place, with free view of performances and happenings from the tiered shopping balconies.

Conventional–length external escalators serve the network of skywalks. The novel use of long escalators is not peculiar by any means to Hong Kong. But it has the distinction of resorting to their use to handle mass movement of pedestrians, in peak situations, over very extensive inclines. Hong Kong Island is "very slanty," as the locals say, and the peak-hour flow of workers from residences to central and back presents the problem of getting masses of people—housed terrace-fashion, in multi-story blocks on these inclines—to their work on the flat land of Central and back again. One of the principle residential areas for office and shop workers is that known as mid-levels (Figure 4). Consultants have recommended utilization of super-long escalators up the mountainsides to cope with morning and evening peaks, connecting to an extended pedestrian way system.

Hong Kong has already and recently introduced the longest external escalator in the world to enable recreational access to its mountain-top oceanarium. Thirty-four meters[11] in unbroken length, these escalators supplement, but do not replace, a previous cable car system which spans from mountain foot to peak. On the other side of the mountains another cable-car,[12] installed in 1885, rises from Central to mountain-top gardens and restaurants. Both Hong Kong government and Hong Kong private enterprise are keen to seize on "state-of-the-art" movement technology to answer the carrier requirements of this heavily peopled, restless place.

The tramway which runs along the Island's reclaimed foreshore for 16.3 kilometers,[13] built in 1903, was at that time a typically extreme answer to demands for low cost public movement (Figure 5). Across the water from the Island, in newly constructed Harbor City, a gigantic commercial and office complex, 234 meters of horizontal travelators[14] convey workers and shoppers, local and tourist, from the ferry, bus and taxi terminals to shops, hotels and offices, flanking the moving belts. Here again, the travelators are at a level above that of the pavement "outside" and here again, one sees few of the lower paid, manual workers enjoying the use of these facilities.

In Central and in Tsim Sha Tsui the pressure of immense density, the availability of technology and finance, join with government purpose to move development of the city towards internalization on a more and more extensive scale. All this appeared to have a certain *tendency*, up to September 1982, one which now may have lost momentum.

One might venture that the city itself, as an aggregate or outcome of focus, was trying to *be* something, by virtue of some innate volition, which could have paid only partial respect to the orthodoxies which constrained and the ad-hoceries which fumbled towards the idea it was beginning to have of itself. In brief, how far might the city have been capable of moving via some evolutionary force of its own had September 1982 not intervened?

Lying in wait to encourage such a move, of course, has been an otherwise apparently negative factor, the future of in-city/cross-city mechanical movement, of personnel and freight, arising from recent crises in availability of petroleum. Increasing scarcity in this field, coupled with increasing costs, might provoke a transfer from automotive to other modes, as the current oil glut inverts into ultimate depletion.

Whatever would be the initially energizing form, coal or nuclear power substituting for oil, it would be likely that the modes concerned would be electrified. Also, given the undeveloped nature of the automotive electric vehicle, these modes would be largely linear and route-powered (RP).

This would divert from a direction in which Hong Kong has been heading as part of its post-war free-wheeling: the ever-increasing resort to individual automotive use for personnel and freight.

It seems clear that, were such a tendency to develop, the major factors excluding petroleum-powered automotive movement from the interiors of our buildings (air and noise pollution, bodily risks and other problems) would disappear. The way seems set, therefore, in Hong Kong for the progressive internalization of mechanical movement of the city.

The signs of this tendency towards route-powered, non-automotive movement, coupled with internalization of pedestrian movement, had been emerging in pre-1983 Hong Kong; and because Hong Kong is more vulnerable than most metropoli to petroleum famine, that planned or *ad hoc* horizontal movement electrification and concomitant "internalization" of the city would have matured to an ultimately conscious, purposive and comprehensive development of these new city forms.

The characteristic of the automobile has been its ability to negotiate fairly abrupt changes in vertical and horizontal directions, because of its detachment from a power source installed continuously along its route. One of the most unfortunate features of the development of cities over the last three quarters of a century has been the almost total predication and thus dependence of their route and access configurations on the infinitely continuing hegemony of the Internal-Combustion-Engined-Vehicle (ICV). Multi-decked clover-leaf intersections, national motorway grids, and the wreckage of city centers at the hands of transport departments of city and state governments throughout the world have represented this faith in the most traumatic way.

Other systems of transport, particularly in the United States, have fallen into disuse and, most critically, exploration of other forms of city or urban region resulting from the logic of such systems, has not been undertaken. *A progressive refinement and sophistication of built city form, that is to say, integrating into a three-dimensional network of linear route-powered transport modes has not been undertaken.*[15] There has been, until recently, no pressure for reorganization of these kind.

Despite the recent and ultimate oil crisis, this essay takes no risks in assuming that no steps are being taken to strategically re-conceive the nature of urban access and movement problems in terms of a post-petroleum, innovative interlacing of "static" and "non-static" (movement based) activities, that is, integration of movement systems with the buildings of the city.

Possibly the most influential book on the relationship between these two kinds of activity, Colin Buchanan's *Traffic in Towns*,[16] deals (significantly) with the problem of relating *automotive* traffic to cities by setting stakes for an expensive "traffic architecture."

In cities where three-dimensional, non-automotive, linear or cross-linear arrangements *have* occurred on any scale, they have been planned, throughout the world, as a conjunction between central city or equivalent rail lines, and interconnection at those rail line stations with elevators or banked escalator systems in multi-story buildings. In Hong Kong, more than anywhere, this development, coupled with non-conventional upper-level pedestrian linkage and mechanical movement, has proceeded, via drift, to the beginnings of internalization.

It seems likely that the transport modes that must, a quarter of a century from now, stand in for the ICV, will be tied mostly, as noted, to dependence on electrical input along route, developed at a distance from urban centers and fed into the state grid. The route configurations and, more seriously, the building/route-and-access relationships that have characterized Hong Kong to date will therefore need to change. There is not long to discover what those relationships must be in the future; but they must be discovered if paralysis is not to overcome the operation of this metropolis. The same problem, as noted, confronts other urban areas, large and small, throughout the world. The question arising can be posited perhaps in the following form.

First, how can the versatility of some version of the elevator be utilized to establish those horizontal line components of the route-powered network currently missing from our cities? Such a conceptualization is not in itself novel. But its conceptualization in conjunction with purposive city internalization is a different matter. Second, in conventionally built cities such as Hong Kong where the logic of the internal layout and support system is ready to hand and frequently more rationalized and reticulated than the street system, where else, except within and between the buildings themselves above ground level, can networks of horizontal route-powered (RP) systems be most easily installed, connected to the elevator systems, equivalent to the automotive vehicle, *but surpassing it in three-dimensional reach*?

What would the implementation of such conjectures imply for our cities of tomorrow? In the main, it would be the conception of buildings as much more vertically and obliquely integrated and connected non-automotive-transport arenas than they have been in the past: an extension of them to a containment of junctions of verticals and obliques with horizontal, elevated and ultimately area-wide, route-powered modes, consistently internalized.

It has been conventional to date to think of RP movement of people and goods in the CBD's only. But the burden of the developing urban crisis imposes the need to install throughout the city, area-wide, such an RP network carried by the buildings and penetrating them at successively more numerous levels—the more intensively developed the land they occupy, the more undulating the ground level and chaotic the street system.

A further outcome—significant, among other things, in architectural terms—would seem to be the development of *continuous building*, either in the less dense areas of the city in linear form, matching and containing the RP networks, or in multi-dimensional form, as land values increase towards the CBD's, the urban centers, and as the usefulness of the post-petroleum street declines (Figure 4).

Such continuous building, linearly or multi-dimensionally, is the antithesis of the type of architectural envelope endemic now in the Western and Westernized world: discrete island development of blocks divided and defined by the existing street grid. Hong Kong is an extreme sample of this fragmented, externalized development. With the peculiarly unhorizontal terrain of Hong Kong and the tangled nature of many of its main streets and access ways, the post-petroleum movement systems must commence, in Hong Kong, with a revolutionary review of the role that buildings must play in connectivity-relation to one another as a means of establishing a three-dimensional movement system area-wide.

Hong Kong is uniquely placed and pressured by population, topography, climate, function and intensive development of land to lead the world in post-petroleum RP city reformation along the lines set out above. The now-caretaker British Government has consistently exhorted the Hong Kong people to have confidence in the political arrangements being made for their future. It should respond itself to these encouragements in demonstration of leadership in positive thinking about the incoming energy crisis and in strategies to deal with it. Not least of these innovations will need to be the very conception of what constitutes a city.

The idea of a city has become confused as the conceptualization of cities has been taken out of the hands of architects and put into the charge of urban planners. A result is that city design now comprises abstractions almost entirely: land use, systems analysis, traffic management, etc. In the process, ability, or even wish, to innovate in the physical formation of the city has been lost.

If land subdivision were not geared to an out-of-date street system in Hong Kong as in central cities elsewhere, opportunities for escape from the pattern of block-by-block building on sites fragmented from one another by past deals would be more easily available and more clearly indicated. But so long as the present ownership fragmentation is reinforced by a combination of near-medieval street network, notions of daylight and fresh air regulations, not to say view, so long will the conception of architecture and city building as a maximization of external form—around minimization of plot size—persist.

Consolidation of many small sites into fewer large ones would enable the construction of buildings without the need to endlessly proliferate the additional expense of external wall as a first cost, and in terms of future maintenance and running costs. The energy costs in summer of protecting inhabitants from the effects of living in buildings that seem specifically designed to expose as much as possible of the interior to the effects of the sun are enormous. Equivalent costs for losing artificially manufactured heat through the same multiplicity of external envelopes in cold weather are no less onerous.

Charles Fourier, the nineteenth century political theorist, in putting forward his ideas for city design at the beginning of the Industrial Revolution, was incredulous of a civilization which, he said, after 3,000 years, had not managed to secure its way of life entirely from the rigors of the external elements. Today, another one and a half centuries on, we have added to those rigors a "fresh air," so-called, which is a plague to physical health in the streets and a hostile visual environment designed by architects trained in the maximization of stridency in external form.

The argument, in the end, of how Hong Kong (and other metropoli) should develop in a climate of increasingly scarce resources, aside from issues of view and clean air, will of course be resolved by the government in concert with the speculators. They will soon become aware of the paradox that amid land scarcity in the centers, at least one-third of the land—the streets—lies undeveloped. Then, a simple twist of the ordinances will permit the fusion of the Central Area buildings in a single entity, giving the architects a new chance for innovative form-making.[17]

Notes

1. Peter Wesley-Smith, *Unequal Treaty 1898-1997*, (Hong Kong, 1980). PRC *amour propre* calls now for the use of the word Territory in place of Colony, prior to 1997.

2. Treaty of Nanking 1842. Hong Kong was ceded to Britain "in perpetuity."

3. British Prime Minister Margaret Thatcher first visited China in September 1982, provoking the PRC to insist on an early settlement.

4. The first New Town in Hong Kong was Kwun Tong. Commencing in 1955, 618 acres of land were developed there. (Source: *Hong Kong 1973*, Hong Kong Government Press, 1973, p. 93).

5. Of the present total population of Hong Kong's New Towns and market towns of approximately 1.6 million, the population of the separate units is as follows:

Tsuen Wan	690,000	Fanling	83,000
Shatin	241,000	Yuen Long	70,000
Tuen Mun	210,000	Junk Bay	7,000
Tai Po	86,000	Tin Shin Wai	2,700

(Source: Technical Secretariat, New Territories Development Department, Hong Kong Government, December, 1984).

6. Date of Commencement of MTR construction: November 1975. Opening of MTR service: October, 1979.

7. There are three parts to the tower, one having 28, another 41, and a third 35 stories.

8. The best current assessable cost of the new Hong Kong Bank Headquarters is HK$ 5 billion (Source: Hong Kong Bank) but there have been many conflicting claims about cost, some predicting as much as HK$ 9 billion at the final count.

9. The cost of the Exchange Square site was HK$ 4,755,000,00. At 16,080 square yards, this gives 35,490 dollars per square yard. or about HK$ 3226 per square foot.

10. Mongkok on the Kowloon peninsula has the highest density, estimated to 61,500 persons per acre. (Source: Jon A. Prescott, *Asian Urbanization: a Hong Kong Casebook*, University of Hong Kong Press, Hong Kong, 1971, p. 11).

11. Maximum single unbroken length of escalator: 112.2 feet. Total length: 742.5 feet.

12. Construction of the Peak Tramway began in 1885. It was officially opened on May 30, 1888. (Source: *Hong Kong's Famous Funicular: The Peak Tramway*, Peak Tramways Co. Ltd., Hong Kong, 1978)

13. The Hong Kong Tramway operates over 9.7 miles of route, involving 18.2 miles of track. Track laying commenced in May, 1903. The Tramway was officially opened at 10:00 A.M. on July 30, 1904. (Source: R.L.P. Atkinson, *Hong Kong Tramways: a History of Hong Kong Tramways Ltd.*, The Light Railway Transport League, London, 1970.)

14. The total length of the Harbor City travelators is 772 feet. Each unbroken length is 257 feet. (Source: G.E.C., Contractor of the project)

15. Gerald Foley, *The Energy Question*, (London, 1978), pp. 140-142.

16. Colin Buchanan et al., *Traffic in Towns* (London, 1963).

17. Research for this article by Carmen Vernon and Hilary Lau Kar Lok.

Conclusions

Ervin Y. Galantay

The metropolis is the highest form of human settlement both in terms of size and complexity of organization. Metropolitan formation is a product of the urbanization process. The speed and direction of this evolutionary process can be influenced to some extent by voluntary intervention.

All science is concerned with the description and the control of phenomena. This volume includes contributions by social scientists interested in a *description* of the metropolitan phenomenon and in formulating theories about its nature as well as articles by planners, architects, and urban managers involved with the *control* of the metropolis as an activity system, as built form, and as an environment.

Our contributors accepted as a premise Hans Blumenfeld's axiom that the metropolis is not just a larger form of the town or the city, but an entirely new type of human settlement which requires for its emergence a minimal critical threshold population. For our purposes we set this lower limit —somewhat arbitrarily—at two million inhabitants.

The authors also agreed to limit their conjectures about the future to the lifespan of two generations and to keep discussion within the time frame of the next 40 years, up to the year 2025.

The traditional definition of the metropolis is based on the *spatial concentration* of a population in a core-city and a surrounding "hinterland" —or metropolitan "field"—forming a well-defined inter-commuting area. However, in our authors' view demographic concentration is a less significant descriptor than the concentration of jobs, wealth, and power. In fact, a far better measure of metropolitan rank that population size is the density and quality of information flow and of exchange: the *degree of "connectivity."*

John Dyckman reminds us that within the newly emerging global division of labor and hierarchically nested services a new system of metropolitan cities is emerging. Leading metropoli are those which are most closely integrated into the world system in terms of controlling a significant share of management, finance, scientific and design innovation. In this international competition some of the smaller national capitals may be too undersized in terms of global interconnectedness but can still act as regional metropoli with the entire nation acting as their hinterland.

Just as interlocking, specialized units within a city permit each unit to carry out its tasks. metropoli can provide higher level services at lower cost among interacting organizations. The new inter-regional spatial division of labor (i.e., separation of the conception, manufacture, assembly, and distribution of a product) leads to domination and dependency relations as in the familiar "center-periphery" model. But above all metropoli are centers which command major decisions either on the international or on the regional level. On the basis of our criterium of "global interconnectedness" it is easy to see why a threshold population of five million inhabitants may be required in a less developed country to be competitive with a metropolis with two million inhabitants in a more developed country.

Melvin Webber has been the first to point out that in less developed countries access to communication media—and thus to vital information-is generally limited to a small core area of the metropolis. By contrast, in post-industrial societies accessibility to critical information is spread out beyond the core and permits spatially dispersed low-density metropolitan structures.

Thus the communication definition of the metropolis permits us to view as "metropolitan" such poly-nuclear agglomerations as the Dutch "Rand-stad" or the Swiss "Mittelland" which both play a significant role in the international system comparable to the role of the more familiar mono-nuclear metropoli such as Paris, Moscow, or Buenos Aires.

The rich background paper on global urbanization provided by Panayotis Psomopoulos permits us to conclude that the transition toward a fully urbanized world may be completed within a century. At this stage metropoli will tend to merge into a large, interconnected system on a global scale. The first elements of such "multi-nuclear band formations" are already discernible in the European "It-Brit Axis", the Japanese Tokaido, the U.S. Atlantic Seaboard, and the Canada/U.S. Great Lakes Megalopolis.

Dennis Dwyer examines the usefulness of a unitary, general theory of urbanization such as Peter Hall's "cyclical model" but finds significant differences in the genesis and structure between metropoli in the more developed and the less developed countries. The centripetal demographic movement which gave rise to the metropoli of the industrial country has been reversed. Dwyer agrees with Bryan Berry's observation that a turning point had been reached around 1970. Since then a centrifugal movement toward non-metropolitan areas has started—a process of "counterurbanization"—due to a preference for lower densities and the economic possibilities permitting greater dispersal.

By contrast, the centripetal movement continues unabated in the less developed countries giving rise to giant metropoli in a system of "subsistance urbanization" unrelated to industrialization. In these "cities of the poor" the underprivileged can no longer be considered as "marginals" since they are the "emerging new urban majority." In a state of economic stagnation further growth is based on "job-splitting" and, although living standards are declining, the "shared-poverty system" can absorb more people almost indefinitely.

Anthony O'Connor finds any analysis based on the binary terms of the "North-South dichotomy" insufficient to account for the great range of development paths in different regions. The metropolis in tropical Africa has little in common with the metropoli of Latin America which may in fact have more similarities with the cities in Southern Europe. O'Connor is worried that present urbanization trends show such inertia that, without massive intervention, metropolitan "primacy" will increase in terms of the concentration of wealth, consumption, and interaction with the international system without any benefit for the underprivileged "majority." He argues that while there may not be any "optimal size" for the metropolis there is no advantage to a very large size—nothing is gained by a population in excess of, say, five million. Due to spatial segregation large metropoli no longer function as "melting pots," in fact, ethnic consciousness is heightened. The population in very large cities loses contact with the rural areas while a more dispersed urban system is more supportive of the integration of the national economy.

Commenting on Dwyer and O'Connor, Ervin Laszlo proposes a general model of societal transformation based on analogy with the non-equilibrium systems in thermodynamics. He states that the rapid growth of giant metropoli places unprecendented stress on regulatory structures, and the urban system is approaching a breakdown point of "ungovernability." The system is close to a "bifurcation" or phase transition as the "muddling-through" and "disaster" scenarios are equiprobable.

Tao Ho concurs in saying that planning has been excessively concerned with deterministic and mechanistic concepts and static images. More attention must be paid to dynamic "chaos-to-order" transitions. He asks for greater awareness of the informal, stochastic processes which have a homeo-static potential for self-organization.

The consensus of our authors is that the *"disaster" scenario* is not convincing since the resiliency of the urban system, the adaptability of humans to stress, crowding, etc. is such that, before a breakdown would occur, autocatalytic mechanisms will take over to bring about a new state of temporary equilibrium. This is indeed already happening in Third World metropoli where the "informal sector" takes care of whatever the "formal sector" is uncapable of providing: housing, jobs, even subsistence-level services.

As to the evolutionary model it is admitted that several paths of development are conceivable. The urbanization process may be characterized by an inherent "genetic" logic and be irreversible. Yet the "arrow of time" can be bent toward a more desirable future; the speed, rhythm and pattern of metropolitan formation can be influenced by voluntary intervention—and this is where planning can play a role.

Anthony Penfold warns that urban ills are national ills: they only appear more visibly exemplified in the metropolis. He considers the metropolis as a systemic schema of linked elements that constitute subsystems. To what extent do the values of the residents impinge on these subsystems? It depends on "who calls the shots." Penfold claims that residents of the "informal sector" in Third World metropoli have more chance to shape their environment than the residents in more developed countries hampered by excessive reglementation.

Talking specifically about the *Western European metropolis*, Klaus Müller-Ibold cites the examples of Germany, Holland, and Switzerland to demonstrate that a high degree of metropolitanization is not a precondition for the rise of a post-industrial society.

In fact, if the social-equity goal is to be optimized, a decentralized system may be preferable. Within a poly-nuclear metropolitan agglomeration revenue-sharing can be achieved by redistribution of the tax-base. Müller-Ibold feels that in ranking metropoli the criteria of population size and density are less important than "quality of life" indicators, which favor poly-nuclear agglomerations.

Michel Bassand emphasizes the political and language barriers to metropolitan integration. In an urban system such as that of the Swiss Plateau such barriers are impeding social mobility but help in fostering local identity and civic pride. In a model of the European metropolis the divergent interests of innumerable "social actors" must be identified and in the search of appropriate policies the questions answered: who plans, who decides, who implements, who benefits, and who pays? Bassand assigns high value to "localism" which is fostered by participation in decision-making.

Among the "social actors" Müller-Ibold identifies an increasingly important group of "guest-workers" of non-European cultural background. A new problem for Europe is the attempt to integrate such groups without social disruption. Adriaan Constandse agrees with Müller-Ibold that attention must be paid to compatibility/incompatibility factors in determining threshold levels of acceptance for these migrant workers to optimize their integration into the dominant culture. In contrast to Bassand, Constandse is weary of participatory exercises since most individuals are self-seeking rather than public-regarding, and they have notoriously short time-horizons. In the interest of future generations the responsibility for decisions must be taken by technically competent public servants.

In analyzing the problems of the *Eastern European metropolis* Ferenc Vidor recalls that the basic structure of these cities has long been established by the same historical development as in the case of the Western European cities, and socialist central planning has only added a new layer. Krysztof Pawlowski concurs in pointing out that the paradigm of the socialist metropolis was created as a vision of the "ideal city" long before the advent of the Socialist State. Nevertheless, basic differences in planning and management now exist due to the absence of private ownership of real-estate as well as the central control of the supply of land and housing. In contrast to the difficulties of land-assembly for large-scale projects in the capitalist countries, great opportunities for rational planning exist. However, as Vidor admits, these opportunities are not fully exploited because of the subordination of spatial planning to production targets and sectoral priorities. Galantay points to successes in the provision of efficient public transport, energy-saving compact urban form, and the adequate provision of basic services and amenities. In this aspect of "planning in a climate of frugality" the socialist model has some lessons to offer to the less developed countries. Milos Perovic provides us with an insider's view of the planning of New Belgrade and of the ideological forces shaping the Yugoslav metropolis. He castigates the Eastern European dogma of hierarchical "rational planning" which he traces to the influence of the early CIAM movement. Perovic pleads for a more humane urban design with more concern for the users' preferences.

Moving to the Metropoli of *North America*, Rebecca Robertson finds that "overreglementation" drives footloose industries and capital out of the metropolitan areas. Similarly, rent control measures killed maintenance and resulted in decaying housing stock, reducing the choice of homes available to lower income groups. The metropolis as a welfare-maximizing mechanism is bankrupt. Although there is some cosmetic "gentrification" municipal revenues continue to decline and thus the ability of the city to pay for essential services. The result is increasing contrast between the showcase areas and the slums; the hollow core, the grey areas and the decaying older suburbs. Loss of security is also driving out families and businesses. Growth is now occuring in non-metropolitan areas. Commenting, Adam Krivatsy states that the metropolitan areas of California and the Sunbelt are still growing and the vitality of the central areas seems to be increasing. In the cycle of land development the rich have first choice of location but housing stock eventually trickles down to lower-income groups, to turn finally into slum areas. Slums perform an essential function, providing low-cost, low-control areas as well as reserves for redevelopment in another phase of the cycle. The fiscal problems of many large cities could be solved by introducing a metropolitan form of government with revenue-sharing.

Percy Johnson-Marshall comments that the new dispersed form of metropolitan pattern in the United States is particularly wasteful of agricultural land and contrary to energy saving and ecologically sound principles of planning. Paolo Soleri also finds the trend toward dispersal an example of conspicuously wasteful consumption and pleads for more frugal urban forms for the metropolis.

Turning to *Latin-America*, Dietrich Kunckel calls attention to the already very high degree of urbanization of the continent. He emphasizes that in each metropolis a population is adapting to an ecological niche—no two problems are quite the same—and finds the attempt to transfer concepts gleaned from European or North American experience of little use. In Latin America, "primate cities" are still growing fast in absolute size but their dominance with respect to the urban system is corrected as ever more medium-size cities grow to pre-metropolitan size.

An essential difference of Latin American cities with respect to North American or European metropoli is the existence and increasing importance of the "informal sector" both in housing and in job provision. There is increased government awareness of the need for investment in this sector. Commenting, both Geraldo Nogueira-Batista and Elias Gomez-Azcarate are worrying about the size-related phenomenon of increasing spatial segregation of income groups and of activities—an "unmixing" depriving the metropolis of a source of its dynamism. The rich elites are increasingly withdrawing in high-security "enclaves." At the same time, poverty reduces the ability of the underemployed to pay for intraurban transportation thus reducing their access to jobs, cultural and environmental amenities. This segregation and income polarization is leading to a decline of social solidarity, and increasing antagonism among social classes, and raises the specter of social instability, the acceptance of dictatorial leadership and restrictions of personal freedom. Both Nogueira-Batista and Gomez-Azcarate consider the financial dependence of Latin America, and particularly the foreign debt burden, as the greatest obstacle to adequate investment in essential infrastructure, and see a possible solution only within the framework of more equitable "North-South" relations.

Talking at the 13th ICUS Conference about the metropolis in Islamic countries, Cyrus Mechkat reintroduced the "Center-Periphery Model" of dependent metropolitanization. He stated that the lifestyle in the traditional Islamic "Medina" is incompatible with modernization and the impact of attitude changes caused by Western technology. Not the size of the metropolis but the speed of change is disruptive. Violent upheavals such as the fall of the Shah of Iran result from the conflict between traditional values and the pressures for greater integration into the international system. Yet Islam used to have an international tradition of its own with considerable mobility between cities of the "Nations of Islam." Abdulaziz Saqqaf calls attention to the currents of international migration particularly in the Gulf States which create conflict between the autochthonous and migrant populations even though they share a common cultural heritage. Social segregation and income polarization occur just as in the European examples described by Müller-Ibold. In a case study of Cairo, the largest Islamic and Arabic metropolis, Saad Eddin Ibrahim highlights the subsequent tidal movements of modernization and traditionalist reaction and the impact of social evolution on the urban environment. He identifies the lower middle classes as the most important social actors shaping future urban policy which will need to be based on a "small-city strategy" to break the excessive domination of the metropolis.

In examining the South-East Asian metropoli, Peter Wyss concurs with Kunckel in finding little use for the transfer of Western models of urban structure and management. He emphasizes the vitality of the informal "bazaar" sector contrasted to the limited impact of formal planning. Not even 10% of the urgent recommendations of the 1970 Master Plans for Karachi, Colombo, Calcutta or Manila have been implemented, yet the urban systems adapted to the increased population pressure. Luckily, in some of the largest metropoli both natural growth rates and migration have slowed down somewhat.

Wyss finds that the interest of international aid organizations in the informal sector is very convenient for the governments who can now claim to be enlightened by *not* intervening and assuming a "laisser-faire" attitude. He calls for greater government involvement in public infrastructure provision, particularly in the creation of efficient mass transportation which the informal sector clearly cannot provide.

Sumet Junsai regrets that in city planning too little attention is being paid to spiritual factors. The metropolis is not just an economic entity and a welfare-maximizing mechanism. It should also be the crucible for innovation, the catalyst of intellectual, social and political change. It must provide the support system for the unfolding of the national genius as a contribution to global culture.

In discussing Jumsai's thesis most authors agreed that the metropolis can only fulfill this creative role if minimal adequate living standards are available for the entire population. Creativity is compatible with a frugal use of resources but not with a lack of social mobility. Other conditions for creativity are social stability and program continuity since nothing is more disruptive than frequent policy changes resulting in the waste of scarce resources.

Finally, Kiyonori Kikutake outlines the specific problems of Japan as a technologically advanced country faced with resource scarcity including a lack of developable land. He proposes a capital-intensive, high-technology solution by the creation of an artificial "Marine Metropolis" on the continental shelf. This permits an alternative to encroachment on prime agricultural land and forest reserves. Commenting, Paolo Soleri concurs with Kikutake on the merits of a high-density solution but favors more frugal urban paradigms based on a modest lifestyle.

The search for a more resource-conserving urban form is also the main concern of Ian Brown. He speculates about a "post-petroleum Hong Kong" which could become a model for a novel type of high-density central city structure optimizing "connectivity" by a multi-level movement system of "travelators" and "route-powered" modular vehicles.

With respect to recommendations for future action, William K. Mackay calls for credible, realizable programs as a guide for investment. The transportation system, infrastructure, and the localization of key institutions are the major shapers of metropolitan macroform. Mackay does not foresee any reduction in travel demand. In the more developed countries, travel time economized through "tele-mobility" will be used to extend the choice of activities and to multiply contacts.

Urban macroform should be restructured from monocentric and radio-concentric forms to multinodal and orthogonal patterns. Mackay supports Galantay's model of alternating high-density/high-rise "activity corridors" with low-density, low-control strips of "urban villages." The metropolis should be broken up into smaller autonomous sub-units or "cells" the size of small towns.

Dudley Leaker enumerates some essential conditions for effective planning actions: an unambiguous legal base; substantial consensus for planning goals; multiparty support to ensure program continuity; administrative/managerial competence and a corps of incorruptible public servants; continuous monitoring of implementation for feedback and goals/means adjustments.

Since in the more developed countries the rate of change of urban tissue is very slow—not more than 1-2% of the stock of physical structures is renewed annually—emphasis can be placed on the *quality* of the enviroment, on the conservation of resources, on more efficient communication, on recycling of water, heat and waste products, and the development of viable subcenters and activity corridors.

However, our authors agree that the real problems and the real opportunities for innovation and creative intervention exist above all in the metropoli of the Third World. This is due to the fact that in the less developed countries the rate of change in land-use is extremely rapid, and in some cases the metropoli are still in a "nascent state" as in tropical Africa.

In dealing with the "cities of the poor" and the stark results of "subsistence urbanization," attempts should be made to assure order and control of development on the level of the urban macroform combined with a minimum of reglementation on the micro-level to foster the free play of self-organization. It will be necessary to "fast-track" the passage from planning and rhetoric to implementation and action, with less room for public participation in long-term decision-making.

At the preparatory symposium for ICUS 13, in Paris, most of our authors participated in discussions on "The Future Metropolis," agreement was reached that *decentralization policies* will be needed, requiring a shift in resource allocation away from the metropolis and against the needs of the metropolitan population and against political pressures. This does not imply an anti-metropolitan bias but simply that more large cities will be needed to counterbalance the domination of the largest metropoli. Decentralization will require decentralization of power, not just of population.

As to conjectures about the future the committee agreed on an attitude of "cautious optimism." It is to be noted that already our time frame to the year 2025 is optimistic since it assumes the survival of mankind to that date, i.e., the abstention of world leaders from thermonuclear war.

The committee found considerable exhortatory merit in "disaster scenarios" but no cause for sinking into neo-Malthusian gloom. Such is the elasticity and resilience of the urban system—and the inventiveness of the human mind to cope with constraints and scarcities—that "doomsday prophecies" have never proved correct in the past.

One may take heart from the fact that around 1830 it had been predicted that London could never reach a size of five million inhabitants because the congestion caused by horse-drawn transport would bring all traffic to a stand-still. Worse yet, the accumulation of horse dung would impede movement, the toxic vapors emanating from the manure would choke the inhabitants, the female sex would suffer intolerably due to the scarcity of smelling salts . . .

More timely is the concern with the gloomy scenarios triggered off by the unchecked rapid growth of such giant cities as Mexico City. However, rather than taking a defeatist attitude, one should be encouraged by the fact that Mexico City has already grown to 17 million inhabitants and so far both the administrators and the inhabitants have coped remarkably well. So, with some luck, the Mexico metropolis might still function with 25 or 30 million inhabitants. In fact, the awareness of the problems increases the likelihood of their resolution and, as Ervin Laszlo remarks: "crises and opportunity are one." Or, as Percy Johnson-Marshall observes: the situation of the metropolis is "desperate but not hopeless."

It is desperate in the short term, because conditions of extreme poverty exist and are becoming more acute year by year, yet not hopeless in the long range, because the slowing down of the urbanization process and of the growth rate of the population creates an opening for intervention. Sensitive planning will permit the further development of the biosphere for human and other species, achieving a more desirable future within our limited "cone of opportunities."

A greater awareness of "global solidarity" will be needed to convince the inhabitants of the metropoli in the more developed countries to reduce their standards of living and to accept a more frugal lifestyle.

Yet only by a massive transfer of resources can the "metropolis of the poor" in the less developed countries provide for the needs of their population even on the level of minimum but adequate standards. To muster the political will toward the goal of greater equity is a moral imperative. In the next century it may become a matter of survival.

Contributors

Abdulaziz Al-Saqqaf, born in Hugarriah, Yemen in 1951, is Chairman of the Department of Economics of Sana'a University, Yemen Arab Republic.

He was educated in Sana'a and at Ohio University in Athens, Ohio. He obtained a Masters degree in Public Administration at Harvard University and a Ph.D. in International Economics and Finance from the Fletcher School.

He has been Director of Public Relations at the Ministry of Information of Yemen 1972-76; and has been teaching since 1980 at Sana'a University.

He is a Fellow of the Salzburg Seminar in American Studies. He has published numerous professional articles and books, among them the seminal *Theories in Public Finance and the Fiscal Systems* (Al-Madani Press, Cairo, 1983).

Michel Bassand, born in Switzerland in 1938, is a Professor of Urban Sociology at the EPFL - the Swiss Federal Institute of Technology in Lausanne.

He studied sociology at the University of Geneva receiving his Ph.D. degree in 1972. After teaching at the Universities of Grenoble, Neuchâtel, Paris and the Department of Sociology of the University of Geneva, he was named full Professor at the EPFL in 1976. Since then he has been Chairman of the Department of Architecture and is at present Director of the IREC - the Institute of the Built Environment of the EPFL. Michel Bassand has published numerous books and professional articles on the urban power structure, youth and family relations, leisure time-use, spatial mobility, the urban power structure, and public policies with respect to regional development.

Hans Blumenfeld, was born in Germany in 1892. He has practiced planning in many countries, including the USSR, the USA, Austria, Germany, and Canada.

He graduated in Architecture from the Polytechnical Institute of Darmstadt in 1921. Hans Blumenfeld was Chief of the Division of Planning Analysis, Philadelphia City Planning Commission, 1945-1952, and Assistant Director, Metropolitan Toronto Planning Board, 1955-1961. Since 1961, he has been on the faculty in urban and regional planning, University of Toronto. Hans Blumenfeld has doctorates from the University of Montreal, University of Waterloo, and the Technical University of Nova Scotia. He was made an Officer of the Order of Canada in 1978. His selected essays have been published by the MIT Press with the title of *The Modern Metropolis.* His latest book is *Metropolis - and Beyond* published by J. Wiley & Sons, New York, 1980.

Ian Brown, born in England in 1940, is an architect and urban planner. He worked for Erno Goldfinger in London and Doxiadis Associates in West Africa, before returning to join the Greater London Council.

He was a member of the multi-authority teams on the Swindon City and Thamesmead New Town projects. In 1972 he was invited to teach in a joint appointment at Princeton's SAUP and Woodrow Wilson School. He was coordinating author of the GLC book on pedestrianized streets published in 1974. Since 1978 he has been teaching architecture and urban planning at the University of Hong Kong where he is senior lecturer. He has published numerous articles in international journals including *Ekistics; New Society; Proceedings of the United States Department of Transportation; Higher Educational Review; Asian Journal of Public Administration* and the *Asian Wall Street Journal.*

Adriaan K. Constandse, born in Holland in 1929, is Head of the Socio-Economic Research Department of the Rijksdienst voor de IJsselmeerpolders (IJsselmeerpolders Development Authority) and Professor in Sociology of Physical Planning at the Agricultural University of Wageningen, The Netherlands.

He studied geography and sociology at the University of Utrecht, and obtained a Ph.D. at the same university in 1960. He was engaged in rural development of the newly reclaimed land of the polders as well as in the development of two new towns: Lelystad and Almere. He has been a visiting professor several times at Louisiana State University, Baton Rouge, USA.

Denis Dwyer, born in England in 1930, has been Professor of Geography and head of the Department of Geography at Keele University, England, since 1974.

He obtained his doctorate from the London School of Economics. In 1967, he was appointed Professor of Geography and Head of the Department of Geography and Geology in the University of Hong Kong. He also served as a member of the Hong Kong Town Planning Board. He has carried out research on the urban problems of developing countries in several countries in South East Asia, in Zimbabwe and in Hong Kong. He has also served widely as a consultant to governments, to aid-giving organisations and to foundations. Denis Dwyer's major publications include *People and Housing in Third World Cities* (1975), which has subsequently been translated into both Spanish and Japanese, *The City in the Third World* (1974), *Asian Urbanisation: A Hong Kong Casebook* (1971) and *The City as a Centre of Change in Asia* (1972).

John W. Dyckman, born in 1922 in Chicago, is Director of the European Center for Regional Planning and Research of Johns Hopkins University in the Nord-Pas-de-Calais, France, and Professor of Geography and Environmental Engineering at Johns Hopkins.

He received his doctorate from the University of Chicago. Prior to going to Johns Hopkins he held the James Irvine Chair in the School of Urban and Regional Planning at the University of Southern California. He has taught at the University of California, Berkeley, where he was first chairman of the Center for Planning and Development Research and was professor of City and Regional Planning. He has also taught at Stanford University, and at the University of Pennsylvania. In 1966 he went to Yugoslavia as the first Field Director of the American-Yugoslav Project in Urban and Regional Planning. He has worked extensively as a consultant both in the U.S. and in numerous foreign countries. He directed a number of studies for the Arthur D. Little company, including an econometric model for the State of California Department of Finance. He is the author of *Capital Requirements for Urban Development and Renewal,* with R. Isaacs, and of more than 100 articles, monographs, and sections of books.

Ervin Yvan Galantay, born in Budapest, Hungary in 1930, is an American architect and planner.

He studied architecture at the ETH- the Swiss Federal Technical University in Zurich, graduating in 1955. He was Greenfield Fellow of the Philadelphia City Commission (1957); received his Masters degree in City Design in 1958 and worked in the office of I.M. Pei in New York, 1958-61. In 1961 he was appointed Assistant Professor at Harvard University, 1964-71 Associate Professor at Columbia University. Since 1971 he has been Professor of Architecture and City Design at the Swiss Federal Institute of Technology, Lausanne, where he has also been, in turn, Chairman of the Department and Director of the Graduate Program in Development Planning.

As a Member of the MIT/Harvard Joint Center of Urban Studies team he contributed to the planning of the Venezuelan New Town of Ciudad Guayana. He acted as Senior Consultant in the planning of Owerri, the new capital of Imo State in Nigeria. He represented the Swiss government at the 1978 U.N. Conference on Human Settlements in Vancouver.

He is the author of numerous articles. His book on *New Towns* has been translated into both Spanish and Japanese editions.

Elias Gomez-Azcarate Ph.D., born in Mexico in 1947, is presently Director of Programming and Budget Planning of Urban Transportation and Infrastructure for the federal government of Mexico.

He obtained his architect's degree at the National University of Mexico in

1970, followed by graduate and post-graduate studies in urban and regional planning in the United States, Holland and the Federal Republic of Germany, obtaining the "Liz.Rer.Reg." (Doctorate in Regional Sciences) from the University of Karlsruhe in 1975. He is a Fellow of the Salzburg Seminar's in American Studies. Since 1975 he has been a senior official in the federal government of Mexico, in charge until 1983 of the research studies, draft and implementation of the National Urban Development Plan.

Tao Ho, born in Shanghai, China in 1936, is a Hong Kong architect. He received his B.A. degree at Williams College in the USA (1960) and his Master of Architecture degree at Harvard University in 1964.

He is a Founding Member and Architect of the Hong Kong Arts Centre, a lecturer at Hong Kong University and at Chinese University: a member of the World Society of Ekistics and of the Eastern Regional Organisation for Planning and Housing.

He is a founder and member of the editorial board of *Vision* Magazine and a consultant of the Chinese government on projects in Tianjin and Beijing. He is a Core member of APAC (Asian Planning and Architectural Consultants) and of GREAT EARTH International founded in Beijing in 1984.

Saad Eddin Ibrahim, born in Egypt in 1938, is Professor of Sociology at the American University in Cairo, and Head of Arab Affairs in Al Ahram's Center for Political and Strategic Studies as well as Secretary General of the Arab Thought Forum.

He graduated from Cairo University in 1960 and holds an M.A. (1964) and a Ph.D. (1968) from the University of Washington-Seattle. He is the author of: "Arab Society in Transition"; "Urbanization in Morocco", "Social Change and Development in Egypt" and numerous other articles in Arabic and English on the sociology of the Arab World.

Percy E.A. Johnson-Marshall, born in India in 1915, is Professor of Urban Design and Regional Planning at the University of Edinburgh.

He studied at the University of Liverpool (CMG, Dip.Arch., MA) and is a Fellow of the Royal Town Planning Institute and Dist.TP. of the Royal Institute of British Architects. During WW II he was in charge of designing the first reconstruction plans for Coventry: '45-46 acted as advisor on planning and reconstruction to the Government of Burma, '46-48 Ministry Planner advising on legislation, '49-56 Senior Planner in charge of London Comprehensive Development areas and responsible for several regional plans. He is an advisor to the Brazilian Government and U.N. consultant on Human Settlements. From 1966-84 he was head of the department of U.D. and Regional Planning at the University of Edinburgh.

His publications include numerous reports, articles, the Development Plan for the Region of Porto, Portugal; and the book *Rebuilding Cities,* 1965.

Sumet Jumsai, born in Bangkok in 1939, is a Thai architect. He studied in England and received his B.Arch., Master of Architecture and Ph.D. degrees at Cambridge University.

His firm, Sumet Jumsai Associates Ltd, founded in 1969, initiated and planned Bangkok's first satellite town for a population of 100,000 people: Nava Nakorn. He has been a member of committees on historic conservation and the environment since 1972 and on national land use and urban policy since 1980.

He is a lecturer at Chulalongkorn and Silpakorn Universities and has published numerous books and articles. He is Chairman of the Fine Arts Commission of Thailand and of the Arts Commission of Siam Society.

Kiyonori Kikutake, born in 1928, is a Japanese architect practicing in Tokyo. He is also a lecturer at Waseda University and at Tokyo University. He has been a guest professor at the University of Southern California (1963) and at the University of Hawaii (1971).

His work has been published in numerous books and periodicals and he has received numerous awards:

1964 the Minister of Education, Japan: Arts award

1964 Pan Pacific Architecture citation of the Hawaii Chapter, AIA

1964 the award of Architectural Institute of Japan

1978 the August Perret award of the U.I.A. - the International Union of Architects.

He has acted as Vice-President of the Japan Architects Association (1982-83) and is a Fellow of the American Institute of Architects.

Adam Krivatsy, born in Hungary in 1929, is an architect and urban planner practicing in San Francisco.

He studied at the Technical University of Budapest, graduating in 1954, and received a Master's degree in Urban Planning at Columbia University, New York, in 1961. He worked as an urban designer with I.M. Pei and Partners in New York; and was Chief Planner of J. Warnecke and Associates in Honolulu. In 1967 he founded, and is presently owner of, the San Francisco Planning firm HKS-Associates. He is a member of the American Institute of Architects and of the A.I.P.

Dietrich Kunckel, born in Berlin in 1938, is a Venezuelan architect and planner.

He studied at the Technical University of Aachen F.R.G. He pursued urban studies at Princeton University in 1966 and worked at the Regional Plan Association in New York on "Urban Design Manhattan" published in 1968. In Venezuela since 1970 he first worked at the Ministry of Public Works (MOP), then as an associate of Estudio Quatorce. In 1971 he founded his own firm LKSA which designed and built the Caracas Opera House and Performing Arts Center.

He is president of INTEPLANCONSULT involved in regional planning and the development of New Towns in Venezuela, and an Adjunct Professor and Director of the Urban Design Program at the Simon Bolivar University in Caracas.

Ervin Laszlo, born in Budapest, Hungary in 1930, is an American futurologist.

He first studied music at the National Academy in Budapest, then acquired the degree of "Docteur ès Lettres et Sciences Humaines" at the Sorbonne in Paris, France (1970). He is a member of the Club of Rome, Editor of "World Futures" (Quarterly) Associate Editor of "Behavioral Science", and has authored or edited numerous books and articles.

He has been Professor of Philosophy at the State University of New York (1968-77), and a visiting Professor of Future Studies at the University of Houston and at Kyung Hee University, Seoul. Since 1977 he has been a Project Director of the United Nations Institute for Training and Research in New York, UNITAR.

Dudley Roberts Leaker, born in South Wales in 1920, is a British planning consultant, Q.R.I.B.A., F.R.I.A.S.

He has been, in turn, Architect of the cities of Bristol, Plymouth and Coventry. He has also acted as the Senior Architect of Stevenage New Town; Chief Architect and Planning Officer of Cumbernauld New Town and of Warrington New Town; Advisor to the Milton Keynes Development Corporation and Executive Director of South Milton Keynes.

He headed the team which gained the Rynolds Award for the "Best Community Architecture" of the American Institute of Architects. He has been joint author of several New Town Plans and Chief Officer responsible for their implementation.

He is at present Advisor to the British New Towns Consortium, Independent Inspector at Public Inquiries for the British Government, a Fellow of Open University of Milton Keynes, and Chairman of the Working Party on New Towns of the International Federation on Housing and Planning.

William K. Mackay, born in Peru in 1931, is a British transportation planner and consultant. Q.H.Sc., C.Eng., F.I.C.E., F.I.T.E., F.A.S.C.E., F.F.B., M.Cons.E.

He has been Transport and Highway Group Engineer for Cumbernauld New Town. He acted as the expert delegated by the United Kingdom to the O.E.C.D. in Paris on "Innovations in Transport Systems" and the "Impact of the Structure and Extent of Urban Development on the Choice of Modes of Transport".

The UK Institute of Municipal Engineers awarded him a medal for his essay on "Roads in Urban Areas" and he received the Wellington Prize of the American Society of Civil Engineers for his paper on "Transportation and Urban Renewal". He is at present Partner of Jamieson & Mackay, International Consultancy Civil, Structural and Transportation Engineers with assignments both in Europe and in developing countries.

Jesus Martin-Ramirez, born in Madrid in 1936, is Professor and head of the Department of Psychobiology at the University of Seville, Spain. He is a medical doctor with a degree in Neurosciences, holds a Ph.D. in the Philosophy of Education, and is a "Licenciado" in Law.

He has worked at the Freie Universität Berlin; the Autonomous University of Madrid; the Ruhr Universität in Bochum, Germany; at Stanford University and in the Research Department of the Ramon y Cajal Center in Madrid in the fields of neuropathology, psychology and psychobiology.

He has been a visiting professor at the Universities of Hawaii; of Hiroshima; the U.N.A.M. at Mexico City; and at Marroquin University in Guatemala. He is the author of seven books and 120 scientific papers published in eight languages.

Cyrus Mechkat, born in Teheran, Iran in 1937, is a Professor at the School of Architecture of the University of Geneva, Switzerland. His previous professional practice in Iran included planning and management of slum clearance and mass housing programs. In Switzerland he is participating in housing and urban design proposals.

His teaching, research and publications focus on the following fields:
—central-peripheral relations in the transition from traditional to modern societies;
—production of the built environment: methods and techniques of rehabilitation in industrialized and in developing countries.

Klaus Müller-Ibold, born in China in 1929, is a German planning consultant.

He studied architecture with emphasis on urban planning at St. John's University, Shanghai and the Technical University of Hanover (Dipl. of Eng. 1954 and Ph.D. 1961). He served on the Board of City-Managers for the city of Kiel (1963-68). He has been a full Professor of Urban and Regional Planning at the Universities of Berlin and Dortmund (1968-72). He is a member of the West-German Reform-Commission for university curricula on planning. Before settling as private consultant in 1981, Müller-Ibold was Director-General of the Public Works Authority of Hamburg (1972-80).

He has been a member of several public committees and councils on the national level, and consultant to the West-German Federal Government, to State Governments to and municipalities. He is a member of national and international professional organizations and Vice-President of the International Federation of Housing and Planning.

Geraldo Sà Nogueira Batista, born in Brazil in 1938, is the supervisor of The Brazilian National Research Program in Housing, Urbanism and Sanitation of the National Council of Scientific and Technological Development (CNPq).

He obtained a M. of Arch. degree at the University of Brasilia in 1964 with a dissertation on shopping development and a M.Phil. at the University of Edinburgh in 1975 with a thesis on "Land Use Control Policies and Instruments in Brazil". He is the author of several papers and documents on architecture, planning, and urban design, including two recent articles dealing with urban design aspects of the plan for the further expansion of Brasilia and the cultural problems and perspectives of the Brazilian urban habitat.

He is also a professor in the Department of Urban Planning at the University of Brasilia where he teaches Planning Law and Urban Planning Practice.

Anthony O'Connor, born in 1936, teaches in the Department of Geography at University College London.

He is a graduate of Cambridge University (B.A. 1960, Ph.D. 1963), and has held appointments in Uganda, Tanzania, Nigeria and Sierra Leone. He is Deputy Chairman of the U.K. Standing Committee on University Studies of Africa, and Secretary of the European Council on Africa Studies. His research has increasingly focussed on post-colonial urbanization. His book, *The African City,* was published by Hutchinson of London and Holmes and Meier of New York in 1983.

Krzysztof Pawlowski, born in 1930, is an architect and urban planner with a Ph.D. degree from the Technical University of Warsaw, Poland. He is a Professor attached to the Polish Academy of Sciences specializing in the rehabilitation of historic areas and in the history of urban design.

From 1974-1982 he served as Adjunct-Director of Historic Monuments of Poland. He has been, in succession, Vice-President of the International Federation for the Conservation of Historic Monuments (ICOMOS), President of the Polish Chapter of ICOMOS, and Expert of UNESCO in charge of projects in Algeria, Iran, Mozambique and Senegal. Since 1982 he has also been attached as Adjunct Professor to the Paul Valéry University in Montpellier (France).

He is the author of numerous publications on the history of planning such as "Tony Garnier et les débuts de l'urbanisme fonctionnel en France" (Paris, 1967) and "La théorie de l'urbanisme français au siècle des lumières" (Warsaw, 1970).

Anthony Penfold, born in Britain in 1930, is a Venezuelan planner.

He studied at the University of Liverpool and in the USA receiving a B.Arch. and a Master of Civic Design degree in 1958, and a Master of City Planning degree at Yale University in 1959. In 1960-62 he worked at the London County Council and collaborated with Colin Buchanan on the volume *Traffic in Towns.* Following this, he enrolled in the Ph.D. program of Harvard University. As a Fellow of the MIT/Harvard Joint Center of Urban Studies he contributed to the planning of the new industrial town of Ciudad Guayana (1962-66).

He was in charge of the planning of the Caracas Metro at the Ministry of Public Works. After acting as Vice-President of Alan Vorhees and Associates, he founded in 1978 his own firm PBSA - involved in planning work in Latin America and the Caribbean. He is also an Associate Professor of Planning at the Central University of Venezuela and an Expert of the World Bank.

Milos Perovic, born in Skopje in 1939, is a Yugoslavian architect and planner.

He studied in Belgrade - Dipl.Ing.Arch. 1963; M.Sc. 1972 and Ph.D. 1984 - and at the Athens Centre for Ekistics: C.R.E. 1971.

He has acted as chief planner of the Town Planning Institute of Belgrade 1972-76 and is at present head of the Metropolitan Planning Unit of the Institute of Planning and Development, in Belgrade.

He has received several prizes for excellence in architecture and for the management of large scale urban projects in Yugoslavia, and published numerous articles and books including the 1976 Computer Atlas of Belgrade and the *Selected Essays of C.A. Doxiades,* 1982.

Panayotis C. Psomopoulos, born in 1928, is a Greek architect and planner.

He studied at Athens Technical University and became associated with the late Constantinos Doxiades doing research from the neighbourhood scale to that of global settlements and being involved with projects in fifty countries worldwide.

He is President of the Athens Center of Ekistics and of the Athens Technological Organization since 1975; Secretary General of the World Society for

502

Ekistics since 1964; and Editor of the journal EKISTICS since 1976.

He has published numerous technical papers and articles including the 1977 "The City of the Future" report for the Ulriksdal seminar in Stockholm, and "Human Settlements 1984-2000" for NACORE, New Orleans.

Rebecca Robertson, born in 1950, is a Canadian city planner.

She obtained her Master of City Planning degree at the University of Toronto in 1974. She first worked at "Urban Systems" in Toronto, then as a Research Associate of the U.N.A.M. - the Autonomous National University of Mexico.

In 1978 she joined the firm LKSA in Caracas and collaborated with D.Kunckel, A. Penfold and E.Galantay on plans for a new industrial city based on the exploitation of bituminous oil, to be built North of the Orinoco in the states of Anzoàtegui and Monegas. At present she is a Principal Planner of the New York City Planning Commission in charge of planning and residential rehabilitation of Manhattan from 14th to 96th streets.

Paolo Soleri, was born in Italy in 1919. He studied at the University of Turin (Torino) where he received the degree of a Doctor of Architecture in 1946.

Since 1956 he lives and works in Arizona dividing his time between theoretical studies, architectural experimentation and conducting design workshops.

He has been a Fellow of the F.L. Wright Foundation, and been awarded Fellowships by the Graham and Guggenheim Foundations. His Mesa-City project has been exhibited in the Museum of Modern Art in New York. He is the Founder and Director of the Cosanti Foundation responsible for the construction of "Arcosanti", a prototype New Town for 3000 residents, 70 miles north of Phoenix, Arizona.

He has written numerous articles and books such as *Arcology: City in the Image of Man,* MIT Press 1970 and *Arcosanti: An Urban Laboratory,* Avant 1984.

Ferenc Vidor, born in Budapest, Hungary in 1924, is a professor at the Graduate Institute of the Budapest Technical University and Chief Technical Advisor in Regional Planning of the Hungarian Academy of Sciences.

He studied at the Budapest Technical University and received his B.A. degree in 1950 and his Ph.D. in Urban Planning in 1965.

He has been a Lecturer and Assistant Professor at the Budapest Technical University 1951-61; Head of the Housing Department at the Hungarian Central Planning Board in 1961-64; Professor of Urban and Regional Planning at Middle East Technical University, Ankara, Turkey, 1965-68; Head of Research at the VATI Urban Planning Institute in Budapest 1968- ; Co-Director of the United Nations' Centre for Urban and Regional Planning in Baghdad, Iraq, 1974-76.

He is the author of numerous publications including "Future Research in Hungary: Planning and Forecasting Within the Urban Realm", Akadémiai Kiadò, Budapest, 1984.

Peter André Wyss, born in Switzerland in 1939, is the President of his private consulting firm established in Singapore.

He studied at the ETHZ - Swiss Federal Institute of Technology in Zurich - and holds a M.Architecture degree and a Dr. of Technical Sciences degree in Urban Planning. He has been a Lecturer and Assistant Professor of the Graduate Program of Development Planning of the ETHZ. After graduation he worked in developing countries as a United Nations Advisor in Karachi, Pakistan, and in Colombo, Sri Lanka, and as a private consultant. He was the Far-East representative of the Electrowatt Group residing in Manila, Philippines, until 1984.

He is the author of numerous technical reports and articles and has lectured at universities in Europe and Asia.

Sources

The primary source of this volume was derived from papers presented in Committee III ("Human Beings and the Urban Environment: The Future Metropolis") at ICUS XIII ("Absolute Values and the New Cultural Revolution"). The symposium, one of seven sponsored by ICUS, of the International Cultural Foundation, Inc., was held at the J.W. Marriott Hotel, Washington, D.C., September 2-5, 1985, and had as its organizing chairman, Ervin Y. Galantay. The honorary chairman was Percy Johnson-Marshall.

Supplemental papers include "Cairo: A Socio-Political Profile" by Saad Eddin Ibrahim, an article based on a paper first read at a Professors World Peace Academy symposium on the "Middle Eastern City," Paris, February 1-5, 1985; "Post-Petroleum Hong Kong: State of the Art as the Art of the State" by Ian Brown, a paper commissioned by ICUS Publications for this volume; and four papers by Ervin Y. Galantay—"Moscow: Model Socialist Metropolis," which was commissioned for this volume; "Metropolitan Planning as an Instrument of Social Stability in Southeast Asia," a paper based on an article written for the International Conference on a New World Order, Taipei, Taiwan, October, 1981; "How Big Should Cities Grow: The Concept of Optimal Size and Its Relevance to Spatial Planning in Developing Countries," a paper first read at ICUS VIII, Los Angeles, November 22-25, 1979; and "Islamic Identity and the Metropolis: Conflict and Continuity," an article based on a paper first read at the PWPA Symposium on the "Middle Eastern City," Paris, February 1-5, 1985.

INDEX

The index is to major topics and names of persons. Tables, figures and footnotes are referred to (in parenthesis) behind their appropriate page number. **Bold Face** numbers refer to section(s) written by the subject or otherwise notable in relation to the subject.

C

D

E

N

O

P

R